The
Free Will Baptists
in History

THE
Free Will Baptists
IN HISTORY

William F. Davidson

PUBLICATIONS • WORLDWIDE MINISTRIES

114 Bush Road • P.O. Box 17306
Nashville, Tennessee 37217 USA

www.randallhouse.com

Unless otherwise indicated, all Scripture quotations in this volume
are from the authorized *King James Version* of the Bible.

The Free Will Baptists in History
by William F. Davidson

ISBN: Hardcover 0-89265-956-4
         Paper 0-89265-955-6

To
Evelyn
September, Joe, Mindy
Don, Kirk
Dawn, Donald, Matt, Bryce, Alex, Connor

Table of Contents

Part I
Searching for Denominational Roots:
The First Two Centuries (1609-1800)

Part II
The Third Century:
From Identity to Organization
(1800-1935)

Part III
A Continuing Witness:
From Organization to Maturity
(1935-1983)

Part IV
Marching into the New Millennium

Preface

When it was first suggested that a revision and second edition of the original text of *The Free Will Baptists* in America was well overdue, it was assumed that the project would involve minor editorial surgery on the earlier content and the addition of a final chapter designed to bring the saga up to the present moment. But the one abiding characteristic of history is that it is never static. The moment a text is published, it is out of date and a candidate for revision. That fact alone would not cause undue difficulty for the historian. Recent events are easily identified, offer readily accessible documentation, and typically are still clear in the minds and hearts of eyewitnesses. Reconstruction of such history is relatively simple.

The larger problem rests in the realization that history of the distant past also is subject to change. While the historical event itself remains the same, newly projected interpretations of the event and newly discovered resource materials demand that accounts of the event be constantly revisited. With that said, it should be no surprise to the reader that the anticipated minor surgery for the original text mushroomed, in some chapters, to the level of major re-write. And this part of the revision task proved to be most difficult. While new technology—e-mail and fax and modem— greatly simplified the process, some resource materials were not to be so easily obtained. Required research trips to Nashville, Tennessee, to Raleigh, North Carolina, and to Moultrie and Macon, Georgia added both time and expense to the revision project, but they also allowed access to important resources that otherwise would not have been available.

An historical study of this type must recognize certain limitations. No attempt has been made to discuss the entire history of individual State Associations. Rather, the work is a general history and has attempted to investigate the major facets of denominational heritage including first beginnings, influence from other groups and movements, missions, theology, polity, and education. Except for a brief chapter on beginnings, the work has been limited to denominational development in the United States.

The history of the General Conference of the Freewill Baptists of New England has been told before and, for that reason, has not been given as much attention here as might be expected. It was at first thought that this part of the denomination's heritage could be ignored altogether, but the most preliminary investigations revealed influences on the present National Association that could not be denied. Limitations and restrictions were in order, but it was recognized that at least a portion of the New England tradition had to be included if the larger story was to be understood.

The work was founded on certain presuppositions of the author, and these will become evident as the story unfolds. It might be good, however, to list them here so that the reader is not surprised in his study. First, it is assumed that the Free Will Baptists and, for that matter, other Baptists cannot be identified before the time of John Smyth, Thomas Helwys, and John Murton in England about 1609. While spiritual kinship can be claimed with movements before that time, especially the Anabaptists of the Reformation, such kinship does not demand historical ties. Any attempt to trace a Baptist group back to the New Testament requires the acceptance of theological aberrations that are too far afield to be condoned.

Second, it is assumed that the denomination cannot be traced to any one background or source. While it seems evident that the first Free Will Baptists in America came out of the old General Baptist movement, other segments of the present denomination can be traced to numerous other backgrounds. The Randallites of New England, the Separate Baptists from Tennessee, and the General Baptists of North Carolina and Illinois all played a part in the history of the present National Association. With this understanding, it was not surprising to find that some associations developed as a result of local theological ferment and could not be traced to outside influence at all.

Again, it is assumed that present theology and polity formulations evolved over a long period of time. While most major theological positions such as general atonement and the work of Christ have remained the same, many peripheral aspects of theology and polity have changed and changed again through the years. It also is assumed, in this respect, that varied opinions in the areas of lesser importance continue to exist within the denominational family and that the agreement to disagree can be both healthy and productive.

Finally, it is assumed that, with the larger evangelical family, Free Will Baptists have begun to cherish and respect their heritage and that a study of this nature will prove a valuable contribution.

No attempt will be made here to speak again of the many individuals that contributed to and made the first edition possible. Credit was duly given in the 1984 text. Mention must be made, however, of new friends who graciously aided in the task of re-vision. George Stevenson must be commended for his continuing research in the history of the General and Free Will Baptists in North Carolina. Articles published in the Dictionary of North Carolina Biography offered a wealth of new information on such important early leaders as Paul Palmer and Benjamin Laker. Herbert (Pete) and Geraldine Waid opened their home to me and made available the documents relating to Free Will Baptist history in Georgia that they have so carefully preserved and catalogued. With their help, it was possible to more accurately tell the story of the denomination's earliest developments in that state. I also must thank Dr. Robert Gardner, Senior Researcher in Baptist History at Mercer College, Macon, Georgia, Dr. John Crowley, Valdosta State University, and Dr. Wayne Faircloth, Clerk of the Tired Creek Primitive Baptist Church, for their kind attention to my repeated requests for help. Dr. Gardner graciously helped with research in the Baptist Collection at Mercer, saving me hours of travel and time, but more importantly, he shared his vast knowledge of people and events in Baptist history in Georgia and Virginia. Dr. Crowley patiently responded to numerous e-mail requests for the conclusions that he had drawn from his study of the Primitive Baptists in South Georgia, and Dr. Faircloth went far beyond my expectations in preparing a typed draft of the handwritten minutes of the Richland Creek, later Tired Creek, Primitive Baptist Church, to be sent along with a copy of the original. Bert Tippett put out the red carpet for me at Free Will Baptist Bible College, providing both housing and access to the excellent Free Will Baptist Historical Collection there. I had the privilege of traveling to Southeastern Free Will Baptist College and personally interviewing President Billy Bevan, but time and travel restraints made it virtually impossible for me to visit the other denominational educational institutions. Carl Cheshier and Tim Eaton at Hillsdale Free Will Baptist College and Wendell Walley and Dr. E. T. Hyatt at California Christian College interrupted busy schedules at the beginning of a new semester to respond to my request for information on the recent history of their particular schools. Dr. Jack Williams trusted me with his personal copies of the annual denominational Yearbooks for the latter part of the century, allowing me, with some fear and trembling on his part, to take them out of the state and out of his sight for the entire time of the revision project. Both Dr. Jack Williams and Dr. Melvin Worthington, Executive Secretary of the National Association, served as my experts on the events and decisions that have shaped the denomination since 1984. Their contributions to this work were invaluable—long telephone conversations, locating and faxing of documents, interpretation of data. And finally, I must express my gratitude to my good wife who tolerated my long hours at the computer and my frequent absences from Columbia. Her encouragement was a necessary ingredient in the writing process.

One thing more is required before we move on to the larger text. Much of the primary resource material used in the telling of the story comes from a distant past and the spelling, wording, and sentence structure used in the documents often looks alien when viewed through our twenty-first century eyes. I must plead the indulgence of the reader in asking that I be trusted to have accurately transcribed the text used in the direct quotes that appear throughout the book. I have chosen not to mark the many inconsistencies that appear—Old English spelling and grammar, broken sentences, obscure references. In the popular appeal of today's younger generation, "Trust Me!"

I pray that the reading of this history of the Free Will Baptists will be as rewarding and enjoyable as was the writing.

—WFD

Part I

Searching for Denominational Roots: The First Two Centuries (1609-1800)

1

The Case for a European Heritage

For the most part, Free Will Baptists have been content to depend on tradition for answers to questions of origin. Up until 1950, it was assumed that Benjamin Randall and the Freewill Baptists of New England were responsible, either directly or indirectly, for all the people, churches, and conferences that make up the present denomination. After 1950, a new tradition traced the beginnings of the movement in America back to Paul Palmer and the General Baptists of North Carolina in the early eighteenth century. Recent research has substantiated the denomination's claim that Palmer formally organized the first American Free Will Baptist Church in eastern North Carolina in 1727, but it also became quite evident that other groups of like faith had sprung from entirely different sources in other parts of the country. It would be a number of years before the various groups would come together in cooperative organization.

Even when the question of American origin was settled, other questions remained unanswered. Were these Free Will Baptists uniquely American? Was the movement begun in a vacuum? Did the spiritual atmosphere of North Carolina in the early eighteenth century with its established church and tempering tendency toward toleration dictate the spontaneous birth of such a movement? Were its leaders American by birth? Is it possible that the movement can be traced beyond 1727 to a European background?

The Problem Stated

It is interesting to note that one of the most popular questions raised in the study of American Christian history is the uniqueness of the American Christian. Some have argued that the wide-open spaces, the pioneer atmosphere, and the time factor demanded a new breed of individual in America. The more prevalent and popular argument has been that the American Christian is deeply indebted to his European background in his development of American Christianity.[1]

This latter conclusion is evidently true in the case of the Free Will Baptist denomination. There is no question but that the Free Will Baptists depended heavily on the General Baptists in England for their theology. Both the General Baptists and the Free Will Baptists in North Carolina used the 1660 English General Baptist statement of faith as a basis for their own theological systems.[2] It would also seem likely that at the early date of 1727, some of the leaders of the General Baptist movement in North Carolina came directly to the work from England. However, it has been impossible to trace the background of any of the early leaders. Much shadow continues to linger around the early years of the lives of Paul Palmer, Joseph and William Parker, and William Burgess. At any rate, recent research indicates that the North Carolina General Baptists and, consequently, the Free Will Baptists can be traced to an English heritage.

The Controversy Concerning the
Origins of the English General Baptists

Until the middle of the twentieth century there seemed to be little question as to the origin of the English General Baptist movement. Since the General Baptists were so much like the Anabaptists on the Continent, it was taken for granted that the two groups were historically linked.

However, soon after the middle of the century, a number of church historians began to question the prevailing theory. Lonnie D. Kliever,[3] one spokesman for the new school of thought, suggested that the documents failed to prove that John Smyth and Thomas Helwys, England's first Baptists, actually were part of the Anabaptist movement in Holland. Rather, he concluded that the English Baptist movement was a logical progression, in the persons of Smyth and Helwys, from Anglican priest to Puritan to Separatist to believer's baptism. While they admitted a spiritual kinship between the English Baptists and the Anabaptists of the Continent, they argued that the roots of the English Baptist denomination were to be found in England itself. The kinship argument rested on the similarities found in the two movements—Lordship of Christ, believer's baptism, authority of the Scriptures, separation of church and state, and religious liberty.

However, in a recent work dealing with the Separatist movement in England, B. R. White argued that while parallel developments did take place, it was not necessarily true that the movements depended on one another for birth and growth. The seedbed of New Testament interest would allow any number of new groups to develop on the basis of their own interpretation of Scripture. White argues that "given the original New Testament source material and the nature of the contemporary Protestant appeal to it, such developments need not imply, and without clear evidence ought not be taken to imply, any direct borrowing. . . ." Further, he says, "Men were to move without any great difficulty from a Presbyterian-Puritan position to a Congregationalist-Separatist position and without any manifest Anabaptist influence."[4]

While White is not specifically concerned with the Baptists at this point, we must remember that the Baptists would be included in the Separatist tradition. It is admitted that they did not meet all of the qualifications for the traditional Separatist position, but it is also evident that they had broken ties with the English church.

Actually, the earlier theory of Anabaptist relationship was a logical one. There is no question but that Smyth and Helwys, with their congregation, spent a number of months in Holland in self-exile. While there, Smyth did indeed woo the Dutch Waterlander Mennonites. But a more careful look indicates that the relationship ended at that point. The Waterlanders did not accept Smyth, and his plan for merger substantially failed.

Smyth's background was an interesting one. In just a few short years, he moved from Anglican priest, to Puritan, to Separatist, to believer's baptism. As early as 1605, Smyth proclaimed himself opposed to separation from the church, but by 1607, he began to entertain serious doubts about the validity of a church as corrupt as the Church of England. By 1607 or early 1608, Smyth became pastor of a small church at Gainsborough. Like other Puritans and Separatists, the little band found itself under constant persecution at the hands of James I. Just a few years earlier, James had promised that the dissenters would conform to the Church of England or be "harried" out of the land and Smyth and his congregation found James to be true to his word. Though there is a good deal of controversy about the time of their departure from England, Champlin Burrage determined that by September 26, 1608, the little church was well settled in Holland. Burrage points to a letter of that date, probably written by Thomas Helwys, a leading member of Smyth's church.[5]

By that same year, Smyth decided that if the church were corrupt then its baptism must also be corrupt. Since he himself had been baptized in the Church of England, his own baptism was suspect and he came to the conclusion that he must be baptized again. This determination left him with a unique dilemma. Since he came to this conclusion on the basis of his own studies of the New Testament and since there were no others who stood with him, there was no one qualified to administer his re-baptism. Burrage explains the difficult position in which Smyth found himself.

> The problem of the proper manner of administering baptism seems never to have troubled his sensitive mind. His chief difficulty appears rather to have been where to find a suitable person to baptize him. The Mennonites did not at that time meet his requirements on account of their peculiar beliefs. To whom then should he turn for baptism, for he demanded an administrator whose own baptism had been such that no one could with fairness adversely criticize it? To his disappointment there appeared to be no such person in all the world.[6]

At first the solution seemed to be quite simple. In late 1608, or early in 1609, Smyth baptized himself and then the rest of his congregation. This type of baptism became known as Se-Baptism and while it was not unique to Smyth, it was rare enough to cause him difficulty for the rest of his life. While he never came to doubt the doctrine of believer's baptism, he continually struggled with his own self-baptism. At least a part of his unrest probably came from the criticism of the Separatists who earlier had been his friends. At this point, he separated himself from those who had been most like him in their dissent from the Church of England. Henry Ainsworth was most outspoken in his criticism of Smyth's Se-Baptism.

> Mr. Sm.(yth) anabaptised himself with water: but a child could have done the unto himself, who cannot performe any part of spirituall worship: therefore Mr. Sm.(yth) anabaptising himself with water, did no part of spirituall worship: and consequently it was carnal wor(sh)ip, and service of the Devil.[7]

The final break with other Separatists was to come in the publication of *The Character of the Beast* in 1609. In this work, Smyth claims that ". . . al that shal in tyme to come Seperate from England must Seperate from the baptisme of Englan, and if they wil not Seperate from baptisme their is no reason why they should seperate from England as from a false church. . . ."[8] Though it is true that the congregation would find others of like faith in Holland, they found themselves in a lonely and unique situation among their English brethren. From this time, they would stand alone in their defense of believer's baptism.

For the next few years, Smyth's Se-Baptism continued to be a source of personal conflict, and Smyth began to court the Waterlander Mennonites, seeking a merger that would establish validity for his own baptism and for his church. The Mennonites, however, were skeptical and Smyth died before an agreement for merger was reached. Two of Smyth's followers, Thomas Helwys and John Murton, had opposed Smyth's defection to the Mennonites from the very first. Along with fellow church members William Pigott and Thomas Seamer, they wrote to the Mennonites to inform them that they did not agree with John Smyth and his followers within the congregation.[9] As soon as possible, this small remnant, still faithful to Baptist principles, returned to England and in 1612, founded the first Baptist church on English soil. The church was located in Spitalfield just outside the city limits of London.

These first Baptists were General or Arminian Baptists, teaching that Christ had died for all men and that all men could be saved if they accepted Christ as Savior. It was from this background that the Free Will Baptists later would spring.

In 1633, another English group left the independent Congregationalist church (still a part of the Church of England) of pastor Henry Jacob to establish a second type of Baptist movement. The split was an amiable one. Henry Jacob remained with the Independent Congregational Church and John Spilsbury and others separated themselves to found a Particular or Calvinistic Baptist church. This new church also was based on Baptist principles and boasted the same believer's baptism, separation of church and state, religious liberty, and Lordship of Christ as did their General Baptist brothers, but their theology was purely Calvinistic. As Particular Baptists, they believed that Christ had died for the particular few—the elect.

Earlier Kinsmen of the English General Baptists
Non-Calvinistic Dissenters in the Reign of Edward VI

EARLIER SOURCES

The publication of Champlin Burrage's history in 1912 shed a tremendous amount of new light on English dissent from the reign of Edward VI until late in the seventeenth century. While Mr. Burrage primarily was interested in Calvinistic dissenters, he was careful to include the discovery of documents concerning a "non-Calvinistic" group in the early history of English dissent. The congregation, meeting at Fabersham and Bocking, was evidently Arminian in flavor. Though their impact was too small for them to be considered the beginning of a General Baptist movement in England, the documents demand that we include them as spiritual brothers.[10]

ATTEMPTS AT CLASSIFICATION

Burrage made no attempt to classify the dissenting Separatists except to say that they were not Calvinistic. More recently, Dr. Barry White, in commenting on the Burrage account of the Separatist group, identified them as "free willers."[11] Though Burrage spoke somewhat disparagingly of the group, and though they were not well enough organized to have lasting impact, it would seem that they fit better into a Free Will Baptist camp than into any other. As far as available records show, this is the first group to be identified as "free willers."

The Free Will Baptist Name in Early Documents

Until recently, it has been impossible to accurately determine a historical relationship between the General and Free Will Baptists in America with the General Baptists in England. However, investigation of available documents indicates that the early General Baptists in England were known as Free Willers and were not above using the title for themselves. Burrage has given significant time to explaining that the term is an acceptable one for the early period. Thomas Helwys published a 96 page pamphlet in 1611 that was entitled *An advertisement or admonition, unto the congregation, which men called the New Frylers (Free Willers), in the lowe Countries written in Dutche.* An earlier work published by Walter Burgess had clouded the issue by arguing that the term "Frylers" used by Helwys was to be translated "Frisian." Burrage gives clear evidence to show that the term should be translated "Freewillers."[12] As far as can be determined, this is the first use of the name in the literature of the early period.

More recent discoveries have given weight to the conclusion that the name was in fairly common use throughout the seventeenth century in England. In 1984, the author made an exciting discovery of two mid-seventeenth century documents that used the term "free will" as a proper title. They were dated 1659 and 1660. One, entitled *A Loving Salutation to all People Who Have Any Desires After the Living God: but especially to the Free-Will-Anabaptists,* seems to have been written by an individual who had at one time been a member of this early "Free Will Baptist" movement, but now had converted to a new position. The salutation was signed by I. Beevan and dated 1660. Beevan reminded his audience of his own background, including a time of seeking and spiritual darkness—probably his Arminian experience—and then very lovingly calls his Arminian readers to repentance. The text indicated that Beevan had "seen the light" and that he could no longer associate with these Baptists who taught a general atonement.

The second document is of much more value because it was written by members of the movement itself and because it clearly outlines the principles and practices of the group. The document is entitled *A declaration of a small society of baptised believers, undergoing the name of Free-Willers, about the city of London.* It is dated January 1659. The manuscript included the text itself and a postscript. It was signed by Henry Adis, Richard Pilgrim, and William Cox. Following the signatures, the statement was added, "In the behalf of themselves and those that walk with them."

While it must be recognized that new documents are being found continually, it would seem that the three articles mentioned—the 1611 advertisement by Thomas Helwys and these two mid-century documents—reveal the earliest use of the term "free-willers" by the General Baptists themselves.

The Occasion for the More Important Document

As usual, the General Baptists of 1659 were under constant persecution by the Church of England, the Presbyterians, and some of the independents. Their adoption of the doctrine of believer's baptism had isolated them from many of their friends as well as from the church. The "Declaration" begins:

We well knowing, that we are and have been misrepresented to the people of this and other Nations, as well as by particular Letters from friend to friend, as by publick intelligence in pamphlets and in newsbooks by which means we have been rendred (sic) odious in the eyes almost of all, and as it were made a by-word and a hissing to all: . . .[13]

These "Free-Willers" were accused of five false persuasions: (1) opposition to magistry, (2) desiring to destroy the public ministry of the nation, (3) countenancing the Quakers in their irregular practices, (4) endeavoring "a toleration of all miscarriages in things ecclesiastical and civil, under pretense of liberty of conscience," and (5) desiring to "murder and destroy those who differed from Baptists in matters of religion."[14]

The First Free Will Baptist Apologetic

The "Declaration" answered each of the five accusations. Concerning the first, on the basis of Romans 13 and other passages, they agreed to obey the government " . . . in all civil things, that are agreeable to the mind of God. . . ."[15] The inference was clear. They would obey the rulers as long as they could do so in good conscience. However, when the government imposed rules contrary to the Word of God, the Baptists would resist. Again, the "Declaration" clearly revealed that the Baptists would not rise in rebellion, but rather, would suffer the consequences of disobedience.

At this point, the Baptists were not different from many of their accusers. The jails were and would continue to be full of those, of different movements, who would suffer at the hands of the government rather than deny or compromise their convictions.

At first reading, their initial effort at defense seems to be conflicting and confusing. They wished to see God-fearing men set up as magistrates who would hate covetousness and guarantee justice, but they refused the office for themselves.

> . . . But for our part to take a carnal weapon in our hands, or use the least violence either to support or pull down the worst, or to set up or maintain the best of men, we look not upon it to be our duty in the least; much less to have a thought of endeavoring to set up ourselves either directly or indirectly; for were we Abillitated and furnished with such endowments as might render us capable of being Rulers, yet we could not allow ourselves to act as Magistrates because we are a people chosen out of the World, John. 15.19.[16]

It would not seem too bold to conclude that these early General Baptists did not deny that a Christian could hold the office of magistrate. If he could hold the office in good conscience, he was free to do so. Indeed, they prayed that such men might hold the office.

In their second defense, the Baptists denied that they sought to destroy the public ministry of the nation. While they recognized the differences between themselves and their accusers, they denied any interest in their destruction. Describing themselves as "the peaceful lambs of Christ," they declared that they prayed for the conversion of their accusers and not for removal.

The space given to the third accusation, that of countenance of the irregular practice of the Quakers, seems to indicate that they felt the accusation was too ridiculous to be worthy of response. They simply argued that their discipline was such that even their own people, indulging in such practices, would be disciplined.

The fourth accusation was a reminder of the continuing Baptist defense of the doctrine of liberty of conscience. But at this point, the accusers declared that the Baptists had used the doctrine as a platform for license. The Baptists, here, saw two avenues of accusation. If the accusers were inferring internal miscarriages in things ecclesiastical, the Baptists argued that the very integrity of their movement demanded that they repair the miscarriages according to the light revealed in the Scripture. "So that we positively say, that if we shall allow of any miscarriages either in Doctrine or Discipline amongst ourselves, to thwart the mind of Christ revealed in the Scriptures of truth, we can expect no better answer from Him than a proclamation of our worship to be a vain worship. . . ."[17]

In one of the few harsh rejoinders contained in the "Declaration," the authors reminded their accusers that if they knew the Scriptures, they would recognize themselves as Libertines rather than the Baptists.

If, on the other hand, the accusers were inferring that the Baptists tolerated ecclesiastical error in other movements of dissent, the Baptists argued that they themselves were clear because they thought of the other movements as "without as to us."[18] The "Declaration" continued by confirming the fact that the Baptists did indeed believe in liberty of conscience. Since it seemed evident that it was the will of God to leave the tares and the wheat together in the church, and because it was evident that it was not God's will that any should perish, they felt they must tolerate others. If God could be longsuffering, they were willing to follow His example.

Adis, Pilgrim, and Cox could have dismissed the final accusation easily with their first paragraph. They simply declared that it was impossible to murder and destroy those who differed in matters of religion and at the same time proclaim religious liberty. These last two accusations contradicted one another.

However, determined to make their position clear, the authors gave more attention to this accusation than to any of the others. They declared that the Scriptures reveal a three-fold sword: (1) the Sword of the Spirit—the Word of God, (2) the Sword of Justice—the magistrate's sword, and (3) the Sword of Steel—the sword of slaughter. Their relation to the three swords already had been defined clearly in the earlier portions of the apologetic. The first sword, that of the Spirit, was their only weapon. They would be subject to the magistrate's sword and not resist it, determined to suffer whatever penalty was inflicted in the case of disobedience for conscience sake. The last sword simply did not have a place in the lives of these General Baptists.

It should be mentioned that the pacifism inferred in the last defense was not typical of all General Baptists. A number of the Baptists served in the army during the English commonwealth.

The "Declaration" and Its Authors

Though recent research has indicated that Free Will Baptists in America sprang from varied sources, it seems evident that the first Free Will Baptists on the American scene descended directly from the General Baptist work of Paul Palmer and Joseph Parker in Eastern North Carolina. Since that is true, it stands to reason that this early General Baptist heritage also could be traced to the General Baptist movement in England. While there is no question but that the name "Free Will" was in general use by 1660, there has been no attempt to prove that there actually was a separate Free Will Baptist movement at this early date. It would rather seem that the General Baptists in England sometimes referred to themselves as "FreeWillers." There seems little doubt but that these FreeWillers were a part of the General Baptist movement in England that had begun with John Smyth and Thomas Helwys in the first quarter of the seventeenth century. It should be remembered that Helwys himself had used the term as early as 1611.

BASIS FOR THE CONCLUSION

The Authors of the "Declaration"—It had been hoped that Henry Adis, Richard Pilgrim, and William Cox could be directly related to the General Baptist movement in contemporary documents. However, available copies of the *1653 General Baptist Confession of Faith* do not include the signatures of these three men.

The problem is increased when we come to the *1660 Standard Confession of Faith*. By this time, a breach had developed within the General Baptist ranks over the question of the doctrine of laying on of hands. The doctrine became a serious bone of contention for the General Baptists. Those who accepted the doctrine as necessary, not only for ordination, but for all believers, were called "Six Principle Baptists." The name was taken from the six principles of the Christian faith found in Hebrews 6:1, 2.

The breach was so great that at least twenty-eight leading General Baptists refused to sign the *1660 Confession*.[19] Since Henry Adis later acknowledged an allegiance to the principles in Hebrews 6:1,[20] it is not unlikely that he was among the twenty-eight men who refused to sign the new *Confession* and that this explains the absence of his name from the list of signatures.

The most solid documentary evidence that the three authors were General Baptists is found in the introduction to their published minutes. The editor of the published minutes, W. T. Whitley, listed all three men as General Baptists in a list entitled, "List of Leaders Till 1661." It does not seem presumptive to assume that he gleaned his list from his own copies of the minutes.[21]

Evidence Within the Text—The "Declaration" emphasized at least four areas of basic concern: (1) the support of magistry, (2) the determination to obey the government except in those things that deny the Scriptures and then to suffer consequences rather than to rebel, (3) the right of freedom of religion and conscience for all men, and (4) the doctrine of general atonement. Even a brief survey of contemporary General Baptist *Confessions of Faith* would indicate that the authors of the "Declaration" were in full agreement with the General Baptist position. The survey also carefully reveals that the authors could not fit into the opposing Particular Baptist camp.

While the *1651 Confession, The Faith and Practise of Thirty Congregations, Gathered According to the Primitive Pattern*, did not reveal a consistent Arminian system, it is clearly a General Baptist document. Evidently feeling that an article on the power of the magistrate should not be a part of the *Confession of Faith* proper, the authors of this early document added a postscript recognizing the necessity of the magisterial office and the duty of the Christian to pray for good government.[22] By 1660, the *Standard Confession* included the statement on the civil magistracy with-

1 0

in the text of the *Confession*. This *Confession* went further to include the determination that the Baptists would not rebel against the government even in areas of conscience in which they could not obey the law of the government. They simply would bear the consequences of disobedience.[23]

In regard to religious liberty, the *Standard or Brief Confession* and the "Declaration" of 1659 were nearly identical.

> That it is the will and mind of God (in these Gospel times) that all men should have the free liberty of their own Consciences in matters of Religion, or Worship, without the least oppression, or persecution, as simply on that account; and that for any Authority otherwise to act, we confidently believe is expressly contrary to the mind of Christ, who requires that whatsoever men would that others should do them, they should even do so unto others. Mat. 7.12. And that the tares and the wheat should grow together in the field (which is the world) until the harvest (which is the end of the world), Mat. 13. 29, 30, 38, 39.[24]

Finally, the doctrine of general atonement appeared in both *The Faith and Practise of Thirty Congregations, Gathered According to the Primitive Pattern* and in the *Standard Confession*. The earlier confession simply stated that "Jesus Christ through (or by) the grace of God suffered death for all mankind or every man; Heb. 2.9."[25] The *Standard Confession* uses the same reference that was found in the "Declaration." This confession would give the more strongly Arminian flavor that would remain with the General Baptists throughout their history. In Article IV, the *Confession* stated:

> . . . for which end Christ had commanded, that the Gospels (to wit, the glad tydings, of remissions of sin) should be preached to every creature, Mk. 16:15. so that no man should eternally suffer in Hell (that is, the second death) for want of a Christ that dyed for them, but as the Scripture sayeth, for denying the Lord that bought them, 2 Pet. 2. 1. or because they believed not in the name of the only begotten Son of God, Jn. 3.18. Unbelief therefore being the cause why the just and righteous God, will condemn the children of men; it follows against all contradiction, that all men at one time or other, are put into such a capacity, as that (through the grace of God) they may be eternally saved, Jn. 1.7. Acts 17.30. Mk. 6.6. Heb. 3.10, 18, 19. 1 Jn. 5. 10. Jn. 3.17.[26]

While it has not been possible to trace the authors directly to the documents of the early General Baptist movement, it is evident from the content of the *General Baptist Confessions of Faith* and the "Declaration" that Henry Adis, William Cox, and Richard Pilgrim were indeed General Baptists and very much in tune with the doctrines of the General Baptist family.

The General Baptists and Their Arminian Theology
General Atonement

Typically, the name "General Baptist" assumes an Arminian theology. But to speak of an official and well-defined Arminianism at the moment when Smyth, Helwys, and Murton were emerging as the first modern Baptists demands the stretching of that theology's influence beyond its historical bounds. In 1609, when Smyth and his followers first gave evidence of their dissatisfaction with other Separatists in England, the issues were believer's baptism vs. that of infants and general atonement as opposed to the more popular limited atonement preached by the reformers. A formal Arminian theology was yet to be formulated. With that said, however, it must be admitted that the core of what would become "Arminianism" was already in place before the new name could be officially added. In fact, the issues that had concerned the General Baptists and Arminius had been boldly addressed by the Anabaptists almost a century earlier.

In an unpublished article entitled, "The Diversity of Arminian Soteriology: Thomas Grantham, John Goodwin, and Jacobus Arminius," J. Matthew Pinson has attempted both to define early Arminianism and to characterize correctly the theology of the English General Baptists. Beginning with the assumption that Thomas Grantham was the ". . . quintessential representative of Arminian Baptist theology, combining classical Arminian soteriology with a distinctly Baptist view of church and state,"[27] Pinson goes on to remind the reader that, even as late as the middle of the century, use of the term *Arminian* for Grantham and his followers is tentative at best. His hesitation comes not because Grantham's doctrine of salvation ". . . differed exceedingly from Arminius's own soteriology, but because of the shape 'Arminian' theology took in the early part of the seventeenth century and in the centuries that followed."[28] His argument suggested that Arminius himself was more Reformed in his understanding of original sin and human depravity than most would admit. Like Arminius, Grantham taught that human reason and will were corrupted in Adam's fall from grace. In this, Grantham reflected a Reformed flavor that was accepted by other General Baptists of the moment but would be rejected by contemporary Arminians and by Arminianism in general later in the modern period.

Working from the assumption that man was totally helpless, it was not surprising that Grantham also adopted Arminius' view of the salvation experience. Arminius assumed that as a righteous judge, ". . . God must punish sin with eternal death unless one meets the requirement of total righteousness before Him."[29] No one, of course, meets the criteria. The righteousness that God requires must come from some other source. Arminius had declared, as had many of the Reformed theologians before him, that it could only have come from Christ. Christ had mediated the penalty for sin by paying ". . . the price of redemption for sins by suffering the punishment due to them"[30] Pinson concluded that Grantham followed Arminius closely in adopting this penal satisfaction theory of atonement. In this case, Christ satisfies both God's demand for righteousness and the Law's requirement of payment. "This view has been called the penal satisfaction theory of atonement, and these were Grantham's sentiments exactly."[31]

John Goodwin, an Arminian independent, on the other hand, followed Hugo Grotius' governmental theory of atonement. Here, God, as governor or sovereign, could simply pardon sinful man

1 2

apart from the fulfillment of the law. "The penalty for sin is thereby set aside rather than paid."[32] In his treatise, *Imputatio Fidei, Or a Treatise of Justification*, Goodwin declared, "The sentence or curse of the Law was not properly executed upon Christ in his death, but this death of Christ was a ground or consideration unto God, whereupon to dispence with his Law, and to let fall or suspend the execution of the penalty or curse therein threatened."[33] Simply speaking, Goodwin denied the imputation of Christ's righteousness to the believer, assuming that God is free to dispense with the law and freely pardon the sinner.

Believer's Baptism

There seems to be little doubt but that John Smyth accepted the doctrine of believer's baptism as a result of his study of the Scripture and through his conviction that rejection of a corrupt English church also demanded rejection of its baptism. But some of his contemporaries suggested other motives. Edmund Jessop had embraced the dogma of believer's baptism and had agreed to join the General Baptist movement. Second thoughts, however, led him to publish a tract in which he denounced his friends, accusing them of rejecting infant baptism based on the presupposition that original sin did not exist. At first glance, Smyth's argument seemed flawless. He had openly and often declared that free will was ". . . a natural faculty or power, created by God in the soul of man, . . . and being fallen he still retained freedom of the will."[34] In his own statement of faith of 1609, he made a strong case for general atonement in Articles Three and Nine.

> That God imposes no necessity of sinning on any one; but man freely, by Satanic instigation, departs from God.

> That men, of the grace of God through the redemption of Christ, are able (the Holy Spirit, by grace, being before them grace prevement [sic]) to repent, believe, to turn to God, and to attain to eternal life; so on the other hand, they are able themselves to resist the Holy Spirit, to depart from God and to perish forever.[35]

So far, this fits very well within Arminian thought in the modern period, as does his definition of believer's baptism included in Article Fourteen. ". . . That baptism is the external sign of the remission of sin, of dying and of being made alive, and therefore does not belong to infants."[36] No problem here. To this point, Smyth's arguments were based on his study of Scripture. Jessop's accusations, however, had not been groundless. In Article Five, Smyth rejected the doctrine of original sin. Here, he argued, ". . . There is no original sin (lit., no sin of origin or descent), but all sin is actual and voluntary, vis., a word, a deed, or a design against the law of God; and therefore, infants are without sin."[37] No wonder Jessop was concerned. Original sin had been assumed by the church at least since the third century and even now, in his century, most all Protestants, including the General Baptists, would admit to man's lostness and need for a Savior from the very moment of birth.

These early General Baptists could indeed look to Smyth for the biblical foundations of their new dogmas, but the task of refining those doctrines and bringing them fully into line with the New Testament would be left to Smyth's successors, Helwys and Murton.

That Other General Baptist Dogma

General atonement and questions of justification and redemption were not the only doctrines that had set these first Baptists apart. Logically, if man could make choices before salvation and grace that were resistible, then it stood to reason that the same freedoms should exist after salvation.

In an article entitled, *Anabaptismes Mysteries of Iniquity Unmasked*, written by an unidentified "I. P.," an opponent of the General Baptists, pointed to the possibility of apostasy as one segment of the doctrine of his enemies. Actually, the report was quite objective, if not complimentary.

> The baptists, in those days, wrote many books in defence of their opinions, and were in the habit of producing great numbers of scriptures to prove their doctrines; and that they maintained an appearance of more holiness than the members of the established church, whose books and conversation they avoided. He [his informant??? or H. H. mentioned below?—question inserted by the author] likewise informs us, that besides the denial of infant baptism, they also denied the doctrine of election, reprobation, and final perseverance.[38]

The tract evidently was written in response to a letter written by a General Baptist identified only as "H. H."

But again, the General Baptists were not in agreement as to how a believer might fail in his attempts at perseverance. Thomas Grantham could no more assume that the believer could maintain salvation by good works than he could believe that man is saved by those good deeds. His conviction that everything rested on the righteousness of Christ prevented any such notion. Rather, he argued, a believer only falls from grace when he reverts to his earlier condition of unbelief. The resultant loss of salvation is irrevocable. Such believers, he argued, are "Trees twice dead, plucked up by the Roots: and consequently uncapable of bearing fruit in God's vineyard forever."[39]

Goodwin, on the other hand, taught that perseverance consisted essentially of the believer's continuance in good works. Pointing to David's sin and repentance in the Old Testament, he asserted that during his time of impenitence David was to be considered apostate, but that confession and repentance returned him to God's favor. In other words, his apostasy was remediable.

Pinson's study sheds light on the diversity that continues to mark Free Will Baptists in the modern period. Questions of human depravity, the nature of justification, and the possibility of apostasy still give rise to lively discussions within the theological arenas of the denomination. But that diversity has its limits. Such foundational concerns as the inerrancy of Scripture, general atonement provided for and guaranteed by the blood of Christ shed at Calvary, a literal heaven and hell, the bodily resurrection of Christ and subsequently that of all believers, and the possibility of apostasy in one form or another all remain firm convictions of the denomination and serve as the glue that assures unity for this small but growing Christian movement.

Summary

Though the name "Free Will Baptist" did not gain popular usage in the United States until the latter part of the eighteenth century, it is evident that the name was used by the General Baptists in England more than 150 years earlier.

Since the first Free Will Baptists in America could be traced to the earlier General Baptist work of Paul Palmer in Eastern North Carolina, it seemed logical that the movement had deeper roots—a heritage in England as well.

A recent historian identified an early group (middle sixteenth century) of English dissenters as "FreeWillers." Though this early group was not strong enough to be considered the beginning of the General Baptist movement, they did reveal a close spiritual kinship.

The English Baptist movement proper, begun by John Smyth, Thomas Helwys, and John Murton, continued to expand as late as the middle of the seventeenth century. By 1659, members of the movement referred to themselves and were referred to as "FreeWillers." Writing in 1818, Adam Taylor reflected on the attitude of those who opposed the young General Baptist movement and, at the same time, affirmed the new name.

Mr. Helwisse succeeded Mr. Smyth in the charge of the church in Holland; in the formation of which he had been his associate and fellowlaborer. Though his labors and writings were instrumental in making a number of proselytes, yet he met with much opposition. The separatists, whom he had left, attacked him and his tenets with great warmth, calling his party heretics, anabaptists and freewillers.[40]

In England, as in North Carolina later, the name was a secondary title, used for more careful identity. Those who used the name have been carefully identified as General Baptists.

When it is understood that the General Baptists in England referred to themselves as Free Will Baptists and that the later Free Will Baptists in North Carolina used the English General Baptist *Standard Confession of 1660*, it seems safe to assume that the Free Will Baptist denomination can now be traced to Paul Palmer in 1727 and beyond—to England's General Baptist movement of the seventeenth century.

Notes for Chapter 1

[1]Sidney E. Mead seems to have developed a balanced theory which recognizes both a European heritage and a degree of uniqueness for the American Christian in his essay, "The American People: Their Space, Time, and Religion." (Sidney E. Mead, *The Lively Experiment: The Shaping of Christianity in America.* [New York: Harper & Row, publishers, 1963]). There is no question but that there were elements of uniqueness—freedom of conscience, separation of church and state, and a growing national spirit. On the other hand, Winthrop Hudson in, "How American is Religion in America?" (Gerald C. Brauer, *Reinterpretation in American Church History.* [Chicago: The University of Chicago Press, 1968]), depicted America as a product of its European heritage.

[2]William F. Davidson, The *Original Free Will Baptists in America: A Continuing Witness From Infancy to Identity, 1727-1830,* published under the title, *An Early History of the Free Will Baptists* (Nashville: Randall House Publications, 1974), 172-173. A full comparison of the *1660 Standard Confession* of the General Baptists of England and *The 1812 Former Articles* of the Free Will Baptists in North Carolina has been included on pp. 93-97.

[3]Lonnie D. Kliever, "General Baptist Origins: The Question of Anabaptist Influence," *Mennonite Quarterly Review* (October 1962), 291-321. Used by permission.

[4]B. R. White, *The English Separatist Tradition From the Marian Martyrs to the Pilgrim Fathers* (London: Oxford University Press, 1971), xii-xiii.

[5]Champlin Burrage, *The Early English Dissenters in the Light of Recent Research,* Vol. 1 (New York: Russell and Russell, 1967 [1912]), 236.

[6]Burrage, Vol. 1, 237.

[7]Ibid., 238.

[8]W. T. Whitley, "The Character of the Beast," *The Works of John Smyth, Fellow of Christ's College, 1594-8* (Cambridge: at the University Press, 1915), 567.

[9]A letter from Thomas Helwys, William Pigott, Thomas Seamer, and John Murton at Amsterdam to the Waterlander Church there, dated March 12, 1609/10, dealing chiefly with the cause of their ejection of John Smyth and his followers. Quoted in Burrage, Vol. 1, pp. 185, 186.

[10]Burrage, 52, 53.

[11]White, 2, 3.

[12]Burrage, xii, 252.

[13]Henry Adis, Richard Pilgrim, William Cox, *A Declaration of a Small Society of Baptised Believers, Undergoing the Name of Free-Willers About the City of London* (London: Printed for the author Henry Adis Uphouldster, living in Princes Street, January 1659).

[14]Ibid.

[15]Ibid.

[16]Ibid.

[17]Ibid.

[18]Ibid. There is little question but that these authors, along with other Baptists, were not anxious to further widen the breach between themselves and other dissenters or to increase the persecution they were already suffering. Both this document and the *Standard Confession of 1660* give evidence of the fact that the writers had the slanders of their opponents in mind when they wrote. The authors of the "Declaration" were so concerned with this matter that they added a postscript to the document to explain the meaning of the term *without.* However, they refused to water down the document so that it failed to clearly present their message. The inclusion of 1 Cor. 5:12, 13, as a definition for the term *without* clearly revealed the differences between the two groups.

[19]William L. Lumpkin, *Baptist Confessions of Faith* (Valley Forge, Pa.: The Judson Press, 1959), 222. Used by permission.

[20]A. C. Underwood, *A History of the English Baptists* (London: The Baptist Union of Great Britain and Ireland, 1947), 91.

[21]W. T. Whitley, *Minutes of the General Assembly of the General Baptist Churches in England, with Kindred Records,* two volumes (London: Printed for the Society by the Kingsgate Press, 1910). Henry Adis is listed on page xxxv with the dates of his three books (no titles), 1648, 1660, 1661. William Cox is listed on page xxvii as from "Sevenoaks." Richard Pilgrim appears on page xi.

[22]*The Faith and Practise of Thirty Congregations, Gathered According to the Primitive Pattern* (London: Printed by J. M. for Will. Larnar, at the Blackmore Neer Fleet-Bridge, 1651), quoted in Lumpkin, 188.

[23]*A Brief Confession or Declaration of Faith.* (London: Printed by G. D. for F. Smyth at the Elephant and Castle, near Temple-barr, 1660), 3, quoted in Lumpkin, 233, 234.

[24]*Brief Confession* as quoted in Lumpkin.

[25]Ibid.

[26]Ibid.

[27]Matthew Pinson, "The Diversity of Arminian Soteriology: Thomas Grantham, John Goodwin, and Jacobus Arminius." Unpublished manuscript, 1999, p. 1. Pinson's article will constitute a chapter in a proposed dissertation on the varieties of English Arminianism in the 17th and 18th centuries.

[28]Ibid. Pinson has concluded that the English General Baptists splintered into three clearly defined groups in the latter part of the seventeenth century—a "centrist prong (the majority of General Baptists at the time) and two lesser, extremist prongs. The centrist prong manifested itself in Thomas Grantham and carried on the orthodox 'Reformed-Arminian' tradition. The left fringe, represented by Matthew Caffyn and limited to Kent and Sussex, began articulating heterodox positions on the person of Christ and the Trinity. The right fringe, (limited to the Midlands), in part reacting to the left fringe and in part seeking more respectability in the English religious community, became more like present-day Southern Baptists and affirmed the final perseverance of the saints, and generally toned down their Arminianism (as in the Orthodox Creed)." J. Matthew Pinson, Personal Letter to William F. Davidson, May 11, 1995.

[29]Pinson, "Diversity of Arminian Soteriology," 7.

[30]Ibid.

[31]Ibid.

[32]Ibid., 10.

[33]Ibid., 11.

[34]Gordon C. Olson. *The Formative Influences, Rise, and Early History of the General Baptists in England,* an unpublished thesis (1957), 127-128.

[35]Ibid.; B. Evans, *The Early English Baptists,* Vol. I. (London: J. Heaton and Son, 1862), 253.

[36]John Smyth, *Statement of Faith,"* 1609. Quoted in B. Evans, *Early English Baptists,* 253.

[37]Ibid.

[38]Olson, *Formative Influences,* 127-128. Champlin Burrage and W. T. Whitley have concluded that "J. P.," the author of the tract, was John Paget of Amsterdam, while Adam Taylor argued that it must have been Dr. John Preston of the Anglican Church (Whitley, *Works of John Smyth,* 44, 368-369; Burrage, *Early English Dissenters,* Vol. I, p. 257; Adam Taylor, *The History of the English General Baptists.* Vol. I, *The English General Baptists of the Seventeenth Century* [London: Printed for the Author, by T. Bore, Raven-Row, Mile–End Turnpike, 1818]).

[39]Ibid., 13.

[40]Taylor, *History of the English General Baptists,* Vol. 1, p. 86.

2

First Beginnings
on the American Scene:
The General Baptists
in North Carolina

The Years of Reaping, 1727-1755
The Criteria for Choosing the Date and Locale

In spite of earlier traditions, there now seems to be little doubt that the Free Will Baptists can trace their earliest beginnings in America to the General Baptist movement begun by Paul Palmer in eastern North Carolina in 1727. This argument, however, has been complicated by the fact that General Baptists were present in America since before 1652.[1] It has been necessary to determine which General Baptist groups had the opportunity to influence the later movement and to indicate why North Carolina should be accepted as the birthplace of the first Free Will Baptists in this country.

The General Baptist movement in Virginia had to be considered because it had reached a point of local church organization thirteen years before Paul Palmer organized the first General Baptist church in North Carolina in 1727,[2] and because some of the Virginia members later became a part of the North Carolina movement.[3]

The South Carolina group began shortly after that of its sister state to the north and the close proximity of the two has demanded that South Carolina be considered.

Finally, because New England gave birth to the northern Freewill Baptists in 1780, and because the General Baptists were present in that area long before Paul Palmer settled in North Carolina, it was evident that the antecedents of the northern movement must be investigated. This larger movement will be considered in a separate chapter.

The Fate of the Virginia Churches

THE BEGINNING

General Baptists were present in Virginia as early as 1699,[4] but the first church was not organized for another fifteen years. Sometime before 1714, the General Baptists in Isle of Wight County wrote to England requesting that preachers be sent to establish churches for the scattered flock. In response, the English General Baptists appointed Robert Norden and Thomas White and provided for their trip to Virginia. White was not destined to complete his journey and died enroute, but

Norden continued to Virginia and began his ministry at Burley, across the James River from Jamestown, in the autumn of 1714.[5] Apart from itinerant work to the north, Norden spent his entire ministry in America at Burley. He ended his earthly ministry April 30, 1725.[6]

In 1727, after two years without a pastor, the church welcomed two new elders from England, Casper Mintz and Richard Jones, making Jones their pastor and sending Mintz to organize a new church in Surry County.[7]

Isaac Backus, editing a paper written by John Leland, mentioned a third church in Prince George County, but few references were made to that work until Clarence Urner began to investigate the records of that county about 1933. He discovered that Robert Norden had traveled north to Prince George and had succeeded in obtaining a license to preach in that area. The application for license was dated June 14, 1715, and declared that:

> Robert Norden an Annabaptist preacher appears in Court and takes the Oaths and Subscribes the Declarations mentioned in the Act of Parliament of the 1st of William & Mary & Entitled an Act for Exempting their Majestys Protest Subjects Dissenting from the Church of England from the penaltys of Certain Laws. Order the sd be recorded.
>
> I Robert Norden do Sincerely promise and Solemnly Declare before God and the World that I will be true and faithfull to his Majesty King George, and I do Solemnly promise and Declare that I do from my heart abhor, detest and renounce, as Impious and Hereticall that Damnable Doctrine and Position that Princes Excommunicated or Deprived by the Pope or any Authority by the See of Rome may be Deposed or Murthered by their Subjects or any other whatsoever, and I do Declare that no foreign Prince, Person, Prelate, State Superiority, Preheminence or Authority, Eclestasticall or Spirittuall within this Realm. Robert Norden.
>
> I, Robert Norden Profess faith in God the Father and in Jesus Christ his Eternall Sonn the true God and in the Holy Spiritt, One God Blessed for ever more, and I do acknowledge the Holy Scriptures of the Old and New Testament to be given by Divine Inspiration. Robert Norden.[8]

Soon after Norden received his license to preach in Prince George County, two private homes were accepted as public meeting houses for the General Baptist faith.

> Matthew Markes having petitioned this court that his house be entered a publick meeting house for those persons called Annabaptists, its Ordered the same be done accordingly.
>
> Att a Court held for the county of Prince George on the second Tuesday in July Anno Domini 1715, being the twelfth Day of said month.
>
> On motion of Nicholas Robertson it's Ordered that his house be recorded a public meeting house for the Sext of Annabaptists.[9]

The Demise of the General Baptist Movement in Virginia

The Prince George Church—After 1725, the Prince George church ceased to appear in the records. The last concrete evidence of the church's existence appeared in the will of Matthew Markes, in whose home the church met. Markes gave two hundred acres of land to Edward Markes on the condition that he not prohibit the meeting held there. The identity of the church was established in the same will in that Robert Norden was made guardian of Markes' plantation until Edward came of age.[10] The disappearance of the church from later records would indicate that it prospered under the ministry of Norden and perished after his death. In 1729, four years after the death of Norden, Paul Palmer wrote from North Carolina to John Comer in New England, telling him of a Yearly Meeting that included the Virginia churches. He listed just two churches—the Burley church, under the direction of Richard Jones, and the Surry church.

> There is a comely little church in the Isle of Wight county, of about thirty or forty members, the Elder of which is one Richard Jones, a very sensible old gentleman, whom I have great love for. We see each other at every Yearly Meeting, and sometime more often. There is another church in Surry County, where my brother Jones lives, I suppose of about thirty more.[11]

The Surry Church—Except for the brief details of its organization, history has left no record of the church in Surry County. The church probably had disappeared by 1756, either rejoining the mother church at Burley, or joining a portion of the Burley congregation in their flight to North Carolina to escape a deadly plague about 1742.[12]

The Burley Church—The history of the church at Burley moved in two directions after Richard Jones became pastor in 1728. Though the plague of 1742 caused part of the congregation to flee to North Carolina, a remnant of the group continued its ministry in the Burley area until 1756, when they petitioned the Philadelphia Association of Particular Baptists for assistance. Morgan Edwards, writing in 1772, dated the end of the General Baptist movement in Virginia and preserved their plea for help:

> . . . The church of Burley was in being about 16 years ago, [1756] as appears by the following letter addressed to the association of Philadelphia. The church of Jesus Christ in Isle-of-Wight county, holding adult baptism, &c. to the Reverend and General Assembly or Association at Philadelphia, sends greeting. We the above mentioned church, confess ourselves to be under clouds of darkness, concerning the faith of Jesus Christ, not knowing whether we are on the right foundation, and the church much unsettled; wherefore we desire alliance with you, and that you will be pleased to send us helps, to settle the church and rectify what may be wrong; and subscribe ourselves your loving brethren in Christ, Casper Minz, Richard Jones, Randal Allen, Joseph Mattgum, Christopher Atkinson, Benj. Atkinson, David Atkinson, Thomas Cofer, Samuel Jones, Wm. Jordan, John Allen, John Powell, Joseph Atkinson—Dec. 27, 1756.[13]

The remainder of the congregation already had become established in North Carolina. Because they settled in the area of the Paul Palmer work and because they predated his efforts by thirteen years, they are of greater concern for this particular study. If those churches continued throughout the eighteenth century and into the transition period when the Free Will Baptists came to the fore, the date of origin for the Free Will Baptists would have to be pushed back to 1714.

In 1742, William Sojourner gathered a part of the Burley congregation and led them to North Carolina to escape the sickness that had invaded their corner of Virginia. The small group of General Baptists settled on Kehukee Creek in Halifax County and soon established a church that was to become the mother of a number of churches in that area.

The Kehukee Church was organized by Sojourner himself, but his influence had as much or more impact through his converts. Working with another General Baptist leader, Josiah Hart, Sojourner was instrumental in the conversion of Thomas Pope, William Walker, John Moore, Charles Daniel, and Edward Brown.[14] Most of these men had been brought up in the established church, but under the direction of Sojourner, they became strong leaders of the General Baptist movement. John Moore later became pastor of a branch of Kehukee at Tar River Falls, while William Walker and Thomas Pope became leaders of a similar arm on Upper Fishing Creek. The church at Tar River Falls was established as early as 1744, and the organization of the Fishing Creek church followed in the next year.[15] In 1749, Edward Brown established a new work at Great Cohara,[16] making a total of four churches that had grown out of the direct influence of the Virginia emigrants.[17]

At least four North Carolina churches then—Kehukee, Upper Fishing Creek, Great Cohara, and Tar River Falls—could trace their heritage back beyond 1727 and the Paul Palmer beginnings in the eastern part of the state.

Fortunately, contemporary records reveal the fate of the four churches. Kehukee joined with the churches in Pitt County, Toisnot, Bertie, and Tar River Falls to become the nucleus of the Kehukee Association[18]—an association based on the Particular Baptist plan. Fishing Creek agreed to reorganize as a Particular Baptist church in 1756 and Great Cohara followed suit in 1759.[19]

All the earlier mentioned converts of Sojourner and Hart were persuaded to join the Particular Baptist movement and were instrumental in drawing their churches into that order. The reorganization of the Great Cohara church in 1759 ended the possibility of any direct influence of the Virginia churches on the continuing General Baptist movement.

The South Carolina Movement

As in Virginia, a few General Baptists probably had entered South Carolina shortly before the beginning of the 18th century. W. T. Whitley and A. H. Newman contended that the first settlers in the southern part of the combined Carolinas included three important Baptists from England: Paul Grimball, Lady Axtell, and Lady Elizabeth Blake.[20] Lady Blake enjoyed a position of significant influence in that she was the wife of Joseph Blake who was soon to become governor of the province. Whitley inferred that these earliest Baptists in South Carolina adhered to the General Baptist faith.[21] Though his assumption may have been correct, this group of early Baptists soon joined the Particular Baptist church which had been established in Charleston by William Screven sometime after 1683.[22] Of more importance to this study is the fact that the General Baptists, though they might have been present in South Carolina earlier, did not reach the state of organization until 1736.[23]

THE BEGINNING AND THE END

The Stono Church—The early General Baptist movement had its beginning and ending in the Stono church, a split from the Particular Baptist church in Charleston. It seems that General Baptists were present in the church for many years and had accepted the leadership of that group throughout the ministry of William Screven. Tension began to build during the ministry of succeeding ministers until finally, in 1733, a total schism was effected. The church at that time was under the ministry of Rev. Thomas Simmons, pastor of the church for almost ten years. His ministry had been a period of sharp contrasts including both expansion through the development of new branches and the near destruction of the church through the succession of the General Baptist faction.[24]

About 1733, William Elliott, Jr., whose father had donated land for the Charleston church building, gathered twenty-one members of the General Baptist faith and left the church to begin an independent work at Stono, about sixteen miles from Charleston.[25] The new church, having no other recourse, struggled without an ordained leader for almost three years before Rev. Robert Ingram, of the English General Baptists, responded to their call to service. The church was organized November 25, 1736, soon after Ingram arrived in the colony.[26]

Through a court case in 1745, the church fell heir to a second meeting house in the city of Charleston. On July 18, 1699, William Elliott, later a member of the General Baptist church at Stono, donated a lot on Church Street that became the site of the first church building by 1700 or 1701. The lot, designated Lot No. 62, had been conveyed in trust to appointed trustees for the "Protestant Disenting Antipaedo Baptists vulgarly called Anabaptists."[27] The trust had been renewed in 1712, but by 1744, it had lapsed due to the death of the trustees. In the meantime, the Charleston church had split for the second time, leaving two Particular Baptist factions in addition to the split that had moved to Stono as General Baptists. The majority of the church, attempting to remove Rev. Simmons from the pulpit and failing, left the church.[28] Then, when the property trust was allowed to lapse, the majority faction filed a petition with the South Carolina General Assembly asking that new trustees be appointed. The petition was presented January 26, 1745, in the name of "Sundry Members of the AntipaedoBaptist Church in Charleston."[29] They argued that William Elliott had been a Particular Baptist when he donated the lot and that he had remained in that persuasion until shortly before 1733. They further contended that when Elliott embraced the General Baptist faith he denied himself the right to continue to determine the use of the property. They felt that the property should continue to be used by the group for which it had been intended—the Screven group which they represented.[30]

In response, the minority group, led by Thomas Simmons, joined forces with the General Baptist group at Stono. This new alliance filed a counter petition in which William Elliott, Jr., the son of the donor, claimed that his father always had been a General Baptist.

The decision of the Assembly was a startling one and probably gave little satisfaction to either of the opposing parties. The trust was renewed with William Screven, John Raven (a minor, whose guardian, Branfill Evance, was to act in his place until he came of age), and Paul Grimball,

Particular Baptists; Elisha and William Butler, General Baptists; Francis Gracia, Particular Baptist representing the minority group; and John Ladson appointed as the new trustees.[31] To further complicate the matter, the Act continued:

> . . . for the preventing any disputes that may hereafter arise . . . all the Antipaedobaptists, as well those distinguished by the name of General Baptists as those distinguished by the name of Particular Baptists, are entitled to and shall have an equal right in the said lot numbered sixty-two, and the appurtenances; and each of the said sects shall and may lawfully make use of the same for divine service. . . .[32]

The problem was solved temporarily when the General Baptist faction agreed to use the church building and leave the Particular faction with the use of the parsonage.[33] The Particular Baptists soon built a new sanctuary, leaving the old structure in the keeping of the General Baptists until they ceased to exist.[34]

Rev. Henry Heywood, the successor to Ingram, led the Stono church in its battle for the Charleston property. Heywood was a native of Franham, England, and had come to the colonies at the request of the Stono congregation. He was the most capable of the Stono leaders, having an adequate education and enjoying some recognition as a writer. He continued to serve the church until his death, October 29, 1755.[35]

After the death of Heywood, the church began a steady decline. Two years passed before Daniel Wheeler was secured as a successor to Heywood. He continued an uneventful pastorate until his death in 1767.[36] Caleb Evans accepted the pastorate in 1768 and by 1772, his congregation had dwindled to eight active members.[37]

The records did not list a resident minister after the death of Evans in 1772. Although a remnant of the congregation asked for a reaffirmation of the property settlement in 1787, the movement was recorded as officially extinct in January 1791.[38] For all practical purposes, the General Baptist movement in South Carolina was dead.

The Failure at Rocky River—In 1790, John Asplund, the traveling Baptist historian, listed a General Baptist church at Rocky River.[39] This attempt to establish a General Baptist work was not classed with the Stono group for two reasons: (1) The church first was organized as a Particular Baptist church, and (2) the church continued on the General Baptist plan for only five years.[40] In 1790, under the leadership of Jeremiah Walker, the church joined with three churches in Georgia to form a General Baptist Association. Upon the death of Walker, the association was dissolved and the church at Rocky River applied for membership in the Georgia Baptist Association. For the sake of convenience, the church was advised to join the Bethel Conference in their own state, but the local conference refused to admit them until a committee could investigate and determine that the church had denounced its General Baptist doctrine. The committee never reported to the conference and the church ceased to exist under the old name.[41]

The last General Baptist effort in South Carolina had failed.

The Early Leaders of North Carolina
Examined From a New Perspective

For the most part, histories of early North Carolina Baptists have tended to center attention on the work of Paul Palmer and, by so doing, they have shown little concern for the General Baptist picture before and after the time of Palmer's influence. At least two factors have pointed to the necessity of a new look at the early leaders of the movement: (1) the brief period of Palmer's influence, and (2) the greater importance of the extended and wider influence of Joseph and William Parker in laying the groundwork for the later Free Will Baptist movement.

The Background and Brief Influence of Paul Palmer

THE MYSTERIOUS EARLY YEARS

The Confusion Surrounding the Ministry of Paul Palmer—Using the character sketch provided by Morgan Edwards in 1772, most historians begin their study of Palmer by contending that he was a native of Maryland, baptized by Owen Thomas at Welsh Tract in 1732, and ordained in Connecticut.[42]

Palmer first appeared on the American scene in 1717 in York County, Virginia, when his marriage to Martha Hansford Hill was listed in county records.[43] Martha's untimely death in the first year of their marriage ended this opportunity for happiness. His spiritual history can be traced beyond 1732 to the first mention of his name in the minutes of the Perquimans Precinct Monthly Meeting of Friends (Quakers) in 1719.[44] He appeared again the next year in the Colonial Records of the state of North Carolina where, on April 3, 1720, he became involved in a court case concerning ownership of a slave named Sambo.[45] The life of Palmer before 1717 has continued to be a complete mystery. No available records shed light on his early youth or on the source of his General Baptist persuasion.

Sometime before 1720, Palmer married Johanna Peterson, the daughter of Julianna Laker and the widow of Thomas Peterson.[46] Peterson owned a plantation of about 500 acres and except for a 100 acre plot reserved for the founding of the town of Edenton, he left the property to his wife.[47]

After their marriage, Paul and Johanna Palmer moved to Johanna's property in Perquimans Precinct where Palmer was to become an important landowner in his own right. By 1729, he had increased the estate to 964 acres.[48]

Before Palmer made any noticeable impact on the religious situation, he became a respected figure in the political arena of the colony. By 1725, probably because of his growing influence as a landowner, he was chosen to serve on the Grand Jury of the Precinct.[49]

The first half of the decade was an important period of preparation. Palmer's marriage into the influential Laker family and his increasing influence as a landowner and political leader combined to set the stage for his debut as a successful General Baptist evangelist.

The greater mystery has revolved around the confusion growing out of Morgan Edwards' dating of Palmer's baptism in 1732. There is no question but that Palmer had established a church in Chowan County, North Carolina, in 1727,[50] and that by 1729, had drawn such attention to his preaching that the governor complained to the Bishop of London of the Baptists' success. In a letter postmarked Edenton, October 12, 1729, Governor Richard Everard reminded the bishop that upon his arrival in North Carolina there was no sect in the state but Quakers. By the year of his writing, however, he complained that Paul Palmer, a Baptist teacher, had gained hundreds of converts and there was no way to stop his progress.[51]

George Washington Paschal, the author of the most exhaustive history of North Carolina Baptists, further confused the issue by concluding that Palmer's last work was in North Carolina.[52] If the 1732 date given by Edwards can be trusted at all, then it must be assumed that Palmer worked first in North Carolina, then traveled north to preach in Maryland, Connecticut, Delaware, and New Jersey and finally returned to his preaching point in the South. It is certain that Palmer was present in the North after he began his work in North Carolina. John Comer, a young Baptist preacher in Newport, Rhode Island, in the entry in his diary for October 6, 1730, reported that Palmer was as far north as Boston.[53] The next month Comer noted that Palmer and a Mr. Drake had ordained Henry Loveall in East New Jersey.[54] The Comer evidence gave some credence to the Edwards' date, but one problem still has remained unsolved. Though it might not have been unusual for Palmer to preach before ordination, it does seem highly unlikely that he would have aided in the ordination of Loveall before that time.[55] It seems the mystery that pervaded the early years of Palmer's life followed him into the later years of his ministry.

The Solutions Offered—The fascinating and elusive story surrounding the ministry of Paul Palmer has encouraged the presentation of a number of solutions to the problem. B. F. Riley, without giving documentation, concluded that Palmer came to America directly from the General Baptists in England,[56] and W. T. Whitley built on his statement in giving an enlarged solution:

> In 1729, Paul Palmer appears at Perquimans in North Carolina. The latest Baptist historian of the South thinks that he came direct from England. There was a Palmer family of General Baptists on the borders of Surrey and Sussex, known from 1660 to 1790. And as Norden's death was reported, it seems likely that Paul went to take up the work. There is a gap in the Assembly records from 1728 to 1731, so that we cannot say whether he was officially ordained as Messenger.[57]

An even more exciting possibility has been revealed through recent research. In 1722, a Paul Palmor (sic) in Perquimans County, North Carolina, asked for a certificate of dismissal from the Quaker congregation in that county.[58] Though the Paul Palmer mentioned in the Quaker minutes cannot be identified conclusively, two things point toward the probability of his being the General Baptist Palmer of 1727: (1) The white population of the entire state at that time was only about 10,000 people,[59] allowing little possibility of two Paul Palmers in the tiny county of Perquimans, and (2) only one Paul Palmer appeared in the official records of the Colonial period. George Stevenson, Archivist for the North Carolina State Department of Archives, has given special attention to Palmer and his spiritual pilgrimage, tracing him through both Quaker and North Carolina Colonial records. It was his discovery of Palmer's 1722 request for a "certificate of clearness" from the Perquimans Precinct Monthly Meeting of Friends that demanded a new look at Palmer and his ancestry.[60]

Stevenson also offered a possible solution to the question of Palmer's ordination. Robert Norden, mentioned earlier, came from England as an ordained messenger, an office of authority much like that of a diocesan bishop. Stevenson supposed that in the absence of ordained ministers in North Carolina, Palmer sought out Norden for his own ordination process. "Since Norden's ordination as messenger was specifically in Virginia, it is likely that he exercised no general superintendence over North Carolina. It is probable, however, that with or without the assistance of Richard Jones, elder of Surry and Isle of Wight churches, he ordained Palmer shortly after his immersion."[61] While there seems to be no clear evidence for this assumption, it certainly is more plausible than that of Morgan Edwards in 1772.

THE PERIOD OF INFLUENCE

Paul Palmer's influence in North Carolina was phenomenal in its instant success, but much briefer than has been recognized. Such a conclusion does not belittle Palmer's contribution to the over-all Baptist picture in the state, but it does recognize the fact that his influence on the General Baptists was cut short and that the destiny of the continuing movement was left in the hands of others.[62] For the most part, the General Baptist group that remained after the Particular Baptist reorganization in the middle of the century was the remnant of the work of two other General Baptist leaders, Joseph and William Parker. The few churches that grew out of Palmer's direct influence did not continue into the later period as General Baptist churches.

A number of factors contributed to the transfer of General Baptist leadership in North Carolina from Paul Palmer to the Parkers: (1) the evangelistic nature of Palmer's ministry, (2) his travels to the northern states, (3) the early death or reorganization of the churches he organized, and (4) his own early disappearance from the General Baptist field of activity.

The Evangelistic Nature of Palmer's Ministry—Like the other leaders in the state, Palmer's ministry combined the evangelistic preaching of the General Baptist tradition with a steadfast conviction that he must reach more than the people of a local congregation. Unlike the others, however, Palmer did not become pastor of any of the churches that he organized.[63] While William and Joseph Parker and their important contemporary of Camden County, William Burgess, could see the importance of remaining with a congregation until it was established, Palmer's burning burden for evangelism left him time for little more than initial church organization.

The Period of Travel in the North—As was mentioned earlier, John Comer gave the first concrete proof of Palmer's later travels.[64] Comer was a contemporary of Palmer and corresponded with him often from September 1729 to March 1730.[65] Comer's account of Palmer's travels in the northern states was based on a personal visit with Palmer at North Kingstown, October 6, 1730.[66]

A recent discovery has established Palmer's presence in Maryland in 1735. The Somerset (Maryland) Court Judicials, 1734-1736 record a petition, submitted by Paul Palmer, for the right to preach in the area.

Somerset Court, Judicials, 1734-1736, pp. 62-3, August Court, 1735: The Reverend Paul Palmer a dissenting Baptist minister came here into Court in his proper person & prays that he may be admitted to preach and teach the Severall Congregations that

Shall Come to hear him in the County of Somerset to wit a Michael Robinsons, Robert Gauts, Geo. Trewitts, Henry Jermans, Capt John Walker's and at William Burton's which is granted him he Complying with the act of parliament in such Case made and provided &c whereupon the said Paul Palmer took & Subscribed the oath of fidelity as by the said act of Parliament is directed and Subscribed to the articles of religion Except what part of the said Articles is Excepted against in favour of Such dissenting Ministers by said act and Likewise took the severall oaths to the Government as by act of Assembly directed with the test and Subscribed the Same Oath of abjuration and Declaration as is by the atsd act of Assembly required &c. Somerset Court, Judicials, 1738-1740, p. 266, Somerset Court, March, 1739/40: Somerset County the first day of May, 1740 Worthy Sir, I hope you remember that when I was Qualified at your Court that I made mention of the following places to be recorded for our meetings (to witt) William Burtons at Indian River and Michael Robinsons, Robert Golts, George Truets, Henry Garmans (Jarman's) at Snow Hill and Capt John Walkers on Swann Gutt and further Humbly pray that on (one) half acre of land on the Land of Luke Watson adjoining on the healing Spring on the west side of Swann Gutt and the House of James Houston may be recorded for our Assembly of Worship to God and your Humble S (servant) and he your assured friend as he hopes shall learn to be thankfull to God and yourself now and at all times—Paul Palmer—to Mr. Thomas Howard [Haward, Hayward] at his Office in Somerset County in Maryland These. . . .[67]

Further information about Palmer's time away from the work in North Carolina must be limited to tentative conclusions drawn from Morgan Edwards' account of the evangelist's baptism and ordination. Unfortunately, Edwards did not give definite dates for Palmer's travels. He did infer that Palmer was in Maryland and Connecticut after 1732 and possibly as late as the last half of that decade. In his account of the ministry of Henry Loveall at Chesnut Ridge, Maryland, he stated:

He took care of them at the time they became a church, Jul. 10, 1742. Before that, Mr. George Eaglesfield preached but baptized none; after him, Mr. Paul Palmer, who baptized 9 persons, then went to North Carolina: he was a native of this province; baptized at Welshtract in Pennsylvania by Rev. Owen Thomas about the year 1732; ordained in Connecticut; died in said North Carolina. . . .[68]

Palmer was the second minister to preach at the church, and the third minister, Henry Loveall, did not become pastor until 1742. Edwards' account was too vague to allow a definite conclusion as to whether Palmer preached in Maryland after his work in North Carolina was in progress or if the church struggled without a preacher until 1742. Since the records have indicated that Palmer was present in North Carolina from 1720 to 1729,[69] his ministry in Maryland necessarily came before or after that decade. Any attempt to date his work in Maryland before his coming to North Carolina would demand the conclusion that the Chesnut Ridge church was without a minister for almost twenty-two years. The more logical conclusion is that Palmer spent his time in Maryland after 1730, following his meeting with Comer, and before 1742 when Loveall arrived at Chestnut Ridge.

In spite of the difficulty in dating Palmer's work in Maryland, it is evident from Comer's contemporary record that Palmer was away from his churches in North Carolina in the critical period following organization.

The Fate of the Palmer Churches—One further evidence of the impact of these factors on Palmer's influence was seen in the fact that only three churches can be traced directly to him. His most productive years were from 1727 to 1729 when he led in the organization of the first two General Baptist churches in the state. Records of the founding of all three churches have been preserved in contemporary documents.

George Stevenson concluded that Palmer continued his ministry through much of the next decade.

> He is known from contemporary records to have gathered a congregation from Broad Creek, Flea Point, and Greens Creek in present Pamlico County, another from Goose Creek in Beaufort and Pamlico counties, one from Pungo River in Beaufort and Hyde counties, and yet another from Swift Creek in present Pitt and northern Craven counties. On the south side of the Neuse River he preached and baptized at Hancock Creek and in the area of Brice Creek; on the upper reaches of the river he made conversions among the settlers of Contentnea Creek. In Onslow County he gathered a church on New River, some families from Chowan church having moved to that place. A generation after his death a place where he had baptized in Trent River near Deep Gully (in present Jones County) was still known variously as 'Paul Palmer's Landing' and 'Paul Palmer's Dipping Hole.'[70]

Even so, there is no evidence that Palmer's churches continued as General Baptist churches into the later part of the century or that they served as a link between the General Baptists of the 18th century and the Free Will Baptists of the 19th.

There is no evidence that the churches in Somerset County, Maryland continued as General Baptist churches.

The first General Baptist church in North Carolina was established by Paul Palmer in Chowan County near the present community of Cisco.[71] John Comer's diary provided an accurate dating for the church and, through the listing of the members, made possible a reliable conclusion concerning its location.

> This day I received a letter from ye Baptist church in North Carolina, settled about two years (in ye year 1727) since, by Mr. Paul Palmer, signed by John Parker, John Jordan, Benjamin Evans, John Parker, John Brinkley, Michael Brinkley, Thomas Darker, James Copland, John Welch, Joseph Parke, William Copland, Joseph Parker.

> This church consists of 32 members, it meets in Chowan.[72]

The location mentioned by Comer has caused some confusion. Chowan was a precinct rather than a town. Comer's diary entry for Friday, November 7, 1730, indicated that Palmer probably had addressed his letters from the precinct without further identification—a technicality that would not have been recognized by an outsider. George Washington Paschal has determined that the problem of location could be solved through a study of the men who had signed the letter to Comer.

> And that the church referred to in Comer's journal was in Chowan Precinct is fully corroborated by a consideration of the persons whose names were signed to the letter. Except for 'Darker' which is almost certainly a mistake for 'Parker,' the names are Chowan Precinct names, and nearly every one of them the name of a man whose activities at this time were taken notice of in papers now found in the Colonial Records and other contemporary documents.[73]

Setting a pattern that he was to follow throughout his ministry, Palmer did not become pastor of the new church, but allowed Joseph Parker to become shepherd of the flock. Unlike the General Baptist churches in Virginia[74] and later in North Carolina, the first church in the state did not record a request to the Precinct courts for a settled meeting house. Since the property of most of the charter members was located near the site of the church,[75] it was not unlikely that the congregation met in the homes of various members for worship.[76]

The second General Baptist church in the state also has been traced to Paul Palmer. On September 5, 1729, Palmer and seven others filed a request with the Pasquotank Precinct Court seeking license to worship as dissenters in the home of William Burgess.[77]

North Carolina

To the Worshipfull Court of Pascotank Precinct Now Setting

The Humble Petition of us the Subscribers Humbly Sheweth That Whereas There is a Congregation of the People Calld Baptis Gathered In this Precinct meeting together for Religious Worship In ye Dewelling House of William Burgess on the North Side of Pascotank on the head of Ramonds Creek, he ye said Burgess having granted ye Same for use of ye said meeting we Pray ye Same may be recorded and we ye humble Petitioners in duty bound Should Pray

W Burgess
Paul Palmer
Frances Brockit
Thomas Heonrton
William Jones
Philip Torksey
Robert Wasson
Charles Leutrough[78]

Morgan Edwards, in his account of the beginnings of the Kehukee Association, listed William Burgess as the founder of the Pasquotank church.[79] It was true that Burgess was the first to sign the application for license and that the other names were listed in a secondary position.[80] This was to be expected, however, since the license asked for permission to use the home of Burgess for a meeting house. Since Burgess did become the first pastor of the church,[81] it would seem that the same pattern developed here as had been true at the church in Chowan County—Palmer led in the organization of the church and then left it in the hands of a permanent shepherd.[82]

One other church has been traced directly to Palmer's evangelistic efforts, but information has been limited to one brief statement by Morgan Edwards. He closed his study of the beginnings of the Kehukee Association by reminding his readers that ". . . Paul Palmer gathered a church at New River, in the borders of South Carolina." [83]

The three churches credited to Palmer's direct influence as well as those identified by Stevenson did not enjoy a long existence as General Baptist churches. The Chowan church soon disbanded, probably due to lack of a permanent meeting house; the removal of their young pastor, Joseph Parker, to Meherrin in what was to become Hertford County;[84] and Paul Palmer's new interest in Pasquotank precinct. By 1732, there was no trace of a Baptist congregation in Chowan Precinct.[85]

The Pasquotank church was lost to the General Baptists through another channel. After the death of William Burgess, his son and successor, John, led the church into an acceptance of the Particular Baptist faith. In 1757, the church was reorganized as a Particular Baptist church[86] and became a part of the reorganization process that was to engulf most of the General Baptist churches by the end of the decade.

The church at New River evidently made little impact on the General Baptist movement. Other than Edwards' passing statement that Palmer had established a church there, no other records have been found. In 1757, another church was established at New River in Onslow County, but no mention was made of the earlier church. The new church was organized on the Calvinistic plan and joined the Kehukee Association of Particular Baptists.[87]

Palmer's Early Disappearance from the General Baptist Field of Activity—After 1729, partly as a result of his travels to the North, Palmer's name temporarily disappeared from the records in North Carolina. Nine full years were to pass before he was to appear again as a leader of the General Baptists in the state. In 1738, Palmer applied to the Court at Edenton, North Carolina, for license to preach as a dissenting minister.

North Carolina

Permission is hereby granted to Paul Palmer of Edenton a Protestant Minister to Teach or preach the Word of God in any part of the said Province (he having qualified himself as such) pursuant to the directions of an Act of Parliament made in the first year of King William and Queen Mary In-titled an 'Act for Tolerating Protestant dissenters.'

Given under my hand at Edenton the 4th day of October Anno Dom. 1738.[88]

Palmer evidently enjoyed the relaxed religious atmosphere in North Carolina throughout his ministry. Before 1738, the absence of interference by the established church allowed dissenters to preach without license. After that time, however, the Church of England took a new interest in eastern North Carolina and began to bring pressure against those who differed from them. Palmer found that a license granted by the government was the only sure guarantee of freedom to preach his gospel of the general atonement.[89]

In spite of his new license and guaranteed freedom, Palmer never regained the degree of influence he had known in the first years of his ministry. The fiery evangelist that had stirred thousands and had brought fear to the heart of the established church caused little commotion following his return to the records in 1738.

A torn sheet from the title page of a family Bible has preserved the last known message from Palmer's own hand where he recorded the death of his son, Samuel, on November 24, 1739.[90] The record indicated that Palmer preached the message for Samuel's funeral. The only other reference to Palmer was Morgan Edwards' statement that the evangelist had organized a church in the southern part of the state in 1742. Damon Dodd, a Free Will Baptist historian, concluded that Palmer continued to preach under the license for ten or twelve years,[91] but the records have failed to prove such a conclusion.

The date of Palmer's death has not been established. The mystery that enshrouded his early life and ministry continued to follow him even in death. Whether it was caused by death or the infirmities of old age, Palmer's ministry was cut short and by 1742, he disappeared from the General Baptist field of action.

Palmer's ministry had been an important one. He established the first General Baptist churches in the state, and he continued to have an indirect influence on the movement through the work of his contemporaries, Joseph and William Parker. His direct influence was ended, however, and the leadership of the General Baptists fell upon the shoulders of the Parkers—a responsibility they continued to bear until the century had almost run its course.[92]

The Laker-Parker Heritage
The General Baptist Picture Prior to Palmer

Contrary to the picture painted by past historians, Paul Palmer did not begin the General Baptist movement in a vacuum devoid of earlier General Baptist influence.

The Influence of Benjamin Laker—Though the Colonial Records for North Carolina have preserved a wealth of material on the political, social, and religious history of the period prior to 1727, there have been few records concerned with the Baptists. Recently, however, a few items of interest and importance have come to light.

Benjamin Laker, formerly known only as Paul Palmer's father-in-law, was a General Baptist before 1700. His social and political background can be traced in the early records of North Carolina. Laker was a resident of Perquimans Precinct as early as 1685 when the Precinct recorded the death of his daughter, Elizabeth.[93] He continued to live in the same location for the rest of his life. Laker quickly gained a place of prominence in the Precinct both as a landowner and as a political figure. By 1690, he was included in the list of Councilmen for the Precinct and in 1694, he served on the Grand Jury for the General Court.[94] He later served as General Court Justice, one of the highest offices in the court system.[95] His political career was enhanced further by the marriage of his daughter, Sarah, to Thomas Harvey. Following Harvey's appointment as deputy governor of Carolina—governor of the northern section of the combined Carolinas—Laker was made a deputy to one of the Lords Proprietors and was accepted on the governor's council of advisers.[96] From 1690 to 1698, Laker's name appeared often in the Colonial Records. In almost every entry, the records indicated a position of importance.

On May 17, 1696, Benjamin Laker married Juliana Tailor.[97] That marriage was to be significant in the continuing General Baptist story for Johanna, Juliana's daughter, eventually married Paul Palmer. No attempt has been made to prove that the Laker family converted Palmer to the General Baptist position, but it was important that he married into a family familiar with General Baptist tradition. At the very least, it made his work in North Carolina an easier task. In fact, George Stevenson concluded that it might be necessary to push the beginning of the General Baptist movement in North Carolina back beyond Palmer to Laker. George Washington Paschal determined that Palmer "gathered" the first church in North Carolina at Chowan, but Stevenson has suggested an alternative interpretation of the documents that Pashcal used.

> As to Dr. Paschal's statement that Paul Palmer 'gathered' the first General Baptist congregation, one must ask where is confirmation of this. What Palmer actually said to Comer and what Comer said in reporting Palmer was that Palmer 'settled' the Chowan congregation. The difference in the terms is very great. Comer gives an example of a church 'gathered' in one of the north-eastern colonies, but not 'settled' until ten years later when its first pastor was secured. Another case in point is the congregation at Cape May, N.J. A congregation was gathered here in 1702 by Abel Morgan; it was served by laymen acting as 'exhorters' for ten years; it was finally 'settled' in 1712 when Nathaniel Jenkins became its regular pastor. I will certainly agree that Palmer 'settled' the Chowan congregation, but to say that he 'gathered' it, or that he founded the first Baptist congregation in North Carolina seems to me repugnant to the known facts of Benjamin Laker and the 1702 congregation (the congregation that appealed to England for leaders and books—author's note).[98]

> Although Palmer is generally given the sobriquet 'Father of North Carolina Baptists,' it seems probable from circumstances that the title properly belongs to Benjamin Laker.[99]

Though the Colonial Records failed to include any information on Laker's religious background, his will did give some insight into his Christian character and into his particular religious persuasion. The type of books he left behind indicated that he was a serious student of the

Scriptures. The fact that he listed the books as separate items at the very first of his will inferred that he considered them among his most valuable possessions. To George Blighten he left his copy of *An Exposition Upon the Five Books of Moses,* and to his daughter, Sarah Harvey, he bequeathed *Church Principles* written by the English General Baptist leader, Thomas Grantham.[100] The wording of his will left little doubt as to his love for Christ:

> I bequeath my Soul into the hands of Almighty God hoping for Salvation thro Christ my Redeemer & my body to a Christian buriall to be buried att the discretion of my Execu-trix hereafter Named. . . .[101]

The new evidence concerning Laker's background has at least given a new picture of the period before formal organization of the first General Baptist church by Paul Palmer in 1727. Baptist historians agree that the Baptists came to North Carolina at least as early as 1695,[102] but they failed to identify the type of Baptists that made their home in the early settlements of old Albemarle.[103] The will of Benjamin Laker provided the first clear evidence that the earliest Baptists in North Carolina included those of a General persuasion.

The General Baptist Plea for Help—One other early source indicated that the first Baptists in North Carolina were part of the General camp and that they worshiped as a congregation even though they had not reached a level of organization. In 1702, twenty-five years before the first church was organized, the General Baptists in Carolina wrote to the General Baptists in England asking for help. They desperately needed a minister, but also asked for books if the more important need could not be met. The association recorded their response to the letter in their minutes for June 1702:

> . . . Whereas our Brethren of the Baptist persevation [sic] and of the Generall Faith who have their aboad in Caralina have desiered us to Supply them wth a Ministry or with books, we being not able at present to doe the former have collected ye Sum of Seven pounds twelve Shillings wch wth wt can be farther obtain'd we have put into the hands of our Bror S Keeling to Supply ym wth ye latter. & yt ye sd Bror Keeling do wright a letter to them in the name of this Assemly.[104]

The plea for help arrived in England less than a year after Benjamin Laker's will was probated in North Carolina. The death of a man of Laker's caliber—a layman of influence in both government and society—very well could have left the struggling group of worshipers in panic and occasioned the desperate cry for help.

Since the two Carolinas had not been divided in 1702, there has been some controversy as to the source of the plea for help. It was mentioned earlier in this study that there also was a community of Baptists in the Charleston area before 1700.[105] Since these two settlements—the Charleston area to the south and the Albemarle regions to the north—were the only settlements in Carolina at that early date, the letter had to originate in one of them. W. T. Whitley concluded that the Baptists in Charleston ". . . naturally looked to the home country for Elders to guide their church."[106] He further argued that the English General Association resolution of 1702 was adopted to meet the needs of the Charleston community.[107]

Whitley obviously was in error for two important reasons: (1) William Screven had been pastor of the Charleston church at least since 1699, and possibly since 1683,[108] and (2) the church at Charleston was decidedly Calvinistic in doctrine.[109] It does not follow that a church with a settled pastor and a Calvinistic majority would send to the General Baptists in England for help. The only logical conclusion must be that the 1702 plea came from the Albemarle region of North Carolina where the small, unorganized group of worshipers struggled without leadership.

These two factors—the General Baptist background of Benjamin Laker and the plea for help from the North Carolina General Baptists—would indicate that Paul Palmer came to his new field to find that it was already prepared to some small degree and that it was ready for cultivation.

THE GENERAL BAPTIST PICTURE IN NORTH CAROLINA AFTER PALMER

The Extended Influence of Joseph Parker—In spite of the fact that Paul Palmer established the first General Baptist churches in North Carolina, Joseph Parker became the more important figure in the continuing General Baptist story. His extended ministry and his missionary travels to the area that was to become the breeding ground for the Free Will Baptists also made him the more probable candidate for a link between the two groups.

Joseph Parker had been a part of the General Baptist movement in North Carolina from its beginning. His signature was included among the charter members on the letter to John Comer in 1729, and he was the only pastor of that first congregation.[110] Like Palmer, he was a part of the initial organization, blessed with a ministry that lasted almost 50 years longer than that of his fellow minister.[111]

In his early ministry, Joseph married Sarah Welch, the daughter of John Welch, another member of the church in Chowan Precinct.[112] The young couple soon left their home and joined others who were leaving the Albemarle region for less thickly settled lands to the west. By about 1730, Parker and his wife had settled at Meherrin near the present town of Murfreesboro.[113] Before five years had passed, the young preacher established a General Baptist church—a church that continued to bear the banner for the General Baptists for 59 years, and the church that became the center of missionary outreach for the movement in eastern North Carolina.[114] In 1735, Parker and his people built their first meeting house at the western edge of the present city limits. Parker donated the property for the church building.[115]

After almost twelve years at Meherrin, Parker again moved his center of operation, this time securing a land grant in Edgecombe County to the west and south of Meherrin.[116] By this time, a pattern had developed in Parker's work that he would follow for the rest of his ministry. Here, as at Meherrin, he secured land, preached his doctrine of general atonement, and made provision for the establishment of a church. By 1748, he had established the Lower Fishing Creek Church near Enfield.[117]

Before Parker's ministry at Meherrin ended, another facet of his evangelistic pattern assumed a clear and permanent identity. The additional aspect was not a new one. It had been at the heart of

General Baptist practice in the state since the first church had been established in Chowan Precinct. Parker continued and improved the practice of making an initial church organization a mission center from which other churches would be established. Paul Palmer left the Chowan church as soon as it gained strength and traveled to Pasquotank Precinct to establish a church in the home of William Burgess.[118] Joseph Parker moved to Meherrin and made it his center of operation. By 1740, the church there had established an "arm" or "branch" at Bertie near what was to become the town of Roxobel.[119] Though it has not been established conclusively that Parker founded the arms of the Lower Fishing Creek Church at Swift Creek and at Rocky Swamp,[120] the two daughter churches fit the pattern Parker had employed earlier and would continue to use for the remainder of his ministry. Some controversy surrounded the dating of Parker's departure from Edgecombe County. S. J. Wheeler, author of a history of the Meherrin church, omitted Parker's work in Edgecombe and contended that he remained at Meherrin until 1773. More recent historians have recognized that Parker was in Edgecombe County by 1742, but they have failed to establish the length of his stay there. Morgan Edwards gave some light on the matter by revealing that Parker had baptized Jeptha Vining at Little Contentnea Creek in 1761,[121] but until recently, no more precise dating was available. Edwards' information, however, did make it clear that Parker again had moved his mission center to a new location.

The discovery of a deed between Jacob Blount and Joseph Parker established an earlier date for Parker's removal from Edgecombe County. The deed was dated December 25, 1756, and recorded Parker's purchase of approximately 100 acres of Blount's land between Little and Great Contentnea Creeks in what was then Craven County.[122]

By 1761, Parker had established a church on Little Contentnea and following his now familiar pattern had made it a mission center from which other churches would be organized. In a short time, Little Creek church had "arms" at Wheat Swamp and Louson Swamp in the present Lenoir County and in the Conetoe settlements (Gum Swamp) of Pitt County.[123]

Joseph Parker continued to serve his churches until his death in 1791 or 1792. Asplund's *Register* revealed he was still at Little Creek in 1790.[124] His ministry extended over a period of 64 years, and he was responsible for the establishment of a possible nine churches in five counties. The sheer magnitude of his work demanded that his contributions to the General Baptist movement in North Carolina be reconsidered.

Whether a definite link existed between Parker and the Free Will Baptists or not, he surely laid the groundwork for their entrance into the religious arena of eastern North Carolina. He opened the area of their first growth to the type of preaching that would characterize their movement from the beginning, preaching there for 30 years on the basis of the same confession of faith that the Free Will Baptists would adopt before 1812.[125] For a history of the Free Will Baptists in North Carolina, Joseph Parker has become the most important figure in the period of development before 1800.

The Influence of William Parker—One other member of the Parker family deserves brief mention. William Parker, probably a cousin of Joseph's,[126] also enjoyed an extended ministry among the early General Baptists. Little information concerning his early ministry has survived, but he probably became pastor of the Meherrin church soon after Joseph left for Edgecombe County in

1742.[127] He still held that office when Morgan Edwards traveled through North Carolina in 1772 and when John Asplund came to the state in 1790.[128]

R. K. Hearn, an early Free Will Baptist historian and a native of the Gum Swamp area in Pitt County, also identified William Parker as the founder of the General Baptist church at Gum Swamp.[129] Hearn grew up within three miles of the church and was familiar with members of the church who had known Parker before his death.[130]

Both Joseph and William Parker preached at Gum Swamp,[131] but the church was a good distance from Meherrin and William's visits were probably few. He remained pastor of the Meherrin church until his death.

Lemuel Burkitt and Jesse Read, co-authors of a history of the Kehukee Association (Regular Baptists), characterized William Parker as an unorthodox, careless minister who baptized the saved and the unsaved alike, arguing that:

> . . . The customary way with him in receiving members, was to baptize all who were
> willing, and requested it. In consequence of which he baptized many, as he required
> no experience previous to their admission.[132]

The charge of negligence had been brought against the General Baptists many times—a charge that their Regular Baptist opponents probably felt was justified. It was true that the General Baptists denied the necessity of a dramatic experience that indicated the moment of salvation and that they received members on the basis of a simple profession of faith in Christ. Their standards did not require the type of experience that the Regulars demanded. Their *Confession of Faith* contended that:

> . . . the way set forth by God for men to be justified in, is by faith in Christ, Rom. 5:1.
>
> That is to say, when men shall assent to the truth of the Gospel, believing with all
> their hearts, that there is remission of sins, and eternal life to be had in Christ.[133]

There was no indication that William Parker fell short of the demands of the General Baptist faith or that he was anything less than a godly, faithful minister of the gospel. His ministry was especially important to the people of the Meherrin vicinity. In 1790, John Asplund listed Meherrin as the only Baptist church in Hertford County,[134] and S. J. Wheeler, clerk of the Meherrin church from 1838 to 1867, has contended that William Parker was the only gospel witness in the county in 1790.[135]

Hearn also credited William Parker with the establishment of churches at Grimsley in Greene County and at Louson Swamp in Lenoir.[136] S. J. Wheeler probably was correct, however, in recognizing Joseph Parker as the founder of the church at Louson Swamp.[137] Both the churches were near Little Creek and probably were arms of that church.

Like Joseph Parker, William became an especially important figure in the preparations for the coming of the Free Will Baptists. He enjoyed a long and fruitful ministry and remained loyal to the

General Baptist faith during the dark days when other General Baptists yielded to reorganization and became Regular Baptists.

The two Parkers set the stage for Free Will Baptist development in eastern North Carolina.

The Extent of Growth
The Factors Leading to Rapid Growth

Colonial Carolina offered a fertile field of opportunity to those dissenting Christians that settled within its boundaries. Carolina was unique, a land of freedom and promise. John H. Wheeler, describing Colonial North Carolina, declared that:

> No freer country was ever organized by man. Freedom of conscience, security from taxation except by their own consent, were their first objects. No one could recover a debt, the cause of action of which arose out of the colony, within five years; the emigrant was exempted from taxation for a year; every emigrant received a bounty of land.[138]

Thomas M. Pittman supposed that the uniqueness of North Carolina was due to its birth in the era of the "new and modern England" that emerged after the restoration of Charles II in 1660.

> . . . The secret of her difference from the states which lie to her north is that she is the child of a new era. She was born free; and the Revolution, the Commonwealth, the Restoration—the transformation of the old 'merrie' England with her narrowness and intolerance and bigotry, into modern England with the seriousness and purity, the spirit of civil and religious liberty wrought into her life and character through the Puritan influence, are our heritage.[139]

Though it is quite certain that one could not establish so great a change in England even as late as the publication of the "Act of Toleration," it was evident that a new flavor of toleration pervaded the early stages of development in North Carolina. Pittman was not far wrong in his final conclusion that the Lords Proprietors had " . . . embodied in their form of government . . . provisions, which would attract dissenters. . ." to their shores.[140]

Three major elements in the unique religious atmosphere of North Carolina contributed to the rapid growth of the dissenting Baptists: (1) the character of the settlers, (2) the guarantees of religious liberty provided by the government, and (3) the failure of establishment by the Church of England.

THE CHARACTER OF THE SETTLERS
IN COLONIAL NORTH CAROLINA

The first settlers in North Carolina made themselves at home in the atmosphere of freedom that their new land offered. They were simple people with simple needs, but they were also a determined people—people that accepted freedom as their heritage and demanded that it be preserved for them. They were characterized as men ". . . who were as free as the air of their mountains; and when oppressed were as rough as the billow of the ocean. They submitted to no unjust laws, they bowed their knee to no earthly monarch."[141] J. D. Huffman added that:

> . . . First of all and above all, they were religious. The desire to be free in the higher concerns of the soul led them to make homes in the wilderness, and the freedom which they craved for themselves they extended to others. Next they loved civil liberty. Those who had not so much as heard of Hobbes or John Locke, held that political power resides originally in the people; that rulers exercise only delegated powers; that exceeding the authority delegated to them, or using it for purposes other than the general weal, they are to be resisted and removed.[142]

The early settlers of the state lived up to part of their description, deposing Thomas Miller, Acting Governor and Collector of Customs, in 1677, when he attempted to enforce an export tax of a penny a pound on their tobacco sales.[143] On the other hand, however, Huffman might have been overly enthusiastic in his description of the religious character of the people. One should not suppose that all the early settlers favored other churches over that of England or even that all were religious. North Carolina had its share of non-Christian inhabitants—men who interpreted "freedom of conscience" to mean freedom to believe nothing. No stretch of the imagination would allow the conclusion that all those who fought establishment in North Carolina were seeking the privilege to worship freely as Baptists or Quakers. The central element in the character of the people was more likely love for freedom than love for Christ.[144] While some were godly and others were godless, all were jealous of their rights and privileges as new men in a new land. Their motives were totally different, but both groups despised and feared establishment. Together they made a majority that was to make an effective establishment impossible. Even after a token establishment was achieved,[145] North Carolina continued to be a land of opportunity for those who could not accept the Church of England.[146]

THE GUARANTEE OF RELIGIOUS LIBERTY PROVIDED BY THE GOVERNMENT

Proprietary Charter—Though their motives might have been monetary rather than religious, the Lords Proprietors asked for and received a charter from Charles II that guaranteed religious liberty for their holdings in America.[147] The charter, dated March 24/April 3, 1662/1663 and entitled "The Proprietary Charter of Carolina," described the freedom that was to be allowed in the new colony:

> . . . And because it may happen that some of the people . . . of the said province, cannot in their private opinions, conform to the publick exercise of religion, according to the liturgy, form and ceremonies of the church of England, or take and subscribe the oaths and articles, made and established in that behalf, and for that the same, by reason of the remoted distances of these places, will, we hope, be no breach of the uni-

formity established in this nation, our will and pleasure therefore is, and we do . . . give and grant unto the [Proprietors]. . . . full and free license, liberty and authority, by such legal ways and means as they shall think fit, to give and grant unto such person or persons. . . . who really in their judgments, and for their conscience sake, cannot or shall not conform to the said liturgy and ceremonies, and take and subscribe the oaths and articles aforesaid. . . . such indulgences and dispensations in that behalf. . . . as they in their discretion think fit and reasonable; . . .[148]

The Degree of Freedom—Though the charter left the degree of freedom in the hands of the Proprietors, they did not seem to abuse the privilege. Except for the simple requirement that settlers stop short of disturbing the peace and well-being of the colony, the religious freedom of Carolina was quite complete.[149] Even after North Carolina became a colony of the crown in 1729,[150] the restrictions on religious liberty were simple and few. In his instructions from the King in 1730, George Burrington, the Royal Governor of the province, was instructed to:

. . . permit a liberty of conscience of all persons (except papists) so as they be contented with a quiet and peaceable enjoyment of the same not giving offence or scandal to the Governt.[151]

The Baptists took advantage of the guarantees provided by the government and used their freedom to develop the largest and most powerful religious group in North Carolina in the first half of the eighteenth century.[152]

THE FAILURE OF ESTABLISHMENT

Last but not least, Baptist growth in North Carolina was phenomenal because they had no competition. David D. Oliver, in "The Society for the Propagation of the Gospel in the Province of North Carolina," has suggested three basic causes for the failure of the Church of England in the state: (1) the lack of a Bishop in North America, (2) the unworthy character of many of the early missionaries, and (3) the lack of encouragement given to the missionaries by the people and by the Society.[153]

The Need for a Bishop—The distance from England's Bishop prohibited any close supervision of the struggling establishment and denied North Carolina the necessary provisions of discipline and a native clergy. The few missionaries that were sent to the colony knew little of the people or of the conditions that were to be faced in a pioneer environment.[154] The hardships of the new colony defeated them before they began.

The Character of the Clergy—North Carolina received more than its share of scoundrels in missionary clothing. Oliver contended that in many cases ". . . those clergymen who were not actually vicious were weaklings."[155] Governor Henderson Walker wrote to the Bishop of London in 1703, complaining about the conduct of the first missionary, Daniel Brett:

... He for about half a year behaved himself in a modest manner, but after that, in a most horrid manner, broke out in such an extravagant course that I am ashamed to express his carriage, it being in so high a nature. It hath been a great trouble and grief to us who have a great veneration for the Church, that the first minister who was sent to us should prove so ill as to give the dissenter so much occasion to charge us with him. . . .[156]

A few years later, Rev. Henry Gerrard took advantage of the more advanced parish in Chowan Precinct and convinced the vestry that he should be allowed to be minister of the one parish. The missionary was so impressive that the vestry added twenty-five extra pounds of yearly salary to the convenience of a settled ministry—a convenience that had not entered the dreams of his predecessors.[157] Gerrard's good fortune was not destined to last, however, and soon the vestry was in an uproar over reports of his "scandalous conduct." In 1706, after he was accused of ". . . debauched practices which tends highly to the dishonor of God and the scandal of the church . . ."[158] the missionary's name disappeared from the records of the colony. The documents have recorded no evidence that he defended himself against the charges.

In 1710, John Urmstone arrived in North Carolina and added a new page to the list of atrocities credited to the English missionaries. Francis L. Hawks, the author of a nineteenth century history of North Carolina, complained that Urmstone ". . . in twelve years, did more to retard the spread of Christianity and the growth of the Church of England in Carolina, than all other causes combined."[159]

It cannot be denied that some of the English missionaries were an asset to their church. Rev. James Adams, the predecessor of John Urmstone, had been characterized as a "true minister of Christ," and his co-worker, William Gordon, could be accused only of the sin of discouragement at the magnitude of his task.[160] The work of a few good men slowed the collapse of the efforts at establishment, but their influence for good could not outweigh the evil influence of their fellows. The worst were so bad that the best were not long remembered.

The Lack of Encouragement Given to the Missionaries by the Society and by the People—It has already been mentioned that the great distance between the Bishop and the colony prohibited any effective degree of communication. When a representative of the Society spent the stipend of twenty pounds allowed all missionaries and the personal donations he had gathered from his friends,[161] he found himself completely on his own. The leaders of the Society could not understand the drastic conditions their missionaries faced, nor could they believe the vestry in the parishes would withhold the salaries that had been established. John Urmstone continuously complained to the Society that his needs were not being met and that he desperately needed the aid of his employers, but his pleas most often were ignored.

The failure of the Society was a small problem compared to the problems the missionary faced on his field of service. The majority of the settlers in North Carolina were antagonistic toward establishment and refused to support the Church of England. More importantly, however, the members of the establishment itself had little concern for the church or for its ministers. William Byrd, a Virginian commissioned to determine the boundary line between North Carolina and Virginia, was astounded at the indifference of the church people in the state to the south concerning the baptism of their children.

> . . . If a parson come in their way, they will crave a cast of his office, as they call it, else they are content their offspring should remain as arrant pagans as themselves. They account among their greatest advantages that they are not priest ridden, not remembering that the clergy is rarely guilty of bestriding such as have the misfortune to be poor. One thing may be said for the inhabitants of that province, that they are not troubled with any religious fumes, and have the least superstition of any people living. They do not know Sunday from any other day, any more than Robinson Crusoe did. . . .[162]

In 1733, Governor Burrington wrote to England concerning the state of religion in North Carolina. His letter revealed the attitude of the people:

> There is not one clergyman of the Church of England, regularly settled in this Government. The former Missionarys were so little approved of, that the Inhabitants seem very indifferent, whither any more come to them.[163]

The greatest complaint was that the parishioners refused to support the missionaries financially. Salaries had been agreed upon, but the vestry either could not or would not collect the taxes that were designed to supply the need. John Urmstone said of the people that ". . . this paying of money puts them quite out of humor; they cannot endure to be at charges upon what they value so little as religion.[164]

The establishment became its own greatest enemy. When the failures of the clergy and the indifference of the parishioners were added to the obstacles faced in the stubborn nature of the settlers, the establishment crumbled. The one opponent that could have slowed the growth of the Baptists had failed. The door to success was left open, and the Baptists passed through to enjoy phenomenal growth and influence throughout eastern North Carolina.

The Churches and Their Spreading Influence

Necessity demanded that most of the churches founded in the first period of concern be considered earlier in conjunction with the leaders that were responsible for their organization. Since repetition of former discussion would add nothing to the study, those churches that were considered in detail simply will be listed in this section of the outline. It will be necessary to look at some churches of later origin, but concern here will be limited to the first years of reaping which continued to the beginning of the period of reorganization about 1755. It should be remembered that during the early years all the churches were General Baptist.

The growth of the General Baptist movement during the period was extraordinary in the number of churches established and in the degree of influence exerted in the colony. A simple list of the churches and the details of their organization would not tell the whole story. J. D. Huffman concluded that from 1700 to 1757 this energetic, evangelistic band of Baptists provided most of North Carolina's spiritual enlightenment:

> . . . For more than fifty years, 1700-'57, they [the Baptists] gave to the people of the State almost all the preaching that they heard. Of Presbyterian and Lutheran preachers there were none. The spirit of evangelization had been dying out among the Quakers since 1715, and they had never been very numerous or generally distributed through-out the State. Under Governor Tryon the Episcopalians had the largest number they ever had at one time, and then only for a little while. . . .[165]

According to Morgan Edwards, the movement had grown to a total of sixteen churches by the end of the period.[166] His total was given in the introduction of his study of North Carolina and did not include a number of the branches of the original churches that he listed in the text. He also failed to include the last church that Paul Palmer organized at New River in Onslow County. Finally, Edwards completely overlooked a General Baptist church that applied to the General Court in 1741 for registration of a meeting house at Flea Point on the Bay and Neuse Rivers. Though Edwards list-ed the branches of the major General Baptist churches, he did not indicate the date of their organ-ization. In many cases, the only date available was that of their constitution as Particular Baptist churches during the reorganization period. Even without the churches of questionable date, how-ever, a more accurate account of General Baptist progress in the early period would include at least twenty churches.

THE EARLIER PALMER-PARKER-BURGESS WORK

The founders of a number of the churches have not been identified, but the majority of those churches that left records were established by Paul Palmer, Joseph Parker, and William Burgess. The churches at Chowan, Pasquotank, Meherrin, Lower Fishing Creek, Swift Creek, Bertie, and New River have been discussed at some length, but at least one other church credited to this branch of the movement should be discussed.

The Church at Swift Creek in Craven County—Earlier discussion indicated that Paul Palmer and Joseph Parker were the more active members of the initial General Baptist movement in eastern North Carolina. Palmer limited himself entirely to evangelistic work, and Parker moved at least three times before he finally settled in Dobbs County. William Burgess, on the other hand, settled at the Pasquotank church and continued to minister there until his death. While Parker con-tinued to engage in extensive itinerant work even after he settled down, the documents recorded only one missionary journey for Burgess. The trip resulted in the establishment of a church on Swift Creek in Craven County, about twelve miles from the city of New Bern.[167]

George Washington Paschal identified this church with a group of New Bern dissenters that applied to the General Court in 1740 for permission to build a meeting house.[168] The petitioners appealed to the court on the basis of English and colony guarantees that Protestant dissenters would be allowed to worship in their own way as long as they pledged their allegiance to the King. The sig-natures of two General Baptist preachers, William and Thomas Fulsher, identified the petition as the work of a congregation of that persuasion.[169] The petition initially was denied, but the decision was reversed after the petitioners accepted the "Test Oath" required of dissenters. The oath, used in conjunction with the oath of allegiance to the King, simply demanded a denial of the Catholic doctrine of transubstantiation—the change of the substance of the bread and wine into the body and blood of Christ in the Eucharist service.[170]

The church at Swift Creek continued as a General Baptist church until it was reorganized on the Particular plan in 1756.[171]

THE WORK OF WILLIAM SOJOURNER AND JOSIAH HART

Josiah Hart had been present in North Carolina for at least nine years before the arrival of William Sojourner at Kehukee[172] and should not be mistaken for a product of the General Baptist movement in Virginia. However, Hart and Sojourner did form an alliance almost immediately; and, for convenience sake, the General Baptist work in their area will be considered under the same division in the outline.

Since the churches at Kehukee, Falls of Tar River, Upper Fishing Creek, and Great Cohara already have been discussed, the study at this point will be limited to the two additional churches that grew out of the influence of these two men.

The Church on Bay and Neuse Rivers—In June 1741, the Bath County Court refused the application of a group of Protestant dissenters for registration of a meeting house on Bay River. On April 25, 1742, the persistent group again submitted their application, this time asking for the registration of two meeting houses.[173] The petition, addressed to Chief Justice Montgomery, reminded the Justice of their earlier failure and continued:

> ..... Therefore as Children to a father, for Relief, so we come to your honour, humbly praying that your honour would be graciously pleased to treat our petition & grant us the house of Mr. Robert Spring & the house of Mr. Nathaniel Draper of Flea Point, formerly belonging to Mr. Amos Cutrel, that we may have the sd houses Registered for places of public Worship; it being a Reasonable request agreeable to the Laws of the Land. . . .[174]

The wording of the petition did not allow a definite conclusion as to whether the group planned to continue as one congregation enjoying the convenience of two houses, or if they had determined to expand into two congregations.

As had been true in the New Bern petition, the Flea Point document was identified as a General Baptist work by its signatures. The signatures included the now important names of Josiah Hart and William Fulsher, plus the name of George Graham who later was to become pastor of the General Baptist church at Bear Creek.[175] The documents did not indicate that Josiah Hart established the church, but it was usually his custom to lead in the task of organization. William Fulsher, whose name appeared on the New Bern petition in 1740, was also a veteran in the field of church planting and probably had a large part in the work at Flea Point. Fulsher spent all of his ministry in the general area of these two churches in Craven and Beaufort Counties.[176]

The Church at Pungo—Morgan Edwards credited one other church to the work of Josiah Hart—the church at Pungo in Beaufort County.[177] This church became an important part of the continuing history of the General Baptist movement as it joined Little Creek (Contantony), Meherrin, and Bear River in refusing to join the swing to the Particular Baptists.[178] The church was organized in 1742,[179] during the productive period between 1740 and 1742 when the Baptists in Craven and Beaufort Counties suddenly came to life and established the churches at Swift Creek, Flea Point, and Pungo.

THE REMAINING CHURCHES IN THE EARLY PERIOD

Six other churches were established before 1755, but the records have not preserved the names of their founders.

The churches at Bear Creek, Grassy Creek, Tar River, and Red Banks demanded little attention, but their two sister churches at Toisnot and Flat Swamp played a somewhat more important role in the history of the movement.

The Church at Toisnot—Lemuel Burkitt and Jesse Read, coauthors of a history of the Kehukee Baptist Association, have contended that the church at Toisnot did not achieve organization until it was organized as a Particular Baptist church in 1756.[180] They did admit, however, that the congregation had gathered earlier on the General plan. The congregation actually had been in existence as early as 1748 when Josiah Hart visited there and baptized John Thomas.[181] Thomas later was ordained as pastor and through his sons, John and Jonathan, became responsible for spreading the General message as far west as the area that was to become Wake County.[182] The Toisnot church was located south of the Tar River and represented the first effort to evangelize the field that was to demand all the attention of Joseph Parker in the last years of his ministry.

The Church at Flat Swamp—Burkitt and Read indicated their attitude toward the General Baptists in their treatment of the early history of the church at Flat Swamp in Pitt County. After revealing that the Flat Swamp church had met with difficulty after becoming Particular Baptist, they added:

> . . . as the love of some of her members began to wax cold, it gave an opportunity to the enemy of the souls to sow seeds of discord amongst them, which caused the Arminians and Universalians [sic] to look out of their dens, where they had been driven by the refulgent beams of gospel truth.[183]

The General Baptist church at Flat Swamp became a victim of Particular Baptist reorganization in 1755,[184] leaving a small, struggling remnant that had neither pastor nor church property. They caused little problem until about 1795 when the unrest in the Particular church gave them courage to surface again.

The church at Flat Swamp was located near an area known as the Conetoe settlement where Joseph and William Parker had established a mission point and where they continued a periodic program of preaching.[185] The Parker work was just fifteen miles from Flat Swamp, and R. K. Hearn has concluded that it was this group that was the source of the Particular Baptist problems mentioned in Burkitt and Read.[186] Hearn further argued that the friction between the General and

Particular Baptists in Pitt County led to the use of a new name for the General Baptists. In scorn, the Particular Baptists termed their opponents "Freewillers"[187]—a name that was to become more and more popular in the closing years of the 18th century.

The Full Extent of Growth—The full extent of General Baptist growth during the first period of concern can best be shown in table form.

Table I

General Baptist Churches in North Carolina in 1755[a]

Church	Date/Location Estab. (County)	Founder
Chowan	1727 Chowan	Paul Palmer
Pasquotank (Shiloh)[b]	1729 Pasquotank (Camden)[c]	Paul Palmer
Meherrin	1735 Hertford[d]	Joseph Parker
Bertie (Sandy Run)	1740 Bertie	Joseph Parker
Swift Creek	1740 Craven	William Burgess William Fulsher
Kehukee	1742 Halifax	William Soujourner
Flea Point	1742 Beaufort	Josiah Hart William Fulsher
Pungo	1742 Beaufort	Josiah Hart
New River	1742 Onslow	Paul Palmer
Falls of Tar River	1744 Nash	(Daughter of Kehukee)
Upper Fishing Creek	1745 Halifax	Josiah Hart
Lower Fishing Creek (Daniel's Meeting House)	1748 Edgecombe	Joseph Parker
Swift Creek	...... Edgecombe	Joseph Parker
Tar River	1749 Granville	
Great Cohara (Rowan)	1749 Sampson	Edward Brown
Toisnot	...... Edgecombe	
Bear Creek	1752 Dobbs (Lenoir)[e]	
Grassy Creek	...... Granville	
Red Banks	...... Pitt	
Flat Swamp	...... Pitt	

ᵃ The table was compiled from the sketches found in Edwards, "Furman MS"; Edwards, "Tour"; Huggins, *History;* Burkitt and Read, *Concise History;* Hearn, *Origin;* Wheeler, *Parker's;* and Paschal, *North Carolina.*

ᵇ The church was called Pasquotank and Burgess Meeting House until 1812 when the name was changed to Shiloh (Wheeler, *Parker's,* p. 5).

ᶜ Camden County was formed from the old Pasquotank Precinct in 1777 (David Leroy Corbitt, *The Formation of North Carolina Counties, 1663-1943* [Raleigh: State Department of Archives and History, 1950], 56. Hereinafter referred to as *Counties*).

ᵈ The church was established in what is now Hertford County. The county was not established until 1759 (Corbitt, *Counties,* 122).

ᵉ Lenoir County was formed from Dobbs in 1791 (Corbitt, *Counties,* 136).

Summary

Though other General Baptist groups were present much earlier, the Free Will Baptist denomination contends that their first witness in America can be traced back to the General Baptist work of Paul Palmer and Joseph Parker in North Carolina in 1727.

A General Baptist work had been organized at Burley in Virginia as early as 1714 and a part of that congregation later moved to North Carolina. At least four North Carolina churches grew out of the Virginia influence and represented the foundation of an older strain of General Baptists in the state. By 1759, however, all four churches had been reorganized as Particular Baptist churches and the Virginia influence was broken.

The General Baptist movement in South Carolina did not reach an organizational stage until 1736 and was limited to one church near Charleston. The work was dead by 1791.

Though Paul Palmer had organized the first General Baptist churches in North Carolina, he soon disappeared from the field of activity. From the viewpoint of the Free Will Baptists, Joseph and William Parker became the more important figures in the continuing history of the General Baptist movement. Joseph Parker had been a part of the first General Baptist church in 1727 and his ministry lasted for more than sixty years. He had introduced the General faith to the area south of the Tar River in Pitt, Greene, and Lenoir Counties where the Free Will Baptists would enjoy their first and most important growth. With his cousin, William Parker, he led the battle to preserve the doctrine that the Free Will Baptists would continue to preach after the name of their earlier counterpart had been forgotten.

Notes for Chapter 2

[1]Henry C. Vedder, *A Short History of the Baptists* (Philadelphia: The American Baptist Publication Society, 1907), 292. (Hereinafter referred to as *Short History*.)

[2]Richard D. Knight, *History of the General or Six Principle Baptists in Europe and America* (Providence, R.I.: Smith and Parmenter, Printers, 1827), 317, 318. (Hereinafter referred to as *Six Principle Baptists*.)

[3]This problem is of particular importance because part of this earlier group moved to North Carolina and became a part of the General Baptists there. It will be necessary to show that these churches did not continue to exist up to the time of the emergence of the Free Will Baptist identity and so predate Paul Palmer and his work.

[4]The entry in the Journal of Thomas Story, a Quaker preacher, for January 23, 1699, stated, ". . . we had a meeting at York City at the house of Thos. Bonger, a preacher among the General Baptists. . . ." Quoted in Garnett Ryland, *The Baptists of Virginia, 1699-1926* (Richmond: The Virginia Baptist Board of Missions and Education, 1955), 1. Used by permission.

[5]David Benedict, *A General History of the Baptist Denomination in America and Other Parts of the World* (2 vols.; Boston: Lincoln & Edmands, 1813), 11, 23, 24. (Hereinafter referred to as *General History*.)

[6]John Hamerstley, Personal Letter to Nicholas Eyres, dated 1742, quoted in Robert B. Semple, *A History of the Rise and Progress of the Baptists in Virginia*. (Richmond: John Lynch, Printer, 1810), 444, 445. (Hereinafter referred to as *Rise and Progress*.) Norden's death in America has been questioned since the General Baptist minutes recorded permission for him to return to England in 1725. Virginia records, however, have recorded the inventory of the estate of "Robert Norden, Dec'd." (W. T. Whitley, "General Baptists in Carolina and Virginia," *Crozer Quarterly*, XIII [January 1936], 26, 27. [Hereinafter referred to as "Carolina and Virginia."])

[7]Benedict, *General History*, 11, 24.

[8]Clarence H. Urner, "Early Baptist Records in Prince George County, Virginia," *The Virginia Magazine of History and Biography*, XLI (April 1933), 98, 99. (Hereinafter referred to as "Early Baptist Records.") Isaac Backus, in his editorial of the Leland work, listed the pastor of the Prince George church as Richard Norden. Leland, on the basis of the editorial note, speculated on the possibility of the two Nordens in the state. Backus had obtained his information from a letter written in 1742 in which the correspondent, John Hamerstley, used the different name (Semple, *Rise and Progress*, 444, 445). Backus evidently had accepted the error and had continued its use in his own writing. The original records have given a final solution. There was only one Norden to serve the General Baptists in Virginia. The correct name was Robert. The date of his application for license, June 14, 1715, indicates that the Burley work came first and was the center of operation. A copy of the application for license also may be found in Whitley, "Carolina and Virginia," 25, 26.

[9]Urner, "Early Baptist Records," 99.

[10]Ibid., 99, 100.

[11]Benedict, *General History*, 11, 24.

[12]Ibid.

[13]Morgan Edwards, "Materials Toward a History of the Baptists in the Province of Virginia." (Furman manuscript). vol. 3 of *Materials Toward a History of the Baptists in the Provinces of Maryland, Virginia, North Carolina, South Carolina, Georgia* (MS, 1772), III, 21, 22. Two sets of manuscripts have been preserved. One remains in the Furman Collection in South Carolina and the other became a part of the Crozer Collection. Since there are a number of differences in the two texts, they will be referred to as "Furman MS" and "Crozer MS."

The presence of Casper Mintz at Burley in 1756 would seem to confirm the fact that the Surry church returned to the mother church and ceased to exist as a separate body.

[14]Morgan Edwards, *Tour of Rev. Morgan Edwards of Pennsylvania, To the American Baptists in North Carolina in 1772-73* (Copied from the original manuscript, in the possession of Mr. Horatio Gates Jones, of

Philadelphia, by J. E. Birdsong, Librarian, for the N.C. State Library, Raleigh: June 24th, 1889), 24-40. (Hereinafter referred to as *Tours*.)

[15]Edwards, "Furman MS," IV, 131, 132.

[16]Ibid., 17.

[17]Lemuel Burkitt and Jesse Read, (in *A Concise History of the Kehukee Baptist Association From its Original Rise to the Present Time* [Halifax, N.C.: Printed by A. Hodge, 1803], 229), have indicated that the church on Upper Fishing Creek was established by Josiah Hart. His close alliance with Sojourner evidently caused Morgan Edwards to include the church as an arm of Kehukee. (Burkitt and Read hereinafter will be referred to as *Concise History*.)

[18]*Minutes of the Kehukee Association, North Carolina, 1769-1778*, MS. p. 1. Morgan Edwards, in (Edwards, "Tours," 28), substituted Pasquotank for the Church in Pitt County. According to Edwards, the Kehukee Association was organized August 3, 1769. By that time, the reorganization of the General Baptist churches as Particular churches virtually was complete. Though Fishing Creek did not become a charter member of the association, it had been a Particular Baptist church since 1756 and had employed much influence in the reorganization process.

[19]The organization of the General Baptist churches will be investigated more carefully in Chapter III.

[20]A. H. Newman, *A History of the Baptist Churches in the United States* (Philadelphia: American Baptist Publication Society, 1894), 222, 223, (hereinafter referred to as *United States*); Whitley, *Carolina and Virginia*, 21, 22.

[21]Whitley, *Carolina and Virginia*, 22. Whitley indicated that these early South Carolina Baptists appealed to the English General Baptists for help in 1702.

[22]Leah Townsend, *South Carolina Baptists, 1670-1805* (Florence, S.C.: The Florence Printing Co., 1935), 5. (Hereinafter referred to as *South Carolina Baptists*.)

[23]Edwards, "Crozer MS," V, 22-23. Edwards contended that the General Baptists first separated from the Charleston church in 1733, but that official organization did not come until November 25, 1736. According to Leah Townsend the original break did not come until 1735 (Townsend, *South Carolina Baptists*, 54).

[24]Townsend, *South Carolina Baptists*, 13-15. Further trouble developed when Rev. Simmons was forced to vacate his pulpit by the majority of the Charleston church. He was restored to office by a small minority. The resulting furor caused some members of the majority group to erase their names from the church books.

[25]Edwards, "Crozer MS," V, 22, 23. "They originated as a distinct church in the year Nov. 25, 1736 when the following persons incorporated. Rev. Robert Ingram, Wm. Elliot, jun., Thos. Elliot, Wm. Elliot, Henry Toomer, Richard Butler, Joseph Elliot, Joshuah Toomer, George Timmons, Bernard Elliot, John Clifford, Thomas Tew, Thomas Davis, Dorothy Jones, Ann Bonwell [Bonneau in "Furman MS"], Ammerrintea Farr, Mary Toomer, Mary Toomer, jun., Ann Chidsey, Frances Elliot, Elizabeth Elliot." Rev. Ingram's name with the charter members of the church would indicate that Edwards' later date for formal organization, 1736, probably was correct. The long wait for organization was not unusual since the church did not have an ordained minister. Rev. Ingram was an English General Baptist. His call to the Stono church could not have come until quite late in 1733, and then probably had to go through the proper channels of the Assembly in England. From 1734 to June 1736, Ingram appeared in the minutes of the English General Assembly as a representative from Webstone in Sussex. His name disappeared from the records after that year. (W. T. Whitley, *Minutes of the General Assembly of the General Baptist Churches in England, with Kindred Records*, 2 vols.: London: Printed for the Society by the Kingsgate Press, 1910, I, 40, 41. [Hereinafter referred to as *General Assembly*.])

[26]Townsend, *South Carolina Baptists*, 15. George Stevenson placed Paul Palmer in South Carolina in 1735, suggesting that the General Baptists in Charleston invited him to speak to them concerning General Baptist theology. Palmer suggested that the small congregation appeal to Rhode Island for ministerial help but that avenue of assistance did not materialize. (George Stevenson, "Paul Palmer" in William S. Powell, ed. *Dictionary of North Carolina Biography*, Vol. V. [Chapel Hill: University of North Carolina Press, 1994], 12. [Hereinafter referred to as "Paul Palmer."])

[27]Ibid.

[28]Ibid., 14, 15.

[29]Ibid, 15.

[30]Ibid., 54, 55.

[31]Joe M. King, *A History of South Carolina Baptists* (Columbia: The General Board of the South Carolina Baptist Convention, 1964), 15, 16. (Hereinafter referred to as *History.*)

[32]Ibid.

[33]Edwards, "Furman MS," V. 8.

[34]Townsend, *South Carolina Baptists*, 57, 58.

[35]Ibid., 66.

[36]Ibid.

[37]Ibid.

[38]Townsend, *South Carolina Baptists,* 57, 58; Elmer T. Clark, *The Journal and Letters of Francis Asbury, 1771 to 1783* (London: Epworth Press, 1859), 484. Asbury stopped in Charleston Thursday, February 24, 1785, and obtained permission to use the empty General Baptist meeting house. That branch of the Stono church evidently ceased to meet even before the death of the main congregation at Stono.

[39]John Asplund, *The Annual Register of the Baptist Denomination in North America to the First of November, 1790,* 41. (Hereinafter referred to as *Register.*)

[40]Townsend, *South Carolina Baptists*, 193.

[41]Ibid.,193, 194.

[42]Edwards, "Furman MS," II, 3; Benedict, *General History*, II, 97; Torbet, *History*, pp. 236-237; Paschal, *North Carolina*, I, 132.

[43]George Stevenson, "Paul Palmer." In William S. Powell. *Dictionary of North Carolina Biography*, Vol. V. (Chapel Hill and London: University of North Carolina Press, 1994), 10.

[44]Stevenson, "Paul Palmer," 10; *Minutes of the Perquimans Monthly Meeting, 1680-1762.* Vol. I. (Indexed by Dorothy Lloyd, Gilbert and Mildred Marlette. Microfilmed from the original by Charles E. Rush, Librarian for the University of North Carolina Library, 1942), old page 19, new page 32. (Hereinafter referred to as *Perquimans MM.*)

[45]William L. Saunders, ed. *The Colonial Records of North Carolina* (10 vols.; Raleigh: P. M. Hale, Printer to the State, 1886), I, 406. (Hereinafter referred to as *Colonial Records*). Nicholas Crisp accused Paul and Johanna Palmer of commanding their slave, Cush, to steal Crisp's slave, Sambo. The case continued in the courts for a number of months but it finally was dismissed because the prosecution failed to appear and establish its case. The Palmers were exonerated completely and suffered no loss of respect. Palmer later served on the jury in the same court.

[46]J. R. B. Hathaway, *The North Carolina Genealogical Register* (3 vols., January 1900—July 1903), III, 284. (Hereinafter referred to as *Register*); *Will of Juliana Laker,* Perquimans Precinct, Files of North Carolina Secretary of State, September 24, 1735.

[47]George Washington Paschal, *History of North Carolina Baptists,* 2 vols. (Raleigh: The General Board, North Carolina Baptist State Convention, 1930), I, 133.

[48]Ibid., I, 132.

[49]Saunders, *Colonial Records*, II, 596.

[50]C. Edwin Barrows, ed., *The Diary of John Comer* (Philadelphia: American Baptist Publication Society, 1892), p. 84. (Hereinafter referred to as *Comer*). The Chowan church will be considered more thoroughly in the latter part of this chapter.

[51]Saunders, *Colonial Records,* III, 48.

[52]Paschal, *North Carolina*, 1, 132.

[53]Barrows, *Comer,* 111.

[54]Ibid., 113.

[55]As early as 1678, the General Baptists determined that ordination could be administered only by a qualified Bishop or Messenger. ("The Orthodox Creed," quoted in William L. Lumpkin, *Baptist Confessions of Faith* [Philadelphia: The Judson Press, 1959], 320, 321. [Hereinafter referred to as Lumpkin.])

[56]B. F. Riley, *A History of the Baptists in the Southern States.* (Philadelphia: American Baptist Publication

Society, 1898), 166.

[57]Whitley, *Carolina and Virginia*, 28. Whitley based his argument on an incorrect date. Palmer had been in North Carolina since 1720, at least five years before the death of Norden in Virginia. See above.

[58]*Minutes and Records, Perquimans Monthly Meeting of the Religious Society of Friends in North Carolina, 1680-1762*, MS, p. 35.

[59]Hugh Talmage Lefler, *North Carolina History as Told by Contemporaries* (3rd ed., rev., Chapel Hill: The University of North Carolina, 1956), 55. (Herinafter referred to as *Contemporaries*.) Copyright 1956, The University of North Carolina Press. Used with permission of the publisher.

[60]The author has read through the minutes of the Perquimans monthly meeting but ground breaking research was done by Stevenson.

[61]Stevenson, "Paul Palmer," 10.

[62]It should be noted that no attempt has been made to discredit Palmer, but rather to show that the pictures usually given of this early period have not recognized the importance of Joseph and William Parker to the later General Baptist movement and, consequently, to the emerging Free Will Baptist denomination. The fact that Palmer founded the first solidly organized General Baptist church in the state has not been denied, nor has there been any doubt but that his fiery evangelistic preaching gave strength and life to the movement's first growth. For the purposes of this study, however, it has been necessary to show the brief nature of Palmer's influence in contrast to the extended influence of the Parkers.

[63]Paschal, *North Carolina*, 1, 156.

[64]See above.

[65]Barrows, *Comer*, 84-102.

[66]Ibid., 111, 112.

[67]*The Somerset Court Judicials, 1734-1736*, pp. 62, 63. Quoted in Clayton Torrence, *Old Somerset on the Eastern Shore of Maryland* (Baltimore: Regional Publishing Co., 1966), 508, 509. Used by permission.

[68]Edwards, "Furman MS," II, 4.

[69]Saunders, *Colonial Records*, II, 406-603; Saunders, *Colonial Records*, III, 48; Paschall *North Carolina*, I, 138; Barrows, *Comer*, p. 84. For the first five years of the decade, Paul and Johanna Palmer often appeared in the Colonial Records either as participants in court cases or, in Paul's case, as a member of the various courts of the state. In 1726, Palmer already had begun to preach and also was busy selling tracts of land near Poplar Run in Chowan County. The Poplar Run area was to be the site of the first General Baptist Church in the state and was near the property of a number of members of that first church. From 1727 to 1729, Palmer enjoyed his greatest influence in North Carolina as he worked with the Parkers and William Burgess in the establishment of the first Baptist churches in the state. Stevenson has Palmer in Maryland in 1730 or 1731 on his return from ministry in New England, and again in 1735. (Stevenson, "Paul Palmer," 12.)

[70]Stevenson, "Paul Palmer," p. 12. Morgan Edwards, in 1772, assigned churches in some of these locations to Palmer's contemporaries, particularly William Fulsher and Josiah Hart (see chart on pp. 46, 47). This is not to say that there was not room for multiple congregations in these areas. Nor should we forget, however, that Palmer was a church planter. He seldom remained long with a church after initial organization. In any case, these churches did not play a significant role in the transition from General to Free Will Baptist sentiment at the turn of the century.

[71]Paschal, *North Carolina*, I, 140; Dodd, *Story*, 38; Torbet, *History*, 236, 237.

[72]Barrows, *Comer*, 84.

[73]Paschal, *North Carolina*, I, 140.

[74]See footnote 9, p. 48.

[75]Paschal, *North Carolina*, I, 141. John Parker, Thomas Parker, John Jordan, and William Copland had adjoining property near the church, while the Parkers owned land further north.

[76]Such a practice was not unusual for the area. The church at Pasquotank did not have a permanent meeting house for the first seven years of their existence (Edwards, "Furman MS," IV, 11, 12) and Meherrin built their first meeting house in 1735, five years after Joseph Parker moved to the area and began to preach. (S. J. Wheeler, *History of the Baptist Church Worshipping at Parker's Meeting House Called Meherrin*, by the Clerk [Raleigh: Printed at

the Recorder Office, 1847], 6, [Hereinafter referred to as *Parker's*]; Paschal, *North Carolina*, I, 165.)

[77]The date was erased from the original, but J. R. B. Hathaway has been able to ascertain the date through magnification (Hathaway, *Register*, I, 293).

[78]Copied from the original, now a part of the Ruth Hathaway Jones Papers in the Southern Historical Collection of the University of North Carolina Library. A copy may also be found in Hathaway, *Register*, I, 293.

[79]Edwards, "Tours," 28.

[80]Paschal included a copy of the petition for license with the names listed together in two columns with Burgess leading the list (Paschal, *North Carolina*, I, 144), while J. R. B. Hathaway has indicated that Burgess was the last to sign (Hathaway, *Register*, I, 283). The original document does have Burgess listed separately, but it was quite evident that his was the primary signature with the others following in secondary position.

[81]Edwards, "Furman MS," IV, 135.

[82]Paschal felt that Palmer continued the same practice that he initiated in the first church. "...The records indicate that William Burgess was the first pastor of the church that met in his house. It is certain, however, that Paul Palmer was the leader in the formation of both these churches. We learn from Comer's journal that such was his relationship to the church in Chowan, and the fact that Palmer's name is on the petition [the 1729 application for license for a meeting house in the home of William Burgess] is sufficient proof of his like relation to the church on the east of Pasquotank River" (Paschal, North Carolina, I, 146).

[83]Edwards, "Tours," 29. George Washington Paschal (in Paschal, North Carolina, I, 153) has shown that the church was located some miles from the South Carolina border in Onslow County. (See also footnote 70 of this chapter).

[84]Wheeler, *Parker's*, 5.

[85]Letter from Gov. Burrington to the Bishop of London (*Colonial Records,* III, 339, 340). Burrington listed the churches in his area and omitted any reference to Baptists. His seat of government was in Edenton and he would have been familiar with the churches in Chowan County (Hugh Talmage Lefler and Albert Ray Newsome, *The History of a Southern State, North Carolina* [Chapel Hill: The University of North Carolina Press, 1954], 162). Copyright 1954, The University of North Carolina Press. Used with permission of the publisher.

[86]Edwards, "Furman MS," IV, 135.

[87]M. A. Huggins, *A History of North Carolina Baptists, 1727-1982* (Raleigh: The General Board, Baptist State Convention of North Carolina, 1967), 411. (Hereafter referred to as *History*.)

[88]Hathaway, *Register*, 11, 195.

[89]Paschal, *North Carolina*, I, 160.

[90]Hathaway, *Register,* III, 475.

[91]Damon Dodd, *The Free Will Baptist Story* (Nashville: Executive Department of the National Association of Free Will Baptists, 1956), 53.

[92]William Parker became pastor of the church at Meherrin about 1748 and continued that ministry until his death in 1794 (Paschal, *North Carolina*, I, 521; Huggins, *History*, 45). Joseph Parker had been a part of the General Baptist church in the state in 1727, and continued his ministry in the movement for sixty-five years. The latter Parker died in 1791 or 1792 (Wheeler, *Parker's*, 7).

[93]Births, Deaths, and Marriages in Berkeley, Later Perquimans Precinct, N.C., quoted in Hathaway, *Register,* 111, 366.

[94]*Colonial Records*, I, 414; Mattie Erma Parker, ed. *The Colonial Records of North Carolina: Higher Court Records*, 2 vols.; (Raleigh: Department of Archives and History, 1963), 13. (Hereafter referred to as *Higher Court Records*.)

[95]Parker, *Higher Court Records*, 269.

[96]George Stevenson, "Materials Towards a History of Free Will Baptists in Lenoir County and Kinston, North Carolina, 1769-1919." Unpublished MS, 1.

[97]Hathaway, *Register*, III, 407.

[98]George Stevenson, personal letter to Ronald Creech, handwritten, March 25, 1968, p. 8.

[99]George Stevenson, "Benjamin Laker," in William S. Powell, ed. *Dictionary of North Carolina Biography*. Vol.

IV. (Chapel Hill, N. C. and London: The University of North Carolina Press), 5.

[100]*Will of Benjamin Lakaro (Laker)*. Perquimans Precinct, Files of the North Carolina Secretary of State, April 7, 1701. Dr. Ernest Payne and Dr. Barry White, two of the leading English Church Historians at this time, have agreed that the Grantham work mentioned in the Will of Benjamin Laker was written by Thomas Grantham in 1678. The proper title of the work is *Christianismus Primitivus* (Letter from Dr. Barry White, postmarked Regent's Park College, Oxford, May 1, 1972).

[101]*Will of Benjamin Lakaro (Laker)*. The form used in the introduction to the wills of the early eighteenth century was fairly standard, but it was evident that the individual reserved the right to use his own words in meeting the requirements of the standard. Laker's statement was much more specific concerning salvation and the work of Christ as Redeemer than was true in the introduction to the will for his wife Juliana and other wills of the period (*Will of Juliana Laker*, Perquimans Precinct, Files of the North Carolina Secretary of State, September 24, 1735; *Will of Churchill Reading*, Bath County, Files of the North Carolina Secretary of State, September 19, 1734).

[102]Edwards, "Furman MS," IV, 125.

[103]Paschal, *North Carolina*, I, 130; Robert G. Torbet, *A History of the Baptists*. (Philadelphia: The Judson Press, 1950), 236; Edwards, "Furman MS," IV, 125. Used by permission.

[104]Whitley, *General Assembly*, 1, 75.

[105]See above.

[106]Whitley, *Carolina and Virginia*, 22.

[107]Ibid.

[108]The traditional date for Screven's arrival in South Carolina is 1683, but Leah Townsend discovered that he was still in New England as late as 1696 (Townsend, *South Carolina Baptists,* 5).

[109]A. H. Newman, in (Newman, *United States*, 224, 225), has established the fact that ". . . in 1700, just as the Baptists were entering their new meetinghouse, they [the Charleston church] adopted the *Confession of Faith* set forth in 1689 by 'the ministers and messengers of, and concerned for, upwards of one hundred congregations in England and Wales (denying Arminianism),' and, by reason of its subsequent adoption (with slight modifications) by the Philadelphia Association, known in America as the *Philadelphia Confession*."

[110]See above.

[111]See above, footnote 92.

[112]Hathaway, *Register*, II, 299.

[113]Paschal, *North Carolina*, 165.

[114]Burkitt and Read, in (*Concise History,* 208), noted that "Elders Joseph Parker, William Parker, Winfield, and others of that order, often preached here. . . ."George Washington Paschal, in (*North Carolina*, I, 171), argued that ". . . this statement is valuable since it suggests that Meherrin was a kind of headquarters from which these ministers went forth on evangelistic tours such as we know were often made by General Baptist preachers in the early days of the Province."

[115]Wheeler, *Parker's,* 6; Thomas C. Parramore, *The Ancient Maritime Village of Murfreesboro, 1787-1825* (Murfreesboro, N. C.: Johnson Publishing Co., 1969), 13, 14.

[116]*Colonial Records*, IV, 619.

[117]Huggins, *History*, 40; Paschal, *North Carolina*, I, 169.

[118]See above.

[119]W. Moore, quoted in Paschal, *North Carolina*, I, 168, indicated that ". . . Joseph Parker and his people at Meherrin dismissed by letter enough of their members to form what was long known as Bertie Church, but later Sandy Run."

[120]These two churches were listed by Morgan Edwards as arms of the church Lower Fishing Creek (Edwards, "Tours," 30). George Stevenson revealed that Paul Palmer also worked in these areas and that he gathered a church near Little Contentnea Creek near the location of Joseph Parker's later church.

[121]Edwards, "Crozer MS," V, 13.

[122]North Carolina, *Craven County Deed Books*. Deed recording the sale of property on Little Contentnea Creek to Joseph Parker by Jacob Blount (Deed Book 10, December 25, 1756). The property later became a part of Pitt

County and now is in the edge of Greene County.

[123]Wheeler, *Parker's*, 7; R. K. Hearn, *Origin of the Free Will Baptist Church in North Carolina*, quoted in D. B. Montgomery, *General Baptist History* (Evansville: Courier Company, 1882), 165; Charles Crossfield Ware, *North Carolina Disciples of Christ* (St. Louis: Christian Board of Publication, 1927), 80. (Hereinafter referred to as *Disciples*). S. J. Wheeler contended that Joseph Parker lived at Wheat Swamp and traveled to Little Creek, but the deed of 1756 has indicated the opposite.

[124]Asplund, *Register*, 38.

[125]The Free Will Baptists of North Carolina adopted a *Confession of Faith* sometime before 1812. The confession closely followed the *Standard Confession* adopted by the English General Baptists in 1660. The same confession had been used by the General Baptists in North Carolina during the eighteenth century (Burkitt and Read, *Concise History*, 29).

[126]Paschal, *North Carolina*, I, 168.

[127]J. D. Huffman, "The Baptists in North Carolina," First Paper, *North Carolina Baptist Historical Papers,* I, (July 1897), 230. (Hereinafter referred to as "First Paper."); Pashcal, *North Carolina*, I, 168.

[128]Edwards, "Furman MS," IV, 169; Asplund, *Register,* 37.

[129]Hearn, *Origin*, 164.

[130]Ibid. Rufus K. Hearn was born in 1819. (Page from the Hearn Family Bible in the possession of Mrs. J. E. Sugg, II. Hereinafter referred to as Hearn Family Bible.) Hearn recorded his interviews with eye witnesses in his history of the denomination. The interviews will be considered later.

[131]Wheeler, *Parker's*, 6; Hearn, *Origin*, 164.

[132]Burkitt and Read, *Concise History*, 208.

[133]*A Brief Confession of Faith*, quoted in William L. Lumpkin, *Baptist Confessions of Faith* (Philadelphia: The Judson Press, 1959), 226. (The Lumpkin work hereinafter referred to as *Confessions.*)

[134]Asplund, *Register*, 37.

[135]Wheeler, *Parker's*, 8.

[136]Hearn, *Origins*, 165.

[137]Wheeler, *Parker's*, 6.

[138]John H. Wheeler, *Historical Sketches of North Carolina from 1581 to 1851* (2 vols., Philadelphia: Lippincott, Grambo and Co., 1851), 30. (Hereinafter referred to as *Sketches.*)

[139]Thomas M. Pittman, "The Preparation for Baptist Work in North Carolina," *North Carolina Baptist Historical Papers*, III (January 1900), 184. (Hereinafter referred to as "Preparation".)

[140]Ibid., 187.

[141]Wheeler, *Sketches*, 30.

[142]J. D. Huffman, "The Baptists in North Carolina," Fifth Paper, *North Carolina Historical Papers,* II (January 1898), p. 73. (Hereinafter referred to as "Fifth Paper".)

[143]Paschal, *North Carolina*, I, 80.

[144]Huffman, "First Paper," 219; John Brickell, *The Natural History of North Carolina* (1743), 37. Brickell revealed the other side of the coin, shattering the rosy and unrealistic picture painted by later historians. "But though they are thus remarkable for their friendship, harmony and hospitality, yet in regard to their morals, they have their share of the corruptions of the age; for as they live in the greatest ease and plenty, luxury of consequence predominates, which is never without its attendant vices."

[145]Lefler, *Contemporaries*, 33. The state officially accepted establishment in 1715, but it was never to have the authority that it enjoyed in other states. David D. Oliver, in "The Society for the Propagation of the Gospel in the Province of North Carolina," *James Sprunt Historical Publications*, IX (1910), 19, [Hereafter referred to as "Society"] has revealed that ". . . in those places where the dissenters were strong, all kinds of expedients were resorted to in order to avoid the payment of parish dues." The establishment could not conquer the will of the stubborn North Carolinian.

[146]This was illustrated by the rapid growth of the General Baptists. The ineffectiveness of North Carolina's establishment was revealed in the fact that Paul Palmer did not find it necessary to obtain a license to preach until he

returned to prominence in 1738.

[147]The proprietors used the guarantee of religious freedom as a drawing card in their advertisements for settlers for the new colony ("Description of the Province of Carolina, 1666," quoted in Lefler, *Contemporaries*, 21).

[148]Lefler, *Contemporaries*, 18.

[149]John Lawson, *Lawson's History of North Carolina* (Richmond: Garrett and Massie, Publishers, 1937 [1714]), p. XXV.

[150]"North Carolina," *Encyclopedia Britannica*, 1969, Vol. 16, p. 611.

[151]*Colonial Records*, III, 110. The Quakers had been accused of conspiracy against the government in 1711 when they supported Thomas Cary in the "Cary Rebellion." In 1715, they lost their right to vote or to hold office and the political power they had enjoyed in the colony was destroyed (*Colonial Records*, II, 213, 884, 885). Their right to worship remained unmolested, however, and the guarantee of religious freedom remained basically intact. This exception to the general rule did not affect the Baptists. Paul Palmer, William Parker, and other Baptists served in a number of public offices after the Quakers were censured.

[152]J. D. Huffman, "The Baptists in North Carolina," Part II, First Paper, *North Carolina Baptist Historical Papers*, II (July 1898), 205, 206. (Hereafter referred to as "Part II, First Paper.")

[153]Oliver, "Society," 12.

[154]Edward Legare Pennington, *The Church of England and the Rev. Clement Hall in Colonial North Carolina* (Hartford: Church Missions Publishing Co., 1937), 27. (Hereafter referred to as *Clement Hall*.)

[155]Oliver, "Society," 15.

[156]*Colonial Records*, I, 572.

[157]*Colonial Records*, I, 616; Paschal, *North Carolina*, I, 104.

[158]*Colonial Records*, I, 616; Paschal, *North Carolina*, I, 105.

[159]Francis L. Hawks, *History of North Carolina* (2 vols.; Fayetteville, N.C.: Published by E. J. Hale & Son, 1858), II, 353.

[160]Paschal, *North Carolina*, I, 107.

[161]The usual allowance for all missionaries was twenty pounds. John Blair, appointed as a missionary in 1704, also received fifty pounds from an interested friend and five pounds from the Bishop of London (Paschal, *North Carolina*. I, 102).

[162]William Byrd, *A Journey to the Land of Eden* (New York: Macy-Massius, The Vanguard Press, 1928), 63.

[163]*Colonial Records*, III, 429.

[164]*Colonial Records*, II, 271; Paschal, *North Carolina*, I, 114.

[165]Huffman, "Part II, First Paper," 205, 206.

[166]Edwards, "Furman MS," IV, 125.

[167]Edwards, "Furman MS," IV, 23, 24.

[168]Paschal, *North Carolina*, I, 182.

[169]William Fulsher continued as a General Baptist preacher until at least 1772 when Morgan Edwards found him serving the General Baptist church at Matchipungo (Edwards, "Furman MS," IV, 169).

[170]Paschal, *North Carolina*, I, 192.

[171]Edwards, "Furman MS," IV, 24.

[172]Josiah Hart was mentioned in a General Court record in 1733 (Paschal, *North Carolina*, I, 173). In 1739, three years before Sojourner arrived in North Carolina, Hart witnessed the will of William Hutson of Craven County (J. Bryan Grimes, ed., *Abstracts of North Carolina Wills Compiled from Original and Recorded Wills in the Office of the Secretary of State* [Raleigh: E. M. Uzzell and Company, 1910], 178).

[173]"Petition from the Protestant Dissenters of Bay and Neuse Rivers," copied from the original in the General Court Records held by the University of North Carolina Library.

[174]Ibid.

[175]Edwards, "Furman MS," IV, 20.

[176]William Fulsher was at New Bern, Craven County in 1740; at Flea Point, Beaufort County in 1742; and at Pungo, Beaufort County in 1772.

[177]Edwards, "Tours," 28, 29.

[178]Edwards, "Furman MS," IV, 169, 170. Edwards called the church Matchipungo in the "Furman MS," but listed it as Pungo in "Tours." The listing of William Fulsher as pastor in both cases and the similarity of the names made it evident that the two names indicated the same church.

[179]Huggins, *History*, 411.

[180]Burkitt and Read, *Concise History*, 284.

[181]Paschal, *North Carolina*, I, 181.

[182]Burkitt and Read, *Concise History*, 285; Paschal, *North Carolina*, I, 181.

[183]Burkitt and Read, *Concise History*, 217.

[184]Paschal, *North Carolina*, I, 181, 182.

[185]Hearn, *Origin*, 167; Huggins, *History*, 46; Ware, *Disciples*, 80.

[186]Hearn, *Origin*, 166, 167.

[187]Ibid., 167

3

North Carolina Continued

The Years of Reorganization (1755-1794)

The year 1755 held a great deal of historical significance for the North Carolina General Baptists. It marked the end of an era of phenomenal growth and the beginning of an era of rapid decline that was to bring the movement to almost total extinction. Though the period continued through 1794 when the Meherrin church was reorganized, the reorganization process was virtually complete by 1760. By that time, fifteen of the original churches either had been reorganized as Particular Baptist churches or had lost so much strength that they had disappeared from the records. Tar River church was added to the Particular camp in 1761 and Meherrin completed the process in 1794. Grassy Creek, Granville County, located in an area of Separate Baptist influence, had joined that movement rather than the Particulars.[1]

The story of the reorganization process has been told before. As was true of the earlier period, however, the story, written from the viewpoint of the Baptist denomination, had little concern for the effects of the process on the General Baptists or on the later Free Will Baptists.

The Factors Leading to Reorganization

At least four factors prepared the way for the coming of the reorganization process and for its success: (1) the national decline of the General Baptist movement, (2) the missionary emphasis of the Particular Baptists following the Great Awakening, (3) the initial loss of leading General Baptist preachers, and (4) the inability of the General Baptist laymen to stand against the invaders.

The National Decline of the General Baptist Movement

Earlier reference has been made to the rapid and wide-spread decline that the General Baptist movement experienced after the Great Awakening. Ruth B. Bordin limited her area of concern by contending that the Arminian Baptists in New England became " . . . firmly committed to Calvinist principles,"[2] but W. T. Whitley argued further after 1742 the progress of all General Baptists in America ceased; and presently a decline set in.[3] Whitley listed the lack of settled meeting houses, the refusal of the General Baptists to pay their ministers, the Calvinistic thrust of the Great Awakening, the lack of emphasis on an educated ministry, and the Revolutionary War as the major causes of the decline.[4] Except for the final one, all of these causes would have applied to the General Baptists in North Carolina during the reorganization period. Though the Great Awakening had its beginning in the Middle and New England colonies, it made its way into North Carolina through the preaching of

George Whitefield,[5] the evangelical zeal of the Separate Baptists[6] and the new missionary emphasis of the Regular Baptists.

The Missionary Emphasis of the Particular Baptists
Following the Great Awakening

THE SOURCE OF THE PARTICULAR MISSIONARY EMPHASIS

After recognizing that the earliest Baptists in North Carolina were of the General persuasion and that this type of Baptist faith promised to be the dominant type in America, William L. Lumpkin added that ". . . their movement was shattered . . . by the twofold offensive of Regular and Separate Baptists after the middle of the eighteenth century."[7] Though the Regular Baptists did not accept the degree of revival spirit that characterized the Separates, they did enjoy some of the fruits of the revival period. Robert G. Torbet argued that the Regular Baptists did not escape the influence of Jonathan Edwards and George Whitefield—an influence that combined evangelical zeal with Calvinistic principles.[8] He added that it was this influence that set the stage for Regular harvests in North Carolina in the reorganization of the General Baptist churches and in the Regular union with the Separates.

> Since the main leaders of the Awakening, with the exception of Wesley, were Calvinists, the success of that movement gave an evangelistic zeal to many who had adhered to Reformed doctrine. At the same time, the adoption of a Calvinist Confession of Faith by the Philadelphia Baptist Association in 1742 and the Charleston Association in 1767 gave to Regular Baptists a theological tradition which was in accord with the best thought of Edwards and Whitefield. As the influence of these associations developed, their point of view provided guidance to the growing number of churches which were the product of the revivals. We have observed how the Separate Baptists united with Regular Baptists, and how the General Baptists, as in North Carolina, were transformed into Particular Baptists, until by 1800, Calvinism was the prevalent theology among them.[9]

THE NATURE OF REGULAR BAPTIST MISSIONARY EMPHASIS

The confessions of the Philadelphia and Kehukee Baptist Associations clearly indicated that the Regular Baptists had not turned from their doctrine of election.[10] Though some initial conversions resulted from their efforts, the Regular Baptist missionary excursions into North Carolina were directed toward the rescue of the elect from General Baptist error rather than toward a mass program of evangelism for the unsaved. George Washington Paschal described the nature and the success of the Regular missionary adventure in North Carolina in his account of John Gano's report to the association.

> . . . On hearing the story told with many interesting details by their young messenger [Gano] the ministers and delegates of this the oldest Baptist Association in America were moved with compassion for the Baptists of North Carolina and they voted that one

ministering brother from the Jerseys, and one from Pennsylvania, visit North Carolina, the several churches to contribute to their expenses. It is well to mark the warm missionary zeal of these Philadelphia Baptists and their readiness to make contributions of money to send messengers to rescue their Carolina brethren from error. But for it we should have a very different type of Baptists in North Carolina from that found there today.[11]

The Initial Loss of General Baptist Leaders

Though David Benedict attributed most of the success of the reorganization process to the work of itinerant ministers of the Philadelphia Association,[12] the defection actually began much earlier among the ministers of the General Baptist movement. As early as 1751, James Smart and Henry Ledbetter yielded to the influence of Robert Williams and Stephen Hollingsworth, and began to preach Calvinistic doctrines in their churches.[13] Smart was pastor of the important church at Upper Fishing Creek and from that vantage point exerted a great deal of influence on the churches in that area. In spite of initial opposition, he continued to preach there until 1755 when he moved to South Carolina. The church eventually followed his example and joined the Particular Baptist movement.

Robert Williams carried the campaign to Kehukee and laid the groundwork for reorganization there. Through his influence, William Wallis and John Moore were persuaded to turn to the Particular Faith. Moore introduced the new doctrine to his church at Falls of Tar River and Wallis was credited with a part in the final reorganization of the church at Kehukee.[14]

Charles Daniel, Edward Brown, and Thomas Pope soon followed their fellow ministers into the Particular Baptist fellowship.

The impact of this factor on the final success of the reorganization process should not be overlooked. By 1760, all the ministers converted through the influence of the Sojourner-Hart alliance were swallowed up by the Particular Baptist invasion. Sojourner himself had died in 1739,[15] and the name of Josiah Hart no longer appeared in the records. The Palmer-Parker-Burgess group suffered as Palmer and Burgess already had passed from the scene. By the end of the decade, the two Parkers and William Fulsher constituted the entire ministry of the General Baptist movement.[16]

The Inability of the General Baptist Laymen to Stand Against Their Invaders

Except for token anger and unrest, the General Baptist people offered little resistance to the process of reorganization. Morgan Edwards indicated that the Calvinistic preaching of James Smart caused grief to the people at Upper Fishing Creek, but he added that ". . . in process of time they also embraced the same sentiments."[17] Though only a small minority in each church accepted the new organization, the majority that was left failed to exercise their rights in retaining the property. In almost every case, the preacher led the defection, and the people that refused to follow were left as sheep without a shepherd. The right of the majority meant little to the untrained, leaderless remnant that, by tradition, had learned to depend completely on the pastor. George Washington Paschal explained the tradition and the desperate plight of those who refused to capitulate:

... We might have expected to find more appeals to the courts to settle the claims to the meeting houses, for it is strange that the General Baptists should have so meekly acquiesced in the loss of their property to the few seceders from their doctrine. It is to be explained partly on the supposition that the ministers were all influential in the churches and in a sense the title to the church was regarded as being vested in the minister. The conservatives, though much the more numerous, had no leader, no religious teacher, no preacher, and if the meeting house, church and all, had been given them they would have been able to make no use of it.[18]

The majority firmly held to the convictions of General Baptist tradition and stubbornly withstood the pressures of invasion. Without leadership and direction, however, they could not achieve the major victory that would spare their churches and their property. The battle was won; the war was lost.

The Motives for Reorganization

Morgan Edwards, writing in 1772, gave birth to a tradition. He contended that of all the Baptists in America, those in North Carolina were "the least spiritually minded."[19] Edwards simply was putting into words the attitude of the Regular Baptists concerning the General Baptists of North Carolina. They considered the General Baptists to be lost, and that attitude provided the foundation for the Regular mission work in the state. During the entire period of reorganization, the interest of the Regular Baptists was directed toward the rescue of the General Baptists from their prison of error.

The Point of Contention

The basic problem could be traced to the different convictions of the two groups concerning the necessity of an "experience" at the time of salvation. The Calvinists contended that a convert should be able to pinpoint the time and nature of his conversion,[20] while the General Baptists demanded only a simple profession of faith in Christ. Since no experience was required by the General Baptists, their opponents accused them of allowing unsaved persons to be baptized. This practice, they concluded, resulted in the development of unregenerate churches, making a mission program justified and necessary.

The Perpetuation of the Tradition

THE REGULAR BAPTISTS AND THE TRADITION

The tradition was to be an abiding one with each new generation accepting it as truth and adding a list of new charges against the General Baptists.

Lemuel Burkitt and Jesse Read, writing in 1813, gave new life to the tradition in their treatment of the Kehukee Association by contending that:

> . . . several of those churches, that at first belonged to the Kehukee Association, were gathered by the Free-will Baptists, and as their custom was to baptize any persons who were willing, whether they had an experience of grace or not, so in consequence of this practice, they had many members and several ministers in those churches, who were baptized before they were converted; and after they were brought to a knowledge of the truth, and joined the Regulars, openly confessed they were baptized before they believed; And some of them said they did it in hope of getting to Heaven by it. Some of their ministers confessed they had endeavored to preach, and administer the ordinance of baptism to others, after they were baptized, before they were converted themselves; and so zealous were they for baptism, (as some of them expected salvation by it) that one of their preachers confessed, if he would get any willing to be baptized, and it was in the night, that he would baptize them by fire light, for fear they should get out of the notion of it before the next morning.[21]

David Benedict, another Baptist historian, added in 1813 that:

> . . . although some of their ministers were evangelical and pure, and the members regular and devout; yet, on the whole, it appears to have been the most negligent and the least spiritual community of Baptists, which has arisen on the American continent. For so careless and indefinite were they in their requisitions, that many of their communicants were baptized and admitted into their churches; and even some of their ministers were introduced into their sacred functions, without an experimental acquaintance with the gospel, or without being required to possess it. . . .[22]

> The faults and errors of this people were probably exaggerated by some of their zealous reformers; but viewing matters in their most favourable light, and admitting as many of their preachers and brethren as we can, to have been worthy of their functions and professions; yet they, as a body, were deeply involved in error. . . . [22]

Recent Baptist historians have made it clear that the tradition is not dead. J. D. Huffman, at the end of the nineteenth century, reminded his readers that the early General Baptists had few requirements for church membership and that "all who made a profession of faith in Christ as their Saviour were baptized. . . ."[23] He further argued that a profession of faith was the maximum requirement and that the Arminians often were satisfied with a person's simple desire to be baptized. More recently, and with fewer reservations, William L. Lumpkin argued that ". . . the North Carolina General Baptist churches, in point of fact, had required no profession of conversion prior to baptism. . . ."[24]

THE TRADITION EVALUATED FROM THE
GENERAL BAPTIST POINT OF VIEW

The Early Leaders Defended—There can be little doubt but that some of the charges against the early North Carolina Baptists were justified and that a number of unregenerate members did become a part of the churches. However, Lumpkin's bold assertion that the General Baptists required no profession of conversion seemed especially harsh and opposed to the character of the early leaders of the movement. Even the Regular Baptist historians found little fault with the major General Baptist leaders and indeed, have been compelled to defend them. S. J. Wheeler, a Baptist historian at the middle of the nineteenth century, described William Parker as a ". . . remarkably pungent and practical preacher—seeking every opportunity to do good, and deeply devoted to the spiritual interests of his flock. . . ."[25] William Washington Paschal, a recent and respected Baptist historian, credited the success of the General Baptists at Meherrin to the fact that Joseph Parker, their preacher, ". . . was walking in all the commands and ordinances of the Lord blamelessly."[26] Finally, Morgan Edwards described William Sojourner as ". . . a most excellent man. . . ."[27]

Again, the problem seems to have stemmed from a difference in conviction and interpretation. The Regular Baptists continually accused the General Baptists of being lax in discipline, but their accusations did not include charges concerning immorality, failure to worship, or any other open sin. The General Baptists were not condemned for a moral sin but for a theological one.[28]

The Arminian Response—Free Will and General Baptist historians have not denied that the early churches might have contained members that actually had not been redeemed, but they have been quick to deny that the churches willingly or knowingly accepted unsaved members. R. K. Hearn argued that the early General Baptists were no more guilty than other denominations—that all churches could find some goats among the sheep. He stoutly denied that the General Baptists accepted members that did not confess Christ as Savior.

> . . . These early churches took the Bible for their guide, they practiced its sacred teach-ings, and as the Apostles never required an experience, and as it was nowhere author-ized in Holy Writ, they practiced what they found the gospel required, that is faith in the Lord Jesus Christ, repentance towards God, and Baptism by immersion; and bap-tized their members on a profession of their faith in the Lord Jesus Christ, and not by experience.[29]

Ollie Latch, a recent General Baptist historian, has been as outspoken in favor of the General Baptists as their opponents have been against them. After admitting that they could have been guilty of neglect and worldliness, a blight which he felt cursed all the churches of the day, Latch denied that the General Baptists were guilty of any serious sin.

> . . . Grand indeed were some of the accounts of how God in his predetermined wis-dom saved the unruly sinner. The General Baptists had no truck with such, and simply led the free person to find Christ in his own way, exercising his own free will. So the chief charge which the Calvinists laid against the Arminians was that 'they did not

require an experience of grace from their members when they received them into the church.' What that charge actually means is that the Arminians did not require a long and often ridiculous account of how one came to know he was elected to grace and was one of the sheep. Outside then, of the probable effect of the worldly spirit of the times that was infecting all Christendom, it does not appear that there was any great error apparent in the General Baptists of which any need be ashamed.[30]

In the final analysis, it is not unlikely that both sides were honest in their evaluations and that both arguments contained elements of truth. The General Baptists admitted that they did not require the experience of grace that the Regulars demanded. On the other hand, the Regulars could not accuse the General Baptists of spiritual sin, but rather had to limit their accusations to the area of theological error. The General Baptists were content that they had met the requirements of the Scriptures, but the Regulars interpreted their refusal to demand an experience as evidence that they were not saved.

The Regular Baptist determination that the General Baptist churches were not true churches—that they were made up of unregenerate members—supplied the motive and the justification for the missionary enterprise in North Carolina.

The Method of Reorganization
The Forces Employed

Two major forces were employed by the Regular Baptists to achieve their capture of the General Baptist churches in North Carolina: (1) an inside force made up of the ministers within the ranks of the General Baptists, and (2) an outside force consisting primarily of itinerant preachers from the Philadelphia Association of Regular Baptists. The two forces joined hands to form an overwhelming army that the General Baptists could not resist. The final success of the reorganization process depended on the crippling desertion by the former force and the superior training and ability of the latter.

THE INNER FORCE

Though David Benedict inferred that the itinerant ministers from the Philadelphia Association had the greater influence in the reorganization process, he did admit that the seceding General Baptist ministers had a part in the success of the program. His major error, it would seem, was in the order he applied to the various influences. After speaking of the powerful influence of the northern ministers, Benedict added that ". . . what was left unfinished by them, was undertaken and carried on, with a very laudable zeal, by the ministers among themselves. . . ."[31] In the same discussion, Benedict admitted that Calvinistic doctrines had been introduced in North Carolina as early as 1751 and that the northern ministers did not arrive earlier than 1754.[32] In spite of Benedict's conclusion, the dates would indicate that the opposite was true. The inner force predated the northern missionary enterprise by at least three years. The latter influence supplied the final blow in a battle that already was well under way.

The Men of the Inner Movement—The outline has demanded an earlier examination of the men of the inner movement, but some mention must be made of them at this point. By early 1751, James Smart and Henry Ledbetter had accepted a Calvinistic position and were preaching the new doctrine in their churches.[33] In the same year, William Wallis, a layman,[34] joined the movement and became a powerful influence at Kehukee. In 1752, William Walker was added to the number of Calvinistic defectors.[35]

Most of these men had been influenced by Robert Williams, a leader difficult to catalogue in either of the classifications of influence. He was a native of North Carolina but had gone to South Carolina in 1745 to receive instruction from the Particular Baptists in the Welsh Neck district.[36] Because he lived in North Carolina before the Particular Baptists had gained control, it seemed necessary that he be included in the list of ministers that wielded influence from within.

By 1755, the list was complete and included Robert Williams, James Smart, and William Walker, Fishing Creek; John Moore, Falls of Tar River; William Wallis and Thomas Pope, Kehukee; Edward Brown, Great Cohara; Henry Ledbetter, Tar River; and Charles Daniel.

The Success of the Inner Movement—The influence exerted from within the ranks of the General Baptist movement laid the groundwork for the reorganization process. None of the churches actually had been reorganized when the first missionaries arrived from Philadelphia in 1754, but the stage had been set and the curtain had been drawn for the second act of the Regular Baptist invasion in North Carolina.

At least three factors combined to give the degree of success achieved by the inner group: (1) the fact that the defecting ministers were leaders of influential General Baptist churches, (2) the degree of control that the churches allowed their ministers,[37] and (3) the special training that some of the ministers had received from the Particular Baptists in South Carolina.[38]

THE INFLUENCE FROM THE OUTSIDE

The Work of John Gano—The missionary program of the Philadelphia Association was initiated by the very able John Gano. He was commissioned by the association to travel in the southern states as a representative of the Particular Baptists, and by the summer of 1754, he was preaching in North Carolina.[39] Gano probably was the most formidable opponent that the General Baptists faced. David Benedict described him as one of the most important ministers of his day.[40] He was welltrained for the ministry, enjoyed the respect and esteem of the Philadelphia Association, and possessed a confident and overpowering personality. Though his reputation and superior training might have put the General Baptists on the defensive, it was his powerful personality that assured his success among them. Morgan Edwards recorded an example of Gano's power of persuasion:

> . . . On his arrival [in North Carolina], he sent to the ministers, requesting an interview with them, which they declined, and appointed a meeting among themselves, to consult what to do. Mr. Gano, hearing of it, went to their meeting, and addressed them in words to this effect, 'I have desired a visit from you, which, as a brother and a stranger, I had a right to expect; but as ye have refused, I give up my claim, and am come to pay you a visit.' With that, he ascended into the pulpit, and read for his text

the following words, 'Jesus I know, and Paul I know, but who are ye?' This text he managed in such a manner as to make some afraid of him, and others ashamed of their shyness. . . .[41]

Gano's work among the General Baptists was successful from two standpoints—he added a number of defectors to the growing list in North Carolina, and he persuaded the Philadelphia Association of the missionary responsibilities that awaited them in the southern state. His report to the association painted such a desperate picture of the situation that they hurried to send representatives to complete the program of reform.

The Work of Miller and Vanhorn—In response to the request of John Gano, the Philadelphia Association sent Benjamin Miller and Peter Vanhorn to North Carolina to finish the work begun by the defecting ministers and continued by Gano. Miller had been pastor of the Particular Baptist church at Scotch Plains, New Jersey, since 1747 and Vanhorn was pastor of the influential church at Pennepek.[42] Apart from Gano, the association probably could not have found more able leaders for the missionary enterprise. The two men left Philadelphia on Tuesday, October 28, 1755, and made their way to the church at Kehukee in the center of the unrest that had been growing since 1751.[43]

In less than two months after their arrival in the state, the two men completed the reorganization of their first church, and the Particular Baptist invasion gained its first tangible victory. On December 11, 1755, the church at Kehukee officially became a Particular Baptist church.[44]

The victory was to be the first of many. By the end of 1761, twelve churches had joined the new movement, and the initial phase of the reorganization process was complete .[45] Miller and Vanhorn personally were responsible for the final reorganization of at least four churches[46] and instrumental in the others.

THE FINAL ANALYSIS

The final step in the reorganization process demanded the dissolution of any former organization, a rigid examination of the individual members of the congregation in which they were to give solid evidence of their experience of grace, and the establishment of a new organization made up of those members that had proven themselves a part of the elect. Burkitt and Read contended that Miller and Vanhorn accepted those members that ". . . in a judgment of charity were born again."[47]

Except for one church that Benjamin Miller established in the Yadkin area of western North Carolina,[48] the Particular missionary enterprise did not direct itself to the task of pioneer missions. The method of reorganization was married to the motive, and together they demanded that all the attention of the Particular Baptists be given to the task of rescuing the General Baptists.

The Scope of the Reorganization Process

While the Particular invasion was almost totally successful in its capture of the ministers and property of the General Baptist movement, it failed miserably in its attempt to reach the laymen. It was at that level of the reorganization process that the General Baptists suffered the greatest degree of tragedy. The hundreds of General Baptists that refused to join the Particulars were left without leaders or property and soon disappeared from the field of Baptist influence.

The Degree of Regular Baptist Success

THE MINISTERS AND CHURCHES

Earlier mention has been made of the churches and ministers involved in the reorganization process. From that standpoint, the Regular Baptists could boast of a magnificent victory. Their conquests included most of the leading General Baptist churches and the majority of their most able preachers. By 1761, the General Baptist movement had been reduced to four ministers and the churches they directed.[49]

THE TRAGEDY OF THE REORGANIZATION PROCESS

The startling and tragic story of the contrasting failure of the Particular invasion has been preserved. In most cases, the reconstituted churches consisted of the minister and a handful of the members of the earlier General Baptist congregation. The large congregation of the church at Upper Fishing Creek contributed only thirteen members to the new organization, and the powerful church at Kehukee could add only ten.[50] This was to be the story in every church that yielded to the missionary zeal of the Particulars. George Washington Paschal determined that no more than five percent of all the General Baptists became a part of the new churches.[51]

The first few years of the reorganization period proved to be the darkest days in the history of the North Carolina General Baptists. Added to the crippling losses of their churches and preachers were the continuous accusations that pictured them as unsaved, untrained, and ignorant people. Though they represented the majority in the congregations to which they belonged, they were deprived of the property they had purchased, the churches they had built, and the leaders they had chosen and commissioned to serve. They had no source of hope. The churches of the Parkers and William Fulsher were too far away to help them, and their convictions would not allow them to join their enemies. Without help and without hope, they soon disappeared and were heard from no more. This was the major tragedy of the reorganization process.

The full scope of the reorganization process can be illustrated best in table form.[52]

TABLE 2

THE GENERAL BAPTIST CHURCHES THAT YIELDED TO THE REORGANIZATION PROCESS[a]

Church	Date of Reorg.	Persons Responsible	No. in New Church
Kehukee	Dec. 11, 1755	William Wallis, Miller, Vanhorn	10
Fishing Creek	Dec. 6, 1755	Miller, Vanhorn	13
Bear Creek	1756	Miller, Vanhorn	15
Swift Creek (Craven County)	Feb. 27, 1756	Miller, Vanhorn	12
Fishing Creek (Lower)	Oct. 13, 1756	Thomas Pope	6
Falls of Tar River	Dec. 3, 1757	John Moore, Charles Daniel	7
Pasquotank (Shiloh)	Jan. 20, 1758	Thomas Pope, Charles Daniel	12
Toisnot	Sept. 7, 1758	John Moore, George Graham	14
Red Banks	Nov. 20, 1758	Thomas Pope, Joseph Willis	
Great Cohara	Oct. 15, 1759	Thomas Pope, Johnathan Thomas, Stephen Hollingsworth	12
Tar River Sandy Run (Bertie)	April 3, 1761	William Walker Thomas Pope	20

[a]The table was compiled from the sketches found in Edwards, "Furman MS"; Edwards, "Tours"; Huggins, *History*; Burkitt and Read, *Concise History*; and Paschal, *North Carolina*.

TABLE 3

**THE DEFECTION OF GENERAL BAPTIST LEADERS
TO THE REGULAR BAPTISTS[a]**

Minister	Date of Affiliation	Church
Robert Williams	1745	Kehukee
James Smart	1751	Upper Fishing Creek
Henry Ledbetter	1751	Tar River
William Wallis (Layman)	1751	Kehukee
William Walker	1752	Upper Fishing Creek
John Moore		Falls of Tar River
Charles Daniel		
Edward Brown		Great Cohara
Thomas Pope		Kehukee
George Graham	1756	Bear Creek

[a] The table was compiled from the sketches found in Edwards, "Furman MS"; Edwards, "Tours"; Huggins, *History*; Paschal, *North Carolina*.

The Remnant of the Reorganization
The Regular Baptists and the Remnant

The attitude of the Regular Baptists toward the remnant of their successful invasion was characterized by an almost total lack of concern and interest. Because the large numbers of displaced General Baptist members were considered unregenerate and apart from the elect, no program of rehabilitation was initiated or even considered. The few souls that made up the body of the elect had been rescued; the missionary enterprise was complete.

Morgan Edwards, in a vivid illustration of his disregard for the remnant, dismissed them effectively with a brief paragraph of introduction and a list of their churches and ministers.[53]

In 1794, John Asplund published a revised register of the Baptists that denominated the entire membership as Regular or Particular Baptists. In his treatment of North Carolina, he omitted the General Baptist churches that had been included in his earlier work in 1790. Though Asplund's omission inferred that the General Baptists no longer existed, a close examination of his list indicates that he left out General Baptist churches that surely remained in the year of his publication. The church at Meherrin especially was conspicuous by its absence.[54] The list contained information for the years 1790 through 1793 and for part of 1794. The church at Meherrin joined the Particular Baptists sometime in 1794, but the reorganization evidently came later than Asplund's publication or he would have included Meherrin as a Particular Baptist church. It is quite certain that Asplund was familiar with the church since he included it in his earlier listings. The indicated conclusion is that the remnant of the General Baptist movement was no longer important and that the churches of that persuasion simply had been dismissed from the area of concern.

In all fairness to the Regular Baptist historians, their attitude was not an unnatural one. Concern for the opposing group had little place in the continuing history of the Regular movement.

The General Baptist Movement Following the Reorganization Process

In 1772, Morgan Edwards identified four churches and their ministers as the entire remnant of the General Baptist movement in North Carolina. He listed William Parker at Meherrin, Joseph Parker at Contantony (Little Contentnea), William Fulsher at Matchipungo (Pungo), and a Wingfield at Bear River.[55]

In the light of the purposes of this particular study, the remnant of the General Baptist movement in North Carolina has taken on a new importance. If it is true that the present Free Will Baptist denomination has its roots in that movement, then the connection must be found in the continuing history of the tiny group that survived the reorganization process. Morgan Edwards told only the beginning of that history.

THE WORK OF JOHN WINFIELD AND WILLIAM FULSHER

William Fulsher entered the General Baptist picture early in its history and became an important figure in the movement's progress. He was instrumental in the organization of the church at New Bern in 1740 and of the church at Flea Point in 1742.[56] His entire ministry was spent in the vicinity of Craven and Beaufort Counties. In 1772, he pastored the church at Pungo in Beaufort County,[57] one of the four churches that remained true to the General Baptist cause.

The later years of Fulsher's life, however, were not so productive. By 1790, John Winfield was pastor of the church at Pungo, and Fulsher had retired into the background. In the same year, he was listed in the census as a resident of neighboring Carteret County,[58] but there is no evidence that he was still active as a minister.

John Winfield appeared suddenly on the General Baptist scene in 1772 when Morgan Edwards listed him as one of the faithful ministers of the General Baptist remnant. At that time, he pastored the Bear River church. The church was located near the stream that served as the dividing line between Lenoir and Greene Counties[59] and was not far from the Parker work at Little Contentnea and Wheat Swamp. By 1790, Winfield had moved to Beaufort County to become pastor of Fulsher's church at Pungo.[60] John Asplund caused some confusion by listing the latter church in Hyde County. Since he listed Winfield as pastor but did not record the name of the church, the possibility of two churches existed. It was more likely, however, that the church was technically on the edge of Hyde County but within an area that commonly was acknowledged as a part of Beaufort. The church was located on the shore of the Pungo River,[61] which was a natural dividing line for the two counties. The more convenient line finally was accepted; and, in 1819, the part of Hyde County lying west of the Pungo River was annexed to Beaufort.[62] From that time, the location of the church officially was a part of the latter county.

Little information has been preserved concerning the later years of Winfield's life, but Burkitt and Read inferred that his church had been absorbed by the Particular Baptists before 1803.[63] Winfield's residence was in Hyde County, and he might have been traced to a later date through the county records except that there were two men there by the same name.[64] One of the men was still in the county in 1810, but the records did not indicate whether or not the preacher had been the survivor.[65]

THE MORE SUCCESSFUL WORK OF THE PARKERS

While Winfield and Fulsher were struggling to hold their own in Beaufort County, William and Joseph Parker were establishing new churches in Pitt, Greene, and Lenoir.[66] Though the churches at Wheat Swamp, Gum Swamp, Louson Swamp, and Grimsley might not have been a part of the remnant at the time of Edwards' writing, they were definitely a later part of the movement. Since Joseph Parker had settled at Little Creek and William was busy at Meherrin, the other communities possibly were preaching points and had not reached a stage of formal organization.[67] The fact remains, however, that Joseph and William Parker evangelized a wide new area for the General Baptists. The remnant was not as harmless as the Regular historians had supposed.

The Significance of the Remnant's Success
to the Later Free Will Baptist Movement

The possibilities of a historical connection between the General Baptists and the Free Will Baptists in North Carolina will be considered in a later chapter, but the section on the remnant of the reorganization process would be less than complete without some mention of the significance of the remnant's success to the later movement. The area the Parkers cultivated became the seedbed for Free Will Baptist growth. In every community south of the Tar River that had boasted a Parker church or preaching point, a Free Will Baptist church appeared soon after the movement was born.[68]

Summary

The national decline of the General Baptist movement, the new attitude of the Regular Baptists toward evangelism, the initial loss of major General Baptist leaders, and the inability of the General Baptist laymen to combat the superior training and ability of the Regulars contributed to the success of the Particular Baptist invasion in North Carolina.

The Regular Baptists made their attempt to initiate a pioneer mission work in the state. Their conviction that the General Baptist churches were made up of unregenerate members gave them their motive for sending missionaries so far from Philadelphia. Their sole purpose in the North Carolina endeavor was to rescue the elect from the error of the General Baptists.

Two forces were employed to complete the rescue—a crippling force of defection from within and a powerful proselyting force from without. By 1751, the General Baptist movement began to crumble from within as James Smart, Robert Williams, Henry Ledbetter, William Wallis, William Walker, and other important leaders defected to the Particular Baptists. In 1754, after the defectors had weakened the movement, John Gano was sent from Philadelphia to continue the plan of reorganization. The following year, Benjamin Miller and Peter Vanhorn arrived from Philadelphia and added the final touch by actually reorganizing the churches as Particular Baptist churches.

In regards to the churches and property of the General Baptists, the Regular invasion was devastatingly successful. The churches at Kehukee, Upper and Lower Fishing Creek, Falls of Tar River, Toisnot, Tar River, Red Banks, Pasquotank, Great Cohara, Swift Creek (Craven County), and Bear Creek yielded to the pressures of the Regular Baptists by 1761. On the other hand, however, the invasion was a miserable failure at the membership level. No more than five percent of the General Baptist laymen joined the new movement. The General Baptists were considered unsaved, untrained, and ignorant, but the large majority were faithful to their traditional convictions.

The initial thrust of the reorganization process left the General Baptists with only four churches and their pastors. Joseph Parker at Little Creek, William Parker at Meherrin, William Fulsher at Pungo, and John Winfield at Bear River refused to be a part of the defection to the Particulars. The Parker churches established arms or preaching points in Pitt, Greene, and Lenoir Counties, and through those outlets they evangelized a large area south of the Tar River in the General Baptist tradition. This remnant of the movement cultivated the ground that was to become the seedbed for later Free Will Baptist development. The Free Will Baptists, accepting the same spiritual tradition as their earlier counterpart, found an eager audience for their doctrine of a general atonement. Free Will Baptist churches quickly sprang up in the communities that had been prepared by the Parkers.

Notes for Chapter 3

[1]Paschal, "Morgan Edwards' Materials," 392.

[2]Ruth B. Bordin, "The Sect to Denomination Process in America: the Freewill Baptist Experience," *Church History*, XXXIV (March 1965), 78.

[3]W. T. Whitley, "The Six-Principle Baptists in America," *The Chronicle*, III (January 1940), 7. Used with permission of the American Baptist Historical Society.

[4]Ibid., 7-9.

[5]Whitefield preached at New Bern as early as 1739 (Paschal, *North Carolina*, I, 197).

[6]The Separate Baptists had come to North Carolina as early as 1754. By 1758, they had organized the Sandy Creek Association (Lumpkin, *Confessions*, 357).

[7]Ibid., 347.

[8]Torbet, *History*, 238.

[9]Ibid., 272.

[10]The Philadelphia Association adopted the 1689 confession of the English Particular Baptists (A. D. Gillette, ed., *Minutes of the Philadelphia Baptist Association from A.D. 1707 to A.D. 1807* [Philadelphia: American Baptist Publication Society, 1851], 46). The articles of faith of the Kehukee Association indicated the continued attitude of the Regular Baptists toward their Calvinistic views of evangelism. "We believe, that God, before the foundation of the world, for a purpose of his own glory, did elect a certain number of men and angels to eternal life; and that this election is particular, eternal and unconditional on the creature's part" (Burkitt and Read, *Concise History*, 48).

[11]Paschal, *North Carolina*, I, 208.

[12]Benedict, *General History*, II, 100.

[13]Edwards, "Tours," 21; Paschal, *North Carolina*, I, 205.

[14]Edwards, "Tours," 35-38.

[15]Ibid., 38.

[16]John Winfield had joined the ranks of the General Baptists by 1772. His name had not appeared in the records before that time (Edwards, "Furman MS," IV, 170).

[17]Edwards, "Crozer MS," IV, 8, 9.

[18]Paschal, *North Carolina*, I, 214.

[19]Paschal, *North Carolina*, I, 203.

[20]Lemuel Burkitt and Jesse Read described the experience (in Burkitt and Read, *Concise History*, 171, 172), indicating that the one who applied for church membership ". . . shall relate his experience, setting forth how the Lord awakened him, and brought him to a sense of his lost state by nature; how he had seen the insufficiency of his own works to save him: And how the Lord had revealed to him the way of life and salvation through Jesus Christ, and the reasons he has to believe that he is interested in this glorious plan; and the evidences that he has become a new creature."

[21]Burkitt and Read, *Concise History*, 42, 43.

[22]Benedict, *General History*, II, 98.

[23]J. D. Huffman, "The Baptists in North Carolina," Fourth Paper, *North Carolina Baptist Historical Papers*, II (October 1897), 35. (Hereinafter referred to as "Fourth Paper.")

[24]Lumpkin, *Confessions*, 354.

[25]Wheeler, *Parker's*, 8.

[26]Paschal, *North Carolina*, II, 170.

[27]Edwards, "Furman MS," IV, 129.

[28]Burkitt and Read, *Concise History*, 42, 43, 208; Huffman, "Fourth Paper," 35; Paschal, *North Carolina*, II, 202. Richard Knight, (in *Six Principle Baptists*, 318), was one of the few historians that indicated that the General Baptists might have been guilty of spiritual laxity. In a very general statement, he commented that ". . . it appears that

many of these southern churches became remiss in their attention to spiritual devotion, lax in their discipline, and rather declining."

[29]Hearn, *Origin*, 169.

[30]Ollie Latch, *History of the General Baptists* (Poplar Bluff, Mo.: The General Baptist Press, 1954), 113, 114. (Hereinafter referred to as *General Baptists*.) In his defense of the General Baptists, Latch actually agreed to more guilt than their opponents had described.

[31]Benedict, *General History*, II, 100.

[32]Ibid., 98, 99

[33]Edwards, "Crozer MS," V, 8, 9.

[34]Morgan Edwards, in (Edwards, "Tours," 26), referred to Wallis as a "private man."

[35]Paschal, *North Carolina*, I, 205.

[36]Paschal, *North Carolina*, I, 205; Huggins, *History*, 43.

[37]See above, 90.

[38]Robert Williams, William Walker, and Henry Ledbetter spent time among the Particular Baptists in South Carolina and then returned to North Carolina to continue the program of reorganization (Benedict, *General History*, II, 98; Paschal, *North Carolina*, I, 205).

[39]Benedict, *General History*, II, 99.

[40]Ibid., II, 306.

[41]Edwards, "Furman MS," IV, 126.

[42]Paschal, *North Carolina*, I, 209.

[43]Ibid., 210.

[44]Edwards, "Tours," 38. Edwards has caused some confusion. He contended that Kehukee was the first church to be reorganized but later gave an earlier date for the church at Upper Fishing Creek.

[45]Edwards, "Furman MS," IV, 7-24; Paschal, *North Carolina*, I, 210, 211; Huggins, *History*, 48.

[46]Burkitt and Read, *Concise History*, 230, 238; Edwards, "Furman MS, IV, 129-142.

[47]Burkitt and Read, *Concise History*, 230.

[48]Miller established a Regular Baptist church in the Yadkin area late in 1754 or early in the following year. The church was especially important because it was the first Baptist church west of Granville County. It had opened a new door for Baptist witness in a pioneer area (Paschal, *North Carolina*, I, 209).

[49]Edwards, "Furman MS," IV, 169, 170. The churches and ministers will be found in the chart below. The remnant of the reorganization will be considered in a later section.

[50]Edwards, "Tours," 25-38; Burkitt and Read, *Concise History*, 230.

[51]Paschal, *North Carolina*, I, 212.

[52]See above, 101.

[53]Edwards, "Furman MS," IV, 164-170. Pages 165-167 contain the names of the churches—one church in the middle of each page. Contantany is listed at the bottom of page 164.

[54]John Asplund, *The Universal Register of the Baptist Denomination in North America, For the Years 1790, 1791, 1792, 1793, and Part of 1794* (Boston: Printed by John W. Folsom, for the Author, 1794). (Hereinafter referred to as *Universal Register*.)

[55]Edwards, "Furman MS," IV, 169, 170. The Wingfield mentioned by Edwards was probably John Winfield who accepted the pastorate of the church at Pungo sometime before 1790 (Paschal, *North Carolina*, I, 235; Asplund, *Register*, 37; Benedict, *General History*, II, 100).

[56]See above, p. 70.

[57]Edwards, "Furman MS," IV, 169.

[58]U. S. Department of Commerce, *U. S. Bureau of the Census. Heads of Families at the First Census of the United States Taken in the Year 1790, North Carolina* (Washington: Government Printing Office, 1908). (Hereinafter referred to as *Heads of Families*.)

[59]Paschal, "Morgan Edwards' Materials," 393.

[60]Asplund, *Register*, 37.

[61]Edwards, "Tours," 28.

[62]David Leroy Corbitt, *The Formation of North Carolina Counties, 1663-1943* (Raleigh: State Department of Archives and History, 1950), 126.

[63]Burkitt and Read, *Concise History*, 225.

[64]*Heads of Families*; Hyde County, North Carolina, *Will Book* I, 172, 249.

[65]U. S. Department of Commerce, Bureau of the Census, *Population Schedules of the Third Census of the United States, 1810 for the Counties of Beaufort, Duplin, Hyde, Lenoir, and Pitt* (Washington: The National Archives, 1957).

[66]Wheeler, *Parker's*, 7; Hearn, *Origin*, 165; and Ware, *Disciples*, 80.

[67]Wheeler, *Parker's*, 6; Hearn, *Origin*, 165.

[68]*Minutes of the Annual Conference of Free Will Baptists of North Carolina, Bethel Conference, 1829*, quoted in Harrison and Barfield, *History*, I, 157, 158; *An Abstract of the Former Articles of Faith Confessed by the Original Baptist Church Holding the Doctrine of General Provision With a Proper Code of Discipline* (2nd ed., Newbern, N.C.: Printed by Salmon Hall, 1814 [1812]). (Hereinafter referred to as *Abstract*.)

4

North Carolina Continued

The Years of Recovery (1794-1812)
The Restatement of the Problem

THE FREE WILL BAPTIST CLAIM TO AN ANCIENT HERITAGE

As early as 1812, the Free Will Baptists in North Carolina indicated they were a continuation of the old General Baptist movement in the state.[1] By 1830, they openly were claiming the older movement as a part of their heritage.[2] From that time forward, the Free Will Baptists have never doubted that they have enjoyed a continuous witness in America since the founding of the first General Baptist church in North Carolina in 1727.

Unfortunately, however, the histories of the denomination have failed to establish their claim. For the most part, the histories were documented poorly and the doubts concerning the claim have not been erased. Because of the failure of the historians, the claim of an ancient heritage for the movement either has been surrounded by clouds of doubt or simply catalogued as tradition.

In spite of the poor documentation, however, a surprising number of respected historians have agreed that the Free Will Baptists have a valid claim. Some of the historians that accepted the validity of the claim wrote their works from the standpoint of a Regular Baptist concern. It naturally would be understood that their fields of interest did not allow a thorough defense of the Free Will Baptist position. Their conclusions were important, however, because of the respect they have acquired as church historians.

The Task at Hand

The primary purpose of this part of the study is to prove, through a thorough investigation of the sources, that there has been a continuing Free Will Baptist witness in America since 1727. The secondary purpose was to investigate the movement's development up to the time that the new identity was established. The secondary purpose has been employed up to this point to lay a solid foundation for the arguments for the primary purpose. Basically then, these chapters have served two purposes: (1) They have supplied the necessary background for the continuing story—the story would have been incomplete and incoherent if it had begun at the end of the reorganization period, and (2) they have established the fact that Joseph and William Parker introduced the doctrine of general atonement in the very area that was to become the heart of the Free Will Baptist movement. Free Will Baptist churches arose early in the communities that were evangelized by the Parkers.

The problem will be approached from two directions: (1) a historical argument recognizing and evaluating the conclusions of recent and early historians, and (2) a theological argument showing the spiritual kinship between the General and Free Will Baptist movements.

The Historical Argument
The Conclusions of Recent Historians

GEORGE WASHINGTON PASCHAL

George Washington Paschal has written a recent history of the Baptists in North Carolina that must be acknowledged as the most exhaustive study available.[3] His careful use of the documents of the early period has made his work especially valuable as a source book for any serious study of the Baptists in the state.

Paschal struggled with some difficulty to the conclusion that the Free Will Baptist denomination grew out of the old General Baptist movement in North Carolina. He presented his conclusion on two different occasions. The treatment of the problem in his history of the Baptists in the state was not so forceful as that found in his article, "Morgan Edwards' Materials Toward a History of the Baptists in the Province of North Carolina." While the former conclusion was tempered with the introduction of the possibility that the General Baptist movement might have ended with the reorganization of the church at Meherrin, the latter was presented without reservation.

In his *History of North Carolina Baptists*, Paschal noted that Joseph Parker had established churches at Little Contentnea Creek in Greene County and at Wheat Swamp in Lenior. He then concluded that ". . . from the churches thus organized in his old age have come with slightly amended teachings the present Freewill Baptists of the State. . . ."[4] Showing some hesitancy, he continued:

> The Calvinists soon built a church near that of Winfield on the Pungo and seem to have absorbed its membership. The church at Meherrin continued in the General Baptist order with diminishing power until the death of William Parker in 1794. Then it became a Particular Baptist church and the General Baptists of North Carolina were no more, unless indeed we regard the Freewill Baptists as General Baptists under a different name.[5]

Because his interests did not include the fate of the General Baptists after the successful invasion by the Particulars, Paschal did not feel it necessary to pursue the question. However, he did pause long enough for a somewhat more favorable conclusion in his study of Edwards' "Materials." In a more positive attitude, he spoke of the remnant of the invasion, arguing that:

> These General Baptist churches were all that were left of the numerous and large churches of this order after the reforms of Miller and Vanhorn in 1755-56. Joseph Parker, who with Paul Palmer had gathered the first Baptist churches in the Province, and his cousin William Parker, and John Winfield retained their Arminian principles.

Joseph Parker had established the church at Meherrin, but at this time had probably moved to Contentney. He gathered other General Baptist churches in eastern North Carolina, and served other weak congregations, which formed the nucleus of the present denomination of Free Will Baptists in this state. . . .[6]

I. D. STEWART

It has been extremely difficult to classify many of the historians that have dealt with the question of the heritage of the Free Will Baptists because their works have fallen in the borderline area between recent and contemporary sources. Though it was published as late as 1862, the work of I. D. Stewart has been considered extremely important for the purposes of this study. He was concerned primarily with the history of the Freewill Baptist movement in New England, but he did present a number of solid convictions concerning the origins of the movement in the South. His access to the early documents of the northern movement, including their correspondence with the group in North Carolina, added weight to the importance of his conclusions.

After recognizing the degree of success achieved by the reorganization process in North Carolina, Stewart added:

> . . . Palmer was no more, but Parker and a few churches declined to unite, and their number continued to increase till Hutchins [Elias] was there, when there were some twenty ministers, as many churches, and 845 members. They were called Freewill Baptists, and in faith and practice did not differ from their brethren of the same name at the North, only many of them were slaveholders.[7]

Stewart had based his conclusion on the information included in a letter from Jesse Heath, a leader of the North Carolina group, to the senior editor of the Freewill Baptist periodical, *The Morning Star*. The letter was dated May 29, 1827, and indicated that Heath had entered the Free Will Baptist movement in North Carolina some twenty years before. Heath revealed that in 1807 the group had consisted of five churches and three ministers.[8] Stewart contended that the few churches and ministers composed the remnant of the Joseph Parker ministry, and they became the nucleus of the Free Will Baptist denomination in the South.

D. B. MONTGOMERY

Though the General Baptist name died out in North Carolina, it continued to be used in other areas of the country. There is still a small group of General Baptists that trace their history back to the work of Elder Benoni Stinson in southern Indiana in 1823.[9] The group has been represented most ably by the historical studies of D. B. Montgomery.

Montgomery summarized his study of the General Baptists in North Carolina by saying:

> However, some of these churches were not transformed until 1794 [Meherrin], and some few of them never yielded to the proselyting influences of the transforming ele-

ment, but maintained their principles and gradually added other churches and their unbroken lineage is in existence in North Carolina at this time (1882). . . .[10]

Montgomery, especially, was impressed with the letter from Jesse Heath to the northern Freewill Baptists in 1827. He felt that the letter gave strong support to the conclusion that the Free Will Baptists in North Carolina had grown out of the General Baptist movement. He evidently did not have access to the entire letter as he referred to an excerpt found in I. D. Stewart's studies. As mentioned earlier, the letter indicated that Jesse Heath became a Free Will Baptist minister in 1807 and that the struggling denomination then consisted of five churches and three ministers. Montgomery evaluated the importance of the letter by saying:

> . . . The above letter is of great importance in establishing a connection between the four churches of the old General or Original Free Will Baptists that escaped the transformation and continued steadfast in their original doctrines, and the present Original Free Will Baptists in North Carolina.

> The reader will bear in mind that in 1807, when Elder Jesse Heath, became a minister among the General Baptists in North Carolina, that this was only thirteen years after the Meheren [sic] Church, of which Elder William Parker had been pastor for many years previous to his death, had been absorbed, and these people then claimed to be the direct descendants of the English General Baptists as organized by Elders Paul Palmer, Joseph Parker, William Parker, William Sojourner and others. . . .[11]

DAMON C. DODD

In 1956, in the midst of a revival of concern for Free Will Baptist history, Damon C. Dodd attempted the first extensive study of the movement since 1897. Because Dodd undertook the monumental task of covering the period from the beginning of the movement up to the year of publication, his study of the reorganization process and of the remnant was limited to less than six pages. Basing his conclusions almost entirely on the work of George Washington Paschal and R. K. Hearn, he argued:

> Meherrin was not the only Free Will Baptist church to survive the reformation. We have definite record of at least three others which came through the trials and are still 'true to the faith of Free Will Baptists today.' Gum Swamp church, in Pitt County, withstood the shocks of proselyting and remains today as a bulwark of the faith. Another is Little Creek church, in Greene County. This church had been quite severely divided at one time over the matter of going over to the Calvinists. The pastor and a large number of its members turned from the old paths, but a few remained firm and saved the church from going over completely.

The church at Wheat Swamp remained Free Will Baptist for several years but finally died for lack of a pastor. . . .[12]

Dodd's work suffered to some degree because the documentation of the study was somewhat weak. Though he mentioned "definite records" concerning the history of the three churches mentioned above, he did not identify the records. His work made a significant contribution, however, as it identified the traditional Free Will Baptist position concerning their relationship to the older General Baptist movement.

G. W. MILLION

In 1958, just two years after Dodd's work was published, G. W. Million gave added evidence of the new excitement concerning Free Will Baptist history by publishing a second study of the movement. Like Dodd, Million attempted to investigate the entire history of the movement from its beginning to the time of his writing. Again like Dodd, his work presented the traditional position of the denomination but failed to give adequate documentation.

Million added two churches to the list presented by Damon Dodd—the Grimsley church in Greene County and the church at Louson Swamp. In a summary of his study of the reorganization process, Million attempted to trace the sixteen churches mentioned by Morgan Edwards.

In 1752 there were sixteen churches. Six of them went into the Kehukee Association; this left ten to be accounted for otherwise. Five of this number can be named and accounted for somewhat. Gum Swamp, organized in 1728, survived the struggle of 1765 and today is doing a great work. Little Creek in Greene County, organized in the same year, was divided by the efforts of the Calvinists just described and although her pastor and several of the members went to the Calvinistic party, a sufficient number stood firm in the old paths to preserve the identity of the church and she is still alive. Grimsley Church, Greene County, is still alive and true to the faith. Lousan Swamp survived the revolution period spoken of but went off with Mr. Hunnicutt in his raid. Wheat Swamp also survived, but possibly died for lack of pastoral services. It is likely that the greater part of the membership of the remaining four churches migrated into Tennessee and Kentucky.[13]

Million was mistaken in his tracing of the churches that had existed before the reorganization period. There were at least twenty churches in existence at that time.[14] Morgan Edwards did not include a number of the "arms" of the various churches in his initial estimate of the size of the movement in North Carolina. He did include them in the text of his study. Twelve of those churches had joined the Kehukee Association by 1761.[15] It is quite certain that Million's date for the churches at Little Creek and Gum Swamp was based on the tradition that has been accepted by the denomination.[16] Though the churches have a long and important heritage and are among the oldest churches in the denomination, the records have not indicated the possibility of such an early date. There are three basic arguments against the early date: (1) Major settlement in the province in 1728 was limited to the eastern counties—it is unlikely that the western reaches of Craven and Beaufort Counties[17] enjoyed extensive settlement by that time, (2) the churches were credited to the work of Joseph Parker but Parker did not arrive in Dobbs (Greene) County until 1756,[18] and (3) the records did not mention any of the five churches considered by Million until the Little Creek church was organized in 1761.

In spite of the arguments, however, the tradition need not be far wrong. If it can be proven that the church organized by Joseph Parker on Little Contentnea Creek was the same church that continued as the Little Creek Free Will Baptist Church, then the church still holds the distinction of being the oldest existing church in the denomination. The problem will be dealt with later as the history of the church is evaluated more thoroughly.

M. A. HUGGINS

M. A. Huggins has contributed the most recent history of the Baptists in North Carolina.[19] Though the work was not as exhaustive as Paschal's earlier study, it has made a number of important contributions to the study of the Free Will Baptists in the state. His painstaking research in the Baptist records has resulted in an excellent table showing the organization date, association affiliation, location, and founders of the churches organized between 1727 and 1829. The table has proven to be a valuable source for a study of this type.

Huggins proved to be the most outspoken "Regular" Baptist in defense of the Free Will Baptist claim to a heritage that dates back to 1727. Many of the reservations noted in earlier Baptist histories were omitted in the new study.

In his treatment of the beginnings of the Free Will Baptist movement, Huggins agreed with the group's contention that the first Baptists in the state were all "Free Will Baptists" in character and doctrine.[20] He also agreed that after the reorganization process, the few churches that remained true to the general order called themselves Free Will Baptists. He considered the new name to be ". . . only another name for General Baptists."[21]

From that common agreement with the Free Will Baptists, Huggins went on to develop his own conclusion that:

> It seems quite clear that the members of the churches, who did not wish to become Particular Baptists, formed the nucleus for the beginning of the new denomination which came in time to be called (Original) Freewill Baptists, while the Particular Baptists came in time to be called by some, Regular, and later, Missionary Baptists....[22]

Huggins further argued that Parker's churches at Little Contentnea, Wheat Swamp, and Gum Swamp (Conetoe settlement) joined together in 1780 to form the Bethel Conference of Free Will Baptists. The early date is significant because it places the organization of the first Free Will Baptist conference before the death of Parker. Unfortunately, Huggins did not indicate the source of his information.[23]

Huggins concluded his study of the movement's heritage by contending that "...gradually the General Baptists became Free Will Baptists and thus a new denomination was established in the state."[24]

CHARLES CROSSFIELD WARE

Charles Crossfield Ware is a past curator of the Historical Collection of the Disciples of Christ at Atlantic Christian College in Wilson, North Carolina. He has done extensive research in the history of the Disciples and in the process of that study has found it necessary to spend much time with background studies in the history of North Carolina Baptists.

Like Huggins, Ware agreed that Joseph Parker's churches were known as Free Will Baptist churches before Parker's death. Working from that premise, he indicated that there were three Free Will Baptist centers in the state when Parker died in 1791 or 1792. He identified the churches as Wheat Swamp in Lenoir County, Gum Swamp in Pitt County, and Pungo in Beaufort.[25] The churches at Little Creek, Grimsley, and Louson Swamp were mentioned, but he seemed to feel that they were arms of the work at Wheat Swamp. Ware closed his argument by contending that five of the churches constituted the group mentioned by Jesse Heath in his letter to the New England Freewill Baptists in 1807.[26]

OTHER PROMINENT CHURCH HISTORIANS

Though the argument for a Free Will Baptist heritage that dates back to 1727 has not been documented satisfactorily, it has gained a wide popularity and acceptance. Robert G. Torbet, Albert Henry Newman, and Henry C. Vedder did not deal extensively with the problem, but they did defend the claim of the Free Will Baptists.[27] The respect that they have attained as historians has demanded that they be included in the list.

The Conclusions of Contemporary Historians

Again the matter of classification of the historians has proven to be a problem. The work of Lemuel Burkitt and Jesse Read was published in 1803, in the middle of the controversial period, and is identified easily. Others, however, were written later and have caused some question as to their right to be accepted as contemporary sources. In the latter case, the decision was made on the basis of the fact that the authors had lived and served during the controversial period. Though their histories came later, the men themselves were involved in the activities of the period. Since the works came out of the period in question and included the personal knowledge of the authors, they bear a greater weight of proof for the argument that the Free Will Baptists have existed since 1727.

LEMUEL BURKITT AND JESSE READ

One of the most important arguments for a continuing witness of the Free Will Baptists has been furnished by their opponents. Lemuel Burkitt and Jesse Read made it quite clear that they considered the General Baptists to be lost. In their opinion, the reorganization process had been both necessary and a blessing to the Baptists of North Carolina. They had few good things to say about the remnant that escaped the invasion. In spite of their antagonism toward the remnant, however, they did make some valuable contributions to the continuing history of those men and churches that escaped the onslaught of the Particulars. Their work proved extremely important from at least three standpoints: (1) the study was published in 1803 and bears the authority delegated to a contemporary source, (2) the entire ministry of the two authors was spent in the area of and during the time of the Parker ministry, and (3) the writers used the term "Free Will Baptists" to refer to the General Baptist remnant. The first two points have established the authority of the work. The final one has confirmed the fact that the Free Will Baptist name was in common use before 1803, and it was used to identify the churches that had survived the Particular Baptist invasion in North Carolina.

The Importance of the Date of the Writing—In 1812, Jesse Heath and James Roach, two early leaders of the Free Will Baptist movement, inferred that the denomination had been in existence for many years. In that year, they were assigned the task of investigating the early documents of the denomination that were "now extant" and using them as a basis for a code of discipline.[28] The Discipline was to be added to their existing *Confession of Faith*.

Jesse Heath came to the denomination in 1807.[29] Though he indicated the denomination included five churches and three ministers at that time, he did not offer further information concerning the history of the group. In the light of the limitations found in the early Free Will Baptist documents, the work of Burkitt and Read became extremely important. Their 1803 publication date indicated that the Free Will Baptists were in existence at least four years before Heath became a minister and their writings pushed the date back beyond the death of the Parkers.

The Background of the Writers—The value of the work for the purposes of this study has been enhanced by the fact that Burkitt and Read lived and worked in the area where the Free Will Baptists were to prosper. The time of their ministry coincided with that of Joseph and William Parker.

Lemuel Burkitt was born in 1751 and grew up in eastern North Carolina during the reorganization period. He became a Christian and began to preach in 1771. Jesse Read was baptized in 1773 and ordained in 1775.[30]

Both men were in the right place at the right time. Read was pastor of the Rocky Swamp church in the county next to William Parker's work at Meherrin. Burkitt was to become Parker's successor when the Meherrin church was reorganized in 1794.[31] Both men traveled extensively over the entire area of Free Will Baptist development in their work with the Kehukee Association. They were familiar with the religious activities of the period and would have known the proper designations for the various religious groups. They were eyewitnesses to the development of the Free Will Baptist movement.

The Use of a New Name for an Old Movement—Two basic facts stood out in Burkitt and Read's treatment of their Arminian opponents: (1) The Free Will Baptist name was in common use before the death of the Parkers, and (2) the name was used to identify the churches established by the preachers of the early General Baptist movement.

Though the authors often referred to churches being organized on the "Free-will order," they also employed the name as a proper title for churches within the Arminian movement.[32]

There can be no question but that Burkitt and Read identified the new name with the old General Baptists. They contended that the first Baptist churches in North Carolina were organized on the Free-will order by Paul Palmer and Joseph Parker.[33] They were more specific in their treatment of the beginnings of the Kehukee Association in admitting that most of the churches first had been gathered by the "Free-will Baptists."[34] William Parker's church at Meherrin and Winfield's church at Pungo, two of the churches that were not involved in the initial reorganization process, also were designated as Free-will churches.[35] William Walker, one of the earlier leaders of the General Baptist movement, was identified as a "Free-will Baptist" minister.[36]

By 1803, the new name was the accepted title for the old movement. The Parker churches were considered Free Will Baptist churches and the ministers were designated as Free Will Baptist preachers.

S. J. WHEELER

Though S. J. Wheeler wrote his history as late as 1847, it has been classified as a contemporary source for the purposes of this study. Wheeler's ministry covered much of the period of concern and in many cases he was able to speak as an eyewitness. He also had access to the minutes of the Pasquotank (Shiloh) church as far back as 1758,[37] as well as those of other churches in the area. In his capacity as Clerk of the Chowan Association, he traveled throughout the area of Free Will Baptist development. He became Clerk in 1838 and continued in the office for twenty-nine years.[38]

Wheeler has made a number of valuable contributions to the study of a continuing Free Will Baptist witness: (1) He provided most of the information available on the later years of Joseph Parker's ministry, (2) he identified the churches that Joseph Parker established after the reorganization process, and (3) he identified the minister who succeeded Parker after his death.

Like Burkitt and Read, Wheeler referred to the Parker churches as Free Will Baptist churches. After tracing the travels of Parker from his first work in Chowan Precinct to his final field of activity in Lenoir and Dobbs (Greene) Counties, Wheeler revealed that Parker was supported in his later years by the Free Will Baptist church at Wheat Swamp.[39] During that period, Wheeler contended, Parker was involved in an itinerant ministry that included preaching points at Gum Swamp and Pungo .[40]

By far, Wheeler's most important contribution was his identification of Parker's successor. By indicating the arrival of a Free Will Baptist minister to continue Parker's work, Wheeler revealed a definite and historical link between the old General Baptists and the new Free Will Baptist movement. Not only did he recognize a continuing ministry through the leaders of the movement, he also has connected the churches of the older movement with the leadership of the new. After revealing that Joseph Parker had died in 1791 or 1792, he added:

> . . . James Roach, a Freewill minister from Craven county, took charge of the churches on Wheat Swamp and Loosing [Louson] Swamp, on the demise of Elder Parker, and under his labors the churches were revived and greatly increased. There are at this time [1847] more than three thousand members of the Freewill churches, who are probably, the descendants of the handful of Wheat Swamp, Pungo and Conetoe [Gum Swamp.][41]

Wheeler's information concerning Parker's successor has been corroborated by the census records for 1790 and 1800. James Roach moved from Craven County to the area of the Parker work sometime after 1790.[42] He was to become one of the most important leaders in the Free Will Baptist movement.

RUFUS K. HEARN

Rufus K. Hearn's work, *Origin of the Free Will Baptist Church of North Carolina*, represented the first successful attempt by the Free Will Baptists to record their history and to defend their claim to an ancient heritage.[43] Hearn's history, like that of S. J. Wheeler, was written shortly after the controversial period. However, since Hearn's ministry continued through much of the period, his work has been classified as a contemporary source. Hearn was born in 1819[44] and spent his entire ministry within the framework of the Free Will Baptist denomination.

Though Hearn's work was not published in book form,[45] and though he was guilty of failing to document his information at times, the work must be considered one of the most accurate histories of the Free Will Baptist denomination. The entire study consisted of only a few pages, allowing little time for the question of a continuing Free Will Baptist witness, but Hearn's arguments, based on interviews with eyewitnesses to the events of the controversial period, have demanded a certain degree of respect.[46]

The Testimony of Eyewitnesses—Hearn's main argument for a continuing Free Will Baptist witness was based on his interviews with eyewitnesses to the events of the transition period. When Hearn was a small boy, he was familiar with old people who told him of their attendance at conferences at the Gum Swamp Free Will Baptist Church when they were children.[47] Since Hearn was born in 1819, the argument indicated that the church was in existence well before 1800. The "old folks" contended that the church was a Free Will Baptist church when they were children and that it had continued to serve in the same denomination.

The second interview, though possibly enjoying less authority, was more complete and of much more interest. Even though Hearn was dealing with a second party rather than with the eyewitness, he felt that the relationship between the two parties made the information a reliable source. Hearn interviewed a Free Will Baptist whose mother had been a member of the Gum Swamp church while the Parkers were living. The church was identified as a Free Will Baptist church during the time of William Parker's ministry.

> An old FreeWill Baptist sister, who lived to be considerably over a hundred years old told her son, and he, also a FreeWill Baptist, told the writer of this that she knew Elder William Parker well, recollected when he first came to the neighborhood and when he preached his first sermon on the plat of ground whereon old Gum Swamp Church now stands. The writer lives within about three-quarters of a mile of said church, and was raised within two miles of it. The old sister referred to was named Teel, by marriage. I think her maiden name was Pollard. She was raised within a few miles of Gum Swamp and lived and died in the neighborhood and was a faithful member of the FreeWill Church at that place up to the time of her death. I do not recollect whether she was

baptized by Elder Parker, or by some other minister who was raised up under his ministry. She said that he soon raised up a church, and was pastor up to the time of his death.[48]

The Final Conclusion—Hearn enjoyed the special privilege of compiling his history during a time when he still could look into the past through the experiences of those who had lived through the transition period. His interviews convinced him that the Free Will Baptists had an ancient and worthy heritage—that the denomination was a continuation of the Parker work and must be dated from 1727.

> We bear the same name,[49] we have the same book of discipline, we preach the old doctrine, we receive members the same way without an experience of Grace, we commemorate the Lord's Supper the same way, we wash the saints feet the same way, we are the same persecuted old FreeWill Baptists that was organized in 1727 by Elder Paul Palmer.[50]

The Backward Look

The review of the conclusions of recent and contemporary historians concerning the Free Will Baptist claim to a definite connection with the old General Baptists has resulted in two further conclusions: (1) The claim has not wanted for supporters but rather for proof, and (2) some of the contemporary sources have given solid evidence of the truth of the claim. The investigation of the conclusions of the historians has prepared a foundation for the study of other arguments for the validity of the Free Will Baptist claim to a continuing witness since 1727.

The Correspondence Between New England and North Carolina Free Will Baptists

Though the Free Will Baptists of North Carolina never became organizationally involved with the Freewill Baptists of New England, they did enjoy a friendly relationship with them through correspondence and through the visits of representatives from New England to North Carolina. The correspondence has been preserved and has offered added evidence of the continuing witness of the Free Will Baptist denomination.

THE CORRESPONDENCE OF ELDER JESSE HEATH

Jesse Heath became a Free Will Baptist preacher in 1807. By 1812, he was one of the major leaders in the young and growing movement. From 1827 through 1830, Heath was involved in a continual correspondence with the Freewill Baptists in New England. The denomination is indebted to Heath for the only contemporary statistics of the southern movement before 1829.

Only one of Heath's letters had a direct bearing on the question of a continuing Free Will Baptist witness. In a letter to the senior editor of *The Morning Star*, a weekly newspaper published by the northern Freewill Baptists, Heath traced the southern movement back to 1807. The letter was written in response to inquiries from the group in New England as to the size, progress, and history of the sister movement in the South. It was dated May 29, 1827. Heath remembered:

> Twenty years ago, when I first came to the ministry, there was but three ministers and five small churches, but bless the Lord, latterly we have been highly favored, and the work at this moment is gloriously reviving amongst us. . . .[51]

Though Heath's letter did not trace the Free Will Baptists all the way back to the Parkers, it did give documentary evidence of the existence of the movement just four years after Burkitt and Read revealed that the General Baptist churches were known as Free Will Baptist churches.[52] Heath indicated that he joined a work that was already in existence. Though the group was small and struggling, it predated the arrival of the new preacher.

Heath's letter made a valuable contribution to the history of the Free Will Baptists. Though it did not complete the link between the General and Free Will Baptists in North Carolina, it did provide an internal, contemporary source that predated the extant conference records of the movement by twenty-two years.[53]

THE CORRESPONDENCE OF ELIAS HUTCHINS

While Jesse Heath served as official correspondent for the southern group of Free Will Baptists, Elias Hutchins accepted the task for those in the North. Hutchins also served the Freewill Baptists as an itinerant evangelist. In that capacity, he traveled extensively in North Carolina and gained a personal knowledge of the men and of the progress of the southern movement.[54] His letters to his own denomination concerning his travels in North Carolina serve as valuable sources for a study of the early history of the denomination.

The Travels of Elias Hutchins in North Carolina—Elias Hutchins was impressed with the importance of an itinerant ministry when he first accepted the call to preach. His first step in preparation for his ministry was the purchase of a horse and saddle. He began his ministry at Wilton, Maine, and was ordained there in 1824.[55] By the winter of 1829, Hutchins was in North Carolina serving as a representative of the Freewill Baptists of New England.[56] The visit lasted more than nine months and gave Hutchins the opportunity to travel throughout the area of Free Will Baptist development. Before the visit was completed he had spent time in Pitt, Beaufort, Craven, Lenoir, Wayne, Duplin, and Orange Counties. Through his travels he became thoroughly familiar with the Free Will Baptists and their history. He again visited the area in late 1832 and early 1833. He selected Greene County as his center of operation, but continued to use the pattern of travel that was characteristic of his ministry. His travels during the latter visit took him as far west as Sampson County where the Free Will Baptists had recently established meeting houses at Piney Grove and Ten Mile.[57]

Hutchins' extensive travels in the area of concern added a degree of authority to his writings that other historians of the northern movement did not enjoy. His conclusions concerning the continuing witness of the Free Will Baptists in the South were based on his own personal research. At the end of his first visit to the state, he was convinced that the Free Will Baptists had their roots in the older General Baptist movement of the eighteenth century.

The Argument for a Continuing Free Will Baptist Witness—In 1830, soon after his first visit had been completed, Hutchins sent a circular letter to the North Carolina Annual Conference of Free Will Baptists expressing his conclusions concerning their ancient heritage. The letter was accepted and entered in the records of the Conference for the year 1830. There can be no doubt but that the Free Will Baptists of North Carolina accepted Hutchins' contention that they had grown out of the old General Baptist movement. They were sure that the churches and leaders of the older group were a part of their heritage. Hutchins encouraged the small denomination by comparing their situation in 1830 with their drastic circumstances many years before. He reminded them:

> Should you contrast your present situation with the standing of your brethren 65 years ago, you will discover abundant cause to be thankful for the favors that God has of late conferred upon you. About that time, the most of the churches and ministers composing the body to which you now belong forsook their original principles and united themselves to a body of Christians whose sentiments their former brethren could not think accorded with the gospel of Christ. The small number that refused to follow the seceding party soon encountered serious difficulties, and their prospects were of a gloomy character. They were illiterate, opposed, considered as heretics, and had all manner of evil spoken against them; and at the expiration of 60 years, this little despised body consisted of only about 800 members. But, O my brethren, what has God done for you in the course of five years that are past! The mouths of gainsayers, in many places, have been stopped; much of the prejudice that formerly existed against you has given place to feelings and sentiments more Christlike and refined; some that were your enemies, have become your friends; and many that were the subjects of the kingdom of darkness and looking on religion with indifference have been translated into the Kingdom of God's Son, and can now cheerfully unite with you in the worship of the living God.[58]

Hutchins received no arguments against his conclusions. The conclusions of the outsider perfectly matched those of the natives of the state. It should be remembered that the recipients of the letter included Jesse Heath. Heath had been a part of the movement since 1807 and had worked with James Roach, the preacher that succeeded Joseph Parker. The acceptance of Hutchins' conclusions by men of Heath's experience indicate that the convictions were a part of the movement from the very beginning.

The Continuing Ministry of the Leaders During the Transition Period

In his letter to the editor of *The Morning Star*, Jesse Heath revealed that the Free Will Baptist denomination consisted of five churches and three ministers in 1807.[59] Because he did not name either the churches or the ministers, it was necessary to look in different directions for clues to their identity. The possibilities proved numerous, but the sources limited positive identification to only one of the leaders.

THE POSSIBLE LEADERS DURING THE TRANSITION PERIOD

Howell Hearn, the father of the first Free Will Baptist historian, was born in 1784[60] and lived through the transition period. He was identified as a Free Will Baptist minister in the first records of the Annual Conference, but the sources did not allow the conclusion that he was one of the three ministers mentioned by Jesse Heath. They only established that he lived during the period in question, that his ministry took place in the area of Free Will Baptist development, and that he was an early leader of the movement. In short, the records made Howell Hearn a likely prospect for one of the three men that were present in 1807.

John Winfield was pastor of a General Baptist church as early as 1772.[61] By 1780, he had moved to Hyde County, became the pastor of the Pungo church in neighboring Beaufort County.[62] Burkitt and Read, the Regular Baptist historians, inferred that the church had been reorganized before 1803 and that all General Baptist influence in the area was ended.[63] Though the Winfield church might have been dissolved, the early establishment of a Free Will Baptist church in the area indicated that the General sentiment was still alive.

As was mentioned earlier, tracing Winfield's continuing ministry met with a unique problem. There were two men of the same name in Hyde County in 1790. One of the two men lived until 1810, but it has been impossible to identify the survivor. The continued General influence in the area and the early establishment of a Free Will Baptist church in the tiny community was the best evidence that the preacher survived beyond the end of the eighteenth century. Winfield became a second likely prospect as one of the three leaders in 1807.

ONE POSITIVE IDENTIFICATION

At least one leader of the Free Will Baptists has been traced from the early period into the nineteenth century when the new name was well established.

James Roach first was mentioned by John Asplund in 1790.[64] Asplund did not identify Roach except to list him as a Baptist minister in Craven County. His name followed that of the pastor of the Goose Creek Regular Baptist Church, and the position of the name seemed to indicate his affiliation with that congregation. However, Roach's name never appeared in the Kehukee Association records,[65] and in 1794, he was chosen to succeed Joseph Parker.[66] It has become evident that he was committed fully to the General faith since he became a leading figure in the Free Will Baptist movement early in the nineteenth century.

Soon after 1790, James Roach moved from Craven County to his new work among the Parker churches in Pitt, Greene, and Lenoir Counties. He settled in Greene County[67] and traveled to the churches at Wheat Swamp, Louson Swamp, Grimsley, and Gum Swamp.[68] The last years of his life were spent at Gum Swamp.[69]

In 1812, Roach and Jesse Heath were chosen to revise the old *General Confession of Faith* and to prepare a new discipline.[70] His long experience gained him the respect of his people.

There can be little doubt but that James Roach was one of the three ministers that Jesse Heath referred to as being a part of the denomination in 1807. He lived through the entire period of transition and in his capacity as successor to Joseph Parker, he became the major figure in the transition process. Through his connections with the Parker churches and his emergence as a Free Will

Baptist leader, James Roach established a solid connection between the old General Baptists of North Carolina and their Free Will Baptist successors.

The Continued Use of the General Baptist Name in the Nineteenth Century

It has been shown in the contemporary writings of Lemuel Burkitt and Jesse Read that the General Baptist remnant assumed a new name before the death of William and Joseph Parker. Burkitt and Read actually shunned the older name in favor of the new.[71] Even the earliest leaders of the Palmer-Parker movement were designated as Free Will Baptists. Though the two names were synonymous, the new name became the more popular title for the movement before the writing of Burkitt and Read's history in 1803.

The name question often proved to be a stumbling block in any attempt to prove that the Free Will Baptist work in North Carolina grew out of the older General Baptist movement. Tradition argued that the older name disappeared before 1800 and that the new name did not appear until the second quarter of the nineteenth century. The gap was considered an obstacle too great to overcome.

Burkitt and Read shattered the latter part of the tradition by revealing that the new name was applied to the Parker and Winfield churches before the turn of the century. In 1812, the Free Will Baptists shattered the first part of the tradition by indicating that they used both names to refer to their body of believers. Though they spoke of themselves as Free Will Baptists, they retained the older name on the title page of their 1812 revision of the old *General Baptist Confession of Faith*. The revised work was entitled, *An Abstract of the Former Articles of Faith Confessed by the Original Baptist Church Holding the Doctrine of General Provision with a Proper Code of Discipline*.

The document was identified as a Free Will Baptist work by the signatures of James Roach and Jesse Heath, two of the most prominent names in the early history of the denomination. R. K. Hearn, the Free Will Baptist historian, made it quite clear that the title identified the new group with the old name. After indicating that he was attempting to prove that the Chowan church of 1727 was the first Free Will Baptist church, he added:

> . . . This is the reason why the title page of our book of discipline calls us the 'Original Baptist Church,' holding the doctrine of General Provision, and this is our true name, and I will, before I get through, show why we are called Free Will Baptists. . . .[72]

No gap existed between the use of the old name and the acceptance of the new. The two periods over-lapped. Again, a solid connection was established between the General Baptists and their successors in North Carolina.

The Continuing Ministry of the Churches During the Transition Period

It must be admitted that few records of a local nature—deeds or church records—were found for the Parker churches. However, new evidence found during the process of research demands that the churches receive some consideration.

In the first place, the emergence of Free Will Baptist churches in communities that had been opened up by the General Baptists happened too often to be attributed to simple coincidence. The first records of the Free Will Baptist Annual Conference of North Carolina revealed that ten of the earliest Free Will Baptist churches sprang up in such communities.[73] Except for New Bern, all the communities were tiny settlements that hardly could have supported two churches of like conviction. Most of the communities today consist of a general store and a service station. Many of them still do not attempt to support more than one church of a particular faith.[74]

Second, S. J. Wheeler and R. K. Hearn revealed that Joseph and William Parker established preaching points at Little Creek, Grimsley, Wheat Swamp, Louson Swamp, and Gum Swamp.[75] Morgan Edwards corroborated the information concerning the church at Little Creek.[76] At the same time, Burkitt and Read established that all the Parker churches as well as the Winfield church at Pungo were called Free Will Baptist churches before the end of the Parker-Winfield period.[77] All the communities mentioned as Parker preaching points continued to support Free Will Baptist churches after the Parkers were dead.

Finally, new evidence has shown that the present Little Creek Free Will Baptist Church is located on the same property that Joseph Parker bought from Jacob Blount on Christmas Day, 1756. Dr. Charles Holloman, serving as a professional researcher for the writer, located the surveys for Parker's property and for the land adjoining his holdings.

The Free Will Baptist denomination has contended for many years that the present church was organized by Parker and that the church still stands on the old property. Up to this time, however, the claim had not been substantiated. The original deed indicated that the property was between Little and Great Contentnea Creeks, but failed to pinpoint the exact location. The recently discovered surveys solved the ancient problem. Parker's initial 100 acre purchase was located near the western bank of Little Contentnea Creek at the crossroads that was to become the present community of Scuffleton. The northern half of the property was enclosed by a narrow grant of forty-two acres that was unowned property until it was granted to Benjamin Hooker in 1797. The Hooker property bordered the creek bank. Its northeastern corner was located at the western end of the Scuffleton bridge. The narrow strip followed the Parker line on the west, north, and east, serving as a buffer between the preacher's property and the creek.[78] The strip did not extend the full length of Parker's large purchase. To the southwest his land bordered a new purchase of two hundred acres he had acquired in 1761.[79] On the south and southeast, the initial purchase was bordered by the land of Jacob Blount and by Mark Sauls' Pocosin (Swamp).[80]

A 1762 Tax List revealed that all of Jacob Blount's land was in Pitt County.[81] Pitt had been formed from Beaufort County in 1760 and included a small tract of land west of Little Contentnea Creek that earlier had been a part of Craven County.[82] This information along with John Asplund's contention that the Little Creek church was in Pitt County,[83] already limited the possible sites of the church property to a narrow strip along the western bank of the creek.[84]

From 1812, when the Free Will Baptist Annual Conference met at Little Creek,[85] the location of the church has been accepted as the present location at Scuffleton. Until now, however, there has been no proof that the church was on the Parker property which had been purchased in 1756. Part of the problem in tracing the history of the church and in pinpointing its location came from the evolution of the name of the creek that gave the church its identity. Morgan Edwards listed the creek as Contantony Creek,[86] but John Asplund changed it to Quotankney.[87] Actually, both men were correct for the name of the creek had passed through a number of changes during the eighteenth century. In addition to the two names above, the creek also has been known as Conneghta, Little Coteckney, Little Cotentnea, and Little Contentnea.[88] In a recent investigation of the early maps, William S. Powell showed that all the names identify the same creek.[89]

The recently discovered surveys completed the picture. The property of Joseph Parker was located near the western bank of Little Contentnea Creek at what is now the community of Scuffleton. The records show that the Little Creek Free Will Baptist Church has been located at the same location since 1812. Since Parker made it his habit to donate his own property for a church,[90] it would seem likely that he did the same at Little Creek. There has been a church of the same type of faith on Parker's property near Scuffleton at least since 1761.[91] Since the church was named after the creek, it is not unlikely that it sat near the creek bank on Parker's property as it does now.

The combined sources indicated that at least five churches became known as Free Will Baptist churches in the late eighteenth century and continued in that denomination into the following century. The continuous ministry of James Roach at Gum Swamp as successor to the Parkers and eventually as a Free Will Baptist minister indicate that that church existed throughout the period of transition, and it formed an additional link between the two groups.

The Theological Argument
The Mutual Use of the 1660 English General Baptist Confession of Faith

The General Baptists and the Free Will Baptists of North Carolina not only grew up in the same general area and followed one another closely in time, they also used the same Confession of Faith. Though that fact alone would not prove that the Free Will Baptists grew out of the older group, it does indicate that they enjoyed a close spiritual kinship. Coupled with the other evidence that has been submitted, the spiritual kinship added another important link in the argument for a continued Free Will Baptist witness.

THE GENERAL BAPTISTS AND THE 1660 CONFESSION

Burkitt and Read, the Regular Baptist historians, again have contributed valuable information to the history of their opponents. In the introduction to their study of the Kehukee Association, they contended that:

> . . . The most of these churches, before they were ever united in an Association, were General Baptist, and held with the Arminian tenets. We believe they were the descendants of the English General Baptists, because we find from some original papers, that their *Confession of Faith* was subscribed by certain Elders, and Deacons, and Brethren, in behalf of themselves and others, to whom they belonged, both in London, and several counties in England, and was presented to King Charles the second.[92]

In their remarks, Burkitt and Read quoted a portion of the introduction to the *Standard or Brief Confession of Faith* drawn up by the English Baptists in March 1660.

The confession was identified by the reference to King Charles the Second. The *Brief Confession* was presented to Charles on July 26, 1660.[93] By 1663, the confession had become the standard for the General Baptists in England. It would seem that it served in the same capacity in North Carolina.

THE FREE WILL BAPTISTS AND THE 1660 CONFESSION

In 1812, Jesse Heath and James Roach were chosen to examine and reprint the "former Confession of Faith" of the Free Will Baptists. The preface to the new edition inferred that the denomination already had achieved a ripe old age by 1812. It made it quite clear that the movement had not had its beginning during the lifetime of the examiners. The two men were to work with the "former Confession of Faith" which had been drawn up by the "former Elders and Deacons." The men were to be given access to all the "former articles of faith and rules of discipline now extant."[94] The finished work revealed that the men had gone beyond a simple examination. They made a number of revisions in the confession and presented them to the people for their approval. The editors prayed that the Free Will Baptists would compare the revisions with the Scriptures and come to their own conclusions. Their plea explained:

> Some things stands without variation and some things with variation, and we therefore desire the reader may be pleased to take the pains to peruse the scriptures, that the grounds of our faith and practice may be better understood, that this impartial account of our principles and practice, may be accompanied with the blessing of God, and be beneficial to men, is the hearty prayer of us, your well wishers and servants in the Lord.
>
> James Roach
> Jesse Heath[95]

The revisions made by Roach and Heath were not extensive enough to disguise the fact that the *Free Will Baptist Confession* had been based on the *1660 Confession of the English General Baptists*. Eight of the articles in the *Free Will Baptist Confession* were almost identical to their counterparts in the *English Confession,* both in the text and in the Scripture references used as foundations for the accepted doctrines. Others, though not identical, were similar in content.

The 1812 Free Will Baptist "Former Articles"
and the General Baptist Confession of Faith

The 1660 Standard Confession[96]	The 1812 Former Articles[97]
I. We believe and are verily confident, that there is but one God the Father, of whom are all things, from everlasting, glorious, and unwordable in all his attributes, I Cor. 8.6. Is. 40.28.	I. We believe that there is but one living, true and eternal God: the Father of whom are all things from everlasting to everlasting, glorious and immutable in all his attributes. I Cor. viii, 6. Isa. xl, 28.
II. That God in the beginning made Man Upright, put him into a state and condition of Glory, without the least mixture of misery, from which he by transgression fell, and so came into a miserable and mortal state, subject unto the first death, Gen. 1.31. Eccles. 7.29. Gen. 2.17. 3.17,18,19.	IV We believe that in the beginning God made man upright and placed him in a state of glory without the least mixture of misery from which he voluntarily by transgression fell, and by that means brought on himself, a miserable and mortal state, subject to death. Gen. ii, 17, & iii, 17, 18,19.
III. That there is one Lord Jesus Christ, by whom are all things, who is the only begotten Son of God, born of the Virgin Mary; yet as truly Davids Lord, and Davids root, as Davids Son, and Davids offspring, Luke 20.44. Revel. 22.16. whom God freely sent into	II. We believe that there is one Lord Jesus Christ, by whom are all things the only begotten son of God, born of the Virgin Mary, whom God freely sent into this world, because of the great love wherewith he loved the world, and Christ as freely gave

the World (because of his
great love for the World)
who as freely gave himself
a ransome for all. I Tim.
2.5, 6. tasting death for
every man, Heb. 2.9. a
propitiation for our sins,
and not for ours only, but
for the sins of the whole
World, I John 2.2.

himself a ransom for all,
tasting death for every
man; who was buried
and rose again the third
day and ascended into
Heaven, from whence we
look for him, the second
time in the clouds of
Heaven, at the last day to
judge both quick and dead.
I Tim. ii, 5 and 8; Heb. ii,
9; 1 John ii, 2; Rev. i, 7;
Acts xxiv, 15.

IV.   That God is not willing
that any should perish,
but that all should come to
repentance, 2 Pet. 3:9, and
the knowledge of the truth,
that they might be saved,
I Tim. 2.4. For which end
Christ hath commanded
that the Gospel, (to wit,
the glad tydings of remission of sins) should be
preached to every crea-
ture, Mark 16.15. So that
no man shall eternally
suffer in Hell (that is, the
second death) for want of
a Christ that dyed for
them, but as the Scripture
saith, for denying the Lord
that bought them, 2 Pet.
2. 1. or because they believe
not in the only begotten
Son of God, John 3.18.
Unbelief therefore being
the cause why the just and
righteous God, will con-

V.   We believe that God is not
willing that any should
perish, but that all should
come to repentance and
the knowledge of the truth,
that they might be saved;
for which end Christ hath
Commanded the Gospel to
be preached among all
nations, and to every creature. Mark xvi, 15; Luke
xxiv, 47.

VI.   We believe that no man
shall suffer in hell, for
want of a Christ that died
for him, but as the scripture has said for denying
the lord that bought them;
because they believe not
in the name of the only
begotten son of God. Un-
belief therefore being the
cause why the just and
righteous God of Heaven,
will condemn the children

94

demn the children of men; it follows against all contradiction, that all men at one time or other, are put into such a capacity, as that (through the grace of God) they may be eternally saved, John 1.7. Acts 17.30. Mark 6.6. Heb. 3.10, 18, 19. 1 John 5. 10. John 3.17.

VI   That the way set forth by God for men to be justified in, is by faith in Christ, Rom. 5. 1.

That is to say, when men shall assent to the truth of the Gospel, believing with all their hearts, that there is remission of sins, and eternal life to be had in Christ.

And that Christ therefore is most worthy their constant affections, and subjection to all his Commandements [sic] and therefore resolve with purpose of heart so to subject unto him in all things, and no longer unto themselves, 2 Cor. 5:15. And so, shall (with godly sorrow for the sins past) commit themselves to his grace, confidently depending upon him for that which they believe is to be had in him: such so believing are justified from all their sins, their faith shall be ac-

of men, it follows against all contradiction, that all men at one time or another, is found in such a capacity as that through the grace of God, they may be Eternally saved. II Peter ii, 1; 1 John i, 17; Acts xvii, 30; Mark vi, 6; Heb. iii, 10; 1 John v, 10.

VIII.   We believe in the doctrine of general Provision made of God in Christ, for the benefit of all mankind, who repent and believe the Gospel. Luke xiv, 16, 17, 18, 19 and 20; Mat. xxviii, 18, 20.

counted unto them for
righteousness, Rom. 4.22,
23, 24. Rom. 3.25, 26.

VII.	That there is one Holy Spirit, the pretious gift of God, freely given to such as obey him, Ephes. 4.4. Acts 5.32. that thereby they may be throughly sanctified and made able (without which they are altogether unable) to abide stedfast in the faith, and to honour the Father, and his Son Christ, the Author and finisher of their faith; I Cor. 6.11.	III.	We believe that there is one Holy Ghost the precious gift of the Father, through his dear Son unto the world, who quickeneth and draws sinners home to God. John xvi, 7 and 8; Acts ii, 4; Eph. iv, 4, 5, 6.
VIII.	That God hath even before the foundation of the world chosen, (or elected) to eternal life, such as believe, and so are in Christ, John 3.16. Ephes. 1.4. 2 Thes. 2.13. yet confident we are, that the purpose according to election, was not in the least arising from foreseen faith in, or works of righteousness done by the creature, but only from mercy, goodness, and compassion dwelling in God, and so it is of him that calleth, Rom. 9.11. whose purity and unwordable holiness, cannot admit of any unclean person (or thing) to be in his presence,	XI.	We believe that God hath before the foundation of the world, chosen or elected unto Eternal life, such as believe in Christ: yet confident we are, that the purpose of God according to election, was not in the least arising from any foreseen faith or righteousness done by the creature, but only by the mercy, goodness and compassion, dwelling in God towards the creature, and so it is of him that calleth, whose purity cannot admit of any unclean person or thing in his presence. Therefore his decree of mercy, reaches only the

therefore his decree of
mercy reaches only the
godly man, whom (saith
David) God hath set apart
for himself, Psal. 4.3.

Godly man; whom saith
David, the Lord hath set
apart for himself. John iii,
16; Rom. ix; Psalms iv.3.

IX. That men not considered
simply as men, but ungod-
ly men, were of old or-
dained to condemnation,
considered as such, who
turn the grace of God unto
wantoness, and deny the
only Lord God, and our
Lord Jesus Christ, Jude 4.
God indeed sends a strong
delusion to men, that they
might be damned; but we
observe that they are such
(as saith the Apostle) that
received not the love of the
truth, that they might be
saved, 2 Thes. 2.10, 11, 12.
and so the indignation and
wrath of God, is upon every
soul of man that doth evil,
(living and dying therein),
for there is no respect of
persons with God. Rom.
2.9,10,11.

XII. We believe that men, not
considered simply as men,
but ungodly men were of
old, ordained to condemnation, considered such who
turn the grace of God, into
lasciviousness, denying
the only Lord God, and
our Lord Jesus Christ that
bought them; and there-
fore shall bring upon themselves swift destruction:
but we observe that they
and such the Apostle saith,
because they receive not
the love of the truth, that
they might be saved; therefore the indignation and
wrath of God is upon every
soul of man that doth evil,
living and dying therein;
for there is no respect of
persons with God. Jude i,
4; 11 Peter ii, 1; 11 Thes. ii,
10, 11, 12; Romans ii, 9.

X. That all children dying in
Infancy, having not actually transgressed against the
law of God in their own
persons, are only subject
to the first death, which
comes upon them by the
sin of the first Adam, from
whence they shall be

XIII. We believe that all children, dying in infancy,
having not actually transgressed against the law of
God in their own person,
are only subject to the first
death which was brought
on them by the fall of the
first Adam, and not that

raised by the second Adam; and not that any one of them (dying in that estate) shall suffer for Adams sin, eternal punishment in Hell, (which is the second death) for of such belongs the Kingdome of Heaven, I Cor. 15.22. Mat. 19.14. not daring to conclude with that uncharitable opinion of others, who though they plead much for the bringing of children into the visible Church here on earth by Baptism, yet nevertheless by their doctrine that Christ dyed but for some, shut a great part of them out of the Kingdome of Heaven for ever.

any one of them dying in that state, shall suffer punishment in Hell by the guilt of Adam's sin, for of such is the kingdom of God. I Cor. xv, 22; Mat. xviii, 2, 3, 4 and 5; Mark ix, 36 and 37; Mat. xix, 14.

XVIII. That such who are true believers, even Branches in Christ the Vine, (and whom he exhorts to abide in him, John 15. 1, 2, 3, 4, 5.) or such who have charity out of a pure heart, and of a good conscience, and of Faith unfeigned, I Tim. 1.5. may nevertheless for want of watchfulness swerve and turn aside from the same, vers. 6, 7. and become as withered Branches, cast into the fire and burned, John 15.6. But such who add unto their Faith Vertue, and unto Ver-

X. We believe that the Saints shall persevere in grace, and never finally fall away. John x, 27, 28 and 29.

tue Knowledge, and unto
Knowledge Temperance,
&c. 2 Peter, 1.5, 6, 7. such
shall never fall, vers. 8, 9,
10. 'tis impossible for all
the false Christs, and false
Prophets, that are, and are
to come, to deceive such,
for they are kept by the
power of God, through
faith unto Salvation, I Pet.
1.5.

XXIII That the holy Scriptures
is the rule whereby Saints
both in matters of Faith,
and conversation are to be
regulated, they being able
to make men wise unto
salvation, through faith in
Christ Jesus, profitable for
Doctrine, for reproof, for
instruction in righteousness,
that the man of God may be
perfect, throughly furnished
unto all good works, 2 Tim.
3.15,16,17. John 20.31. Isa 8.20.

VII. We believe the whole Scriptures are infallibly true,
and that they are the only
ruler of faith and practice.

It has been suggested earlier that the use of the *1660 Confession* by both groups did not prove that the Free Will Baptists grew out of the older movement. However, it did show that the two groups were alike in theology. The Free Will Baptists were the logical successors to the General Baptists in North Carolina.

Summary

The thesis that the Free Will Baptist denomination grew out of the General Baptist movement in North Carolina is not a new one. Though it formerly has lacked proof and has been classified as tradition, the thesis has gained the support of a number of prominent church historians. Recent and respected historians such as George Washington Paschal, W. T. Whitley, M. A. Huggins, Albert H. Newman, Robert Torbet, and Henry C. Vedder have agreed that the Free Will Baptists can be traced back to the Paul Palmer work in 1727.

Lemuel Burkitt, Jesse Read, and S. J. Wheeler were contemporaries of the early Free Will Baptists. They also acknowledged the relationship between the older movement and the new. Burkitt and Read grew up in the area of Free Will Baptist growth. They served in the area while the Parkers were still living and were familiar with the religious groups that inhabited eastern North Carolina. These contemporary historians revealed that the new name was popular in North Carolina before the end of the 18th century and that the General remnant of the Particular invasion became known as Free Will Baptist churches.

The Free Will Baptists also defended their claim to an ancient heritage. Rufus K. Hearn, the first Free Will Baptist historian, was born in 1819. He interviewed individuals who had lived during the ministry of the Parkers. They testified that the Gum Swamp church in Pitt County had served the Free Will Baptists throughout the transition period. The church had been established by the Parkers. The personal membership of the witnesses in the churches throughout the period added strength to their testimony. Jesse Heath and Elias Hutchins served as correspondents between the Free Will Baptists in North Carolina and those in New England. Heath, representing the North Carolina group, was in constant touch with the New England movement from 1827 through 1830. His letters extended the internal records of the southern movement back to 1807—twenty-two years earlier than the records of the Annual Conference that are now extant. In his most important letter, he reminded his readers that the denomination consisted of five churches and three ministers when he was ordained in 1807.

Elias Hutchins, an itinerant minister for the New England Freewill Baptists, spent many months in North Carolina between 1829 and 1833. He traveled throughout the area of Free Will Baptist growth and did extensive research on the history of the movement. He concluded that the Free Will Baptists of North Carolina were the descendants of the General Baptist movement of the eighteenth century. He also revealed that these early Free Will Baptists considered the history of the older movement a part of their heritage. Hutchins did his research while many eyewitnesses were still alive and when the documents of the period were probably still available. His conclusions were valuable because he worked so soon after the period of concern.

James Roach was the only leader that could be traced through the transition period. He succeeded Joseph Parker in the General Baptist work at Little Creek, Grimsley, Wheat Swamp, Louson Swamp, and Gum Swamp. He became a leading figure in the continuing history of the movement as a Free Will Baptist minister. He ended his ministry as pastor of the Gum Swamp church in Pitt County. Roach represented a solid link between the old movement and the new.

Tradition contended that a long gap existed between the demise of the old name and the acceptance of the new. The gap was considered a formidable enemy to the thesis that the two groups were connected. Available evidence, however, shattered the tradition. Burkitt and Read revealed that the new name virtually replaced the older title before the end of the eighteenth century. They referred to all the General Baptist churches as Free Will Baptist congregations.

As late as 1812, the Free Will Baptists were using the two names synonymously. They entitled their Confession of Faith, *An Abstract of the Faith Confessed by the Original Baptist Church Holding the General Provision*. The supposed gap between the two names suddenly disappeared.

S. J. Wheeler and R. K. Hearn identified five preaching points that were established by the Parkers before their death. James Roach moved from Craven County after the death of Joseph Parker and continued the work that the Parkers had started. He finally settled at the Gum Swamp church in Pitt County. The first available records of the Annual Conference revealed that Free Will Baptist churches appeared in all the communities that the Parkers had evangelized and left in the hands of James Roach. The fact that all the Parker communities were involved has made a theory of coincidence less than tenable. Recently discovered evidence shows that a church of the General persuasion has stood on Joseph Parker's property at Scuffleton, North Carolina, from 1761 to the present time.

Both the General Baptists and the Free Will Baptists of North Carolina used the *1660 English General Baptist Confession of Faith* as a basis for their doctrines. The mutual use of the Confession confirmed that there was a definite spiritual kinship between the two groups. That kinship made the Free Will Baptists the natural heirs to the heritage established by the older group. The conclusions of the contemporary historians, the solid link found in the continuous ministry of James Roach through the transition period, the continuing ministry of the Parker churches, the use of the same Confession of Faith by both groups, and the synonymous use of the two names before and after 1800 have pointed to the validity of the Free Will Baptist claim. Except for the conclusions of recent church historians, the evidence came from contemporary sources. That evidence indicated that the Free Will Baptists have had a continuing witness in America since Paul Palmer and Joseph Parker established the first General Baptist church in North Carolina in 1727.

Notes for Chapter 4

[1]*Abstract*, Title Page, Preface.

[2]Elias Hutchins, personal letter to the North Carolina Free Will Baptist Conference, quoted in Harrison and Barfield, *History*, I, 163-168.

[3]Paschal's work was published in 1930.

[4]Paschal, *North Carolina*, I, 223.

[5]Ibid.

[6]Paschal, "Morgan Edwards' Materials," 393.

[7]I. D. Stewart, The *History of the Freewill Baptists for Half a Century* (Dover, N.H.: Freewill Baptist Printing Establishment, 1862), 463.

[8]Jesse Heath, personal letter to the Senior Editor of *The Morning Star*, May 29, 1827, in *The Morning Star,* June 28,1827. The letter will be considered more carefully in a later section. (Hereafter referred to as *Letter*, May 29, 1827.)

[9]D. B. Montgomery, *General Baptist History* (Evansville: Courier Company, Book and Job Printers, 1882), 139. (Hereafter referred to as *General Baptist History*.)

[10]Ibid., 136.

[11]Montgomery, *General Baptist History*, 144, 145. Montgomery caused some problems by publishing an incorrect copy of the letter from Heath. He indicated that by 1827, Heath had been in the ministry for twenty-five years. The copy of the letter in *The Morning Star* indicated twenty years. Montgomery corrected the error in his subtraction by recognizing that Heath had entered the ministry in 1807.

[12]Dodd, *Story*, 53.

[13]G. W. Million, *A History of Free Will Baptists* (Nashville: Board of Publications and Literature, National Association of Free Will Baptists, 1958), 121. (Hereafter referred to as *History*.) Million offered no support for his early date for Little Creek and Gum Swamp. Joseph Parker did not purchase the property for the Little Creek church until 1756 and there is no evidence that the Gum Swamp church appeared until late in the eighteenth century.

[14]See above (Table 1, p. 46).

[15]See above (Table 2, p. 67).

[16]The church at Little Creek has a sign on the front lawn that lists the organization date as 1730.

[17]Little Creek church is in Greene County and Gum Swamp in Pitt. As late as 1740, these areas were part of Craven and Beaufort Counties. Dobbs (later Greene) was formed in 1758 and Pitt was established in 1760 (Corbitt, *Counties*, 89, 176).

[18]See above.

[19]Huggins' *History* work was published in 1967.

[20]Huggins, 45.

[21]Ibid.

[22]Ibid., 45, 46.

[23]Attempts were made to contact the author through his publishers, but it was found that Dr. Huggins died in 1971.

[24]Huggins, *History*, 393.

[25]Charles Crossfield Ware, *North Carolina Disciples of Christ* (St. Louis: Christian Board of Publication, 1927), 80.

[26]Ibid.

[27]Torbet, *History*, 273, 274; Newman, *United States*, 500; Vedder, *Short History*, 385.

[28]*Abstract*, 3.

[29]Heath, *Letter*, May 29, 1827.

[30]Burkitt and Read, *Concise History*, 185, 186, 242-244.

[31]Ibid., 209.

[32]Ibid., 43.

[33]Ibid., 28.

[34]Ibid., 43.

[35]Ibid., 209, 225.

[36]Ibid., 232.

[37]Saunders, *Colonial Records,* V, 1180.

[38]James A. Delke, comp., *History of the North Carolina Chowan Baptist Association*, 1806-1881 (Raleigh: Edwards and Broughton, 1882), 30.

[39]Wheeler, *Parker's*, 6.

[40]Ibid., 6, 7.

[41]Ibid., 7.

[42]*Heads of Families, 1790*; U. S. Department of Commerce, U. S. Bureau of the Census, *Population Schedules of the Second Census of the United States, 1800 for the Counties of Beaufort, Duplin, Hyde, Lenoir, and Pitt* (Washington: The National Archives, 1957), 598. (Hereafter referred to as *Second Census*.)

[43]The Free Will Baptists had authorized the writing of a history in 1833, but the project was not completed until Hearn wrote his history after the middle of the century (Elias Hutchins, Letter to the Editors of *The Morning Star*, January 22, 1833, in *The Morning Star*, February 14, 1833). (Hereafter referred to as *Letter*, January 22, 1833.)

[44]Page from Hearn Family Bible.

[45]Hearn loaned his original copy to D. B. Montgomery who included it in his history (Montgomery, *History of the General Baptists*, 146).

[46]Two attorneys, one familiar with North Carolina law and the other having special training in the field of "Evidence," have agreed that materials such as Hearn's interviews would be acceptable as evidence in present day court situations. The evidence would fall under the classifications of "Ancient Documents" and "Exceptions to the Hearsay Rule." In cases dealing with ancient documents or in situations where living witnesses cannot be called, hearsay evidence has been accepted by the courts as corroborative proof along with other evidence. This especially has been true in cases concerning property boundaries and family history.

Such an argument would indicate a new value for Hearn's interviews with eyewitnesses. Though it is true that they could not stand alone, they can be used as corroborative evidence. Used in conjunction with other evidence, they have formed an important part of the argument for a continuing Free Will Baptist witness (Personal interview with Mr. Ashton Phelps, Sr., Attorney at Law, New Orleans, Louisiana, April 21, 1972; Telephone interview with Dr. Charles Holloman, Raleigh, North Carolina, April 1972).

[47]Hearn, *Origin*, 170, 171.

[48]Ibid., 164, 165.

[49]Hearn earlier referred to the use of the General Baptist name on the first *Free Will Baptist Confession*, indicating that the two names were used interchangeably during the transition (Hearn, *Origin*, 150).

[50]Ibid., 176, 177.

[51]Heath, *Letter*, May 29, 1827.

[52]Burkitt and Read, *Concise History*, 43.

[53]Heath referred to records for the year 1825, but the Minutes for 1829 are the earliest records now available.

[54]In 1832, the Free Will Baptists in North Carolina officially appointed Hutchins to work with Jesse Heath on the development of a history of their denomination (*Minutes of the Free Will Baptist Annual Conference of North Carolina*, 1832, quoted in Harrison and Barfield, *History*, I, 175). Unfortunately, the work was never completed.

[55]"Biographical Sketch of Rev. Elias Hutchins," *The Morning Star*, XXXIV (October 5, 1859), 1; J. Woodbury Scribner, "Elias Hutchins," Centennial Paper for the New Hampshire Yearly Meeting, MS, 1892.

[56]*Minutes of the Free Will Baptist Annual Conference of North Carolina*, 1829.

[57]Elias Hutchins, *Letter*, dated June 20, 1830, *The Morning Star*, (July 28, 1830), 50, (hereafter referred to as *Letter*, June 20, 1830); Hutchins, *Letter*, January 22, 1833; *Minutes of the Free Will Baptist Annual Conference of North Carolina*, 1832.

[58]Elias Hutchins, Personal Letter to the North Carolina Free Will Baptist Conference, quoted in Harrison and Barfield, *History*, I, 164, 165.

[59]Heath, *Letter*, May 29, 1827.

[60]Hearn Family Bible.

[61]Edwards, "Furman MS," IV, 170.

[62]Asplund, *Register*, 37.

[63]Burkitt and Read, *Concise History*, 225. John Rippon, (John Rippon, *The Baptist Annual Register* [4 vols.; London: Button and Conder], II, 64, 65), indicated that the Pungo church applied for acceptance by the Kehukee Association in 1792.

[64]Asplund, *Register*, 36.

[65]*Minutes of the Kehukee Association, North Carolina, 1769-1778*, MS; Burkitt and Read, *Concise History*. Job Thigpen was listed in the same manner. The name was on a separate line, but appeared to be connected to the Regular Baptist church at New River (Asplund, *Register*, 36). Burkitt and Read identified Thigpen as a Free Will Baptist minister. He did not become a Regular Baptist until 1793, three years after the publication of the *Register*.

[66]Wheeler, *Parker's*, p. 7. Wheeler's information was corroborated by the Census of 1800. James Roach moved from Craven to Greene County shortly after 1790 (*Second Census*, 265).

[67]*Second Census*, 256.

[68]Wheeler, *Parker's*, 7; Hearn, *Origin*, 171, 172; Ware, *Disciples*, 80.

[69]Hearn, *Origin*, 171, 172.

[70]*Abstract*, Preface, 3.

[71]In almost every case, Burkitt and Read referred to the General Baptist churches as Free Will Baptist churches or churches organized on the Free Will plan.

[72]Hearn, *Origin*, 150.

[73]Harrison and Barfield, *History*, I, 157, 158.

[74]The communities are near the home of the writer. The reference has been based on the writer's personal knowledge of the area.

[75]Wheeler, *Parker's,* 6; Hearn, *Origin*, 164, 165.

[76]Edwards, "Furman MS," IV, 169.

[77]Burkitt and Read, *Concise History*, 43, 225.

[78]Survey for Benjamin Hooker, November 8, 1797.

[79]Survey for Joseph Parker, 1761.

[80]North Carolina, *Craven County Deed Books*. Deed Recording the Sale of Property on Little Contentnea Creek to Joseph Parker by Jacob Blount (Deed Book 10, December 25, 1756).

[81]"Pitt County: 1762 Tax List," *North Carolina Genealogy*, XIV (Winter, 1968). Also see Joseph Blount Cheshire, ed., *Sketches of Church History in North Carolina* (Wilmington, N.C.: Wm. L. De Rosset, Jr., Printer, 1892), 122.

[82]Corbitt, *Counties*, 176, 177.

[83]Asplund, *Register*, 38.

[84] *United States Coast Survey. Virginia, North Carolina, South Carolina* (H. Lindenkohl & C. G. Krebs, Lith., 1865). Pitt County extended only a short distance west of Little Contentnea Creek. The line was changed in 1895. The creek became the dividing line between Pitt and Greene Counties and the property that had belonged to Parker became a part of Greene (Corbitt, *Counties*, 178).

[85]The church was known as A. Jones' Meeting House in 1812, but R. K. Hearn, who had lived during the period, identified it as Little Creek (Hearn, *Origin*, 165).

[86]Edwards, "Furman MS," IV, 169.

[87]Asplund, *Register*, 38.

[88]William S. Powell, *North Carolina Gazeteer* (Chapel Hill: University of North Carolina Press, 1968), 118, 286. Copyright 1968, The University of North Carolina Press. Used with permission of the publisher.

[89]Ibid.

[90]See above.

[91]See above.

[92]Burkitt and Read, *Concise History*, 28.

[93]Tho. Crosby, *The History of the English Baptists, From the Reformation to the Beginning of the Reign of King George I* (4 vols.; London: Printed for the Author, 1739), 11, 19.

[94]*Abstract*, 3.

[95]*Abstract*, Preface.

[96]*A Brief Confession of Faith*, quoted in Lumpkin, *Confessions*, 224-235. The right-hand column has retained the numbers found in the *1812 Articles*, but the items have been rearranged to correspond with their equals in the *1660 Confession*.

[97]*An Abstract of the Former Articles of Faith Confessed by the Original Baptist Church Holding the Doctrine of General Provision with Proper Code of Discipline* (Newbern, N.C.: Printed by Salmon Hall, 1814 [1812]). The Abstract has represented the first attempt by the later movement to establish its identity and to clarify its theological position.

5

Tennessee

The Free Will Baptists of Tennessee, like their counterparts in New England, were a product of American Christianity. Though some historians try to trace their heritage back to England, it seems more likely that they are the direct descendants of the Separate Baptists that emerged out of the First Great Awakening of the mid-eighteenth century and migrated first to Virginia and North Carolina and then to Kentucky. In fact, it is possible to trace the Separate Baptist leaders as they traveled to the wilderness of Kentucky and to show that the first Free Will Baptists in Tennessee were directly related to this earlier movement.

Interestingly enough, though the Separate Baptists of Kentucky gave birth to the first Free Will Baptists of Tennessee, they did not have the same impact in their own state. Kentucky must look to other influences for origins of a Free Will Baptist heritage there. Both Tennessee and Kentucky then give weight to the argument that the Free Will Baptists cannot point to any one point of origin but that they must look to various sources of strikingly different backgrounds.

The Coming of the Separate Baptists
The Aftermath of the First Great Awakening

THE FIRST LEVEL OF SEPARATION

The First Great Awakening (1726-1742) produced a number of both immediate and far-reaching results. Two of the results constituted an unexplainable paradox that has continued to be characteristic of revivalism to the present time. On the one hand, revivalists were willing to cross over denominational lines in order to cooperate in revival effort while, at the same time, many denominations divided over the question of revival. The Presbyterians split into Old Side (anti-revivalists) and New Side (revivalists), and the Congregationalists divided into Old Lights (anti-revivalists) and New Lights (revivalists). Though division seemed to be related more closely to polity with the Presbyterians and to theology with the Congregationalists, the revival was the catalyst in both cases.

The Presbyterians soon settled their differences and made peace, but the Congregationalists continued to splinter and their rupture was never to find healing. In fact, the two parties within the Congregational framework would soon become three and then four.

THE SECOND LEVEL OF SEPARATION

Contending that the Revivalist churches were still accepting non-regenerate members and that they continued to be controlled by the laws of the established church, the more extreme New Lights determined that they could no longer be Congregationalists. Their first complaint spoke to the tradition of receiving into church membership those who could not testify to a personal salvation experience. The second spoke to the Congregationalists' determination to subscribe to the Saybrook Platform. It restricted the ordination of ministers to a clerical association and required that the churches be dependent on the state for their existence and support.

Actually, this concern for a regenerate church was not new. Rather, it was an attempt to return to Congregational policy of an earlier day. Until 1662 and the introduction of the Half-Way Covenant, the Congregationalists and other Puritans had demanded evidence of a conversion experience as a prerequisite to church membership. But, in the midst of spiritual decline in the latter half of the seventeenth century, they had compromised that requirement in order to replenish their dying congregations.

The Half-Way Covenant allowed children to be baptized into the church on two conditions: (1) The parents or grandparents had given verbal assent to the covenant and (2) the parents had not lived lives that would be considered "scandalous." The requirement for evidence of a conversion experience had been abandoned. At first, those brought into the church via the Half-Way Covenant were indeed half-way members—they were considered to be a part of the church body but could not partake of the Lord's Supper. In just a short time, through the influence of Solomon Stoddard, this restriction also was removed. Stoddard declared that the Sacrament, in some sense, drew men to Christ and for that reason, could not be denied to any who were part of the covenant. Finally, the Brattle Street Church in Boston removed all bars to membership in the church for those who had entered as Half-Way members.

Since the Awakening placed so much emphasis on the conversion experience, it would be expected that the revival would bring an end to support for the Half-Way Covenant, This, however, was not to be. Instead, "in churches which seemed to share most deeply in the Awakening, the Half-Way Covenant continued with unabated vigor after the revival ceased."[1] C. C. Goen suggested that this question of regenerate membership was a leading cause of separation and that separation was more likely to occur in churches that had been most touched by revival spirit. The initial separation that drew the battle lines of revivalism and anti-revivalism did not carry the reformation to its logical conclusion. Revivalism, in itself, was not enough. The extreme New Light could not condone the acceptance of non-regenerate members.[2]

THE FINAL LEVEL OF SEPARATION

Like the Anabaptists two centuries earlier, there were some within the separating ranks who were convinced that the new reformation still had not fully run its course. If the separation fell short of the regenerate church ideal, then its baptism also was suspect. The only sure guarantee of a regenerate church must include believer's baptism.

The experience of Isaac Backus probably best illustrates the rapid development of Baptist sentiment that grew out of the New Light movement. Backus was converted as the result of New Light preaching in his home town of Norwich, Connecticut, in 1741. Though concerned that the local church still accepted Half-Way members, he finally joined the church in order to gain access to the Lord's Supper. He found comfort in the hope that the church soon would see the error of its ways and demand regenerate membership. His hopes were groundless and the more extreme New Lights were ejected from the church.

In October 1745, they established a Separate Church at Bean Hill and appointed Jedediah Hyde as their pastor. In 1746, Backus announced to the church that he was called to preach the gospel and immediately set out on a fourteen month evangelistic mission that took him through Connecticut, Rhode Island, and Massachusetts. In 1747, while on a preaching mission with Separate pastor Joseph Snow, Backus accepted an invitation to settle permanently as pastor of the church in Titicut, Massachusetts.

Though Baptist principles had been introduced into the church the year before by Ebenezer Hinds and Jonathan Woods, Backus would struggle long and hard with the issue before accepting a Baptist position. The next few years saw a continued waffling between infant and believer's baptism. Commitment to a particular position would immediately be retracted with apologies to the church. Even when Backus finally accepted believer's baptism as his personal conviction, he did not ask the church to reorganize on Baptist principles. For five years, the church allowed members to exercise their personal preference regarding baptism. Those who wished to have their children baptized simply called in a Separatist pastor to perform the ceremony, while those who accepted believer's baptism looked to the pastor for administration of the rite.

As would be expected, the church could not long exist under such circumstances and Backus could not long rationalize acceptance of a "false" baptism. On January 16, 1756, Backus, his wife, and five others covenanted together to establish a new church. The six signed a statement of faith written by Backus, and a new Baptist church was born.

C. C. Goen has summarized the factors that undergirded Backus' position on believer's baptism.

> There were three main points which he made again and again in various ways: (1) Infant baptism falsely supposes that the NT church is grafted into the OT Israel with no distinction between the old covenant, based on the family and the nation, and the new covenant, based on individual personal response in faith. (2) Infant baptism leads naturally to a territorial church which becomes so intermingled with society in general ('the world') that it loses its distinctive character as a fellowship of the redeemed. (3) Infant baptism is cruel to children because engenders a false sense of security and thus endangers their opportunity to realize their sinful condition and need for personal faith in Christ. In breaking with both the standing churches and the pedo baptist Separates, Backus simply followed New Light theology and Strict Congregational ecclesiology to their logical conclusions.[3]

It probably is safe to assume that these same factors were primary in leading others to a Baptist persuasion. In any case, whatever their reasons, many Separates rejected the limited reformation of the Strict Congregationalists (the Separate Church) and moved on to the final level of separation—believer's baptism and a truly regenerate church.

The Separate Baptists in Migration: South and West

Two men, Shubal Stearns and Daniel Marshall, were basically responsible for the spread of the Separate Baptists from New England to Virginia, North and South Carolina, Georgia, Kentucky, and Tennessee. Stearns, a native of Boston, responded to the New Light message quite early and served as a preacher in that order until 1751 when he adopted the principles of the growing Separate Baptist movement. He was rebaptized by Rev. Wait Palmer in Tolland, Connecticut, May 20, 1751, and soon afterwards was ordained as a Baptist minister by Palmer and Joshua Morse.

Like many of the Separates, Stearns believed in the immediate direction of the Holy Spirit in the revealing of God's will for the individual.[4] In 1754, believing that he was obeying the inner voice of the Spirit, Stearns collected his family, his belongings, and a few members of his congregation and headed south and west to minister to the more spiritually destitute on the frontier. At Opekon, Virginia, the small band of migrants found a Baptist church where they were well received by the pastor, John Garrard. Here, too, they found Daniel Marshall, the second figure to play a large role in the spread of the Separate Baptists. Marshall was a native of Windsor, Connecticut, who, like Stearns, had been converted near the end of the Awakening and had quickly separated from his local church. In 1747, he married Martha Stearns, Shubal's sister, and five years later moved south to minister among the Mohawk Indians. When confronted by Stearns and his crew of Separate Baptists, Marshall agreed to be immersed and became a part of the group. Though Stearns had numerous opportunities to preach in Virginia, he was not satisfied with the success of his work. Letters from his friends in North Carolina added to his restlessness. The letters told of a spiritually hungry people, "… that preaching was greatly desired by the people of that country (North Carolina); that in some instances they had rode 40 miles to hear one sermon."[5]

Stearns, Marshall, and the others again broke camp and traveled some 200 miles to Sandy Creek, Guilford County, North Carolina. The group now consisted of sixteen members: Shubal Stearns and wife, Shubal Stearns, Jr., and wife, Peter Stearns and wife, Ebenezer Stearns and wife, Daniel Marshall and wife, Jonathan Polk and wife, Joseph Breed and wife, Enos Stimson and wife.[6]

The first task was that of establishing a church. The sixteen Baptists built a meeting house, chose Shubal Stearns as their pastor, Daniel Marshall and Joseph Breed as his assistants, and set about the business of evangelizing their new neighbors.

> The inhabitants about this little colony of Baptists, although brought up in the Christian religion, were grossly ignorant of its essential principles. Having the form of godliness, they knew nothing of its power. Stearns and his party, of course, brought strange things to their ears. To be born again, appeared to them as absurd as it did to the Jewish doctrine, when he [Nicodemus] asked, if he must enter the second time into his mother's womb and be born. Having always supposed that religion consisted in nothing more than the practice of its outward duties, they could not comprehend how it should be necessary to feel conviction and conversion. But to be able to ascertain the time and place of one's conversion, was, in their estimation, wonderful indeed.[7]

Stearns and his congregation of sixteen arrived at Sandy Creek on November 22, 1755, and in just a few short months the church had increased to a membership of 606. By 1758, just three years after the founding of Sandy Creek Church, the Separates boasted three churches—Sandy Creek, Abbott's Creek, and Deep River—and more than nine hundred communicants. It should not be supposed, however, that these statistics indicate three local churches of 300 members each. As was true of other Baptist groups at the time, Separate churches ordinarily established "arms" of the church in nearby areas and included the membership of the daughter churches in the statistics of the founding church. It also was not unusual for the pastor of the original church to serve as pastor of the smaller congregations as well. At any rate, with such a large membership, Stearns and his fellow ministers became increasingly aware of the need for an organizational body that would be able to coordinate the activities of the growing movement.

Stearns visited each of the churches in the area, explained his plans for an association, and asked them to send delegates to Sandy Creek in January 1758. At that time, the Sandy Creek Association was formed and for twelve years all of the Separate Baptists in Virginia and North and South Carolina continued to be a part of this first Separate Baptist Association.

Growth of the Separates in the Sandy Creek area was to be representative of their experience wherever they traveled. Led by Samuel Harris, James Read, Dutton Lane, John Waller, and Reuben Ford in Virginia, and Daniel Marshall, Joseph Breed, and Philip Mulky in South Carolina and Georgia, Separates soon were to be found throughout the Southeastern states.

Ironically, the original church at Sandy Creek, partly because of the members that had left to establish other churches and partly in response to Governor Tryon's attempt to destroy the Separate Baptists at the Battle of Alamance, had been reduced from 606 to 14 members. The Battle of Alamance was fought within twenty miles of the church, and the Separate Baptists were prime targets for Tryon's armies. The church's local disaster, however, was destined to be the catalyst for Separate Baptist growth in other parts of the country. Morgan Edwards, a Regular Baptist historian, testified to the influence of the Sandy Creek Church in 1772.

> It is a mother church, nay a grandmother and a great grandmother. All the Separate Baptists sprang hence; not only eastward towards the Sea, but westwards towards the great river Mississippi, but northward to Virginia and southward to South Carolina and Georgia. The word went forth from this Zion, and great was the company of them who published it, in so much that her converts were as the drops of morning dew.[8]

The Coming of the Free Will Baptists to Tennessee
Background: The Separate Baptists

THE LEADERS IDENTIFIED

It was mentioned earlier that the Separate Baptist leaders in Kentucky could be traced directly to the Separate Baptist ministry that had grown out of the Sandy Creek Association in North and South Carolina and Virginia. For that reason, it was impossible to deal with the Free Will Baptists in

Tennessee simply as a derivative of the Separate Baptists in Tennessee. Because of this unusual history, it was necessary that extensive background be given.

It has been quite simple to prove that the South Kentucky Association of Separate Baptists was directly related to the old Sandy Creek Association of North and South Carolina, Virginia, and Georgia. Minutes of the South Kentucky Association are full of names that would have been familiar to Shubal Stearns and Daniel Marshall. In fact, of the first 25 Baptist preachers that settled in Kentucky, 20 are known to have been Separate Baptists earlier in Virginia and North Carolina.[9] Elijah Craig, Thomas Chilton, Joseph and Moses Bledsoe, and others all began their ministries in Virginia.

THE THEOLOGICAL BACKGROUND

The discovery of a second Baptist heritage for the Free Will Baptists of Tennessee comes as something of a surprise. At the outset, the Separate Baptists were Calvinistic in their theology and were in full agreement with the Congregationalists and the Strict Congregationalists from whom they had separated. In explaining the scope of dissent in the years immediately after the First Great Awakening, Stephen Marini argued:

> Dissent existed in the form of Baptists and remaining Separates, groups that did reject the New England way of Church and State, but that also continued to endorse the corpus of Calvinist religion. Indeed, the Separates claimed that their polity was the true Cambridge norm, while the Baptists embraced the *Savoy Confession of 1688*, a virtually verbatim version of the *Westminster Confession* with changes in the mode of baptism and the definition of ecclesiastical organization. Organized dissent remained Calvinist before the Revolution.[10]

Limited almost entirely to a frontier ministry, whether in central North Carolina or eastern Kentucky, the Separates quickly found that a doctrine of limited atonement did not meet the needs of their congregations. By the time the Separates reached the wildernesses of Kentucky, the doctrine of general atonement had become a primary characteristic of the movement. Many of the Separates rejected the *Philadelphia Confession of Faith* and its Calvinistic theology quite early. In fact, they hesitated to adopt any rigid confession of faith for fear that it would take precedence over the Scriptures in the minds of the people. Writing in 1790, John Asplund characterized the South Kentucky District Association by saying: "This association was constituted about 1785. Adopted no articles of faith, only the Bible; they hold to general provision."[11]

Even though a formal confession of faith was not available, two entries in the minutes clarify and define the theological stance of this early Separate Baptist Association. Both of the entries speak to the continuing question of union with the Regular Baptists in the area. In 1793, delegates from the Elkhorn Association (Regular Baptists) met with the South Kentucky Association of Separate Baptists at Marble Creek to discuss the possibility of union. When the Elkhorn delegates adamantly demanded acceptance of the *Philadelphia Confession of Faith*, it became evident that a union was not possible at this point in time.

After the Separates rejected the terms of union, five of their ministers along with four churches seceded from the association. If the dissenters thought their action would force the association into union with Elkhorn, they quickly found themselves to be mistaken. Rather, the association, in the same meeting, decided to reaffirm its original principles.

The minutes for that year reveal that the Separates considered themselves a part of the union that had been consummated between the Regular and Separate Baptists in Virginia in 1787 and that they did not plan to remove themselves from that union at this time. From the wording of the minutes, it seems quite clear that union with the Regular Baptists of the Elkhorn Association would not have been impossible had they been willing to be more compromising in their demands.

1. What was the Separate Baptists first constituted into a society upon, in Kentucky? Ans. The Bible.

2. How did we become united with the Baptists in Virginia, called United Baptists? Ans. On a letter the Committee of Baptists, in Richmond, directed to be written to us, in Kentucky, bearing date, October 2, 1788, from under the signature of Reuben Ford and William Webber.

3. Did those terms oblige us to receive any part of the *Philadelphia Confession of Faith*? Ans. No.

4. Do we agree to abide by the constitution in terms of union with United Baptists of Virginia? Ans. We do.[12]

Without additional information, this entry in the minutes with its rejection of the *Philadelphia Confession of Faith* would not be enough to identify the Separates as Arminians. As the struggle for union continued, however, their position became increasingly clear. In 1801, the proposed union finally came to pass. The minutes of the South Kentucky Association for that year outlined the terms of the union. Article 9 stated, "The preaching that Christ tasted death for every man, shall be no bar to communion."[13] The report was signed by a joint committee appointed by the Elkhorn and the South Kentucky Associations—Ambrose Dudley, John Price, Joseph Redding, David Barrow, Robert Elkin, David Ramey, Thomas J. Chilton, Moses Bledsoe, and Samuel Johnson.

Finally, the minutes for August 27, 1803, contain a circular letter to the South Kentucky Association, attempting to clarify the earlier terms of union and the theology of the Separate Baptists within the union.

Recalling to mind that we are now in the more immediate presence of the great searcher of hearts in this conference, that we have met together for the solemn and glorious purpose of advancing truth in religion, renouncing that craftiness, guile, and deceit whereby some lie in wait to catch and deceive the followers of our Lord Jesus Christ, we do call on our brethren who hold to believe in the doctrine of eternal unconditional election and reprobation as they are contained in the *Regular Baptist*

Confession of Faith, to remind themselves that the generality of the members and churches that compose this Association do most sincerely now, and did at the time the union was entered into, believe that those points were inconsistent with, and contrary to the glorious and benevolent purpose of the gospel of Jesus Christ our Lord. In short, it was known that our views of the gospel were that its provisions were free, etc.; that salvation is freely offered to all, and every one of the guilty and fallen sons of Adam's race.[14]

OTHER PREPARATIONS FOR THE TRANSITION
TO FREE WILL BAPTIST TRADITION

Theology was not the only arena in which the stage was being set for the coming of the Free Will Baptists of Tennessee in the late eighteenth and early nineteenth centuries. The Separate Baptists also prepared the way in the areas of polity and practice.

The associational structure itself would continue to have influence until after member church-es in the Cumberland Association began to call themselves Free Will Baptists. J. H. Spencer, writing in 1885, concluded that the South Kentucky Association of Separate Baptists was dissolved after the union with the Regular Baptists of Elkhorn in 1801, but it must be remembered that both groups within the union retained their identity. It was true that they no longer used the names Regular and Separate Baptists.

In 1802, the year after the union took place, the association became so large that it became necessary to make some sort of division. As nearly as possible, the association was divided into two divisions of equal size. Those churches on the north side of the Kentucky River became the North District and those to the south became the South District Association.

In 1803, the South District began dividing over the question of universalism. It seems that John Bailey had been accused earlier of preaching "hell redemption" in 1791, and now the problem had surfaced anew. The majority of the association argued that if Bailey submitted willingly to the asso-ciation and to church government, he should be retained. At that point, the minority withdrew and applied to other churches that remained in the 1801 union. This faction of the South District Association renewed their ties to the old Separate Baptist tradition and emerged as the only true Separate Baptist group in the South.

In 1804, the association included 22 churches and 827 members. They assumed the name of South District of Separate Baptists. By 1819, the association again had become so large that it became necessary to divide into two associations. The daughter association was called the Nolynn Association of Separate Baptists and began its existence with 15 churches and 800 members. These two associations would set the stage for the soon arrival of the Cumberland Association of Free Will Baptists in Tennessee.

The Nolynn Association was much more open in its defense of a general atonement. While it was necessary to search for the doctrine in the minutes of the South Kentucky Association of Separate Baptists, the minutes are clear as to the position of this new association. In a circular let-ter to the association in 1820, its leaders responded to accusations of Arianism, Socinianism, Universalism, and Arminianism. After dispensing with the first three of the accusations, the writers dealt more specifically with the question of Arminianism.

> So likewise doth the Arminian plan oppose the experience of every enlightened Christian if it be what Calvinism say it is, but we believe Jesus Christ our divine Saviour in person tasted death for every man and thereby made an atonement for the sins of the whole world. Or in other words, made salvation possible for all the fallen family and that all men may be saved by repentance toward God and faith in our Lord Jesus Christ.[15]

Finally, the Separate Baptists of Kentucky and Tennessee set the stage for the coming Free Will Baptists in the areas of church ordinances and polity. Though the Separate Baptists earlier had advocated nine different ordinances—baptism, the Lord's Supper, feet washing, laying on of hands, love feasts, anointing the sick, right hand of fellowship, kiss of charity, and devoting children—they soon settled upon the three ordinances that the Free Will Baptists would continue to use later. In the minutes of the South Kentucky Association of Separate Baptists for 1788, the association considered a number of questions including that of the ordinances of the church. Question: "Whether the washing of saints feet is a duty, enjoined on Christians? Ans. It is."[16] By this time, baptism, the Lord's Supper, and the washing of the saints' feet had become the three basic ordinances of the church. Though some of the other nine, mentioned above, were still practiced, they did not retain the status of ordinances. It is interesting to note that the practice of laying on of hands has continued among the Free Will Baptists to the present time. It has changed only in the limitations that have been placed upon it. In the beginning, it enjoyed the same status as baptism and was administered to all new Christians as they joined the church. In more recent years, it has been limited to the ordination of ministers and deacons as they prepared for ministry in the church.

The minutes of 1788 also mentioned the church office of "ruling elder." Question: "Is there any officer in the church besides Bishop and Deacon? Agreed, there is."[17] It is evident that bishop is synonymous with pastor and that the third office is that of ruling elder. The Separates had included ruling elders in the list of officers from the very beginning. It is not unlikely that the office was carried over from the old New England background at the time of the Great Awakening. Actually, the Separates in North Carolina and Virginia had at one time tried to revive the New Testament office of apostle. For one year, two apostles of the church served in Virginia. It was quickly recognized, however, that the office was not workable outside of the New Testament framework. No new apostles were appointed at the end of the first term. Ruling elders would quickly become part of the Free Will Baptist movement and would continue to be an active office until late in the nineteenth century.

The Birth of the Free Will Baptists in Tennessee

THE FOUNDING FATHER

Though others were important in the early history of the Free Will Baptists in Tennessee, Robert Heaton must be considered the founding father of the new movement.[18] Heaton was born March 15, 1765, to Amos and Elizabeth Heaton. His family was among the earlier settlers of middle Tennessee and settled at Heaton's Station near the present route of Highway 41. In 1809, at the age of 44, Robert Heaton responded to the call of God for full-time ministry and in that year preached his first message. His diary gives record of that first sermon as well as his ordination.

> August 22 in 1809 was the first time that Robert Heaton stood on the stage to indeavor to preach the gospel & to spread the tidings of salvation & on the 10 day of May in the year of our Lord 1812 was ordained & authorized to preach the gospel & to administer the ordinences of the house of the Lord.[19]

There is no record of Heaton's educational background, but it is unlikely that the frontier offered opportunities for more than the barest of educational essentials. In that sense, Heaton probably related well to the frontiersmen that made up the Separate Baptist congregations. But in other ways, Heaton was nothing like the Baptist farmer preacher that was characteristic of the Baptist movement during this frontier era. Ordinarily, the preacher bought a small plot of land, gave a portion of that land for the construction of the church, and then struggled for survival along with his people. Heaton, on the other hand, evidently had taken advantage of his early arrival in Tennessee. Between 1787 and 1794, he had acquired three grants from North Carolina (North Carolina still had control of the area at this early date) that totaled 1,280 acres. In the next 30 years, he was involved in real estate negotiations with at least eight individuals and the state of Tennessee.[20] This information, along with the fact that Heaton owned at least two slaves,[21] would indicate that he was quite wealthy.

Since Heaton's wheeling and dealing in real estate extended far into the era of his ministry, it is evident that he did not take a vow of poverty. It should be realized, however, that the other Baptist ministers did not take vows of poverty either. They simply did not have the opportunities that came to Robert Heaton.

If his property holdings do indicate wealth, it does not seem to have affected his ministry adversely. His journal reveals a committed minister of the gospel whose primary concerns were the Lord's church and the Lord's people. It seems quite evident that Heaton gave himself completely to the task of ministry for the rest of his life. There seems little doubt but that his call to the ministry was considered a life-time commitment to Christ.

THE FIRST CHURCH

Goodspeed's *History of Tennessee* reported that "The Free-will Baptists have had an organization in the western part of the county (Robertson), near Turnersville, since 1798, when Nathan Arnett and Jonathan Darden gathered the members of that denomination into a church. After a few years the organization was allowed to lapse but later was revived, and is now known as Head's Church, the land upon which the church is built having been donated by George Head."[22]

While Goodspeed's history was written in 1886 and is usually considered a reliable source, there is no documentary evidence that the Arnett and Darden church ever existed. Ralph Winters in a genealogical study,[23] concluded that Goodspeed's reference is to Miller's Creek Baptist Church of Christ. It seems that Caleb Winters was a part of that church in 1808 when he represented the

Miller's Creek Church at the Union Association at Long Creek Church in Muhlenburgh County, Kentucky. Mr. Winters suggested that Caleb Winters was a charter member of that congregation when it was reorganized as Head's Church. Robert Picirilli, who has done extensive research in these matters, expressed serious doubt that Winters' claims can be substantiated.[24] Though Head's Church became a part of the Cumberland Association of Free Will Baptists later, no records are available before 1840. In that year, the Head's Church presented itself to the Concord Association of Separate Baptists for membership in their organization.[25]

Since it has proven impossible to trace the Head's Church to the earlier date suggested by Goodspeed, it has been necessary that we date the first church in Tennessee in 1812, the year of Robert Heaton's ordination. Even this work might be dated earlier since Heaton's diary mentions eight "former members" who were received into the church in 1813. He does not identify the earlier church from which these members came.[26]

In 1812, Heaton baptized 25 new converts and the church was on its way. In 1813, an additional 14 were baptized, and the eight former members mentioned earlier also were added to the list. On September 25, 1813, the church was formally organized with Robert Heaton as pastor, William Cradock and Benjamin Drake as deacons, and Thomas Heaton as clerk. Though the church is not identified at that point in Heaton's diary, he does identify it later as the Zion Church in Davidson County, White's Creek, State of Tennessee.[27]

The journal entry for September 3, 1820, revealed that an arm of the Zion Church had been established at Sykemore (Sycamore). It is quite evident that Heaton served as pastor for both churches at this time, but in 1823, when the Sycamore church on Sycamore Creek in Robertson County was established as an organized church, John Chaudoin was listed as pastor of the church at Zion. By this time Heaton probably had taken responsibility for the one church at Sycamore.[28] By that year, the new church was known as Sycamore Church at Sweet Spring Meeting House, Robertson County.

The record of the constitution of the Sykemore Church in Heaton's journal indicates that at least one other church, besides Zion and Sykemore, was already in existence. William Boldry of Macadoo Church joined Chaudoin, Cradock, and Drake in the constitution services. The church had been in existence at least since 1813. In that year, the South Kentucky Association minutes indicate that the Macadoo Church had written to the association seeking ordination for "Brother Boldra." The minutes also revealed that two other churches in Tennessee, White's Creek and Sam's Creek, Davidson County, Tennessee, had presented letters to the association, and it seems quite evident that they were interested in membership.[29] Robert Picirilli, in his recent study of these early churches, determined that the White's Creek Church mentioned in the minutes was not the same as Heaton's Zion Church which was also on White's Creek.[30] In 1815, Sam's Creek, Zion, and Spring Creek reported to the South Kentucky Association. This is the first time Spring Creek was mentioned, but since Robert Heaton was listed as the messenger, it seems likely that it was a part of the growing movement of Heaton related churches. White's Creek and Macadoo did not report that year. By 1817, the list of Tennessee churches was reduced to four. Spring Creek did not report to the association and was not to be mentioned again. The church probably ceased to exist, but there is no evidence to indicate the nature of its difficulties. It would be more than presumptuous to suggest that

Heaton just could not handle both Zion and Spring Creek since we find him again involved in an arm of the Zion Church at Sycamore in 1820.

FROM SEPARATE TO FREE WILL

The relationship of the Tennessee churches with the South Kentucky Association always had been inconvenient at best. The few churches in the state to the south were quite isolated from their sister churches in southern Kentucky. The question of convenience would be the first factor leading to a series of associational changes over the next few years. The first change came as a result of a division in the South Kentucky Association of Separate Baptists. The division was both amiable and practical. The association had grown in number of churches, but, more importantly, in the territory in which the churches were found. It was almost impossible for all of the churches to be represented in the mother association. In 1819, the Nolin (Nolynn) Association of Separate Baptists was born. Nolynn not only offered an associational home closer to Tennessee but, being smaller, also offered opportunities for leadership for Heaton's small circle of friends. In 1819, the association voted to meet the next year at "Loes Meeting House" in Tennessee, the house of worship for the Sycamore arm of Zion Church.[31] When the association met at Loes in 1820, Robert Heaton was chosen moderator; Heaton and Alexander Rasco (a preacher and a member of Zion) were appointed to write the circular letter for the association; and William Boldry, John M. Chaudoin, and Rasco were on the business committee.[32] By the time the association met at Loes again in 1823, the Sycamore arm of Zion had been constituted into a church, with Robert Heaton as its pastor. John M. Chaudoin took responsibility for the mother church.

In 1824, only three Tennessee churches reported to the association: Sweet Spring (formerly Sycamore), Zion, and Liberty.[33] In the minutes, Sweet Spring listed 74 members and was represented by Benjamin O'Donnell, H. D. Felts, and N. A. Williams. Zion reported 70 members and was represented by Alexander Rascoe, Reubin Chadowen (Chaudoin), Braxton Lee, Kindred Jackson, and John M. Chadowen (Chaudoin). The third church, Liberty, reported to the association for the first time. The church was represented by Anthony Hinkel.

Evidently, the Tennessee churches were again feeling the strain of travel to the Nolynn Association. Zion and Sweet Spring requested permission to form a new association in Tennessee. Though a committee was appointed to look into the matter, no decision was recorded in the minutes, and the new association did not come into being.[34] The association attempted to accommodate the Tennessee churches by meeting in their area as often as possible. The association met at Loes Meeting House in 1820 and 1823 and then at Zion in 1826. Until 1826, the little group of churches in Tennessee seemed to constitute a closely knit fellowship of believers. Most of the churches and many of the leaders were related to Robert Heaton in one way or another. John M. Chaudoin and Alexander Rascoe were members of Zion while Heaton was still pastor there and Felex Demumbro, the 1825 delegate to the association from Liberty Church, was baptized by Heaton in 1812.[35]

In 1826, however, difficulties arose that were destined to break the bonds of fellowship that had developed among these churches. In January, Robert Heaton established a new church at Marrowbone, later to be called Charity. The founding of the new church, in itself, was not out of the ordinary nor was it unusual that Heaton chose this particular location for the new congregation. In the first place, Heaton had been involved in a church-planting ministry since at least 1812. He simply continued to do what he did best—plant new churches. The location of the new church was a natural one. It very possibly was influenced by the fact that Heaton had been involved in real estate negotiations in the area since 1815 with his most recent acquisitions on Marrowbone coming in 1824 and 1825.[36] But as natural as these elements were, there was one difficulty. According to Heaton's journal, it seems that most of the members for Marrowbone came from Sweet Spring (Sycamore) and Zion. It also is evident from the minutes of the Nolynn Association for 1826 that not everyone was happy with the exodus from the two earlier churches.

Dr. Robert Picirilli, in hand-written notes developed as preparation for an article entitled, *A Study of Separate, Free Will Baptist Origins in Middle Tennessee*, compared the minutes of the Nolynn Association with the membership list of Marrowbone found in Heaton's journal.

> . . . the 1826 minutes of the Nolin Association (meeting at Zion, October 7-9) [1826] show reports from Zion (53 members), Sweet Spring (27 members), Liberty (38 members), and Macedo (26 members). So we can tell where Heaton's Marrowbone group had come from. Zion, since the previous year, has dropped from 70 to 53 (a loss of 17) and Sweet Spring from 73 to 27 (a loss of 46). These two losses combine to equal 63, almost exactly the number at Marrowbone![37]

Marrowbone petitioned the association for membership and immediately found itself in the spotlight when John M. Chaudoin, pastor of Zion, objected to admitting the new church. Supposedly, his objection centered around the damage done to his own church by the exodus to Marrowbone, though other factors could have been involved. At any rate, the new church was received into the association over his objections.[38]

When the association met the next year, a committee was appointed to decide on the difficulties that still existed between the churches in Tennessee. The committee decided in Heaton's favor and Chaudoin was held responsible for the breach in fellowship. The churches were warned that any church that supported Chaudoin's position could be in danger of being removed from the association.[39] This raises an interesting question. Since Chaudoin was handled so harshly, there is a good possibility that his charges against Heaton had gone beyond the spiriting away of members from Zion to more important questions of doctrine or discipline. Of course, the handling of the whole matter could as well be an indication of how much respect Heaton had developed over the years. After all, he had been with Nolynn from its first beginnings and had been a part of the old South Kentucky Association since 1815. Chaudoin was a newcomer to the group and simply could have overstepped his bounds of influence. It is a question that probably will not be answered. The records do not give enough information for a firm conclusion.

On the other hand, it is possible to determine the result of the disagreement. Zion and its pastor disappeared from the minutes, and there is no evidence that the church continued to exist for more than a brief time. The church at Marrowbone continued to prosper. A deed dated April 9, 1840, reveals that they purchased property from A. F. Carney on Marrowbone Creek for the purpose of permanently locating the church. The deed mentions that the property included a meeting house, a church, that was already in existence. The trustees for the church were John Demumbro, Dennis Dozier, Cordy C. Peoples, Wilson L. Gower, and George S. Allen. By this time the name of the church had been changed to Charity.[40]

The entry in Heaton's journal for 1839 seems to indicate that the Zion Church had collapsed and that he was trying to revive the work there. In that year, he mentions 69 members at "The Church of Christ Called Separate Baptist at Charity & Zion Meeting Houses in Davidson County."[41]

By 1828, the Marrowbone church was the only one from Tennessee reporting to the Nolynn Association. One new church at Kerr's Creek appeared in the minutes for a brief time. The church was represented by Felix Demumbry, probably the same Demumbro mentioned earlier.[42]

After 1830, Marrowbone was again left as the only Tennessee representative in the Nolynn Association and after 1833, Heaton himself no longer reported to the body. Heaton's absence could very well have been related to the inconvenience of distance that plagued the Tennessee churches all along. The records do not indicate that Heaton had found difficulty with the association. At any rate, a new opportunity for fellowship became available, and Heaton quickly moved in that direction.

In 1827, the Concord Baptist Association split over the question of general atonement. The Calvinists accepted the name "United Baptist" and became known as Concord #1, and the Arminians dubbed themselves "Separate Baptists" and became Concord #2.[43] At last the Separate Baptists in Tennessee had an associational home located nearby. In 1837, Blue Springs Church, represented by W. L. Gower, a member of Heaton's Marrowbone Church, reported as a member of the association. Heaton also attended the association and preached during the session.[44] In 1838, both Goodsprings (evidently a recent addition to the churches that Heaton had organized) and Charity joined the association,[45] and in 1840, Head's Church, represented by Charles Lankford and George Head, also petitioned for membership.[46] Finally, in 1841, Liberty in Stewart County (another of W. L. Gower's projects) was added to the group.[47]

It will be remembered that the Separates and Regular Baptists had struggled for union almost from the time of their arrival in Kentucky and Tennessee. Some unions had been achieved as early as 1801. For some reason, Heaton and the five churches related to him had never been involved in a merger that related them to the regular Calvinistic Baptists. When news of a reunion between Concord #1 and #2 began to surface in 1840, the churches found themselves facing a new dilemma. When the merger was finally consummated in 1842, Charity, Liberty, Blue Springs, Goodsprings, and Head's churches petitioned for letters of dismissal. They were dismissed for the purpose of establishing a new association.[48]

In 1843, in what possibly was the second session, the Cumberland Association of Separate Baptists met at Head's Meeting House in Robertson County, Tennessee. The new association consisted of the five churches that recently had been dismissed from Concord Association of Separate Baptists #2 plus two new churches—Mount Zion and Sycamore—that had joined the group since that time.

Liberty was represented by James M. Cherry, W. W. Cherry, and J. R. Williams; Blue Springs by J. Darrow, W. L. Gower, and B. F. Binkley; Good Springs by A. Williams, J. Dowlen, and J. Walker; Charity by John Martin and Robert Heaton; Mount Zion by William Barton, W. D. Hamlin, and L.

Hollin; Head's by M. Woodrough, W. Head, and G. Head; and Sycamore by W. Railey, Thomas Smith, and J. Wingo.[49] This new body was destined to be the beginning of the Free Will Baptist movement in Tennessee.

WHAT'S IN A NAME?

We are left with just two questions. How and when did this Separate Baptist Association adopt the new name, Free Will Baptist? Morgan Scott, a Separate Baptist historian, concluded that in 1823, the Nolynn Association was approached by a mixed group of Free Will Baptists and United Baptists in the interest of union. He draws his information from a circular letter attached to the Nolynn minutes for 1823. With tongue in cheek, Walter Williams, the author of the letter, used contemporary names and churches that placed the whole story in a New Testament setting. His sarcasm suggested that he never expected such a union to occur and that he expected his people to laugh with him at the ridiculous offer.

There is a good possibility that Williams' use of satirical prose misled Scott so that he identified three groups rather than two. The letter actually seems to identify the Separates as "Free Willers" rather than suggesting that the Free Willers constituted a separate group.

> . . . At that time much people were assembled together, and the Lord opened the hearts of the disciples called free willers insomuch that they said surely tis right that all the disciples of Jesus should have Union and Communion together. And it came to pass when the disciples had met at a little synagogue in the province of Hardin (Kentucky, author's conclusion), that they took council together and sat themselves down. And there came three men in _____ clothing, who appeared to be of the sect called Calvinists, and the free willers in Council gave them audience. . . .

> The three men reminded the free willers (we suggest that the letter here is referring to the Nolynn Separate Baptists) that there had never been union but that they, the United Baptists, were willing to make the first overtures. They presented their Book of Order and said union could be consumated if the Separates would agree to obey and conform to the book.[50]

The response was expected. After the book was read aloud, ". . . the disciples and elders said, this is not the book of the law nor of the prophets. Therefore, we can have nothing to do with this little book."[51]

The Nolynn Association offered an alternative. They agreed to union if the United Baptists were willing to obey and conform to the book called the Old Testament and the New Testament. The United Baptists responded that they had come with no authority to make such a concession.

As far as the Free Will Baptists of Tennessee are concerned, the circular letter was more than an exercise in satire. It indicates that the Separate Baptists were aware of the name given them by their opponents and that they did not object to using the name "free willers" for themselves.

An even more important source concerning the name appeared in 1825. Lucretia Patterson, a member of Heaton's circle of churches, published an autobiographical pamphlet entitled, *The Experience of Lucretia Patterson, a Religious Tract Written by Herself*. Of much more interest was the subtitle in which she identified herself as a part of Heaton's circle—"The experience and religious exercises of Lucretia Patterson of the Society of Free Will or Separate Baptists."

The pamphlet is a beautiful testimony of Mrs. Patterson's struggle with a call to public ministry at a time when women simply were not allowed to speak in church. The larger part of the pamphlet is given to her struggle with the Lord and the argument she raised with Him against making her call known to the congregation. The rest of the article is a message in itself dealing with numerous spiritual subjects such as salvation, unity, and advice for other ladies who have faced a struggle similar to that of Mrs. Patterson.

The testimony reveals two important facts: (1) The new and alternative name was being used formally by the society as early as 1825 and (2) the society in question was composed of Heaton's group of churches in middle Tennessee. In the text of the pamphlet, Mrs. Patterson mentions that she was baptized by John M. Chaudoin.[52] Since that is true, she probably was a member at Zion. Her relationship to Heaton's group, however, is best illustrated by a recommendation that was included as a preface to the pamphlet. In that statement, almost all of the leaders of the middle Tennessee churches are mentioned by name.

> This work was brought forward by the Authoress, and read/Kitt for the purpose of inspection of the committee of Ministers and laymembers of the society to which she belongs. After having examined the same we do believe it to be the spirit of the Gospel; and hoping it will be productive of much Good, we do advise the Authoress to commit the work to the public.

Ministers
Wm. Bauldry
Jno. M. Chaudoin
Thomas Scaggs
Jno. Chaudoin
Rueben Chaudoin
Robert Aeaten.
Lay Members
Benjamin Drake
Kittie Bauldry/Jessie Atherley
Polly T. Felts/Susannah Drake[53]

In spite of the fact that the new name—Free Will Baptist—was familiar to the Separates quite early, it did not come into common use until much later. When the Cumberland Association was organized in 1842/1843, only the older name was used. By 1854, however, the new name was being used interchangeably with the older one.[54]

Notes for Chapter 5

[1]S. Leroy Blake, *The Separatists, or Strict Congregationals of New England* (Boston: Pilgrim Press, 1902), 55; quoted in C. C. Goen, *Revivalism and Separatism in New England, 1740-1800* (Anchor Books, 1969), 37. Used by permission.

[2]Goen, *Revivalism and Separatism,* 37.

[3]Ibid., 223. "Pedobaptist" refers to those who baptize infants and "Strict Congregationalists" was the proper name given to the Separates who demanded evidence of a conversion experience.

[4]David Benedict, *General History of the Baptist Denomination in America,* Vol. II (Boston: Printed by Manning & Loring, 1813), 37.

[5]Ibid., 38.

[6]Ibid.

[7]Robert B. Semple, *History of the Baptists in Virginia.* (Richmond: John Lynch, Printer, 1810), 15.

[8]Morgan Edwards, "Tour of Rev. Morgan Edwards of Pennsylvania to the American Baptists in North Carolina in 1772-73." (Raleigh: Copied from the original manuscript, in the possession of Mr. Horatio Gates Jones, of Philadelphia, by J. E. Birdsong, Librarian for the N.C. State Library, June 24th, 1889), 8.

[9]J. H. Spencer, *A History of Kentucky Baptists From 1769 to 1885,* Vol. I (Cincinnati: J. R. Baumes, 1885), 107.

[10]Stephen Marini, *Radical Sects of Revolutionary New England* (Cambridge, Mass.: Harvard University Press, 1982), 5. Copyright 1982 by the President and Fellows of Harvard College. All rights reserved. Reprinted by permission.

[11]John Asplund, *The Annual Register of the Baptist Denomination in North America,* 1790, 51, 52.

[12]*Minutes of the South Kentucky Association of Separate Baptists,* 1793. (Hereinafter designated SKASB.)

[13]Ibid., 1801.

[14]Ibid.

[15]*Minutes of the Nolynn Separate Baptist Association,* "Circular Letter," 1820. (Hereinafter designated NASB.)

[16]*Minutes,* SKASB, 1788.

[17]Ibid.

[18]Robert E. Picirilli, "A Study of Separate, Free Will Baptist Origins in Middle Tennessee," *The Quarterly Review,* Vol. 37, No. 2 (January-March 1977), 45. It should be noted that Dr. Picirilli has done a careful analysis of the Separate-Free Will Baptist relationships that centered around the ministry of Robert Heaton. Dr. Picirilli's study compared Robert Heaton's diary with the minutes of the South Kentucky Association of Separate Baptists and those of the Nolynn Association. Copyright 1976, The Sunday School Board of the Southern Baptist Convention. All rights reserved. Used by permission.

[19]Robert Heaton, "Unpublished Ministerial Record," original in the Free Will Baptist Historical Collection at Free Will Baptist Bible College, Nashville, Tennessee.

[20]*Deed Index, 1784-1871,* held by Tennessee Historical Commission, Nashville, Tennessee; *General Courts: Davidson and Robertson Counties* (Early Tennessee 1787-1871), held by Tennessee Historical Commission, Nashville, Tennessee.

[21]*Tax Lists, Davidson County, Tennessee, 1798 and 1805,* held by the Tennessee Historical Commission, Nashville, Tennessee.

[22]*History of Tennessee, From the Earliest Time to the Present, Robertson, Humphries, Stewart, Dickson, Cheatham, and Houston Counties* (Nashville: Goodspeed Publishing Company, 1886), 864.

[23]Ralph Winters, *Historical Sketches of the Winters Family,* I (Clarksville, Tenn.: Ralph Winters, 1965), 13; quoted in Picirilli, "Separate/Free Will Baptists," 45.

[24]Robert Picirilli, handwritten notes used in preparation of article, "A Study of Separate/Free Will Baptist

Origins in Middle Tennessee," 1.

[25]*Minutes of the Concord Association of Separate Baptists, #2*, 1840. (Hereinafter designated CASB #2.)

[26]Heaton.

[27]Ibid.

[28]Ibid.

[29]*Minutes*, SKASB, 1813.

[30]Picirilli, "Separate/Free Will Baptist Origins in Tennessee," 47.

[31]*NASB*, 1819.

[32]*NASB*, 1820.

[33]Picirilli, "Separate/Free Will Baptist Origins in Tennessee," 46. Robert Picirilli has concluded that Sweet Spring was the name given to the arm of Zion at Sycamore after it was constituted into a church.

[34]*NASB*, 1824.

[35]Though the Nolynn minutes list the delegate from Liberty as F. Demumbreum, it seems almost certain that he was the same Felix Demumbro listed in Heaton's Journal in 1812. See *NASB*, 1825, and Heaton, entry for 1812.

[36]*Deed Index, Davidson County, 1784-1871,* Book Q, 431; Book L, 34; and Book Q, 787.

[37]Picirilli, handwritten notes, "Separate/Free Will Baptist Origins in Tennessee."

[38]*NASB*, 1826.

[39]*NASB*, 1827.

[40]*Deed*, Trustees of Charity Church from A. F. Carney, April 9, 1840, *Deed Index, Davidson County, 1784-1871.*

[41]Heaton.

[42]*NASB*, 1828.

[43]*CASB #2*, 1836.

[44]*CASB #2*, 1837.

[45]*CASB #2*, 1838. Robert Picirilli speculated that since the new Good Springs Church was located at Sycamore, it might possibly be a replacement for the old Sycamore/Sweet Spring Church. The speculation has merit but is complicated by the fact that the Minutes for the Cumberland Association (founded 1842, 1843) lists churches both for Good Springs and at Sycamore.

[46]*CASB #2*, 1840.

[47]*CASB #2*, 1841.

[48]*CASB #2*, 1842.

[49]*Minutes of the Cumberland Association of Separate Baptists*, 1843.

[50]*NASB*, 1823.

[51]Ibid.

[52]*The Experience of Lucretia Patterson, a Religious Tract, Written by Herself* (Nashville: Printed at the Republican Office, 1825), 16.

[53]Ibid., preface.

[54]Handwritten minutes (1847-1866), Bethlehem Free Will Baptist Church, Ashland City, Tennessee.

6

The Freewill Baptists in New England

In the past decade, a good deal of controversy has developed around the importance of the Freewill Baptist movement in New England to the present denomination. The two schools of thought that emerged tend to take rather extreme positions with one arguing that the group in New England had no bearing at all on the present and the other that most all of the Free Will Baptists in the United States must admit some relationship with their brothers to the north. The first school points to the fact that the entire northern movement merged with the Northern Baptists in 1911 and the latter argues that remnants of that merger have had impact on the present denomination especially in Ohio, Kentucky, Illinois, Arkansas, and in states further west. While either of these positions could be defended, it seems more likely that there is a balance between the two positions that is nearer to the truth.

Others argue that the story of the northern group already has been told and it would be redundant to tell it again. While it is true that a number of secondary sources deal with the New England movement, none have done so in the context of the larger denominational picture. Their interest has been limited to New England, and they have failed to recognize the influences of the New England segment on the present denomination and the relationship between North and South that developed before the merger of 1911.

Actually, the importance of the Freewill Baptists (spelling used by the group in New England) to the continuing history of the denomination is not a new question nor is it limited to denominational circles. The growth of the northern group was so phenomenal that they often have overshadowed the developments in the South. Their rapid expansion and the national attention they received during the preparations leading up to their union with the Northern Baptists in 1911, have given them such prominence that historians often have accepted this group as representative of the whole movement.

Ruth B. Bordin, in an article entitled, "The Sect to Denomination Process in America: The Freewill Baptist Experience," has done an excellent job in showing the development of the northern group from sect to denomination. In her article, however, Miss Bordin gave the impression that her work included the entire movement. She developed her article around the Troeltsch-Niebuhr Thesis, arguing that when a religious group matures it leaves behind the sect-type characteristics of a lay ministry and a voluntary body of believers requiring a personal religious experience as a requisite for fellowship, and adopts the church-type characteristics of an educated ministry and a conventionalized conversion experience which makes church membership relatively automatic.[1]

In the development of her argument, she limited her examples and illustrations exclusively to the New England movement.

In her only statement about the movement in the South, Miss Bordin added insult to injury by saying that "... many small Freewill Baptist churches served by one of their own members had been gathered among the ex-slaves."[2] At the time of her concern—the decade from 1880 to 1890—Free Will Baptists in the South numbered 11,864 and boasted 167 churches.[3] At the time Miss Bordin wrote her article, the denomination embraced about 450,000 members.[4]

Norman Allen Baxter also limited his *History of the Freewill Baptists* to the northern segment, but has qualified his title by adding the subtitle, *A Study in New England Separatism*. His work, however, also tended to picture the group as the entire movement. Like Miss Bordin, he argued that the denomination had begun with the work of Benjamin Randall in 1780.[5] His only mention of the southern group came in a brief concluding statement that indicated the size of the present organization. Though he did not say that the Free Will Baptists in North Carolina actually had their origin in the New England movement, he left that impression by dealing with them along with the remnants of the merger with the Northern Baptists and by failing to differentiate between them.[6]

As mentioned earlier, the attitude was not a new one. The denomination had struggled with the problem in the late 19th century when some of the New England group attempted to take credit for the founding of the southern movement.

> Some of our Northern brethren have tried to prove that Elder Elias Hutchins, who visited our conference in 1829, was our founder. We can't see how they could make that mistake, when brother Hutchins was sent here as a delegate to visit our conference. When he arrived here, he found that we had over 30 churches, thirty-three preachers, and a membership of 1,910.[7]

For a number of years the Freewill Baptists actually included the two North Carolina conferences in the statistical tables prepared for each General Conference. In 1839, it finally was admitted that the North Carolina Free Will Baptists had never united officially with the New England group.

> It will be seen by the minutes that by a vote of the General Conference the Conferences in North Carolina are not inserted in our statistical table as they have never formally united with us and have made no returns to the Conference for several years. . . .[8]

The Birth of a New Movement
The Setting

The struggle for survival in a new land in the seventeenth century had brought spiritual decline in the colonies that was at least partially responsible for the First Great Awakening. That struggle finally came to a happy conclusion when most of the population was touched by revival. But the revival ended in 1742, and by 1780, the colonies again found themselves in a struggle for survival—this time against the outside enemies of taxation and foreign control. As was true in the earlier struggle, the colonies soon found their attention turned from heavenly things to the more immediate concerns of independence and freedom. Although many of the churches had returned to their pre-revival complacency, at least one influence of the revival remained. George Whitefield returned from England again to attempt to bring America back to God.

New England Freewill Baptists
Introducing Benjamin Randall

THE LONG PROCESS OF METAMORPHOSIS FROM UNCONVERTED PIETY TO FREEWILL BAPTIST SENTIMENT

The founding of the Freewill Baptist movement in New England resulted from the long process of metamorphosis that occurred in the theology of Benjamin Randall. Following the example of another great Baptist, John Smyth,[9] Randall allowed his own personal study of the Scriptures to determine the direction of his theological development. By the time he founded the first Freewill Baptist Church in New Durham, New Hampshire, in 1780, his theology had passed through four major changes: (1) the period of unconverted piety, (2) the period in the Congregational church, (3) the period in the Calvinistic Baptist tradition, and (4) the period of Freewill Baptist sentiment.

The Period of Unconverted Piety—Benjamin Randall was born in New Castle, New Hampshire, in 1749. His father was a sea captain and a member of the Congregational Church. Though his home life might not have been the deciding factor, he was impressed with the necessity of a godly life at a very early age.[10] In his journal, he said:

> . . . I well remember my mothers putting me to bed, and of my trying to say, what I call my prayers. "Now I lay me down to sleep, I pray the Lord my soul to keep, & c."

> I felt as if I wanted something more than I could express in those words. And my heart was so affected that I covered up my little head and wept; and tryed to pray in other words, which would more fully express my feelings. From that time I practiced praying in secret, on my knees, or prostrate on my face, altho' I had never known that kneeling was joined as a duty. . . .[11]

It seems at that point in his experience, Randall's desire for righteousness was based more on fear than on any kind of mature understanding of God's requirement. He saw God ". . . as a great monarch dwelling in an admirable city. . . ."[12] empowered with the right to deny sinful man entrance into the "glorious place" after death. His view of the wrath of God caused him to adopt a rigid standard of conduct that directed his young life even before his conversion. He faithfully attended worship in the Congregational Church, showed his dislike for the coarse language of the sailors on his father's ship, and made a daily habit of Bible reading and prayer.[13] His self-imposed righteousness, however, was to no avail. His early years were distressing years, failing to bring the confidence and contentment that he desired.

The Period of Converted Congregationalism—Randall's early training had made a deep impression. He was so determined that the order and reverent atmosphere of the Congregational service were proper worship that he was reluctant to even listen to George Whitefield when he arrived in the neighboring city of Portsmouth in 1770. In his journal, he remembered his attitude:

> . . . He spoke from Revelations 2:4, 5. The power with which he spoke was a torment to me. When he began to be engaged, and his blessed soul to be inflamed with love, and his heart with pity and grief for poor sinners—and began to expand his arms— and the tears began to roll down from his eyes, it immediately raised an evil spirit within me. Ah, thought I, you are a worthless, noisy fellow! All you want is to make the people cry out! My good old minister does not do so, and he is as good a man as you, and much better.[14]

Fortunately, Randall's inquisitive young mind would not allow him to refrain from hearing Whitefield preach.

> . . . I felt enough of the spirit of persecution to have all such preachers whipped out of town; though I should not like to have been seen in it myself, I should have been willing to see others do it. Although Mr. Whitefield's coming was so disgustful to me, yet as almost everybody else turned out to hear him, I also went; but more as a spectator, than with a desire to reap any benefits, for I was resolved that his preaching should have no effect on me. . . .[15]

Randall heard Whitefield preach three times and was on his way to a fourth service when he heard that the evangelist was dead. The shock of the tragic news caused the young man to pause and to review the last messages that Whitefield had preached. For the first time, Randall saw the futility of his own life and recognized the truth of the great man's preaching. In that moment, his former religion seemed worthless and he recognized his need for salvation. While meditating on his lost condition, Randall's thoughts continually were turned to the words of the Scriptures ". . . but now once in the end of the world hath he appeared to put away sin by the sacrifice of himself."[16] As the truth of the passage finally became clear in his heart, Randall found relief from his burden of sin and knew the peace he had sought all of his life.

After his conversion, Randall felt the need of Christian fellowship and, following his natural inclinations, joined the Congregational Church. His experience with his family's church, however, was not a happy one. His recent conversion had strengthened his earlier convictions, and he was dismayed at the corruption he found in his new church home. It was not enough that the people lived godless lives; the church ignored their sin and failed to employ discipline. Randall was so depressed that he could neither eat nor sleep. While the city slept, he stood before the homes of his friends and prayed for their salvation.[17]

In a final attempt to help his church, Randall began to hold open meetings in which interested members would have the opportunity to hear the reading of printed sermons and to join in prayer and singing. After a brief period of success, the meetings drew the disapproval of the pastor and had to be discontinued. Randall recognized that his failure was complete and that further ministry in the Congregational church was impossible. In May 1775, he ended his association with the church that he had known and loved since childhood.[18]

The Period in the Calvinistic Baptist Tradition—The second step in Benjamin Randall's spiritual development—through conversion to Congregationalism—had been a natural one, but the third was to be totally out of character. While serving as an orderly sergeant in the Revolutionary Army, Randall began to study the Scriptures concerning the validity of infant baptism. His study resulted in the firm conviction that the Scriptures taught believer's baptism and that he himself should be immersed.[19] To his surprise, he found that the group of worshipers that had followed his ministry also had turned to the Baptist position. The discovery removed Randall's fears, and on October 14,1776, he was baptized by Rev. William Hooper. Following baptism, Randall completed the third step in his spiritual development by joining the Calvinistic Baptist Church at Berwick, Maine.[20]

Randall had struggled with a call to the ministry since the early days of his Christian experience, but he had used every available excuse in order to refuse the responsibility. As time passed, however, his followers looked more and more to his leadership, and in March 1777, Randall yielded himself to the call of Christ for full-time ministry.[21]

The importance of this third stage in Randall's spiritual development must not be underestimated. This was a time of valuable preparation for his coming experience in a new and unique ministry preparation that spanned many levels of progress from baptism to the steps of the gospel pulpit.

The Period of Freewill Baptist Sentiment—The final stage in Benjamin Randall's theological metamorphosis—the conviction that Christ had died for every man—came as no surprise. It was the natural conclusion to his spiritual development. At the time of his conversion, he had experienced an attitude of heart that would have been totally alien to the Baptists around him. His reaction to conversion has been recorded:

> I saw an universal atonement—an universal love—an universal call—and that none would ever perish, only those who refused to accept . . . O what love too I felt for all mankind, and wanted that they all might share in that all fullness, which I saw so extensive, and so free to all. . . .[22]

John Buzzell, Randall's earliest biographer, revealed that the young preacher had little problem with his different views when he first began to preach. Randall's conviction was so complete that he felt as though everyone shared his sentiment. All had been peace and harmony since his acceptance of the Baptist faith and ". . . nothing had been said about Calvinism or Arminianism."[23]

Peaceful co-existence, however, was temporary and one of his Baptist brothers finally asked why he did not preach the doctrines of Calvin. Randall's answer set the stage for a sure and permanent break with the Calvinistic Baptists. He simply replied, "Because I do not believe it."[24] In July 1779, Randall was called to meet with the Calvinistic Baptist leaders at Gilmanton, New Hampshire, and there fellowship was broken with his old friends in the faith.

In the fall and winter of the same year, Edward Lock and Tozier Lord also left the Calvinistic Baptists and began to preach the doctrines of the general faith in their churches in Loudon-Canterbury and Barrington, New Hampshire.[25] These two men, along with John Shepard, ordained Benjamin Randall, April 5, 1780. The final stage of metamorphosis was complete. The stage was set for the birth of a new movement in New England.

BENJAMIN RANDALL: A CLOSE UP

A historical narrative of this type tends to emphasize historical fact and neglect personalities and individual contributions. Since Benjamin Randall played such a large part in the development of the Freewill Baptist movement in the North, it seems imperative that some attention be given to the man himself. In fact, in Randall's case, the simple story of his theological evolution threatens to leave the reader with an image of a whimsical, misguided, sectarian preacher "carried about by every wind of doctrine." A closer look reveals exactly the opposite. It should be remembered that Randall's first searchings came as a result of the dismay he felt when he closely examined the lives of the Congregational church members in his hometown, and that his acceptance of believer's baptism came as a result of careful study of the Scriptures. A brief close-up reveals a committed, determined leader for the new denomination.

A Glimpse at the Man Himself—Enoch Place, a Freewill Baptist minister from Stafford, New Hampshire, and a contemporary of Benjamin Randall, describes Randall in a diary entry dated March 24, 1807.

> Benjamin Randall stood five feet, nine inches and a half. Very straight and delicately formed, with long slim fingers. Light complexion . . . black hair that hung in ringlets on his shoulders. Sharp penetrating eyes, rather darker than a common blue eye, inclining to gray. Large mouth but thin lips . . . He was unusually dignified in his manner . . . had a loud, clear voice . . . He usually dress (sic) in black singlebreasted coat without buttons, the fastenings being hooks and eyes . . . for many years he wore small clothes and long boots, but in the last of his days, he wore pants. . . . He usually wore a broad lightweight black hat . . . travelled in warm weather on horseback, and in a sleigh in the winter.[26]

Place evidently had become a good friend of Randall late in the older minister's lifetime. He was so impressed that he often mentioned Randall in his diary. Unlike the typical biography, Place gave attention to personal detail, and Benjamin Randall comes alive again for a later audience.

A Glimpse at the Man's Commitment—Sacrifice and commitment always have been key characteristics of the minister of Jesus Christ, but there is still excitement to be found in the example of one who has gone far beyond the call of duty—that one who literally has burned himself out for God. Benjamin Randall was such a man. During his long ministry, he sacrificed his health, his vocation, and his time to the higher calling of the gospel ministry. Place's diary refers to that commitment in the account of a winter-time baptismal service.

> . . . Then all repaired to a river nearby. The ice on the river was 15 inches thick, and steps were cut into it to favor elder Randall, as he was then very feeble and sick of consumption . . . . When the baptism was over, on account of elder Randall's feeble health, they retired to the house to give the hand of fellowship. After which the elder prayed again, but could not rise from his knees until two young men . . . helped him to his feet.

> Randall continued to preach for the next few nights though he was so weak he had to lean against the wall for support.[27]

A Glimpse at the Man's Lifestyle—Randall modeled the Christian experience in lifestyle as well as in commitment. Even in the light of the rigid standards of his day, his example was above the ordinary. The diary included Randall's personal testimony:

> . . . I have always tried to follow Jesus . . . to be holy, separated from sin and the company of sinners—only when I could do them good. No man has ever seen my horse tied at a store or tavern any longer than I could possibly do my business and be off. . . . I have always avoided all public places of amusement and the like. I was never in a court of justice in all my life. Everything like jockeying, trafficking, and trading for gain, I have studiously avoided.[28]

Benjamin Randall was a disciple of Christ, careful in his lifestyle, not an idler, not materialistic, committed to his task.

The First Church

In 1778, two years before his ordination, Benjamin Randall accepted the invitation of the citizens of New Durham, New Hampshire, to preach in their city. His ministry in New Durham continued through the period of trial with the Calvinistic Baptists and up to the time of his ordination. After his ordination, Randall moved quickly to organize his congregation into a church. On June 30, 1780, the *Church Covenant and Articles of Faith*, prepared by Randall, were accepted and signed by four men and three women. The church at New Durham was the first Freewill Baptist Church in that area. It signified the birth of a new denomination in New England.

The Covenant that Randall prepared probably would not have been out of place in any Baptist church in New England. It was rather his *13 Articles of Faith* with their emphasis on general atonement that would set a new course for the small group.

As would be expected, Randall's new theology and his break with the Calvinistic brethren made numerous enemies for the small congregation. In fact, even after Randall became convinced of the validity of the doctrine of general atonement, he personally continued to struggle with a number of Biblical passages that seemed to speak to the doctrine of election. His opponents were quick to recognize his difficulty with the passages and often used them in their arguments with him. But if his enemies were looking for a battle, they would be disappointed. He simply admitted that he did not yet understand such passages as Romans 8:29, Ephesians 1:4, and Romans 9:13. His strongest argument suggested that the verses also failed to prove the opponent's position completely and that if "fully understood they contained a sense which run parallel with a universal call of the gospel."[29]

Early Growth

Though Randall at first stood alone as a Freewill Baptist, he continued to draw strength from Tosier Lord, Edward Lock, and John Shepard. Lord had established an anti-Calvinistic church at Berwick-Crown Point in Barrington and another at Shapleigh, Maine. In June 1779, the Baptist Church at Loudon and Canterbury also rejected the doctrines of Calvinism. These churches never formally united with the Freewill Baptists and afterwards became extinct. They were important, however, at a time when Randall and his few church members needed fellowship with others of like faith.

At first, newly developed Freewill Baptist churches were considered branches of the mother church at New Durham. Each congregation had its own monthly meeting, but members of the other congregations were expected to attend. Randall was responsible for baptizing individuals who joined the different congregations on profession of faith. For a number of years, in the interest of unity, Randall and his closest co-laborers personally visited each of the churches at least once every twelve months.[30]

The phenomenal growth of the denomination in New England is best seen in the number of ministers added and in the number of churches organized. By 1800, the denomination boasted 31 ordained ministers with a good number of them coming from Calvinistic Baptist churches after being converted to an Arminian position. In the first ten years, 20 churches were planted in the New England area. A statistical table for 1790 indicates that two of the churches had already become extinct, but the others remained to form a strong nucleus for continued growth. The table listed the churches by the names of the cities in which they were found, but also included the original name of the church. Both Strafford, New Hampshire, and Bristol, Maine, had two churches within the confines of the city.

STATISTICAL TABLE IN 1790[31]

	Churches	Ministers	Ruling Elders and Unordained Preachers.
1780	New Durham, N.H.,	Benjamin Randall.	Joseph Boody, Jr., Nathaniel Buzzell, Samuel Tasker, James Runnells, Isaac Townsend.
"	Hollis, Me. (Little Falls.)		
1781	Tamworth, N.H.*		
"	North Strafford, N.H., (1 Barrington.)	Joseph Boody.	
"	Woolwich, Me.,		Eben. Brookings, Jr.
"	Georgetown, Me., (Parker's Island.)		Thomas Stilluwll. David Oliver
"	Westport, Me., (Squam Island, part of Edgecomb.)	Daniel Hibbard,	John Dunton.
"	Bristol, Me.		
"	Gorham, Me.,	James McCorson,	John Cotton. Samuel Thombs.
"	Scarborough, Me.* (Dunston.)		
"	Durham, Me., (Little River.)		Levi Temple.
1782	Gray & New Gloucester, Me.,	Nathan Merrill.	William Irish.
1783	Strafford, N.H., (Barrington, C'n Pt.)		Micojah Otis.
"	Parsonsfield, Me.,	Samuel Weeks.	
1785	Lincolnville, Me. (New Canaan.)		
"	Paris, Me. (Number Four.)		
1786	Edgeeomb, Me.,	John Whitney.	
1788	Canaan, Me.		
"	2 Bristol, Me. (Redford's Island.)		
"	Cambden, Me. (Seguntecook.)		
		Pelatiah Tingley, (of Waterboro, Me.)	Daniel Philbrick, (of Pittsfield, N.H.) Joseph Hutchinson, (of Windham, Me.)
	20 Churches.	8 Ministers	9 Ruling Elders. 7 Unord. Preachers.

*Probably extinct

The Organizational Structure

THE QUARTERLY MEETING

By 1782, twelve churches had come into existence, and Randall was beginning to recognize the necessity for some sort of organizational structure. He spent the first nine months of that year close to his home while he cared for his dying father-in-law. During that time, it was impossible for him to keep close touch with the growing number of churches. Increasing difficulties with Shaker missionaries in the area and the growing difficulty of administration for so many churches convinced him that the churches needed to enter into an organizational agreement that would provide mutual help.

In September 1782, Randall met with Pelatiah Tingley, Daniel Hibbard, and several laymen at the Little Falls Church in Hollis, Maine, to discuss the possibility of establishing a new central conference. Randall submitted a plan of organization and suggested a name for the new body of churches. The plan provided for the inclusion of all of the Freewill Baptist churches and outlined the pattern for a quarterly meeting. The quarterly meeting would meet four times a year and consist of delegates and others from the constituent churches. Its stated purpose was to devise ways and means that would lead to united church effort and the highest degree of efficiency in the task of the gospel ministry.[32]

These plans were sent to the various churches with the understanding that the congregations would consider the proposals and then meet together on Saturday, December 7, 1782, to determine their future course of action.

At the appointed time, the delegates met at the Little Falls Church and agreed to organize a quarterly meeting. Benjamin Randall was chosen moderator and Pelatiah Tingley, clerk. The body was to be known as the Baptist Quarterly Meeting. At the end of the session, Randall was chosen Quarterly Meeting clerk, and he was to hold the position for the remainder of his life. The regular session was to be held on the first Saturday in March (at New Gloucester), June (in New Durham), September (in Woolwich), and December (in Little Falls). The order was to remain the same until the quarterly meeting decided to make other arrangements.[33]

At first, the quarterly meeting was regarded as the church, while the local churches were called branches or monthly meetings.[34] This central organization accepted and rejected members for the churches and handled any difficult questions of discipline.

THE YEARLY MEETING

Before a decade had passed, the denominational leaders recognized that the quarterly meeting system was not adequate to meet the needs of the growing denomination. In 1792, Randall submitted a new and complicated organizational proposal that was designed to keep the churches in constant contact with one another. The local church conference would continue to be called the monthly meeting, the old quarterly meeting would become known as the yearly meeting and would still meet four times a year, and new quarterly meetings would be established that would meet in between the four yearly sessions. The local churches (monthly meetings) were to send their messengers and letters to the quarterly meetings, and the quarterly meetings were to send their messengers and letters to the yearly meetings.

It should be noted that, since the ordained ministers were expected to attend all of the meetings, they were on the road constantly. It seems this was by special design. The meetings were so arranged as to keep the ministers almost continually traveling, and spreading the news of free salvation, and accounts of the wonderful works of God from one extreme of the "Connexion to the other."[35]

On May 23, 1792, Randall met with representatives from New Durham, Pittsfield, Middleton, and Barrington at the home of James Lock, in Barnstead. The yearly meeting was organized with a yearly meeting convening four times a year and the new quarterly meetings gathering every three months. It was agreed:

> That each church attend to all its local business, maintain good discipline, take scriptural steps with delinquents, to the last admonition; then, if unsuccessful, refer the matter to the quarterly meeting. That each church, as now, have a clerk to keep its records, full and plain. That the church send its clerk to each session of the quarterly meeting, with his book of records, with several others as messengers. That through its clerk and messengers, each church report its condition to each session of the quarterly meeting.[36]

The quarterly meeting also was instructed to appoint a clerk and to keep careful records of all its transactions. These minutes would be presented at each yearly meeting.

As mentioned earlier, the yearly meetings would serve a higher purpose than that of simple business transaction. John Buzzell, in his *Life of Elder Benjamin Randall*, mentioned the importance of the yearly meeting as an evangelistic tool.

> . . . These meetings, also, called the attention of thousands to hear the word of God, who perhaps would have remained ignorant of those things if their attention had not been excited by these means. I have known persons of respectability to travel nearly twenty miles to attend a monthly meeting; and have seen as many as a hundred spectators to a church conference, when the church consisted only of ten members. At quarterly meetings, I have often seen thousands flocking from different parts to hear the Word; and when we have been under the necessity of repairing to groves for the want of room, I have frequently seen them even climb the trees, like Zaccheus to see and to hear, and as I may say, hazard their lives for the sake of information. . . .[37]

The first yearly meeting was held at New Durham from June 9-11, 1792.

After the successful organization of the first yearly meeting, it was recommended that the same plan be adopted by the churches at Edgecomb, Gorham, and Parsonsfield, Maine. For more than fifty years, until the organization of the General Conference, the yearly meeting was the highest ecclesiastical body within the denomination.

THE GENERAL CONFERENCE

By 1827, the denomination again found itself struggling with the limitations of the yearly meeting structure. By that year, the denomination had seen the development of seven yearly meetings and thirty quarterly meetings with at least five as far away as Ohio. At this point, the denomination reached its final level of organization in the establishment of the General Conference. The new system simply added one level to the existing pattern—the monthly meeting (local church) reported to the quarterly meeting, the quarterly meeting to the yearly, and the yearly meeting to the new General Conference.[38]

The Choosing of a Name

For the first number of years, the new movement in New England found itself called by many names—Church of Christ, General Provisioners, and Free Willers. It was not until 1799 that the name "Freewill Baptist" appeared as an official title in the minutes. Even then, there were a number of denominational leaders that objected to the new name.[39] But by the turn of the century the name was well established, and in 1804, the state of New Hampshire confirmed the name by legislative act.

STATE OF NEW HAMPSHIRE

In the House of Representatives, December 7, 1804

Resolved, that the people in this State, known by the name of the Freewill Anti-Pedobaptist Church and Society, shall be considered as the distinct religious sector denomination, with all the privileges as such, of the Constitution.

Sent up for concurrence

John Langdon, Speaker

In the Senate, December 8.

Nicholas Gilman, president.

Not approved nor returned by his Excellency, the governor, it therefore becomes a law

Joseph Pearson, Secretary of State[40]

It is interesting to note that though the name was not officially adopted in the South until 1828, it already was in use at least as early as 1803. In both New England and in the South, the name seems to have been applied at first by outsiders in an attempt to identify these opponents of the traditional Calvinistic system.

The Matter Concluded

The Freewill Baptist movement in New England grew out of the unique spiritual development, drive, and vision of one man—Benjamin Randall. Though he was not the first to arrive at new levels of spiritual conviction through his own study of the Bible, his spiritual metamorphosis was unique in its direction. Rather than developing through the expected channels of the General Baptist movement which had been present in New England for many years, it had passed from Congregational to Calvinistic Baptist Sentiment before finally ending in the new Freewill Baptist doctrine. The lack of General Baptist influence might be explained by the decline of the movement which had begun about the time of the Great Awakening. W. T. Whitley dated the decline from the adoption of the *Calvinistic Baptist Confession of 1677* by the Philadelphia Association in 1742. He argued that ". . . from this time the progress of all General Baptists in America ceased; and presently a decline set in."[41] Ruth B. Bordin also indicated the decline:

> Before the Awakening New England Baptist churches had almost all been Arminian, but by 1780 the large flocks of Calvinistic Separatists into the denomination, plus the closer association of the Calvinist Baptists of the middle colonies had changed the picture completely, and most New England Baptist churches were firmly committed to Calvinistic principles.[42]

Whatever the reason for the lack of General Baptist influence, it has been quite evident that the Freewill Baptist movement in New England had its beginning through a spiritual development that began in the Congregational background of its founder, and that it cannot be dated before 1780.

Summary Part I

In Part I, we have attempted to trace the earliest roots of the denomination from its beginnings in Europe to its first developments here in the United States. For the most part, the study has been limited to the first two centuries of growth which ended in 1800. In some cases, it was necessary to extend the study beyond 1800 in order to clearly identify a particular movement as Free Will Baptist. Some of the earliest groups waited until quite late to adopt the new name.

In England, the first Baptist congregation accepted the doctrine of general atonement. Though the earliest congregations were commonly known as General Baptists, their leaders did speak of themselves as Free Will Baptists as well. The alternative name appeared in the documents as early as 1611. By 1659, the General Baptists often spoke of themselves as Free Will Baptists in their official documents.

On the American scene, the first two centuries of denominational history saw the birth of three different Free Will Baptist movements that originated from three entirely different backgrounds. In New England, Benjamin Randall experienced a denominational and theological evolution in which he moved from Congregational to Baptist to Freewill Baptist sentiment. The first Freewill Baptist church in that area was established in New Durham, New Hampshire, in 1780. The influence of Randall's group quickly spread throughout the New England states. By the end of the 18th century, the movement was well organized on an associational plan that included both quarterly and yearly meetings. The end of the century also saw a growing interest in the name, Freewill Baptist. In 1804, the denomination officially adopted the name and it was confirmed by an act of the Legislature.

In North Carolina, the Free Will Baptists had a much older heritage through the work of the General Baptists in the eastern part of that state. Paul Palmer, an evangelist and church planter, established the first General Baptist church in the area in Chowan County, near the present community of Cisco.

In 1729, Palmer established a second church in Pasquotank Precinct at the home of William Burgess, but because of the nature of his ministry—church planting and evangelism rather than settled pastorate—and because of his travels, Palmer did not have continued influence on the eastern North Carolina churches. The responsibility for the growing movement rather was left to Joseph and William Parker. Like Palmer, Joseph Parker established a number of churches, but he ordinarily stayed with one church for a number of years before moving on to a new field of service.

The growth of the General Baptists between 1727 and 1755 was phenomenal. The first church in Chowan Precinct ceased to exist a few years after its organization, but before its death it gave birth to churches at Pasquotank and at Meherrin. By the end of the first period of its history, the movement had developed 20 churches in 14 counties. By 1755, the influence of the General Baptists stretched as far west as Granville County, as far north as Hertford County, and as far south as Onslow.

Tragedy struck the Parkers and their General Baptist churches in 1755 when representatives from the Philadelphia Baptist Association (Calvinistic) infiltrated the ranks and converted many of the churches to a new theological position. By 1772, Morgan Edwards could list only four churches and their ministers as the entire remnant of the General Baptist movement in North Carolina. These included William Parker at Meherrin, Joseph Parker at Contantony (Little Contentnea), William Fulsher at Matchipungo (Pungo), and a Mr. Wingfield at Bear River. Meherrin finally entered the Calvinistic camp sometime in 1794 after the death of William Parker.

When Joseph Parker died in 1794, James Roach, formerly a Regular Baptist related to the Goose Creek Baptist Church but now a General Baptist convert, was chosen to succeed Parker at Little Contentnea. Roach would be one of two leaders to sign the first *Free Will Baptist Confession of Faith* early in the 19th century. Little Contentnea along with Wheat Swamp, Louson Swamp, Grimsley, and Gum Swamp—churches that had been established late in the

Parkers' ministry, became the nucleus of the Free Will Baptist movement at the close of the General Baptist era.

There can be no doubt but that the Free Will Baptists were the direct descendants of the Old General Baptists of eastern North Carolina. The Parker churches that became Free Will Baptist, James Roach and his transition from General Baptist to Free Will Baptist, and the mutual use of the *General Baptist Confession of Faith of 1660* clearly revealed the relationship between the two groups.

Finally, the Free Will Baptists in Tennessee can be traced as far back as 1785. Here again, the denomination must recognize relationship to a new and different source. The Free Will Baptists in Tennessee can be traced back to the Separate Baptists of Kentucky.

Robert Heaton, the founder of the movement in Tennessee, was a member of the South Kentucky Association of Separate Baptists, the Nolynn Association of Separate Baptists, the Concord Association of Separate Baptists, and finally, Cumberland Association of Free Will Baptists. Though the group did not become known as Free Will Baptists officially until mid-century, the new name was in use as early as 1824.

And so ends the history of the first two centuries of Free Will Baptist development. A number of things have become clear: (1) The Free Will Baptist denomination can claim an ancient and worthy heritage that dates back to at least 1727 here in the United States and, through relationships with the General Baptists, back to 1609 in England and (2) a history of the Free Will Baptists cannot be limited to any one particular area or background. The present denomination must recognize that there is no common source for the many groups that make up the National Association of Free Will Baptists.

Notes for Chapter 6

[1]A. Leland Jamison, "Religions in the Perimeter," in *The Shaping of American Religion*, Vol. I: *Religion in American Life*, ed. by James Ward Smith and A. Leland Jamison, 4 vols. (Princeton: Princeton University Press, 1961), 167-172, has given the clearest summary of the Troeltsch-Niebuhr thesis.

[2]Ruth B. Bordin, "The Sect to Denomination Process in America: the Freewill Baptist Experience," *Church History*, XXXIV (March 1965), 92.

[3]H. K. Carroll, *The Religious Forces of the United States* (New York: Charles Scribner's Sons, 1912), 38.

[4] *Contact* (December 1953), 4-6. This periodical is the official publication of the National Association of Free Will Baptists.

[5]Norman Allen Baxter, *History of the Freewill Baptists* (Rochester, N.Y.: American Baptist Historical Society, 1957), 1. Used with permission of the American Baptist Historical Society, Valley Forge, Pennsylvania, 1948.

[6]Ibid., 181, 182.

[7]Thad Harrison and J. M. Barfield, *History of the Free Will Baptists in North Carolina*, Vol. I (Ayden, N.C.: The Free Will Baptist Press, 1897), 162. Elias Hutchins was an elder in the northern group. His name appeared often in their minutes both as a representative from Ohio and as an itinerant preacher (*Minutes of the General Conference of the Freewill Baptist Connection* [Dover, N.H.: Published by the Freewill Printing Establishment, 1859], 30-32; *The Freewill Baptist Register*, 11 [1832], p. 48; "Rev. Elias Hutchins," *Free Baptist Cyclopaedia* [Chicago: Free Baptist Cyclopaedia Co., 1889], 283, 284).

[8]*Minutes of the General Conference, 1839*, 158.

[9]W. T. Whitley, *The Works of John Smyth*, Fellow at Christ's College, 1594-8 (2 Vols.; Cambridge: at the University Press, 1915), 11, 564. Smyth first had been a Puritan, but was later a Separatist, a Baptist, and an Anabaptist.

[10]I. D. Stewart, *The History of the Freewill Baptists for Half a Century*, Vol. I (Dover, NH: Freewill Baptist Printing Establishment, 1862), 32.

[11]John Buzzell, "An Extract of the Experience of Elder Benjamin Randall. (Taken from a manuscript) Written by Himself, Corrected by the Editor," *A Religious Magazine*, VI (February 1822), 206.

[12]Ibid., 206, 207.

[13]Frederick L. Wiley, *Life and Influence of Rev. Benjamin Randall* (Philadelphia: American Baptist Publication Society, 1915), 12; C. Raymond Chappell, "Benjamin Randall-Frail but Unafraid," *The Chronicle*, IV (July 1941), 98.

[14]"Apostolic Succession and Religion of the Spirit, Exemplified in the Life and Times of Benjamin Randall," *The Morning Star*, XXXIV (April 12,1859), 1.

[15]John Buzzell, *Life of Elder Benjamin Randall* (Limerick, Maine: Hobbs, Woodman & Co., 1827), 11; "Apostolic Succession," *The Morning Star*, XXXIV (April 27, 1859), 1.

[16]Hebrews 9:26; "Apostolic Succession," *The Morning Star*, XXXIV (May 18,1859), 1.

[17]"Apostolic Succession," *The Morning Star*, XXXIV (July 20, 1859), 1.

[18]"Apostolic Succession," *The Morning Star*, XXXIV (July 27, 1859), 1; Stewart, *Half a Century*, I, 39.

[19]Baxter, *Freewill Baptists*, 9.

[20]Wiley, *Life and Influence*, 41; Raymond J. Bean, "Benjamin Randall and the Baptists," *The Chronicle*, XV (July 1952), 102; Robert G. Torbet, *A History of the Baptists* (Philadelphia: The Judson Press, 1950), 274. Norman Baxter listed the city as Madbury, arguing that other historians had mistaken the words of Isaac Backus when he said, ". . . Madbury contains a part of the Berwick Church." Baxter, *Freewill Baptists*, 9.

[21]Wiley, *Life and Influence*, 46.

[22]Buzzell, "Extract," 216; Buzzell, *Life of Elder Benjamin Randall*, 20, 21; "Apostolic Succession," *The Morning Star*, XXXIV (May 18,1859), 1.

[23]Buzzell, *Life of Elder Benjamin Randall*, 75.

[24]Ibid.

[25]Baxter, *Freewill Baptists*, 21-24; Wiley, *Life and Influence*, 78, 79. Wiley listed the Barrington Church as the church at Crown Point. It was evident that both Baxter and Wiley were referring to the same church as Tozier Lord was identified as the pastor and Benjamin Randall was said to have joined the church after his release from the Calvinistic Baptists. Earlier records would indicate that Baxter was correct (Buzzell, *Life of Elder Benjamin Randall*, 80,81).

[26]Enoch Place, *Journal, The Free Will Baptist* (Wednesday, May 27, 1896), 2.

[27]Ibid.

[28]Ibid.

[29]Buzzell, *Life of Elder Benjamin Randall*, 85.

[30]G. A. Burgess and J. T. Ward, *Free Baptist Cyclopaedia* (Chicago: Free Baptist Cyclopaedia Co., 1889), 208.

[31]I. D. Stewart, *The History of the Freewill Baptists for Half a Century* (Dover, N.H.: Freewill Baptist Printing Establishment, 1862), 95.

[32]Wiley, *Life and Influence*, 105, 106.

[33]Ibid., 107.

[34]Burgess and Ward, *Cyclopaedia*, 208.

[35]Buzzell, *Life of Elder Benjamin Randall*, 139, 140.

[36]Wiley, *Life and Influence*, 141.

[37]Buzzell, *Life of Elder Benjamin Randall*, 140.

[38]*A Treatise on the Faith of the Freewill Baptists* (Dover, N.H.: Published by David Marks, 1834), 9.

[39]Burgess and Ward, *Cyclopaedia*, 209.

[40]Wiley, *Life and Influence*, 190.

[41]W. T. Whitley, "The Six-Principle Baptists in America," *The Chronicle*, III (January 1940), 6, 7.

[42]Bordin, "Sect to Denomination," 77, 78. Also see C. C. Goen, *Revivalism and Separatism in New England*, 1740-1800 (New Haven: Yale University Press, 1962), 240-242 and Edwin Scott Gaustad, *The Great Awakening in New England* (New York: Harper & Brothers, 1957), 120. Used by permission.

Part II

The Third Century:
From Identity to Organization
(1800-1935)

By the end of the eighteenth century, the name "Free Will Baptist" had become popular both in New England and in North Carolina. In 1804, the name was officially adopted in New England and was confirmed by legislative decree. In 1828, the new name was accepted as the formal title for the movement in North Carolina.

In spite of the fact that the Free Will Baptists in different parts of the country sprang from different backgrounds, it became evident quite early that there were numerous similarities beyond the common name. This section of the text will attempt to show those similarities as they developed during the nineteenth century. Though the different segments of the movement developed independently in different parts of the country, they were bound together by their common theology, polity, and church government. New England and North Carolina Free Will Baptists had been in correspondence since 1825 and by the beginning of the 20th century, most of the Free Will Baptists of the United States were in constant contact either through correspondence or through associational alliances.

7

Early Nineteenth Century Growth

Revival in North Carolina (1812-1830)

The year 1812 marked the beginning of a new era for the Free Will Baptists in North Carolina. Though they still depended heavily on the direction given by the leaders of the transition period, James Roach and Jesse Heath, they had revised the old *Confession of Faith* to meet their own needs. It still bore the old name, but the confession was unquestionably a Free Will Baptist document. Few changes were necessary as the new identity matured.

The period also gave birth to a new brand of leadership. Jesse Heath came to the movement at the end of the old period and was instrumental in executing the final steps in the development of the new identity. At the same time, however, Heath was the first of the new leaders. He had contact with the old movement through his work with James Roach, but he was known as a Free Will Baptist minister from the beginning. Roach would soon pass from the scene; Heath would set the pace for the new identity.

New growth was to come slowly. Years were to pass before the Free Will Baptists in eastern North Carolina would enjoy any great degree of prosperity, but the years of decline were over. In 1807, Jesse Heath had found five churches and three ministers in the entire movement. In forty-six years, the remnant of the old General Baptist movement had lost three churches and had gained but four. Before twenty-three more years had passed, however, they had added twenty-six churches to the five that Heath had found. As the period progressed, the tempo increased. The last years of the period were full of excitement and growth. Revival was in the air.

The Development of an Identity

By 1830, the new identity was established. The new name had come to wear like a well-fitting glove and the new leaders were in full command. The problems of recovery were becoming dim memories. The denomination had made a name for itself. The Free Will Baptists of North Carolina had arrived.

An adequate explanation of the new identity demanded that at least four aspects of the identity be considered: (1) the organizational development of the early Free Will Baptists, (2) the first signs of new growth, (3) the acceptance of the new name, and (4) attitude toward identity.

The Organizational Development of the Early Free Will Baptists

THE EARLIEST EFFORTS AT ORGANIZATION

The First Yearly Meeting—As early as 1729, Paul Palmer revealed the existence of a Yearly Meeting of General Baptists that had included the churches in Virginia.[1] For some reason, however, the Yearly Meeting found little place in the records of the early history of the movement. David Benedict concluded that the Yearly Meeting continued through the early years of General Baptist growth,[2] but there has been no evidence that it enjoyed the same degree of strength and authority that characterized the Kehukee Baptist Association and the later Bethel Conference of the Free Will Baptists.

At any rate, the remnant of the General Baptists had little opportunity for such formal organization. The few churches probably were held together by the itinerant ministries of the Parkers rather than by the ties of a continuing Yearly Meeting.

The Court of Union—The records of the Pasquotank church revealed that the congregation had developed a system of self-government sometime before 1758.[3] The Court of Union first had been established to deal with the secular matters of the members. The Court was made up of the ministers of the local church and six laymen. The business matters of the church were handled by the Elders. Eventually, the Court of Union was discontinued, but the people were so displeased that it was reinstated with a number of revisions. Nine Elders were elected on a permanent basis to serve as the local Court of Union. The new system extended beyond the private church, from problems of the members to the business of the church, and this type of Court continued until the time of Lemuel Burkitt near the end of the eighteenth century. S. J. Wheeler, the Baptist historian of the early nineteenth century, concluded that all the churches employed this complex system.[4]

The Remnant and Organization—As was mentioned earlier, the records do not reveal that the few churches of the General Baptist remnant gave much attention to organization. It was more than likely true that relationships between the churches were limited to the visits of the Parkers and their followers as the Parkers fulfilled their preaching obligations. It was the custom of the period for the Elders of the mother church to deal with the business problems of the arms of that church.[5]

The poor government of the General Baptists spurred the later movement to an early concern for an effective organization. They recognized the importance of direction and discipline as requisites for growth and stability.

R. K. Hearn evaluated the situation of the General Baptists following the reorganization process, by saying that " . . . they were not disciplinarians, and were in some sense like fragments of a routed and dispirited army after its principal officers and soldiers had gone over to the enemy."[6]

The Free Will Baptists were ready for a solid and dependable program of organization.

THE PROGRAM OF ORGANIZATION
UNDER THE NEW IDENTITY

The Code of Discipline—The preface to the *Free Will Baptist Confession of Faith and Code of Discipline of 1812* indicated that though scattered disciplinary materials were available, no efforts had been made to draw up a complete code that would serve as a foundation of government for the churches.[7] A conference evidently had been in existence before 1812, but it had been organized so loosely that new methods of organization were demanded. The new Code was quite complete. It set the guidelines for the conference, dealing with matters of discipline, the duties and qualifications of church officers, the ordinances of the church, transfer of members from one church to another, and the proper constitution of a new church.[8] *The Code of Discipline* was a first step toward effective organization.

The Bethel Conference—M. A. Huggins, author of the most recent history of the Baptists in North Carolina, contended that the Bethel Conference of Free Will Baptists was organized in 1780.[9] Though Huggins did not document his argument, R. K. Hearn confirmed the fact that conferences were held at the Gum Swamp church before the turn of the century.[10]

By 1812, the Bethel Conference had established a solid identity with scheduled meetings, rules of decorum, and a revised *Confession of Faith* that indicated both the ties with the old movement and the direction of the new.

By 1825, the conference had attained a new degree of maturity—formal minutes, adequate representation for the member churches, and a new system for determining denominational statistics had been added to the older program of organization. Jesse Heath described the conference machinery in 1827. He indicated that his information had come from the records for 1825. He reported to *The Morning Star:*

> . . . Our annual conference is composed of two delegates from every church, and all the preachers both ordained and licensed, and the general treasurer. The conference meets annually, and returns are made from all the churches so that once a year we know the state of the whole connexion. Our minutes are taken and printed and distributed among our members. . . .[11]

The Bethel Conference had made large strides of progress since the time of five small churches and three ministers. However, the progress made by 1825 could not be measured in the numbers of new converts or new churches. It was a progress in maturity, in organization, and in denominational spirit. These were the years of concern for identity. The growth in numbers followed quickly.

The records for 1825 revealed that the tiny conference had grown to a total of 800 members, but the increase in membership did not tell the full story of progress. In 1807, Jesse Heath became the fourth minister in the denomination. In eighteen years, the number had increased to twelve.[12]

With the earlier problems of identity, organization, and the struggle for existence becoming dim memories, the denomination was ready for the revival that was to gain its greatest strength between 1825 and 1830.

> The earliest available minutes for the Bethel Conference were those printed and distributed in 1829. The minutes and other records revealed an astounding measure of growth since 1825. The conference now boasted thirty-three ministers and twenty-six churches in eleven counties.[13] By 1830, the membership had grown to 1,892—an

increase of more than 1,000.[14] Revival had touched the Free Will Baptists of North Carolina.

The First Signs of New Growth

By 1829, there were too many churches, separated by too many miles, and the Bethel Conference no longer could give adequate guidance to the growing denomination. The first solid evidence of the magnitude of the growth was the necessary development of new conferences to meet the needs of the new churches.

THE FREE-WILL BAPTIST ASSOCIATION

The second Free Will Baptist Conference to be established in North Carolina was the result of addition rather than division. Before 1830, the movement had not had success west of Orange County in the center of the state. Even then, Frederick Fonville continued a lonely existence as the only Free Will Baptist preacher in the area.

In 1827, a group of United Baptists in the mountains of the state began to question their Calvinistic doctrines. On October 13, 1827, they separated from the French Broad Association of United Baptists, and declared themselves to be an independent conference.[15] The unsettled situation remained until the annual association in October 1830, when they accepted the Free Will Baptist denomination as their home. In the sixteenth item of business, they resolved that ". . . in the future our Churches represent themselves as Free-Will Baptists."[16]

The minutes of the new association gave no clue as to the source of the Free Will Baptist influence that led to their final decision. They spelled their name like that of the group in the eastern part of the state, but they organized on the basis of associations like the Freewill Baptists in New England. The latter characteristic, however, probably was a carryover from their United Baptist background, rather than the result of influence from the North. This is another example of the patchwork character of the denomination. The Free Will Baptists must acknowledge another ancestor. The United Baptists (Calvinistic) join the Separate and General Baptists and the Congregationalists as grandparents of the present movement.

At the time of organization, the new association consisted of seven churches at Caney River, Middle Fork, Liberty, White Oak Creek, Union, Tow River, and New Found.[17] By 1834, they had grown to a total of twelve congregations.[18]

The Free-Will Baptist Association represented a new witness[19] in an area that had not been reached by the movement in the eastern part of the state. It was to be an important addition to the continuing witness of the Free Will Baptists.

THE SHILOH CONFERENCE

The division between East and West was not sufficient to meet the problems that arose during the period of rapid growth. The churches in the eastern part of the state could no longer be serviced by one conference. The minutes for 1830 recorded the division of the Bethel Conference. "On motion, by Elder Heath, the conference agreed that a division be made in the annual conference, on account of convenience."[20] The conference appointed Elder Henry Smith, Jesse Heath, Jesse Alfin, Brinson Hollace, Nathaniel Lockhart, William Latham, and William Isler to draw up the plans for division.[21] The committee decided that the new conference should include all the churches in the far eastern portion of the state. Though the division was to be made on the basis of churches rather than on a designated line, the choice of churches indicated that a fairly definite boundary had been set. The line passed through central Pitt County. All the churches east of that line were to be a part of the new conference. The new group consisted of the churches at: New Bern, Spring Creek, Little Swift Creek, Bay River, Brice's Creek, Goose Creek, and Piney Neck, Craven County; Pungo, Concord, North Creek, and Beaver Dam, Beaufort County; Welch's Creek, Martin County; and Clay Root, Pitt County.[22] The conference voted that ". . . for distinction, the eastern division shall be called the Shiloh Conference. . . ."[23]

Moving West

Until about 1830, most Free Will Baptist activity in North Carolina was limited to the eastern portion of the state. For a number of years only one church was to be found between Greene County in the East and the new Free-Will Baptist Association in the mountains to the West. Frederick Fonville was the only Free Will Baptist minister who was willing to face the task of preaching the gospel beyond the denominational stronghold in the East.

On the surface, it seems simple to suggest that the long history of the church in the eastern counties and the larger population in the area made it both convenient and practical to limit the scope of activity. Why ask preachers to uproot their families and move to the West when the task in their own part of the state was not yet complete?

But the answer is not found so easily. The nature of the people themselves has to be considered. In two letters written during his travels in North Carolina, Elias Hutchins, the representative from New England, gave some idea of the attitudes and openness of the people in different parts of the state. In a letter dated November 25, 1829, he told of a visit into the rural areas of eastern North Carolina.

> The week after Conference, I rode with the above mentioned preachers and eld. Heath, about sixty miles back into the country, where we attended several meetings. On week days we generally met from two to three hundred people, and on the Sabbath nearly one thousand. They generally heard with great attention; many were deeply affected, and some made to rejoice under the Word; some were received as candidates for baptism, and others will probably submit to that ordinance soon.[24]

Hutchins went on to say that on the following two nights he had set aside time to rest, but as the day ended, the house of his host began to fill with people, and it became necessary for him to preach again. In fact, he was to get very little rest during his visit to North Carolina.

About six months later, in June 1830, Hutchins began a trip westward that took him past the home of Elder Frederick Fonville in Orange County. At this late date, this church at Strong Creek was the most westward church in the state for the denomination. Here, Hutchins found an entirely different attitude. Though he was welcomed by Fonville himself as a brother in the ministry, he quick-ly recognized that the people in the area were not nearly so excited about his coming. "It is a dull time with professors in this place; iniquity is abounding, and the love of too many has already waxed cold. Yet, I trust, that there are some who mourn over the desolations in Zion, and are yet praying for her prosperity."[25]

It probably should be noted that Hutchins' evaluation of the people in the western regions was based on their lifestyles rather than on their attendance at his services. The thing that seems to have impressed him most about the eastern part of the state was that many of the people were turning away from worldly amusements. At any rate, whether the difficulty lay in neglect of worship or in lack of godly living, the Free Will Baptists and their message of salvation were not nearly so well-accepted in the middle and western parts of the state as they had been along the seaboard.

In spite of the lack of excitement in the area, Fonville and his small congregation had estab-lished a foothold, and by 1833 churches had been added at Salem in Duplin County by Elder Lewis Hartsfield and in Samson County by Elder McNab. Of course, it should be remembered that a new Free Will Baptist association had emerged out of the United Baptists in the mountain areas of the state. But they had come from another denomination and could not be considered a part of the mis-sion activity of the Free Will Baptists in the East.

At last, the Free Will Baptists of North Carolina were moving westward, and the movement was showing new signs of growth.

The Acceptance of the New Name

The new identity had demanded a new name. The old faces were gone, the new leaders had taken their places of responsibility, the organizational machinery had acquired a new maturity, and the *Confession of Faith* had been updated to meet the needs of a nineteenth century denomination. The organization, the revised *Confession*, the *Code of Discipline*, and the leaders belonged to a new movement. There was a keen awareness of the new identity.

THE FIRST USE OF THE NEW NAME

Two sources indicate that the General Baptists yielded to the new name before the end of the eighteenth century, but only one attempted to explain why they came to be called Free Will Baptists. Both sources contained contemporary information and were vitally important in the study of the new name. Lemuel Burkitt and Jesse Read, historians of the opposing Regular Baptists, made it clear that the name was in common use before the end of the century and that the name was used to identify the congregations established during the General Baptist period. Because they were concerned with their own denomination, they did not attempt to trace the source of the name. That task was left to the Free Will Baptist historians.

The Source of the Name—R. K. Hearn, the Free Will Baptist historian, contended that the new name was given to the General Baptists by their enemies and it was intended to be a title of scorn and ridicule—a constant reminder that the General Baptists were considered unorthodox and unregenerate.[26]

The name was applied first to the General Baptists in the Conetoe settlements of Pitt County. Burkitt and Read, in their study of the Flat Swamp church in Pitt County, noted that the church had begun to have difficulty and the resulting decline allowed the Arminian Baptists to gain new ground. The problems of the Regular Baptist church encouraged the ". . . Arminians and Universalians to look out of their dens, where they had been driven by the refulgent beams of gospel truths. . . ."[27] Hearn then argued:

> From this statement it is manifest that there was a people in this section that gave them considerable trouble, who according to the figurative language of their enemies, were driven into seclusion by the glorious light of Calvinistic decrees, election, reprobation, etc., and owing to the trouble this people gave them, they called them, by way of reproach, 'Free-willers.'[28]

Hearn continued to argue that the people that caused such trouble for the Flat Swamp church were the members of the Parker church at Gum Swamp. The two churches were fifteen miles apart, and the Flat Swamp church was located on the road William Parker would have traveled on his return trip to Meherrin. Hearn contended that members of Parker's church met him at Flat Swamp and that he preached in the shadow of the Regular Baptist church. In scorn, the Regulars called the General Baptists "Free-willers" because they preached the "heresy" that Christ had died for all men.[29]

The Official Adoption of the New Name—As early as 1803, Burkitt and Read ignored the old name, indicating that the new name already had become more popular. However, it would seem that the name had some difficulty in gaining formal or official acceptance. Possibly the conference hesitated because the people remembered the scorn and ridicule that first had accompanied the new name, but probably, the name had become so widely used that official adoption seemed unnecessary.

Elias Hutchins, the historian of the New England Freewill Baptists, has indicated that the name was adopted officially by the North Carolina Annual Conference in 1828.[30] Conference minutes for that year are not available, but the first published minutes of the denomination clearly indicated that the new name was the official title for the new identity.

The Evolution of the New Name—In a relatively short period of time, the new name passed through three phases of change. Burkitt and Read, writing in 1803, combined the first two words, calling the Arminians "Free-will Baptists."[31] When the group published its first minutes in 1829, the hyphen was retained, but the first letter of the second word was capitalized.[32] For a short period of time, they were to be called "Free-Will Baptists." Finally, the hyphen was dropped altogether. When the first history of the denomination was compiled by R. K. Hearn, he called his people "Free Will Baptists."[33] The final spelling has been used since that time.

The Attitude Toward Identity

The Free Will Baptists were proud of their heritage and of the new identity. They carefully guarded the doctrines and disciplines they felt made them unique. The best example of their fierce protection of their identity was found in a letter to *The Morning Star* from Thomas Latham of Pantego, North Carolina. Latham, in a long letter, responded to an article that evidently questioned the nature of the practice of washing the saints' feet. He admitted that the practice should be discarded if it fell short of the Scriptural requirements of an ordinance, but he made it clear he had not entertained such doubts about this particular practice of his denomination. The *Free Will Baptist Confession of Faith* included the practice as an ordinance,[34] and Latham felt himself compelled to defend the position. He argued that the ordinance had been commanded by Christ in the thirteenth chapter of John's Gospel and that the practice was accepted as an ordinance by the early church.[35]

Latham agreed to further discussion in an attitude of love, but the letter indicated that, in his own heart, the matter was closed.

Many elements of the established identity set the Free Will Baptists apart. The new name itself indicated their difference from other Baptists. The identity made them a special people. It deserved their loyalty and their determined defense.

The New Leaders and Their Contributions

By 1829, there were thirty-three Free Will Baptist ministers in the Bethel Conference. All of them were important because they were involved in the revival and phenomenal growth that occurred after 1825. However, even a brief look at all of them would be impractical. Three of the leaders were chosen as representatives of the early movement as it continued under the new identity.

The Contributions of Jesse Heath

Jesse Heath had served as a bridge between the old General Baptist movement in North Carolina and the Free Will Baptist denomination. Though he was tied to the old movement through his work with James Roach, he was to be the first minister to represent fully the new identity. Jesse Heath was a Free Will Baptist.

Though his first contribution might have been the most important, it was not to end his usefulness to the denomination. His ministry and influence extended into the third decade of the nineteenth century. The records revealed that his advice was sought after and respected. He led in both the theological and the organizational development of the new identity. Along with James Roach, Heath gave the denomination its first organized code of discipline and a revised program of doctrine that was to serve the new movement for decades. It was at his suggestion that the Bethel Conference divided in order to meet the needs of the growing movement.[36] His touch was evident throughout the period of development for the new identity.

Finally, Jesse Heath preserved much of the history of the denomination that occurred before official records were kept. Though he did not attempt a formal history, his correspondence with the

Freewill Baptists in New England provided the only statistics for the denomination between 1807 and 1825.

Without question, Heath was the foremost leader of the early Free Will Baptist denomination. His contributions as preacher, administrator, historian, and theologian were vital to the success and prosperity of the new movement. No other early leader was to contribute so much or to gain such a degree of respect.

However, there were other leaders that made unique contributions—contributions that gave the movement a new outreach and a recorded history of their progress.

The Contributions of Frederick Fonville

Frederick Fonville was listed as a Free Will Baptist minister as early as 1825. Though it is impossible to determine how long he served before that year, it has been established that he was one of the earliest Free Will Baptists preachers in the state. His name appeared on an old page of minutes that came into the possession of historian, R. K. Hearn. Hearn found the single sheet of minutes attached to the back page of an old hymnbook. The book was yellowed with age and printed in a style no longer used in Hearn's day. The Conference attendance at that time did not compare with the large numbers of people that attended during Hearn's ministry. The entire offering for the day was $14.25, and only 200 copies of the minutes were ordered to be printed.[37] Only four ministers were listed, but these fell at the bottom of the page and could have been part of a longer list. Hearn was convinced that the minutes were old and revealed the names of the earliest Free Will Baptist preachers after the death of James Roach. Hearn knew two of the ministers personally. Levi Braxton had served at Gum Swamp since the death of Roach and for as long as Hearn could remember.[38] The other minister, Jesse Heath, had been with the movement since 1807. Hearn only knew the other two men, Frederick Fonville and Isaac Pipkin, as old ministers of the faith.

Fonville added one other contribution to the early ministry and guidance of his denomination. He chose to serve in Orange County, an area to the west that had not been touched by the Free Will Baptists. Yielding to his pioneer spirit, he began the move West, finally spreading the Free Will Baptist witness from one end of the state to the other.

Fonville's ministry was a difficult one. In his early years, he attended conferences and enjoyed the fellowship of his people, but the distance and his age soon limited his experience with other Free Will Baptists. At times, the minutes of the conferences were mailed to Orange County to keep him in touch.[39] For a large part of his ministry, the difficulty was magnified because his wife could not help him or give him the encouragement he desperately needed. She did not become a Christian until 1830.[40]

Frederick Fonville overcame his difficulties and established a successful ministry in Orange County. His perseverance finally paid dividends as other Free Will Baptists began to follow his example and move West. By 1829, a conference was established in the far western regions of the state, and by 1833, the central section began to feel the impact of the Free Will Baptist witness. By the latter year, three churches were established as far west as Sampson County.[41]

The Contributions of Rufus K. Hearn

Though the Annual Conference authorized the writing of a denominational history in 1833, the work was not completed until many years later. Rufus K. Hearn finally was chosen to develop an accurate study of the movement's heritage and progress.

The historian was selected carefully. Born in 1819 into a Free Will Baptist family, he grew up a few miles from the Gum Swamp Free Will Baptist Church and was familiar with eyewitnesses to the events that had taken place when the movement first was called by the new name.[42] His own father, living in the area since 1784, had been a Free Will Baptist preacher for many years.[43]

The younger Hearn joined the church at Gum Swamp and was ordained as a Free Will Baptist minister August 1, 1853.[44] He continued to serve the denomination until his death.

Hearn became a powerful preacher, noted for his able defense of the doctrines of the movement, but his greatest contribution was his history of the denomination. It was brief and often poorly documented, but it was the first serious attempt to write a denominational history.

Expansion in New England
The Changing of the Guard

THE DEATH OF BENJAMIN RANDALL

The founder of the New England segment of the denomination served 31 years and seven months before his death on October 22, 1808. He was 59 years old at the time of his death and had been confined at home for some nine months with consumption.

If Randall was not satisfied with the progress of the denomination, he surely had no regrets about his own life and ministry or about the quality of the denominational leaders that had grown up under his direction.

John Buzzell, one of those new leaders and a personal friend of Randall, spoke of the founder's death and the loss the denomination was experiencing.

> His wife lost a kind and benevolent husband—his children an affectionate parent—the church a faithful servant and minister of the gospel—the town an amiable member of society—the state of New Hampshire one of its most useful and respected citizens; and this poor benighted world, a burning and shining light.[45]

Randall left detailed plans for his burial, and his requests were carried out to the letter. John Buzzell preached the funeral message from 2 Timothy 4:7 and 8, "I have fought a good fight, I have finished my course, I have kept the faith: Henceforth there is laid up for me a crown of righteousness, which the Lord, the righteous judge, shall give me at that day: and not to me only, but unto all them also that love his appearing."

THE NEW LEADERS

One accurate measure of the growth of a new denomination is found in the number of leaders and ministers that grow out of the ministry of the new movement. Seventeen ordained ministers attended the funeral of Benjamin Randall, representing just a small part of the growing fellowship of ministers now involved in the Freewill Baptist work. By 1800, the denomination boasted thirty-one ordained ministers. Though three or four of that number never officially joined the denomination, they were a vital part of the fellowship early in its history.[46] By the time of Randall's death in 1808, a number of capable leaders were ready to carry on the work he had started.

Any number of men—David Knowlton, Winthrop Young, Joseph Quimby, Joseph Boody, Joseph Boody, Jr., David Knowlton, Jr.—could have taken over the reigns of leadership from Randall, but that task was to be left to John Buzzell, Randall's close friend and long time colleague. Buzzell had been ordained on October 25, 1792, and quickly assumed a position of importance in the rising denomination. He served as a traveling preacher until 1798 when he became pastor of the church at Parsonsfield, Maine.

> If Randall had a successor, it was John Buzzell. During the testing and sifting time that followed the death of Randall, he stood like a rock for the old landmarks, and more than any other one prevented our denomination from drifting away from foundational principles.

> Buzzell compiled and published our first hymn book, was the editor of our first periodical literature and was the prime mover, if not the founder, of our first denominational school, Parsonsfield Seminary. He helped establish *The Morning Star* and was for a while its editor. He helped organize the Foreign Mission Society and was its first president, serving 14 years. During his ministerial life the denomination which he helped to establish grew from 20 churches to more than 1200; from 8 or 10 ministers to over 1200, and from a membership of about 400 to more than 60,000. His Parsonsfield pastorate, which was severed by death, was of 65 years duration. . . .[47]

As mentioned in this early testimonial, Buzzell was a part of the denomination from its earliest years until late in the nineteenth century. He lived to be 96 years of age and was involved in ministry with the Freewill Baptists most of those years.

Had Benjamin Randall lived just a few more years, he would have had the privilege of seeing most of his dreams for the denomination realized. Under the leadership of Buzzell and a number of new converts, including John Colby and David Marks, the denomination was to begin a period of phenomenal growth.

The Years of Expansion

In 1808, at the time of Randall's death, the denomination reported four Yearly Meetings and eight Quarterly Meetings with none further west than Vermont. In fact, up until that time, all Freewill Baptist activity was located in Maine and New Hampshire. But growth for the denomination was just around the corner. In 1830, at the time of the denomination's fiftieth anniversary, seven Yearly Meetings reported to the General Conference and during the next 50 years, 36 other Yearly Meetings would be added as the Freewill Baptists extended their ministry as far west as Nebraska and as far south as Texas on the southern Gulf.[48] Few of the northern states were left without a Freewill Baptist witness after 1850.

By 1888, the New England group recorded 148,082 members. It should be noted, however, that they included a number of associations and yearly meetings that were only loosely related to the General Conference, if at all. Of these, Nebraska, West Virginia, and Tow River Association in Tennessee had the closest ties to the work in New England. Others, like the Original Free Will Baptists in North and South Carolina, the Cape Fear Association in North Carolina, Chattahoochee Association in Georgia, Mount Moriah Association in Alabama, Cumberland Association in Tennessee, and the General and Separate Baptists had little or no organizational relationship. For some of the associations mentioned, relationship was limited to correspondence and possibly the adoption of the *New England Treatise of Faith*. A more accurate measure of denominational growth is seen in the following chart. These statistics are limited to growth within the movement itself.

DENOMINATIONAL GROWTH[49]

Date	Y M's.	Q M's.	Churches	Ministers	Members	Increase
1780			1	1	7	
'83		1	13	4	280*	273*
'90		1	18	8	400*	120*
1800	4	6	51	28	2,000*	1,600*
'10	4	8	130	110*	5,000*	3,000*
'20	4	15	220	175*	9,000*	4,000*
'25	6	23	273	190	16,000*	6,000*
'30	7	30	434	375	21,499	5,499*
'35	10	55	753	459	33,876	12,377
'40	13	74	857	720	41,797	7,921
'45	24	107	1,193	801	58,174	16,377
'50	26	120	1,126	867	50,223	Decrease
'55	27	128	1,150	913	50,457	234
'60	31	145	1,286	1,022	58,441	7,984
'65	31	147	1,252	1,076	54,076	Decrease
'70	34	155	1,386	1,145	66,909	12,833
'75	38	164	1,399	1,185	72,128	5,219
'80	41	166	1,432	1,213	78,012	5,884
'85	46	186	1,490	1,262	77,827	Decrease
'88	57	204	1,619	1,414	86,201	8,374

*Estimated

Even though the chart indicated that growth leveled off after 1850, it must be recognized that early growth was astounding. It also should be noted that growth had to be measured in the influence expressed in geographical expansion as well as in numbers.

Notes for Chapter 7

[1]Benedict, *General History*, II, 24.

[2]Ibid., II, 98.

[3]Saunders, *Colonial Records*, V, 1180. S. J. Wheeler had access to the records of the Pasquotank church that went back as far as 1758. His account of the Court of Union was published in the Colonial Records.

[4]Ibid.

[5]Ibid.

[6]Hearn, *Origin*, 158.

[7]*Abstract*, 3.

[8]Ibid., 10-19.

[9]Huggins, *History*, 46.

[10]Hearn, *Origin*, 170, 171.

[11]Heath, Letter, May 29, 1827.

[12]Ibid.

[13]The ministers in 1829 were Frederick Fonville, Isaac Pipkin, Levi Braxton, Reading Moore, Jesse Hawarin, James Moore, Jesse Heath, Jeremiah Heath, Jesse Braxton, James Price, Caleb Spivy, John Creekman, Briant C. Wood, Richard Witherington, Brinson Hollace, Mark Andrews, Jeremiah Rowe, Henry Smith, Jesse Alfin, Nathaniel Lockhart, Robert Bond, Everet David, John Gurganous, William Latham, Howel Hern, Samuel Modlen, Roderick Powel, Jacob Utley, Enoch Cobb, Jebediah Dixon, Thomas Reaves, Daniel Daughety, Wilson Daniels (*Minutes of the Free Will Baptist Annual Conference of North Carolina, 1829*). The churches included North East, Duplin County; Beaver Creek, Jones County; Louson Swamp, Wheat Swamp, and Bethel, Lenoir County; Stony Creek, Orange County; Clay Root, Gum Swamp, and Tar River, Pitt County; Little Creek and Grimsley, Greene County; Stony Branch, Bachelor's Creek, Spring Creek, Little Swift Creek, Bay River, Brice's Creek, Beard's Creek, Newbern, and Piney Neck, Craven County; Pungo, Beaver Dam, and North Creek, Beaufort County; Long Ridge, Washington County; Indian Springs, Wayne County; and Sumpter District, South Carolina (Harrison and Barfield, *History*, I, 157, 158).

[14]Jesse Heath, Letter to Elder John Buzzell, November 18, 1830, quoted in *The Morning Star*, December 22, 1830.

[15]*Minutes of the Free-Will Baptist Association, 1830* (Salisbury, N.C.: Printed by Philo White, 1830), 3.

[16]Ibid.

[17]Ibid., 4.

[18]*Minutes of the Free-Will Baptist Association, 1834* (Rutherfordton, N.C.: Roswell Elmer, Printer, 1834), Table on "State of the Churches."

[19]There is a good possibility that this phase of the continuing Free Will Baptist witness was a new discovery. The Free Will Baptist Association in the mountains was not mentioned by the earlier historians of the Baptists in the state. The minutes for the association were discovered by the writer in the middle of a collection of Southern Baptist papers that had been microfilmed as a part of the Mercantile Collection which was housed in a library in St. Louis.

[20]*Minutes of the Free Will Baptist Annual Conference of North Carolina, 1830*.

[21]Ibid.

[22]Ibid.

[23]Ibid.

[24]Letter from Elias Hutchins to *The Morning Star* dated November 25, 1829. *The Morning Star*, Vol. 4 (1830), 134.

[25]Letter from Elias Hutchins to Elder John Buzell dated June 20,1830. *The Morning Star*, Vol. 5 (1831), 50.

[26]Hearn, *Origin*, 167.

[27]Burkitt and Read, *Concise History*, 213.

[28]Hearn, *Origin*, 167.

[29]Ibid., 167, 168.

[30]Ibid., 169.

[31]Burkitt and Read, *Concise History*, 43.

[32]*Minutes of the Free-Will Baptist Annual Conference of North Carolina, 1829.*

[33]Hearn, *Origin*, 148.

[34]*Abstract*, 9.

[35]Thomas J. Latham, Letter to *The Morning Star*, December 23, 1830. *The Morning Star*, January 19, 1831, 151.

[36]*Minutes of the Free Will Baptist Annual Conference of North Carolina, 1830.*

[37]Hearn, *Origin*, 171. As early as 1830, 1,000 copies of the minutes were printed for distribution.

[38]Hearn was born in 1819 and lived in the immediate area of Braxton's ministry.

[39]*Minutes of the Free Will Baptist Annual Conference of North Carolina, 1829.*

[40]Hutchins, *Letter*, June 20, 1830.

[41]Hutchins, *Letter*, January 22, 1833.

[42]Hearn, *Origin*, 170, 171.

[43]Page from the Hearn Family Bible.

[44]Harrison and Barfield, *History*, II, 354.

[45]Buzzell, *Life of Elder Benjamin Randall*, 298.

[46]Burgess and Ward, *Cyclopaedia*, 208.

[47]*Centennial Souvenir of the New Hampshire Yearly Meeting of Free Baptists*, 1792-1892 (Laconia, N.H.: Published by the Board of Directors, 1892), 43, 44.

[48]Burgess and Ward, *Cyclopaedia*, 211.

[49]Ibid., 212.

8

The Local Church in the Nineteenth Century

A history of this type tends to develop into a catalog of facts, dates, and statistics that become somewhat sterile and difficult to read. Since the denomination has never had a history that told the story completely, the facts and figures are indeed important and must be included. Such a history would not be complete, however, without some look at the people themselves. This chapter will attempt to describe the local church and its people in the nineteenth century.

In 1827, Jesse Heath attempted to describe the Free Will Baptists of North Carolina for the benefit of their sister denomination in New England. Recognizing the spiritual kinship that existed between the two groups, he explained:

> . . . As to principle, there is not the least difference, and I hope there will be none in practice. We baptise none but such as confess their sins, believe in Jesus, and consider baptism by immersion as the duty deeply impressed. We think that no person can feel baptism deeply impressed on their minds as a duty, and still be in an unprepared state to comply with it. We have not been in the habit of practicing Open Communion because, no application has been made for liberty to eat and drink with us; but if any in good standing were to ask that liberty, they would not be denied. At our meetings we often invite others to the stage, and when invited labor amongst them—We practice the imposition of hands on all newly baptized members, according to the example of St. Peter, John, and Paul. We also practice washing of feet, believing it to be a gospel ordinance, but there is no compulsion if any are not disposed to wash with us, we do not compel them. We sometimes commune and wash feet in the day and sometimes at night. We have a book of discipline which contains a few articles of faith and rules of discipline—the constitution of our annual conference—the ordination of a minister—and the form of matrimony. The principle use that we make of this book, is in the government of our annual conference—the ordination of our ministers—the constitution of our churches, and in the solemnization of matrimony. Our annual conference is composed of two delegates from every church and all the preachers both ordained and licensed, and the general treasurer. The conference meets annually, and returns are made from all the churches so that once a year we know the state of the

whole connexion. Our minutes are taken and printed and distributed among our members. . . .[1]

Heath's description painted a fairly complete picture of the denomination touching on theology, polity, and practice. His outline plus a few additional areas of interest set the direction for this part of the study.

A Glance at the Nineteenth Century
Free Will Baptist Church Member

Except for New England where many of the churches were founded in established communities, the typical Free Will Baptist of the nineteenth century—and, indeed, far into the twentieth century—would be of rural background. For the most part, he would be less than well educated and would own little property.

Because the movement grew more rapidly in New England, it would seem that patterns for the future would be established there. But on the contrary, it was the farmer of the South and the frontiersman of the Near West that would establish the direction of the denomination for the next 100 years. Though most of the Free Will Baptists in the Far West were directly related to New England historically, the individual church member was much more akin to his denominational brothers in the South. When the New England movement merged with the Regular Baptists in 1911, most of the remnant—those that remained Free Will Baptists—were located in the West from Ohio to Nebraska and, except for theology, had little in common with those who were involved in the merger.

From the very beginning, the Free Will Baptists of New England drew from the more wealthy elements of society and most often their churches were to be found within the city limits of the hill towns in northern New Hampshire and southern Maine. The town inventory for New Durham, New Hampshire, in 1784, contained the names of nine men who were original signers of Randall's *New Durham Church Covenant*. Stephen Marini, in an analysis of the statistics included in the inventory, determined that these men were leading citizens of the community both in responsibility and in wealth. This is shown in the following table:

	Oxen	Cows	Horses	Tillage	Mowing	Pasture	Wild[2]
Free Will Baptists	2	1.67	2.75	1.22	4.6	1.88	90.3
New Durham Per Capita	1.15	1.57	1.33	1.1	3.15	2.25	83.35

Some of New Durham's wealthier citizens were members of Randall's congregation—Shadrack Allard, Ebenizer Bickford, Colonel Thomas Tash, and Joseph Boody. All four men served as selectmen for the township and Tash was elected as State Representative in 1778. Boody's home was one of the largest in New Durham and served as a meeting house for Randall's religious services. It was here on June 30, 1780, that Randall organized the first Free Will Baptist church in New England. "In a hill town like New Durham, early settlers like Tash, Bickford, Allard, and Boody constituted the social and economic infra-structure. Through their carefully calibrated evangelism, Benjamin Randel and other Freewill itinerants were able to attract such leaders as well as average subsistence farmers, creating a sectarian community of respectable rural citizens."[3]

It must be understood that "rural" in this context is used differently than would be true in the South. These men were farmers but owned large amounts of property and wielded significant influence in the communities in which they resided.

In sharp contrast is the testimony of Jesse Heath found in a letter written to the editor of *The Morning Star* in 1827, where he confessed, ". . . I must tell you something of our situation in the ministry; we are all men of families, of little property and not a single scholar amongst us, so that the work is of God and not of us."[4] It is interesting to note that the editor felt compelled to attach an editorial note to Heath's letter when it was published on June 28, 1827, "We presume that their privileges to obtain a common school education have not been so great in that country, as ours have been in this."[5]

Unlike the experience in New England, few if any of the churches in the South bore the names of the towns near which they were situated. Those church buildings that still remain remind us that most of the churches were located in rural settings, in small communities, or at a crossroads that afforded easy access. The individual church member here would be far different from his counterpart in the North. He would have enjoyed few of the privileges of education and wealth that were available in New England.

Ransom Dunn, a New Englander, visited the Free Will Baptists in Georgia and Alabama in the latter part of the nineteenth century and found that the churches had not changed a great deal.

> Their churches are still scattered and weak, and located away from large towns and railroads. Their ministers, without classical education, support themselves largely or entirely by secular employment, and in spite of poor s_____, small profits, and low wages, by faith, zeal, and sacrifice, are marvelously successful. And this too without schools, periodicals, or denominational prestige. Their churches and associations are independent, with only a limited correspondence even among themselves, and yet their doctrinal ecclesiastical uniformity and denominational identity are very satisfactory.[6]

But if the typical Free Will Baptist in the southeastern seaboard states lived somewhat below the level of his brothers in New England, he still fared far better than many of the frontiersmen of western North Carolina, Tennessee, and Kentucky. The frontier created a new breed of American. The struggle for survival against both the wilderness and the Indian nations developed a hardened, rough, totally self-dependent individual. In an attempt to help us understand the atmosphere of the frontier revivals of the early eighteenth century, Sydney Ahlstrom described the frontiersmen as hardened frontier farmers, tobacco chewing, tough spoken, notoriously profane, famous for their alcoholic thirst, and always surrounded by their large broods of children. He further suggests that the immense loneliness of the frontier farmer's life and the opportunity of participation in a large social occasion like the early nineteenth century camp meetings explained both the popularity and the spirit of response that swept across these frontier areas from 1800 to 1805.[7]

To suggest that all Free Will Baptists of the nineteenth century were alike would be more than naive. Preaching style, message, and educational requirements for the ministry were shaped as much by the social, cultural, and geographical factors as by the religious.

More will be said of this in a later chapter especially as it relates to the development of that group of Free Will Baptists that makes up the present-day denomination.

Attitude Toward Worship

Elias Hutchins, a Free Will Baptist from New England, often paused during his North Carolina travels to write to his own wing of the denomination in the North. His letters preserved much of the history of the early movement in the South and gave a number of vivid pictures of its character. Hutchins especially was impressed with the reverence evident in the worship service of the Free Will Baptists. He spoke often of the well-behaved, solemn, and attentive audiences. In one of his letters, he described a baptism service held at the Pungo Free Will Baptist Church in May 1830, in which 20 persons were baptized. "The scene was solemn and impressive, well calculated to animate the Christian, and fill the minds of sinners with sensations of a favorable character; and the large congregation that witnessed the performance by a commendable decorum evinced great respect for the ordinance. . . ."[8]

Lifestyle

In lifestyle, the Free Will Baptists of the eighteenth century were not far removed from America's Puritan heritage of the sixteenth and seventeenth centuries. True to their evangelical background, they lived by rigid standards of conduct that became almost as important as salvation itself. While the rules of conduct were not equated with the salvation experience, obedience to the rules determined the degree of commitment of the individual Christian.

Since theological difficulties did not constitute a major problem, much attention could be given to this secondary concern. Most nineteenth century associations and conferences developed a program of standards designed to guide the daily lives of their members. The earliest *Discipline* published in North Carolina set the stage for other Free Will Baptists in this important area.

> If any member shall be found frequenting the race grounds, the ballroom, the card table, shooting matches, or any other place of disorder, without lawful business, they by the Church may be considered and in that case they shall make the Church satisfaction, or be dealt with as the Church may think proper.[9]

By the middle of the century, dramatic plays became not only popular but accessible to most everyone. After dealing with a number of disciplinary problems in the church that included dancing and drunkenness, Mt. Moriah Church, in Alabama, determined that local plays were at least one source of the difficulties they were facing.

> Resolved that we the members of the Mt. Moriah Free Will Baptist Church, believe that the common fashionable party playes of our day is morally wrong and Resolved fur-

ther that we concider (sic) it a breach of order for any member of our church to participate in the playes and that in doing so they subject themselves to the discipline of
the church and shall be excluded for such violations unless they give marks of
Repentance and reformation. Dancing can by no means be tolerated.[10]

The last statement is clear evidence that the church saw evil influences in the theater that went
far beyond the play itself.

The question of lifestyle was not addressed as often or as candidly in the North as it was in the
South and West, but there is ample evidence that New England Free Will Baptists were just as concerned with lifestyle as their brothers in other parts of the country. Benjamin Randall himself was a
strict model of the lifestyle expected in Free Will Baptist churches. Our glimpse of Randall in an earlier chapter revealed that he was careful to avoid the very appearance of evil. Not only did he refuse
to attend public places of amusement, he also made sure that his horse was not tied at the store or
tavern any longer than necessary so people did not think him to be an idler. The store served not
only as a source for supplying daily needs, but often was the gathering place for the men of the village and allowed opportunity for gossip, drinking, and the planning of mischief.

Elias Hutchins, another New England preacher, traveled often in North and South Carolina and
quite often spoke of the ungodliness among the people in the two states. One of his greatest concerns was the attitude of the people toward the Sabbath, and he could not hide his excitement as he
saw changes being made. "And the Sabbath, formerly a day of revelry, drinking, gambling, fighting,
horse racing, &c. is now religiously observed; and the salutary influence of the religion of Jesus is
too obvious to be denied by its most inveterate enemies."[11] Though his testimony was limited to one
small community, it was the beginning of a series of revivals in the area. Other communities would
begin to enjoy the same type of reformation.

The patterns of lifestyle established in the nineteenth century continued to have impact on the
denomination throughout that era and up to the present time. The denominational message continues to include a strict and conservative lifestyle that touches every phase of the Christian experience—dress, amusements, and language.

The Ministry

ITINERANCY

From the very beginning, itinerancy characterized the ministry in New England as Randall and
his closest associates traveled constantly to the increasing number of growing churches and quarterly meetings in the area. Randall was convinced that this type of ministry was necessary if unity was
to be achieved among the churches in the fledgling denomination. It was not unusual for Randall
himself to be away for weeks at a time. His biography mentioned that on one occasion he was away
for 57 days, had traveled about 500 miles, and had attended 61 meetings.[12]

Actually, the preachers were not the only ones who traveled from church to church. As mentioned earlier, most of the initial congregations were considered branches of the mother church in
New Durham, though each had its own monthly meeting. The individual congregations were expected to attend monthly meetings at local churches other than their own, so travel was very much a part

of the Christian experience for the Freewill Baptists in New England. Though this would change after the beginning of the nineteenth century, Randall continued to travel from church to church and from quarterly meeting to quarterly meeting for most of his ministry.

In the South, itinerancy was to take a different tact. For the most part, settled pastors served individual churches, but itinerants were elected to meet the needs of failing churches or to preach in areas where churches had not been established. In 1866, the General Conference in North Carolina appointed elders R. K. Hearn and Joseph Sauls as itinerants for the year. They were instructed to raise support for their ministry through periodic preaching, on invitation of the settled pastor, in the stronger churches.[13]

In less than twenty years, the financial base for itinerant ministry had changed, but the basic character of the work remained the same. By this time, the "evangelists" were allowed $1.50 a day while actually engaged in evangelistic work. They were required to keep a careful account of all money received by them from the churches in which they preached as well as expenses from their own pocket when they were not met by donations. The records at least infer that any money above the allotted amount for them was expected to be placed in the Conference treasury.[14]

The itinerants evidently took their jobs seriously. In 1890, W. H. Slaughter, the appointed evangelist, reported he had been away from home 152 days and had organized one church. His report included that he was unable to serve for 30 days because of bad weather. He had received $51.82 from the churches during the year, and the Conference voted to add $103.72 to that amount, a tidy stipend for the South at this time in the nineteenth century.[15]

In the final analysis, itinerancy was important both in the North and the South, but it was to serve as a foundational characteristic for the former and as a secondary concern for the latter.

INSTRUCTIONS FOR YOUNG PREACHERS

In the early years, extemporaneous preaching was the order of the day in both the North and the South, but by 1834 the pattern had begun to change in New England. In a series of articles begun in *The Morning Star* in that year, the paper's editor attempted to prepare young denominational preachers for a life time of ministry. The young men were encouraged to attain a higher degree of preparation. "After all, the burden of ministry soon would fall on their shoulders and was it not therefore desirable that they should be prepared to fill their places in the best possible manner?"[16] After further encouragement to consider home mission work in the West (Ohio) or mission work overseas, the editor listed a number of instructions that would ensure success and God's pleasure.

1. Consider the desk (pulpit) sacred. (This instruction included a warning against humor in the pulpit or speaking out against other denominations.)
2. Avoid any preaching by note.
3. Your text should be meditative and well understood.
4. Accustom yourself to frequency of writing.
5. Let your preaching be simple, grave, warm.
6. Be punctual.
7. Give your whole time to the ministry.

8. Have little to do with worldly goods.

9. Avoid engaging in political affairs.

10. Do all to the glory of God.[17]

The change in preaching method should be noted. Though the preachers still were to preach without notes, they were to be well prepared when they entered the pulpit. Instruction three recognized the importance of advanced study and preparation. In the newspaper article, instruction eight suggests that interest in material goods should be replaced by reading and study of doctrine. The ministry, at least in the North, was growing up.

The exhortation to "give your whole time to the ministry" infers a full-time ministry. If so, the local church seemed intent on making sure the preacher obeyed instruction eight and did not give too much attention to worldly goods.

In New England, the denomination attempted to increase support for the ministry through literature. In a pamphlet entitled, "Sustaining the Christian Ministry," the writer used Galatians 6:6, 1 Corinthians 1:21, and 2 Corinthians 4:7 to establish the responsibility of the minister in proclaiming the gospel. He then continues to argue that ". . . in this great and difficult work, His (the pastor's) time and talent are to be employed. To know and clearly comprehend God's word, to successfully explain it to the darkened minds of sinful men, and defend its doctrine before intelligent and hardened skeptics, demands much time for careful and critical study of the Bible."[18]

It is evident the article was concerned with a "full-time" ministry. The writer recognized the minister must have time to go from house to house to bear the burdens of others and to spend time in prayer and study. He suggested that even the unsaved have a responsibility to support the ministry because it would be by that preaching that they receive the opportunity to accept Christ as Savior. Since God called the minister to a full-time ministry and since it was impossible for him to meet God's requirement and still sustain his family, support was the responsibility of his people. "Once more, private Christians should sustain Christian ministers in their labors because God requires it of them. It is as much their duty as it is the minister's duty to preach."[19]

It soon became evident, however, that literature was not enough. Support for the ministry continued to be a major problem. In the middle of the century, the editor of *The Free-Will Baptist Quarterly* decried the fact that Free Will Baptist preachers were paid far less than those in other denominations. He listed the average salary as $200 a year and then suggested that the estimate might be somewhat high. "Now, while this is so, in other denominations, which we acknowledge evangelical, and invite to our communion table, are given double this sum and are not able to supply vacancies at that, can we expect with us a sufficiency of well-qualified pastors, such as the present time the cause of God demands?"[20] The solutions suggested were quite interesting: (1) The people were to be instructed, (2) churches were to rent pews or tax pew owners in order to support the ministry, and (3) the denomination was to establish a Free Will Baptist Building Society with a large capital so that congregations would not have to use local monies for church buildings. This would allow the church to pay the pastor an adequate salary.

But, if support for the ministry was a problem in the North, it was magnified in the South. Here, the individual church members themselves struggled for daily existence, and it simply was not possible to supply the needs of a full-time pastor. The $200 salary in New England seemed a fortune to pastors in the South. In 1853, the Pantego-Concord Church in North Carolina raised the pastor's salary from $10 to $25 per year.

Even after the coming of better times and after the denomination began to minister to different classes of people, the old pattern of limited support continued to be a problem. The established pattern was hard to break. It would be late in the twentieth century before the denomination again became concerned about the financial needs of the local pastor.

Education

By the middle of the nineteenth century, the New England segment of the denomination had established a number of schools and encouraged their young preachers to attend them. In the South, however, it was a number of years before an educated ministry was attained. Here again, economic and cultural factors postponed a concern for education for the ministry. It was not until the early part of the twentieth century that the group in the South would begin to push in the direction of education for all ministerial candidates. In North Carolina, in 1913, the education committee for the Central Conference of Free Will Baptists recommended that ". . . every man called to the ministry be required to take the advantage of literary education as far as opportunity permits."[21] This was at least a step in the right direction. However, even those who were able to attain some level of literary training had few opportunities to go on to theological training in preparation for ministry.

The Message

A later section of this chapter will deal thoroughly with Free Will Baptist theology of the nineteenth century, but this section on the ministry would be less than complete without some word about the message the denomination sought to proclaim.

From the beginning, Benjamin Randall's message included three major ingredients—free will (his concern for the universal call of the gospel), entire sanctification, and the millennial expectation of the second coming of Christ. For most twentieth century Free Will Baptists, the first and the last of these key ingredients would be not only expected but required, but Randall's interest in Christian perfection would be totally alien and unacceptable.

In order to understand his concern for either the millennial kingdom or perfection, one must have some knowledge of the religious milieu in which Randall lived.

In an excellent study of the sectarians that emerged in New England as a result of the First Great Awakening, Stephen Marini suggested that while these groups enjoyed the heritage of great awakening millennial preaching, they approached the millennium from an entirely different viewpoint. "It was a conflict between pre-millennialism and postmillennialism—whether the thousand-year reign of the saints should precede or follow the cataclysmic Second Coming of Christ."[22] The Great Awakening preachers like Jonathan Edwards continued with the traditional message of American Puritanism that focused on America as the chosen nation of God. Edwards and his followers looked for an earthly millennial kingdom in America and saw themselves as God's instruments in preparation for the Lord's coming. On the other hand, New Light sectarians looked for an imminent return of Christ in which God would again crash into human history and set right the ills of a world in chaos. While the traditionalists saw great promise in America's military triumph in the Revolution, the sectarians sought "the signs of the times" in both political events and natural events to determine the Lord's coming.[23] Marini mentions the "Dark Day of 1780" which occurred on May 19, 1780. All of New England was plunged into darkness. Ezra Stiles, a Congregationalist divine, observed that "the Obscurity was so great that those who had good eyesight could scarcely see to read common print; the birds and fowls in many places retired to roost as tho' it had been actually night, and people were obliged to light candles to dine by."[24]

This miraculous event along with the continuing millennial signs of war and revival encouraged the sectarian to anticipate and to proclaim the soon second coming of Christ.

It is not surprising that Randall was influenced by the revivalism of the day. As a convert of Whitefield, he was, in a very real sense, a product of revival. Maybe more importantly, however, was the fact that his earliest days of Christian commitment coincided with a new revival that swept across rural New England between 1776 and 1783.

Whitefield's death in 1770 ended the last ties with the First Great Awakening, and growing concern for independence and revolution again turned men's eyes from heavenly things to the more pressing concerns of survival. By 1776, though often for different motives, most of New England longed for a new revival. The New Light Congregationalists sought renewal as a guarantee of God's aid in the struggle with England (the next phase in the struggle of bringing in the kingdom) while the more radical New Lights sought revival that would lift mankind above the temporary struggles of their world.[25]

It was soon evident that the more radical approach to revival was also the more popular. Two experiences in Randall's life—his conversion in 1770 and his "corn field" experience ten years later—prepared him for the more radical approach. Immediately after conversion, he realized the Old Light congregation in New Castle fell far short of God's requirements and his later renewal—the corn field experience—which ended his struggle with the question of universal atonement, finally and completely severed his relationship with the Old Light ministry. At this point, two elements of his message were complete. He preached in anticipation of the imminent second coming of Christ and never wavered, even in the face of constant opposition, from the doctrine of free will and universal atonement.

Randall's emphasis on entire sanctification is somewhat more difficult to understand. The doctrine prevailed for a very brief time in Randall's own movement but has no place in the present denomination at all. Again, Randall was the product of his times. Though the golden age of perfectionism in the mid-nineteenth century was still more than fifty years away,[26] it was not unusual that Randall should be interested in a doctrine of entire sanctification. The New Light Stir had produced a number of perfectionist movements. If Christ was expected to return immediately, then His followers were compelled to make themselves ready for His appearing.

Randall's own experience might have contributed to his interest in this doctrine as well. In his personal experience with the Spirit some ten years after his conversion, he found himself so completely in the Spirit's control that he had no real sense of reality. In a moment when "I never could tell whether I was in the body or not," he says, "when I was then stripped, I saw a white robe brought and put over me, which covered me all over. I looked down all over me and I appeared as white as snow."[27] If such an experience was available to Randall, then it was available to his disciples as well.

Finally then, Randall's unique contribution to New England in the late eighteenth century was his emphasis on universal atonement. While other New Light radicals were willing to adjust traditional Calvinism, few were ready to totally cast it aside.

In the South, the old General Baptists and their successors, the Free Will Baptists, had long been accused of having little message at all. Lemuel Burkitt and Jesse Read, in their *Concise History of the Kehukee Baptist Association*, described the older General Baptist movement:

> They preached, and adhered to the Arminian, or Freewill doctrines, and their churches were first established upon this system. They gathered churches without requiring an experience of grace previous to their baptism; but baptized all who believed in the doctrine of baptism by immersion, and requested baptism of them. The churches of this order were first gathered here by elders Paul Palmer and Joseph Parker, and were succeeded by a number of ministers, whom they had baptized; and some of whom, we have no reason to believe, were converted when they were baptized, or first began to preach. . . .[28]

The accusation continued to be a source of difficulty for the Free Will Baptists into the nineteenth century. In a letter to the leaders of the denomination in New England in 1827, Jesse Heath found it necessary to defend the orthodoxy of the southern group. ". . . We baptize none but such as confess their sins, believe in Jesus, and consider baptism by immersion as a duty deeply impressed. We think that no person can feel baptism deeply impressed on their minds as a duty, and still be in an unprepared state to comply with it. . . ."[29]

Except for sermon titles in the minutes of the different Free Will Baptist groups in the South, little is said about the message that they preached. However, the accusations of opponents like Burkitt and Read, the correspondence of Jesse Heath, and available statements of faith from the period, it is evident that the heart of the message was found in the doctrines of general atonement and believer's baptism. In an era when general atonement was rejected by most Baptists, constant preaching of the doctrine became necessary. Like Randall in New England, preachers in the South came to the conclusion that the universal call of the gospel was primary in the teachings of the Scripture. Only those who responded freely to the call were worthy candidates for baptism. To preach anything less than general atonement and baptism by immersion was to neglect the proclaiming of the whole counsel of God.

Theology

Like other new movements, the Free Will Baptists experienced an evolution in the development of their theology. Only the most basic doctrines were considered sacred and non-negotiable—general atonement, believer's baptism, authority of the Word, the deity of Christ, and the unity of the Trinity. Beyond those basics, a number of changes occurred during the first few years of the denomination's existence.

General Atonement

The doctrine of general atonement was to separate the Free Will Baptists from most other Baptists in the United States and proved to be the one major bar to cooperation and reunion among the Baptists during the nineteenth century. It also brought open opposition from Calvinistic Christians in every area that Baptists were to be found. Randall was ejected from the Madbury church in New England because he rejected the doctrine of election. The Free Will Baptists in the South were termed heretics because they preached general atonement. But, in each case, they were willing to bear persecution in order to meet the demands of the gospel as they saw them. Ellis Gore, the founder of the Free Will Baptist movement in Alabama, described the attitude of the denomination toward the doctrine.

> . . . We assume ground which forbids any compromise with the Calvinistic doctrines (sic), or with those that believe them. They could have no confidence in our veracity were we to accede to any compromise upon Calvinistic principles. We have freed ourselves from their fetters never again to be entangled by them, and we will suffer no vestige of fatalism to be introduced into the articles of faith by which we are to be governed. . . .[30]

Gore then continued to ask for a "revolution" ". . . to expurge the doctrine of unconditional, eternal election with its concomitant reprobation, eternal passing by or non-election, by a firm and persevering stand against it. . . .[31]

In spite of the fact that different groups of Free Will Baptists originated from different backgrounds, they all came to the same conclusion in this area of doctrine. The language of the statement changed from one area to another, but the message remained the same.

In New England—

> By virtue of the atonement, which is designed to counteract the effects of the fall, man is placed in a salvable state; the grace of God, the influences of the Holy Spirit, and the invitations of the gospel are given to all men, and by these they receive power to repent and obey all the requirements of the gospel. Hence it appears a perfect inconsistency to suppose that God would provide salvation for a less number than He really loved. As His love extended to all mankind, if He provided salvation for one, He must necessarily for all, there being nothing in His nature, nor in man's nature, whereby this provision should be limited.[32]

In North Carolina—

> We believe that God, is not willing that any should perish, but that all should come to repentance and the knowledge of the truth, that they might be saved; for which end

Christ hath commanded the Gospel to be preached among all nations and to every creature.

We believe that no man shall suffer in hell, for want of a Christ that died for him. . . .[33]

In Tennessee—

We believe that Jesus Christ has come and made a full atonement for all and all may come by the Gospel and be Saved.[34]

Since the doctrine of general atonement caused the Free Will Baptists so much pain, they were careful to answer their opponents in their statement of faith. For that reason, the question of atonement often comprised the larger part of the statement. The accusations ranged from the acceptance of unsaved church members to the heresy of a "works salvation." In response, the Free Will Baptists reminded their opponents that it was necessary for the Holy Spirit to draw men to Christ, that God had chosen before the foundation of the world those who should be saved (in this case, those who willingly responded to the gospel call), that God did not accept men on the basis of their own righteousness or works, that good works were pleasing to God only after salvation, and that men apart from Christ were dead in their sins.[35]

Believer's Baptism

While believer's baptism further alienated the Free Will Baptists from many Calvinists, it tended to align them more closely with other Baptists. For that reason, numerous attempts were made in both North and South to reunite the Baptist brethren into one denomination. Whether Benjamin Randall, who came to accept believer's baptism through his own study of the Scriptures, or the Free Will Baptists in the South, who inherited the doctrine from the older General Baptists, all saw the doctrine as basic and primary. Though not considered essential to salvation or part of the plan of salvation, it quickly became the sign and seal of church membership.

The rejection of Covenant theology and its attendant infant baptism left the Free Will Baptists with one major question—the question of God's provision for those children that did not reach an age of accountability. What happened to a child that died before he was old enough to understand the gospel and willingly accept Christ as Savior? The question arose early and was settled, at least in the minds of the denominational leaders, by 1812.

We believe that all children, dying in infancy, having not actually transgressed against the law of God in their own persons, are only subject to the first death which was brought on men by the fall of the first Adam, and not that any one of them dying in that state, shall suffer punishment in Hell by the guilt of Adam's sin, for of such is the kingdom of God.[36]

Entire Sanctification

Stephen Marini, in his *Radical Sects of Revolutionary New England*, labeled the Freewill Baptists in New England a sect. But while he used a fairly traditional definition of sectarianism, his applications were quite new.[37] Lumping together the Universalists, Shakers, and Freewill Baptists into one category, he identified their sectarian characteristics as visionary experiences (remember Randall's corn field experience), reaction to the accepted Calvinism of the day and, in the case of the Freewill Baptists, entire sanctification. In an accompanying statement, Marini implied that Benjamin Randall preached salvation by works, "he . . . appealed to a visionary experience in proclaiming that God did not damn or save souls, that humans were free to decide their eternal destiny for themselves."[38] Admittedly, the author could have been pointing to Randall's doctrine of general atonement.

While he might have misunderstood Randall on the latter doctrine, he is correct in his conclusion that the early movement advocated entire sanctification. This was touched on earlier in this chapter.

Such a dogma seems out of place within the larger framework of Free Will Baptist theology. Entire sanctification and the possibility of apostasy appear totally incompatible, but incompatible or not, the two doctrines appeared side by side in the denomination's statement of faith at least for the two decades between 1834 and 1854.

> Sanctification is a work of God's grace, by which the soul is cleansed from all pollutions of sin, and is renewed after the image of God. Though in regeneration the soul is sanctified, yet, while the Christian continues in the state of trial, he has to contend with the corruptions of nature, and is liable again to be defiled. Sanctification is also a setting apart the soul and body for holy service. It is a progressive work, by which the Christian obtains victory over every temptation, corruption, and sinful inclination; and in which the will is brought into entire resignation to the will of God. The attainment of entire sanctification in this life, is both the privilege and duty of every Christian. For as sin is odious in the sight of God, Christ died to save His people from it, and the gospel has sufficient power to complete the work during this probation.[39]

The Church Member's Book, published in 1847, attempted to clarify the doctrine for the layman.

> As men grow in grace, they will rise superior to the corruptions of human nature, and power of temptations. But O, how many appear to think that their 'inbred corruptions' are so many clogs, that must necessarily embarrass them all through life. How many talk of their 'besetting sins' as if there were no remedy. But is it so? No, praise God: 'the blood of Jesus Christ his Son cleanseth from all sin.' . . . Not the complaining of evil propensities or sore temptations, but the gaining of victory over them, is a true sign of growth in grace. Here is the warfare, the striving, the wrestling, of vital, living piety. Grace shall triumph; and there is no necessity that we run uncertainly or fight as one

that beateth the air. God is to be sought unto, to do this thing for us: and He will give
to faith and prayer glorious victory.[40]

Randall and his followers argued that entire sanctification was more than a privilege for the
individual Christian; it was a necessity for the church. A sinful world could not be won by a sinful
church. Holiness was championed as the normal state of the body of Christ and anything less was
considered an ". . . abnormal institution and an awful burlesque on sacred things."[41]

As one reads, he has to be reminded of Randall's own "corn field" experience some ten years
after his conversion experience. The statement of faith gives no indication of a second work of grace
or a crisis experience. The combination of a progressive format with entire sanctification is somewhat unusual. Other groups who have advocated entire sanctification or other systems of victorious
living ordinarily point to a particular experience that initiates victory. While this seems to have been
the case in Randall's own experience, the denomination's 1834 statement of faith did not require it
of others.

In any case, the doctrine was to have a short life span within the theological framework of the
denomination. By 1874, the language of the statement softened and the section on sanctification was
reduced to a single paragraph. Entire sanctification yielded to a more practical, progressive trans-
formation into the image of Christ.

> Sanctification is a work of God's grace, by which the soul is cleansed from all sin, and
> wholly consecrated to Christ. It commenses at regeneration, and the Christian can and
> should abide in this state until the end of his life, constantly growing in life and the
> knowledge of our Lord Jesus Christ.[42]

Perseverance of the Saints

In the latter part of the twentieth century, the Free Will Baptists' approach to perseverance constituted the only major difference between this group and others within the Baptist family. From the
beginning, the New England congregations were warned of the possibility of apostasy. The statement
of the doctrine in the first treatise of 1834 is quite simple and would require some revision, but for
all practical purposes, the content of the statement would remain the same. Eventually, the revised
statement was accepted by other Free Will Baptist groups both in the South and in the West and continued to express the position of the denomination until it was revised again just recently. In spite of
the importance of the doctrine because of its uniqueness to the denomination—the doctrinal statement in 1834 was handled in two brief sentences. "As the regenerate are placed in a state of trial
during this life, their future obedience and final salvation are neither determined nor certain. It is,
however, their duty and privilege to be steadfast in the truth, to grow in grace, persevere in holiness,
and make their elections sure."[43]

It should not be imagined, however, that the denominational leaders were slack in their defense
of the doctrine. Three full pages of footnotes in small print were required to explain the position
and to fully support it with Scripture texts.

The final wording was included in the treatise by 1869:

There are strong grounds to hope that the truly regenerate will persevere until the end, and be saved, through the power of divine grace which is pledged for their support; but their future obedience and final salvation are neither determined nor certain, since through infirmity and manifold temptations they are in danger of falling; and they ought therefore to watch and pray, lest they make shipwreck of faith and be lost.[44]

By this time, the doctrine was fully accepted and the compilers of the treatise did not feel that their editorial comments were necessary. Instead, they listed only the Scripture passages that the denomination used to defend the position. It is interesting that many of the verses used were the same verses that the Calvinists called upon in their attempts to develop a doctrine of perseverance. Beyond those verses, 2 Chronicles 15:2, 2 Peter 1:10, John 15:6, 1 Corinthians 9:27, and Ezekiel 33:18 were used as the Scriptural basis for the doctrine.

The latter statement—the final revision—was later adopted by North Carolina (at least from 1916 to 1920 and after 1949), the Co-operative General Association, the Tow River Association in Tennessee, and the American Association in western North Carolina and eastern Tennessee.

In the South, development of the doctrine was not quite so clear cut and predictable. For a moment in time, this segment of the denomination differed from other Free Will Baptists and, indeed, from their own earlier General Baptist background. It was at this point in his research that the author recognized how difficult it is to set bias aside when researching his own denominational background. When reading the earliest available statement of faith for the Free Will Baptists in North Carolina, he suddenly was confronted with a doctrinal position that was totally out of character.

In 1812, Jesse Heath and James Roach were appointed as a committee to "examine and reprint the former *Confession of Faith*, put forth by the former Elders and Deacons. . . ."[45] It can only be supposed that this was the confession used by Joseph and William Parker and their General Baptist colleagues in the latter part of the eighteenth century. It will be remembered that the confession was used in an earlier chapter to prove that the Free Will Baptists of the nineteenth century were the direct descendants of the earlier General Baptists. The document was signed by James Roach, who had taken over the last remaining General Baptist church in 1794—Joseph Parker's Little Creek Church—and by Jesse Heath, an early Free Will Baptist leader. Though the title page still used the older name, the signatures made it evident that this was a Free Will Baptist document. In fact, the title page was not changed by North Carolina Free Will Baptists until many years later. The newer name was used on the cover of printings after 1901 and finally was substituted for "General Baptists" on the title page of 1912. There can be no question but that the *Confession* served as the first statement of faith for the new Free Will Baptists in the South.

As expected, the new confession was primarily a verbatim copy of the English General Baptists' *Standard Confession of 1660*. But one article in the new confession offered the totally unexpected. This first confession included the doctrine of eternal security.

While the articles in the two confessions did not always follow number by number, it was possible, in most cases, to identify the identical articles in both. Article X in the *Free Will Baptist Confession* was different. The sister article in the *1660 Confession* read:

> That such who were true believers, even Branches in Christ the Vine (and whom he exhorts to abide in him, John 15:1, 2, 3, 4, 5) or such who have charity out of a pure heart, and of a good conscience, and of Faith unfeigned, I Tim. 1:5, may nevertheless for want of watchfulness swerve and turn aside from the same, verses 6, 7, and become as withered Branches, cast into the fire and burned. . . .[46]

The article continued to agree that those who remained faithful would not fall, though the necessity of personal faith was evident.

On the other hand, Article X of the *North Carolina Abstract* read, "We believe the Saints shall persevere in grace, and never finally fall away. John 10:27, 28, and 29."[47]

In 1835, Windsor Dixon, John A. Fonville, Robert Bond, Reuben Barrow, and Daniel Cox were appointed a committee of five to revise the *Discipline*—the rules of discipline and polity attached to the *1812 Abstract*—and to have the confession itself reprinted. Though this particular printing is not available, the 1855 edition indicates that the wishes of the Conference were carried out and that only the *Discipline* was revised. In fact, this seems to have been the practice throughout the remainder of the nineteenth century. At least one revision was made, however, by the committee in 1835. Article X, the article advocating perseverance, was deleted and Article XII, dealing with condemnation of the ungodly, was used to replace the original statement.[48]

In less than one generation, the theological atmosphere changed, and the new group committed itself firmly to the older General Baptist pattern that would continue to be an important point of doctrine for the denomination from 1835 forward.

Without supporting documents, it becomes almost impossible to recreate the discussion that deleted the old statement. Jesse Heath wrote in 1827 that when he came to the denomination in 1807, there were only five preachers. Except for James Roach, who can be traced to Little Creek Church in Greene County, North Carolina, the preachers appeared suddenly on the Free Will Baptist scene, and we know nothing of their background. It is at least possible that they were converts from the Calvinistic Baptists in the area and that they simply brought part of their denominational baggage with them.

Whatever their background, it seems evident that they initially believed in eternal security and since they outnumbered James Roach four to one, their voice carried the day. But the victory was a brief one, and by 1827, the General Baptist argument regained the upper hand. In 1835, the growing church erased the doctrine of eternal security from its confession, and the North Carolina group found itself in full agreement with other Free Will Baptists in the North and West. As mentioned earlier, this doctrine came to constitute the unique difference between the Free Will Baptists and others in the Baptist family.

Biblical Authority

While it is true that the doctrines of entire sanctification and eternal security might have confused and divided the Free Will Baptists for the first few years, they were always one on the question of Biblical authority.

Though the first treatise for New England did not include the question of authority in the text of the confession itself, a good number of pages were given to the subject in the introduction to the treatise. The Scriptures were defined as the only rule of faith and practice for Christian people, were considered fully inspired, and were to be accepted as final authority without addition, deduction, or alteration.[49]

On the other hand, both Arkansas and North Carolina included the matter of authority in the statement of faith itself from the very beginning. Though they had far less to say about the issue than did the New England Treatise, they clearly presented a position of infallible authority.[50]

Other groups of Free Will Baptists came from different backgrounds and rejected the idea of a statement of faith of any sort arguing that the Bible alone was sufficient for guidance and direction. Free Will Baptists in Tennessee waited some years before accepting a formal statement of faith. They received the tradition honestly. The Separate Baptists, from whom the middle Tennessee Free Will Baptists came, never used a statement of faith. As far as they were concerned, the use of any type of formal statement suggested that the Bible was less than adequate.

In an interesting discussion concerning union with the United Baptists, a Calvinistic group, the Separates in the Nolynn Association refused to consider union because the other group demanded that they accept their confession of faith. A committee of three from the United Baptists Association reminded the Free Willers that though there had never been union, they were willing to make the first overtures. They presented their book of order and said union could be consummated if the Separates would agree to obey and conform to the book. The response was expected. After the book was read aloud ". . . the disciples and elders said, this is not the book of the law nor of the prophets. Therefore, we can have nothing to do with this little book."[51] The Nolynn Association did agree to an alternative. If the United Baptists were willing to obey and conform to the book called the Old Testament and New Testament, then union was possible. The meeting ended when the United Baptists said they had come with no authority to make such a concession.

Ordinances

Morgan Scott, in his *History of the Separate Baptist Church*, listed baptism, the Lord's Supper, feet washing, laying on of hands, love feasts, anointing the sick, right hand of fellowship, kiss of charity, and devotion to children as the ordinances practiced by the Separate Baptists. The reader should remember that the Separates were the forebears of the Free Will Baptists in middle Tennessee. Scott goes on to explain that in 1901, at the time of the writing of his book, the movement had reduced the ordinances to three—baptism, the Lord's Supper, and foot washing.[52] This influence, coupled with that of the General Baptists, had its impact on most of the Free Will Baptists in the South. In the *Confession of Faith* printed in 1855 in North Carolina, the list of ordinances was almost the same as that of the early Separates.

We believe, as touching Gospel ordinances, in believers' Baptism, laying on of the hands, receiving of the sacrament in bread and wine, washing the saint's feet, anointing the sick with oil in the name of the Lord, fasting, prayer, singing praises to God, and the public ministry of the word, with every institution of the Lord we shall find in the New Testament.[53]

In New England, the ordinances were limited to four—believers' baptism, the Lord's Supper, foot washing, and public worship. But here by 1835, foot washing was eliminated and deemed unnecessary to include public worship in the list.

Baptism

This particular ordinance had been a distinctive of the Baptist movement since the founding of the first church in London in 1612, and, indeed, could be traced back to the Anabaptists of the Reformation. By this time, of course, immersion was the accepted mode of administration and as indicated in the title of the ordinance, believers only were worthy of participation in the ordinance.[54]

Individuals who were old enough to understand the call of the gospel and had made a public profession of faith in Christ became members of the church through the ordinance of baptism. Baptism was not considered essential to salvation, and therefore, it was not necessary that the individual be baptized immediately after confession of faith. However, in the early days, practical factors demanded immediate baptism. Quite often the churches had services only once a month, and their pastor probably found himself at other locations throughout the remainder of the month. Baptism was important. It was not unusual for pastors to go to great lengths in order to make baptism possible. At least on one occasion, it was necessary for the church members to cut steps in the ice at the local baptizing spot so Benjamin Randall could administer the rite of baptism to new converts.[55]

Baptism, like the Lord's Supper, was considered a symbolic act. In this case, it was a sign of regeneration. Since the symbolism was of such an important nature, the churches constantly warned against baptizing those who had not had a personal experience of faith. "It is admitted by all to be a sign of regeneration, or the sanctifying influence of the Spirit, and it does not seem proper to affix a sign where there is no evidence that the thing signified does really exist."[56] The symbolism further included "…death to the world, the washing of their souls from the pollutions of sin, the resurrection to newness of life, the burial and resurrection of Christ, their resurrection at the last day, and their engagement to serve God."[57]

The Lord's Supper

Free Will Baptists of the nineteenth century were little different from other Baptists of the day in the celebration of the Lord's Supper. The exception was that the Lord's table was open to all those who were "true believers." Denominational background was unimportant. The practice of "open communion" was typical wherever Free Will Baptists were found. The records are full of accounts of cooperation in worship with Methodists, other Baptist groups, and the Disciples of Christ. The lowering of the bars of access to the table allowed fellowship that would not have been possible otherwise. This open approach to communion became a distinctive of the Free Will Baptists within the Baptist family.[58]

Washing of the Saints' Feet

This ordinance, as well, has a symbolic character, but rather than symbolizing death and resurrection, it speaks of the humility of Christ and of that of the believer who participates. Though misunderstood and frowned upon by outsiders, the celebration of the ordinance traditionally has been a reverent, spirit-lifting service in which individual members of the church attested to their humility before Christ and before their brothers in the body. Unfortunately, there is little information about the actual format of the service in the nineteenth century. All of the statements of faith mention the ordinance, but then go on to simply defend it scripturally, with little attention given to the service itself.

In more recent times, the service has followed immediately after the Lord's Supper and has been considered an integral part of the worship service. Ordinarily, the benediction is not given until after the ordinance has been completed. Christians are invited to participate but are not coerced if they decline. The men and women of the church are separated, basins of water are made available, and one individual ties a long towel around his waist and then kneels to wash his brother's feet before wiping them with the towel. The recipient, in turn, takes the towel and washes the feet of another. The women are involved in the same type of service in another part of the church. The service is accompanied by singing and rejoicing as individual Christians submit themselves to one another in humility.

The 1834 treatise for the New England segment of the denomination included foot washing as an ordinance, but even at this early date, the treatise committee included a note that indicated that the ordinance was losing its influence in that area.

> Though the washing of the saint's feet, as a religious ordinance, was practised by Randal and by our connexion in its rise, many have doubted whether it was practised by the apostles, or designed to be perpetuated in the church. At present, it is not practised by a majority of our churches. At the General Conference in 1831, it was resolved, that every member in connexion with us has a free and lawful right to wash feet or not, as he can best answer his conscience to God; and that neither the practise, nor the omission of it, should cause a breach of Christian fellowship.[59]

Though the 1831 decision allowed for an individual member to continue the practice of washing feet, he would have some difficulty in finding access to the ordinance if the local churches ceased to practice it. In 1848, when the treatise was revised, the ordinance had completely disappeared.

In other areas, however, the ordinance of foot washing continued to be a distinctive of the denomination. Though the format of the service and the time of the service (morning or evening after worship) differed, many Free Will Baptists continued to accept this ordinance of the church as required by the Scriptures.

Laying on of Hands

The ordinance of laying on of hands was practiced by most Free Will Baptists in the South and on the near frontier for most of the early part of the nineteenth century. In the beginning, the ordinance was administered to every new believer,[60] but by the end of the century, it was limited to the ordination of ministers and deacons.

Polity
Ruling Elders

For twenty-first century Free Will Baptists, the office of ruling elder would be completely out of place. However, it is evident that the office was in popular usage at least until late in the nineteenth century.

The office ceased to exist entirely in New England by 1834, but there is no question but that ruling elders were elected during the life time of Benjamin Randall. In his biography of Randall, John Buzzell contrasted the election of Joseph Boody as ruling elder with that of John Whitney as teaching elder or pastor.[61] In the *1834 Discipline*, however, the terms of bishop, elder, and pastor were used synonymously. "Bishops are overseers, who have the charge of souls to instruct and rule them by the word. They are called elders, and they perform the duties of pastors, teachers, and evangelists."[62]

In the South, the office was more carefully developed and was destined to have a much longer life span. In North Carolina, ruling elders were used at least as early as 1812. Since the *Discipline* was new in that year, it is not possible to tell if the office also was new or was simply the continuation of an older tradition. The task of the ruling elder seems to have been, for the most part, limited to difficulties between members in the local church.

> The ruling Elders must be appointed and qualified in like manner as the Deacons are, and shall serve the Church according to their appointment.

> The business of the ruling Elders after their qualification to that office, is to settle controverted points between their brethren, if they shall be informed of any business of this nature, then they shall issue their order and appoint the time and place to meet the parties, and it shall be legal for them to take such testimony both in and out of the Church as shall to them (seem) meet, and so shall enable them to pass a true and right judgment.

> When the Elders have full information of any matter respecting controversy between their brethren, should they find a fraud intended they shall be at liberty to give the injured party liberty of the common law, and make report thereof to the next conference.

And if any member shall fly from the judgment of the Elders, it shall be open excommunication.[63]

In the first available revision of the *Discipline* in 1855, requirements for the office remained the same except that the pastor was enjoined to reveal the excommunication publicly before the local church.[64] The *Discipline* inferred that the office was a powerful one, and no mention was made of an appeal to a higher authority.

In South Carolina, the Conference carried the office of ruling elder one further step and introduced, as far as can be determined, the first "bishop" for the Free Will Baptists. Of course, his jurisdiction was limited to South Carolina, but he was given a great deal of power within the General Conference of that state. In 1876, the Conference records included the following motion:

> On motion agreed that we appoint an Elder of government to preside over all the ministers belonging to the South Carolina Confurrance. Motion was agreede to that the Elder of Government has the full oversight of all the ministers belonging to the South Carolina Confurrance. He shall have the authority to Call on any of the Elders or ministers belong(ing) to any of the Churches and appoint a plase of trial and try any case of disorderly walk among the ministers and they Shall Consider them Selves subject to his decision and he shall have the authority if they will not hear him and abide by his Judgment he shall be at Liberty and have the power to deman there papers untill Satisfaction is given or untill the next General Confurrance Shall investigate the Case . . . .[65]

N. Hall was elected as elder of government. The use of the term "bishop" might not have been too far from the truth. In 1882, the minutes remind us that ". . .on motion Elder W. B. Flowers was elected bishop. . . ."[66] No explanation was given. It is more than likely true that the term was used in lieu of "elder of government."

In any case, the office was soon abandoned. In 1883, the Conference agreed to abolish that office, and instead, appointed J. B. Moore as a ruling elder. At this point, he was the only ruling elder and replaced the older elder of government and bishop. He was required to visit each quarterly conference during the year.

The office of ruling elder continued in North and South Carolina for a number of years. In fact, it was not deleted from the *Discipline* in North Carolina until 1948, though the office itself had been inactive for a number of years.

There is little evidence of the use of the office in other areas. It seems that Georgia, Alabama, Arkansas, and Tennessee used the terms of elder and pastor synonymously.

Presbytery

The use of an ordaining presbytery seems to have been the pattern from the very beginning and though the system would become more sophisticated during the years, it has changed relatively little to the present time.

In the beginning, the southern churches handled the entire ordination process at the local level. After a candidate was set aside for ordination, the pastor assigned a time of prayer and fasting for the church, chose individuals from the church as an ordaining council, and then presided over the ordination and the imposition of hands. At this time, the records give little evidence of a theological examination. The congregation allowed an individual to preach and, if the gift of preaching was evident, he was recommended for ordination. Five simple questions at the time of ordination, led to a final statement of approval.

1. Do you, in the presence of God and this assembly, believe the whole Volume of the Scriptures, both of the Old and New Testament, to be infallibly true?

2. Do you believe the Faith and Order of this Church to be altogether consinant with the Holy Scriptures as far as you be acquainted with them?

3. Do you feel divinely called of God, to take upon you the office of the public Ministry of the Word?

4. Are you at this time on your part, in the full fellowship of the brethren of this church?

5. Do you propose in your heart, to earnestly contend for the faith and order of this Society and to serve the brethren as far as respects Ministerial function in the order of this Society?

6. If the answers be discreet and satisfactory, he shall receive Ordination and his credentials.[67]

In both New England and in the South, the responsibilities of the presbytery were later passed over to the quarterly meeting. This was true as early as 1834 in the North and certainly by the middle of the century in the South. A note in the *New England Discipline* in 1834 mentioned that quite often the ordination service itself was held at the quarterly meeting.[68]

South Carolina developed a more complex presbyterial system called a "committee of investigation." The new committee probably was a substitute for the old "elder of government." Each quarterly conference appointed a committee and gave it the responsibility of settling difficulties between ministers within the ranks of the quarterly meeting as well as the task of ordaining new ministers. In this case, a candidate for ordination was carefully examined as to personal character and his understanding of the doctrines of the church.[69]

A 1914 revision of the *North Carolina Church Discipline* established a pattern that has continued to serve the denomination until the present time.

After which if either of those persons (that is, either the licentiate or exhorter) is found useful, the church shall recommend him to an ordaining council consisting of five men set apart for the Conference for this special work. The candidate shall appear before the council some time during the regular session of the Conference, and if after a careful examination as to his orthodoxy and other qualifications he is found qualified, the council shall recommend his ordination which shall be attended to by prayer and fasting and the laying on of hands by the presbytery appointed by the moderator.[70]

Fasting has been discontinued. Both the examination and the ordination service are often held in the candidate's local church. The committee now serves for long periods of time rather than for just one conference session but, otherwise, the presbytery's task has remained much the same.

By the twentieth century, the use of a presbytery at a quarterly meeting level was standard for the denomination. In Arkansas and some other states, at the beginning of the century, the presbytery was responsible for the ordination of both pastors and deacons for the local churches.

Monthly Meetings

In both North and South, many of the churches met only once a month. A Saturday night service included the opportunity for settling the business of the church as well as worship and the Sunday services were given entirely to worship. When a particular church was not having its own services, its ministers and members were expected to attend the monthly meetings of other churches. The system gave opportunity for fellowship between churches, for one minister to serve more than one church, and for the availability of a number of preachers for each worship service.[71]

While the system seems untenable to the twenty-first century Christian who has long enjoyed the luxury of a full church program, it was quite practical in the nineteenth century. In many cases, the local church could not pay a pastor a living wage. His limited church responsibility allowed him to work at a regular job for family support.

Distance and travel difficulties also became factors. Robert Wilkinson, the clerk for the Pantego-Concord Church in North Carolina, reported in 1851 that "Ower meetings is quartley. Comensing on satterday befor the 3rd Lord's day february, maye and, august and November. Ower monthley metings we have nun. The Reson is ower pastur lives so far of that he can attend us onley quartley."[72]

The monthly meeting system continued to have its impact on the denomination well into the twentieth century. For many years, in most parts of the South, the churches continued to exist on a part-time basis. Churches met twice a month, allowing the pastor to minister to at least two churches. In parts of eastern Kentucky and other nearby mountain regions, the monthly meeting system has continued to the present day in its original form. Though most of our pastors have only one church, they and their members are actively involved with the other churches at their monthly meeting times.

Church Attendance

For all practical purposes, church attendance was mandatory in the early nineteenth century. Careful records were kept and absentees were summoned to the next monthly conference to give excuse for their failure to attend. In most cases, it was expected that they also attend other churches when their own monthly meeting was not scheduled. Much of the discipline of the nineteenth century had to do with absenteeism.

It was not long, however, before the churches realized they could not dictate faithfulness. Though some attempt was made to call members to task as late as 1860, most of the churches had given up the struggle by the middle of the century. The Pantego-Concord Church expressed the prevailing attitude after that time, ". . . and the absent Brothern and Sistrs heretofor was not taken up as it was thought it woold doe no good as wee can't compel no person to be a Christian against their Will."[73]

Discipline

Free Will Baptist discipline in the eighteenth century could be characterized as loving but strict. The discipline process included the traditional evangelical concern for rehabilitation, but repeated offenses spelled sure excommunication. In fact, in some instances, even one offense could lead to excommunication if repentance was not evident.

The two major areas leading to discipline were the abuse of alcohol and failure to attend monthly meetings. The records reveal that disciplinary action for theological aberration was rare indeed.

Actually, the Free Will Baptists were not out of character. By this time, discipline had become an important part of frontier life all across the South and as far west as the frontier.

> The frontier Baptist Churches held monthly congregational meetings at which all members were required to be present. It was here that the life of each member came under the scrutiny of the Church. It was the duty of each member to watch over the conduct of fellow members and to bring charges against anyone guilty of any infraction of the rules of Christian conduct or church order. Indeed a good share of the business of these congregational meetings was devoted to the hearing of charges, and unrepentant members were excluded without fear or favor. Intoxication was the most frequent cause for church discipline, though such things as adultery, unChristian business dealings, gambling, immoral conduct, stealing, removing land marks, tale-bearing, quarreling, dishonest horse trading, cruelty to slaves, misusing wives, are some of the other causes.[74]

Though William Warren Sweet, in the quote above, did not mention theological difficulty at all, it should not be supposed that the churches ignored theological heresy. The problem simply did not occur on a regular basis. Any training the pastors received came at the feet of older pastors in the denomination. In fact, most of what they knew about the Scriptures was learned through the preaching of others of their own persuasion. Limited opportunities for education, lack of access to seminaries and Bible colleges, and limited travel gave little opportunity for the young preachers to develop new ideas or different opinions.

As mentioned in the above quote, no one was above discipline, even to the point of excommunication. In Alabama, a pastor's son was accused, on a number of occasions, of attending parties where dancing provided the entertainment. Ellis Gore, Jr., son of Elder Ellis Gore, admitted his dancing to the church and declared that he saw no harm in it. Though the church continued to work with him from 1855 to 1858, he refused to repent or to abandon the practice. The church records for Mt. Moriah Free Will Baptist Church indicate that he was excluded from the church in November 1858.[75] This was not an isolated incident. Preachers, as well as the most affluent members of the churches, were subject to censure if charges against them could be proven.

Proof was necessary. In fact, false accusations were considered as much a sin as were excessive drinking, adultery, or unexcused absences from church. Immediate excommunication was the price an individual paid for unsubstantiated charges against a fellow church member.[76]

Discipline was a careful and serious business. It served the dual purpose of punishing the guilty and protecting the innocent.

Even though discipline was strict, it was not vindictive. The element of rehabilitation was never forgotten. When an individual was forgiven, the church was willing to forget as well. This is best illustrated in the records of the Pantego-Concord Church, in North Carolina, in 1852. In May of that year, the church appointed a consistory[77] from its own membership to try a case of controversy between Ransom W. Harness and William R. Wright. The consistory was composed of Silvester F. Carrow, Joseph Bell, Franklin Ange, Robert R. Wilkinson, and Elder Albritton, the pastor of the church. In an earlier monthly conference, the church excommunicated Harness for falsely accusing Wright of spending time with his (Harness's) wife. Now, Harness was appealing the case and asking that Wright be disciplined. After a lengthy discussion, Wright again was exonerated, and it was evident the church did not hold the accusations against him. In the same minutes, Wright was chosen as a ruling elder of the church.[78]

In other cases, even the guilty, upon repentance, were allowed to return to full fellowship and to hold office in the church.[79]

The churches attempted to follow carefully the disciplinary guidelines outlined in Matthew 18. In 1868, the South Carolina General Conference approved the following motion:

> Moshion agreed that hereafter no members Shall be at liberty to separate a Brother or a Sister untill he or she has went and seen the offended Party and if they will not hear then he or she shall tak one or two and if they will hear them [probably should be 'shall not hear them'—author's note] he or she shall lay the Case before the Church for investigation.[80]

The Churches and Free Will Offerings

The author of this work will never forget the first time he attempted to borrow a large sum of money for a building program for an urban Free Will Baptist church. A committee of bank officials offered the privacy of a plush board room and were open and friendly until, as pastor of the church, the author reminded them that the church was supported totally by free will offerings, no subscription and no pledges. The bankers were absolutely dumbfounded. They could not imagine the audacity of these church officials who were asking to borrow a huge sum of money without the collateral of pledges.

At that time, it was assumed that the tradition of free will offerings was as old as the denomination itself, but church records for the nineteenth century indicate that denominational leaders had not yet come to this level of maturity. Assessment plans were developed by local churches to meet expenses at the local level, such as pastors' salaries or for the education of ministers, and at the quarterly meeting level, for emergency funds set aside for aid to desperate churches. In some cases, monetary goals were set (25 cents from each male member in South Carolina) and in other cases, "contributions were left to the individual member's ability to contribute."[81]

By the mid twentieth century, the pattern had changed completely, and most Free Will Baptist churches asked free will offerings of their members.

The Local Church and the Conference

In church government, the Free Will Baptists have found themselves in complete agreement with others within the Baptist family. The structure was Congregational in nature, and each church was considered to be completely autonomous. The clearest statement of the position was prepared by the Chattahoochee Association of Georgia.

> That gospel churches are the only ecclesiastical bodies authorized by the Scriptures; that each church has the unrestricted right to administer its own government, without suspension or interference, being under Christ, essentially independent and absolute; and that if this right be surrendered by delegation or otherwise the assembly then ceases to be a gospel church.

> That churches may nevertheless, we suppose, meet by delegates, formal association, and declare the term upon which they will keep up a friendly correspondence; but that the rights and authority of churches, being unalienable are in no wise compromised or hindered by entering into an association; and therefore that associations have no shadow of authority over churches or individuals, their sole design being to promote mutual intercourse and to give that advice which might be given by any delegate in this individual capacity.[82]

North Carolina seems to have taken Congregational government and local church autonomy for granted until the General Conference faced a dispute concerning membership in secret societies in 1853. In an attempt to open the church doors to members of the Free Mason and Odd Fellow societies, Elder Alfred Moore introduced a resolution that would have refused churches the liberty to reject any person applying for membership or to excommunicate any member on the grounds that he belonged to a secret society. The Conference divided over the issue with the majority reaffirming the traditional position of local autonomy. Article IX of the *Constitution of the Annual Conference* stated simply that "all matters shall be decided by a majority" and on that basis, the conference resolved "that we believe the Rules of Discipline gives to each individual Church its own key—the privilege of transacting its own business independent of the General Conference."[83]

As soon as two churches were organized in any given area, an association was formed. In all parts of the country, the denomination moved quickly from monthly to quarterly to yearly meetings and from there to annual or general conferences. In each case, the higher body assumed an advisory character recognizing that the local church had final authority in matters of local polity. Discipline of constituent bodies within the general and annual conferences or within the associations was limited to expulsion from membership.[84]

Even though the local churches enjoyed autonomy, they often delegated authority to their associations when satisfaction could not be found at home. This was most clearly seen in the early establishment of a presbytery at the quarterly meeting level which had the responsibility of ordaining both pastors and deacons through the local churches. Beyond that, the churches occasionally called for help in collecting money for building churches and, on rare occasions, for dealing with local problems of discipline. In those situations where the local church asked for funds from the Conference for their church building, it was not unusual for the Conference to involve themselves in the building process even to the point of placing a representative on the building committee to supervise the work.[85]

On at least one occasion, the annual conference intervened in a local church dispute that had divided the church into two factions with each having its own pastor. A committee from the annual conference was sent to the church, and after thorough investigation, decided that it was best to remove both pastors. A new pastor, who was acceptable to both factions, was appointed by the committee. The committee reported to the annual conference that the dispute had been settled and that reconciliation had been gained.[86] This drastic intervention seems to have represented an isolated case, but it does give some idea of the power the conferences and associations could muster when invited to do so by the local churches. Actually, there seems to be some variation in the way the Conference involved itself in the work of the local churches. In the controversy mentioned above, regarding difficulties between ministers, the Conference stepped in and took charge, but in many other situations of a lesser nature, the Conference remained aloof and allowed the local church to deal with its own problems.

New England spoke the mind of most of the Free Will Baptists when in the General Conference of 1841, they resolved "that the strict independence of the churches in all matters related to the transaction of their own business, is indispensably necessary in order to promote the uninterrupted enjoyment of religious liberty in our denomination."[87]

Music

Stephen Marini has suggested that in New England, the period 1775 to 1815 was the golden age of hymnody as hymn singing in worship began to replace the Psalter in many churches. In evangelical circles, hymnody became a strong rival to preaching and public prayer because the hymns gave the laity an opportunity to be actively involved in worship and because the hymns allowed a new structure for the articulation of evangelical faith.[88]

Free Will Baptists began to compose their own hymns soon after the first church was founded, and the first published hymnal, in 1823, included some 35 hymns that were written by Free Will Baptist clergy and laity, most of them either by Benjamin Randall or John Buzzell. Randall often composed short verses at monthly, quarterly, and yearly meetings which were sung during the conferences.[89] For the most part, the hymns spoke to the questions of Free Will Baptist origin and background, distinctive doctrines, contemplation of Christ, or the Christian experience after conversion. The Freewill Baptists often sang a song that proclaimed their radical evangelical beginnings. "Come all who are New-Lights indeed, / Who are from sin and bondage freed; / From Egypt's land We've took our flight, / For God has giv'n us a New-Light."

The hymn continued to speak of the sacrifices made by those who adopt a radical life style and the protection that God offers to those who are faithful. "Though by the world we are disdain'd / And have our names cast out by men; / Yet Christ our captain for us fights, / Nor death, nor hell, can hurt New-Lights. / Thus guarded by the Lord we stand, / Safe in the hollow of His hand; / Nor do we scorn the New-Light's name, / The saints are all New-Lights, Amen." Marini declared that "such hymns stated the ecclesiastical and social rootage of the Freewill community. They functioned as statements of public identity, anthems calling worshipers to awareness of their particular background and pietistic style."[90]

The doctrinally oriented hymns spoke to the matters of free will and free grace, often taking the scenario all the way from the first yearnings of salvation to sanctification and perfection. John Buzzell's 1812 hymn is a classic example of this type of hymnody.

Once I was going on in sin,
All filled with pride and unbelief!
Refus'd to let the Savior in,
And often did His Spirit grieve.

But Oh! At length, my state I saw,
And felt a load of guilt with sin;
I found I'd broke God's righteous law,
And lay expos'd to Hell by sin.

At last I smote upon my breast,
And did to God for mercy cry;
And soon He answered my request,
I found His pardoning mercy nigh.

From dark to light, from hate to love,
From death to life, He rais'd my soul;
He placed my mind on things above,
And all the powers of sin controll'd.[91]

As early as 1829, the New England General Conference decided that musical instruments had no place in the church.[92] Music in the church was to be "lined out" by the song director and then sung by the congregation. David Marks, who published a number of hymnals for the denomination in the first part of the nineteenth century, agreed with the Conference decision and stated in 1830, "I made a solemn covenant with the Lord, that I would not approbate this practice by reading hymns knowingly to be sung in connection with the use of musical instruments; but would give my testimony against this innovation in gospel worship.[93]

The first formal Free Will Baptist hymnal was published by John Buzzell in 1823 and was entitled, *Psalms, Hymns, and Spiritual Songs*. The collection included lyrics from a number of now famous hymn writers—Watts, Doddridge, and Toplady plus a number of hymns written by Free Will Baptists.

From that time various hymnbooks were published for the denomination beginning with the *Conference Meeting Hymnbook For the Use of All Who Love Our Lord and Savior Jesus Christ*. The selections for this hymnal were compiled by David Marks in 1828. The book contained the words for 93 hymns.

In 1832, Marks published *Hymns for Christian Melody*. In an introduction, he defended the need for a new hymnbook for the denomination. The hymnal offered words without notes, in keeping with the editor's covenant with the Lord, but the names of the tune were included below the individual song titles. An even one thousand hymns were included plus an addendum of doxologies and anthems. They were arranged according to subject under such heads as conviction, grace, and worship. *Christian Melody* was reprinted in 1841, but without revision.

Sometime before 1839, the denomination began to publish a small hymnbook entitled, *Sacred Melodies for Conference and Prayer Meetings and for Social and Private Devotion*. The 1839 issue was the third edition. It is not possible to speculate that new editions were published every year and that, consequently, the first edition had been printed in 1837. Rather, it appears that new printings were made available upon demand. Subsequent printings actually were revised editions. Though similar, the hymnals changed from printing to printing.

A new hymnbook containing 1,232 hymns and 15 doxologies was published in 1853. Like its earlier counterparts, its hymns were arranged according to topic.

The South also had an interest in music and did not need to depend entirely on the Randall movement for their hymnody. In 1832, just four years after David Marks had published the *Conference Meeting Hymnbook* in New England, Jesse Heath (North Carolina) and Elias Hutchins (from New England but a frequent visitor to North Carolina) published a hymnal for Free Will Baptists in the South. The hymnal entitled, *Psalms, Hymns and Spiritual Songs, Selected for the United Church of Christ, Commonly Called Free Will Baptists, in North Carolina; and for Saints in All Denominations*, was quite similar to its New England counterpart. It is not unlikely that the decision to publish and the format were influenced by New England through Hutchins, their personal representative in the South. The entries were presented without notes and were divided into three large categories mentioned in the title. Each larger category was then broken down into individual topics such as worship, ordinances, morning and evening hymns.

A number of hymns were given over to praise and to the question of salvation. If the southern hymnbook differed in content from those published in New England, it was in the area of space given to songs relating to the ordinance of foot washing. It will be remembered that while the ordinance was mentioned in the *1834 Treatise* published in New England, the practice soon disappeared in that area. Another difference was found in the New England use of "New-Light" hymns which were unfamiliar to Free Will Baptists in the South.

Before too much credit is given to New England, it must be noted that William Lumpkin and Enoch Cobb published *The Free Will Baptist Hymnbook* in 1832. The manuscript had been registered with the circuit court in September 1831, a good six months before the work published by Heath and Hutchins. It is admitted that Hutchins had been visiting in the area since 1828, that his preaching and advice were well received by the North Carolina brethren, and that he could have influenced Lumpkin and Cobb as well.

In 1841, Cobb published a new edition of *The Free Will Baptist Hymnbook*, and in 1854, Rufus K. Hearn, Joseph Bell, and Jesse Randolph followed with *Zion's Hymns*. Though similar to the 1832 publication by Heath and Hutchins, these newer works were different enough to offer a variety of songs to the Free Will Baptists of the South. At this point, the denomination in the South does not appear to be far behind their brethren in the North in meeting the musical needs of their people.

Hymnals with accompanying music were introduced in New England at least by 1868, but the southern group would wait a number of years before publishing similar volumes. By 1901, the Triennial Conference recommended *Zion's Free Baptist Gospel Voices* which had been copyrighted the same year. D. E. Dortch was listed as editor and the hymnal boasted shaped notes and traditional Free Will Baptist hymns. The preface indicated this was a first for the southern group. It evidently was published because the old Zion hymnbook did not offer the convenience of notes. The conferences in North Carolina requested the new edition and also asked that it contain as many of the old Zion hymns as possible.[94]

In 1921, R. F. Pittman and Floyd Loftin introduced *Hymns of Praise* and in 1928, Pittman and R. E. Tripp added *His Service Songs*.

Summary

This is the Free Will Baptist church of the nineteenth century. It is the history of beginnings, of evolution, and of a maturing process. It is a history of stage setting for the Free Will Baptists of the twentieth century.

Notes for Chapter 8

[1]Jesse Heath, Letter to the Senior Editor of *The Morning Star* dated May 19, 1827, *The Morning Star* (June 28, 1827).

[2]Stephen Marini, *Radical Sects of Revolutionary New England* (Cambridge, Mass.: Harvard University Press, 1982), 97.

[3]Ibid.

[4]Jesse Heath, Letter to the Senior Editor of *The Morning Star,* May 29, 1827.

[5]Editorial Note in *The Morning Star,* June 28, 1827.

[6]Ransom Dunn, "Letter to the General Conference," *Minutes of the General Conference* (1889), 14, 15.

[7]Sydney E. Ahlstrom, *A Religious History of the American People* (New Haven: Yale University Press, 1972), 433. Copyright 1972, Yale University. Used by permission.

[8]Elias Hutchins, Letter to *The Morning Star* dated June 20, 1830, *The Morning Star* (July 28, 1830).

[9]*An Abstract of the Former Articles of Faith, Confessed by the Original Baptist Church, Holding the Doctrine of General Provision, with A Proper Code of Discipline* (Newbern, N.C.: Printed by Salmon Hall, 1812), 12.

[10]*Minutes of the Mt. Moriah Free Will Baptist Church, Alabama* (1850-1871), handwritten manuscript held by M. P. Gore, McShan, Alabama, 38.

[11]"Letter, Elias Hutchins to Elder Samuel Burbank, January 1830," *The Freewill Baptist Magazine*, III (March 1830), 233.

[12]Buzzell, *The Life of Elder Benjamin Randall,* 118.

[13]*Minutes of the North Carolina Original Free Will Baptist General Conference* (1866), 4.

[14]*North Carolina General Conference* (1883), 7.

[15]*Minutes of the Annual Conference of the Original Free Will Baptist Church of North Carolina* (1890).

[16]"The Ministry," *The Morning Star,* Vol. IX, No. 12 (July 23, 1834), 46.

[17]"The Ministry," *The Morning Star,* Vol. IX, No. 27 (November 5, 1834), 106; "The Ministry," Vol. IX, No. 28 (November 12, 1834), 110.

[18]"Sustaining the Christian Ministry," a pamphlet (Rochester, N.Y.: The American Baptist Historical Society, n.d.), 2.

[19]Ibid., 4.

[20]"Support of the Ministry in the Freewill Baptist Denomination," *The Freewill Baptist Quarterly,* Vol. 2, No. 8 (October 1854), 413.

[21]*Minutes of the One Hundred and Sixty-fifth Annual Session of the Central Conference of the Original Free Will Baptists* (1913), 7.

[22]Marini, *Radical Sects,* 46, 47.

[23]Ibid.

[24]Ezra Stiles, *The Literary Diary of Ezra Stiles,* ed. by Franklin Bowditch Dexter (New York: Charles Scribner's Sons, 1901), 2:424, quoted in Marini, *Radical Sects,* 47.

[25]Marini, *Radical Sects,* 40.

[26]The Perfectionism of Charles Finney, Asa Mahan, and John Humphrey Noyes did not develop fully until after 1835.

[27]Buzzell, *Life of Elder Benjamin Randall,* 88.

[28]Burkitt and Read, *Concise History of the Kehukee Association,* 28.

[29]Jesse Heath, Letter, May 29, 1827. *The Morning Star,* June 28, 1827.

[30]F. H. Smith, *"Rise and Progress of Mt. Moriah Church and Mt. Moriah Association with Some of their Labor"* (Handwritten manuscript held by M. P. Gore, McShan, Alabama), 10.

[31]Ibid.

[32]*A Treatise on the Faith of Freewill Baptists* (Dover, N.H.: Published by David Marks for the Free-will Baptist Connexion, 1834), 63, 64.

[33]*An Abstract of the Former Articles of Faith Confessed by the Original Baptist Church, Holding to the Doctrine of General Provision* (Newbern, N.C.: Printed by Salmon Hall, 1812), 6.

[34]*Minutes of the Tow River Association of Free Will Baptists, 1851-1886* (Original Minutes held by the Free Will Baptist Historical Collection, Free Will Baptist Bible College, Nashville, Tennessee.)

[35]*Abstract,* 7, 8.

[36]Ibid., 8.

[37]See A. Leland Jamison, "Religions in the Perimeter," in *The Shaping of American Religion,* Vol. 1: *Religion in American Life,* ed. by James Ward Smith and A. Leland Jamison (4 vols., Princeton: Princeton University Press, 1961), 167-172, for the clearest summary of sectarian characteristics as developed in the Troeltsch-Niebuhr theory.

[38]Marini, *Radical Sects,* 1-7.

[39]*A Treatise of the Faith of the Freewill Baptists* (1834), 80-83.

[40]*The Church Member's Book—Or Admonitions and Instructions for all Classes of Christians* (Dover, N.H.: Published by the Free-will Baptist Printing Establishment, 1847), 24.

[41]B. Minard, *A Remarkable Experience of Elder Benjamin Randall* (Houlton, Maine: Published by the Author, 1890), 24.

[42]*A Treatise of the Faith and Practice of the Freewill Baptists* (Dover, N.H.: Published by the Free will Baptist Printing Establishment, 1874), 32.

[43]*Treatise—Freewill Baptists* (1834), 84-87.

[44]*Treatise of the Faith and Practice of the Free-will Baptists* (Dover, N.H.: The Freewill Baptist Printing Establishment, 1869), 33, 34.

[45]*Abstract,* Preface.

[46]*A Brief Confession of Faith,* quoted in William L. Lumpkin, *Baptist Confessions of Faith* (Philadelphia: The Judson Press, 1959), 230. This is the English *General Baptist Confession of 1660.*

[47]*Abstract,* 7.

[48]*An Abstract of the Former Articles of Faith, Confessed by the Original Baptist Church, Holding the Doctrine of General Provision, With a Proper Code of Discipline* (New York: Printed by D. Fanshaw, 1855), 7.

[49]*Treatise—Freewill Baptists* (1834), 10-14.

[50]*Abstract* (1812), 6; *Minutes of the Sixth Annual Session of the Arkansas State Association of Free Will Baptists* (1903), 6.

[51]*Minutes of the Nolynn Association of Separate Baptists* (1823), 6.

[52]Morgan Scott, *History of the Separate Baptist Church* (Indianapolis: Printed at the Hollenbeck Press, 1901), 107.

[53]*Abstract* (1855), 8.

[54]Ibid.

[55]Enoch Place, "Journal," *The Free Will Baptist* (Wednesday, May 27, 1896), 2.

[56]*Treatise—Freewill Baptist* (1834), 108n.

[57]Ibid., 108, 109.

[58]Ibid., 110. "It is the usual practice of our connection, at the time of communion, to invite all Christians of good standing in any evangelical church, to partake with us; as, in general, such persons only are known as 'true believers'"; G. W. Million and G. A. Barrett, eds. *A Brief History of the Liberal Baptist People in England and America from 1606 to 1911* (Pocahontas, Ark.: Liberal Baptist Book and Tract Company, 1911), 17.

[59]*Treatise—Freewill Baptist* (1834), 112.

[60]Jesse Heath, *Letter* dated May 29, 1827 in *The Morning Star* (June 28, 1827).

[61]Buzzell, *The Life of Elder Benjamin Randall,* 121.

[62]*Treatise-Freewill Baptist* (1834), 94, 95.

[63]*Abstract* (1812), 15, 16.

[64]*Abstract* (1855), 11.

[65]*Minutes of the South Carolina General Conference of Free Will Baptists, 1883 to 1922* (original minutes held by the Free Will Baptist Historical Collection, Free Will Baptist Bible College, Nashville, Tennessee), 50.

[66]"South Carolina General Conference" (1882), 77.

[67]*Abstract* (1812), 16, 20.

[68]*Treatise—Freewill Baptists* (1834), 143; *Minutes of the South Carolina General Conference* (1882), 78; *Minutes of the Tow River Association of Free Will Baptists.*

[69]*Minutes of the South Carolina General Conference* (1882), 78.

[70]*Minutes of the One Hundred and Sixty-sixth Annual Session of the Central Conference of the Original Free Will Baptists* (1914), 3.

[71]*Minutes of the Bethlehem Free Will Baptist Church, Tennessee* (1847-1874); "Freewill or Free Baptists," *Free Baptist Cyclopaedia,* 208.

[72]*Minutes of the Pantego-Concord Free Will Baptist Church* (1851), original Minutes held by the Free Will Baptist Historical Collection, Mount Olive College, Mount Olive, North Carolina, 21.

[73]Ibid.

[74]William Warren Sweet, *Revivalism in America* (Gloucester, Mass.: Peter Smith, 1965), 133.

[75]*Minutes, Mt. Moriah Free Will Baptist Church* (1850-1880), original Minutes held by M. P. Gore, McShan, Alabama, 36.

[76]*Minutes, Pantego-Concord Church* (1850).

[77]This is the only time "consistory" appeared in the nineteenth Century records. It evidently was local in nature (limited to members of the local church) and had temporary authority. More than likely, a new consistory was chosen for each case brought before the church. There is no way to tell if this was a denominational process or if it was unique to the Pantego-Concord Church. In the North Carolina General Conference, by 1855, the Church was required to call two or more elders and three of their own members as a committee to investigate charges against the settled pastor. This would seem to indicate that if Pantego-Concord's "Consistory" was not the model, it was at least one type of investigating committee common to the day.

[78]*Minutes, Pantego-Concord Church* (1852), 15, 16.

[79]*Abstract,* (1812), 17-18; *Abstract* (1855), 15; *Minutes, Mt. Moriah* (1852), 3; *Minutes of the Tom's Creek Free Will Baptist Church, Kentucky* (1915), original Minutes held by the Tom's Creek Church, Paintsville, Kentucky, 73; *Minutes, North Carolina General Conference* (1884), 2, 3.

[80]*Minutes of the South Carolina General Conference* (1868), 44.

[81]Ibid., *1882,* 79; *1899,* 113; *Minutes, Mt. Moriah Church* (1851), 6.

[82]"Minister's Meeting, United Baptist." *The Christian Index,* Vol II, No. 33 (August 18, 1843), 583. This Association later became the Chattahoochee Association of Free Will Baptists.

[83]*Minutes of the North Carolina Original Free Will Baptist General Conference* (1853), 4.

[84]*Minutes of the Twenty-fourth General Conference of Freewill Baptists* (1880), Vol. II. (Boston: F. B. Printing Establishment, 1887), 401.

[85]*Minutes of the General Conference of the Original Free Will Baptists of North Carolina* (1884), 6.

[86]Ibid. (1892), 6.

[87]*Minutes—New England Freewill Baptists* (1841), 335.

[88]Marini, *Radical Sects,* 158.

[89]Ibid., 158, 159.

[90]Ibid., 159.

[91]John Buzzell, *Religious Magazine,* I, 141, 142, quoted in Marini, *Radical Sects,* 160.

[92]*Minutes of the General Conference of the Freewill Baptist Connection, Third General Conference, 1829.* (Dover, N.H.: Published by the Freewill Baptist Printing Establishment, 1859), 45, 46.

[93]David Marks, *Life of David Marks* (Limerick, Maine; Printed at the Office of *The Morning Star,* 1831), p. 364.

[94]D. E. Dortch, ed., "Preface," *Zion Free Will Baptist Gospel Voices* (Ayden, N.C.: Free Will Baptist Publishing Co., 1901).

9

New Beginnings to 1875

Attitudes toward and difficulties over slavery, to be discussed later, would deny unity to the Free Will Baptists until late in the nineteenth century, and even then, alliances were weak and sensitive. Though New England was directly responsible for the founding of Free Will Baptist churches in the Midwest and as far west as Nebraska and Texas, distance from the larger part of the General Conference allowed many groups to develop a cooperative but independent spirit.

Other factors also contributed to the uneasy alliance with New England and, at the same time, dictated limited numerical growth in most every area except New England proper. The lack of an educated ministry, isolation, social and economic factors, the rural nature of the movement outside of New England, and the lack of a missionary vision doomed much of the denomination to a continual struggle for survival until after the founding of the National Association in 1935. It must be admitted, of course, that both the tentative unity and the struggle for survival constituted the salvation for the remnant of the denomination when New England finally merged with the Northern Baptists in 1911. Had the bonds of unity been more tightly bound or had the southern and Western groups been more dependent on New England, the merger would have had the potential for destruction for the entire denomination. As it was, it had little impact on those who wished to remain Free Will Baptists.

In spite of limited numerical growth, expansion was an exciting aspect of Free Will Baptist life in the nineteenth century. New groups, though most often quite small, began to spring up both south and west. In fact, by the end of the period under investigation in this section of the text, there were so many new groups it has been impossible to deal with each one individually. This chapter then, by necessity, has been limited to the larger new beginnings that developed before 1875. New movements after that time will be mentioned later in less detail.

South Carolina

As mentioned earlier, Free Will Baptists can trace their heritage to a number of different backgrounds including the Congregationalists, the General Baptists in North Carolina, the General Baptists in Illinois, and the Separate Baptists. But most often, new groups were born as a result of the missionary zeal of older Free Will Baptist associations. Such was the case in South Carolina.

Reading Moore—a Pioneer Missionary in South Carolina[1]

Reading Moore was one of the earliest preachers in the denomination. He was born in 1781 and grew up in the vicinity of the Grimsley Free Will Baptist Church in Greene County. He became a member of the Grimsley church and received his early training from the Free Will Baptists in that area. He was ordained as a Free Will Baptist minister in 1816.[2] It would be difficult to find a better choice for the first missionary to South Carolina. Moore was a part of the denomination during its transition from General Baptist to Free Will Baptist and so was well-acquainted with the doctrines of the church and its struggle for identity. He also enjoyed the privilege of sitting at the feet of Jesse Heath and James Roach, the recognized leaders of the denomination. His ordination provided the final credential needed for his own work in a new territory. He soon left the now settled field of service in North Carolina and traveled south to the state where two General Baptist missions had failed earlier. More than twenty-five years had passed since the last General Baptist congregation had disappeared and Moore now found an eager audience for his message of general atonement.[3] Recently discovered documents suggest that Moore already had begun his pioneer mission work in South Carolina before he was officially ordained. Elder J. B. Moore, who probably served as the clerk for Bethel Church in Marion County, spoke of Reading Moore's early ministry in the state in a Preface to the Records of Bethel Church.

> . . . we Can Safely Say that the Bethel Church was orgernized by Eld. Redding Moore Between the dats of <u>1820</u> and <u>1830</u>. Elder Redding Moore who was onced a citizen of green County North Carolina, and came to South Carolina in the year 1816 who was then a member of Grimsley church in green county North Carolina and at that time was a Licinuate Preacher and in the fall of 1816 he Redding Moore went back to North Carolina at the sitting of the Eastern Conference, and was ordained to the Minerstry then return home to South Carolina. . . .[4]

In their earlier work, *History of the Free Will Baptists of North Carolina*, Thad Harrison and J. M. Barfield placed Moore in South Carolina in 1816, but failed to include adequate details. For some reason, the missionary preacher did not appear in the state's census for 1820, but other documents clearly substantiated his early presence there. He was present in the 1830 census and the Equity Records of Marion County, South Carolina, include notice of a land purchase by Reading Moore on March 5, 1816. The land was purchased from William Alsobrook and the sale was probated before Turner Bryan, the local Justice of the Peace, on June 1 of the same year.[5] These sources suggest that J. B. Moore was correct in his assumption that Reading had already been busy in South Carolina some months before his ordination in North Carolina.

Later in the *Preface*, J. B. Moore identified three churches as the first fruits of Reading's work in the state—Mother Church, Little Sister, and Pine Grove. The first church was planted in Clarendon County and the other two in the county of Williamsburg. J.B. Moore suggested that Reading Moore drew these three churches together in 1818 to form the South Carolina Conference.[6] This early date would seem to be difficult to substantiate. *The Minutes of the Free Will Annual Conference in North Carolina*, 1831, indicated that the South Carolina churches were not formally released from that organization until 1831.[7] In any case, the new conference prospered both in the number of churches and in membership. In 1830, while still part of the North Carolina conference, South Carolina boasted three churches, 50 members, and three ministers—Reading Moore and two new workers who had joined him from North Carolina just that year.[8] Beyond this limited information there is little known of the Free Will Baptists in South Carolina from the birth of the first conference in 1818 to the founding of the of the South Carolina General Conference in 1858.

The South Carolina General Conference

The state's General Conference was organized in 1858 when 13 churches met together at Ebenezar church in Williams Berg District. Moab Hewit was elected moderator, and C. F. Osborn and I. F. Cook were appointed "clarks." Other leaders included B. Rishberg, W. R. Johnson, J. H. Johnson, W. T. Walters, John Wilson, I. Willson, Right Willson, and S. More. At this point, the churches were not identified by name but rather by district. Letters were read from two churches in Clarendon District, seven in Williams Berg, two in Darlington, one in Marion, and one in Sumter.[9] In the 1859 minutes, 13 individual churches reported by name, and the districts were identified as counties. In that year, the General Conference boasted 4,538 total members,[10] and in 1860, the list of ordained ministers included John Wilson, Samuel More, Moab Hewit, Samuel McKinsey, Right Willson, J. R. Lloyd, and Benjamin Joiner. J. N. Ridgeway was added to the list as a licensed minister.[11]

The War Between the States had a dramatic impact on the General Conference and, after the war, only 671 members remained. The first signs of recovery appeared in 1874 when it was agreed that there should be two General Conferences in the state, one on either side of Black River. Since the minutes for both that year and the following year were silent concerning the actual establishment of a new conference, it is supposed that the division of convenience did not come until 1876 when the Santee Conference was organized. The mother conference continued to be known as the South Carolina General Conference.[12]

Organization and discipline for the churches in the South will be covered more thoroughly in a later chapter; but it should be mentioned here that South Carolina tended to be more strict in its discipline, and that organization in the Conference was much more complex. In 1876, an "elder of government" was chosen by the South Carolina General Conference and was to have jurisdiction over all of the members belonging to that association.

A few years later, the terms "bishop" and "elder of government" seemed to be used synonymously. In 1882, each Quarterly Meeting was asked to appoint a committee of investigation "whose duty it shall be to investigate reports of inconsistency with ministerial usefullness and propriety and to settle difficulties between ministers which are connected with their respective Conferences."[13] From this time, the office of elder of government became less and less important and in 1883, was abolished. For at least a few years, a "ruling elder" was chosen to oversee the different quarterly meetings. But this office, as well, seems to have been short-lived.

In 1897, in an attempt to confirm their long and fruitful heritage, the South Carolina Conference changed the title of its minutes to read *Minutes of the Seventy-Ninth Session of the Annual Conference of Original Free Will Baptists of South Carolina*. This was the first attempt to trace the heritage of the South Carolina Free Will Baptists back to Reading Moore's arrival in the state in 1816.

The final step of organization came in 1912 when the State Convention was organized at Horse Branch Church.

Georgia
Theories of Origin

FROM CALVINIST TO ARMINIAN

The Free Baptist Cyclopaedia suggests that Free Will Baptists in Georgia had their beginnings at least as early as 1826, and possibly earlier, in what is now Muskogee County near the city of Columbus. When the *Cyclopaedia* was published in 1886, and when it was revised in 1889, the editors knew nothing of a Free Will Baptist ministry there before 1826. They point back to a series of revivals about 1826 that included the preaching of a general atonement that upset a number of the Calvinistic brethren in the area. In 1831, several churches from the Flint River and Ocmulgee Calvinistic Association rejected the *Philadelphia Confession of Faith* and organized into the United Baptist Association. This occurred at Sharon in 1831. The new association was Arminian in belief and allowed each church to practice either open or closed communion at its discretion. Open communion ordinarily was related to Arminian bodies. The association continued a few years and then disbanded.[14] J. H. Campbell, writing in 1874, attributed the founding of the association to Cyrus White. He, too, described the new group as "Arminian" in theology.[15]

This early introduction of Arminian theology on the Georgia scene should not be surprising. The same Virginia exodus that had sent Separate Baptist preachers to Kentucky and Tennessee also had provided a new brand of ministry for Georgia. Had this Separate movement not experienced failure, Georgia Free Will Baptists would be able to claim the same heritage as that of Tennessee.

Some time before 1788, Jeremiah Walker moved to Georgia in an attempt to overcome two moral difficulties that had occurred during his ministry in Virginia. In 1788, he returned to his church in Virginia and asking forgiveness, was restored to full membership. On his promise of future faithfulness, he also was allowed to resume his ministry. Returning to Georgia, he soon adopted an Arminian position and began to preach his new doctrine throughout the Georgia Baptist Association, a Calvinistic organization. By 1790, at least three other ministers had joined him. David Tinsley, Matthew Talbot, and Nathaniel Hall also had served in Separate Baptist circles in Virginia and, in the light of recent Separate history, were likely candidates for conversion to Arminianism.[16]

Unlike the Separates in Tennessee, Walker and his colleagues formed an entirely new General Baptist Association, leaving the old Separate tradition behind. The association only met six times— 1790 to 1795[17]—and then disbanded, but the ground had been cultivated for the coming of other Arminian enterprises in days to come.

The first harvest of that cultivation came in the founding of the United Baptist Association in 1831. *The Free Baptist Cyclopaedia*, published in 1889, concluded that the United Baptist Association had disbanded prematurely and that some of its leaders continued to dream of a new association based on Arminian principles. The result of those dreams was the Chattahoochee United Free-Will Baptist Association, organized in the fall of 1836. The organization was held at the Newtemon Church in Henry County, the same church in which the old United Baptist Association had been organized in 1831. Elder Cyrus White, who had been one of the leaders of the earlier movement, was elected moderator and Priar Reaves was appointed clerk. C. C. Martin, who later became a major leader among the Free Will Baptists, was a licensed preacher at the time of organization.[18] The organization was described as Arminian in belief and open communion in practice.

THE JOHN BROADNAX AND MUSKOGEE COUNTY THEORY

Damon Dodd, in *Marching Through Georgia*, suggested an earlier and totally different beginning for the Free Will Baptists in the state. Using materials provided by the family of an early Georgia preacher, Dodd concluded that John Broadnax left South Carolina some time before the beginning of the nineteenth century, traveled through Florida and into Alabama, and eventually settled in what is now Muskogee County, Georgia. After settling in the small town of Columbus, Broadnax began a prayer meeting in his home that grew so rapidly the congregation found it necessary to move to a large shed that serviced a sawmill in the city. Broadnax, preaching free will, free grace, and free salvation, so excited his parishioners that they asked to be organized into a Free Will Baptist church. According to Dodd, the first Free Will Baptist church in the state of Georgia was organized between 1793 and 1795 in Columbus. The name chosen for the new church was Providence. Mr. Broadnax donated a part of his own land for a building, and soon the congregation had made provision for a meeting house on the new property. Admitting that there are no extant written records to substantiate this fact, Dodd stated that he received the information from living descendants of John Broadnax. An old family Bible identified Broadnax as the founder and organizer of Providence church.[19] Dodd went on to say that Elder Cyrus White, the moderator of the United Baptist Association, became acquainted with John Broadnax and was converted to a Free Will Baptist persuasion. It should be remembered that White had already begun to preach an Arminian message.

WHEN THEORIES BREAK DOWN

There are a number of difficulties with both theories of the birth of the Free Will Baptists in Georgia—that proposed by *The Free Baptist Cyclopaedia* as well as the one by Dodd. While it is more than likely true that the old United Baptist Association later added the "Free Will Baptist" designation to its name, this seems to have come much later than the 1836 date suggested by the *Cyclopaedia*. The minutes for the association still used the "Chattahoochee United Baptist Association" title at least as late as 1854. The new name probably was not added until about 1860.

Unfortunately, there are a number of years for which minutes are not available, and it is impossible to date the addition of the new name to the United Baptist title. Later they were known as the Chattahoochee United Free Will Baptist Association.[20] Even so, newly discovered documents have revealed that the newer name was used in informal conversation quite early. John Crowley, in the process of researching Primitive Baptist history in Southwest Georgia, found references to the Free Will Baptists in that area as early as the decade between 1820 and 1830. Crowley reports that in 1830, Lewis St. Johns, a licensed preacher, was ejected from the Tired Creek Primitive Baptist Church for heresy. The church had worked with St. Johns for about two years. In 1835, several members were expelled from Richland Creek Primitive Baptist Church, a daughter church of Tired Creek, for heretical beliefs. Later, this group was identified as Free Will Baptist.[21] Crowley's study offered exciting new light on earlier theories about Free Will Baptist beginnings in Georgia, but one or two points need to be clarified. It would seem that Lewis St. Johns was dismissed from Tired Creek in October 1828, but that he was forgiven and restored to fellowship in 1830.

> Saturday before the first Sunday in October, 1828. The Church met in conference took up Brother St. Johns case being the unfinished business of last conference and being fully convinced that Brother St. Johns was in error labored to convince him of it but failing to so (sic) and he persisting in the error it was on motion agreed that he be excluded from this church—[22]

The church records did not define the exact nature of St. Johns' error. He was a member of the church in good standing and had served on its Presbytery as late as August of the year of his excommunication.[23] While one might assume that the error was theological, it has proven difficult to confirm that conclusion. In any case, St. Johns was reinstated to full membership just two years later.[24] Crowley probably was correct in his assumption that the group excluded from Richland Creek in 1835 was Free Will Baptist. On July 10, 1835, John, Wiley, and David Blewett, Reuben Dubose, Wiley, Nancy, and Lucy Horne, and Mary Ricks were excommunicated for heresy. Again, the exact nature of their error was not included. But on April 11th of that year, Huldah St. Johns was excluded for ". . . violation of the 11th Article of our Decorum," a statement speaking to the eternal nature of both blessing and judgment, and on October 15, 1838, Rebecca Blewett was publicly accused of being a Free Will Baptist.[25] Two of the 1835 group, John Blewett and Wiley Horne, came to Richland Creek from Tired Creek and were charter members of the newer church. It does not seem too far-fetched to assume that Rebecca Blewett was influenced by members of her family and that she was guilty of the same sin for which they had been excluded three years earlier. It is somewhat more difficult, however, to determine that Lewis St. Johns was party to the same heresy.

Crowley's work proved to be especially valuable in its discovery of the early use of the Free Will Baptist name in Southwest Georgia. In addition to the church records, Crowley also unearthed a reference to the name in a letter to *The Primitive Baptist*, dated March 1, 1838. There, Wiley Pearce speaks of Free Will Baptists in Southwest Georgia and of their increasing popularity. He identifies them as ". . . Whiteites, or . . . Free Wills, or soft shells, who appear to be walking in their silver slippers as it is a pleasant time for them."[26]

Finally, on June 9, 1843, the editor of *The Christian Index* recorded the receipt of minutes from various associations including a set from the Chattahoochee United (Free Will) Baptist Association.[27]

However, in a chart of Baptist associations in Georgia published in *The Index* on August 4, 1843, the Chattahoochee Association was listed only as United Baptist. In a personal letter to the author, Dr. Robert Gardner has attempted to shed light on the mystery of the names. ". . . Let me draw a conclusion for you. The association was Free Will, but did not use that term for itself. *The Index* editor applied that term to the association, to be sure his reader knew which association he was talking about. This material does NOT provide information concerning when the association first used Free Will [to identify itself]."[28]

The other problem is doctrinal. In 1843, the minutes for the ministers' meeting of the United Baptist Association were published in *The Christian Index*, a Calvinistic Baptist paper and in that issue, the association advocated a general atonement, "that the blessings of salvation are made free to all by the gospel, that it is the immediate duty of all to accept it by cordial and obedient faith, and that nothing prevents the salvation of the greatest sinner on earth but his own voluntary refusal to submit to the Lord Jesus Christ. . . ."[29] In the article on perseverance, however, the statement of faith waffled to some degree.

> That such only are Christians as endure unto the end; that their persevering attachment to Christ is the grand mark that distinguishes them from superficial professors; that a special providence watches over their welfare and they are kept by the power of God, through faith, unto salvation.[30]

But waffle or not, the gist of the statement leaned toward the doctrine of perseverance of the saints. The problem was compounded in the minutes of 1850 when the revised statement gave unusual attention to the doctrine of original sin, supported election, and defended a strong statement on perseverance.[31]

Dodd and others were correct in identifying Cyrus White as an Arminian. As early as 1830, Jesse Mercer, a Calvinistic Baptist preacher, exposed White's Arminian tendencies in a series of letters printed and made available for public distribution.[32] But from that point, the waters become extremely muddy. Unanswered questions become the order of the day. Did the Chattahoochee United Baptist Association reconvert to Calvinism after the death of White, and eventually, turn to Arminianism for a second time? If Broadnax and White did meet and strike an alliance (such a relationship would have had to have been early since Dodd suggested that Broadnax had died by 1821), why did the Chattahoochee Association fail to adopt the Free Will Baptist name until as late as 1860?

Since there was another United Baptist Association in Georgia, it would be easy to assume that the two were confused and the other United Baptist Association, rather than the Chattahoochee, gave birth to the Free Will Baptists in the state. That simple solution, however, proved unworkable. A brief statement in the January 13, 1843, issue of *The Christian Index*, identified some of the churches of the Chatthoochee Association as "Whiteite" in background. In fact, the association itself was tied to White in the article. There is no doubt but that the Chattahoochee United Baptist Association, that taught election and perseverance in 1850, was the same association identified by the *Free Baptist Cyclopaedia* as the United Free Will Baptist Association begun by White in 1836.[33] The *Cyclopaedia* was correct in assuming that the Chattahoochee Association could be dated as early as 1836, that it was related to Cyrus White and his ministry, and that it eventually would assume the newer name— Free Will Baptist. It was in error in supposing that the newer name could be superimposed on the association as early as 1836.

Dodd's theory also presents difficulty. The early date that Dodd has suggested for the founding of the Providence Church—1793-1795—cannot be substantiated. At that time, the area was still in Indian hands and Muskogee County did not exist. In fact, Columbus did not become a town until 1828.[34] John H. Martin, in a survey of the early newspapers of Columbus, concluded that "there were no churches here during this year. There would occasionally be preaching by some missionary to the frontier heathen, or by some traveling preacher...."[35] Martin's work was published in 1874, and he had access to the original publications.

Nancy Telfair, in her *History of Columbus, Georgia, 1828-1928*, has concluded that "the first churches in Columbus were organized in 1829, the Methodists and the Baptists."[36]

Finally, John Broadnax proved to be something of a mystery man. He has been identified as John T. Broadnax by his great-great granddaughter, and Land Lottery records placed him in Hancock County as late as 1807. Hancock is east of Macon, some one hundred miles from Columbus and Providence Church. It must be recognized, of course, that census records for Georgia are not available for either 1800 or 1810 and that searches for individuals during this time frame are hampered by the fact that the Columbus area was still Indian territory and federal records were not kept. The researcher then is left with Georgia's first and second Land Lotteries in 1805 and 1807. In the earlier year, John T. Broadnax, identification No. 1210, applied for a grant in the Lottery but drew a blank ticket. Even though he did not receive the grant, the second Lottery in 1807 found him living in Hancock County on Lot No. 157, District No. 17. This time he applied for a grant in Wilkinson County and it was granted.[37]

The family Bible that Dodd mentioned finally has surfaced but it tends to disprove rather than prove Dodd's assumptions. The Bible actually belonged to another member of the family, James Edward Broadnax. The inscription on the flyleaf read, "James E. Brodnax, his Bible, January the 7. 1850. Given him by a friend. James E. Brodnax was born the 11 day of December 1822. Charity Annamenica(?) was born the 21 day of December."[38] Geraldine Waid, Archivist for the Georgia Free Will Baptist Historical Society determined that John T. Broadnax was not a minister at all. That task was left to James Edward Broadnax, who began preaching in 1850. He served for 35 years as an ordained minister in the Chattahoochee United Free Will Baptist Association.[39] Broadnax family members today credit James Edward with the gift of land that served as home for Providence Free Will Baptist Church.[40] In 1849, James purchased a one and one-fourth acre plot of land adjacent to his grandmother's property. Her property was listed as Lot 191 and James Edward's as Lot 192. Family tradition contends that this is the property that was donated by James for the construction of Providence church. Realizing it is difficult to determine the exact boundaries of the property today, it is assumed that this is the property on which the church now stands.[41]

Though all of our questions have not been answered, the Georgia picture has become somewhat clearer. Dodd's argument for a late eighteenth century birth for the Free Will Baptists in the state has proven unacceptable, but there is now strong evidence that the name "Free Will Baptist" was used as early as 1830 to identify those United Baptists who had rejected Calvinism in favor of the doctrine of general atonement. It is quite clear that the Chattahoochee United Baptist Association was a forerunner of the Free Will Baptists, but it also is clear that the new name was not formally used until well after the middle of the century.

Mid-Century Developments

By the middle of the century, a number of churches began to show interest in Free Will Baptist work in the western part of the state, and some had gone so far as to make overtures that eventually would lead to conversion to Free Will Baptist sentiment. In 1857, a group of Arminian Baptists from Savannah sent representatives to the Chattahoochee Association to investigate their doctrinal structure and the operation of the church at both local and associational levels. The investigating team was impressed and returned to Savannah with a favorable report. The visit finally resulted in the founding of the South Georgia Association of Free Will Baptists.

Soon after, in the early 1860's, new churches were organized in Cedartown, Rome, LaGrange, Newnam, and Carrolton and these new congregations became the nucleus for the Liberty Association of United Free Will Baptists.

No other Associations were formed until the Ogeechee in 1878. Martin followed in 1887 and Georgia Union, representing Pulaski, Dodge, Laurens, and Bibb counties, was organized in 1895.[42]

The Georgia State Convention

The first mention of a State Convention for the Free Will Baptist churches in Georgia is found in the minutes of the Chattahoochee Association. In its fifty-seventh session, held with Trinity Church, the body voted to send delegates to the State Convention which was to meet with New Shiloh Church, Erwin County, Georgia, Friday night before the second Sunday in November 1892.

The 1919 minutes attested: "Sister G. A. Fuller came before the Convention and gave a report of the Free Will Baptist Church at LaGrange. This church had been connected with a State Association of Free Will Baptists that had existed from approximately 1885 through 1905 and had been forced to disband because of lack of cooperation. . . ."[43] Records for this early organization are not available and nothing more is known of its history.

The second State Association was organized in December 1917. The idea for the new association had been promoted for at least two years by Neal H. Pharrish, A. L. Davidson, J. B. Little, S. Ealy, A. D. Emanuel, and J. A. Blanton. Laymen involved in the promotion were W. H. Holmes, W. M. Wilson, Sr., P. G. Harvey, T. J. Fort, and F. M. Mosely. In the organizational meeting in 1917, Pharrish was elected as moderator, T. J. Fort as secretary, P. G. Harvey as treasurer, and H. L. Lumpkin as corresponding secretary. At that time, the new State Convention consisted of Chattahoochee, Georgia Union, Little River, Midway, Ogeechee, and South Georgia Associations. The Martin Association joined in 1919, and Liberty was added in 1921.[44] The State Convention existed until 1932, when decreasing attendance and lack of interest caused its demise.

The present State Association was not organized until five years later. On Tuesday, August 31, 1937, representatives from South Georgia, Midway, Ogeechee, Union, and Chattahoochee met at the Alabama Church in Blackshear to discuss the possibility of forming a new State Association. K. V. Shutes was elected moderator, and T. B. Mellette was appointed secretary.[45] The new state association boasted a full program of activities. Initial organization included the appointment of a Board of Missions (responsibilities included both home and cross-cultural outreach), a Board of Education, a State Evangelist, and plans for an annual camp meeting. During the same meeting, the women of the state organized the State Auxiliary Convention.[46]

By 1940, K. V. Shutes, the new state evangelist, was traveling long distances to meet the needs of the churches in the state. In his report to the association that year he spoke of both tent and local church revivals, radio programs with the potential of reaching 100,000 homes, 110 converts, the founding of one new church and firm prospects for four additional ones.[47]

The first education committee appointed by the new State Association encouraged Georgia Free Will Baptists to support Zion Bible School. This Bible institute was founded by T. B. Mellette, a Free Will Baptist pastor who came to Georgia from South Carolina after completing studies at Duke University. The school disbanded in 1942 after Free Will Baptist Bible College in Nashville became the focus for educational concerns in the denomination. Until that time Zion served as the only option for young Free Will Baptists who desired training for ministry. Two earlier educational institutions, Tecumseh College in Oklahoma and Eureka College (formerly Ayden Free Will Baptist Seminary) in North Carolina had burned and were no longer available.

Zion offered a three year program of study that included English, World Literature, Bible Synthesis, Evans' Great Doctrines, the Book of Romans, the Book of John, the Pauline Epistles, Psychology I and II, and Systematic Theology. The school never had more than five students at one time and its life span was brief. Even so, its graduates would make a significant mark on the denomination's history in the state over the next two or three decades. Zion scholars included Daniel and Chester Pelt, Jim Barnes, Luther Norris, "Scottie" Driggers, W. F. McDuffie, K. V. and S. T. Shutes, and J. B. Lovering. Education at the school was free. No tuition or living expenses were required of the student. The school depended entirely on the generosity of churches and friends in the state.[48]

Alabama
The First Church

REGULAR BAPTIST BACKGROUND

The history of the Free Will Baptists in Alabama, like that in Georgia, is steeped in tradition, but, unlike Georgia, accessible documents and second generation testimony offer a better opportunity to transform tradition into history. Early minutes are available for the first churches established in Alabama as are the organizational minutes for the first association. In addition, the grandson of the founder of the Free Will Baptist movement in Alabama is still living and well remembers his uncle's account of the grandfather's early exploits. This unique opportunity revolved around an unusual and true story. Ellis Gore, the founder of the Free Will Baptists in Alabama, was still fathering children at the ripe old age of 75. His son, Ellis Burdine Gore, was born after Ellis was seventy years old, and a number of other children would follow him. Ellis Burdine's son, M. P. Gore, is still living and enjoys telling the stories of his grandfather's ministry in western Alabama.[49] He not only has served as a second generation link with the origins of the Free Will Baptists in Alabama but also has done an excellent job of preserving documents from the early period.

The first Free Will Baptist church in the state was organized on November 6, 1838. Though not Free Will Baptist at the outset, this church set the stage for the founding of the denomination in the area. A meeting house, dubbed Kingcade after a nearby creek, had been built in the area sometime in 1835 or 1836. Following a tradition established not only in Alabama but in Arkansas and other Southeastern states, the meeting house was built by the community and was "free for any body to preach or worship God."[50] Then in 1838, members from Providence and South Carolina churches (later Yorkville and now Ethelsville Baptist Church, Ethelsville, Alabama) under the leadership of Elders Samuel McGowan and Christman, joined together to organize the Kingcade Baptist Church. The two sponsoring churches were Calvinistic in background, and Kingcade was instituted as a Calvinistic Baptist church. McGowan, pastor at Providence,[51] was the leading force in the founding of the new church.

Only two resolutions were deemed necessary at the time of organization, but one gives some idea of the number of slaves in the area and the attitude of the church toward slavery and slave-holding members. After setting the monthly meeting date in the first resolution, the congregation turned to more important business and resolved that they should ". . . admit slaves in the Church as Members. . . ."[52] The church continued to abide by the resolution until 1869 when the association encouraged the freed slaves to begin their own conference.

In just a few months, the congregation became dissatisfied with the name of the church and young Ellis Gore suggested that its name be changed to Mt. Moriah.[53] This is the first time Gore was mentioned in the Alabama records. His father, Thomas Gore, moved to Alabama in 1817 from Chester County, South Carolina, and settled in the western part of their new state. By 1841, the younger Gore had gained a place of prominence in the church, and when Samuel McGowan left Mt. Moriah in 1841, Gore was elected as pastor. He served the church from September 1841, to September 1883, a ministry of 42 years.

FROM REGULAR TO FREE WILL BAPTIST

The transition from Regular to Free Will Baptist sentiment in Alabama offers one of the most interesting traditions in the denomination's history. Elder Gore's preaching of a general atonement immediately brought him to the attention of his Calvinistic Baptist Association. S. L. Smith, writing in 1888, remembers:

> Nov., 1845, the Difficulty according to the Church Book known as the Split, begun, charges having been brought against him, Elder Ellis Gore, the Pastor for Preaching Spurious doctrin, was reighened [arraigned?] before the Tuskaloosa Association, where he maintained himself as he always did, Preached the doctrin of Free Salvation, of open Communion to his Church, and a large Majority of his Church acceded to the doctrin, & cededed from the mision [missionary?] Church, & declared them Selves Freewill Baptist.[54]

Smith goes on to say that a conference was held, and the new Free Will Baptists were given right and title to the church. The association, however, did not give up the property without a struggle. Before the conference, a committee of twelve, including two ordained ministers, were assigned the task of sitting in conference at Mt. Moriah Church. When Brother S. and Brother L. tried to hold conference, Gore objected and asked on two occasions which church they planned to call into conference. When they finally agreed that it was their purpose to call Mt. Moriah into conference ". . . Brother Gore then Shook his fist in his Face and said, Brother S., I am Moderator of the Mt. Moriah Church, & you had as well try to Put me out of my house, as to attempt to sit in Conference here today or any other time. . . ."[55] Remembering Baptist policy and recognizing that the majority of the church had agreed to withdraw from the conference, Brother L. agreed that he and Brother S. had no right to be in the church, the three men made friends, and Mt. Moriah was left to go its own way.

Only two things are amiss in Smith's report. For some reason, he left out the most interesting part of the story. M. P. Gore, the grandson of Elder Ellis Gore, repeats the tale, told by his father, of Mt. Moriah's evolution from Missionary Baptist to Free Will.

Elder Gore preached free salvation and open communion for a number of years and his church had supported the change in theology, but his Calvinistic ordination left him less than qualified for ministry under the new circumstances. Recognizing the need for new credentials but finding no one in the area who could help him, Gore, according to tradition, traveled to Fayetteville, North Carolina, by horseback in order to obtain Free Will Baptist ordination. When he returned, he reconstituted Mt. Moriah as a Free Will Baptist church.[56]

The second difficulty with Smith's account of the transition related to the timing. As mentioned above, Smith dated the break with the Missionary Baptists in 1845, but Mt. Moriah remained with the Missionary Baptists at least until 1849. In 1845, after being dismissed from the Columbus Association, the church petitioned for membership with the Baptist Union Association. The church was represented by Ellis Gore, W. W. Guyton, and J. Eddins. In 1846, Gore was chosen to preach the introductory sermon at the second district meeting of the Union Association meeting at Oak Ridge Church, and the association's annual conference was held at Mt. Moriah in 1849.[57] Unfortunately, the minutes are missing for 1850 through 1852. There is a good possibility that those notes would have given documentary evidence both of Gore's travels to North Carolina for ordination and of Mt. Moriah's break with the association, but as it stands, we are left with second-generation testimony of these important events. When the minutes resumed in 1853, Gore and Mt. Moriah were no longer a part of the association.

The First Association

Mt. Moriah Association was organized ". . . Fryday the 8th and before the 2nd Sabath, in Nov 1850."[58] Elder Ellis Gore was elected moderator and William C. Easterwood was appointed clerk. Three churches—Mt. Moriah, Macedonia, and New Salem—comprised the membership of the new association. Macedonia and New Salem were organized in 1850, both through the preaching and encouragement of Ellis Gore.[59] Besides a constitution and statement of faith, the organization was based on three early resolutions that included a covenant for the church and statements of personal commitment for the individual members.

> 1st Resolved That having been as we trust, brought by divine Grace to embrace the Lord Jesus Christ, & to give ourselfs, wholy up to him, we do Solemnly and Joyfully covenant with Each other, to walk together, in him with brotherly Love, as our common Lord. We do therefore, in His Strength, engage to exercise a mutual care as members one of another, to promote the growth of the whole body in Christian knowledge, holiness & comfort in all the will of God.

2nd Resolved That we will Cheerfully contribute of our property for the Maintainance of the Poor, and suport of the Gospel.

3rd Resolved That we will neither omit Family and Closet religion at home, nor the too common neglect of religiously training of our Children with others under our care, & and that we will Frequently exhort one another in the Spirit of meekness, according to St. Mathew 18 ch.[60]

The New Salem church burned soon after 1850 and the church disbanded shortly thereafter. By 1869, following The War Between The States, the association was limited to the two churches at Mt. Moriah and Macdeonia.

In 1874, Shiloh in Pickens County, Alabama; Union Chapel and Detroit in Sanford County, Alabama; Bethlehem in Monroe County, Mississippi; and Shiloh in Lafayette County, Mississippi, all petitioned for membership. At that time, the association appointed three union meetings. The Bethlehem Union meeting was to meet the Saturday before the first Sabbath in September 1875. Shiloh was assigned the fourth Sabbath in July 1875, and Mt. Pleasant determined to meet the Saturday before the second Sabbath in August 1875. The articles of faith included general atonement, open communion, and the free moral agency of man before and after conversion.[61]

Recent Developments

Except for Ellis Gore's trip to North Carolina for ordination, the Mt. Moriah Association was purely an Alabama product, but Free Will Baptists in the northern part of the state were closely related to Tennessee, and those in the east were originally part of the Chattahoochee Association in Georgia. Churches along the northern border of the state found it convenient to become a part of either the Tennessee River Association or the Flat Creek Association of Tennessee. By 1881, there were enough of the Alabama churches to form their own association and these, along with churches in Colbert, Lawrence, and Morgan counties, joined together to found the Flint River Association. All of the churches were located in Alabama. By 1884, there were eight churches and five hundred members in the association.[62]

In the eastern part of the state, in 1882, the Alabama churches withdrew from the Chattahoochee Association of Georgia and established their own organization called the South Eastern Association. Within a few years it had 25 churches and over a thousand members. In 1887, the new association gave birth to the State Line United Freewill Baptist Association. This daughter association grew to a total of 14 churches within two years.[63]

The Alabama State Conference was organized in 1911. Though organizational minutes are not available, the minutes of the sixth annual session in 1916 pinpoint the date. The 1916 session was held at Blockton Church in Bibb County. Woods Springfield was moderator, J. E. Hodgins was assistant moderator, and C. B. Searcy was appointed secretary and treasurer. Nine associations reported to the Conference—Bear Creek, Kahaba, Jasper, Liberty, Mt. Moriah, Vernon, South Eastern, State Line, and Morning Star. By 1929, Flint River, Muscle Shoals State Line, and the State Line of Alabama and Mississippi Associations were added to the list.

In a new constitution and set of by-laws, the association adopted the name "The Alabama State Conference of the Original Free Will Baptist Church of Jesus Christ." The name was changed again in 1931 when the minutes speak of the "State Association of Free Will Baptists." In 1931, the State Association boasted 79 churches and 6,852 members. The 1929 and 1930 minutes included the names of state leaders that would eventually have impact on the denomination at large—J. B. Bloss, J. M. Haas, S. T. Shutes, and J. T. Quick.

The name of the State Association was changed again in 1936 to include churches in Mississippi. For at least a few years, the Association was known as the "Alabama and Mississippi State Association of Free Will Baptists."[64] Mississippi would not have its own State Association until 1942.

Arkansas

Free Will Baptist traditions in Arkansas also bear some scrutiny. There are two primary sources of information for the history of the denomination in the state in the early period—*The American Baptist Register, 1851*, and the *Goodspeed Biographical and Historical Memoirs of Northwestern Arkansas*. The latter work was published in 1889. Even with these early sources, there are a number of problem areas. These will be defined as the story continues.

Early Churches

According to Goodspeed, the first Free Will Baptist church west of the Mississippi River was constituted in 1832 by Samuel Whitley. The congregation met at the home of David Pickett on War Eagle, with seven members—Ann and Sallie Whitley, Polly Pickett, Melinda Combs, John Clarke, Ann Perott, and one other that could not be identified. Though the congregation might have met at Pickett's home because of Mrs. Pickett, it is more likely that both were involved and had opened their home as a meeting house for the new church. In other words, there is a good possibility that the unidentified member was David Pickett himself. Goodspeed goes on to add Big Fork Church, near Aurora, as the second church, this one constituted either by Isaac or Samuel Whitley in 1833. F.W. Blackburn and Robert Lee were among the early preachers who aided the Whitleys. Both churches were in Marion County.[65]

Goodspeed probably was correct in everything but the dates of the two churches in the assumption that the Marion County churches were the first Free Will Baptist churches established in Arkansas. It is recognized that Goodspeed's was published quite early and that they probably used eyewitnesses. The reader understands, of course, that even eyewitness accounts, when they are repeated forty years after the fact, are subject to error in date and some of the finer details. Two more contemporary documents now available allow a more accurate dating of the work of Samuel and Isaac Whitley in Marion County. The U.S. Census for 1850 identified Isaac, Charles B., and Samuel V. (?) Whitley in Carroll County, near Marion. The three were about the same age—Isaac 47, Charles 50, and Samuel 46—and probably were brothers. They came to Arkansas from Virginia. Charles arrived in the new state first and established the Union United Baptist Church in Marion County at least by 1838. Isaac was still in Virginia in 1840 and did not arrive in Arkansas until 1842. Samuel preceded him to the new state by some two years. Isaac traveled through North Carolina where he married Elizabeth, and then settled briefly in Missouri where Elizabeth gave birth to their first daughter, Louisa(?). Samuel went instead to Tennessee, married Priscilla, and then arrived in Marion County, Arkansas, about 1841.[66] Samuel quickly responded to his brother's preaching and was accepted into the church by experience on Saturday before the fourth Lord's Day, June 1841. Isaac followed suit and was received by experience and baptized on Saturday before the fourth Lord's Day, July 18, 1842.[67]

The late arrival of Samuel and Isaac and their professions of faith after 1840 negated the earlier date suggested by Goodspeed, but the Whitley churches in Marion County still number among the earliest churches established by the Free Will Baptists in the state. The churches and their United Baptist background also further illustrate the argument that the Free Will Baptists must point to many sources as points of origin.

The mystery of dating, background, and personnel has been solved to some degree by a committee report authorized by the Union United Baptist Association in 1916. The committee included two of the Whitley descendants who were still related to the United Baptist work. I. J. Whitley, A. B. Carlock, and John W. Whitley served on the committee. They were given the task of reviewing the history of the Union Association of United Baptists up to 1916. Using minutes and other materials available at that time, they concluded that the United Baptist churches in Arkansas were directly related to the Primitive Baptist Church established at Middle Ridge, Tennessee, in 1847.

In that same year, an association of Primitive Baptist churches was organized. Reverend Wess, age 75 years, was moderator. Almost immediately, difficulties developed over the questions of "fore ordination" and "free salvation." Wess and his followers represented the old Primitive Baptists and Reverends Goodman, Stubblefield, and C. B. Whitley and their followers represented the new or "United Baptists."[68] The committee reminded its readers that "the doctrine of the United Baptist Church was adopted in 1801 at Old Province Meetinghouse, Clark County, Kentucky, by a joint committee of Elkhorn and South Kentucky Associations."[69] In that case, these United Baptists of Arkansas were not strangers to Free Will Baptist history at all but were a part of the Separate Baptist tradition of Kentucky which had given birth to the Free Will Baptists in Middle Tennessee.

C. B. Whitley, Goodman, and Stubblefield continued to serve in the Middle Ridge, Tennessee area until 1835. At that time, according to the committee report, these three men gathered their families, and with Isaac Boren and Joel Plumley left Tennessee for a new beginning in Arkansas. On the fourth Sunday in July 1838, they organized a church at Plumley's home, the Presbytery consisting of Elders C. B. Whitley, David Stanley, and William C. Reed, a deacon. Other churches were soon organized and on the Friday before the second Sunday in September 1850, the Union Association of United Baptists was formally organized.[70]

This new information answered a good number of the questions raised by Goodspeed's account. The minutes of the Union United Baptist Church clearly indicate that C. B. Whitley was in Arkansas long before his brothers Samuel and Isaac. Those minutes, when compared with the 1850 census and the 1916 committee report place the Whitleys in their proper roles, clearly identify the United Baptist background, and clarify the questions of dating.

Goodspeed probably was correct in suggesting that Samuel and Isaac Whitley were the first to call themselves Free Will Baptists, and there is little question but that they organized the churches at War Eagle and Big Fork. Their 1832 date is not acceptable and must be moved up to at least 1842 and probably to as late as 1845. It also must be agreed that these two early churches were direct by-products of C. B. Whitley's earlier work at Union. In fact, the Union Association itself was closely related to the Free Will Baptists throughout the remainder of the nineteenth century. The association reported to the New England Free Will Baptist General Conference as early as 1883.

> The Union Association was reported as early as 1883 when it had a membership of 507, in ten churches, vis: Big Spring, Center Point, King's River, Liberty, Mt. Pleasant, Mt. Zion, Mulberry Hall, New Bethel, Union, and Walnut Grove. It now reports 876 members. This Association is located in Carroll, Boone, Newton, and Madison Counties, East of the old Mt. Zion Association of Free Will Baptists, with which it keeps up a friendly correspondence by letter.[71]

The above report was published in the *Free Baptist Cyclopaedia*, in 1889, just a few years after the Union Association began to report to the General Conference.

Before leaving the early period, at least two other groups should be mentioned. The Old Mt. Zion Association probably had the same roots as the Union Association. Both were in the same area and date from about the same time. *The American Baptist Register of 1851*, reported that "an Old Mt. Zion Association was organized in 1840, with eleven Arkansas Churches in it. Two of the churches, Prospect and Brush Creek, were organized in 1840. There were seven pastors in the Association."[72] It must be admitted that the *Register* did not identify Mt. Zion Association as Free Will Baptist in 1851. However, *The Free Baptist Cyclopaedia*, published in 1889, identified the Old Mt. Zion Association in the same area of western Arkansas and included two of the churches listed in 1851—Mt. Zion and Sugar Creek. These two churches were organized in 1847 and 1848.[73] Since the Regular Baptists also had established churches in the area by 1840,[74] there is a good possibility that Mt. Zion and Sugar Creek were a part of that association when *The American Baptist Register* was published in 1851. If that were the case, then the two churches, like the United Baptist, had broken with their brethren on the questions of free salvation and open communion.

Franklin County traditionally has been considered another early site for Free Will Baptist ministry. Charles R. Kelliam (Kellum-iam) appeared in the southern part of the county at least as early as 1846. In that year, he served as the postmaster for the area and officially opened the Post Office for Charleston on August 10, 1846.[75] According to the 1850 census for Franklin County, Kelliam came to Arkansas from Vermont by way of North Carolina where he married his wife, Susan. Two children, Charles and Edward, were born in Arkansas. The census listed Kelliam as a dry goods merchant.[76] He exerted a significant amount of influence in the early days of the new community, and eventually it was named Charles Towne. It was not until later, when Kelliam's business failed, that the name was changed to Charleston.[77]

In the same year the post office was commissioned, Kelliam organized a Free Will Baptist church in the community. He remained as its pastor until 1850. Goodspeed, in *The History of Northwest Arkansas*, referred to the church as a Missionary Baptist Church, but did give Kelliam credit for its organization. The editors of Goodspeed's history were aware that both Missionary and

Free Will Baptists existed in the area, for they mentioned the Corinth Free Will Baptist Church in the same discussion.

At least two factors help to explain Goodspeed's failure to recognize Kelliam's Free Will Baptist background. First, the church itself changed hands on a number of occasions and probably was a Missionary Baptist Church by the time Goodspeed's was published in 1889. After Kelliam's ministry ended in 1850, the church remained without a regular pastor until 1857. Darius Buckley assumed the pastorate in that year and continued until 1859 when Reverend T. H. Compere took charge of the congregation and continued with them until the church was disbanded in 1862. It was reorganized in 1876 by Reverend E. L. Compere, who continued to serve the church for the next 12 years.[78] The final reorganization probably was based on Missionary Baptist principles. The second factor is directly related to the social and ecclesiastical atmosphere of this particular time in northwest Arkansas. For the most part, individual congregations did not build their own house of worship, but rather worshiped in community meeting houses that were used by various denominations. Under such circumstances, confusion was not uncommon. The practice is illustrated by statements of the Assistant Marshall in Benton and Marion Counties in 1850.

> The Houses of Publick Worship are generally built by Neighborhoods Free for every denomination. Therefore they cannont be named for any particular denomination.

> There are some 5 or 6 Log Cabbins that have been built by Common labor and for the accomodation of no one sect to the exclusion of another. These will generally accommodate some 150 to 200 each. . . . [79]

Even though Kelliam's ministry in Franklin County was quite brief, his work did not go unnoticed. It was in this area that the Arkansas District Association was organized in 1869.

Pope County also served as an early preaching point for the denomination. Francis M. Hutson (Hudson) came to Arkansas from Alabama sometime before 1850. He was 21 years old at that time and had a son Jeremiah, now five-years old, born in Arkansas.[80]

Little is known of this first church in Pope County except that it was established in 1850 and that Hutson served as one of the deacons.

Later Associations

Most of the later associations will simply be mentioned, but Social Band, because of its uniqueness, must be discussed in some detail. Here again, the denomination's patchwork background is illustrated.

The association was formed at Sugartree Grove Church in Ripley County, Missouri, September 17, 1875. The new association included three churches—Sugartree Grove, 40 members; Brier Creek, 26 members; and Macedonia, 22 members—and chose the name Social Band General Free Will Baptist Association. Elder D. L. Poyner, who had organized both Sugartree Grove and Brier Creek in 1871, was chosen as moderator for the association. I. Whittenburg was appointed clerk.

D. L. Poyner, Samuel Davis, Eliphaz Davis, and L. J. Thornbury were listed as ordained ministers, and G. A. Barrett was added as a licensed preacher.

The association's unusual name must be attributed to Elder Poyner's earlier background in Illinois. Poyner came to the Missouri-Arkansas area from southern Illinois and had presented papers from the Central Illinois Association of General Free Will Baptists in that area. This unusual alliance came about in 1862 or 1863 when a number of Free Will Baptists of the Cumberland Association in middle Tennessee joined a small congregation of General Baptists from Kentucky and moved to Franklin County in southwestern Illinois. There they found other General Baptists and established a number of churches including Friendship, New Hope, Springdale, Union Free Will, and Freedom. Soon after, they joined together in the Central Illinois Association of General Free Will Baptists.[81]

For the most part, Poyner found nothing but opposition from the other churches in the area. Unlike tradition in northwestern Arkansas, local congregations in the northeastern part of the state and in southern Missouri, owned their own buildings. The Missionary Baptists and Methodists were among the more prosperous churches and constructed and controlled their own meeting houses. Almost without fail, they refused to allow the new General Free Will Baptists to use their facilities. When the association was organized in 1875, none of the churches had their own buildings and only two school houses were available for services.

Poyner did find one colleague in the person of Elder Greaf Williams, formerly of the Liberty Association of General Baptists of Missouri. After moving into Poyner's area of ministry, Williams joined the older preacher in founding a new church at Springhill in Randolph County, Arkansas. Charter members included Ellis Wright and Kinsey Hare. The new church was organized in 1874.

This new alliance was destined to be short lived. In early discussions concerning the possibility of an association of churches, both Poyner and Williams were adamant in their determination to retain elements of their own heritage. The most important disagreement centered on the question of a name for the new association. Williams was determined that the new group be called General Baptists while Poyner pushed for the original name, General Free Will Baptists. When the churches met in conference in 1874, the longer name was accepted. Williams left the church in anger and took a large part of the Springhill congregation with him. The Springhill church disbanded and those that remained loyal to Poyner changed their membership to Sugartree Grove. At the time of organization of the new association in 1875, the organization was limited to three churches.[82]

By the time for the second session of the association held at Brier Creek in October 1876, Social Band had added one new church, New Prospect, and had ordained G. A. Barrett and M. R. Langley. F. M. Bates had been licensed to preach. The membership of the four churches totaled 122 at that time. The association continued to prosper, and by 1902, included 14 churches—Sugartree Grove, Macedonia, Grandview, Mountain Grove No. 1, Springhill, Warm Springs, Hickory Grove, Shiloh, New Union, Mount Zion, Walnut Grove, Bethlehem, Little Zion, and New Harmony. That year, Elder D. N. King was elected moderator and N. Y. Gary was appointed clerk.[83]

The Arkansas State Association

The Arkansas State Association was organized in 1898 at Moreland Free Will Baptist Church in Polk County. Local associations included in the initial organization were Antioch, New Hope, Old Mt. Zion, Arkansas District, and Tyronza. Reverend Jesse Jeffrey served as moderator and George W. Burris as clerk. Burris traditionally has been considered the founder of the association.

Some earlier local associations, including Old Mt. Zion, found it difficult to come to terms with Free Will Baptist doctrine. Both Old Mt. Zion and a later Mt. Zion Association had, as late as 1891 and 1898, prescribed to a statement of election and perseverance of the saints. The latter association is now extinct and denominational leaders were not aware of its existence until David Joslin, Executive Secretary for the Arkansas State Association of Free Will Baptists, discovered a set of minutes dated 1898. At that time, the *Articles of Faith* included, "We believe in the corruption of the human nature and the inability of man to recover himself by his own free will and ability," and "we believe that saints who persevere in grace until the end will be saved and not one of them will be finally lost."[84] Admittedly, the language could be interpreted in a number of ways and might not have been as antagonistic to Free Will Baptist doctrine as it sounded. However, minutes of the Old Mt. Zion Association for 1891 were much more dogmatic in the statement on perseverance. "We believe that saints persevere in grace and not one of them will finally be lost."[85]

By 1903, the new State Association had revised the confession so that it included a careful statement of general atonement and a statement, although somewhat confusing, relating to the possibility of falling from grace. At this time, the association suggested that Christians would persevere until the end if they were to inherit eternal life.[86]

By the thirty-first annual session of the State Association in 1928, all questions of theology had been settled and the association had adopted a carefully worded statement of faith that was in full agreement with Free Will Baptist practice elsewhere. Recognizing that true believers had access to God's help in godly living, the statement agreed that they should persevere in divine grace until the return of Christ. It was understood, however, that those who willfully refused or neglected to perform their duty would backslide and find themselves in danger. If they persisted in the backslidden condition, they could be eternally lost.[87]

Free Will Baptists in Arkansas were among the first in the denomination to organize a State Association, but they were slow to accept other larger organizational schemes. George W. Burris, who had masterminded the organization of the State Association, attended the first session of the Co-operative General Association in 1917 at Pattonsburg, Missouri, but was displeased with some of the decisions that were made and discouraged Arkansas from uniting with the larger organization.

Though representatives from Arkansas were present at the organizational session of the National Association in 1935, they did not encourage membership at that moment. It was not until 1946 that Arkansas finally petitioned the National Association for membership.[88]

Kentucky
The Story Behind the Story

Arminian Separatists established a strong ministry in southern Kentucky as early as 1785 and, eventually, gave birth to the Free Will Baptist denomination in the state of Tennessee. For some reason, the new influence did not touch Kentucky, and the Separates that remained in Kentucky continued with the older denomination.

Until recently, it was supposed that the Free Will Baptists did not appear in Kentucky until late in the nineteenth century. Even reliable sources such as *The Free Baptist Cyclopaedia*, published in 1889, failed to identify a Free Will Baptist ministry in the state before 1879, and it must be admitted that the present day movement cannot be dated before that time.

A recently discovered letter indicates that the old theory has to be discarded. Elder Jesse Lane, in a letter dated Evansville, Vanderburg County, Indiana, August 29, 1829, described a flourishing Free Will Baptist community in the state by that time. Though Lane himself spent most of his time in Indiana, he evidently traveled extensively in Kentucky. After describing the scope of the work in Indiana, he reminded his readers that Kentucky also boasted an association of about 1,200 members. The association met regularly in October.[89] This earlier Free Will Baptist movement was doubtless the product of the missionary effort of Randall's General Conference in New England. Even so, the presence of a missionary so far west at this early date was at first surprising.

But then, David Marks, one of the most respected preachers of the New England segment of the denomination, traveled as far as Ohio in 1822. In his memoirs, he spends a great deal of time describing the difficulties of travel between New England and the Midwest. In spite of his difficulties, he found that other preachers had preceded him. John Colby visited the area as early as 1815, and Elder J. N. Hinkley founded a church in Milan, Ohio, in 1819. Marks also found churches in Greenfield, Clarksfield, and Portsmouth. The Portsmouth church already had gained a membership of 112.

Marks eventually visited the northern shores of Kentucky but found the crossing of the Ohio River a frightening experience. He did not find a Free Will Baptist ministry in the area.[90]

In any case, obstacles notwithstanding, Lane and others found their way from New England to the wilderness regions of Ohio and Kentucky.

This early Free Will Baptist Association in Kentucky never made the records of the General Conference, and by 1889, it had disappeared from the state and from the denomination's memory. Its discovery, however, has changed the Free Will Baptist story for the state of Kentucky.

Starting Over

Though the older movement disappeared quite early, origins of the present Free Will Baptist ministry in the state can be traced back to at least 1879. Here again, history and tradition tend to find themselves in conflict. Both New England and Kentucky agreed that the Johnson County Quarterly Meeting was organized about 1879 and was made up of churches at Hager Hill, Little Blain, and Tom's Creek churches. They also agreed that Mud Lick Church was added in 1881. At that point, the agreement ended. New England assumed the first churches in the state were organized by William Calhoun, a New England missionary with headquarters in southern Ohio.[91]

Kentucky, on the other hand, claimed that the churches there already had declared themselves Free Will Baptists in theology and policy and that Calhoun was asked to visit them and to give instruction in their new-found faith.

Their story was not unlike the traditions we have discovered in other states. According to tradition, the first Free Will Baptist church in the state had been organized as the result of a disagreement at the Mingo United Baptist Church. This first church was organized in Johnson County at the mouth of Rush Fork of Tom's Creek. The disagreement centered around the question of discipline rather than theology, but it was serious enough to encourage a minority of the membership to withdraw from the church. The numerical loss was quite small, but Mingo suffered because some of the dissenters numbered among the church's most valuable members.

At the outset, the smaller group intended to organize another United Baptist Church and join the same association that gave counsel to Mingo. They soon found that associational rules demanded reconciliation with Mingo before membership was possible. When that door closed, the new church approached the Free Will Baptist churches in Ohio and asked for advice and instruction.

The major leaders in the transition from United Baptist to Free Will Baptist were James, Nathan, and Eliphus VanHoose.[92]

In this particular case, tradition finally took on the character of factual history. At least three early sources point to the historical accuracy of the story as told by Kentucky's Free Will Baptists. Two of the sources are published histories, and the other is the Record Book for Tom's Creek Church, a primary source in every sense of the word.

Unfortunately, the first record book for the church has not been located, but the second book, offering records beginning with July 19, 1893, does refer to the earlier book and to the organization of the church. The records made it clear that eyewitnesses to the organization were still alive. T. S. Williams was still pastor, and both Eliphus and James VanHoose were still active in the church. With this in mind, there is no reason to doubt the reference to the earlier church book and to the organization was correct and accurate.

The note recorded on the flyleaf of the second *Book of Records* (original handwritten copy) read, "Tom's Creek freewill baptist church was organized in April 1876 by T. S. Williams and a preacher by the name of William Chalhoun from Ohio under a oak tree near the mouth of Sycamore."[93]

By 1893, when the second Record Book was begun, the list of members at Tom's Creek included T. S. Williams, his wife Melissa, Eliphus VanHoose, Free Love VanHoose, Jasper Daniel, Charlie and Jefferson Castle, James Staggs, and James VanHoose. Nathan VanHoose, one of the leaders in the break with the United Baptists in 1876, must have died soon after the new church was organized. His name did not appear in the 1893 list of members.[94]

In the latter days of the nineteenth century and in the early 20th century, Tom's Creek Church produced a number of early Free Will Baptist leaders for the denomination's continuing story in the state. Burns Conley, Frew VanHoose, Daniel Wheeler, Wiley Williams, John Elliott Conley, and others offered leadership and counsel to the denomination for the next several years.

The other two sources, though secondary in character, proved important because they were written almost immediately after the Johnson County Association was organized. J. H. Spencer published his *History of Kentucky Baptists, from 1769 to 1885*, in 1886. Though he was less than generous in citing the Free Will Baptists as a local sect, his contemporary account did give credence to the heritage claimed by the Free Will Baptists.

> There was no church of this sect in Kentucky until within the last few year, and even now its numbers in the State are insignificant. Some few years past, a disturbance originated in Paint Union Association, which resulted in a division of some of the churches, or, at least, in the exclusion of some prominent members. These expelled members were gathered into one or more churches which took the name of Free-Will Baptists. Under the ministry of Thomas S. Williams, these churches increased to the number of four, and, in 1880, aggregated 180 members. They associated under the style of 'Johnson County Quarterly Meeting.' The fraternity is located in the county from which it takes its name, and is a constituent of Ohio Yearly Meeting, an association located in the State whose name it bears. . . .[95]

In a somewhat friendlier account in his 1887 publication of *Big Sandy Valley*, William Ely retold the story of Williams and his split with the United Baptists, but this time in more detail. It was Ely who pinpointed the Mingo Church as the source of the disagreement between Williams and the United Baptists.

In both cases, these early authors confirmed the Kentucky account of the origins of the Free Will Baptists in eastern Kentucky.

The Kentucky State Association

Kentucky was quite late in organizing a State Association. But finally, on May 6, 1939, representatives from Quarterly Meetings in Lawrence County, Johnson County, and Floyd County, met at Tom's Creek Church to discuss the possibility of such an association.

At this first session, Rev. Burns Conley, who had been closely related to Tom's Creek for more than 57 years, explained the purpose of the organization. For the first time, the delegates determined to bring together "all the quarterly meetings of the Free Will Baptist denomination in Kentucky and to unify more completely the work of the denomination."[96] Once the organizational structure was established, Millard VanHoose was elected moderator; Scott Castle, assistant moderator; William W. Moore, clerk; and Irvin Rice, treasurer.

Eventually, other associations within the state joined the new association: Pike County Conference (1942), Boyd County Conference (1948), Kosciusko County (Indiana) Conference (1955), Northern Ohio Quarterly Meeting (1957), Martin County Conference (1959), Blue Grass Conference (1959), Big Sandy Valley Conference (1961), and Green River Association (1965). The Indiana Conference soon withdrew from the association and was involved in the task of establishing a State Association in Indiana.

Ohio

The Early Days

Free Will Baptists in Ohio will not find it necessary to depend on tradition. The state boasts some of the best kept records in the entire denomination. Yearly Meeting records are available at least as far back as 1833. In addition, Ohio exerted a strong influence early in the history of the New England segment of the denomination and, for that reason, General Conference records are more plentiful and accurate.

Even so, there has been controversy concerning the founding of the first church in the state. *The Free Baptist Cyclopaedia* pointed to the work of Eli Stedman and the organization of the Rutland Free Will Baptist Church in Meigs County in 1810. Stedman came to Ohio from New England. He was converted at the Free Will Baptist church in Turnbridge, Vermont, and ordained by the Strafford Quarterly Meeting on October 26, 1802.[97] In 1805, after serving three years in New England, he moved to the Midwest and settled in southern Ohio.[98]

Two other churches, both of which still exist and are part of the denomination, claim to be the oldest existing churches in the state. Porter Church, near Wheelersburg, was founded by Rev. Rufus Chaney in 1817. Arguing that the history of the other church, Old Kyger, is shrouded in confusion, Porter claims to be the oldest Free Will Baptist church in the state existing at the present time.

But Old Kyger also has claimed antiquity. This congregation rejected Porter's heritage and insisted that their church was established by Eli Stedman in 1811, just one year after he began his initial ministry in Rutland.[99] An article published at the beginning of the twentieth century introduced the possibility that Kyger is even older. The article, entitled, "Ohio Free Will Baptist State Convention" and "Ohio River Yearly Meeting," suggested that Kyger was the first Free Will Baptist church founded in Ohio, predating both Rutland and Porter. In this account, the church was founded by Elder Stedman at the home of Paul Darst in 1805.[100] While it seems almost impossible that the earlier date escaped the notice of earlier historians, we do know that Stedman had moved to Ohio by that time. It would seem more likely that he needed five years to establish his ministry and that the organization of the Rutland Church in 1810 was his first. But, on the other hand, it is not far-fetched to suggest that he found a ready audience for his Arminian doctrine and that the Kyger Church was established in his first year in the new state. The church is located just outside of Cheshire, Ohio, ten miles from Rutland and right in the middle of Stedman's parish.

Quarterly and Yearly Meetings

By the middle of the century, Free Will Baptists in Ohio boasted 17 Quarterly and five Yearly Meetings, all of them related to the Randall movement in New England. All of the organizations were important, but many of them joined New England in its merger with the Northern Baptists in 1911 and were lost to the continuing Free Will Baptist witness. Only those that continued to be a part of the present denomination demand our attention at this time.

By 1814, Elder Stedman had organized several churches, including Rutland and Kyger, and in that year these churches joined to organize the Athens Quarterly Meeting. The Quarterly Meeting grew rapidly and soon divided, giving birth to the Muskingum Quarterly Meeting in the same area.

No records remain to indicate the existence of a Yearly Meeting although the two associations probably corresponded and spent time in fellowship. In 1818, a number of the churches within the two associations became discouraged, and many of them consolidated with the Christian Church (Disciples). When David Marks visited Ohio in 1822, he found just a few scattered churches—Alexander in Athens County, a new church at Rutland, and the Porter church some fifty miles away. Reverend John Sleeper had just organized a church at Alexander, and James E. Brown assumed the pastorate of the new church at Rutland. In the fall of 1822, the second Athens Quarterly Meeting was organized with these three churches represented. The Morgan and Columbia churches were added in 1823, and at that time, the association reported a total membership of 186.[101]

This new association continued for just a few years, but its member churches joined forces again in 1831 to organize the Meigs Quarterly Meeting. In that year, the association included First Alexander, Second Alexander, Rutland, Chester, and Morgan churches, with 90 members. Asah Stearns, James Shurtleff, Samuel Thorn, and John Sleeper were the ministers of record.[102]

The Porter church found itself inconvenienced in its association with the Old Athens Quarterly Meeting. The distance simply was too great to make travel for Conferences practical. The church later associated with both Meigs County and the Miami Quarterly Meetings, but finally, in 1833, joined the Madison and Harrison churches to establish the Little Scioto Quarterly Meeting.

Meigs County and Little Scioto Quarterly Meetings joined in 1833 to form the Ohio River Yearly Meeting. This probably was the second Yearly Meeting to be organized in Ohio. The Ohio Yearly Meeting was established in 1824, and the Ohio and Pennsylvania Yearly Meeting had its origin in 1833, the same year as Ohio River. Ohio River becomes especially important to this study because a number of its Quarterly Meetings later refused to join the merger with the Northern Baptists and have remained a part of the denomination to the present time. The Athens Quarterly Meeting (thought to be a second organization for Athens, but actually the third) joined the Yearly Meeting in 1844. Shiloh was begun in 1869 and Jackson was added in 1873. The Hocking Valley Quarterly Meeting and Adelia became a part of the Quarterly Meeting in 1880 and 1882 respectively. Pine Creek Quarterly Meeting was organized in October 1879, and at that time Little Scioto withdrew from the Ohio River Yearly Meeting and with the new Pine Creek Quarterly Meeting established the Ohio and Kentucky Yearly Meeting.

Finally, the Porter Quarterly Meeting was organized December 7, 1901. This Quarterly Meeting was composed of Madison and Porter churches. Ministers present at the time of union were William Shunkwiler, Ezra Shunkwiler, James Brant, J. W. Tillon, I. Smith, and J. Shepherd.

From this group of Quarterly Meetings—Meigs, Jackson, Pine Creek, and Porter—there emerged a continuing Free Will Baptist witness in the state of Ohio. As far as can be determined, all the other Free Will Baptists in the state joined the Randall movement in its merger with the Northern Baptists. The influence of these associations also touched Kentucky. Johnson County Quarterly Meeting in Kentucky joined the Ohio River Yearly Meeting some time after 1879 and this Conference, as well, has remained faithful to the denomination.[103]

Little need be said here about the New England merger with the Northern Baptists as it will be covered more carefully in the next chapter. In the light of Ohio's past relationship with the General Conference, it is somewhat surprising that the four associations, mentioned earlier, remained with the denomination rather than following the Randall movement's example. Ohio was always closely related to the General Conference in New England. The General Conference met in Ohio in 1839, 1856, 1886, and in 1907.[104] The next chapter will attempt to answer this question, but at least part of the answer might be found in the first *Constitution of the Ohio River Yearly Meeting*, published in 1833. "No Quarterly Meeting or Church can be admitted into this body who entertains opinions contrary to the body known as Freewill Baptists, or who may not be willing to be subject to his or their brethren or Gospel principals (Sic)."[105]

First State Association

Free Will Baptists in Ohio might well have been the first to draw all of its constituent bodies together into a State Association. Though this association did not survive, it was significant because of its character and its early date. The association was proposed by a Brother Whitacre at the Ohio River Yearly Meeting on August 8, 1873. The minutes for the next day mentioned that a committee considering the State Association reported, but the report was not concluded. It is certain, however, that the association was organized because the Yearly Meeting session ended with the election of delegates to the new state meeting.

In the same Yearly Meeting, the delegates agreed to cooperate with Ohio Free Communion Baptists, and it is possible that the new State Association was designed to implement this cooperation. Such a theory, however, stretches the interpretation of the minutes beyond ordinary limits. It was much more likely that the Free Will Baptists within the state agreed to draw all of their Yearly Meetings together into one session at least one time during the year.[106]

The association continued at least until 1895 when the Ohio River Yearly Meeting met at First Kyger Church and delegates again were elected to represent that organization at the state level. They also passed a resolution that quite possibly was encouraged by struggle within the state organization. ". . . Resolved that we as a Yearly Meeting express our approval of the work being done by our State Association and we pledge the Executive Board and Field Secretary our hearty cooperation in the work being done to build up our cause in the state."[107]

The discovery of this early state organization was surprising, not only because of its date, but also because of its character. New England influence was prevalent in Ohio from the very beginning, and the organizational structure there was patterned after that of the General Conference. "Associations" and "Conferences" were unknown to these congregations. The use of the term "Association" did not appear until the State Association proposal was made in 1873. The introduction of the new organizational structure might be partially explained by the fact that Free Will Baptists in Ohio began to correspond with congregations of similar nature in the South. In 1880, delegates at the Ohio River Yearly Meeting appointed Rev. D. Powell, T. P. Taylor, and W. J. Fulton to correspond with, and if possible, visit the brethren in the South. In fact, the appointment included an additional task. "Resolved that three persons be appointed to correspond and if possible visit brethren in the South and enlist them in uniting with us. . . ."[108]

The discovery of this early State Association has added a new dimension to Free Will Baptist history in Ohio. Until now, it was supposed that the Free Will Baptists in the state did not organize at this level until 1939.

Ohio and the Twentieth Century

As mentioned earlier, most of the Free Will Baptists in Ohio were involved in the merger with the Northern Baptist Convention in 1911, but at least four Quarterly Meetings continued to cling to their Free Will Baptist heritage. These four were Meigs County, Jackson, Pine Creek, and Porter. By 1915, the old State Association had disappeared, and Ohio churches were looking for new alliances. Pine Creek and Porter, along with Lawrence County Quarterly Meeting, formed the Scioto Yearly Meeting, and joined with the Big Sandy Yearly Meeting of Kentucky and the West Virginia Yearly Meeting to form the Tri-State Association of Free Will Baptists. The association lasted for just a short while and then disbanded.

The present State Association was organized on June 13, 1939 in a meeting held at Porter Church in southern Ohio. Representatives of both the Ohio River and the Scioto Yearly Meetings were present. Gus Graham was elected moderator; Jesse Sizemore, assistant; Grace Peach, clerk; and John Kemper, treasurer. A constitutional committee consisting of William Shepherd, G. D. Webb, and Melvin Dunn penned a preliminary constitution that was offered to the two Yearly Meetings. It was agreed that the churches within the Yearly Meetings would review the constitution and that final organization would be completed on October 7, 1939, again at Porter Church.[109]

Notes for Chapter 9

[1]Varied documents use different spellings—Redding, Reddin, Reading.

[2]Thad Harrison and J. M. Barfield, *History of the Free Will Baptists of North Carolina,* 2 vols. (Ayden, N.C.: The Free Will Baptist Press [1897]), II, 341.

[3]The date for Moore's first preaching in South Carolina had been confirmed in a letter to Samuel Burbank (New England) from Elias Hutchins who was traveling in the South in 1830. "He moved from his brethren in this State, and took up his abode among strangers, that knew nothing of the Free Will Baptists, and began to preach free salvation in South Carolina, about 13 years ago." Elias Hutchins, Letter to Elder Samuel Burbank, Jan. 30, 1830. *The Free Will Baptist Magazine,* III (March 1830), 232. (Herein after referred to as Huthchins Letter). Recent documents have suggested that Moore was active in South Carolina a year earlier, in 1816. (See footnote 4.)

[4]Elder J. B. Moore, "Preface," Records of Bethel Church, July 14, 1901.

[5]Marion County, *South Carolina Deed Book 1* (March 5, 1816), 109, 110, 122, probated June 1, 1816, before Turner Bryan, JP (No recording date); Fifth Census of the United States, 1830; *Population Schedules, South Carolina, Vol. 4. File Microcopies of Records in the National Archives:* No. 39, Roll 172 (1944), 33; Will-Reading Moore, *Transcript of Wills, Marion County, S.C.,* Vol. I, 66-67.

[6]Moore, "Preface."

[7]*Minutes of the Free Will Baptist Conference of North Carolina, 1831,* quoted in Harrison and Barfield, *Free Will Baptists in North Carolina, I,* 168.

[8]Hutchins, *Letter,* 232, 233.

[9]*Minutes of the South Carolina General Conference of Free Will Baptists* (1858), original minutes held by the Free Will Baptist Historical Collection, Nashville, Tennessee, 1, 2.

[10]Ibid. (1859), 7.

[11]Ibid. (1860), 12.

[12]Ibid. (1874), 46; (1876), 50.

[13]Ibid. (1882), 78.

[14]Burgess and Ward, "Georgia," *Free Baptist Cyclopaedia,* 227.

[15]J. H. Campbell, G*eorgia Baptists: Historical and Biographical* (Perry, Ga.: J. W. Burke & Company, 1874), 110, 111.

[16]Benedict, *History of the Baptist Denomination, II,* 389-392; Robert G. Gardner, "The Forgotten General Baptist Association in the South," *The Quarterly Review,* Vol. 39, No. 1 (Oct.-Dec., 1978), 63, 64. Copyright 1978. The Sunday School Board of the Southern Baptist Convention. All rights reserved. Used by permission.

[17]Gardner, "The Forgotten General Baptist Association in the South," 71, 72.

[18]Burgess and Ward, "Georgia," *Free Baptist Cyclopaedia,* 227, 228.

[19]Damon C. Dodd, *Marching Through Georgia—A History of the Free Will Baptists in Georgia* (Published by the author, 1977), 30, 31.

[20]*Minutes of the Nineteenth Annual Session of the Chattahoochee United Baptist Association.* (Columbus, Ga.: DeWolf, Barrett & Wilson, 1854), 1.

[21]*Minutes of the Richland Creek and Tired Creek Baptist Church,* 1830, 1835; John Crowley, *Primitive Baptists of the Wiregrass South, 1815 to Present* (Gainesville, Fla.: University of Florida Press, 1998), 69.

[22]*Minute Book of the Tired Creek Primitive Baptist Church,* Decatur County, Georgia, Saturday before the First Sunday, October 1828, p. 17. [Hereinafter referred to as "Tired Creek".]

[23]*Richland Creek Primitive Baptist Church Book,* Decatur County, Georgia, August 16, 1828, p. 3. (Hereinafter referred to as "Richland Creek.")

[24]"Tired Creek," April 1830, p. 21. Dr. Wayne Faircloth, the present Clerk of the Tired Creek Primitive Baptist Church, has expressed doubt that St. John's problem was doctrinal. "If so," he says, "he recanted for he was

restored to fellowship in April 1830, and then lettered out in August of the same year." (Wayne Faircloth, "Personal Letter to William F. Davidson," November 19, 1999). The latter note is interesting. While Lewis St. Johns never appears in the Richland Creek minutes, a Huldah St. Johns was dismissed from that church on April 11, 1835. Is it possible that Lewis St. Johns joined Richland Creek after leaving Tired Creek and that Huldah was a member of his family?

[25]"Richland Creek," (March 7, 1835); (July 10, 1835), 37; (October 15, 1838), 48. Huldah St. Johns had been accused of "violation of the 11th Article of our Decorum." No document entitled "Decorum" is found in the *Church Record Book*, but the 11th Article of their "Abstract of Principles" speaks to the question of the eternal nature of both judgment and blessing. It is possible that Huldah was guilty of defending annihilation of the wicked dead. In the context of the Arminian/Calvinist focus inferred in the other incidents of excommunication, it would be assumed that Huldah's guilt would be the same as that of the others, but the text is not clear enough to allow a firm conclusion. There is little question but that Arminianism is present in the two churches and that it has caused stress in the church, but there is a good possibility that other doctrinal conflicts had surfaced as well.

[26]Wiley Pearce, "Letter to the Editor" *The Primitive Baptist,* Vol. 3, No. 6 (March 1, 1838). John Crowley gives additional background on the Georgia "Whiteites." "The 'Free Wills,' or 'Whiteites,' originated with Cyrus White, a Baptist minister in Middle Georgia. In 1829, White published a pamphlet contending for the Arminian doctrine of universal atonement. The Columbus Association expelled White and his followers for having 'published a faith differing from the orthodox Baptists.'" (Crowley, *Primitive Baptists,* 69).

[27]*The Christian Index* (July 9, 1843), 361; (August 4, 1843), 493.

[28]Robert G. Gardner, E-mail memo, September 6, 1999.

[29]"Minister's Meeting, United Baptist," *The Christian Index,* Vol. II, No. 33 (August 18, 1843), 537.

[30]Ibid.

[31]*Minutes of the Chattahoochee United Baptist Association* (1850), 1.

[32]Jesse Mercer, *Ten Letters, Addressed to the Rev.Cyrus White, in Reference to his Scriptural View of the Atonement* (Washington, Ga.: Printed at the News Office, 1830).

[33]"Chattahoochee United Baptist Association," *The Christian Index,* Vol. II, No. 2 (Friday, January 13, 1843), 25.

[34]Nancy Telfair, *A History of Columbus, Georgia, 1828-1928* (Columbus, Ga.: The Historical Publishing Co., 1929), 24.

[35]John H. Martin, Compiler, Columbus, GA., *From Its Selection as a "Trading Town" in 1827, to Its Partial Destruction by Wilson's Raid in 1865,* Vol. 1 (Columbus, Ga.: Published by Thomas Gilbert, 1874), 14.

[36]Telfair, Columbus, Georgia, 41.

[37]Virginia S. Wood and Ralph V. Wood, Transcribers, *1805 Georgia Land Lottery* (Cambridge, Mass.: The Greenwood Press, 1964), 40; *The Second or 1807 Land Lottery of Georgia.* (Vidalia, Ga.: Georgia Genealogical Reprints, The Rev. Silas Emmett Lucas, Jr., 1968), 17.

[38]*Broadnax Family Bible,* "Fly Leaf."

[39]*Minutes of the Fiftieth Annual Session of the Chattahoochee United Free-Will Baptist Association,* October 3rd and 4th, 1885 (Savannah, Ga.: Morning News Team Printing House, 1885), 12.

[40]Personal interview granted to Geraldine Waid by Broadnax family member. Deed Records for Muscogee County, Georgia. "Indenture between Champaign Travis Turner and James Edward Broadnax (copy held by Mrs. Geraldine Waid, Archivist, Georgia Free Will Baptist Historical Society).

[41]Ibid.

[42]Damon C. Dodd, "Free Will Baptists in Georgia," (unpublished manuscript held by the Stetson Memorial Library, Special Collections, Mercer University, Macon, Georgia, N.D.), 10, 11.

[43]*Minutes of the Chattahoochee Association of Free Will Baptists,* quoted in Dodd's unpublished manuscript, 12.

[44]Damon C. Dodd, "The Georgia State Association," in Robert E. Picirilli, ed., *History of Free Will Baptist State Associations* (Nashville: Randall House Publications, 1976), 27.

[45]Ibid., 28.

[46]*Minutes of the First, Recess, and Second Sessions of the Georgia State Association of the Original Free Will Baptist Church of Jesus Christ,* Alabaha Church, Blackshear, Ga. (August 31, 1937); Ebenezer Church, November 2-3, 1937; Midway Church, Moultrie, Ga., November 9-10, 1938, pp. 2, 14.

[47]*Minutes of the Fourth Annual Session of the Georgia State Association of the Original Free Will Baptist Church of Jesus Christ,* Greenwood Church, Mitchell County, Camilla, Ga., November 12-14, 1940.

[48]Steven R. Hasty, "Zion Bible School," *The Time Machine,* Occasional Newsletter of Georgia Free Will Baptist Historical Society, Vol. I, No. 1 (1982).

[49]Personal Interview with M. P. Gore, McShan, Alabama (February 23, 1983).

[50]F. L. Smith, "Rise and Progress of Mt. Moriah Church and Mt. Moriah Association with some of their Labor," (Handwritten manuscript held by M. P. Gore, McShan, Alabama, dated July 10, 1888). These notes are especially important because of their date and because Smith was personally related to the church and the Association at least by the early 1850s.

[51]Hosea Holcome, *A History of the Rise and Progress of the Baptists in Alabama* (Philadelphia: King and Baird, Printers, 1840), 211.

[52]Smith, "Rise and Progress," 1.

[53]Ibid. Smith states, ". . . Elder Ellis Gore suggested the name Mt. Moriah, which, according to the first church book, was adopted." Unfortunately, that first book is not available but Smith's note does indicate that he had access to the first minutes that the church produced.

[54]Ibid., 2.

[55]Ibid., 3.

[56]M. P. Gore, Personal Interview, February 23, 1983; M. P. Gore, Letter dated McShan, Alabama, November 12, 1971.

[57]*Minutes of the Union Baptist* (Later Pickens County) *Association,* 1836-1967. Minutes available at the Samford University Library, Birmingham, Alabama, and on microfilm in the Southern Baptist Historical Collection, Nashville, Tennessee.

[58]Smith, "Rise and Progress," back of p. 1.

[59]Ibid., 3.

[60]Ibid., back of p. 1.

[61]*Minutes of the Seventeenth Annual Session of the Mt. Moriah Free Will Baptist Association, 1874.* (Carrollton, Alabama: Printed at the West Alabamian Office, 1874), 1-7.

[62]J. D. O'Donnell, "The Alabama State Association" in *History of Free Will Baptist State Associations,* Robert E. Picirilli, ed., 2.

[63]Ibid.

[64]Ibid., 4.

[65]*The Goodspeed Biographical and Historical Memoirs of Northwestern Arkansas* (Chicago: The Goodspeed Publishing Company, 1889), 481.

[66]*U. S. Census, Carroll County, Arkansas, 1850.* (Held by the Arkansas Historical Commission.)

[67]*Minutes of the Union United Baptist Church, 1838-1931.* Microfilm held by the Arkansas Historical Commission. There can be little doubt but that these are the Whitleys referred to by Goodspeed. Even coincidence would not allow three other Whitleys in the area with the same first names. In addition, there were no Whitleys listed in Marion County even as late as 1850. Samuel and Isaac probably lived in Carroll County and ministered in neighboring Marion.

[68]"Church History, To the Union Association of United Baptists to be held at Liberty, Madison County, Arkansas, September 22, 1916" in *Proceedings of the One Hundred Twenty-Ninth Annual Session of the Union Association of United Baptist* (September 21, 22, 23, 1979), 36.

[69]Ibid.

[70]Ibid.

[71]"Arkansas." *Free Baptist Cyclopaedia,* 22.

[72]*American Baptist Register* (1851), J. Lansing Burrows, ed., (Philadelphia: American Baptist Publication

Society, 1853), 34, 35.

[73]"Arkansas." *Free Baptist Cyclopaedia*, 22.

[74]Goodspeed, *North Western Arkansas*, 132.

[75]David Joslin, "The Arkansas State Association," in Robert E. Picirilli, ed; *History of Free Will Baptist State Associations*. (Nashville: Randall House Publications, 1976), 8.

[76]*U.S. Census, 1850, Franklin County, Arkansas*, transcribed from microfilm by Ted R. Worley (held by Arkansas State Historical Commission).

[77]"Medals on Sale in Charleston," *Southwest Times Record*, Fort Smith, Arkansas (April 7, 1974), 8a.

[78]Goodspeed, *Northwestern Arkansas*, 667, 668.

[79]*Social Statistics, U.S. Census, Arkansas, 1850-1870* (microfilm held by the Arkansas State Historical Commission), 927, 983.

[80]*U.S. Census, 1860, Pope County, Arkansas* (Published by Capitola Glazner and Bobbie J. McLane, 1966).

[81]G. W. Million and G. A. Barrett, *A Brief History of the Liberal Baptist People in England and America from 1606-1911* (Pocahontas, Ark.: Liberal Baptist Book and Tract Company, 1911), 219, 220.

[82]Ibid., 235-238.

[83]Ibid., 256. Also see Abby Brown Williams, editor, *100 Years with the Social Band Association of Free Will Baptists*, N.D., 16.

[84]*Minutes of the Thirtieth Annual Session of Free Will Baptists* [Mt. Zion Association], (Conway, Ark.: Arkansas Free Will Baptist Publishing House, 1898), 5.

[85]*Minutes of the Old Mt. Zion Association of Free Will Baptists* (Bentonville, Ark.: The Sun Print, 1891), 9.

[86]*Minutes of the Sixth Annual Session of the Arkansas State Association of Free Will Baptists* (1903), 6, 7.

[87]*Minutes of the Thirty-First Annual Session of the Free Will Baptist Association* [Arkansas] (October 4, 1928), 12.

[88]Joslin, "Arkansas," 9.

[89]Elder Jesse Lane, Letter to *The Free Will Baptist Magazine* dated August 29, 1829 (Evansville, Vanderburg County, Indiana), *The Free Will Baptist Magazine*, Vol. 3, No. 5 (October 1829), 116, 117.

[90]Mrs. Marilla Marks, editor, *Memoirs of the Life of David Marks, Minister of the Gospel* (Dover, N.H. Published by the Free Will Baptist Printing Establishment, 1846), 75-80.

[91]Burgess and Ward, "Kentucky," *Free Baptist Cyclopaedia*, 319.

[92]William Ely, *Big Sandy Valley* (Catlettsburg, Ky.: Central Methodist, 1887), 430

[93]*Tom's Creek Church Records, 1893-1909, Book 2*, (Original Book) inside front cover.

[94]Ibid., 1-5.

[95]J. H. Spencer, *A History of Kentucky Baptists From 1769 to 1885*, Vol. II, 670, 671.

[96]Mrs. E. O. Griffith, "The Kentucky State Association" in *History of Free Will Baptist State Associations*, Robert E. Picirilli, ed. (Nashville: Randall House Publications, 1976), 45.

[97]Alton Loveless, "Brief History of Ohio Free Will Baptists," *The Ambassador* (July-Aug., 1975), 4.

[98]Mrs. Marilla Marks, editor, *Memoirs of the Life of David Marks* (Dover, N.H.: Published by the Free Will Baptist Printing Establishment, 1846), 81.

[99]Telephone interview with Rev. Price, Pastor of Old Kyger Free Will Baptist Church (July 19, 1983).

[100]"Ohio Free Will Baptist State Convention and Ohio River Yearly Meeting," *The Free Will Baptist*, Vol. 29, No. 29 (September 6, 1911), 1.

[101]Burgess and Ward, "Ohio." *Free Baptist Cyclopaedia*, 493.

[102]Ibid.

[103]Loveless, "Brief History," 4. Also see Burgess and Ward, "Ohio," *Free Baptist Cyclopaedia*, 493-500.

[104]*Minutes of the General Conference of the Free Will Baptist Convention*, Vol. 2 (Boston: F. B. Printing Establishment, 1887); Loveless, "Brief History," 5.

[105]"Records of the Ohio River Yearly Meeting Called Free Will Baptist," Vol. 1 (1833-1897), microfilm (orig-

inal held by the Ohio Historical Society).

[106]Ibid. (1873).

[107]Ibid. (1895).

[108]Ibid. (1880).

[109]Loveless, "Brief History," 81, 82.

10

The Free Will Baptists and Society in the Nineteenth Century: Missions, Education, Slavery, Temperance

Missions

For all practical purposes, the story of Free Will Baptist missions in the nineteenth century is limited to the New England segment of the denomination. That story has been told on a number of occasions, and it is not necessary that a new in-depth study be attempted. But, on the other hand, almost nothing has been written since that group merged with the Northern Baptists in 1911, and no attempt has been made to tell the story in the context of a full Free Will Baptist history. This work would not be complete without some reference to the denomination's early approach to the task of the Great Commission.

The South's late arrival on the missions scene is not surprising. Lack of education, less emphasis on an itinerate ministry, frontier isolation, whether in Kentucky or eastern North Carolina, and the magnitude of the local task gave little opportunity for either knowledge of or interest in the needs of the lost in distant lands.

Home Missions

"In a very real sense the entire work of the Freewill Baptists was a home mission labor. Perhaps their problem was that ministers wanted to be free to be itinerate preachers instead of serving in settled pastorates. Coupled with this was the difficulty of securing ministers for the city churches for they much preferred the opportunity to go on tours in the country."[1] This tendency toward wanderlust was illustrated over and over again in the lives of the Freewill ministers. John Colby had traveled as far as Indiana and Ohio by 1810, and Elias Hutchins was preaching in North and South Carolina by 1828. But personal preference was not the only force that shaped an itinerant atmosphere and eventually spawned the home mission movement. In response to a growing number of cries for help from destitute churches, the denomination determined that an organized itinerant program offered the only solution. In 1833, the Holland Purchase Yearly Meeting suggested that the Conference establish an itinerant ministry and the business committee presented a recommendation to the conference that would: (1) allow the appointment of enough ministers to supply all the churches in the Yearly Meeting with preaching at least once in two weeks, (2) designate each Quarterly Meeting as a distinct circuit, (3) provide support based on the size of the itinerant's family and the location of his work, and (4) place the responsibility of raising support on the different Yearly Meetings within the General Conference.[2]

The Home Mission Society was organized at Dover, New Hampshire, July 31, 1834. This was done in an off-year for the conference in a called meeting for the purpose of organization. David Marks called for the meeting in *The Morning Star* dated July 9, 1834. The Society was officially adopted by the General Conference the following year. Total receipts for the first year were $209.98 and for the first decade—1834-1844—$5,525.78 .[3]

Rather than have independent mission boards in each state, the Conference named the society the "Freewill Baptist Parent Home Mission Society of North America" and suggested that the different states establish auxiliary societies that would be governed by the larger body. The Holland Purchase Yearly Meeting asked permission to establish an independent and incorporated society, but the Conference urged them to form an auxiliary with the understanding "that if they cannot obtain an incorporation for an auxiliary Society, they had the approbation of Conference to obtain an incorporation for an independent State Society."[4]

At the outset, the newly-appointed missionaries were not expected to establish new churches but rather were involved in the tasks of meeting the needs of destitute congregations and helping to establish state or district auxiliaries. Their first work was limited to their own area in New England, but expansion came quickly. In late 1835, F. J. Pitman was sent to Ohio as a home missionary. His work at this time was to be among the churches that were already established and was patterned after home missions in New England. In 1835, B. F. Nealy was assigned to the state of Michigan with the assigned task of planting new churches. He soon established the Randalian Seminary at Howard, Michigan, and the Howard Quarterly Meeting. At about the same time, S. L. Julian, Miss Amy Lord, Miss Alice Abbott, and Jerusha Darling were sent out as teachers to the Michigan vicinity, and by 1838, Asa Dodge had arrived and organized a church in Decatur. S. L. Julian moved from Michigan to Illinois and was instrumental in gathering the Fox River Quarterly Meeting. In 1841, A. C. Andrus and R. M. Cary followed Julian to Illinois where they were joined by C. M. Sewall the following year.[5]

Since the establishment of a mission board created an entirely new area of expense for the denomination, the General Conference found it necessary to develop new means of support. At first, individual members simply were encouraged to give "some sum of money" to missions each year, but by 1844, it was evident that something more was needed. In Conference that year, the denomination introduced the "cent-a-week system," a subscription program that was designed to handle all benevolent expenses within the denomination. It also offered an opportunity for "enlisting the great mass of our membership in the act of Christian benevolence of the Gospel of Jesus Christ."[6]

With a sound financial backing, a job description based upon evangelism and church planting, and a growing participation on the part of individual Freewill Baptists, the Home Mission Society met with increasing success. In October of 1892, the denomination listed churches, Yearly Meetings, and associations in New Hampshire, Maine, Vermont, Massachusetts, Rhode Island, Connecticut, New York, Pennsylvania, Ohio, Indiana, Kentucky, Michigan, Illinois, Wisconsin, Minnesota, Kansas, Virginia, West Virginia, Mississippi, and Nebraska.[7]

Foreign Missions

As would be expected, the first attempt at foreign missions was centered in Quebec, New Hampshire's neighbor to the north. In 1800, Christopher Flanders, a Freewill Baptist layman from Newberry, New Hampshire, attended a funeral in Quebec, and finding no minister present, agreed to lead in the committal prayer. The following year, Flanders returned, settled in the area and established a Freewill Baptist prayer meeting. Reverend Joseph Boody of Stafford, New Hampshire, was one of the first ministers to labor on this new mission field.[8]

Interest in an overseas missions endeavor was first encouraged by the General Baptist Missionary Society of England. Reverend Amos Sutton, a General Baptist missionary to Orissa, India, found that the Freewill Baptists of New England were akin to him in theology, especially in the areas of full and free salvation, open communion, and free will. After some correspondence, the Freewill Baptists invited Reverend Sutton to come to America. Recognizing that this was an opportunity to gain new support for the work in Orissa, both financially and in personnel, Sutton accepted the invitation and spent a number of months encouraging the Freewill Baptists to become actively involved in the Lord's work in India.

The Freewill Baptist Foreign Mission Society was organized June 23, 1833, and was incorporated by the Legislature of the state of Maine. On September 22, 1835, Reverend Jeremiah Philips and wife and Reverend Eli Noyes and wife sailed from Boston as commissioned Freewill Baptist missionaries.

After some time of orientation and language study at Cuttack, Sutton's headquarters, they made their way inland to Sumbalpore. This city was on the Mohanudice River some 250 miles west of Cuttack. Dr. Noyes' daughter died and both Dr. and Mrs. Noyes were stricken with fever. The illness made it necessary for them to return to Cuttack. After their departure, Mrs. Philips, the wife of the other missionary, also contracted the fever and died. Philips' careful nursing of his wife left him susceptible to the fever and he, too, soon lay near death. Silas Curtis, a young orphan, who later would become an important Freewill Baptist preacher in America, wrote on a palm leaf these words. "Mama Philips is dead. Papa Philips is very ill, and unless you come quickly and get him he will die also."[9] The palm leaf was passed from mail carrier to mail carrier until it reached Cuttack. Philips was brought out from Sumbalpore and his life was spared.

In February 1838, Philips began a new work in Balasore in the province of Orissa. The work in Sumbalpore was not restored until 1846 when Dr. O. R. Bachelor, traveling by pony, in the company of a native preacher, moved west from Jellasore through the jungles to Sumbalpore, the earlier preaching point of Philips. The native preacher's name was Rama. He was to prove an important part of the Freewill Baptist ministry in that area. In 1846, Miss Sarah Merrill arrived in India, and in 1847, married Bachelor. They served together in India for 53 years. The early work begun by Philips in Sumbalpore continued to pay dividends. In 1909, on two successive Sundays in June, 500 people accepted Christ and were baptized.

After their recovery, Dr. and Mrs. Noyes continued to work with Philips in Balasore, but in 1841, they were required to return to America because of their poor health. In 1840, Miss Hannah W. Cummins, soon to be the new bride of Reverend Philips, arrived in Orissa and in 1844, Reverend and Mrs. Dow and Reverend and Mrs. Reul Colley arrived to join the team. Like Dr. and Mrs. Noyes, a good number of the missionaries enjoyed very brief ministries overseas. The Dows were limited to 4 years, and the Colleys' entire ministry totaled 12 years.

Z. F. Griffin, a later missionary, observed, "Our earlier missionaries made the mistake of taking too little recreation. Pressing work and open doors made them forget the needs of the body, but their minds and bodies should not have been so neglected."[10]

Though most of the foreign mission work attempted by the denomination was limited to India, their efforts should not be belittled. By 1879, the denomination had commissioned and dispatched 39 missionaries to ministry on foreign fields. This was quite an accomplishment for American missions in the nineteenth century.

A good deal of the literature of the New England Freewill Baptists in the mid-nineteenth century was directed toward missions. Considering missions an important benevolent enterprise and a mandate from God, Freewill Baptist leaders took advantage of every opportunity to overcome objections to missions, to raise support for mission endeavors, and to recruit personnel for foreign service. A good example of the literature is found in *Thoughts on the Benevolent Enterprises Embracing the Subjects of Missions, Sabbath Schools, Temperance, Abolition of Slavery, and Peace*, by John J. Butler. Written in 1840, the tiny text served as a valuable tool in the denominational task of reaching the world for Christ.[11]

Missions in the South

An early interest in missions among Freewill Baptists in New England was quite natural. The earlier work of the Triennial Convention, the ministry of Adoniram Judson, and the travels of Luther Rice had done an excellent job of setting the stage for expanded interest. On the frontier and in the South, however, these factors had far less influence and the difficulties mentioned earlier demanded that the Southerner direct his undivided attention toward matters at home.

Even in the home missions arena, evangelism and planting of churches in new areas were limited to moves of convenience or economic necessity. When Free Will Baptists traveled to new areas and became part of new communities, they carried their faith with them, but planned attempts to develop mission enterprises were few. The most noted attempts to establish new churches in areas that were unreached by the Free Will Baptists were those of Frederick Fonville in central North Carolina and Reading Moore in South Carolina. Both of these church planting adventures seem to have been motivated by the lack of Free Will Baptist witness available in those areas.

Tradition contends that South Carolina gave birth to the Free Will Baptist movement in Georgia and in parts of Alabama (see chapter 7). If that is true, Elder John Broadnax left South Carolina, traveled through parts of Florida, and finally settled in Muscogee County near the town of Columbus, Georgia. It has been suggested that he established the Free Will Baptist Church in Columbus between 1793 and 1795. Even if this could be established, the trail in South Carolina is too cold to pursue. The census records fail to give evidence of Broadnax's background before he arrived in Georgia, and more recent studies (see chapter 9) have largely discredited any contributions that he might have made to Free Will Baptist growth in Georgia.

A number of Yearly Meetings in the Midwest and the Far West began to support missions by the beginning of the fourth quarter of the nineteenth century, but these were related, in one way or another, to the mission programs in New England.

The Central Conference of North Carolina finally organized a mission board in 1918. The Board consisted of B. C. Davenport, Rosa Sutton, W. J. Braxton, and G. L. Rouse. The Conference was exhorted to raise funds for mission work through the local churches, and to divide all funds collected so that 50 percent would be designated for state missions, 30 percent for home missions, and 20 percent for foreign missions. The part for home missions was to be retained in the local treasury and the amounts set aside for state and foreign missions were to be sent to treasurers directed to hold such funds.[12] The treasurer for foreign missions was not identified, and the reference gives some basis for confusion.

The old Triennial General Conference ceased to exist about 1910, and the new General Conference was not organized until 1921. In other words, the Central Conference of North Carolina did not belong to any national organization at this time, and the records do not indicate that they were personally responsible for missionaries on a foreign field. It is best to surmise that interest in foreign missions was growing and that the monies were being set aside for future opportunity of ministry.

By 1918, the New England segment of the denomination no longer existed, the old Triennial Conference had expired, and the Co-operative Association in the West was brand new. Missions would have to be placed on a back burner until the organization of the National Association in 1935.

Education
New England

When Jesse Heath reminded the denomination that there was not a single scholar among the Free Will Baptist preachers in the South in 1827, he might not have been aware that his words were both contemporary and prophetic. The same description could have been given at most any point in time in the nineteenth century. Preachers later in the century might have had increased opportunity for common school education, but opportunities for college or seminary training were few and far between. With that in mind, it is not difficult to understand why Free Will Baptists outside of New England did not develop an interest in theological education until the end of the century.

But, on the other hand, New England was not immune to difficulties. In fact, attitudes toward education were both complex and paradoxical. The first seven ministers related to Randall probably were at least as well educated as their Calvinistic brethren, and one of them, Pelatiah Tingley, was a graduate of Yale University. When Asa Rand, an opponent, published a sermon in which he accused the Freewill Baptists of ignorance and love for that ignorance, John Buzzell responded with a balanced attitude that viewed both education and spiritual growth in proper perspective.

> I have no reflections to cast, but I am very positive he (Asa Rand) labored under a great mistake. I know of no people who strive harder to obtain useful instruction. It is

a good thing for a minister to be well stocked with human learning, but when we place learning instead of sound abilities, or of grace, we always do wrong.[13]

Buzzell's argument seemed sound, but the balance was difficult to attain. A continuing denomination-wide aversion to prepared messages constantly brought education and preaching into conflict. As late as 1837, the General Conference resolved "that this Conference recommends to the ministry of this connection to avoid the use of skeletons, notes, or written discourses in preaching the Gospel, as a general practice, believing that extemporaneous discourses are more scriptural, interesting, and useful. . . ."[14] At this point, the resolution committee did agree that preachers should be left to their own conscience as to the method of their preaching.

It was evident that times and attitudes were changing. In 1810, Ebenezer Chase, a convert from the Calvinistic Baptists, was censured for using notes in his preaching. In fact, objections were raised at the time of his ordination as a Freewill Baptist minister. Though he capitulated and had preached extemporaneously for some eleven years, he finally returned to his earlier practice of writing out his sermons and using notes in the pulpit. Recognizing that the practice was causing dissension among his brethren, he left the denomination and rejoined the Congregational church.[15] Had he been patient, he would have found a growing interest in education among the Freewill Baptists and would have been completely at ease with his own style of preaching.

On January 15, 1840, in a called session of the General Conference in Acton, Maine, the Freewill Baptist Education Society was born. After Elder Z. Jordan called the session to order, J. M. Harper was elected moderator and Silas Curtis was elected clerk. The entire agenda was concerned with the question of education. In 17 resolutions, the Conference outlined the need for education within the denomination. But even here, the resolutions were full of warnings against an over emphasis on a good thing. Selected resolutions show the tension between desire for education and concern for orthodoxy.

Resolved, that the Scriptures accompanied by the aids of the Holy Spirit are the only source, which the servant of God can derive or desire that instruction which is requisite to qualify him for teaching the great truths of Religion. . . .

Resolved, that there are many writings left by false and good men, which properly consulted may assist the mind to the acquirement of a clear knowledge of intricate portions of the Bible. . . .

Resolved, however, that as all uninspired writings are liable to contain error, though the productions of pious men, they should be consulted with great caution, lest errors be imbided with truth. . . .

Resolved, in case one wishes to consult any of these helps on any significant point, he should first examine the Scripture thereon, carefully comparing Scripture with Scripture, and thus get as good understanding upon it as possible himself, unaided by any book other than the Bible. He will then be prepared to read to advantage men's views: and will know far better to receive his truth and reject his error. . . .

Resolved, that the religious interests of our denomination, and the future prosperity of the Redeemer's Kingdom among us as a people, requires that a suitable Biblical Library be procured and placed in the care of some approved brother in our connection for the above purpose. . . .

Resolved, that while we are making greater effort for the increase of knowledge in the sciences and the Scriptures, that there is great danger that we lose that Spirituality and warmth of heart so conspicuous in our fathers, and become cold and lifeless in our communications against which the eternal welfare of souls and the awful responsibilities of the Gospel require studiously to guard. . . .

Resolved, that in the opinion of this convention, the establishment of a Theological School which shall require any given amount of knowledge to be acquired, and any specific length of time, to be spent in Biblical studies, will not tend to promote the scriptural prosperity of the connection. But that opportunity for acquiring a correct knowledge of the Scriptures and other qualifications for the work of the ministry as proposed in the preceding resolution for establishing a library under the care of the approved brother, is loudly called for by the present wants of our denomination.[16]

Recognizing the wisdom of the founding of the Educational Society, the Annual Conference, meeting a year later, officially recognized the Society as a Freewill Baptist institution. But recognition was not enough to halt opposition, and immediate steps were taken to satisfy both the fears and the objections of those who continued to question the advisability of an educational program. The same Conference that gave official sanction to the Educational Society included a guarantee that would protect the denomination from an overemphasis on education.

. . . Agreed, that whereas some of our beloved brethren entertain fears, that a certain course of study or amount of knowledge will ultimately be required of candidates for admission to the Gospel ministry in this denomination, therefore,

Resolved, that it is the opinion of this Conference, that no such test should ever be required for admission to ordination in this denomination.[17]

Later opposition developed around three major concerns: (1) that many who were being helped in the ministry, after graduating from the denomination's theological schools, left the denomination to preach in other churches, (2) that some of the men educated in the theological institutions left the ministry altogether and returned to secular pursuits, and (3) that financial aid for young men entering the ministry constituted a false kindness in that it fostered in the young men a spirit of dependence which was "hostile to success, and robbed them of the strength they would gain in the struggles for themselves. . . ."[18] Like earlier objections, these were carefully handled and, little by little, opposition disappeared.

Despite the fears and the objections, numerous schools began to appear on the New England denominational scene quite early. The first school was founded in Parsonsfield, Maine, in 1832 and has had a continuous history from that time to the present. While it was a denominational school, the name, Parsonsfield Seminary, is somewhat misleading. It began as a high school and continued in that capacity up to 1949. After that time, the school's memory has been retained in the city's consolidated school system.[19] A number of other schools were dubbed "seminary," but in most cases, they were grade or high schools which included theological training in the curriculum.

A second school, Strafford Academy, was organized at Strafford, New Hampshire, in 1834, under the instruction of Joshua D. Burry.

Other schools followed quickly, and by the end of the century the number included three schools of academic grades—New Hampton Literary Institution, Maine Central Institute, and Manning Bible School; six colleges—Bates, Hillsdale, Geauga, Parker, Rio Grande, and Storer; and two theological schools—Cobb Divinity School, a department of Bates College, and the theological department of Hillsdale College.[20] Other schools existed for short periods of time and then disappeared from the scene.

By the twenty-sixth General Conference of 1886, the denomination boasted a progressive educational system that gave opportunity for training to all of its ministers. At that time, the committee on education recommended ". . . that we deem it the duty of Free Baptists to patronize their own schools, and that even when State institutions and other schools possess more material advantages. Personal independence and enterprise, with larger opportunities for usefulness while in school, and the accomplishment of more efficient work ultimately in their own fields of labor, furnish abundant motives for 'providing for our own' in the support and patronage of Free Baptists institutions."[21]

The denomination had come a long way since the founding of the Educational Society in 1840.

The South

In the South, of course, education had known no such prosperity. While the New England segment of the denomination found itself in the golden age of educational development, the South remained much as it had been from the very beginning.

AYDEN SEMINARY AND EUREKA COLLEGE

Finally, in 1890, the Annual Conference in North Carolina appointed its first educational committee. In 1891, George Dees was added to the committee which now included Elders P. T. Lucas, J. W. Valentine, D. Davis, J. B. Russell, J. W. Linton, W. H. Slaughter, and Brothers B. P. Oliver, E. S. Dixon, J. B. Nichols, J. R. Calloway, J. F. Heath, W. R. Sawyer, T. J. Sawyer, and Dees.[22] The Committee was requested to respond to overtures from Free Will Baptists in Morehead City about the possibility of establishing a school in that area. The response was to include a personal visit to Morehead City and investigation of the prospective school site.

The committee recommended that the proposal be rejected and the South's first serious attempt to provide education for its ministers was postponed until the establishment of the Ayden Seminary at Ayden, North Carolina, in 1898.

The school actually was conceived two years earlier at a Union Meeting held with the Spring Branch Church, Pitt County, in March 1896. At that time, both a board of directors and a building committee were appointed and charged with the task of raising funds, purchasing property, and constructing a classroom building for the new school. The Board of Directors consisted of J. M. Barfield, president; T. F. Harrison, secretary; W. F. Hart, treasurer; and E. H. Craft, E. E. Dail, A. L. Harrington, and W. H. Harris as members at large. Hart, Harrington, and Barfield also served on the building committee.[23]

The initial building, consisting of classrooms, a library, and a society hall, was completed early in 1898 and, in that same year, the first students were enrolled under the direction of the institution's first principal, J. E. B. Davis. The property was located on Lee Street in Ayden, a small railroad town some 90 miles east of the state's capital.

Under the name, Free Will Baptist Theological Seminary, the school offered training for primary and high school students as well as for those who were involved in ministry. The theological course included Theology, Free Will Baptist Faith, Church History, Luke in Greek, and Homiletics, a heavy course load for this level of study.[24]

Before 1898 was over, the Board of Directors secured the services of Thomas E. Peden as principal and as Bible professor. Peden served the New England Freewill Baptists for years and was instrumental in preserving a remnant for the continuing denomination in Ohio and West Virginia. Three or four conferences from that area had escaped the 1911 merger with the Northern Baptists and joined the General Conference of Free Will Baptists in the South. Peden's employment at the Seminary not only offered excellent educational leadership but also gave the school the potential for support from areas outside eastern North Carolina. He continued his role as principal until 1910.

The school did not achieve the denominational support and respect that was anticipated, and it was never to assume a true seminary character; but its impact on the churches in the Southeast was significant. The 1904 Minutes for the Triennial General Conference reported:

> Free Will Baptist Theological Seminary has succeeded far beyond the most sanguine expectations of its friends. Forty-two churches are supplied with preaching by its students.[25]

For a few years, the Seminary enjoyed a healthy prosperity: 133 students in 1905; transfer of ownership to a Board of Trustees representing seven southeastern conferences in 1910; and an addition to the main campus building, including one of the largest auditoriums in the area, in 1911. But the prosperity was temporary. By 1916, the school was operating in the red and the student population had dwindled to 69. The popularity, convenience, and quality of the public schools began to infringe on the need and the justification for schools like the Seminary.[26] It was evident that only a college level program could offer salvation for the school.

The Seminary closed in 1920 while school officials and denominational leaders gave all of their attention to the construction of a new college campus on the eastern edge of Ayden. It reopened in the fall of 1922 and again offered one track of studies for high school and another for ministerial students. But by 1925, it was evident that the Seminary could no longer exist unless its students could be assured of the privilege of college training upon completion of their high school studies. Though the new campus was not yet ready for use, the board agreed that a college curriculum could no longer be delayed. The Seminary facilities were to serve the needs of the new college until the new campus was available.

On September 6, 1926, Eureka College opened for business on its own campus. The administration building, though still under construction, included enough finished classrooms to allow classes to begin. The new school was prepared to offer a two-year college curriculum as well as a four-year high school program.

Response to the new school was less than expected, and it immediately found itself in difficulty. Too few college students were enrolled the first year to make a sophomore class feasible and those students who had completed their first year on the old Seminary campus had to transfer to other colleges.[27]

In addition, while some were avid in their support of the new college, many preachers and laymen failed to catch the vision for or sense the need for a denominational school. The school failed to meet its budget in the 1927-28 school year and finances would continue to be a major obstacle to success.

During the 1928-29 academic year, the high school program was dropped, and in 1929, Eureka College closed its doors. On November 4, 1931, the administration-classroom building was destroyed by fire, and the last hopes for a denominational school at this location disappeared in the flames. The nation's economic depression, denominational apathy born out of the anti-intellectualism of conservative Christianity, and finally, the fire, all made their contribution to the death of both the dream and the reality of a school in eastern North Carolina.

The two schools had served the denomination well for more than thirty years and while their early demise was a tragedy, the loss surely played a role in a growing interest in a centrally located college that would meet the needs of the entire denomination.

During the life of the two schools, seven men emerged as leaders to give direction to the educational enterprise. Principals and Superintendents of Ayden Seminary included J.E.B. Davis, 1898; Thomas E. Peden, 1898-1910; J. E. Sawyer, 1910-1920; R. B. Lee, 1922-1924; and C. E. Prescott, 1924-1925. R. B. Spencer served as the first president of Eureka College (1925-1928) and L.R. Ennis (1928-1929) held that office when the school ceased operation.[28]

THE FREE WILL BAPTIST UNIVERSITY IN NASHVILLE

Failure to establish a post-secondary educational institution for the denomination evidently did not come as a result of lack of effort or interest. On February 3, 1908, John W. Morton, Secretary of State for Tennessee, filed a charter for the Free Will Baptist University of Nashville. The charter was recorded on a standard form and completed by hand. Murton accepted the charter and went so far as to apply his own signature over the Seal of the State of Tennessee. Dell Upton witnessed the official transaction.

> Be it known, That Rufus Manners, W. M. Brumit, M. S. Wyatt, W. A. Brown, J. H. Roberts and Dell Upton are hereby created a body politic by the name and style of the Free Will Baptist University of Nashville, Ten.

> The particular purposes for which this charter is sought are: To establish a school of universal learning in which to impart instruction, examine students, grant diplomas, and confer degrees in the arts, sciences and professions, and incidental thereto to establish a publishing house for the publication of books, periodicals, and magazines of general educational and religious character.[29]

The charter was signed by those mentioned in the text. Dell Upton was pastor of Cofer's Chapel Free Will Baptist church at the time. The charter was recorded by John E. Shelton, Clerk for Davidson County, Tennessee, and was filed in Corporation Record Book 04, page 150.

History reminds us that this ambitious endeavor never bore fruit. But it tells us two things about the Free Will Baptists in the South in the early part of the twentieth century: (1) education was becoming more and more important in the planning of the denomination; and (2) a Liberal Arts program of study was the preferred pattern for training for Christian ministry.

TECUMSEH COLLEGE

The next attempt at the establishment of a denominational school did not come until well after the turn of the century and the founding of the Co-operative General Association to serve Free Will Baptists in the West and Midwest. In the first Triennial session in December 1916, the new association agreed to adopt the existing Freewill Baptist Biblical Correspondence School, formerly conducted under the auspices of the Nebraska Yearly Meeting in the Missouri State Association as a part of the new regional organization. Rev. John Wolfe was elected Dean of the Correspondence School, and G. S. Lattimer was appointed secretary. The two men, along with Ira Waterman, constituted the first faculty for the school.

In the same session, a motion was made and carried that a resident denominational school be established. John H. Wolfe was elected president of this proposed school as well.[30]

In the first adjourned session of the Co-operative General Association held in December 1917, the new president reported he had met with business leaders in Tecumseh, Oklahoma, and they had agreed to purchase the now defunct Indianola Business College for the denomination as an enticement to establish a new school there. The purchase included five acres of ground just east of the city of Tecumseh, one three-story brick building, 40 by 60 feet, and a frame building, 30 by 40 feet. They also agreed to add a $1,000 cash gift to help in the remodeling of the building for school use.[31] All of this was to be a free will offering to the denomination for college purposes. The city received a double portion for its investment when the recently purchased *The New Morning Star*, a denominational paper, was purchased by the Conference and moved to the college property.

As a result of the generosity of the city leaders, the property was renovated and turned over to the denomination debt free, but the school was left with absolutely no operating capital. This difficulty was compounded by a "no debt" policy negotiated between the school and the Co-operative Association. The first major obstacle to overcome was the locating of a faculty for the fall semester and the difficulty of hiring qualified professors without a guarantee of income. The first teachers came without any assurance that even living expenses would be met. Even so, by fall, 1917, the president had added nine members to the faculty—six of them on campus and another three to come before the year was through. The first faculty included: John H. Wolfe, President, head of the department of theology, philosophy, and Fuller Professorship of Systematic Theology; Rev. S. L. Morris, secretary and lecturer in department of sacred history, apologetics; Rev. Delia S. Wolfe, department of history and languages; Mrs. Grace I. Morris, department of mathematics and physics; Mrs. Pearl K. Smith, dean of women and head of department of preparatory work; Rev. Samara Smith, department of chemistry and biology and department of expression; Rev. Ellen A. Coop, Professor George W. Lawrence, and Angelica Lawrence.[32]

The first curriculum offered seven different programs of study—Classical, Philosophical and Scientific, Literary, Classical Theology, English Theology, Department of Expression, and a Normal School curriculum. The first four required three years of preparatory work in addition to four years for the program itself. The English Theology and Department of Expression courses required four years, and the Normal School program required three years and was designed for teachers rather than preachers.

William Fuller, a layman from Elk Creek, Nebraska, gave $500 for the school's first endowment, and the first professorship was named in his honor.[33]

The school opened for business on September 12, 1917, and the president attributed a small beginning class to factors he felt were beyond the administration's control—lack of advertisement due to the monumental job of getting the college ready for class, the war now at its height, and the large crop of cotton just being harvested in the local area.

The administration determined from the very beginning that the school would be more than an outlet for Biblical training. Recognizing that a good number of Free Will Baptist young people needed training in other areas, the school took shape as a Christian liberal arts school rather than a Bible College. Initial plans allowed room for the development of a school of business and an agricultural school as soon as finances and faculty were available.

For those who could not attend or were not qualified to attend, the Biblical Correspondence School continued to serve their needs. The school provided three full courses including Systematic Theology and History of the Bible, Church History and Evidences of Christianity, and Pastoral and Practical Theology. Tuition was free, and the only expense related to the three courses was for books, a total of $6.75. Twelve students were enrolled in the three courses in its beginning year.[34]

Tecumseh College continued to serve the West and Midwest until 1927 when the campus was burned to the ground. In 1922, fees for theological students totaled $119.75 per semester, and every effort was made to relieve this burden. Ordained ministers were charged one-half tuition and children of ministers, licensed ministers, and children of missionaries were charged only three-fourths of the tuition rate. Of course, the break was not as helpful as expected when the reader understands that tuition constituted only about one-fourth of the semester fees. Students were required to attend Sunday School and church, either at the college church or a church of their choice. Chapel service met at 8:15 each morning and attendance was mandatory. Student attendance was checked by seat captains. The school library contained 3,000 volumes including several hundred copies dealing with ministry. It is interesting to note that athletics were already an important part of school life. The Tecumseh Bulletin for 1921-22 reminded the students that "the College authorities believe athletics to be an important part of student life and, properly directed, a means of culture."[35] Tennis, basketball, and baseball were provided on campus and were encouraged. All students were expected to be involved in some sort of exercise.

By this time, the faculty numbered 14 full-time instructors and the school offered the Bachelor of Arts, the Bachelor of Christian Letters, and the Bachelor of Letters. The B.A. degree required the traditional courses in Greek, Latin, mathematics, literature, history, science, and philosophy. The school also offered high school training for those not yet qualified for college.

ZION BIBLE SCHOOL

T. B. Melette came to Georgia from his home in Turbeville, South Carolina. His journey included time at Duke University where he had trained for a career in education. After spending a few years in teaching and educational administration, he purchased land in Southwest Georgia where he would found a new school dedicated to the task of training young Free Will Baptists for vocational Christian ministry. The school was situated near Zion Free Will Baptist Church and would adopt the name of the older institution. The school was totally dependent on the support of churches and friends in the area. No fees were required for tuition, room, or board. The curriculum included English, World Literature, Bible Synthesis, Evans' Great Doctrines, the Book of Romans, the Book of John, the Pauline Epistles, Psychology I and II, and Butler and Dunn theology.

The school was to have a short life, beginning classes in 1935 and closing its doors in 1942. It was felt that the school was needed no longer after the denomination established a central denominational school in Nashville, Tennessee.

Even so, the school had made its mark. Its Bible oriented curriculum would set a pattern that would be followed by the new Free Will Baptist Bible College and Zion's graduates would become well known in denominational circles over the next few decades—Daniel and Chester Pelt, Jim Barnes, Luther Norris, "Scottie" Driggers, W. F. McDuffie, K. V. and S. T. Shutes, J. B. Lovering.[36]

At last the South and West had come of age and were prepared to offer training for their ministerial students. These four schools—Ayden Seminary, Eureka College, Tecumseh, and Zion Bible School—set the stage for educational development in the soon coming National Association.

Benevolence
Slavery

As early as 1837, long before the political secession of the southern states from the Union, the churches already were divided over the question of slavery. Using identical passages of Scripture, the Northern ministers cried out against the evils of slavery while southern ministers declared it to be both Biblical and practical.

Some southern churches, finding themselves outnumbered in their national organization, quickly decided the only way to escape the "oppression of the majority" was to secede from the national organization and to establish a new denomination in the South. The Presbyterians split in 1837, and the Southern Baptist Convention was founded in 1845. Though some of the denominations would point to other factors, the primary conflict was slavery.

At first glance, it would seem that the Free Will Baptists did not suffer the agonies of division that touched other denominations; and, indeed, they did not experience the same degree of hurt that fell to the Presbyterians, Baptists, and the Methodists that left northern and southern segments of the denominations totally isolated and bitterly opposed to one another. In fact, rupture of this nature was not possible among the Free Will Baptists because they had never enjoyed the unity that had long been the heritage of the other denominations. Rather than division, the impact of slavery among the Free Will Baptists was the postponement of unity until late in the nineteenth century.

Though New England continued to make overtures of union to the South throughout the mid nineteenth century, no such union was possible until the slavery question was settled. Northern Freewill Baptists were almost unanimously opposed to slavery while it was fully tolerated by the denomination in the South. This conclusion is well illustrated by an incident that occurred at the New England General Conference in 1839. At that session, Dr. William Housley, a minister and slaveholder, petitioned the Conference for membership for his churches in Kentucky. He suggested that a large number of other churches would follow his example and become a part of the denomination. Upon investigation, however, he was discovered to be a slaveholder, and when he refused to give up his slaves, the delegates voted to deny his petition.

The Freewill Baptist Anti-Slavery Society was organized at Sugar Hill Church, Lisbon, New Hampshire, June 8, 1843, but formal organization of the society was preceded by years of strong support for the anti-slavery movement. By 1834, *The Morning Star* was speaking out forcefully in favor of abolition, and in June 1834, the New Hampshire Yearly Meeting was the first to endorse the paper's position.[37] The Eighth General Conference in 1835 declared slavery an infringement on the rights of the slave, an unwarrantable exercise of power on the part of the master, and the potential ruin of the country.[38] But it was 1841, two years before the founding of the Anti-Slavery Society, before the denomination clearly expressed its opposition to slavery.

> Resolved, that we not only regard slavery as a moral, physical, intellectual, social, religious and political evil in its inception, duration and catastrophe;—but we record our solemn testimony against slave holding, as a legalized system of man-stealing, as a deep and soul-destroying sin in the sight of God, which no circumstances can justify or excuse. . . .
>
> Resolved, that in the opinion of this Conference, the sin of slave holding consists not so much in the physical suffering of the victims, as in its elementary and intrinsic principle which removes the distinction that God has made between a man and a thing;—

reduces a free agent to a chattel;—makes merchandise of immortal souls;—robs the human being of the right to himself;—and converts personal, inalienable ownership into a marketable commodity. . . .[39]

The Slavery Committee continued to argue that the South's imputation of slavery to the Bible was both false and slanderous. Arguing that the servants of the patriarchs were not slaves but members of the families of their masters with rights to inheritance, that the commandment, "thou shalt not steal" denied an individual the right to steal personal ownership from another individual, and that the law of Moses commanded that none should be held in servitude against his will, the Committee agreed that the original kidnapper, the slave trader, and the slaveholder were alike worthy of God's censure. Quoting Exodus 21:16, "He that stealeth a man, and selleth him, or if he be found in his hand, he shall surely be put to death," the Committee concluded that no man could be enslaved or held as a matter of property without causing the slaveholder to be guilty of sin and worthy of death. In response to the Committee's study and their conclusion, the General Conference resolved "that if the Bible upheld slavery, it would sustain a system of the most atrocious wickedness, and could not be confided in as a holy book, condemning all sin. . . ."[40]

The action of the General Conference then made any defense of slavery a spiritual crime of moral treason against God's Word, "tending directly to the overthrow of all confidence in the Bible, and the God of the Bible, and to make infidels of the rising generation."[41] The Conference closed with its members resolved to "come out from among" those who supported the sin of slavery. The decision of the General Conference was not surprising nor unexpected. The Freewill Baptists of New England were well prepared for the anti-slavery discussions of 1841 and the founding of the Anti-Slavery Society in 1843. John J. Butler, in an interesting series of essays entitled *Thoughts on the Benevolent Enterprises, Embracing the Subject of Missions, Sabbath Schools, Temperance, Abolition of Slavery, and Peace*, published in 1840, set the stage for the discussions with a vivid exposé of slavery abuses in the South. In addition, he responded to the objections to abolition that were voiced by church-related slaveholders. In fact, the language of the resolutions of the 1841 General Conference sounds surprisingly familiar to the readers of Butler's earlier essay.

The 1835 General Conference rejoiced in the knowledge of an almost unanimous support of the anti-slavery movement within the denomination. At this point, the unity of spirit in opposition to slavery in the northern segment of the denomination left no room for cooperation with the South until long after the slavery question was settled.

Unless the twenty-first century reader is made aware of the magnitude of the tension and the hostility that developed between northern and southern Christians over the slavery question, the growing anger and the eventual ruptures are incomprehensible. In the North, laymen and church leaders alike knew little of slavery except for the accompanying abuse which was magnified in political speeches, in the media, and from the pulpit. In the South, on the other hand, both Christian and non-Christian slaveowners saw abolition as the inevitable ringing of the death knell for both the economy and the culture of the entire South.

Butler, in the essay mentioned earlier, characterized all slavery as a torturous, inhuman form of existence. Using Christian slaveholders, preachers, and an occasional law as examples, the author gave more than half of his essay to the task of denouncing slavery as the most heinous of sins. Beginning with the least offensive, Butler tells of the laws which established fines for either black or white who taught a slave to read and then continued to increasingly gruesome tales of the abuse slaves suffered. Quite often the examples included personal testimonies of contemporary ex-slave-holders. William Ladd wrote on November 29, 1838:

> While I lived in Florida, I knew a slaveholder whose name was Hutchinson, he had been a preacher and a member of the Senate of Georgia. He told me that he dared not keep a gun in his house; because he was so passionate; and that he had been the death of three or four men. I understood him to mean slaves. One of his slaves, a girl, once came to my house. She had run away from him at Indian river. The cords of one of her hands was so much contracted that her hand was useless. It was said that he "Hutchinson" had thrust her hand into the fire while he was in a fit of passion, and held it there, and this was the affect . . .[42]

Other stories told of extensive beatings (the "moderate punishment" was 39 stripes), exposure to the elements, and in one case, the public execution of a slave in which a live man was hacked into small pieces with an ax beginning with the feet and continuing until the entire body had been dismembered. In the latter case, the slaves were warned that if news of the execution leaked out, they would suffer the same fate. By the time the author arrived at the Biblical argument for abolition, his readers were well-prepared to accept his position. There is little doubt but that Butler's description of slavery became a powerful tool in the Freewill Baptist's struggle for abolition.

The *Fifth Annual Report of the Freewill Baptist Anti-Slavery Society* began:

> The freedom of the will is one of our denominational characteristics. But our faith stops not here: it includes the freedom of the entire man; ever subject, however, to the restraints of the 'higher law.' We claim this freedom for ourselves, and we grant it to others. Aye, more, we demand it for others; and for all others. Especially do we plead for the enslaved of our race in this boasting 'land of the free and home of the brave.'
>
> We do it because they are not allowed to speak for themselves. We do it the more earnestly because the rod of the oppression is held by the American people.[43]

Claiming that more than three million blacks were now enslaved, the report contended that the "slimy folds" of slavery now touched both church and state. In an almost prophetic foresight, the compilers of the report saw slavery rapidly moving toward the dissolution of the Union. Their strongest opposition was directed toward national laws that required Christian men to return fugitive slaves to their owners. "And more than all this, it calls upon us to disobey God in the return of fugitives, and threatens us with fines and imprisonment, if we obey Him rather than men."[44] The report, compiled by Silas Curtis, H. P. Wellington, M. W. Burlingame, M. J. Speere, D. P. Silley, I. D. Stewart, William Burr, D. S. Frost, William Hurlin, E. G. Knoles, L. B. Tasker, and E. True, called for complete and immediate emancipation. "Resolved, that the principles of immediate abolition are derived from the unerring word of God; and that no political circumstances whatever can exonerate Christians from exerting all their moral influence for the suppression of this heinous sin."[45]

Though the denomination rejoiced earlier that most of its members were united in their views on slavery, it continued to face opposition both from within the church family and from without. Quite often opposition came from government agencies. In 1836, the Free Will Baptist Printing Establishment was twice refused an act of incorporation because *The Morning Star* was so outspoken on the subject of abolition. For several years incorporation was denied the Home Mission Society, "lest, as was then said, it would send forth 'missionaries to preach abolition.'"[46] From 1836 to 1838, the subscription list of *The Morning Star* constantly decreased. A good number of the subscribers, most of them probably related to the denomination, refused to pay subscription fees, and the paper quickly found itself some $15,000 in debt.

But denominational leaders were unwavering and decreed that *The Morning Star* would continue its defense of abolition. It was about this time that the General Conference rejected overtures from Dr. William M. Housley which could have led to the addition of 20,000 new members to the denomination. Housley was a slaveowner and defended slavery before the General Conference. In addition, all ties with Free Will Baptists in North and South Carolina were broken, and the statistics of the two states were no longer included in General Conference reports.[47]

Looking back, the editors of the *Free Baptist Cyclopaedia* concluded, "It was a bold step at that early date for a denomination to thus cut itself off from all connection with slavery. . . ."[48] They went on to say that by 1846, the political position in the North had changed and the change had come largely through Freewill Baptist influence. It could well be that they were right. There can be no question but that the Freewill Baptists and other northern churches exerted a strong influence on changing attitudes toward abolition.

If the North was united in its opposition, the South was just as united in its defense, and that defense was voiced by church, clergy, political officials, and laymen alike. Again, the twenty-first century reader has difficulty in understanding the explosiveness of the issue as it related to the churches. For a generation brought up in an atmosphere of ecumenism, the interchurch struggles that developed around the issue of slavery are almost inconceivable. In fact, even when denominations have divided, the issues have been less volatile and the participants have, for the most part, simply agreed to disagree. The hostilities seldom continue beyond the final parting of the ways. But slavery offered no easy solutions and no compromises. With its Biblical, social, economic, and humanitarian implications, it proved to be far more than a mere difference of opinion that could be solved by organic division. Even after division came, slavery's continued existence nurtured the open wound and denied the possibility of healing. The wound was so deep that our own generation, more than a century later, has been witness to some of the first attempts at reunion. C. C. Goen, in an animated paper presented at the American Society for Church History, in Washington, D. C., and later published in *Church History*, has illustrated the bitterness that developed between churches North and South in the testimonies of a Louisiana minister and Mr. Black, a Northern Methodist minister from Newport, Kentucky, just across the river from Cincinnati. The Louisiana minister warned his brothers in the North:

I am one of five ministers of three different denominations, in a single company [of the Confederate Army] armed for the defense of our rights and liberties, three of whom are between fifty and sixty years old. And I tell you in candor, and in the fear of God, that if you or any of the brethren that have urged on this diabolical war, come on with the invading army, I would slay you with as hearty a good will, and with as clear conscience, as I would the midnight assassin. . . . You are my enemy, and I am yours.

Mr. Black's judgment on the South was no less harsh:

On one sabbath he had his church ornamented with U.S. flags and brass eagles; his hymns were the "Star-Spangled Banner," "The Red, White, and Blue," and "Hail, Columbia." He prayed that the Union may be preserved, "even though blood may come out of the winepress even unto the horses' bridles . . ." [Revelation 14:20]. In the course of his sermon he said: "I trust our troops will rally and wipe out the disgrace of Manassas, though it cost the life of every rebel under arms. Let Davis and Bauregard be captured to meet the fate of Haman [Esther 7]. Hang them up on Mason and Dixon's Line, that traitors . . . may be warned. Let them hang until the vultures shall eat their rotten flesh from their bones; let them hang until the crows shall build their filthy nests in their skeletons; let them hang until the ropes rot, and let their dismembered bones fall so deep into the earth that God almighty can't find them on the day of resurrection."[49]

In the light of such open and vehement hostility, one would expect that the minutes of the southern Free Will Baptists would speak often of the slavery issue. But, surprisingly, such was not the case. If they became embroiled in the slavery controversy at all, they did not feel that their defense of slavery was important enough to record for later generations.

Because the Free Will Baptists in the South typically minister to a less-than-wealthy rural population, the obvious conclusion is that there were no slaveholders, and the controversy simply did not touch the denomination. While that probably was the case for the larger part of the denomination, the records indicate that some slaveholders did exist among the Free Will Baptists.

Robert Heaton, founder of the Free Will Baptist movement in middle Tennessee, owned at least two slaves,[50] and the records often speak of blacks being received into the church as members. In most cases, they were identified as the property of white members of the congregation. It is more likely true that their particular brand of ministry isolated them from the influential arena of political, economic, and theological struggles that were growing between North and South.

For most of the Free Will Baptists in the South, the slavery controversy did not exist. Slavery was an accepted part of the Christian experience, and the church was responsible for the salvation and the Christian welfare of the slave. Blacks in the church heard the same preaching, enjoyed the privilege of baptism, and suffered the same discipline as their white masters. But to suggest that they were accepted as equals, would be more than naive. A brief, cryptic statement in the *1855 Abstract of Faith* for the North Carolina Free Will Baptists indicates the entirely different worlds that existed side by side in the Free Will Baptist Church of the mid nineteenth century. "No person of color within the pale of the Church shall give testimony against any person but those of color."[51]

The first real impact of slavery on the southern Free Will Baptist churches came as a result of the War Between the States. A number of churches and associations were almost wiped out as their members became actively involved in the slavery controversy and went off to war, never to return. The Concord-Pantego Free Will Baptist Church in North Carolina boasted some 81 members before the war; but, by 1865, the congregation dwindled to 21.[52] The Mt. Moriah Association, in Alabama, did not even keep records from 1860 to 1869 and later records attribute the gap in the records to the war. There is a good possibility that the association did not even meet during the most difficult war years. The South Carolina General Conference offered the best illustration of the impact of the war on the church. In 1859, the Conference boasted 4,538 members; but by 1864, they were down to 671 members even though a few more churches were involved in the associational ministry.

The breakdown of the churches came as the result of the War Between the States and was only indirectly related to slavery itself. In the South, the real struggle in the slavery controversy came after emancipation. Up until that time, blacks were received into the church as members, but after the war, white church leaders found that the old rules and regulations that had controlled the slaves could not be applied to free blacks. Either they had to be accepted as equals or some new provision had to be made. The Free Will Baptists were not alone in their dilemma, and the provisions that they made were not unlike those of other denominations.

A query presented to the Mt. Moriah Free Will Baptist Association in Alabama indicated the fears of the white Christians and the association's response indicated the direction that most churches in the South would take.

> Is it right as things are now all the negroes being free that we receive them into our Churches with Equal rights and privaleges with us to attend all the business and deciplin of the Church and Assoc! And after discussion we Answer No and recommend that to prevent amalgamation, the negroes should have their own Church houses and churches and should be properly taught by men of Ability. . . .[53]

While North Carolina was somewhat more lenient in their solution, there was no question but that their preferences were much like those in Alabama.

> Resolved, with this Conference advise the colored members of this Connection to unite and form Churches to themselves: (but if any of them wish to remain enrolled amongst the white members, they can do so as private members,) and we also advise them to form a general conference to themselves.

> Resolved, that we appoint a committee of ten ministers belonging to this Connection or Conference to have the oversight of them and to advise and instruct them until they become competent to act for themselves.[54]

In both cases, white church leaders were expected to work with the black churches until competent ministers could be raised up from their own membership. As mentioned earlier, this provision was adopted by a number of southern denominations and gave birth to black denominations all over the South.

Temperance

The frontier, whether west of the Alleghenies in Kentucky, Tennessee, and Ohio or in rural North Carolina, produced a hardworking, hard-living, lonely individual for whom whiskey often seemed the only source of relief. It became a staple for social gatherings and was used to blur the fears and the heartbreaks of everyday frontier life. William Warren Sweet, in his *Revivalism in America*, depicted homemade whiskey as the "greatest single curse of the whole country at this period, and especially of the raw frontier. . . ."[55]

> It was considered on the frontier almost as much of a necessity as bread and meat. Everybody indulged—men, women, and children, preachers, and church members, as well as the ungodly. Stores had open kegs of whiskey with cups attached for all to help themselves. It was freely served in all the social gatherings, log rollings, corn huskings, and house raisings. At the loading of flatboats there was always a keg of whiskey on the bank with head knocked and a gourd ready. As a sad consequence of the abundance of the firey liquid, a large section of frontier society was debauched and whiskey-sodden. . . .[56]

The struggle for survival on the frontier with its accompanying dangers, loneliness, and the ready availability of whiskey might explain, to some small degree, the frontiersman's dependence on alcohol. But Sweet spoke of the impact of alcoholic abuse on the entire country. I. D. Stewart pictured the problem in the context of a more settled and civilized New England society.

> Company could not be entertained without it, and never was the beverage absent at birth, marriages, or funerals. Towns had usually provided rum at the raising of a meeting house, and at the ordination of a minister legally settled. . . . The drinking habits of the people were such that the sale of distilled spirits was one of the invariable appendiges of all public gatherings.[57]

Among New England Freewill Baptists, the first attempts at temperance were found in the examples of Benjamin Randall and John Buzzell. In fact, most of Randall's earliest colleagues joined him in his support of total abstinence. At this point in time, abstinence was a difficult position to hold. Besides the obvious economic and social support for the manufacturing and sale of alcoholic beverages, they often were used as cheap medicine and, therefore, were found in almost every home. Randall, in poor health, often found himself in need of relief on his many travels. In most cases, some sort of alcoholic beverage was offered and, in every case, he refused, willing to suffer rather than to compromise his conviction.[58] In spite of preaching and example, however, Freewill Baptists in the North, as a whole, did not join the temperance movement until long after Randall's death. New Durham Church records indicate that local churches were still serving cider (evidently intoxicating and potent at this time),[59] that rum was purchased to serve at Randall's funeral, and a number of deacons and ministers maintained distilleries.[60]

For a good number of years, churches were satisfied with the policy of moderation that separated the more potent "ardent spirits"—distilled liquors—from the less intoxicating beverages such as wine, cider, and beer. But, as alcoholic abuse increased, they quickly recognized that total abstinence was the only policy that could effectively deal with the social problems they were facing. Many churches, including the Freewill Baptists, were not willing to impose total abstinence on their congregations when it was first introduced. Instead, a system of pledges was developed that allowed those who drank the less intoxicating beverages to continue their practice pledging to stay away from distilled liquors, and asked those who did not drink to sign a pledge of total abstinence. It is supposed that the term "teetotalers" came out of this pledge system. Those who wished to be a part of the temperance movement and were willing to fight against distilled liquors but were not ready for total abstinence marked their pledge O.P. (old pledge) while those favoring total abstinence marked theirs T (total). The latter were designated "tee-totalers."[61]

When the General Conference first introduced total abstinence in 1832, the resolutions were carefully worded so that local churches were left with the final responsibility of accepting or rejecting abstinence for their members.[62] But this, too, proved less than effective, and by 1837, the Conference agreed that total abstinence was the only solution to the problem of alcoholic abuse and asked its members to set the necessary example of total abstinence from all kinds of intoxicating drinks. For the denomination, the old categories of distilled or ardent spirits and less dangerous fermented beverages ceased to exist. By 1850, the General Conference, still recognizing its role as an advisory body, advised all of its churches to admonish any members who used intoxicating drinks and, if they persisted, to withdraw from them the hand of fellowship.[63] The battle against intemperance became a serious business for the Freewill Baptists.

In the beginning, the argument for total abstinence was based on purely practical criteria. Sweet's commentary on alcoholic abuse on the frontier, mentioned earlier, gave some idea of the monumental problem the church faced. Broken homes, economic waste, and growing crime demanded that a solution be found. The first New Testament argument for abstinence did not appear until 1841 when the Temperance Committee agreed that the New Testament did not confirm that Jesus either made or used wine. Even then no Biblical support was given. When J. J. Butler, the denomination's chief theologian, struggled with the problem of intemperance in 1840, he completely ignored the Biblical approach to a total abstinence platform. He argued rather that intemperance makes a fool of the imbiber, that it was an unnecessary evil (here Butler argued that even moderate or social drinking and the use of ardent spirits for medicinal purposes was unnecessary), that it was a fruitful source of crime, that it was an expensive evil, and that it was a destructive evil. Butler carefully illustrated each of his points with case studies.[64] The development of a Biblical argument would have to wait.

As time passed, the denomination became more and more practical, recognizing that the economic waste involved in alcoholic abuse was having disastrous impact on the church and its worldwide task. From that discovery, they moved on to other areas of waste and suggested, in 1844, that Freewill Baptists also give up their coffee, tea, and tobacco, and that they send the proceeds from those savings to the different mission enterprises.[65] By this time, temperance emphasis had evolved from mere moderation, to total abstinence, and finally, to other areas of unnecessary habit and waste.

Because New England became involved in the temperance movement so early and because of Randall's early example, Freewill Baptists there did not feel the same measure of impact of nineteenth century intemperance as did their brethren in the South. In Sweet's earlier statement, he mentioned that most church discipline at this time related to alcoholic abuse in one way or another. This was especially true among the Free Will Baptists in the South. Being more closely related to the frontier, preachers and laymen alike in this area were less outspoken against intemperance and, indeed, often defended their right to drink. George Syles, a layman in the Mt. Moriah Church, in Alabama, appeared before the church in April 1852, and submitted a confession of drunkenness along with a plea of forgiveness. A motion was immediately made and seconded to forgive, but when Pastor Ellis Gore exhorted Syles publicly to stop his drinking, Syles became angry and asked for his name to be erased ". . . that if he was to be put up as a target to be shot at he wanted his name erast from our Church book. . . ."[66] Syles was excommunicated but as much for "contempt of the church" as for his drunkenness.

The most serious offense was that of running a "grog" shop or retailing distilled liquors under other circumstances. Even this was forgiven if penitence seemed real. But, at this point, repentance did not include the promise of turning away from the besetting sin. The same ministers and laymen returned to the church for censure time after time as they yielded to the temptation of strong drink. In almost every case, the censure came as the result of public drunkenness and the shadow that this cast upon the church.

Like their brothers in the North, Free Will Baptists in the South were concerned about the practical implications of intemperance. As late as 1889, little had been mentioned about a New Testament argument for total abstinence in the battle still directed toward the social disorders that were considered a direct result of the liquor traffic. In that year, the Annual Conference resolved that:

> First, that no whiskey, brandy of any kind, rum, gin, cider, wine, ginger snaps or anything that intoxicates shall be sold within two miles of Reedy Branch Church during the sitting of this Conference. That those who are selling confections on Thursday may continue until Saturday night when they shall close. There shall be no new stands erected. There shall be no racing or any disorder. Nothing shall be sold within 400 yards of the sitting of the Conference; and the order of the spirits two miles of the same.

> That Jesse Braxton and R. L. Griffing be appointed as Martials to keep order and carry out these rules during the sitting of the Conference.[67]

By 1913, the Free Will Baptists in the South were strongly involved in the temperance movement, and most of the older problems of discipline disappeared from the minutes. That year the Temperance Committee submitted a platform that included total abstinence, support for prohibition, and the denunciation of those who were openly proclaiming the temperance movement to be a failure.

They recommended that church members who refused to abide by the church's total abstinence policy be censured by their local church.[68]

As was true in New England, the Biblical argument for abstinence was left to a later time. The overwhelming social difficulties related to alcoholic abuse left their churches and their leaders with more than enough fuel for firing the furnace of temperance and total abstinence.

Notes for Chapter 10

[1]Raymond J. Bean, "Social Views of the Freewill Baptists," *The Freewill Baptist Centennial Papers, 1780-1980* (The Bicentennial Committee, The American Baptist Churches of New Hampshire, 1980), 25. Used by permission.

[2]*Minutes of the Freewill Baptist General Conference* (1833), 97, 98.

[3]"Home Missions," *Free Baptist Cyclopaedia*, 272.

[4]*Minutes of the Freewill Baptist General Conference* (1835), 121, 122.

[5]"Home Missions," *Free Baptist Cyclopaedia*, 272.

[6]*Minutes of the Freewill Baptist General Conference* (1844), 241.

[7]*Original Minutes of the Freewill Baptist General Conference* (1892) (Held by the American Baptist Historical Society, Rochester, N.Y.), 7.

[8]I. D. Stewart, *The History of the Freewill Baptists for Half a Century*, Vol. 1. (Dover, N.H.: Freewill Baptist Printing Establishment, 1862), 258, 259.

[9]Z. F. Griffin, *History of Our India Mission Field* (Sixteen page pamphlet held by the American Baptist Historical Society, Rochester, N.Y.), 2; Also see "The Mission in India," *Free Baptist Cyclopaedia,* 414, 429.

[10]Griffin, *India,* 4. Most of the notes for this section, "Foreign Missions," were taken from Griffin's pamphlet.

[11]John J. Butler, *Thoughts on the Benevolent Enterprises, Embracing the Subjects of Missions, Sabbath Schools, Temperance, Abolition of Slavery, and Peace* (Dover, N.H.: Published by the Trustees of the Freewill Baptist Connection, 1840.)

[12]*Minutes of the One Hundred and Seventieth Annual Session of the Central Conference of the Original Free Will Baptists of North Carolina* (1918), (Held by the Free Will Baptist Historical Collection, Mt. Olive College, Mt. Olive, N.C.), 1.

[13]Stewart, *Freewill Baptists for Half a Century,* 470.

[14]*Minutes of the Freewill Baptist General Conference* (1837), 142.

[15]Bean, "Social Views of the Freewill Baptists," 23.

[16]"Proceedings of the Freewill Baptist Convention." Original minutes of a called conference which met at Acton, Maine, Jan. 15, 1840. (Held by the American Baptist Historical Society, Rochester, N.Y.)

[17]*Minutes of the Freewill Baptist General Conference* (1841), 201.

[18]*Thirty-Seventh Annual Report of the Freewill Baptist Education Society* (Dover, N.H.: Freewill Baptist Printing Establishment, 1876), 7.

[19]"History of Parsonsfield Seminary." *Parsonsfield Seminary Sesquicentennial,* August 21, 1982, 41; Burgess and Ward, *Free Baptist Cyclopaedia,* 509.

[20]"The General Conference of Freewill Baptists: Information Respecting the Action of the General Conference in Regard to the Union of Baptists and Free Baptists in Missionary Work and in Other Denominational Activities," (Issued by the Committee on Conference with Other Christian People, by Order of the General Conference of Free Baptists, 1910), 4, 247 .

[21]I. D. Stewart, compiler, *Minutes of the Freewill Baptist General Conference* (1886), Vol. II (Boston: F. B. Printing Establishment, 1887), 516.

[22]*Minutes of the Annual Conference of the Original Free Will Baptists of North Carolina* (1891), 8, 9.

[23]Michael Pelt, *A History of Ayden Seminary and Eureka College* (Mount Olive, N.C.: 1983), 3.

[24]Ibid., 4, 5.

[25]*Minutes of the Thirty-Second Session of the Free Will Baptist Triennial General Conference, 1904*, 15.

[26]Pelt, *Ayden Seminary,* 9.

[27]Ibid., 14.

[28]Ibid., 18.

[29]*Charter for Free Will Baptist University of Nashville, Tennessee* (Copy held by the Free Will Baptist Historical Collection, Free Will Baptist Bible College, Nashville, Tennessee, Loose Collections, "C-18").

[30]*Minutes of the First Triennial Session of the Co-operative General Association of Freewill Baptists, 1916.* (Weatherford, Texas: *The New Morning Star,* 1917), 3-7.

[31]*Minutes of the First Adjourned Session of the Co-operative General Association of Freewill Baptists, 1917* (Tecumseh, Okla.: The New Morning Star Publishing House, 1918), 14.

[32]Ibid., 16.

[33]Ibid., 16.

[34]Ibid., 20, 21.

[35] *Tecumseh College Catalogue and Announcements* (1921-22), 11.

[36]Steven R. Hasty, "Zion Bible School," *The Time Machine*, Vol. 1, Number 1 (1982), 2, 3.

[37]Burgess and Ward, "Anti-Slavery," *Free Baptist Cyclopaedia*, 19, 20.

[38]*Minutes of the Freewill Baptist General Conference, 1835,* 123.

[39]*Minutes of the Freewill Baptist General Conference, 1841,* 208, 209.

[40]Ibid., 209-211.

[41]Ibid., 211.

[42]"Slavery As It Is," quoted in Butler, *Thoughts on the Benevolent Enterprises*, 103.

[43]*Fifth Annual Report of the Freewill Baptist Anti-Slavery Society* (Dover, N.H.: Wm. Burr, Printer, 1851), 1.

[44]Ibid., 1, 2.

[45]Ibid., 7.

[46]Burgess and Ward, "Anti-Slavery," *Free Baptist Cyclopaedia*, 20.

[47]Burgess and Ward in the *Free Baptist Cyclopaedia*, p. 20, have suggested that the Free Will Baptists in North and South Carolina were members ("in fellowship") of the New England group and that they were dismissed over the slavery issue. There is no evidence that this was true. The two groups corresponded and the General Conference included the South in its statistics but there were no formal ties.

[48]Burgess and Ward, *Free Baptist Cyclopaedia*, 20.

[49]Frank Moore, ed., *Rebellion Record: A Diary of American Events*, 12 Vols. (New York, 1861-1868), vol. 3, p. 13; vol. 4, p. 22. Quoted in C. C. Goen, "Broken Churches, Broken Nation: Regional Religion and North-South Alienation in Antebellum America," *Church History*, Vol. 52, No. 1 (March 1983), 34, 35.

[50]*Tax Lists, Davidson County, Tennessee, 1798 and 1805* (Held by the Tennessee Historical Commission, Nashville, Tennessee).

[51]*An Abstract of the Former Articles of Faith, Confessed by the Original Baptist Church Holding the Doctrine of General Provision.* (New York: Printed by D. Fenshaw, 1855).

[52]*Minutes of the Concord-Pantego Free Will Baptist Church* (1849-1874), 48, original minutes held by the Free Will Baptist Historical Collection, Mt. Olive College, Mt. Olive, N.C.

[53]*Minutes of the Mt. Moriah Free Will Baptist Association* (1869), 15, original minutes held by Mr. M. P. Gore, MeShan, Alabama.

[54]Minutes of the General Conference of Free Will Baptists, 1867, 4, 5.

[55]W. W. Sweet, *Revivalism in America*. (Gloucester, Mass.: Peter Smith, 1965), 118.

[56]Ibid.

[57]Stewart, *History of the Freewill Baptists for Half a Century*, Vol. 1, p. 466.

[58]Frederick L. Wiley, *Life and Influence of the Rev. Benjamin Randall*. (Philadelphia: American Baptist Publication Society, 1915), 248. *The Free Baptist Cyclopaedia* was not quite so dogmatic as Wiley concerning Randall's total abstinence, suggesting that he was "almost, if not quite, a total abstainer. . . ." *Free Baptist Cyclopaedia*, 638.

[59]"New Durham Church Records." Original Minutes held by New Durham Library. The churches and their leaders differentiated between "ardent spirits"—hard liquor and other fermented drinks, but it was recognized that wine, beer, and cider were capable of making one intoxicated. In fact, J. J. Butler argued that the less fermented drinks were more dangerous because they were deceptively potent and because they were available to everyone. "Some seem to think that if they refrain from use of ardent spirits, they are temperate of course, no matter how much of other intoxicating liquors they use. They can join in the wine revel, or get drunk on cider or strong beer, and yet be temperate? Strange. It is worse, far worse, both from the example exhibited, and from its debasing effects, to get intoxicated on wine, cider, or beer, than on rum, brandy, or whiskey. . . ." Butler, *Thoughts on Benevolent Enterprises*, 69.

[60]Burgess and Ward, "Temperance Society," *The Freewill Baptist*, 638.

[61]Donald Barr Chidsey, *On and Off the Wagon: A Sober Analysis of the Temperance Movement from the Pilgrims Through Prohibition*. (New York: Cowles Book Company, Inc., 1969), 14.

[62]*Minutes of the General Conference of Freewill Baptists* (1832), 75.

[63]Ibid., (1837), 148; (1850), 340.

[64]Butler, *Thoughts on Benevolent Enterprises*, 49-79.

[65]*Minutes of the General Conference* (1844), 244.

[66]*Minutes of the Mt. Moriah Free Will Baptist Church* (1852), original minutes held by Mr. M. P. Gore, McShan, Alabama, 9-11.

[67]*Minutes of the Annual Conference of the Original Free Will Baptist Church, of North Carolina* (1889), 8.

[68]*Minutes of the One Hundred and Sixty-Fifth Annual Session of the Central Conference of the Original Free Will Baptists* (1913), 6, 7.

11

Coming Together—Organization in the Latter Part of the Period

The last days of the nineteenth century and the first of the twentieth found the Free Will Baptists concerned about growth, education, theology, and maturity, but the primary concern was that of alliance and organization. From new local associations to alliances with other denominations to area-wide conferences, the period was characterized by organizational ferment. And while other matters must be considered, it is this primary area that demands most of our attention.

Relationships North and South

It already has been established that the question of North-South relationships is represented by two schools of thought within the denomination. The one contends that the New England segment of the denomination had no continuing impact on the present picture while the other implies that without Benjamin Randall there would be no Free Will Baptist history.

Research for this particular study indicates that a more practical position is found in a balance between the arguments of the two schools. Ohio, Kentucky, Texas, Missouri, and probably Florida can trace their roots back to the home mission efforts of New England's General Conference, and Indiana and Illinois received their first Free Will Baptist witness from that same source. In all these cases, it becomes impossible to ignore that early heritage.

But there is more to the story. Most of the southern states, where Free Will Baptist origins were varied and often spontaneous, eventually became involved in an organizational relationship with New England. A footnote attached to the statistical tables for the tenth General Conference in 1839 indicated the attitude of the southern associations at that early time and, indeed, throughout the entire period of slavery struggle between the North and South. "It will be seen by the minutes that by a vote of the General Conference the Conferences in North Carolina are not inserted in our statistical table, as they have never formally united with us, and have made no returns to the Conference for several years...."[1] In the light of that statement, recent historians have assumed that North Carolina and other southern states continued to exist in isolation from direct New England influence.

But late in the century, for some reason, most of the associations applied for admission to the General Conference. Even at that late date, some associations struggled with the new alliance. An interesting confrontation developed in the Tow River Association in eastern Tennessee. D. W. Adkins, a member of the association, was angered by that body's decision to reject the New England Treatise as a statement of faith for Tow River. The northern treatise had been adopted earlier, but it had caused unrest within the association.

> Rsoled (sic) to investigate a Difficulty in our denomination wheras ther is disfellowship among us. The adoption of the treaties of the Free will Baptist north taken place at the Association held in Johnson County, Tennessee, and was Refered to a set meeting to Be held in Bakersville the next October for Ratification or Rejection and was Rejected and wheras D. W. Adkins Refused to Be governed By that meeting and went on and Declared himself no more of us and thanked his god that he had gone out from among the horse swapers, hore mongers, and drunkards, ther fore upon thees grounds we disfelowship him in our denomination. . . .[2]

Tow River, along with Union and American Associations in Tennessee and North Carolina, applied for membership in the General Conference in 1874,[3] and were included in statistics for that year. The relationship was a brief one as the difficulty illustrated above seems to have ended Tow River's interest in alliance. They did not appear in General Conference minutes after 1874.

Though Tow River did not remain with the General Conference, their early entry into the larger body might well have encouraged others. (By 1886, most of the southern groups had applied for and gained admission: North Carolina (1880), Kentucky (1880), Cumberland Association, Tennessee (1883), Mississippi (1886), Georgia (1886), and South Carolina (1886). Lest some may doubt that these southern groups attained formal union with New England, North Carolina's request for admission should be noted:

> . . . By vote of our Conference . . . we respectfully ask that the General Conference admit us to Christian and denominational fellowship as a yearly meeting in your body, if you shall think it proper so to do. From our present knowledge of Freewill Baptist doctrines and usages, we believe ourselves essentially in agreement with you. To justify our uniting with you, we assure you of our warmest Christian and brotherly love.[4]

The General Conference responded by unanimously receiving eastern North Carolina and the Ohio and Kentucky yearly meetings.[5]

The Mt. Moriah Association in Alabama made overtures to the General Conference as early as 1870, predating even Tow River and the American and Union Associations. There is no evidence, however, that formal request for admission was made or that the association was received into the larger body. The attitude of the Alabama Association at the beginning might have made union impossible. In 1870, Ellis Gore and Thomas Maloy were appointed as a committee to correspond with the Freewill Baptists in the North "upon terms of coming together, . . ." but a resolution the following year limited their authority. At that time, their colleagues declared they were to "sacrifice no principal (sic) or usage in forming this relation."[6]

In summary, almost all of the southern states either officially joined the General Conference of New England or at least made serious inquiry into the possibility of alliance. At the same time, it should be noted that the alliances were tenuous and of short duration. Few of the southern associations reported to the General Conference meetings and delegates were seldom exchanged. Whether distance made the union unworkable or the southern churches already had some hint that the General Conference was seeking other, unacceptable alliances, Free Will Baptists in the South began to look elsewhere for fellowship and cooperation.

Other Influences from the North

As far-reaching as the organizational influence was, the Randall movement probably had more impact on the present denomination through its theological terminology and its statement of faith. This conclusion does not infer that the denomination simply adopted New England theology. Though leaders in the South were less educated than their northern brethren, they were men of the Word and had hammered out their own theological principles long before they felt the influence of New England. But the end of the century brought increasing interest in cooperation and union, and it was recognized that the fragmented South and the remnants of the New England movement needed a clear, accurate statement of faith that would be agreeable to all the parties interested in union.

As would be expected, Ohio and other individual states in the Midwest and West continued to use a revision of the 1869 *New England Treatise*. In fact, Ohio Free Will Baptists continued to reprint that treatise at least until 1949.[7] But use of the treatise went beyond the local state level. Yearly meetings in the Far West—Nebraska and Kansas—were firmly committed to New England both organizationally and theologically, and the General Conference treatise set the pace for their existence. The Southwestern Association, which included Texas and Oklahoma churches, also looked to New England as the parent conference, and understandably made use of their treatise.

Later, when the Western states combined forces and formed the Co-operative General Association of Freewill Baptists, the new body adopted a treatise that was copied almost verbatim from New England's 1869 revised statement of faith. An introduction to the Co-operative treatise indicated their dependence on New England. In that statement, they pointed to New England as the birthplace of the denomination and recognized their own Yearly Meetings were directly tied to Randall's organization.[8]

Because of its ancient heritage and tradition, North Carolina resisted adoption of the New England statement. *The Former Articles of 1812*, a slightly revised copy of the old *English General Baptist Confession of 1660*, served eastern North Carolina well for more than a hundred years. After the organization of the State Convention in 1913, however, the union of conferences from different backgrounds caused some difficulty. The Central, Eastern, and Western Conferences used *The Former Articles of 1812* while the Cape Fear Conference was governed by the New England treatise.

In 1915, a committee of four men—one from each Conference—was appointed and assigned the task of developing a unified statement of faith. The committee, consisting of R. F. Pittman, S. H. Styron, W. J. Braxton, and W. A. Jackson, reported at the 1916 State Convention and made available a new statement of faith that included articles from both backgrounds. The new treatise was accepted by the different Conferences and was published in 1916 along with a revised church discipline. In spite of initial acceptance of the new treatise, however, all was not well within the State Convention. In 1919, Elder D. W. Alexander asked that a committee of one be chosen to prepare a treatise suitable for North Carolina Free Will Baptists. Elder J. W. Alford was assigned the task. In 1920, the Convention returned to the old *Articles of Faith* and continued to reprint them until 1941.[9]

Michael Pelt, a professor and administrator at Mount Olive College in North Carolina, concluded that the State Convention's brief adoption of the *New England Treatise* came as the result of influence from the Cape Fear Conference and from the Co-operative General Association. In a letter to George Stevenson, Pelt expanded a conclusion he had drawn in a 1960 article published in *The Free Will Baptist.*

> The treatise which I call to your attention was adopted by the State Convention in 1916 and was later set aside in 1920. During this period in the history of the State Convention, North Carolina Free Will Baptists were influenced by the Cape Fear Conference (Free Will Baptist) and the Co-operative General Association both of which developed from the Randall movement. I think this accounts for the 1916 treatise.[10]

Whatever the influences, the State Convention returned to the "Former Articles" and continued to be guided by that treatise until they were received into the National Association. That alliance again returned the state's allegiance to the more widely accepted treatise. A note at the beginning of the 1949 printing of the *North Carolina Statement of Faith* reminded the readers that this edition was a revision of the *1949 National Association Treatise.*[11]

Finally, when the scattered churches, associations, and conferences were united through the organization of the National Association of Free Will Baptists, the denomination adopted a statement of faith that closely followed the wording of the old *New England Treatise*. Though the statement would be revised on a number of occasions, its content would remain essentially the same.

New England's influence was still a part of the continuing Free Will Baptist story.

The End of an Era—The Loss of New England

In the beginning of the second decade of the twentieth century, the Randall segment of the denomination completed its plans for merger with the Northern Baptist Convention and, in 1911, officially joined that organization. At this point in time, it is useless to bemoan the loss of New England or to speculate as to what might have happened had this large and well established group remained Free Will Baptist and become a part of the 1935 National Association. But New England's potential was enormous and the losses were staggering. Most all of the denomination's educational institutions were in the North, and the merger engulfed major colleges, Bible institutes, and seminaries in Maine, Michigan, and Ohio. Beyond this, and possibly even more damaging, was the loss of educational leaders who were included in the union. The merger also ended all mission activity for the Free Will Baptists. New England had supported missionary endeavor in India since the early years of the nineteenth century, but the entire missions program was lost in the new relationship with the Northern Baptists.

The impact of the merger probably is best illustrated by the statistics involved. Seventeen Yearly Meetings were included in the union, and except for local Quarterly Meetings in Ohio, Kentucky,

Texas, and other Western states, all segments of the General Conference gave up their identity and became a part of the Northern Baptist Convention.[12] In 1908, the denomination had 1,292 churches, 68 Yearly Meetings and Associations, and 87,015 members. At that time, they had three schools of "academic grade, New Hampton Literary Institution, Maine Central Institute, and Mannon Bible School. There were six colleges: Bates, Hillsdale, Geauga, Parker, Rio Grande, and Storer. They also had two theological seminaries: Cobb Divinity School, connected with Bates College, and the Theological Department at Hillsdale College."[13] The 1911 *Free Baptist Register and Yearbook* reported well over a hundred thousand members in the Randall camp.[14] It should be noted that this was the year of formal merger.

Looking Back: The Anatomy of a Merger

How do you consummate a merger between diametrically opposed bodies—the one Arminian and the other Calvinist?

The Freewill Baptists had exhibited an ecumenical spirit from the earliest days of the nineteenth century. In 1834, they were involved in a union meeting that sought to combine three or four denominations in evangelistic ministry. ". . . The Lord put it into their hearts to call a general union meeting; accordingly the Presbyterian, Baptist, Methodist, and Free Baptist churches agreed to commit and conduct a union meeting."[15]

The Second Great Awakening had already run its course, but American revivalism, with its cooperative spirit, was still alive and well, especially through such evangelistic leaders as Charles Grandison Finney. In that sense, the union meeting was not unusual. But for some of the Freewill Baptists, this was not a temporary cooperative effort. H. Whitcher, a Freewill Baptist elder, wrote to *The Morning Star* praising the union meeting. "My dear brethren, effect this union as far as possible, for by a united exertion the world will be converted to God. "[16]

For most of the rest of the century, the denomination limited its overtures toward union to those churches that were of similar nature. They frequently corresponded with the Free Christian Baptists of New Brunswick, certain General Baptist bodies, and the Free Baptists of Nova Scotia. In 1880, however, interest in cooperation with other unrelated bodies was revived. In the twenty-fourth General Conference, a committee was appointed to "consider the propriety of cultivating a better acquaintance and closer union of all open communion Baptist bodies. . . ."[17] By this time, the conference was already in correspondence with Regular Baptist bodies, and later discussions indicated that the Freewill Baptists were convinced that the Baptist position on open communion had been modified enough to allow both cooperation and union. By the beginning of the twentieth century, interest in union with the Northern Baptists was growing rapidly, and in October 1904, the General Conference appointed a committee of 12, designated as "the committee on conference with other Christian people."

The decision to establish a committee at that point in time was based on two factors: (1) delegates from the Disciples Church were present to encourage the Freewill Baptists to join their movement and (2) the denomination was convinced that their particular theology, originally preached by the founders of the denomination, "had been so far adopted by other Christian churches as to make the separate testimony of Free Baptists less important, if indeed necessary at all as in former years."[18] The latter factor was especially applied to the Northern Baptists:

> During this century and a quarter, the Baptists have been greatly modified. The yielding of rigid Calvinistic feeling recorded itself when in 1832 the New Hampshire Confession was adopted by the New Hampshire State Convention. In the middle states where the old Philadelphia Confession is nominally held it has either been expurgated of its strongest expressions or allowed to fall into 'innocuous disservitude.' The Baptists today have little, if any, more sense of restrictions in their Calvinism than Benjamin Randall had in 1780.[19]

The Freewill Baptists were not alone in their evaluation. A committee was appointed at the Baptist Conference in St. Louis in 1905 to meet with a like committee from the Freewill Baptists. These two committees presented the following resolution which was approved by both Baptist societies in Washington in May 1907.

> Resolved, that the Baptists and Free Baptists are so closely related by history which was long common, and have always been kindred, that they enjoy closer fellowship and a greater similarity in genious and spirit than are common between two Christian bodies. It is recognized as a fact that the original occasion and cause of separation between our two bodies have practically disappeared, and that in all the essentials of Christian doctrine as well as church administration and polity we are substantially one.[20]

The next year, the joint committee added one statement to the agreement. "Differences, if still existing, may be left where the New Testament leaves them, to the teaching of the Scriptures under the guidance of the Holy Spirit."[21] For all practical purposes, the basis for union was now established and remaining negotiations needed only to work out the machinery necessary for such a huge undertaking.

Actually, until the agreement of 1908, the Freewill Baptists had found themselves faced with a number of options. They struggled, not so much with the question of union, as with the question of the partner in union.

Four factions within the denomination demanded audience. The first continued negotiations with the Disciples of Christ and were calling loudly for union with that body. The second spoke of earlier ties with the Baptist fellowship and reminded the denomination that these two groups had much in common and were preaching the same gospel messages, in many instances, to people of the same communities. The third faction pleaded for an even older heritage and suggested union with the Congregational churches of New England. And finally, the fourth option offered a continued witness as a Freewill Baptist denomination. Advocates of this latter option argued that the mission of the denomination was not completed and that the ministry begun by Benjamin Randall was more urgent and necessary than it ever had been.[22]

The final decision involved a process of elimination. The invitation from the Disciples was declined quickly as denominational leaders recognized that these two groups were too far separated geographically and that while union would be gratifying in the areas of pride and a sense of growth, such union would not meet the needs of the local congregation. Union with the Congregationalists was deemed impractical because it would demand that the Freewill Baptists totally dispose of their heritage. Not only would the name be changed, but they would be subjected to an entirely new set of traditions and inheritances. In spite of these difficulties, interest in union was not abated. The faction interested in a continued Freewill Baptist witness simply was ignored. Because the Baptists agreed to open their doors to the Freewill Baptists, because the Freewill Baptists could retain at least a part of their name, and because the Baptists guaranteed that Freewill Baptists' identity would not be destroyed, alliance between the two groups seemed the only workable solution.

Unfortunately, ecumenism, then as now, was not kind to the smaller denomination. The two bodies agreed prior to union that each should take the other without requiring alteration in faith or practice and that the Freewill Baptists would continue to enjoy their identity and heritage. It quickly was recognized that those agreements were ideal rather than practical. The smaller denomination disbanded their home mission society and made their accumulated funds and property available to the American Baptist Home Mission Society. Activities of the Freewill Baptist Home Mission Society were transferred to the American Baptist organization, and *The Morning Star*, the weekly paper published by the Freewill Baptists for more than 75 years, was consolidated with *The Watchman*, which was later combined with *The Examiner* as *The Watchman-Examiner*. The Sunday school periodicals and general publications were acquired by the American Baptist Publication Society. Educational interests which had been, for the most part, under the control of independent bodies, were left to adjust their plans of cooperation with the Northern Baptists as seemed best for each school.[23]

Looking back on the merger in 1924, Alfred Williams Anthony, joint secretary for the two denominations and a Freewill Baptist in background, listed the advantages of the merger: (1) The Freewill Baptists as a small body gained the confidence and enthusiasm of a larger body, (2) the Freewill Baptists enjoyed economic relief as the larger body took over the financial responsibility for missions and education, and (3) competing churches—Baptists and Freewill Baptists—in local communities united and became one large, progressive church.[24] Whatever the advantages, the Freewill Baptists of New England paid an exorbitant price. From this point, identity was lost and the denomination simply ceased to exist.

The Remnant: Getting Ready—Experimenting in Organization

The loss of New England vividly reminded the Free Will Baptist remnant of the dangers of fragmentation and isolation. If survival was at all possible, it would depend on the cooperation of churches and associations in a united denomination.

The Triennial General Conference

At least some associations were aware of the need for unity even before the merger of 1911. Representatives from Cumberland Association in Tennessee, the North Dakota Yearly Meeting, Horry Conference in South Carolina, Cape Fear Conference in North Carolina, Hamburg Association in Arkansas, the Mt. Moriah Conference in North and South Carolina, the Stone Association in Tennessee, the Ohio River Yearly Meeting, and the Western, Eastern, and Central Conferences in North Carolina, met in Nashville, Tennessee, in 1901 for the "Thirty-first" session of the Triennial General Conference. The fact that the 1901 conference was recorded as the Thirty-First Session was somewhat confusing. A quick glance at the minutes, however, solved the mystery. Thomas E. Peden, clerk of the General Conference and professor at the Free Will Baptist Seminary in Ayden, North Carolina, came to the South from Ohio. In the earlier context, he was related to the Randall movement in New England, and his handling of the minutes indicated that he brought much of his earlier denominational baggage with him. The dating scheme for the Triennial Conference simply picked up the dates used by the larger General Conference in New England. Peden evidently saw the new Triennial Conference as an extension of the older conference in the North. His statistics for the year further illustrated this conclusion. He not only included all of the associations in the South but added all the New England Yearly Meetings and the mission field in India.[25]

The Midwestern Remnant

This information brings the discussion to an interesting point. Until recently, historians had ignored Ohio's relationship with the South, possibly because they were unaware that such a relationship existed. Since there was no documentary evidence to suggest otherwise, it was assumed that four Quarterly Meetings in southern Ohio discussed and rejected the 1911 merger and chose instead to remain Free Will Baptist. They then were left to struggle in isolation until they joined the National Association some years later.

Triennial minutes for 1901 made it clear that Ohio was seeking new alliances at least as early as the beginning of the century. Ohio then, negotiated with another General Conference 11 years before New England's merger with the Northern Baptists and at least three or four years before the first merger committees were reported. One questions why they became restless at this early date. The link probably was Thomas Peden. His long tenure in Ohio not only allowed him to make friends in high places within the denomination, but also offered access to inside information concerning new directions for the General Conference. Actually, Peden did not need a crystal ball to know that the denomination was moving rapidly toward a merger with other Christian bodies. His alliance with the new Triennial Conference in 1901 does not suggest he had specific information about the merger with the Northern Baptists because the denomination itself had not yet moved that far in its negotiations. He did know that union was a primary theme of the day and that loss of identity for the General Conference was a definite possibility.

As early as 1886, the conference clearly outlined its position on union.

> We, the delegates of the Free Baptist General Conference, acknowledging the manifold
> blessings with which God has favored the people we represent, recognizing the impor-

tance of the work still before our people, taking into consideration the fact that God is moving his children of every name to closer relationships with each other, as well as with himself, and in order that our position on the question of Christian union may not be misunderstood, hereby set forth the following declarations:

1. We believe in the spiritual unity of all the followers of our Divine Lord, and desire so to manifest his spirit as to evince our unity with him and with all who love him.

2. We are ready to form such alliances with other Christian bodies as may promise larger results in advancing our Lord's kingdom.

3. We are ready to join in organic union with such Christian bodies as may so far agree with us in doctrine and usage as to give assurance of continued harmony and peaceful relations in Christian work.

4. We regard loyalty to Christ and the Bible, and the independence of the local church, as suggesting a basis on which closer relationships with other Christian bodies may be attained.

5. We direct the Conference Board to take into consideration, and report upon at the next General Conference, such opportunities for closer relationships with other Christian bodies, as may, in their judgment, give promise of increasing our own usefulness in helping bring the world to acknowledge Christ as King of kings and Lord of lords.[26]

It is not really surprising that Peden and the Free Will Baptists in southern Ohio found they could not tolerate so radical an ecumenical spirit. Indeed, it is amazing that out of all the Yearly Meetings closely associated with New England, only a few were willing to reject the will of the conference. The denomination had existed for more than a century and was extremely proud of its Freewill Baptist heritage. Now, only four Quarterly Meetings in the Midwest and a few Yearly Meetings in the Far West were determined to retain that heritage.

For these few, the General Conference had been "weighed and found wanting" and the Ohio brethren acted quickly. The Triennial General Conference in the South met at least once before the beginning of the new century. *The Free Will Baptist*, the official publication for the South, advertised a meeting in Nashville in 1896.[27] Since no records are available for the 1896 session, there is no way to know if Peden and his Ohio brethren were present, but Peden was conspicuously present for the 1901 sitting of the conference. By that time, he had gained enough respect to be chosen clerk of the new association. Part of that respect came as a result of his move to Ayden, North Carolina, to assume the principal's task at the Ayden Free Will Baptist Seminary. This small rural town, which housed the Free Will Baptist Publishing Company and the Seminary, became a focal point of interest for the Triennial Conference. From this vantage point, Peden projected himself into the center of denominational activity.

The solution seemed quite simple. There was no mystery at all in Ohio's decision to bypass the merger of 1911. In fact, they made their decision at least 10 years earlier and had, in their own minds, ceased to be a part of the New England General Conference at that time. The Ohio Free Will Baptists anticipated the merger and gave Peden the task of finding a new denominational home that would allow them to retain their Free Will Baptist heritage. Peden performed his task admirably. He not only located a body of believers that would offer fellowship and cooperation to the New England remnant, but became an active part of the new organization in order to ensure Ohio's acceptance into the new conference.

Dr. Michael Pelt, a professor at Mount Olive College in Mount Olive, North Carolina, and a diligent researcher in North Carolina Free Will Baptist history, suggested another possibility. Working from Peden's position of influence in the 1901 session, his use of New England dating for the new General Conference, and the inclusion of all the New England Yearly Meetings in the Triennial's statistics, Pelt concluded that Peden was present at the 1896 meeting and was largely responsible for its organization. In other words, Peden, aware of merger talks in New England and fearful for the denomination, took the initiative in organizing a new conference that would carry on the tradition of the Free Will Baptists in America. Pelt goes on to say that it was at the Nashville meeting that Peden was introduced to the brethren from North Carolina and, as the result, was offered the principal's office at the new seminary in that state.[28]

There is some merit to Pelt's theory. It is evident Peden and the Ohio Free Will Baptists were uneasy about proceedings in the General Conference for a good number of years. The first official dissent came in 1887, just one year after the General Conference so graphically expressed its position on union. In that same session, the conference proposed a revision of the constitution and the Ohio River Yearly Meeting strenuously objected. They ". . . unanimously disapproved the proposed new constitution of General Conference and emphatically protested against its adoption."[29] The proposed constitution called for the name of the denomination to be changed from the General Conference of Freewill Baptists to the General Conference of Free Baptists, and this well might have upset delegates from Ohio. It is more likely, however, that the second article was the point of contention. It was here the constitution attempted to enforce the agreements on union that had been presented earlier. The article redefined the character of the General Conference.

> It shall be composed of Yearly Meetings, Associations, and other bodies of evangelical piety that believe in a general atonement, the necessity of regeneration, baptism by immersion, and the communion of all Christians; said bodies to be received by two-thirds vote of the members present.[30]

The door was now open for ecumenical dialogue and Ohio's response indicated it was in this area that they had difficulty.

Consideration must be given also to Peden's long relationship with the Triennial Conference. He continued to serve in that body until it was disbanded in 1910.[31] Pelt's assumption that Peden's leadership during the 1896 Triennial Conference so impressed leaders from eastern North Carolina that they asked him to be head of the seminary is not entirely unlikely. At the same time, however, they could not have discovered his educational capabilities had he been a simple delegate from the state of Ohio.

In summary, both theories demand attention and deserve additional research. One further matter needs to be considered as conclusions are drawn. Ohio was directly linked with New England from the first decade of the nineteenth century and was never involved in Free Will Baptist activity in the South. On the other hand, eastern North Carolina, with the Free Will Baptist Press and its Seminary, exerted influence across the entire South. Many of the churches used Sunday school literature published by the Press and many individual members in the South were subscribing to its paper, *The Free Will Baptist*. The possibility that leadership and organization began here and later "adopted" Peden must be given consideration.

Whatever its role, Ohio was firmly entrenched in the new Triennial General Conference by 1901. That session found the Ohio River Yearly Meeting duly represented by letter and by delegates. Thomas Peden already had assumed the position of clerk.

The Demise of the Triennial General Conference

The General Conference met again in Dunn, North Carolina, in 1904; in Nashville in 1906 (possibly 1907); and in Florence, Alabama, in 1910. By the latter year, interest in the association began to wane and the Florence Conference proved to be the last. The delegates did not make an official decision to disband, but it was evident that the conference could no longer exist under present circumstances.[32]

The Southwestern Association

The Southwest Free Will Baptist Convention was admitted to the General Conference of New England in 1907 and, more than likely, eventually became a part of the 1911 merger. Alfred Williams Anthony, joint secretary for the Freewill Baptists and the Northern Baptists, reported in 1913 that he attended the Southwestern Convention the previous year and removed their misapprehensions about the merger.[33] Though a small remnant of the Southwestern General Convention remained to establish later twentieth century Free Will Baptist work in the area, the association itself did not remain with the denomination and, therefore, does not have claim to space in this segment of the story. In spite of that, it was felt that some comment should be made. This early Convention was noteworthy in at least two or three respects. In the first place, though these churches and associations were a part of the New England General Conference, their fellowship in the General Convention was much more akin to Free Will Baptist polity and government in the Southeast. In 1913, the conference included 17 associations in Texas, Oklahoma, and Missouri, and boasted some 5,000 members.[34] This organizational structure was quite different from the typical Yearly Meeting made up of Quarterly Meetings in a given district.

The association also must be noted because of its contributions in leadership for later years. I. W. Yandell, who served as president of the old Southwestern Convention, offered advice and counsel to the remnant and eventually wrote a popular history for the continuing denomination. Lizzy McAdams, a popular evangelist, soon made her influence felt far beyond her Texas home and went on to have an outstanding ministry throughout the denomination.

The association was small and its life was short, but its impact continues to be felt among Southwestern Free Will Baptists.

The Co-operative General Association

When the National Association of Free Will Baptists was organized in 1935, the Co-operative General Association in the Midwest and Far West was one of the two major bodies involved in the union. The first Triennial Session of the proposed Co-operative Association of Free Will Baptists met at the Philadelphia Church near Pattonsburg, Missouri, on Wednesday, December 27, 1916. Delegates with authority to organize the new association came from the Nebraska Yearly Meeting, the Northwest Missouri Yearly Meeting, the Central Western Missouri and Southeastern Kansas Association, the Northern Kansas Association, the Laclede County Association, the Niangua Association, and the Central Brazos Association of Texas. On Thursday, the delegates were seated and a motion was carried to enter into permanent organization. J. H. Wolfe of Nebraska was elected moderator; J. F. Duckworth of Northwest Missouri, assistant moderator; Ira Waterman of Laclede County, Missouri, clerk; and W. E. Dearmore, of Nebraska, assistant clerk.[35]

Before the Convention was adjourned, the delegates accepted a constitution containing nine articles and a set of by-laws containing sixteen articles; voted to purchase *The New Morning Star*, edited by S. L. Morris; established a Free Will Baptist Biblical Correspondence School; and agreed to establish a resident denominational school. Before the association met again in 1917, a gift of property and cash from the city of Tecumseh, Oklahoma, provided facilities for both the correspondence and the resident schools. Offices and printing facilities for *The New Morning Star* also were moved to the new location.

The Co-operative General Association finally brought together the Free Will Baptists of the West and Southwest into one body. It was to continue to meet every three years until after the entire denomination was brought together in the National Association in 1935.

As mentioned earlier, the first statement of faith adopted by the Co-operative General Association in 1917 was virtually a verbatim copy of the 1869 revision of the *New England Treatise*. The similarity between the two statements of faith extended to footnotes and Scripture texts used as support for the various doctrines. The newer treatise included foot washing as an ordinance of the church. It should be remembered that New England also included the practice in their first treatise in 1834. Later statements of faith instructed the local churches to make their own decisions concerning the practice, and the Co-operative Association simply exercised that prerogative. As would be expected, there were some differences in the book of discipline that accompanied the Treatise, but the association was careful to retain the distinctives of the denomination—the universal call of the gospel, open communion, and the possibility of apostasy.

The Tri-State Association of Free Will Baptists

Ohio played an active and important role in the first Triennial General Conference from 1901 to 1910, and joined the New General Conference after 1920. But their interest in this later regional body soon became less intense. By 1924, they were represented only by letter, and in 1928, they asked E. T. Phillips, a North Carolina minister, to serve as a proxy for their delegate, M. B. Hutchinson. After that year, they no longer were represented.

From the very first, Ohio was geographically separated from other associations in the South, and active participation in their ministry was difficult. Even so, Ohio remained faithful throughout the 10 years of existence of the earlier General Conference. This new conference simply developed a year too late. The long pause between the demise of the first General Conference and the birth of the second caused Ohio to seek fellowship from other sources. Their failure to become involved in the new conference was not as much a lack of interest as it was conflict of interest. Ohio was already a part of a new association.

The Tri-State Association was organized on October 4, 1919, and included the Scioto Yearly Meeting, Ohio; Big Sandy Yearly Meeting, Kentucky; and the West Virginia Yearly Meeting. By 1931, the Tri-State Association embraced seven Quarterly Meetings with 45 member churches. Leaders for that year included H. B. Conley, F. S. VanHoose, Millard VanHoose, Burns Castle, Scott Daniel, Irvin Rice, and Alonzo Dickson of Kentucky; I. N. Russell, Jess Sizemore, Henry Messer, W. J. Shepherd, J. A. Kemper, J. S. Yealey, Sullivan Persell, James Shunkwiler, and Milford Riddlebarger, of Ohio; and T. S. Young, L. D. Ridenor, N. C. Cremens, and C. F. Ferguson of West Virginia.[36]

The Tri-State existed for almost fifteen years and served an urgent need for fellowship and cooperation in the Appalachian area.

The Second General Conference of the South

The first Triennial General Conference of the Original Free Will Baptists ceased to exist in 1910. Thomas Peden, one of the driving forces in the organization, attained a ripe old age and other leaders were growing old as well. Ohio and Nebraska found themselves far removed from center stage and travel was difficult. These and other factors led to a lack of interest that finally destroyed the conference.

During the next ten or eleven years, associations and churches in the South continued to struggle independently, without central leadership or national organization.

For a brief moment, it looked as though 1918 would be the year of solution. In that year, key representatives from the South and East visited the first Triennial session of the Co-operative General Association being held in Paintsville, Kentucky. The representatives were well received and J. L. Welch of Tennessee and F. H. Styron and P. E. Beaman of North Carolina soon found themselves involved in committee work for the Co-operative. The southern representatives were so impressed with the Co-operative that they invited the body to hold its next session in their territory in Nashville, Tennessee.[37]

The honeymoon was a brief one. Tennessee and North Carolina were received officially by the Co-operative, but Free Will Baptists East and West came from different backgrounds and had established different identities. The time was not right for merger.

The harmony of 1918 was shattered when the Co-operative met in Nashville in 1919. John H. Wolfe, formerly of Nebraska and by this time president of Tecumseh College, proved himself a strong foe to change. He almost single-handedly rescued the Nebraska Yearly Meeting from the merger of

1911 and was known throughout the Northern General Conference as an enemy to merger negotiations. Now, in 1919, he championed a new cause.

Representatives from the East found that Wolfe and two of his colleagues, Samra Smith and Ira Waterman, not only failed to preach footwashing as an ordinance of the church, but were openly antagonistic toward the practice. It should be remembered that the practice was listed as an ordinance in the *1917 Co-operative Treatise*, but it must also be recognized that, in this case, preaching and practice did not agree with theological statement. On the other hand, the churches in the South taught that the church practiced three ordinances and they asked that the Co-operative take the same stand. When Wolfe and his followers refused, Tennessee and North Carolina seceded from the association, setting the stage for a new organization for the South and East.

John L Welch, the delegate from Tennessee and the host pastor for the Nashville session of the Co-operative, remembered the struggles and the results of that 1919 meeting.

> . . . When we met at Nashville, we found that the Co-operative General Association would not take a definite stand on the matter of feet washing. John H. Wolfe, you know about him from Nebraska. He was a part of the old Northern Free Will Baptists. He refused to join in with the others. He fought the whole movement. He was at the head of this Co-operative Association and he didn't practice feet washing, the Free Wills of the North didn't. Well he had a man named Samuel (Samra) Smith. He was his right-hand or left-hand man in that movement and Smith wouldn't agree. And they had another man named Waterman, Ira Waterman. He didn't go along with it so they wouldn't agree to take a stand on it. They wanted to leave it an open question. The North Carolina and Tennessee people wanted it as an ordinance you see. Well, the result of the argument was that the North Carolina group and our group (Tennessee) pulled out from the Co-operative because we had been accepted in this 1919 meeting at Cofers, but we pulled out over this question of feetwashing.[38]

On Thursday, May 26, 1921, a delegation of Free Will Baptists from Tennessee, Alabama, Georgia, and North Carolina met at Cofer's Chapel Church in Nashville for "the purpose of entering into a national organization." Since the participants represented the same churches that made up the first General Conference of the Original Free Will Baptists of the United States, it was decided that this newest association should bear the old name and be considered a revival of that heritage.

The conference organized, drafted a constitution, and elected its first officers. John L Welch of Tennessee was elected president and was to serve with D. W. Alexander of North Carolina, vice president; J. E. Hodgins of Alabama, treasurer; Neal H. Parrish of Georgia, field secretary; J. W. Alford of North Carolina, chairman of the executive committee; and Parrish, B. P. Armstrong, M. B. Hutchinson, and J. E. Hodgins as executive committee members.[39]

In the beginning, the new conference was more limited in scope than its predecessor, serving only those churches and associations in the Southeast. The picture changed dramatically by 1935, the year that would bring national organization, as the General Conference recorded twenty associations in nine states—Alabama State Convention, Alabama-Florida State Line Association,

Southeastern Conference of Alabama, Liberty Association of West Florida, Salem Association of West Florida, Martin Association (Ga), Midway Association (GA), Union Georgia Association, Union Association (GA), Nebraska/Northern Kansas, Cape Fear Conference (NC), Central North Carolina State Convention, Eastern North Carolina Conference, North Carolina State Convention, Ohio River Association, South Carolina Conference, Cumberland Association (TN), Union Association (TN), and the Texas State Convention.[40]

At last the Free Will Baptists were drawing near to national organization. The Co-operative Association, working largely from a New England background had unified the West and the General Conference; their name—the Original Free Will Baptists—pointing back to their 1727 origin, had unified the South and East. The National Association of Free Will Baptists was now just a brief step away.

The Denomination on the Eve of Final Organization—a Pattern Confirmed

In the first three decades of the twentieth century, the federal government conducted and published a series of religious surveys that were amazingly thorough and valuable. Unfortunately, as is true of many government documents, few know that they exist. Only the determined researcher will locate them in the dark recesses of the various state archives and historical collections.

The surveys were published every ten years beginning in 1906, and the 1906 and 1926 issues included limited statistics from an earlier survey conducted in 1890. Well-organized charts and tables offered comparisons and contrasts in each ten-year period, indicated growth patterns, and revealed something of the character of the various American denominations. In addition, the editors included a brief overview of each denomination including history, doctrine, polity, and religious activity.

The government admitted that the work often was frustrated by lack of response from individual churches and associations and were sometimes guilty, especially in their study of the South, of adding churches that should have been listed with other organizations. At the same time, these surveys constitute the most exhaustive and accurate records of denominational growth and activity in the early twentieth century that are available.

Whether or not the government survey overestimated the number of Free Will Baptists after the merger of 1911, the growth rate was phenomenal. From 1890 to 1906, the denomination gained 441 organizations (churches and associations), and 28,416 members whose influence was now felt in 13 states as against two at the beginning of the period. In 1906, the denomination reported 608 churches, 263 Sunday schools, and 12,720 Sunday school pupils. The denomination experienced significant growth in all but two areas—ministerial housing and salaries. Statistics indicated that only eight parsonages existed at the turn of the century and that as late as 1916, the average salary for pastors was $476 per year. Only 36 pastors in the entire denomination reported a full salary. Three hundred and forty-five supplemented their salaries by other occupations, and of these, 257 were reported as farming.[41]

A comparative summary, published in 1926, revealed the unusual growth that the Free Will Baptists had enjoyed from 1890 until the summary publication. The years surveyed were 1890, 1906, 1916, and 1926. (See table on following page).

The greatest growth came between 1890 and 1906. Of course, it must be recognized that this first period consisted of 16 years rather than the typical ten, but the growth was so dramatic that the time element cannot be considered totally responsible. The number of local churches increased by 264.1%, membership increased by 239.5%, and the number of Sunday schools increased from 0 to 263.

The 1926 total of 79,592 members included 46,790 females and 31,910 males. Eight hundred ninety-two members were not identified by sex.[42]

The churches continued to show a lack of interest in housing for the pastors. The small growth enjoyed in housing in 1916 was lost before the next survey ten years later.

The period was one of rapid and significant growth, and it should be remembered that this was a time of theological turmoil and difficulty for many denominations. The fundamentalist-liberal controversy was everywhere evident. On the other hand, it could very well be possible that the controversy benefited rather than harmed this small, conservative denomination.

COMPARATIVE SUMMARY, 1890 to 1926: FREE WILL BAPTISTS[43]

ITEM	1926	1916	1906	1890
Churches (local organizations)	1,024	750	608	67
Increase over preceding census:				
Number	274	142	441	—
Per cent	36.5	23.4	264.1	—
Members	79,592	54,833	40,280	11,864
Increase over preceding census:				
Number	24,759	14,553	28,416	—
Per cent	45.2	36.1	239.5	—
Average Membership per church	78	73	66	71
Church edifices:				
Number	770	656	556	125
Value—Churches reporting	9	14	8	—
Amount reported	$1,156,743	$517,240	$296,585	$57,005
Average per church	$1,512	$788	$535	—
Debt—Churches reporting	69	42	37	—
Amount reported	$32,564	$6,260	$3,536	—

Parsonages:

Value—Churches reporting	765	656	554	—
Amount reported	$18,400	$9,630	$3,400	—
Debt—Churches reporting	2	—	—	—
Amount reported	$2,800	—	—	—

Expenditures during year:

Churches reporting	872	612	—	—
Amount reported	$252,613	$75,935	—	—
Current expenses and improvements	$179,730	$64,182	—	—
Benevolences, missions etc.	$66,557	$11,653	—	—
Not classified	$6,326	—	—	—
Average expenditure per church	$290	$124	—	—

Sunday schools:

Churches reporting	643	390	263	—
Officers and teachers	4,202	2,547	1,440	—
Scholars	38,199	22,421	12,720	—

In addition, the surveys revealed information far more important than mere statistics. They touched on the character of the denomination as well. Traditionally, especially in the South, the denomination was rural in nature and typically ministered to the lower middle and lower classes of society. It was true at the beginning, in 1727, and it would continue to be true until the mid twentieth century. Unlike many larger denominations, the Free Will Baptists continued to move horizontally rather than vertically in social development. It is entirely possible that the denominational leaders of 1929 did not recognize the rural character of their organization, but statistics for that year revealed how thoroughly that characteristic captivated the entire movement.

Of the 1,024 churches in the denomination at the end of the first quarter of the twentieth century, only 41 were in urban situations,[44] while 983 were located in rural areas. This translated into 96% rural and 4% urban. At that time, the denomination could be characterized as small, Arminian and ultraconservative in theology, rural in nature, Congregational in government, and associational in structure. Most of these characteristics continued to be descriptive of the movement at least until the middle of the century. Some were to be non-negotiable and would continue to be a part of the future of the Free Will Baptists. Still closely related to the fundamentalist movement, the denomination jealously guards its conservative Arminian theology and the autonomy of the local church. When compared with mammoth organizations like the Southern Baptists with their 15,851,756 or the United Methodists with their 8,400,000, the group is still extremely small. The *1999 National Yearbook* reported a total membership of 206,397 for the 1997-98 reporting period. This number reflected a loss of 37,261 members since the 1981-82 report. The discrepancy could well be explained by new and more accurate accounting methods.[45]

But the denomination did not remain completely static. One aspect of its character did change significantly. Government statistics published between 1906 and 1926 confirmed that the denomination was predominantly rural in its orientation. Only a few churches were located in urban areas, and these often proved to be small towns of less than 3,000 inhabitants. Little change could be noticed during the next two decades, but the late 1950's introduced dramatic changes both overseas and in the United States.

In the late 1930's and throughout the 1940's, most of the churches were at rural crossroads or in small communities, pastors served at least two churches with each church enjoying pastoral ministry twice a month, and many pastors found it necessary to accept secular employment in order to meet the needs of their families. The denomination continued to minister mostly to the lower middle and lower classes of society. In 1955, when a small congregation meeting in the national offices building decided to build in a fairly affluent neighborhood, it met instant opposition. Free Will Baptists seldom had ministered in this type of community, and there was much doubt that such an endeavor could be successful. In spite of the concern, the Horton Heights Church did build in the area and continues its ministry to the present time.

By the end of that decade, new denominational mission strategists prescribed the planting of churches in large urban areas that were to become mission centers for outreach into less populated areas. Successful ministries were begun in Campinas, Jaboticabal, and Ribeirao Preto in Brazil and in Tokyo, Abashiri, and Bihoro in Japan.

The denomination broke a pattern that had prevailed for more than two hundred and thirty years and now found that urban ministry was not only possible but effective and rewarding.

In almost the same breath, the urban flavor made its influence felt in the United States. Large city churches sprang up in Tidewater, Virginia, in Michigan, and in other areas. While the typical church still would retain elements of the old rural character and few would have more than one hundred members, it was not unusual for urban churches to include doctors, lawyers, and other professionals in their congregations. A few would amass more than a thousand members. The old pattern was broken and the denomination's limited ministry finally was expanded to meet the needs of the city.

Finally, the statistics revealed one additional pattern that has continuing impact on the denomination. For most of the early years and up through World War II, women have far outnumbered men in the total membership of the denomination. Government surveys for 1916 and 1926 indicated that the pattern was well-established by the early twentieth century. In 1916, there were 32,764 females in the movement as compared to 22,013 males and in ten years, the numbers had grown to 46,790 females and 31,910 males.[46] The imbalance became even more pronounced during the second World War and in a denomination that traditionally was ruled by men, women, by necessity, found themselves cast into roles that earlier were not open to them. Many served in the teaching ministries of the church, some became choir directors and Sunday school superintendents, and at least a few found themselves responsible for the preaching ministry of the church as well.

Looking Back—The End of an Era

The year 1935 found the denomination on the brink of national organization. The Free Will Baptists had learned their lesson well—isolation and divisiveness tend to spell disaster and survival depended on their joining forces in one national body.

By this time, a modified version of Arminian theology was firmly entrenched, most of the churches were in agreement on church polity and government, and the denomination already had tasted the potential of union in the success of the Co-operative Association in the West and the General Conference in the East. The doctrines were hammered out and streamlined during the nineteenth century, the lifestyle was adopted and defended, the struggles that were common to the various groups of Free Will Baptists across the country, and the shared grief at the loss of the New England segment of the movement in the 1911 merger combined to draw together the Free Will Baptists of the twentieth century into one body—one in purpose, doctrine, ecclesiology, and spirit.

Notes for Chapter 11

[1]*Minutes of the Tenth General Conference of the Free Will Baptist Connection* (1889), Vol. I (Dover, N. H.: Published by the Freewill Baptist Printing Establishment, 1859), 158.

[2]*Minutes of the Tow River Association of Free Will Baptists, 1851-1886* (1882), original Minutes held by the Free Will Baptist Historical Collection, Free Will Baptist Bible College, Nashville, Tennessee.

[3]*Minutes of the Twenty-Second General Conference of Free Will Baptists* (1874), 281.

[4]*Minutes of the Twenty-Second General Conference of Free Will Baptist Connection* (1880), Vol. II. (Boston: F. B. Printing Establishment, 1887), 383.

[5]Ibid., 390.

[6]F. C. Smith, "Rise and Progress of the Mt. Moriah Church and Mt. Moriah Association with Some of Their Labor," 1888. Handwritten manuscript held by Mr. M. P. Gore, McShan, Alabama.

[7]*Treatise on the Faith and Practice of the Free Will Baptists* (Portsmouth, Ore.: Compton Engraving and Printing Company, 1949).

[8]*A Treatise on the Faith and Practice of the Free Will Baptists, adopted by the Co-operative General Association* (Tecumseh, Okla.: The New Morning Star Printing Co., 1917).

[9]Michael Pelt, "The Former Articles of Faith and the Present Statement of Faith of Original Free Will Baptists in North Carolina." *The Free Will Baptist,* Vol. 75, No. 29 (July 27, 1960), 8. Used by permission.

[10]Michael Pelt, "Letter to George Stevenson, June 29, 1960," held by the Free Will Baptist Historical Collection, Mt. Olive College, Mt. Olive, North Carolina.

[11]*A Treatise of the Faith and Government for the Original Free Will Baptists of North Carolina (1949),* 7.

[12]*Minutes of the Thirty-Fifth General Conference of Free Baptists* (Auburn, Me.: Merrill & Weber Company, Printers and Bookbinders, 1913), 6.

[13]"The General Conference of Free Will Baptists: Information Respecting the Basis of Union and Proceedings Related Thereto" Pamphlet (1908), 2-5.

[14]*Free Baptist Register and Year Book, 1911* (Hillsdale, Mich.: General Conference Free Baptists, 1911), 65.

[15]"Religious Intelligence," *The Morning Star,* Vol. 9, No. 1 (Wednesday, May 7, 1834), 3.

[16]Ibid.

[17]*Minutes of the Twenty-Fourth General Conference of Free Will Baptists, 1880,* Vol. II, 28.

[18]Alfred Williams Anthony, "Twenty Years After: The Story of the Union of Baptists and Free Baptists During the Period of Negotiation and Realization, 1904-1924," Reprint from *Christian Work* (October 18, 1924), 1.

[19]"The General Conference of Free Will Baptists: Information Respecting the Basis of Union and Proceedings Related Thereto," (pamphlet held by the American Baptist Historical Society, Rochester, New York, 1908), 4, 5.

[20]Ibid., 5.

[21]Ibid.

[22]Anthony, "Twenty Years After," 2.

[23]This information taken from Anthony, "Twenty Years After," 4, 5.

[24]Ibid., 6, 7.

[25]*Minutes of the Thirty-First Session of the Free Will Baptist Triennial General Conference,* (Ayden, N.C.: The Free Will Baptist Publishing Company, 1903), 13-15. Dating scheme suggested by Michael Pelt, Mount Olive College, Mount Olive, North Carolina.

[26]*Minutes of the Twenty-Sixth General Conference of Free Will Baptists,* Vol. II, 507.

[27]"Free Will Baptist General Conference," *The Free Will Baptist Advocate,* Vol. 15 (Wednesday, May 27,1896), 1.

[28]Michael Pelt, telephone interview, July 21, 1983; Michael Pelt, personal interview, February 3, 1983.

[29]"Records of the Ohio River Yearly Meeting Called Free Will Baptist, 1887," Vol. 1—1833 to 1897.

[30]*Minutes of the Twenty-Sixth General Conference of Free Will Baptists,* Vol. II, 493.

[31]John L Welch, personal interview conducted by Robert Picirilli (Transcribed from tape; original held by The Free Will Baptist Historical Collection, Free Will Baptist Bible College, Nashville, Tennessee; April 25, 1971), 12, 13.

[32]Ibid.

[33]Alfred Williams Anthony, *Getting Together: Baptists and Free Baptists for Two Years,* pamphlet, Report of Special Joint Secretary (October 15, 1913), 11.

[34]*Minutes of the Thirteenth Annual Session of the Free Will Baptist—South West Convention* (Normangee, Tex.: Star Print, 1913), 27.

[35]*Minutes of the First Triennial Session of the Co-operative General Association of Free Will Baptists, 1916.* (Weatherford, Texas: *The New Morning Star,* 1917), 2.

[36]*Minutes of the Tri-State Association of the Free Will Baptists, West Virginia, Kentucky, and Ohio, 1931,* 1-12.

[37]*Minutes of the Second Adjourned Meeting of the First Triennial Session of the Co-operative General Association of Free Will Baptists, 1918* (Tecumseh, Okla.: New Morning Star Publishing House, 1919), no pagination.

[3]John L Welch, personal interview conducted by Robert Picirilli (Transcribed from tape; original held by The Free Will Baptist Historical Collection, Free Will Baptist Bible College, Nashville, Tennessee; April 25, 1971), 11.

[39]*Minutes of the First and Second Annual Session of the General Conference of the Original Free Will Baptist of the United States, 1921, 1922* (Ayden, N.C.: Free Will Baptist Printing Co., 1922), 4.

[40]*Minutes of the Fifteenth Annual Session of the General Conference of the Original Free Will Baptist of the United States, 1935* (Ayden, N.C.: Free Will Baptist Press, 1935), 2.

[41]*Religious Bodies, 1906,* Vol. II, *Separate Denominations* (Washington: United States Government Printing Office, 1910), 125; *Religious Bodies, 1916,* Vol. II, *Separate Denominations* (Washington: United States

Government Printing Office, 1919), 113.

[42]*Religious Bodies, 1926,* Vol. II, *Separate Denominations* (Washington: United States Government Printing Office, 1929), 153.

[43]Ibid., 154.

[44]Urban areas included in all cities and other incorporated towns of 2,500 or more inhabitants. Status as towns or cities was based on the 1920 Census of the United States.

[45]*1983 Free Will Baptist Yearbook* (Nashville: Published by the Executive Office, National Association of Free Will Baptists, 1983), 137; *1999 Free Will Baptist Yearbook* (Nashville: Published by the Executive Office of Free Will Baptists, 1999), A-247. Additional analysis of these statistics will be found in Chapter XV.

[46]*Religious Bodies, 1916,* 152; *Religious Bodies, 1926,* 115.

Part III

A Continuing Witness:
From Organization to Maturity
(1935-1983)

12

The National Association of Free Will Baptists—Birth Pangs

The stage was set for national organization long before 1935. Memories of the huge losses experienced through the New England merger with the Northern Baptists as well as the more positive success enjoyed by the Co-operative Association in the West and the General Conference in the East combined to spur the Free Will Baptists toward national union. The cooperative spirit that had developed in the early part of the century continued to play a major role in on-going negotiations as a number of independent groups began to actively seek membership in one or the other of the larger bodies.

E. C. Morris, who served the Free Will Baptist Church in Bryan, Texas from 1929 until 1932, claimed to be the author of the first formal proposals for discussion between the Co-operative Association and the General Conference.[1] After leading the State Convention of Texas into a formal relationship with the Eastern General Conference, Morris, along with M. L. Sutton and J. L. Bounds, attended the Co-operative Association and invited the Western group to send representatives to the next Eastern Conference which was to meet at the church in Bryan in June 1932. The invitation was accepted, and the committee's visit was the first of a number of exchanged visits over the next few years.

If, indeed, Morris did initiate the first step toward formal negotiations, he simply took advantage of an atmosphere and spirit already evident both in the East and West. In 1930, R. F. Pittman, moderator of the General Conference, addressed the question of union in his annual message to conference delegates and admonished them to "lay aside selfishness and look beyond our Associations and conferences, into a National view."[2] The delegates had an opportunity to exercise that "national view" as Texas petitioned for membership and was warmly received.[3]

Two years later, in his annual report, J. L. Welch, field secretary, reminded the conference that Free Will Baptists in the East had dreamed of a national organization since they themselves had reorganized in 1920.

Whether or not Morris was the first to call for formal discussion is debatable, but the Cooperative Association accepted his invitation and sent a committee on union to the General Conference in 1932. This group, along with a committee of five appointed by the host conference, was instructed to submit a plan of merger the following year. The committee, consisting of J. L. Welch, J. W. Alford, K. V. Shutes, Henry Melvin, A. D. Ivey, and M. L. Morse[4] of the General Conference, and G. W. Scott, Jr., B. F. Brown, Selph Jones, Melvin Bingham, Noel Turner, and

Winford Davis of the Co-operative Association, drafted a proposal for union that was acceptable to both parties.

> We the Joint Committee of the General Conference and the Co-operative Association, agree to the following:
>
> We agree to accept the *Articles of Faith of the 1901 Treatise*, also the Church Covenant contained in the same Treatise, together with all the forms and usages set forth in same, with such amendments as may be made and approved by the body when perfected into one organization.
>
> We heartily agree to the merging of the General Conference and Co-operative General Association into one body, and we urge that steps be taken immediately for the final consummation of such a union.[5]

The document was signed by J. W. Alford and B. F. Brown as representatives of the two participating organizations.

Though two more years passed before formal organization was achieved, most of the ground work was completed by the two committees in that 1933 agreement.

The veteran Free Will Baptists who still remembered the unsuccessful attempts at union in 1919 and 1920 must have felt that the new accord came almost too easily. But times had changed and a new spirit of cooperation overshadowed, at least for the moment, the earlier disagreements that kept East and West apart for more than a decade. The direction taken by these two major bodies in the last few years made that union almost inevitable. If the final agreement produced any surprise at all, it was limited to the simplicity of the document. In three brief paragraphs, the two committees mutually agreed to abide by one statement of faith and one discipline. Provision was made for either conference to introduce amendments, but no exceptions or exclusions were included in this first report, and conference minutes published between 1930 and 1935 do not reveal any serious discussions demanding prejudice by either side.

The agreement was a product of a collective attitude and atmosphere that demanded union of an increasingly warm relationship between East and West. For a number of years, fraternal delegates had been exchanged, and each organization made room in its conference programs for institutional reports from the sister conference. Visiting ministers were often asked to preach, and both organizations continued to encourage union negotiations. By 1933, the denomination was ready for formal union.

By the time of union, both segments of the denomination began to keep statistical records, but, at best, the records were less than accurate. As best can be determined, initial membership in the new body totaled at least 80,000. A statistical report published by the General Conference just before union indicated that the larger conference had churches in North Carolina, South Carolina, Tennessee, Virginia, West Virginia, Georgia, Alabama, Florida, Arkansas, Texas, Mississippi, and Ohio. The report included 817 churches, 721 ministers, and 64,126 members. The Co-operative

Association added more than 16,000 members, 291 churches, and 563 ministers. The states represented were Ohio, Kentucky, West Virginia, Oklahoma, and Missouri.[6]

The statistics reflected at least one difference in practice for the two conferences. In the East, the number of churches far outnumbered the number of ordained ministers pointing to a system that required one minister to serve at least two churches and sometimes four on a part-time basis. Typically, church practice called for formal worship in a particular church on two Sundays of the month while the other two were limited to the Sunday school hour. Fifth Sundays were reserved for area-wide Union meetings. On the other hand, Western practice, at least in Ohio, Kentucky, and West Virginia, encouraged ministers to visit various churches in their area and gave many of them an opportunity to preach even though they were not responsible for a particular congregation.

In Kentucky, churches ordinarily met one Saturday night and one Sunday per month, much like early Randall practice in New England. Members were expected to travel to other churches on subsequent weekends. A Saturday night or Sunday morning service in any given church might include as many as five to ten ministers. It was not unusual for as many as three or four to preach during the time of worship. In that setting, the Tri-State Association's 300 ministers and 100 churches did not indicate an unworkable imbalance.

By 1934, final plans were complete for formal union. In November of that year, the joint committee for union met in Denison, Texas, to outline the parameters for organization. In addition to the terms established in Nashville in 1933, the committee agreed to add two additional conditions: (1) that the two bodies would continue to operate under their present organizations without becoming in any way responsible for each other's present obligations and (2) that the terms of union would not infer jurisdiction of one conference over the other.[7] In practice, the two bodies would retain their identity while cooperating under the umbrella of a national organization. As its final act, the committee designated the East Nashville Church in Nashville, Tennessee, as the site for the organizational meeting for the National Association of Free Will Baptists and appointed J. L. Welch, of the General Conference, as temporary moderator, and Winford Davis, of the Co-operative Association, as temporary assistant moderator of the first session of the new national body.

The Birth of the National Association

The Eastern General Conference and the Co-operative General Association of the West met together in joint session for the first time on Tuesday evening, November 5, 1935, in Cofer's Chapel Church in Nashville, Tennessee. Though formal organization was delayed until additional delegates could be present, this Tuesday evening meeting constituted the first official session of the new National Association of Free Will Baptists.

The following day, I. J. Blackwelder, serving as secretary pro tem, led in the seating of delegates from six State Conventions and 14 local associations. The list included representatives from Alabama, North Carolina, Georgia, Mississippi, Oklahoma, Missouri, Texas, Nebraska, Tennessee, Kentucky, West Virginia, and Ohio. Three delegates from the Arkansas State Conference also attended, but served only as observers since Arkansas Free Will Baptists were not yet ready to commit themselves to the new organization.

In spite of the cooperative spirit that had prevailed as early as 1925, it was natural that some fear should remain on both sides,[8] and the first election of officers reflected the association's concern for fairness and for equal representation. Major officers included J. L. Welch, moderator (General Conference), Winford Davis, assistant moderator (Co-operative Association), I. J. Blackwelder, secretary-treasurer (General Conference), and B. P. F. Rogers, assistant secretary-treasurer (Co-operative Association). The same careful provision for each organization continued in the appointment of committees and in the choosing of preachers for the plenary worship sessions of the association.

One of the first and most important items of business was the drafting of a constitution and by-laws for the new organization. Henry Melvin, E. S. Phinney, M. L. Hollis, A. D. Ivey, E. A. O'Donnell, J. E. Hudgens, J. M. Haas, and B. F. Brown served as the committee responsible for this important task. L. C. Doyle from Arkansas also served in an advisory capacity. "Article I" officially declared the new group to be the National Association of Free Will Baptists and subsequent articles redefined the parameters of the old General and Co-operative Conferences. For all practical purposes, the two bodies would retain their identity and would continue to carry on their own business activities.

The old General Conference was renamed the Eastern Association of Free Will Baptists, and the Co-operative became the Western Association of Free Will Baptists. The parent body was to meet every three years with the member bodies continuing to meet annually.

The National was designed as an advisory body, but reserved the right to settle questions of discipline, doctrine, and usage that were brought before it by member organizations. Its offices included a moderator, assistant moderator, recording clerk, assistant recording clerk, a treasurer, and an executive board. National Executive Secretaries were appointed for major departments within the denomination including foreign and home missions, young peoples' work, women's work, and Sunday school.

The Eastern and Western Associations continued to function for another three years, but ceased to exist after 1938. The minutes of the two subordinate associations do not record discussion of the dissolution, but their demise probably was precipitated by the 1938 decision to call the National Association together yearly rather than triennially. That decision came at the recommendation of the Eastern Association during their last meeting in 1938. A delegation was appointed to deliver the recommendation to the Western Association which was to meet in Paintsville, Kentucky, the following month.[9] Once the recommendation was adopted, there was little reason for the Eastern and Western Associations to continue their existence.

Though the Western Association had been quite successful in its educational endeavors, it had not given a great deal of attention to women's work or to the youth of the church. For the most part, the new National Association looked to the old General Conference for organization in those areas. In its organizational meeting in 1935, the National Association adopted the Free Will Baptist League, the Woman's Auxiliary, and the Sunday school work of the General Conference.

The Choosing of an Organizational Structure

The new National body organized along the lines of an associational structure and adopted a series of standing boards which were to bear the responsibility of handling associational business.

All of the boards would have responsibilities that continued throughout the interim between National meetings.[10]

The duties of the various boards included the responsibility to plan programs and to supervise operations in their respective fields. The members of the boards were to be elected at the National level, but individual boards were responsible for internal organization such as election of officers and the establishment of regulations and guidelines necessary for the successful accomplishment of their ministry. All boards were limited to a total of five members by the Constitution, and these were elected on staggered terms of 1 to 5 years. Once organization was completed and all five members were elected, one member was to be elected each year for a term of five years to fill the vacancy of the retiring member.[11]

The executive board was granted the power to act in behalf of the National Association from one regular session to another and was to allow a continuity that had not been present in earlier organizations.

The new board system not only offered a more efficient system for associational business, but also gave relief from the cumbersome committee structure that had been a part of the denomination's tradition both East and West. Except for a committee on credentials and one on program, the new boards would meet the needs of the denomination for the next number of years. The elected boards included the Executive Board, Foreign Missions, Home Missions, Sunday School, Free Will Baptist League, Education, Superannuation, and the Woman's Auxiliary.

In the 1940 session of the National Association, a new General Board was created to replace the existing Executive Board. The new board was designed to better represent individual associations and was to meet prior to each annual session of the National Association to consider business that would come before the larger body. This representative body was to screen such business and anticipate areas of difficulty. Discussion at this level was to result in resolutions that would be considered in the plenary business sessions later. This new system offered the potential for increased efficiency during National sessions. The new board included an Executive Committee that was to serve in between sessions much like the original Executive Board had served in the early years of the National Association. In addition, the plan called for the appointment of an Executive Secretary who would set up a permanent office and coordinate the many responsibilities assigned to the General Board.

Sometime during the following year, the Executive Committee employed L. R. Ennis of Goldsboro, North Carolina, at a salary of $50 per week. Though the committee accepted responsibility for the weekly salary, it was understood that any income that the new Executive Secretary accumulated from evangelistic meetings and pastorates should be applied to the salary. In that first year, the committee found itself responsible for just $1,056 of the Secretary's total salary.[12]

The choice for an Executive Secretary proved to be a good one. Though Ennis served three churches of approximately 800 members in three different associations in North Carolina, he still found time to travel more than 12,000 miles for the denomination.

The responsibilities of the office quickly multiplied, and in 1943, the General Board recommended that the denomination elect a full-time Executive Secretary and that a permanent office be established in Nashville, Tennessee.[13] Eventually, it was determined that the Secretary should be elected every two years, but a number of these key leaders served for extended periods of time.

L. R. Ennis, 1940-42	W. S. Mooneyham, 1953-58
Robert Crawford, 1943-47	Billy Melvin, 1959-66
Ralph Lightsey, 1948	Rufus Coffey, 1967-78
Damon Dodd, 1949-52	Melvin Worthington, 1979-

Representation

At its inception in 1935, the National Association consisted of the Western and Eastern General Associations, and representation in the larger body was limited to these two organizations. The two associations were to continue to handle their own business, meet annually, and then send delegates to the National which would meet triennially. It was quickly recognized that this structure was less than adequate, and in 1938, delegates to the National body introduced resolutions of change in the areas of composition and representation to the National. At that time, it was decided that the National Association should be composed of State Associations, and of District Associations in those states that had no state organization.

Representation to the National Association was to be by states. Each State Association was entitled to five delegates to be elected from the laity, regardless of the number of District Associations in the state. In addition, each state was then allowed one delegate for each of its District Associations. These delegates were to be elected by their respective associations. District Associations having no State Association were to elect delegates and send them directly to the National Association.[14]

As years passed, the denomination continued to adjust and refine the representation system, but for the most part, representation continued to be by states. Under its present charter, delegates are of two kinds: (1) standing delegates, who are the ordained ministers and missionaries in good standing with an affiliated organization, the officers of the National Association, and members of the various boards, commissions, and committees of the National Association; and (2) lay delegates who are elected representatives of the various organizations and churches affiliated with the National Association.[15]

The Question of Funding

With organization at the national level came added expenses that ranged far beyond the experience of the denomination's past organizations. In 1942, in order to meet those needs, the General Board recommended a "unified program fund" that would be monied by the denomination and allocated monthly to meet the expenses of the different boards of the denomination. The schematic for the first funding year included 10% for superannuation, 20% for home missions, 30% for foreign missions, and 40% for Christian education.[16]

The large amount allocated for education gave clear testimony to the denomination's growing concern for progress in that area. In 1943, the first full year of unified giving, the income totalled $3,841.44, and $2,973.50 was allocated to the respective Boards during the year.[17]

The unified plan served well for a number of years, but as the denomination grew, the need for improvement was evident. In 1954, the Executive Committee of the General Board recommended the adoption of a new "Cooperative Plan of Support." The new program was to become effective July 1955, and would include financial provision for the growing responsibilities of the Executive Department. Recognizing that denominational needs would increase dramatically over the next few years, resolutions reintroduced the following year encouraged the churches to give at least 10% of their general offerings to the Cooperative Fund and encouraged individual Boards to promote their own particular phase of the work in the area of giving by individuals, groups, and churches.[18] By this time, the educational program was well underway and it was now possible to cut the Cooperative pie into more equal slices. Under the new program, funds for education were reduced, and those for Foreign and Home Missions were increased accordingly.

Patterns of Growth

Final union accomplished through the organization of the National Association did not result in phenomenal growth for the denomination, but it did mark the inauguration of a steady, healthy growth pattern that would continue to be typical for the next five decades. A brief investigation of the internal vitality of the denomination serves as the best measuring rod for growth.

Organizational Adjustments

The appointment of an Executive Secretary in 1941 gave early warning that the simple organizational plan that had been introduced in 1935 was already in need of revision. The dissolution of the Sunday School and Woman's Auxiliary Boards (the latter at the request of the Auxiliary Convention) in 1939 gave testimony to the denomination's determination to retain a simple organization. But growing responsibilities at the national level would soon dictate the establishment of a larger and more complex structure.

The demise of the Sunday School Board isolated the National Association from its two major publishing houses, limiting its ability to initiate publication and leaving it without authority over the work that already was being done. Recognizing the importance of a well organized denominational literature program, the association quickly offered solution to the dilemma through the introduction of a new board, that of Publications and Literature. The new board was appointed in 1942 and took its place among the other standing boards of the National Association.

As time passed, denominational growth could be measured by the number of new committees, boards, and commissions that were added at the national level. By 1952, the two original committees had been increased to seven, and growing crowds and programs at the annual meeting demanded a Committee on Committees, as well as Credentials, Resolutions, Temperance, Placement, Program, and Nominating Committees. Changing needs and constant growth continued to direct the evolution of the organizational structure to its present form which includes seven boards and two continuing commissions dealing with theological liberalism and denominational history.

The Family Begins to Grow

Kenneth Scott Latourette, in his study of Christian history, determined that revival and growth within the church are at least partially determined by a particular movement's inner vitality. Again, in part, that internal vitality is measured by the number of new organizations added to the larger body. This type of growth prevailed for the last number of decades before the organization of the National Association and would continue to be a part of its growth pattern after 1935.

Earlier chapters have traced the origins of those state organizations that developed before 1875, but those studies told just a small part of the story of Free Will Baptist progress.

Missouri

As was true for many of the Western states, Free Will Baptist work in Missouri was a product of the General Conference in New England. The movement that developed in the late nineteenth century grew rapidly. By 1890, the state boasted enough Yearly Meetings and local associations to merit the formation of a State Conference. Under the direction of J. H. Culley, president of the conference for at least five years, the new state meeting prospered briefly and then began to decline. By 1896, the conference was reduced to two Yearly Meetings and four or five Quarterly Meetings. By the end of the century, the State Conference disbanded. But in spite of its short life, this first attempt at a state level organization gave testimony to the early maturity Missouri Free Will Baptists had achieved.[19]

At least a few of the leaders of the original State Conference continued their ministries into the twentieth century, and by 1905, they began to spark interest in a new State Association. C. S. Lattimer, William McKown, and C. E. Mann of the old conference, joined T. C. Ferguson, R. W. Watterman, J. J. Wood, S. B. Lewis and others of the younger ministers in a campaign that would result in the birth of a new Missouri State Association in 1914.[20] The new association embraced seven associations and one independent Quarterly Meeting. Most of the associations included at least a few churches in Kansas and the Indian Creek Association listed one congregation in American Falls, Idaho.[21]

The cooperative spirit that found expression in the two earlier State Associations continued to be characteristic of the Free Will Baptist movement in the state, and Missouri found itself represented in the old Southwestern Free Will Baptist General Convention, the initial meeting of the Co-operative General Association in 1916, and in the National Association when it was organized in 1935.

At least one source suggested that a history of the Free Will Baptists in Missouri must date back to as early as 1865. In an interesting paragraph, the source included dates, names, and a list of the pastors who served the church until its demise in 1872.

> . . . The Free–Will Baptist society was first organized at Kirksville, June 4, 1865, by Reverend J. H. Wesscher, with James Phoebe Hayes, William, Jane, Minemoh and Mary Smith, Jay McMorrow, Eleanor Dennis, Charles and Nancy Scoville, Guy and Sarah A. Chandler, Eliza Middleton, H. Young, Jupiter Webb (a colored member), Mrs. M. N. Wesscher, Mary Jones, Cary Ferguson, Nell Mathews, and Mrs. Dunham. This society erected the first house of worship ever built in Kirksville, in May 1866. In 1867

Reverend Mr. Cooley was pastor; after him came Revs. Wesscher, D. C. Miller and A. Sell. In 1872 the church disbanded, ultimately the little pioneer church building was sold to the Southern Methodists in 1875, was torn down in 1881, and sold to Bernard, who used the lumber in burning brick.[22]

Though the author did not include documentation to support his account, the book was first published in 1888 and it was quite likely that eyewitnesses to the event were still alive and available for interview.

Illinois

Illinois, like Missouri, could boast of an early Free Will Baptist heritage that traced directly to the General Conference of New England. Like Ohio, the state would include a few churches that escaped the 1911 merger with the Northern Baptists and retained their original identity.

Since Illinois did not organize a State Association until 1960, little attention has been given to the state's denominational historical significance. But their role in the Free Will Baptist story is an important one. In the first place, this state gives the best example of the impact of the merger. When the Central Illinois Yearly Meeting convened in 1915, the delegates agreed to dissolve the conference and to change the constitution so that the entire Yearly Meeting would henceforth be represented by seven trustees that would meet with the Southern Illinois Baptist Association.[23] That brief benediction fell far short of telling the full story. Except for a few churches in the Franklin and Wayne County Quarterly Meetings in the south central portion of the state, all of the Free Will Baptists of Illinois were swallowed up in the merger. Fifty-four churches were received into the Southern Illinois Baptist Association as charter members.[24]

Campbell Hill could be traced back to 1850 through the ministry of Henry S. Gordon, the first Free Will Baptist missionary in the area. At that time, the church ministered under its original name, the Looney Springs Free Baptist Church. Ava, Pipestone, Sato, and Camp Creek also could point to Free Will Baptist tradition that served them for sixty-five years.[25]

After the merger, the Franklin and Wayne County Quarterly Meetings joined forces in the organization of the Southern Illinois Yearly Conference. After adding the Freedom Quarterly Meeting some time later, the conference continued to represent the largest number of Free Will Baptists in the state until the organization of the State Association in 1960.[26] The State Association was formed August 20, 1960, at the state Camp Ground Tabernacle in Benton, Illinois. Some forty-four churches related to the Canaan District and the Southern Illinois Yearly Conference met together for the purpose of organization. George W. Waggoner served as temporary chairman and supervised the election of the first officers for the association. The delegates elected Leon McBride, moderator; Claude Hampleman, assistant moderator; Jesse Boswell, clerk; and Betty Hampleman, treasurer. The state was represented at the National level for a number of years before the State Association was formally organized.

Texas

Texas was mentioned earlier but little was said about its actual history. This state, too, must trace its earliest beginnings back to the missionary endeavor of the General Conference of New England. The first church was organized in Clayton, Penola County, in 1876 by A. M. Stewart. Stewart also was responsible for the founding of four other churches in the same area and for the organization of the Texas Association of Free Will Baptists in 1878. The first Quarterly Meeting in the Dallas-Fort Worth area was organized in 1883 and included the Randall church, the first Free Will Baptist church in North Texas. The West Fork District Association, still in existence, was organized in 1889 and now serves churches in the Dallas-Fort Worth area.

By 1886, the ministry had spread to the central part of the state with the organization of the Bright Light Church near Bryan. The Central Texas District, organized in 1905, included sixteen churches in two Quarterly Meetings.

Free Will Baptists in Texas expressed an early interest in organizational union with others of like faith. They were represented in the old Southwestern Free Will Baptist General Convention which included associations from Oklahoma and Missouri, and remnants of the 1911 merger. They began to court the Eastern General Conference as early as 1930. Their delegates were officially seated with the conference in the session that met in Nashville in 1933.[27]

It is interesting to note that the stage was set for alliance with the General Conference when, in 1930, the Texas State Association formally rejected the continued wooing of the Northern Baptists. A resolution introduced in 1929 accused the Northern Baptist Convention of teaching Darwinian evolution and of modernism. The resolution asked that the Texas State Conference no longer recognize connection or relationship with the larger denomination.[28] In 1930, the resolution was approved and Free Will Baptists in the state ended a fraternal relationship with the Northern Baptists that began in 1910. It was at this meeting that the State Association determined to seek new relationships with other Free Will Baptist groups.[29]

The State Association was organized at Bradley Junction, October 8, 1915, and has been in continuous operation since that time. E. L. Hill served as the association's first moderator, and W. E. Dearmore was their first clerk.[30] The state was represented at the first National Association when it met in Nashville in 1935.

Nebraska

The Free Will Baptist movement in Nebraska did not survive until the birth of the National Association and technically should not be included in this chapter, but recent Home Mission endeavors and the establishment of new churches there have revived interest in the state's contribution to the denomination's history. Two points of interest speak of an exciting background and demand at least a cursory investigation.

First, where Illinois gave the best illustration of the impact of the 1911 merger with the Northern Baptists, Nebraska gives the best testimony of the attitude of the small remnant that refused to give up its heritage. The testimony could have been repeated in most of the states that were affected by the alien union.

A few of our pastors have felt that they could not void the prospects of a denominational union with the Baptists So have packed baggage and moved over into the Baptist camp. This has weakened our forces, Scattered our flocks, and brought discouragement into our otherwise courageous churches. To rally our forces, man our churches, and bring back hope, are the problems we have today and must Solve. The field is still here, good churches and parsonages, building opportunities untold, and we are able to go up and possess it.[31]

The account also indicates that at least a few churches had accepted union before 1911.

The second area of interest centered in a system of cooperation that was introduced by the Nebraska Yearly Meeting in 1906 and predated the cooperative system of the National Association by some forty-eight years. In this case, the system extended beyond simple finances and included a constitution designed to regulate the life of the Yearly Meeting along with its various boards and committees. But, at the same time, the system spoke often to the question of finance and giving. The Executive Board was instructed to encourage every member and friend of the Yearly Meetings to contribute toward the support of the gospel and each Quarterly Meeting was required to report its contributions on an annual basis. Article 8 encouraged each church to participate in the building of new church buildings and parsonages across the state arguing that it was "the duty of the whole body to assist each church in turn, under the direction of the Executive Committee, concentrating for the time on one place, or a few places, and so making the work lighter and easier for all, and also surer of success."[32]

As unique and as innovative as the cooperative system might have been, it was not enough to ensure the survival of the Yearly Meeting. The dreams of John Wolfe, W. E. Dearmore, R. V. Whitaker, and others were not to be realized in their generation. Perhaps the recent revival of Free Will Baptist ministry in the state will continue the work begun by those pioneer missionaries who served the denomination so well in the early part of this century.

Oklahoma

Tradition claims that Oklahoma is one of the few states in the Midwest and Far West that can trace its Free Will Baptist heritage to sources other than New England.

By 1884, Elders J. M. Roberts and R. J. Townsend found their way from Arkansas to the Indian Territory of Oklahoma. Roberts settled at McClain in the present Muskogee County, and Townsend made his home in the area known as Southern Indian Territory. Both of these men were related to Free Will Baptists in Arkansas, and their early work in Oklahoma produced a number of churches of that order. Concord Church was established in 1892 and soon was followed by Fields Chapel Church near Porum, and Mountain Home Church near Webbers Falls. The Central Association, the oldest district association of the state, was organized in 1893. The organizational meeting was held at Center, Indian Territory, and the new association consisted of four churches founded by Townsend.[33] This earlier association was followed quickly by the forming of the Territorial Association of Free Will Baptists in August 1894.

Churches at Concord, Liberty, New Hope, Shahan, and Pleasant Ridge, with a total membership of 145, constituted the membership of the new organization. Eventually, the association was divided into two bodies, separated by the Canadian River, and by 1903, became known as the Grand River and Roberts-McGee Associations.[34]

In 1908, the Canadian, First Oklahoma, Grand River, Roberts-McGee, Gaines Creek, Southern, and Southeastern District Associations joined together to form the Oklahoma State Association of Free Will Baptists. Leaders of this new state level organization included I. W. Yandell, J. E. Yandell, Jake Smith, J. D. Kimbrough, T. J. Townsend, D. J. Davis, and Elders Hutchinson and Sledge.[35]

Oklahoma, like Texas and Missouri, had been a part of the old Southwestern General Conference and the Co-operative Association. When the National Association was organized in 1935, Oklahoma was represented by both the State Association and the Dibble Association.

Mississippi

The Mississippi State Association consists of three District Associations, all three of which have ministered to Free Will Baptists in the eastern part of the state. Though the Northeast Mississippi Association dates only to 1935, the others are much older. The Little Brown Creek Association was organized in 1891 and was composed of churches in Prentiss and Tishomingo Counties. The South Mississippi Association, originally called the Zion Rest Association, was organized in 1907.[36]

As early as 1942, the Zion Rest and Northeast Associations joined hands to form the first Mississippi State Association. Little Brown Creek was represented by D. W. Jones but did not petition for membership.[37] This first state level organization embraced a nucleus of twelve churches, but the minutes for the organizational meeting listed only five ministers: M. L. Hollis, G. M. Pearson, J. M. Haas, George C. Lee, Sr. and C. M. Jenkins.[38] The following year, the two associations reported 2,468 members, 14 ordained ministers, and 19 churches.[39]

Though the small organization seemed to prosper for a number of years, financial difficulties soon forced its dissolution. In 1948, the state found it necessary to borrow money to meet its obligations, and the credentials committee for the State Association sought financial help from member churches. But help did not come, and the association did not meet in 1949.[40]

No further attempts at state organization were made until November 7, 1964, when Free Will Baptists in Mississippi joined at Lee's Chapel Church near Laurel for the purpose of organizing a new State Association. The officers of the new organization included Luther Gibson, moderator; John Haisten, assistant moderator; Daniel Gaskins, clerk; Billy Sharpston, assistant clerk; and John Reed, treasurer. Though the Little Brown Creek Association did not send delegates to the 1965 session, they have participated at the state level since 1966.[41]

In spite of their late organization at the state level, Mississippi did not hesitate to become involved in the National Association. The first session included delegates from the Northeast Association, and by 1938, Mississippi state leaders were serving in official capacities at the National level.

Virginia

The minutes for the New England General Conference spoke of a Virginia Association in 1870, and later minutes included both the Clinch River (present Clinch Valley) and the John Wheeler Associations. However, there is no evidence that the earlier churches survived, and the relationship between New England and the John Wheeler and Clinch Valley Associations seems to have been of short duration.

The Clinch Valley Association, located in the Southwestern portion of the state, was organized in 1876 and is the oldest in the state.[42] The John Wheeler Association had its origin in the Tow River Association of eastern Tennessee. That association was organized in 1880 and included churches in southwest Virginia and in Sullivan County, Tennessee. Early ministers included R. P. Moore, J. W. Pannel, J. W. Chatham, J. E. Holden, S. D. and A. A. Cox, M. Simmerly, T. J. Russell, and W. Miller.[43] All of the early work was in this portion of the state as Tidewater would not begin to have impact until the mid-twentieth century.

In 1939, representatives from Sandy Valley, Southwest Virginia, and Clinch Valley Associations were involved in an organizational meeting for a State Association. The group met at Mary's Chapel Church in Coeburn. Again, all of the participants were from the southwestern part of the state. John Wheeler Association was added to the number in 1949, and in 1952, the East was represented for the first time when the Tidewater Quarterly Meeting joined the Southwest Virginia Association and, consequently, became a part of the State Organization. Tidewater did not become a fully recognized District Association in the state until 1964. The first leaders of the State Association included James Boatright and B. W. Presley.[44]

Virginia was received into full membership in the National Association in its second meeting at the East Nashville Church in Nashville, Tennessee, in 1938.

West Virginia

Denominational history in West Virginia is similar to that of its sister state, Ohio, and could rival Ohio's heritage in antiquity. But, unfortunately, there are too few documents and sources available to allow the structure of an accurate history.

The origins of the work in the state cannot be traced. *The Free Baptist Cyclopaedia*, published in 1889 in New England, suggested that the state's Free Will Baptists of the nineteenth century came from three different sources, all within the confines of the state and all related to the General Conference of New England. These included the Harper's Ferry Quarterly Meeting, organized in 1868; the Taylor Quarterly Meeting; and the First Kanawha Quarterly Meeting, organized in 1883. After 1873, the Taylor Quarterly Meeting existed under the new name, the West Virginia Association.

The founding of two colleges early in the second half of the nineteenth century confirmed New England influence and reveal as much about the character of the movement in the state as is possible without supporting documents. Storer College, a school for blacks, was founded in 1867 and West Virginia College followed the next year. The General Conference was actively involved in the struggle for emancipation and continued their ministry to the black community after the War Between the States. That ministry extended as far West as Illinois, and it is not surprising that their missionary spirit produced a school for the blacks in West Virginia soon after the war ended.

The first Kanawha Quarterly Meeting, begun about 1877, grew out of the work of W. J. Fulton. At that time, he had baptized Mr. and Mrs. E. M. McVey and James Shaver and instituted meetings that would finally result in the founding of the Kanawha church in 1879. By 1883, churches were organized at Christian Bride, Liberty, Lewiston, Palestine, Winifrede, Alderson, Clear Creek, Dry

Branch, Nazareth, New Salem, Rock Creek, Slaughter Creek, West Charleston, Sand Fork, Fifteen Mile, Mt. Carbon, and Union and these had joined with Kanawha to form the First Kanawha Quarterly Meeting. In 1889, the Raleigh, Boone, and Lincoln Quarterly Meetings, which developed out of First Kanawha, combined forces to establish the West Virginia Yearly Meeting. The new organization included 25 churches and 875 members.

Robert Picirilli, in a brief investigation of the West Virginia State Association, concluded that all of the churches in the Harper's Ferry and Taylor Quarterly Meetings eventually were swallowed up in the 1911 merger between the General Conference and the Northern Baptists and that the present work in the state must be traced back to the younger West Virginia Yearly Meeting where a few Free Will Baptists refused to become a part of the new union.[45] It is true that the Harper's Ferry Quarterly Meeting was included in the minutes of the New England General Conference after the merger with the Northern Baptists.[46] Picirilli did go on to at least entertain the possibility that the Taylor Quarterly Meeting might have had some influence on the merger's rejection in the person of Thomas E. Peden. Peden served as president of West Virginia College, a product of the Taylor Quarterly Meeting in 1889, and then moved to Ohio where he had openly resisted union with other denominational bodies.

At any rate, a few West Virginia Free Will Baptists rejected the merger and retained their original identity. In 1919, the remnant joined with Ohio and Kentucky in the founding of the Tri-State Association of Free Will Baptists and, through that organization, became actively involved in the Co-operative Association of the West.

The earliest minutes for the West Virginia State Association are for 1949. The minutes indicate that the association was organized in either 1945 or 1946.[47] As part of the Tri-State and Co-operative Associations, West Virginia was represented at the first National Association.

Kansas

Indiana, Kansas, and Michigan all became a part of the National Association quite late, but need to be mentioned because of their earlier roots before the 1911 merger of the New England General Conference with the Northern Baptists. Work in Kansas was closely related to that of Nebraska and was largely due to the work of John Wolfe who worked tirelessly to preserve a Free Will Baptist witness in the Far West. The Kansas-Nebraska Yearly Meeting resisted the merger and maintained its identity as Free Will Baptist. Unfortunately, neither of these states could maintain their ministry, and the Yearly Meeting soon disbanded.

New work was not attempted in Kansas until 1954, when Dave Casteel organized the first Free Will Baptist church in Wichita. In that same year, Jack Ledbetter organized the Westside Church in the same city.[48] Fellowship between the two churches began immediately, and in 1962, these two joined Liberty and Wellington churches to form the First Kansas Quarterly Association. A mission at Ulysses also participated in the organizational procedures. By that time, five other churches were organized in the eastern part of the state and joined together in organizing the East Kansas Quarterly Meeting. This Association included Topeka, Timberlane, New Hope, Bethel, and Skyline.

Finally, in 1962, First Kansas and East Kansas Associations met to organize the Kansas State Association of Free Will Baptists. W. T. Turnbough was elected moderator, James McAllister his assistant and Wayne Bookout was appointed treasurer, with Gary Snow as his assistant.[49] In 1963, the State Association petitioned the National for membership.

Indiana

A recently discovered letter revealed that the Freewill Baptists of New England established a mission station in Indiana at least as early as 1829. In fact, by that time, the settled missionary could report twenty-seven churches, twenty ordained preachers, thirteen licensed preachers, and two associations with a total of eighteen hundred members.[50] But that exciting beginning was not to produce a continuing history for the denomination in the state. Two Quarterly Meetings were still included in the minutes of the General Conference as late as 1856, but disappeared from the records by the turn of the century.

The present Free Will Baptist ministry in the state did not begin until the second half of the twentieth century when Clarence Bailey of Pikeville, Kentucky officially organized a church began earlier, as a prayer meeting, by Melvin Staggs. The church united with the Floyd County Conference of Kentucky in 1952.[51]

The Free Will Baptists of Indiana continued to be related to Kentucky associations until 1961 when, in July, they organized the Wabash Valley Association of Free Will Baptist Churches in Indiana. Though other organizations were developed later, it was the Wabash Valley Association that gave birth to the State Association in 1970. In June of that year, the association voted to change its name to the Indiana State Association of Free Will Baptists. In the same year, they petitioned the National Association for membership and the petition was granted.

Michigan

Michigan, like Kansas and Indiana, cannot point to a long and continuing relationship with the denomination that can be traced back to the nineteenth century, but their recent history does not tell the full story. Missionaries from the General Conference in New England traveled to Michigan at least as early as the third decade of the nineteenth century and, finding a warm reception, they immediately began to plant churches in this new field of mission enterprise. During the next few years, this segment of the movement was to have significant impact on the denomination through its emphasis on education. Hillsdale College was founded in 1855 and from that educational headquarters, Freewill Baptists in the state continually offered advice and counsel in the areas of educational development and theological expression.

Though Michigan enjoyed the ministry of Thomas Peden and others who survived the 1911 merger, they were more closely related to the Freewill Baptists of Northern Ohio who openly and willingly embraced the merger. Whatever their motivation might have been, denominational loyalty or sympathy with their closer brothers, Michigan joined the merger and its entire ministry, along with Hillsdale College, was lost to the continuing denomination.

Denominational work was not revived in the state until the early 1940's. In 1941, Hazel Park, Highland Park, Ecorse Church, and the First Church of Flint joined together to organize the Wolverine Association of Free Will Baptists. The new association was represented by seven ordained ministers including N. P. Gates, C. E. Riggs, Maurice Roach, James Grisham, Raymond Riggs, Virgil Greenway, and George T. Warren. The entire membership for the association totaled 208.[52]

From 1941 to 1956, the Wolverine Association served as the only denominational organization in the state. During those years, they represented Michigan in the National Association as an independent association.

The State Association was organized in June 1956, when representatives of the Wolverine and Metropolitan Associations met at the Free Will Baptist Temple in Detroit. The first officers were Charles Thigpen, moderator; N. P. Gates, assistant moderator; William T. Newsome, clerk; Paul Robinson, assistant clerk; and George Butler, treasurer.[53] The following year, the Michigan State Association petitioned for membership in the National Association and was received in July 1957.

California

The Union Square Baptist Church, founded in 1876 in San Francisco, has been identified as the first Free Will Baptist church in California. Though it had its origins in the Baptist denomination, it did practice open communion and in 1881, when N. L. Rowell became its pastor, it began negotiations with the Free Baptists and finally identified itself with that body in 1883. In 1886, Professor Meads, who served at Bates Theological School (probably the Theological School in Maine), organized a mission in Oakland. The congregation of fifteen members built a chapel in 1886 and it was duly organized as a church in 1887. C. F. Penny was installed as pastor. By 1889, the church had sixty members and it continued to exist until at least 1911 and the merger between the New England General Conference and the Northern Baptists. In 1889, the Union Square Church and Oakland joined together to form the Golden Gate Association. By 1911, these two churches and a number of others had formed the Pacific Coast Free Baptist Union.[54]

As would be expected, these churches and associations were lost in the merger, and it was necessary for California Free Will Baptists to begin anew later in the twentieth century.

It is interesting that history offers more light on the birth of the earliest churches in California than it does on those that make up the present denominational family. A number of churches claim to have been the first Free Will Baptist church established in the state in the modern period. It has been suggested that the East Los Angeles Church was founded by 1939, but since that church no longer exists, the Porterville and Turlock churches are the strongest contenders in the battle for first place.[55]

Fortunately, subsequent history of denominational work in the state is more easily documented. The first Free Will Baptist Association of California was organized in May 1944, at the Turlock Church. Ralph Geiger was elected moderator, and J. W. Waltman was appointed as his assistant. The new association embraced churches at Turlock, Porterville, and Winters.[56]

California is noted for its phenomenal growth. When the association met for its third session in 1946, the association appointed George McLain as state evangelist and then accepted a mandate from the Home Mission Committee that recognized the importance of expansion of the work in the state and called on every church to organize a Home Mission enterprise.[57] The association responded admirably and by 1950, the original list of four churches had been increased to twenty-five. By 1955, the churches had almost doubled, with records of that year identifying forty-eight individual congregations. In the next six years, the number increased to seventy-two.[58]

Although growth tapered off during the next twenty years, the association has continued to grow in the number of ordained ministers, interest in education—California has supported a denominational college for a number of years—and in personal giving.[59]

Florida

Florida also can point to an early heritage. According to *The Free Baptist Cyclopaedia*, the first church was organized in 1878, and the first Quarterly Meeting followed in 1885. The Putnam County Quarterly Meeting probably was the only organization that was limited to Florida churches. A number of other state churches were included in State Line United Freewill Baptist Association in Alabama.[60]

Florida churches did not become involved in a larger organizational scheme until 1944 when the Liberty, State Line, Salem, and Union Hill Associations organized the Florida State Association. The new association was named the South Alabama and West Florida Association in order to give recognition to member churches in the two states. The name was changed to the Florida State Association of Free Will Baptists the following year when the conference held its first annual session.[61] Leaders in the two-year organizational development included D. F. Pelt, J. M. Rich, Ernest Owen, D. W. Poole, and J. C. Eldridge.

Other State and District Associations

The National Association continued to grow both in the addition of local churches and State and District Associations. By 1983, the National had added Arizona (1960), New Mexico (1960), Mexico (1961), Northeastern Association (1961), Northwestern Association (1962), Idaho (1963), Maryland (1968), Colorado (1982), and Atlantic Canada (1982).

Statistics

While there are many criteria for measuring growth and all are important, the most objective measuring rod is that of statistics. Though the denomination had few periods of phenomenal growth in the twentieth century, it did show steady increases in membership, associations, ministers, and in churches. In 1934, the Eastern General Conference reported a total of 60,291 members in eleven states. The membership was divided among 775 churches that reported a property value of $882,195. Six hundred seventy-one ministers served the churches. At this early date, though these statistics were impressive, the most significant statistic was that of annual increase. The churches in the Eastern Conference gained a total of 2,281 members during the church year. Unfortunately, this number was not broken down to indicate the relationship between new converts and members gained from other sources.[62]

Though the minutes for the Co-operative Association are available for 1934, their statistics were not nearly so complete as those of their brothers in the East. Oklahoma did not report and Texas had, by this time, become a part of the Eastern Conference. The associational letter from Tri-State reported 3,000 members, two hundred ordained ministers, and fifty church buildings having a total value of $75,000. Missouri reported 10,000 members, 120 churches, and church property valued at $72,000.[63] A more accurate report in 1937 included Oklahoma and listed a total membership of

16,210.[64] During these same years, the Eastern Conference enjoyed a period of unusual growth and now numbered 80,344 members in 878 churches.[65] The conference had enrolled fifteen thousand members since 1936.

The next fifteen years saw limited growth in membership, but did offer encouragement in the number of new churches established, financial increases in the areas of missions and pastoral salaries and in increases in Sunday school and training service enrollments. Membership in 1950 totaled 116,921 members in 1,788 churches.

As mentioned earlier, Free Will Baptists have not experienced the phenomenal growth that has characterized other similar denominations. A firm commitment to conservative theology, the rejection of membership through "easy believism," and the denomination's late entry into the task of urban evangelism tended to limit rapid growth. The denomination has not been willing to lower the bars of church membership in order to gain the prestige that comes with rapidly increasing statistics.

But growth has come—steady and healthy growth that is revealed not only in statistical tables but also in the new fields open to missions, the number of young people that continue to respond to the call for full-time ministry, increased giving that allows larger and larger budgets with which to implement the Great Commission, and in the number of new areas that have been touched with the gospel message.

Statistics do have their place and tell an interesting story. The 1982 denominational report revealed a total membership of 243,658 members and 2,505 churches in 196 associations. The most encouraging statistic related to the number of new converts during the 1981-82 church year. Eight thousand six hundred seventy-nine baptisms were recorded and many of the states within the National Association did not report in this statistical area. Finally, the report indicated one adjustment in denominational tradition that is entirely new. For most of its history, the denomination has had fewer pastors than churches. Smaller churches have struggled for long periods of time without leadership or one pastor has served two or more churches. In more recent times, the tradition has been broken and most denominational churches have a resident pastor. In fact, in the 1983 statistical report ordained ministers outnumbered the churches by a ratio of 2 to 1.[66]

Another interesting statistic is the growing concern the denomination is developing toward the welfare of its ministers In 1969 the Department of Retirement and Insurance, Rev. Herman Hersey, Director, was organized as a National Association ministry. Since its beginning the retirement and insurance fund has grown to an amount in excess of seventeen million dollars.[67]

And so grows the denomination—an increasingly effective Free Will Baptist witness not only in the United States but across the world.

Notes for Chapter 12

[1]Morris accepted the pastorate of the Bryan Church in December 1929, and upon investigation, learned that the church had mistakenly considered itself a part of the 1911 merger with the Northern Baptists by virtue of their relationship to the old Freewill Baptist General Conference of New England. Upon confirmation of their freedom from Calvinistic Baptists, Morris led them into a relationship with the General Conference of Free Will Baptists in the East (E. C. Morris, Personal Letter to the Editors of "The History Corner," *Contact* [December 18, 1971], 2).

[2]*Minutes of the Tenth Annual Session of the General Conference of the Original Free Will Baptists of the United States*. (Ayden, N.C.: Free Will Baptist Press, 1930), 5.

[3]Western Texas had joined the Co-operative Association earlier, but the State Convention's confusion about their merger status and their reservations about the Co-operative had hindered an alliance with the western segment of the denomination (Morris, *Letter*, 1). Some confusion developed during these proceedings as well. The Texas State Convention was invited to join the General Conference again in 1931 and when the conference met at the Bryan Church in 1932, Texas delegates were not included in the official list prepared by the credentials committee. Instead, they were received as fraternal delegates. It was not until 1933 that the matter was concluded and Texas was fully received (*Minutes of the Twelfth Annual Session of the General Conference of the Original Free Will Baptists of the United States, June 15, 1932*, 3,16; *Minutes of the Thirteenth Annual Session of the General Conference of the Original Free Will Baptists of the United States* [Ayden, N.C.: Free Will Baptist Press, 1933], 6.)

[4]Though the official Conference Resolution called for five members, six were appointed (*Minutes—General Conference* (1932), 5, 16).

[5]*Minutes—General Conference* (1933), 12.

[6]*Minutes of the Fifteenth Annual Session of the General Conference of the Original Free Will Baptists of the United States, 1935* (Ayden, N.C.: Free Will Baptist Press, 1935), 16; *Minutes of the Second Regular Session of the Western General Association of Free Will Baptists, 1937* (Purdy, Mo.: Free Will Baptist Gem Print), 13. No statistics were available for 1935.

[7]*Minutes of the Seventh Triennial Session* of the General Co-operative Association of the Freewill Baptists, 1934. (Wanette, Okla.: Wanette Printing Co., 1934), 6.

[8]John L Welch, transcription of personal interview conducted by Robert Picirilli (April 25, 1971), 17. In speaking of the fears and reservations on both sides, Welch remembered, "It was almost like the Paris Peace Conference. Our preachers were afraid of each other, our members were afraid of each other. They thought we were trying to steal each other's property and going to take us in the Northern Baptist or somewhere else. They were just suspicious and treated us with suspicion at every move we made. Finally we gained the confidence of the fellow members." This personal memory gives a glimpse behind the minutes and official records and reveals the concerns that must have surfaced over and over again in committee but were not to be included in final agreements. It also reveals the commitment to union that the two organizations had made. The prevailing spirit of cooperation demanded solution for the obstacles that hampered the final union of East and West.

[9]*Minutes of the Eighteenth Annual Session of the Eastern General Association of the Original Free Will Baptists of the United States* (Ayden, N. C.: Free Will Baptist Press, 1938), 9; *Minutes of the Third Regular Session of the Western General Association of Free Will Baptists* (Purdy, Mo.: Free Will Baptist Gem Print, 1938), 7.

[10]*Minutes of the First Session of the National Association of the Original Free Will Baptists of the United States*. (Ayden, N.C.: Free Will Baptist Press, 1935), 6-8.

[11]*Minutes of the Second Session of the National Association of the Original Free Will Baptists of the United States, 1938*. (Ayden, N.C.: Free Will Baptist Press, 1938), 14.

[12]*Minutes of the Free Will Baptist Bodies of the United States, 1941* (Ayden, N.C.: Free Will Baptist Press, 1941), 21.

[13]*Minutes of the Seventh Annual Session of the National Association of the Free Will Baptists of the United States, 1943* (Ayden, N.C.: Free Will Baptist Press, 1943), 19.

[14]*Minutes, National Association of Free Will Baptists* (1938), 13.

[15]*The 1983 Free Will Baptist Yearbook* (Nashville: Published by the Executive Office, National Association of Free Will Baptists, Inc., 1983), 43,44.

[16]*Minutes of the National Free Will Baptist Bodies of the United States, 1942* (Ayden, N.C.: Free Will Baptist Press, 1942), 18.

[17]*Minutes, National Association of Free Will Baptists* (1943), 14.

[18]*Minutes of the Nineteenth Annual Session of the National Association of Free Will Baptists* (1955), 28.

[19]*Minutes of the Sixth Annual Session of the Missouri State Conference of Free-Will Baptists* (1896). (Minneapolis: Western Free Baptist Publishing Society, 1896.)

[20]C. E. Mann, personal letter to B. F. Brown, N. D., p. 1. C. E. Mann was appointed clerk of the new State Association when it met at Philadelphia Church near Pattonsburg, Missouri, November 25, 1914. Letter includes organizational minutes.

[21]*Minutes of the Second Annual Session of the Missouri State Association* (1915), 4-6.

[22]*History of Adair, Sullivan, Putnam and Schuyler Counties, Missouri* (Astoria, Ill.: Stevens Publishing Co., 1972 [1888]), 397.

[23]*Minutes of the Sixty-fifth Annual Session of the Central Illinois Yearly Meeting of Free Baptists* (1915), 4.

[24]J. W. McKinney, *A Brief History of Free Baptists in Southern Illinois* (Marion, Illinois, 1939), 21, 22.

[25]Ibid., 4, 21, 22.

[26]George Waggoner, "The Illinois State Association," Robert E. Picirilli, ed., *History of Free Will Baptist State Associations* (Nashville: Randall House Publications, 1976), 31.

[27]*Minutes of the Tenth Annual Session of the General Conference of the Original Free Will Baptists of the United States, 1930* (Ayden, N.C.: Free Will Baptist Press, 1930), 14; *Minutes of the Thirteenth Annual Session of the General Conference of the Original Free Will Baptists of the United States, 1933* (Ayden, N.C.: Free Will Baptist Press, 1933), 6.

[28]*Minutes of the Texas State Association of Free Will Baptists* (1928), 10. Quoted in Eugene Richards, "The Texas State Association," Robert E. Picirilli, ed., *History of Free Will Baptist State Associations* (Nashville: Randall House Publications, 1976), 102, 103.

[29]Ibid., 103.

[30]Ibid., 102.

[31]"Minutes of the Nebraska Yearly Meeting of Free Baptists, 1908." Handwritten minutes held by the Free Will Baptist Historical Commission, Free Will Baptist Bible College, Nashville, Tennessee.

[32]"System of Co-operation of the Nebraska Yearly Meeting of Freewill Baptists" (May 1, 1906), 1.

[33]Delbert Akin, "The Oklahoma State Association" Robert E. Picirilli, ed., *History of Free Will Baptist State Associations* (Nashville: Randall House Publications, 1976), 85.

[34]Ibid., 84.

[35]Ibid., 85.

[36]Paul Long, "The Mississippi State Association." Robert E. Picirilli, ed., *History of Free Will Baptist State Associations* (Nashville: Randall House Publications, 1976), 58, 59.

[37]Ibid., 59.

[38]*Minutes of the First Session, Mississippi State Association of Free Will Baptists,* 1942 (April), 2.

[39]*Minutes of the First Annual Session, Mississippi State Association of Free Will Baptists,* 1942 (October), 3.

[40]Long, "Mississippi State Association."

[41]Ibid., 61.

[42]James Myers, Jr., "The Virginia State Association." Robert E. Picirilli, ed., *History of Free Will Baptist State Associations* (Nashville: Randall House Publications, 1976), 106.

[43]*Paul Woolsey, God, A Hundred Years and a Free Will Baptist Family* (Chuckey, Tenn.: The Union Free Will Baptist Association, 1949), 21. Used by permission.

[44]Myers, "The Virginia State Association," 106.

[45]Robert Picirilli, "The West Virginia State Association." Robert Picirilli, ed., *History of Free Will Baptist State Associations.* (Nashville: Randall House Publications, 1976), 110, 111.

[46]*Minutes of the Thirty-Sixth General Conference of Free Baptists, 1917.* (Auburn, Me.: Merrill & Webber Company, Printers and Bookbinders, 1917), 4.

[47]Ibid., 111.

[48]Grover V. Terry, "The Kansas State Association." Robert E. Picirilli, ed., *History of Free Will Baptist State Associations* (Nashville: Randall House Publications, 1976), 40.

[49]Ibid., 42.

[50]Elder Jesse Lane, "Letter to *The Freewill Baptist Magazine*" (dated Evansville, Vanderburg Co., Ind., August 29,1829), *The Freewill Baptist Magazine,* Vol. 3, No. 5 (October 1829), 116.

[51]W. H. Patterson, "The Indiana State Association," Robert E. Picirilli, ed., *History of Free Will Baptist State Associations* (Nashville: Randall House Publications, 1976), 35.

[52]*The Wolverine Association of Free Will Baptists* (1941), 11.

[53]Raymond Riggs, "The Michigan State Association." Robert E. Picirilli, ed., *History of Free Will Baptist State Associations* (Nashville: Randall House Publications, 1976), 63.

[54]G. W. Million and G. A. Barrett, *A Brief History of the Liberal Baptist People in England and America From 1606 to 1911* (Pocahontas, Ark.: Liberal Baptist Book and Tract Company, 1911), 128.

[55]Jack L. Williams, "The California State Association." Robert E. Picirilli, ed., *History of Free Will Baptist State Associations* (Nashville: Randall House Publications, 1976), 14.

[56]Ibid., 14, 15; *Minutes of the Third Annual Session of the First Free Will Baptist Association of California* (1946), 1.

[57]*Minutes—California* (1946), 8.

[58]Williams, "The California State Association," 15.

[59]*The 1983 Free Will Baptist Yearbook* (Nashville: The Executive Office, National Association of Free Will Baptists, Inc., 1983), 137.

[60]Burgess and Ward, "Florida," *Free Baptist Cyclopaedia,* 197.

[61]Chester Huckaby and Ernest Owen, "The Florida State Association," Robert E. Picirilli, ed., *History of Free Will Baptist State Associations* (Nashville: Randall House Publications, 1976), 20.

[62]*Minutes of the Fourteenth Annual Session of the General Conference of the Original Free Will Baptists of the United States* (Ayden, N.C.: Free Will Baptist Press, 1934), 20.

[63]*Minutes of the Seventh Tri-ennial Session of the General Co-operative Association of Freewill Baptists.* (Wanette,Okla.: Wanette Printing Co. 1934), 7, 8.

[64]*Minutes of the Second Regular Session of the Western General Association of Free Will Baptists* (Purdy, Mo.: Free Will Baptist Gem Print, 1937), 13.

[65]*Minutes of the Seventh Annual Session of the Eastern General Association of the Original Free Will Baptists of the United States* (Ayden, N.C.: Free Will Baptist Press, 1937), 19.

[66]*The 1983 Free Will Baptist Yearbook,* 137.

[67]*The 1999 Free Will Baptist Yearbook* (Nashville: The Executive Office, National Association of Free Will Baptists, 1999), A-68. These statistics are for 1997.

13

Missions, Education, the Church, and Its Auxiliaries

Foreign Missions

At the time of its organization in 1935, the National Association of Free Will Baptists could not point to an illustrious history in the area of mission enterprise. In fact, it could not speak of a foreign mission program at all except through its link with the old General Conference of New England. Mission efforts within the continuing movement were limited to the task of planting churches in the homeland. This absence of mission activity, however, should not be construed as a lack of missionary spirit, but rather should be attributed to limited denominational economic resources and to the struggles for organizational unity that would continue to demand the time of the movement's leaders until final organization was accomplished.

The denomination's concern for worldwide missions was outlined as early as 1901. In that year, the Eastern General Conference gave the following report of the Committee on Missions.

. . . The Book of all books commissions us to go and teach all nations. The sacred pages are freighted with the spirit of missions. This spirit is seen in the Father for he so loved the world that he gave his only begotten Son that whosoever believeth in him should not perish but have everlasting life. It was also manifested in the Son for while we were yet sinners Christ died in this far away mission field to save the lost sons and daughters of our fallen race. The Holy Spirit is a missionary among us, reproving the world of sin, of righteousness and of a judgment to come. The Spirit of the triune God is manifestly missionary. God's children having his nature and spirit are missionaries. We read in the Book that if any man have not the Spirit of Christ, he is none of his. The anti-mission spirit that is often seen in our own ranks, is not the Spirit of God but the spirit of selfishness, narrowness and ignorance. The spirit of the whole Christian religion is missionary, for when one finds Christ like Andrew of old he goes to find his brother that he may bring him to Jesus. That the missionary work in the churches is at a very low ebb is certainly evident. Therefore, Resolved that we urge the ministers to preach on missions whenever and wherever in their Judgment they may deem it expedient. That we ask the church to take this matter into prayerful consideration and that they talk missions, sing missions, pray missions and live missions. That we entreat the deacons to see to it that collections are taken in their respective churches for missions at least once a quarter. That the Association take steps to send out missionaries as soon as in the providence of God they can possibly do so.[1]

Both home and foreign mission societies existed at this early date, but for all practical purposes, the task of the Foreign Mission Society was limited to that of yearly exhortation to the body.

By 1930, the Foreign Mission Society was disbanded and replaced by a General Secretary who was given the task of raising funds and identifying personnel for an active foreign missions program. The 1931 session of the General Conference asked each state within the conference to contribute at least $25 to the support of a foreign missionary within three months of the session's closing.[2]

The first stumbling steps were made toward the establishment of a workable foreign missions program. A committee was chosen to determine the location of the first field of service, and I. J. Blackwelder was elected as the first secretary of foreign missions. In 1935, the year of union between East and West, the entire income for foreign missions in the Eastern Conference totalled $281.93. R. Paul, a native preacher in India, was the lone recipient of foreign mission funds for the year.[3]

After final union between East and West was accomplished in 1935, the first items of business included that of adopting the foreign mission program already established. I. J. Blackwelder, Foreign Missions Secretary for the General Conference, was appointed to the newly-developed position of National Secretary-Treasurer of Foreign Missions. When the National met for its second session in 1938, the Foreign Mission Board was ready to recommend support for three missionaries already on the field.

The recommendation included $150 per month for Thomas Willey, working with Indian tribes in the interior of Panama; $50 per month for Miss Laura Belle Barnard, originally related to the International Union Mission and now serving in Kotagiri, South India; and $50 for Miss Bessie Yeley who had already served for two years in Venezuela under the auspices of the Ohio Free Will Baptists. An additional $50 was allotted to Miss Barnard to meet the needs of a current illness. Total income for the three years that had passed since the first National totaled $7,228.03. Disbursements included $4,631.79 to Thomas Willey, and $1,555.60 to Miss Laura Belle Barnard. An additional $390 was sent to the native missionary mentioned earlier.[4]

Miss Barnard's support actually started early in 1935 before the National was formally organized. In its fifteenth annual session, the General Conference agreed to pay $150 for Miss Barnard's travel expense to India and $20 a month to supplement a salary of $10 already programmed for her work in the new country. An additional offering of $86 constituted her entire resource pool above the fare for the freighter that would provide transportation to the field.[5]

Miss Barnard's commission included the task of expanding denominational mission potential in its new field. She was instructed to "search a needy field in India where Free Will Baptists would be invited to send further missionaries, develop a work and establish churches."[6]

When the National Association was organized later that same year, the new body agreed to adopt the foreign mission work already established by its member group. At this point, the entire program consisted of the work in India by Laura Belle Barnard and the native missionary, Paul. In 1936, the Eastern General Association approved Rev. and Mrs. Thomas H. Willey as missionaries to

South America, and they, too, were adopted by the National. At last, the denomination was actively involved in the task of evangelizing the world.

Expanding Fields

In 1943, the Foreign Mission Board was officially organized as a working body of the denomination. A constitution and denominational by-laws were drafted to guide mission efforts under the Board's supervision. Winford Davis was chosen chairman-treasurer of the Board and supervised the work of the Mission's department from his home. In 1950, Raymond Riggs was elected Promotional Secretary-Treasurer. He also operated out of his home until 1953 when he was hired on a full-time basis and an office was opened in the headquarters building in Nashville, Tennessee.[7]

Cuba

By 1943, Thomas Willey, Sr., and his wife had left Panama and moved their mission operation to Cuba. In February of that year, the first Free Will Baptist Association was organized as the Free Will Baptist Association of Pinar Del Rio. The association ministered in an area covering more than one hundred miles in western Cuba. The report for the year recorded six native preachers, five organized churches, thirty-four additional preaching points, seventy-six baptized believers, and two hundred probationers awaiting baptism.[8]

From this beginning, the work in Cuba continued to grow until 1960 when the new Communist regime forced the Free Will Baptists to remove their missionaries and leave the work in the hands of Cuban nationals. During American tenure on the island, a number of missionaries served with the Willeys for a brief time. These included Olive Van Syoc, Rev. and Mrs. Damon C. Dodd, Rev. and Mrs. Robert Wilfong, and Mr. and Mrs. Herbert Phenicie. The Phenicies entered Cuba in 1948 under another mission agency and officially became a part of the Free Will Baptist work in 1953. Rev. and Mrs. Thomas Willey, Jr., also joined the ministry in 1956 and Lucy Wisehart was added in 1957.[9]

Japan

The Wesley Calverys spent a number of years in preparation for ministry in India, but after their visa was refused for the second time, they were rerouted to a new field in Japan. Arriving in Japan in October 1954, they established a Sunday school that met weekly in the garage of their home in Tokyo. This ministry continued during the two years in which they were involved in language study. The first formal mission station was established on the island of Hokkaido where congregations were founded in Abashiri, Koshimizu, and Bihoro. Fred and Evelyn Hersey arrived in Japan in 1956 and, following language study, also moved to Hokkaido to minister with the Calverys. The two couples were joined by the Herbert Waids in 1958 and Jim and Olena McLain in 1964. As had been true in Cuba, the mission in Japan gave primary attention to the task of training nationals for leadership roles in the church. By 1978, Airin Chapel, the largest Free Will Baptist church in Sapporo, was led by its Japanese pastor, Gombei Uchikoshi.[10]

The Herseys and the Waids eventually established new churches in the Tokyo area and continued to serve in that city for a number of years. Statistics for 1983 indicated that the field now included six organized churches and eleven missionaries.[11] Most of the work was centered in Tokyo and in Sapporo, the capital of Hokkaido.

Ivory Coast

Initial ministry in Africa was begun by Lonnie and Anita Sparks in 1956 in the area known as Ivory Coast. This pioneer couple was soon joined by the Daniel Merkh family and then in 1960 by Bill and Joy Jones. The denomination's first medical missionary, Dr. LaVerne Miley, arrived in 1962 with his wife, Lorene, and set up a medical clinic in Doropo that was to serve both the missionaries and the Lobi nationals. In the same year, the Lonnie Palmer family opened a mission station in Laoudi-Ba in the Koulango area. By 1975, the African mission reported 1,000 converts, 25 congregations, 35 additional preaching points, one organized church, ten church buildings, three ordained nationals, and at least five licensed nationals who were in training for pastoral ministry.[12]

Brazil

Thomas Willey, Sr., made a survey trip to the Campinas area of Brazil in preparation for Dave Franks opening the field for Free Will Baptists. Franks arrived in Brazil in 1957. Ken and Marvis Eagleton joined him in 1958 and Sam and June Wilkinson and Eula Mae Martin were added in 1959. Initial ministry was begun in Campinas, but the work soon spread to the city of Jaboticabal under the ministry of the Wilkinsons and Dave Franks and then to Araras and Ribeirao Preto. The latter works were begun by the Bobby Aycock and Bobby Poole families respectively.[13]

As mentioned earlier, pioneer work in this country was quite different from that practiced by the Free Will Baptists in North America. Here, the rural nature of the denomination was rejected, and pioneer work was begun in urban locations. That shift in missions policy was to have its impact on the denomination in the States as well.

Uruguay

Two families, those of Bill Fulcher and Paul Robinson, opened the country of Uruguay to Free Will Baptist mission activity. Both families arrived in early 1962 and established their ministry in Rivera, a border town located near Livramento, Brazil. In 1965, the Walter Ellisons arrived to begin a new work on the Brazilian side of the border. This work was placed in national hands at the end of 1977. Finally, Molly Barker, a registered nurse, arrived in Uruguay in 1966 to establish a ministry in teaching, counseling, and evangelism.[14]

France

Dan and Margaret Merkh, who had been involved in the earlier Free Will Baptist work in Africa, eventually re-directed their interest to the country of France and initiated a Free Will Baptist witness in that new area. After language study, their first mission point was established in the city of Nantes. In 1970, Joe Haas and family began a new work in the city of Rennes, and by 1974, property had been purchased and a building constructed to meet the needs of the new congregation.

Here, as in other mission arenas, the ministry was to be urban in orientation and was to have its first impact in the cities.[15]

Spain

Finally, in 1971, the doors of Spain that were closed by Roman Catholic control for centuries, were opened to Free Will Baptists. In May 1972, Dock and Norma Jean Caton were appointed as the first missionaries for the new field. The Foreign Missions Board, recognizing the success of the work in Africa, again called on two of its veteran missionaries to join the Catons in Spain. In August 1973, Lonnie and Anita Sparks were transferred to the new field. The Sparks initially opened a work in Alcala on the eastern side of Madrid while the Catons moved to Majadahona, a suburb west of Madrid. When a third couple, Ron and Linda Callaway, joined the team in 1977, the work was well-established, and a Free Will Baptist ministry was firmly entrenched on Spanish soil.

Summary

The story of foreign missions within the denomination is an exciting one. From those first beginnings in India, Panama, and Cuba the missions program has grown steadily. Almost every year after 1954 saw the opening of new fields or the addition of new missionaries. By 1970, the fields were opening more rapidly than the denomination could supply missionaries. That year, a cry went out from the denomination for new personnel, "…we have more open doors than we can enter. We have an urgent need for more missionaries—Panama, France, Japan, Ivory Coast, and Brazil. We need missionaries now!"[16]

And the denomination responded! In the 1983 statistical report, the Foreign Missions Board recorded forty-two missionary families and nine single missionaries on eight foreign fields.[17] At that time, the denomination was represented in Brazil, France, India, Ivory Coast, Japan, Panama, Spain, and in Uruguay.

The same statistics reveal that the $281.93 that was received for foreign missions in 1935 was dwarfed by the 1983 budget totalling $2,527,807.

During this period of the department's history, it was ably guided by General Directors, Raymond Riggs, Reford Wilson, and Rolla Smith.

Home Missions

Earlier chapters indicated that New England developed a more complex and extensive program of itinerant ministry than was true in the South, but it would be less than fair to suggest that Free Will Baptists in the Southeast had neglected this important area of ministry. In fact, this segment of the denomination could point to a much older heritage than that claimed by their brothers in the North. Joseph and William Parker established a working model of church planting and itinerancy in North Carolina before Benjamin Randall preached his first sermon. The model, that of establishing a central church that was to serve as a point of mission outreach, served the Free Will Baptists in the South for a number of years, finally resulting in the establishing of new churches in central North Carolina and in South Carolina as well. Though most of the ministers served settled pastorates during the nineteenth century, the denomination did not neglect the task of church planting.[18]

But by the early twentieth century, the home mission efforts were more complex and far reaching. The minutes for the Eastern General Conference of 1904 indicated that the Home Mission

Society supported both local itinerants and at least two national evangelists. Elder H. F. Wogan served in the Far West from his headquarters in North Dakota, and Elder S. B. Stephens traveled in the East. Stephens' report for 1904 revealed the heavy responsibilities assigned to the missionaries and the phenomenal response to their ministry.

> . . . Labored seventy-three weeks, preached 474 times, baptized 429, reclaimed 98, received from other denominations 34, total 569, preached 16 funeral sermons, married 14 couples and secured 49 subscribers for *The Free Will Baptist*. . . .[19]

That section of the minutes closed with the observation that none of the local societies had reported and that the denomination had no way of estimating the total work done by their itinerant missionaries.

The National Association and Home Missions

The first National Home Missions Board was established when the National Association met for its second session in Nashville, in 1938. The new Board included chairman M. L. Hollis, J. K. Warkentin, Mrs. J. E. Frazier, the Reverend Mrs. Lizzie McAdams, and George Dunbar.[20]

Hindered by limited opportunities for Board contact and by lack of income, the Home Missions Department saw little progress in the first few years of its existence. But eventually, through continued interest in the task of home missions and through new and qualified leadership, the Home Missions Board began to exercise an impact on the denomination.

In 1947, Harry Staires was elected as Promotional Secretary for the Board on a part-time basis. His primary task was that of raising income for implementation of the Board's programs. Damon Dodd was appointed as the first full-time Secretary in 1953, and in the following year, the first home missionaries were sent out with pay. These included Rev. and Mrs. Robert Wilfong as missionaries to Tampa, Florida; Rev. and Mrs. G. C. Lee, Jr., to Nebraska; and Rev. and Mrs. Sylvester Crawford to California. In 1955, Bessie Yeley, who served earlier with the Foreign Missions Board in Venezuela, was assigned to the work in Tampa, and Rev. and Mrs. J. J. Postlewaite introduced the first Free Will Baptist witness in the states of Oregon and Washington. That same year, Rev. and Mrs. James Timmons entered Mexico as representatives of the National Home Missions Board.[21]

Other than Staires and Dodd, only three individuals served as General Directors (Promotional Secretaries) for the Board during this period of time, Homer E. Willis (1956-1973); Robert Shockey (1973-1978); and Roy Thomas (1978-1995). More recently, a former associate director, Trymon Messer, succeeded Brother Thomas as director. Upon Brother Messer's retirement in 2001, Larry Powell assumes leadership of the department.

Contemporary Development

In 1958, the Free Will Baptists finally returned to New England. In that year, Rev. and Mrs. Mack Owens settled in Littleton, New Hampshire, and accepted the responsibility for organizing or reopening churches in New Hampshire, Vermont, Maine, Nova Scotia, New Brunswick, and

Massachusetts. The new churches soon organized as the Northeast Association of Free Will Baptists.[22]

In the next two years, both Alaska and Hawaii were opened to the ministry of the Free Will Baptists.

When the Home Missions Board reported to the National Association in 1983, their statistics recorded forty-nine missionaries in twenty-seven states as well as mission points in Canada, Mexico, Puerto Rico, and in the Virgin Islands. In addition, twenty-seven State or District Associations had appointed State Promotional Secretaries whose responsibilities included an interest in both home missions and church extension. Finally, though the office of national evangelist disappeared before the National Association was organized, the denomination continued to enjoy the ministry of a number of full-time evangelists. Denominational minutes for 1983 noted eight men that had committed themselves to full-time evangelism.

Education

When the General Conference of New England merged with the Northern Baptist Convention in 1911, all of their colleges and seminaries were lost to the continuing Free Will Baptist denomination. At the same time, the problem was compounded by the limited and unsuccessful attempts at education in the South. In almost every case, the schools were designed for high school or early college level, and their ministries were cut short either by disaster or by lack of support. The seminary at Ayden, North Carolina, had burned early in the century; and by 1935, both Eureka College in North Carolina and Tecumseh College in Oklahoma were no longer in operation. When the National Association was organized, Zion Bible School in Blakely, Georgia was the only educational institute to report.

It should not be assumed, however, that the denomination had lost interest in education. Both the Co-operative General Association of the West and the General Conference of the East established standing boards of education quite early, and cooperative efforts to establish a national institution of education began as early as 1934. When the National Association was organized in 1935, the new organization elected J. L. Welch as National Secretary of Education and appointed Selph Jones, Henry Melvin, J. C. Griffin, M. F. Vanhoose, and E. A. O'Donnell as trustees for a school that did not yet exist. During that same session, the joint educational committee consisting of J. L. Welch, Melvin Bingham, E. E. Morris, A. D. Ivey (acting for T. B. Mellette), and Selph Jones introduced a series of ambitious recommendations that called for the establishment of a new school that was to begin classes in September 1936. The school was to be located in Nashville, Tennessee. Additional recommendations provided for an intensive and nationwide campaign that was to provide financial support for the new undertaking.

But, if the committee was more ambitious than practical in its desire to have a school in operation in little more than a year, it did recognize the limited scope of the program in its first years of ministry. They suggested "that we begin our school work on a small scale, confining the work to a Bible course and add other courses to the same as the Lord prospers us."[23]

Free Will Baptist Bible College

Prior to the founding of Free Will Baptist Bible College in 1942, formal education in the denomination was limited to a series of Biblical institutes sponsored by the Educational Board, led by chairman J. R. Davidson and supervised by the new Executive Secretary of the denomination, L. R. Ennis. Again, the agenda was an ambitious one. In 1941, the Board called for the establishment of pastors' institutes in all of the states in which Free Will Baptists were represented. In an effort to see their ambitions fulfilled, members of the Board offered to serve as instructors for the new institute programs. Early institutes were taught by J. R. Davidson, Robert Crawford, Damon Dodd, and J. L. Welch.[24]

But the more important concern was the centrally located school that had been the dream of the denomination for a number of years.

Property Purchase—Moving from Dreams to Reality

As early as 1939, the Board of Education agreed that the school should be located in Nashville, Tennessee, but at that time the Board had no authority to purchase and hold property in trust and had no access to funds that could be used to initiate an educational program. Both of these needs were met in 1941 when the National Association established a Board of Trustees for the school and agreed to spend as much as $15,000 for an initial property purchase. Annual payments on any unpaid balance were to be limited to $3,000. Understanding that these demands were absolute, the Board began the almost impossible task of locating and purchasing property that would serve the needs of the new school. The Board now included J. R. Davidson, J. R. Bennett, Winford Davis, George Dunbar, and Melvin Bingham.[25]

The limitations placed on the Board were to lead to an interesting experience. After unanimously agreeing that the property and building at 3609 Richland Avenue in Nashville were ideal for their purposes, the men found that though the owner was willing to sell, their offer fell $1,000 short. Since they had no authority to offer more, the negotiations seemed doomed to failure. The owner refused to reduce his price, but did agree to donate $1,000 toward the school's purchase. The first large donation came from a Presbyterian.[26]

A Dream Come True

In 1942, the National Association appointed L. C. Johnson, a graduate of Bob Jones University, as President of the proposed school. J. R. Davidson, who had served as chairman of the Board of Education, was appointed Business Manager and Treasurer. During that session, the association instructed the Board to open the new school on September 15, less than two months away.[27]

The school opened for classes on schedule with nine students enrolled. By October 13, 1942, the final payment was made on the property and the school was presented to the denomination, debt free.

The first faculty for Free Will Baptist Bible School[28] included L. C. Johnson, President; J. R. Davidson, Business Manager; Miss Laura Belle Barnard, Secretary and Instructor in Missions; and Henry Melvin, Instructor. The first academic program offered a two-year curriculum and the first four graduates were ready for ministry in 1943.

The school was incorporated in 1945 and the Board of Education was officially restructured as a Board of Trustees. The new Board consisted of nine members and included R. B. Spencer, J. L. Welch, Floyd B. Cherry, Ralph Lightsey, Henry Melvin, K. V. Shutes, Melvin Bingham, James F. Miller, and J. R. Davidson. The Board was given the authority to create its own by-laws, giving solid testimony of the respect the denomination had for these educational leaders.[29]

Coming of Age

As Free Will Baptists became more aware of the importance of the Bible College and as the number of students multiplied, the school found curriculum expansion to be both possible and necessary. The Evangelical Teacher Training Association Diploma was added in 1946 as a supplement to the regular two-year program, and in 1949, a third year of study was provided for students involved in the standard curriculum. By 1950, the school was ready to offer a four-year Bachelor degree, the faculty and staff numbered ten (seven faculty and three staff members), and enrollment had reached one hundred students.

The decade between 1950 and 1960 was a period of unusual and exciting growth, and that growth was evidenced in every facet of school life. By the end of the decade, the physical plant included seven buildings, the student body had more than doubled (210), and the faculty had increased to fifteen.

During the school's history *to this point*, only three men had served as President. L. C. Johnson, the first President, completed his initial term in 1944, served a brief pastorate, and then returned to the school in 1947. L. R. Ennis served as President during the brief interim. Charles Thigpen succeeded Johnson in 1979. Without question, the school and its philosophy reflected the ministry and the thinking of L. C. Johnson as Johnson, in turn, reflected his training at Bob Jones University. His long tenure allowed time for the molding and shaping of an educational program that has trained hundreds of young men and women for denominational service.

Free Will Baptist Bible College has served the denomination well for more than half a century. While notable changes have occurred in its educational philosophy and its approach to training, it continues to exert significant influence on the denomination of which it is a part. A large number of the denomination's pastors and most of its missionaries have received at least a part of their training from this institution. In 1983, enrollment totaled 467 students from 29 states and 7 foreign countries, including 10 students enrolled in a new, but relatively short-lived, graduate program.[30]

California Christian College

Though the Bible College in Nashville played a significant role in denominational education since its first sessions in 1942, it was not possible that the one school could meet all the needs of the growing denomination. In 1955, first steps were taken toward the establishment of a Free Will Baptist Bible college in the state of California. In June of that year, a temporary Board of Christian Education was elected by the State Association and given the task of investigating the possibility of establishing a new school in the state. In the following year, a permanent Board of Education was elected, and the educational program was kicked off with a six-week Bible Institute held in the First Free Will Baptist Church of Richmond, California, and offered by Dean Moore and Wade Jernigan.

The new Board consisted of Pete Conners, Gene Rogers, F. A. McCage, E. E. Morris, and B. J. Brown.[31]

For the first six years of its existence, the school operated on a part-time basis, and classes were taught first in the Richmond First Church and later in the Sherwood Forest Free Will Baptist Church of El Sobrante.

In 1961, the State Association authorized the Board of Christian Education to establish a full-time college. This directive was carried out in September 1962, when the school opened on a full-time basis with a total of 39 students.[32] In the fall of the next year, the California State Board of Education granted permission for the institute to increase its two-year program to a three-year diploma granting curriculum. The school continued to work within the confines of an institute structure and a three-year diploma until the fall of 1968 when it received approval for the granting of a four-year "Graduate of Theology" diploma. At that time, California Bible Institute became California Christian College. In 1969, the school was given permission to grant the Bachelor of Science degree in theology.

For almost a decade, the school struggled for survival on temporary campuses provided by local churches but continued growth demanded a more stable situation. In 1964, the Board of Education decided that the state would be better served if the school moved to a more central location. The city of Fresno was chosen and in just a few years a permanent campus was purchased and structured to meet the needs of a growing student body.[33]

Since its inception, six Presidents have offered direction and guidance for the school: Dean Moore (1957-1965), C. Eugene Rogers (1965-1968), Odus K. Eubanks (1968-1969), Wade T. Jernigan (1969-1978), Daniel W. Parker (1978-1980), and John Smith (still in office in 1984). Parker had earlier served as President of Oklahoma Bible College.

Hillsdale Free Will Baptist College

Hillsdale Free Will Baptist College is a four-year Christian liberal arts institution located in Moore, Oklahoma, just south of Oklahoma City. The college began its operations as Oklahoma Bible College on February 3, 1959. First semester classes were held in the First Free Will Baptist Church of Tulsa. Final plans for those first classes had been completed as late as January 8, 1959, by the Board of Education which included John West as Chairman, and Wade Jernigan, Melvin Bingham, Weldon Wood, and Marlin Bivins as members at large. Jernigan was instrumental in the founding of California Christian College a few years earlier, and Melvin Bingham served on the National Board of Education as early as 1941. The first faculty included Roy Bingham, Don Payne, N. R. Smith, Mrs. N. R. Smith, and Bill Sherrill.[34]

Before settling in permanent quarters in the city of Moore, in 1962, the school enjoyed temporary homes in Tulsa, Wagoner, and in Oklahoma City. The school's administration and Board of Trustees had an early vision for the need of Christian liberal arts training for its students. By 1962, the curriculum included not only Bible, pastoral training, missions, and Christian education, but also English, social science, science, and history.

The President of the school explained the varied purposes of the institution in a letter to the Oklahoma State Association of Free Will Baptists in 1963. He pointed out that the sixth academic year was "a strategic, pivotal year for Oklahoma Bible College. We recognize our identity as a Bible college, a religious school with undergraduate theological training with a core curriculum of general education in the arts.[35] The school has continued to honor those early convictions and has, through the years, attempted to balance offerings in liberal arts and in theological studies.

The 1982-84 catalog included courses in business, business administration, secretarial preparation, elementary education, secondary education, history, English, and physical education at the Associates (two-year) level and Christian education, Bible, missions, and Christian music at the Bachelor's level. The school also offers the Evangelical Teacher Training Association (ETTA) certificate.[36]

In 1970, for a brief moment, Oklahoma Bible College became Trinity College. The new name was designed to identify the school as a Christian liberal arts institution as well as a Bible college and to recognize the multi-state support that the school enjoyed. But the name was destined to live a short life. The Oklahoma Secretary of State ruled that it infringed on the rights of Trinity Bible College, another Oklahoma school, and that it could not be used. The new name was dropped and finally, on July 1, 1971, the school became Hillsdale Free Will Baptist College.[37]

Like California Christian College, Hillsdale progressed under the direction of a number of institutional presidents: Danny Parker (1961), Don Payne (1961-1966), J. D. O'Donnell (1966-1971), Bill Jones (1971-1979), Don Elkins (1979-1982), and Edwin Wade (1982-still in office in 1984).

The original property purchase included thirty-nine acres of land, and that large holding has allowed the school to grow not only in student body but in physical plant as well. Enrollment for fall, 1983, totaled 175 students, and the school could boast of adequate classroom and administration buildings, dormitories for both men and women, and housing for married couples who wished to live on campus.[38]

Southeastern Free Will Baptist College

The denomination's newest educational institution came into being on April 30, 1982. At that time, final plans were drawn for the establishment of Southeastern Free Will Baptist College. Like Hillsdale, the school was designed as a Christian liberal arts college with the stated task of ". . . training and equipping Christian workers for preaching, pastoral, missionary, church school and other related ministries. . . ."[39]

The school's first catalog included a number of particular emphases that would be used in the task of reaching the school's goals and purposes: (1) developing a strong local church acknowledging pastoral authority; (2) soul winning and revival; (3) equipping to minister in a church school; (4) the adherence to fundamentalist separatist position (personal and ecclesiastical); (5) high academic standards with emphasis on the practical; (6) missions both home and foreign.[40]

The school opened for the first time in August 1983, using the facilities of Gateway Free Will Baptist Church in Virginia Beach, Virginia. The first degree programs included a Bachelor of Arts degree with a double major in Bible and pastoral training and a Bachelor of Science degree with a major in teacher education and a minor in Bible.

Enrollment for the first semester totalled eighty-nine students. Rev. Randy Cox was appointed the first President of the school and was to give primary guidance for its early development and direction.

Mount Olive Free Will Baptist College

The Mount Olive Free Will Baptist College was organized in the middle of this century, and though it no longer serves the denomination, it must be mentioned because of its early influence. The school is located in Mount Olive, North Carolina, and continues to represent the North Carolina State Association of Original Free Will Baptists. That segment of the movement, along with the school, left the denomination in 1962 in a dispute related to church government. Before that time, the school had been instrumental in the training of a number of Free Will Baptist leaders in the eastern United States. Today, the school sponsors one of the largest and most complete historical collections relating to Free Will Baptists in North Carolina. The collection also houses materials that speak to the history of the larger denomination. The collection constitutes a vital research and resource depository of Free Will Baptist history.

The Church and Its Auxiliaries
Free Will Baptists and the Sunday School

In the North, Sabbath school activity was a part of the denominational program since at least 1828. During the second session of the General Conference, the Maine Western Yearly Meeting submitted the following question for the body's consideration: "Shall we encourage Sabbath schools in the Connection?" The question was referred to a committee and the following report was adopted: "We advise our brethren who are convinced of the utility of Sabbath schools, to form them independent of any other, and have religious instructors."[41] The response indicated an evident lack of denominational agreement on the importance of the Sabbath schools, but that attitude was adjusted by 1835, when the General Conference trustees were instructed to organize a Sabbath School Union that would represent the Sabbath school movement within the denomination. During the 1835 session of the General Conference, it was reported that Sabbath schools were established in many of the churches and that interest in the movement was growing. The report, balancing optimism with reality, admitted a less than adequate progress but also expressed a vision for the establishment of Sunday schools in every part of the denomination.[42]

In 1845, the movement was strengthened by the publication of *The Myrtle*, the first Free Will Baptist Sunday school periodical. The semi-monthly paper grew to a circulation of 10,000 by 1856.[43]

The Sabbath School Union was lost to the denomination when the New England General Conference merged with the Northern Baptists in 1911, but the Sunday school movement continued to live through the influence of the Triennial General Conference in the South. The first available minutes for that body, 1901, included the following report prepared by the Sunday School Committee.

... Realizing the fact that the Sunday School is the right arm of power in the church and the germ from which many of our most successful churches have sprung, and the mold in which moral and Christian character is cast, we therefore deplore the great falling off in attendance of our young people and especially of young men. We recommend that all our schools be superintended, taught and officered by Godly men and women who are apt to teach. That we request our ministers to use their influence and as much of their time as practicable in the interest of Sunday Schools. We urge our schools to use Free Will Baptist Literature. . . .[44]

When the National Association was organized in 1935, convention delegates elected Winford Davis as National Sunday School Secretary, and in 1938, the first Sunday School Board was elected. For a brief period between 1959 and 1962, the National Sunday School office ceased to function and literature for the denomination was printed by the Free Will Baptist Press in Ayden, North Carolina. During those years, the Oklahoma State Association began their own Sunday school literature program and gained a good deal of the denominational market. In 1962, they relinquished their literature program to the National Association, and the Sunday School Board accepted responsibility for literature publication. In that year, the office in Nashville was reopened and Roger Reeds, a pastor from St. Louis, Missouri, was appointed as the first full-time Director of the Sunday School Department.

In 1965, the Sunday School Department announced the development of a Sunday school curriculum that was uniquely Free Will Baptist. The curriculum, up through adult level, was completed by 1969. For the last few years, the Department has been responsible for a number of areas of denominational ministry: the publication of Sunday school literature and other related books and educational aids, the promotion of Sunday school activity within the denomination, teacher training, a bookstore operation, and the task of tract distribution. Randall House Publications serves as the publishing arm of the Sunday School Department and has enjoyed an increasingly important role in the Department's ministry.[45]

The Sunday School Department was housed with the National Association executive offices from 1952 until 1965 at the original location at 3801 Richland Avenue, Nashville, and again from 1965 until 1972 at the new offices then located at 1134 Murfreesboro Road. The Department now enjoys separate quarters in a well-appointed building that meets the needs of both publication, administration, and a full-service retail Christian bookstore. The offices now are located at 114 Bush Road in Nashville, Tennessee.

Church Training Service

Unlike the Sunday School Department, the Free Will Baptist League, later to be the Church Training Service, was a product of that portion of the denomination that had its birth and heritage in the South.

The Free Will Baptist League was first mentioned in the 1922 minutes of the newly-organized General Conference of the Original Free Will Baptists of the United States. The record infers that the

League was established earlier in both North Carolina and in Tennessee and that the General Conference simply agreed to accept responsibility for the organization.

> Since it is the sense of this General Conference that we as a national body are in need of a young people's organization,
>
> Be it Resolved, 1st, That this body go on record as approving and adopting the Free Will Baptist League as agreed upon and adopted by North Carolina and Tennessee, and that we recommend it to our people everywhere.[46]

Another auxiliary organization, the Little Workers' League of the East, also was approved and adopted as a primary department of the Free Will Baptist League. The same minutes called for a permanent national young people's organization as early as it could be established. J. L. Welch was elected editor of Free Will Baptist League literature, and L. E. Ballard and Alice E. Lupton were appointed as associate editors.[47] The highly organized structure of the movement indicated that it had been in business for a number of years before official adoption by the General Conference.

From that time, development moved rapidly. In 1923, the Committee on Young People's Work encouraged the denomination to appoint state youth chairmen who would make up a national board of young people's work, and by 1925, the Board was appointed and at work. The initial Board included T. B. Mellette, Ruth Stewart, Dorothy Harvey, L. E. Ballard, and Terry Pettit.[48] Alice E. Lupton had served as treasurer for the League since 1923 and by 1927 assumed the office of General Secretary. She continued in that position until succeeded by Henry Melvin in 1930.

Melvin was still General Secretary when the League was adopted by the National Association in 1935. At that time, he was elected as National Secretary for the Free Will Baptist League.[49]

By the early 1960's, denominational leaders recognized the need for a training program that would meet the needs of adults as well as those of the young. They also wished to coordinate various youth organizations under the direction of one national office. Up until this time, youth activities were the product of three different organizations: the Free Will Baptist League, the Woman's National Auxiliary Convention, and the Master's Men.

In 1963, the National Association charged the National League Board with the responsibility of developing the new unified program. Basic proposals, as a result of the Executive Committee study, were presented to the National when it convened in Kansas City, Missouri, in July 1964. One of the first items of business was the question of name change. At that time, the Free Will Baptist League was transformed into the Church Training Service, and the name has continued to serve the denomination to the present time.[50]

Under the direction of its first General Director, Samuel Johnson, and the later guidance of Malcolm C. Fry, the CTS introduced an entire graded curriculum as training materials for the family. After 1971, the curriculum included a thirty-six unit core cycle and a series of elective offerings. In 1972, Dr. Malcolm Fry succeeded Johnson as General Director and continued to serve in that capacity until 1978 when the CTS Department was merged with the Sunday School Department.[51] CTS struggled financially for a number of years and the merger seemed the only source of salvation.

Women and the Church

A 1901 statement relating to Free Will Baptists and their Sunday school set the stage for the role that women would play in the ministry of the denomination over the years. In that statement, church leaders recommended that ". . . all our schools be superintended, taught, and officered by Godly men and women who are apt to teach. . . ."[52] Though typically women would serve through their own organizations, the twentieth century also would find them serving as evangelists, Sunday school superintendents, choir directors, national leaders for Sunday school and Church Training organizations, and as teachers in the local Sunday schools of the denomination. World War II, especially, opened doors of opportunity for ministry as more and more women were called upon to fill vacancies left by those men who were away at war. Our interest at this point will be limited to the women's organizations that have played such a vital part in the denomination's history during the twentieth century. Most often, their work would be related to the mission program of the church.

The Early Days

The second Triennial General Conference of the South, meeting in 1904, in Dunn, North Carolina, included an anniversary celebration for the Free Will Baptist Woman's Missionary Society. Though a number of men were involved in the celebration, it was evident that the Society came into being at the insistence of the women and through their genius. It is especially interesting that the leadership for the Society came from every part of the country, carefully representing all of the states and districts existing in the Triennial Convention. The officers included: Addie J. Logan, North Dakota; Mrs. L. M. Peden, North Carolina; Mrs. S. H. Norman, West Virginia; Laura Hobstetter, Ohio; Lovie Cashwell, North Carolina; Hattie Dowty, North Carolina; and Allie Harrington, North Carolina.[53] Since the General Conference had its origin in the Southeast, it was not unusual that a number of the ladies were from North Carolina, but it was amazing that other states were so well represented at this early date.

The women's organizations survived the long decade of pause between the death of the first General Conference and the birth of the second. There is a good possibility that these organizations continued to function even though the umbrella conference had ceased to exist. By 1923, two organizations began to appear in conference minutes—the Ladies' Aid Society and the Home Mission Society.

The 1925 session of the General Conference gave attention to the establishment of a Board of Women's Activities that was to promote the organization of Ladies' Aid Societies and Home and Foreign Mission Societies in the churches. It also called for women's home mission conventions in local conferences and associations and in Yearly Meetings. The Board was to include five members consisting of both ministers and women leaders, and it was instructed to elect a field secretary who would be responsible for the leg work of the promotional program.[54] Though the leaders of 1904 had long since disappeared from the scene, new leaders came to take their place and the names of Fannie Polston, Alice E. Lupton, Mrs. J. E. Frazier, and Mary Ann Welch would become familiar to the Free Will Baptists that made up the General Conference.

The objectives that directed the work of the women in the earliest days of organization included the resolve: (1) to deepen spiritual life of the women, (2) to stress the importance of the educational departments of the denomination, (3) to train leaders for the women's movement, and (4) to enlist every woman possible in the organization.[55] The larger purpose of the organization involved the task of leading the women of the denomination into a larger share of the winning of the world to Christ. Missions and missionary education constituted an essential part of the Auxiliary programs from the beginning.

The Woman's National Auxiliary Convention

When the General Conference met in 1935, Fannie Polston, Field Secretary for the Woman's Auxiliary, asked that a committee be appointed to organize a National Woman's Auxiliary Convention. In response to the request, the conference appointed fifteen women representing Alabama, Florida, Georgia, North Carolina, South Carolina, Tennessee, and Texas. On Thursday, June 13, these women, working with Mrs. Polston as chairman of the committee, were excused by the conference to organize a national body.

By this time, women in the West also had organized a number of home mission groups. For example, in 1935, Missouri reported twenty-seven women's organizations with a total of four hundred fifty-one members.[56]

By the time the National Association came into existence, the women's work within the denomination was already highly organized and was ready for acceptance into the national body without adjustment. One simple sentence in the organizational minutes indicated the denomination's respect for the women and the work they already had accomplished, ". . . the Woman's Auxiliary work was also accepted by the Association."[57] The WNAC has continued to serve as an Auxiliary of the National Association since that time and has met in conjunction with the National at least since 1939.

Officers elected at the first National Convention included Alice Lupton, Mary Welch, Mrs. Sterl Phinney, Lizzie McAdams, Mrs. J. E. Frazier, Mrs. J. R. Bennett, Lola Johnson, Mrs. T. B. Mellette, Mrs. M. H. Mellette, and Fannie Polston. Since 1949, the WNAC has received its direction from an Executive Committee and from an Executive Secretary who has served out of an office in the National Headquarters in Nashville, Tennessee. These have included Agnes B. Frazier (1949-1954), Gladys Sloan (1954-1956), Eunice Edwards (1956-1963), and Cleo Pursell (1963-1985), Mary R. Wisehart (1985-1998), and Marjorie Workman (1998-) .

Men of the Church—"The Master's Men"

The men of the denomination were slow to organize and the present Master's Men movement dates only to 1956. A number of factors probably contributed to the late interest in formal organization, but two stand out as the most likely culprits. In the first place, men were the visible leaders of the denomination for years, and there seemed to be little need for another national movement that would require time that simply was not available. The problem was, of course, that most of the men involved were ministers, and the laymen of the church were offered little opportunity to make contribution to denominational enterprises. There is also the possibility that the men did not share the vision of the women of the church and were perfectly happy to allow their male representatives, the clergy, to do their share of the work.

The second and more practical factor was related to the availability of laymen for ministry. The two world wars that the nation had faced tended to drain the local churches of their manpower; and, quite often, ministers and women were forced to carry additional work loads in the religious arena.

The Master's Men organization was first envisioned by W. S. Mooneyham, Executive Secretary of the denomination. In his annual report to the National Association in 1955, Mooneyham recommended that a special committee be selected to investigate the possibilities of setting up a layman's organization within the Free Will Baptist Church. The committee (Committee on Men's Organizations) was elected and charged to report to the Convention the following year. The committee included O. T. Dixon, Luther Gibson, and Robert Hill. In 1956, the committee presented a proposed constitution and by-laws to the National Convention that provided for local church chapters and district conventions. The constitution stipulated that this organization be called "The Master's Men."[58]

After a brief period of rapid growth, the organization began to suffer significant losses, and by 1963, a number of organized chapters failed to re-charter. That difficulty, the absence of new charters, and a lack of finances demanded that the entire operation be reevaluated and finally resulted in a major reorganization process. In July 1964, laymen from twenty-four states met in Kansas City to participate in the reorganizational meeting. Those present were elected as "congressmen" and were to serve two-year terms. The congress was scheduled to meet at least annually and more often if it became necessary. An executive committee of seven was appointed to carry on the business of the congress between sessions, and Robert C. Hill was elected as Executive Secretary. Hill would continue to give guidance to the organization for a number of years while continuing to serve as pastor of a local church.

In 1969, Ray Turnage was named the first full-time General Director of the Master's Men, but he served for only one year and the organization again was left without a national leader from 1970 until 1975. During most of those years, the work was directed by the National Laymen's Board chaired by Kenneth Lane. Finally, in 1975, Loyd Olsan was employed as a part-time General Director.

In 1977, the offices of the laymen's movement were moved from the home of the General Director to the Sunday School Department's new building in Nashville, Tennessee. Olsan continued to serve as General Director until May 1983. In August of the same year, James Vallance assumed the office and served for the next several years.

The offices of the Master's Men are now located in the national offices building in Antioch, Tennessee. Ohio native, Tom Dooley has served as General Director since 1998.

Notes for Chapter 13

[1]*Thirty-First Session of the Free Will Baptist Triennial General Conference, 1901*, 5.

[2]*Minutes of the Eleventh Annual Session of the General Conference of the Original Free Will Baptist of the United States, 1931* (Ayden, N.C.: Free Will Baptist Press, 1931), 6, 7.

[3]*Minutes of the Fifteenth Annual Session of the General Conference of the Original Free Will Baptist of the United States, 1935* (Ayden, N.C.: Free Will Baptist Press, 1935), 15.

[4]*Minutes of the Second Session of the National Association of the Free Will Baptist of the United States.* (Ayden, N.C.: Free Will Baptist Press, 1938), 9.

[5]*Minutes of the Fifteenth Annual Session of the General Conference of the Original Free Will Baptist of the United States* (Ayden, N.C.: Free Will Baptist Press, 1935), 5, 6.

[6]Laura Belle Barnard, "Joy on a Rugged Path" (Manuscript being prepared for publication, 1983), ch. 4, p. 4.

[7]Harrold D. Harrison, ed., *Who's Who Among Free Will Baptists* (Nashville: Randall House Publications, 1978), 407,408.

[8]Jerry Ballard, *Never Say Can't* (Carol Stream, Ill.: Creation House, 1971), 116; *Minutes, National Association* (1943), 20.

[9]Harrison, *Who's Who*, 409.

[10]Ibid., 410.

[11]Phone interview with personnel in the National Association of Free Will Baptists, Foreign Missions Office, December 22, 1983.

[12]Harrison, *Who's Who*, 410, 411.

[13]Ibid., 411.

[14]Ibid., 412.

[15]Ibid., 413.

[16]*Minutes of the National Association of Free Will Baptists, 1970* (Nashville: Executive Department, National Association of Free Will Baptists, 1970), 36.

[17]*The 1983 Free Will Baptist Yearbook* (Nashville: Executive Office, National Association of Free Will Baptists, 1983), 11, 12; "Financial Summar," *Heartbeat*, Vol. 23, No. 7 (September 1983), 11.

[18]They served settled pastorates in that they seldom traveled long distances for preaching appointments. They might, however, have served three or four pastorates in a given area.

[19]*Thirty-Second Session of the Free Will Baptist Triennial General Conference, 1904* (Ayden, N.C.: Free Will Baptist Print, 1905), 5. The discrepancy in addition was in the original report.

[20]*Minutes of the Second Session of the National Association of the Original Free Will Baptists of the United States, 1938* (Ayden, N.C.: Free Will Baptist Press, 1938), 5.

[21]*Free Will Baptist Home Missions Survey* (Nashville: Board of Home Missions-Church Extension, National Association of Free Will Baptists, 1979), 4.

[22]Roy Thomas, "A Brief History of the Home Missions Department." Harrold Harrison, ed., *Who's Who Among Free Will Baptists* (Nashville: Randall House Publications, 1978), 420.

[23]Handwritten Notes of the Joint Committee Education Meeting held during the first National Association in 1935. Original held by the Free Will Baptist Historical Society, Free Will Baptist Bible College, Nashville, Tennessee.

[24][Mary, Welch], "Early Efforts Toward a Centrally Located School for Free Will Baptists," N. D., 6. Unpublished manuscript held by Free Will Baptist Historical Collection, Free Will Baptist Bible College, Nashville, Tennessee; *Minutes of the Free Will Baptist Bodies of the United States* (Ayden, N.C.: Free Will Baptist Press, 1941), 24.

[25]*Minutes, National Association* (1941), 6, 24.

[26]J. R. Davidson, "Some Experiences in Early History of Free Will Baptist Bible College," N. D., 2. Unpublished manuscript held by the Free Will Baptist Historical Collection, Free Will Baptist Bible College, Nashville, Tennessee.

[27]*Minutes, National Association* (1942), 10; Welch, "Early Efforts," 8.

[28]Welch, "Early Efforts," 9. The name was later changed to Free Will Baptist Bible College.

[29]Mary Ruth Wisehart, "A Brief History of Free Will Baptist Bible College," Harrold D. Harrison, ed., *Who's Who Among Free Will Baptists* (Nashville: Randall House Publications, 1978), 475.

[30]*Free Will Baptist Bible College Bulletin,* Vol. 31, No. 5 (September-October 1983).

[31]E. T. Hyatt, "A Brief History of California Christian College," Harrold D. Harrison, ed., *Who's Who Among Free Will Baptists* (Nashville: Randall House Publications, 1978), 467.

[32]"History of the College," *California Christian College Catalog* (1972-1974), 13.

[33]"Brief History of California Christian College," 469.

[34]"A Brief History of Hillsdale Free Will Baptist College," Harrold D. Harrison, ed., *Who's Who Among Free Will Baptists* (Nashville: Randall House Publications, 1978), 485.

[35]Ibid., 486.

[36]*Hillsdale Free Will Baptist College Catalog* (1982-1984), 35-43.

[37]*Contact* (November 1970), 13; (December 1970), 13; (May 1971), 13.

[38]*Contact*, Vol. XXX, No. II, (November 1983), 21; "Brief History of Hillsdale," 490.

[39]*Southeastern Free Will Baptist College Catalog, 1983-1984,* 7.

[40]Ibid.

[41]*Minutes of the Second General Conference of the Free Will Baptist Connection, 1828* (Dover: N.H.: Published by the Free Will Baptist Printing Establishment, 1859), 34, 35.

[42]*Minutes of the Eighteenth General Conference of the Free Will Baptist Connection, 1835* (Dover, N.H.: Published by the Free Will Baptist Printing Establishment, 1859), 120, 127.

[43]Roger C. Reeds, "A Brief History of the Sunday School Department" Harrold D. Harrison, ed., *Who's Who Among Free Will Baptists* (Nashville: Randall House Publications, 1978), 450.

[44]*Thirty-First Session of the Free Will Baptist Triennial General Conference, 1901* (Ayden, N.C.: The Free Will Baptist Publishing Company, 1903), 6, 7.

[45]Most of the information used in the latter comments in this section were based on Reeds, "A Brief History of the Sunday School Department," 450-453.

[46]*Minutes of the First and Second Session of the General Conference of the Original Free Will Baptist of the United States, 1921-1922* (Ayden, N.C.: Free Will Baptist Printing Company, 1922), 10.

[47]Ibid., 12.

[48]*Minutes of the Third Annual Session of the General Conference of the Original Free Will Baptist of the United States, 1923* (Ayden, N.C.: Free Will Baptist Printing Co., 1923), 8; *Minutes of the Fifth Annual Session of the General Conference of the Original Free Will Baptist of the United States, 1925* (Ayden, N.C.: Free Will Baptist Printing Co., 1925), 8.

[49]*Minutes of the First Session of the National Association of the Original Free Will Baptist of the United States, 1935.* (Ayden, N.C.: Free Will Baptist Press, 1935), p. 7.

[50]"A Brief History of the Church Training Service Department," Harrold D. Harrison, ed., *Who's Who Among Free Will Baptists.* (Nashville: Randall House Publications, 1978), 385.

[51]*Minutes of the National Association of Free Will Baptists, 1978* (Nashville: Published by the Executive Office of the National Association of Free Will Baptists, 1978), 25.

[52]*Minutes, Triennial General Conference, 1901,* 7.

[53]*Thirty-Second Session of the Free Will Baptist Triennial General Conference, 1904.* (Ayden, N.C.: Free Will Baptist Print, 1905), 10.

[54]*Minutes, General Conference* (1925), 9.

[55]*Minutes of the Twelfth Annual Session of the General Conference of the Original Free Will Baptist of the United States, 1932* (Blackshear, Ga.: *The Times,* 1932), 12.

[56]Mary R. Wisehart, "A Brief History of the Woman's Auxiliary" Harrold D. Harrison, ed., *Who's Who Among*

Free Will Baptists (Nashville: Randall House Publications, 1978), 459.

[57]*Minutes, National Association, 1935*, 6.

[58]*Minutes of the Nineteenth Annual Session of the National Association of Free Will Baptists* (1955), 14, 56; "A Brief History of the Master's Men," Harrold D. Harrison, ed., *Who's Who Among Free Will Baptists* (Nashville: Randall House Publications, 1978), 432, 433.

14

The Church in the Twentieth Century

For the most part, the problems and controversies of earlier days had been settled by the late nineteenth century and the church of the twentieth century would offer little that was new whether theological, political, or relational.

Theology

The Statement of Faith that was adopted by the National Association at the time of its organization in 1935 was almost identical to the earlier *New England Treatise* revision of 1869. The same statement was used earlier by the western segment of the denomination and would be adopted by most of the State Associations by 1949.[1]

Since the statements of faith both North and South changed little in over two hundred years, it is not surprising that the cardinal doctrines of the Scripture—Trinity, Christology, Biblical authority, general atonement, justification and sanctification, believer's baptism, symbolic Lord's Supper, and the second coming of Christ with its subsequent judgment—have remained non-negotiables. The statement of the deity of Christ in the 1973 revision of the *Treatise of the Faith and Practices of the Original Free Will Baptists* differs little from the 1869 revision of the northern Treatise.

At the same time, however, the diversified backgrounds represented in the denomination have tended to encourage discussion and revision where change was possible.

Backsliding and Apostasy

A recommendation presented to the National General Board by the Oklahoma State Association in 1968 illustrates the types of disagreement that exist within the denomination. The questions of backsliding and apostasy always offered fertile ground for discussion and, at times, disagreement. The recommendation read:

> BACKSLIDING AND APOSTASY—A person who has been regenerated or born again and is living in unconfessed, unforgiven sin, is rebellious to the principles of the Kingdom of God and His righteousness, and therefore is a backslider in a lost condition who must repent and be restored to the right relationship with God or be eternally lost.

We recognize, according to Hebrews 6:4-6, that it is possible for a person to get in the condition that he could never return to Christ. This, we believe, is Apostasy. However, we also recognize that a regenerate person can fall into sin, be in a lost condition and still not be an Apostate. This person, through repentance, can be reconciled to God.[2]

The controversy focused on the doctrine of backsliding. Free Will Baptists East and West agreed on the possibility of apostasy as defined in Hebrews 6. Traditionally, however, in the East, backsliding was a reversible state within the Christian experience that did not indicate a "lost" condition. In other words, as long as the individual's conscience reminded him of the need of repentance, he had not lost his salvation and needed reconsecration and repentance rather than salvation. In this case, a "lost condition" and apostasy were synonymous and the condition was irreversible. This understanding of apostasy, by its nature, did not assume that man could determine the point of no return between backsliding and apostasy.

In the West, however, a large number of Free Will Baptists understood backsliding to constitute a lost condition resulting in eternal punishment if death occurred before repentance had been exercised. The Oklahoma resolution pointed to that difference of opinion.

The resolution was placed before the national body by the General Board, and a committee, representing both sides of the issue, was appointed and given the task of initiating discussions that would result in a statement acceptable to both positions. In 1969, the National Association agreed to add an appendix statement to Chapter XIII of the Treatise as follows:

1. We believe that salvation is a present possession by faith in the Lord Jesus Christ as Savior and that a person's eternal destiny depends on whether he has this possession. This we hold in distinction from those who teach that salvation depends on human works or merit.

2. We believe that a saved individual may, in freedom of will, cease to trust in Christ for salvation and once again be lost. This we hold in distinction from those who teach that a believer may not again be lost.

3. We believe that any individual living in the practice of sin (whether he be called "backslider" or "sinner") must be judged by that evidence to be lost should he die in his sins. This we hold in distinction from those who suggest that pernicious doctrine that a man may live in sin as he pleases and still claim Heaven as his eternal home.

4. We believe that any regenerate person who has sinned (again, whether he be called "backslider" or "sinner") and in whose heart a desire arises to repent may do so and be restored to favor and fellowship with God. This we hold in distinction from those who teach that when a Christian sins he cannot repent and be restored to favor and fellowship with God.[3]

Footwashing

The 1968 recommendation that called for changes in the Treatise statement on perseverance also encouraged revision of the document's treatment of the doctrine of the washing of the saints' feet. In that recommendation, the Oklahoma State Association asked that the National Association delete one statement from the Treatise. The statement read ". . . and reminds the believer of the necessity of daily cleansing from sin. . . ."[4]

Though the minutes of the regular sessions of the association seemed to indicate that this part of the recommendation was adopted along with the request concerning perseverance, the statement continues to remain the same in the official Treatise of the denomination.[5]

Since the 1968 recommendation for change, areas of interest in the ordinance of footwashing have shifted in other directions. Though the denomination clearly continues to consider the practice to be one of the three ordinances of the church and though most Free Will Baptists still support the practice verbally, churches in many parts of the country have ceased to include the ordinance in their practice. Among those who continue to encourage footwashing, the questions have changed to "how often"? "when" (after the Sunday morning or evening service)? and "should it be separate or in conjunction with the Lord's Supper?"[6]

There seems to be no evidence that the denomination is interested in relaxing its position on this third ordinance of the church.

Biblical Authority

Recognizing that a number of traditionally conservative denominations were moving further and further away from their earlier heritage, the denomination determined, in 1959, to establish a Commission on Theological Liberalism that would accept the dual tasks of study and of warning in the areas of liberalism, secularism, and worldliness.

One of the basic areas of concern was that of Biblical authority, and the issue was spoken to on a number of occasions during the next few years. By 1977, the issue gained the attention of the entire National Association, and when the body met in the summer of that year, the Resolutions Committee included a lengthy and detailed resolution calling for a reaffirmation of the denomination's traditional position on inspiration and authority. In fact, the resolution gave new strength to the historical statement. In response, the association instructed its Executive Committee to write acceptable statements on inspiration and inerrancy and present them to the association the following year. The new statement reaffirmed the denomination's traditional commitment to a plenary, verbal inspiration of the Scriptures and, in keeping with the times, added a statement on inerrancy.

Inspiration Statement

Free Will Baptists believe in the plenary, verbal inspiration of the Bible. By plenary we mean "full and complete." We hold that all parts of the Bible are inspired and that inspiration extends to all its subjects. By verbal we mean that inspiration extends to the very words of the Scriptures, not just to the thoughts and ideas expressed by human authors.

We believe the Scriptures are infallible and inerrant. The Bible is without error and trustworthy in all its teachings, including cosmogony, geology, astronomy, anthropology, history, chronology, etc., as well as in matters of faith and practice. Being the very word of God, it is God's final revelation and our absolute authority.[7]

Given a year to reflect on its content, the body quickly adopted the strong resolution, without change, in its 1979 session. The resolution has continued to guide the denomination in the areas of inspiration and inerrancy since that time.

Free Will Baptists and the New Charismatic Movement

Free Will Baptists, like other denominations, had to recognize the exceptional growth in the New Charismatic Movement in the second half of this century, and to determine what relationships, if any, should develop between the denomination and this new phenomenon in American Christianity. The denomination's traditional non-charismatic stance and a number of unhappy experiences that resulted in broken churches, set the stage for a firm rejection of the new movement.

The rejection came in the form of a resolution presented to the 1978 session of the National Association. The resolution argued that the "tongues" used on the Day of Pentecost represented distinct foreign languages which were readily understood by the nationalities present; that tongues were given as a special gift to the early church as only one sign which confirmed the witness of the Gospel to unbelievers; that while tongues were bestowed by the sovereign will of God on some believers, all did not speak with tongues; that this gift was abused and became a source of disturbance in the congregational meetings (this argument had significant meaning for the Free Will Baptists); that the gift of tongues was neither an evidence of the baptism of the Holy Spirit, nor does it bring about sanctification.

The final summary statement closed the door on any relationship between the denomination and the new charismatic movement. "…We believe that speaking in tongues as a visible sign of the baptism of the Holy Spirit is an erroneous doctrine to be rejected. Any implication of a 'second work of grace' has never been tolerated in our fellowship of churches."[8]

Polity

In large measure, most polity questions for the denomination were settled by the time the National Association was organized in 1935—congregational government (implied in the name "Baptist"), a two-fold system of church leadership (pastor and deacon), local church relationship with advisory bodies at the state and national levels, and the use of a presbytery in the task of ordaining ministers and, occasionally, even deacons.

Despite the fact that denominational leaders had hammered out policies in these areas in earlier years and the fact that most of the churches traditionally had accepted and been guided by these policies, the denomination recognized that "Baptistic church polity" is a nebulous term at best and is often misunderstood by both clergy and laity. A special polity committee appointed during the 1955 National Association called for a careful study of this important topic in the light of Scriptural and historical evidence. Among other things, the results of the study were to include clear definitions of "church and polity," a sharp distinction between the three major forms of church government popular at that time, a Scriptural refutation of the views which opposed Baptistic principles and beliefs, and a brief history of the progress of Baptistic principles. In addition, the study sought to offer concrete and specific explanation for the character and function of the church, offices of the church, mutual relations of churches, and the relationship of the local church to civil government.[9]

The polity committee attempted, in a second part of their report, to outline the present stance of the denomination. The main thrust of this segment of the report was that of the autonomy of the local church. Beginning with the presupposition that, historically, Baptist groups were characterized by their democratic form of government, the committee reaffirmed that characteristic for their own denomination. The body of the report contained most of the elements that make up congregational government—the independence of the local church with its accompanying right to transact its own business, the right of the local church to hold and retain legal title to all property owned by the congregation, and the right of the local church to call its own pastor.[10]

While agreeing that voluntary relationships with district and national bodies were valuable in the areas of fellowship and cooperative endeavor, the committee was careful to warn that local congregations should not confer undue power upon the larger organizations. Such action, they concluded, led to the loss of democratic privilege.

But unfortunately, the groundwork that was laid in 1955 and the warnings that were issued were not enough to assure the denomination of continued unity. An internal conflict in the Edgemont Free Will Baptist Church in Durham, North Carolina quickly drew the attention of the North Carolina State Convention. The Convention, claiming a historical practice of connectional church government, rejected the arguments of the majority of the congregation and proclaimed a small minority to be the true church.

Though the question of local church property was settled in civil court, the larger difficulties of unity and denominational character were not to find solution until the 1961 and 1962 sessions of the National Association. When the association met in Norfolk, Virginia, in July of 1961, the body of delegates formally adopted the policy statement that had been introduced six years earlier and, in so doing, reaffirmed their historical acceptance of congregational church government. The association then called on the North Carolina Convention to ". . . repudiate any and all forms of connectional church government and reaffirm its position in our historic and established form of congregational church government as set forth in the *Treatise of Faith and Practice of the National Association of Free Will Baptists. . . .*"[11]

But reconciliation was not to be accomplished. In the November 1961, issue of *Contact*, the official publication of the denomination, the Executive Committee of the National Association issued a statement that was designed both to establish the position taken by the National and to issue an additional plea for reconciliation to the North Carolina State Convention. The stated purposes of the published article were:

(1) to make it known that we did not regard the action of the Convention as reflective of the entire constituency of Free Will Baptists within the State; (2) to indicate that we

were not going to be rushed into the hasty action of withdrawing fellowship from North Carolina or even of attempting to tell the North Carolina Convention where it stood— it was our position that the North Carolina Convention should be the one to tell the National Association where it stood; (3) primarily to exhort the people of North Carolina to reconsider and take the action requested by the National Association; and (4) specifically to offer to meet with the leadership of the North Carolina Convention if they were interested in offering any specific proposals aimed at achieving a solution to the problems which would bring about such a reconsideration.[12]

North Carolina did not respond to the invitation and on March 29, 1962, in a special called session, voted to withdraw from the fellowship of the National Association and to set up a new denominational program.[13]

At this point, the National Association of Free Will Baptists demonstrated its allegiance to a program of congregational church government. It had no authority to overrule the decision made by the North Carolina State Convention. It could only express its regrets and look to the future. In 1962, those North Carolina Free Will Baptists who wished to remain with the National Association formed a new State Association and petitioned for membership in the larger body.

Alliances

The continuing denomination's debt to the old New England General Conference did not include the ecumenical spirit that characterized Freewill Baptists in the North from the beginning.

Huge losses to the Particular (Calvinistic) Baptists in the mid-eighteenth century and to the Christian Church (Disciples) in the mid-nineteenth, coupled with the loss of New England in 1911, left the remnant with a skeptical spirit that mitigated against interest in discussions that might lead to union with other fellowships.

Records for the late nineteenth century occasionally mentioned negotiations with the Disciples, and it was not unusual for the Free Will Baptists to exchange visiting delegates with that group during their conferences. Free Will Baptist preachers often were asked to minister to local Methodist, Baptist, and Disciple churches while attending conference sessions, but by the twentieth century, relationships were limited to friendly encounters that allowed conference attendance and exchange of pulpits. Discussions related to union were a thing of the past.

The fact that concern for union ended early in this century might point to an even more important factor in the demise of ecumenical spirit. Free Will Baptists always have been conservative in their theological structure, and it was not surprising that they were identified with the fundamentalist movement quite early in the twentieth century. That relationship not only tended to discourage ecumenism but also encouraged an increasing isolationism that led to the dissolving of relationships with a number of evangelical cooperative organizations. The attitude of isolationism was enhanced by the strong influence of Bob Jones University on the educational philosophy of the denomination during the middle decades of the twentieth century. The denomination voted in 1967 to end its long relationship with the American Bible Society, and in 1972, the same decision was made regarding membership in the National Association of Evangelicals.

As time passed, the National Association moved from first degree separation (separation from individuals and organizations not acceptable to the ones separating) to a standard of second and third degree separation (separation from acceptable individuals or organizations who are guilty of associating with other individuals or associations that are not acceptable). The latter standard eventually would lead to rejection of the ministry of Billy Graham, Columbia Bible College, and others within the evangelical family. The graduate school of Columbia Bible College earlier was responsible for the training of a good number of the present generation of Free Will Baptist missionaries and, interestingly enough, the school has regained a degree of favor in the past half decade.

The Local Church Member at the End of the Twentieth Century

An earlier chapter depicted the Free Will Baptist church member in the nineteenth century as severe in lifestyle, from either a rural or small town background, and probably related either to the lower or lower middle class of his society. The local church member in the twentieth century was both like and unlike his nineteenth century counterpart. The examples of Benjamin Randall, Jesse Heath, James Roach, and others that dictated a quasi-ascetic lifestyle for the earlier century have continued to exercise their influence on the existing denomination. Though some of the characteristics of lifestyle have changed in keeping with the times, the principles of separation that kept nineteenth century Free Will Baptists from the race tracks, the dances, and the theater continued to set the parameters for life-style in the late twentieth century and into the next.

While the denominational standard for the individual church member has remained much the same in the area of lifestyle, the member himself has experienced dramatic change in his social status. When the character of the denomination itself evolved from rural to urban-rural, it became necessary that adjustments be made in ministry. The man in the pulpit had to be different because the man in the pew was different. The most immediate and evident response to the new church member was an interest in education. A simple message from an uneducated minister could no longer meet the needs of a changing congregation. While the denomination would continue to retain some of the characteristics of its old nature and the influences of anti-intellectualism from its relationships with conservative Christianity, the cry of the early twentieth century was the cry for an educated ministry. The transition, as expected, was a slow one and continues to the present day. As late as 1950, few local associations required formal training as a prerequisite for ordination, but increased concern for education, the availability of four-year Bible colleges in different parts of the country, and the changing character of the local congregation have encouraged a new attitude toward an educated ministry.

The twentieth century Free Will Baptist can be characterized as severe in lifestyle, either rural or urban in background, and mobile in his social relationships. No longer imprisoned in a horizontal social structure, the local church member found himself capable of vertical mobility that allowed him to pass from one social level to another. Even in rural areas, opportunities for education and training produced a new kind of church member. The methods and ministry of the nineteenth century were no longer acceptable or practical.

The recurring theme in the last half of the twentieth century was that of dramatic change. The church has changed. The farmer has been joined by the lawyer, the doctor, the accountant, the banker, the teacher. And in response, the denomination has changed. This section of the text was entitled, "A Continuing Witness: From Organization to Maturity." Though we might question that any denomination reaches full maturity, the Free Will Baptists have struggled diligently to meet the challenge. The development of a strong national organization that has respected the autonomy of the local church, an increasing interest in education that has spawned a growing educational system, an effective missions program both overseas and at home, and adjustments in methodology to meet the needs of a growing and changing denomination have all been elements of the maturation process.

Notes for Chapter 14

[1]The 1949 Printing of the *North Carolina Treatise* was a revision of the *1949 National Treatise*.

[2]*Minutes of the Thirty-Second Annual Session of the National Association, 1968.* (Nashville: Published by the Executive Department, National Association of Free Will Baptists, 1968), p. 21.

[3]*A Treatise of the Faith and Practices of the Original Free Will Baptists. 1973 Revision.* (Nashville: Published by the Executive Office of the National Association of Free Will Baptists, 1974), pp. 41,42; *Minutes of the National Association of Free Will Baptists, 1969.* (Nashville: Published by The Executive Department, National Association of Free Will Baptists, 1969), p. 20.

[4]*Minutes of the National Association, 1968,* p. 21.

[5]*A Treatise of the Faith and Practices of Free Will Baptists. 1973 Revision.* (Nashville: Published by the Executive Office of the National Association of Free Will Baptists, 1974), p. 38.

[6]Jack Williams, Telephone Interview (November 17, 1983). Mr. Williams is Editor of *Contact*, the official publication of the National Association of Free Will Baptists. His office allows him the advantage of constant dialogue with the membership of the National body.

[7]*Minutes of the National Association of Free Will Baptists, 1978.* (Nashville: Published by the Executive Office, National Association of Free Will Baptists, 1978), p. 86.

[8]Ibid., pp. 8-86.

[9]*Minutes of the Nineteenth Annual Session of the National Association of Free Will Baptists, 1955,* p. 10.

[10]Ibid., pp. 20, 21.

[11]*Minutes of the National Association of Free Will Baptists, 1961.* (Nashville: Published by the Executive Department, National Association of Free Will Baptists, 1961), p. 18.

[12]*Minutes of the National Association of Free Will Baptists, 1962.* (Nashville: Published by the Executive Department, National Association of Free Will Baptists, 1962), p. 17.

[13]Ibid., p. 18.

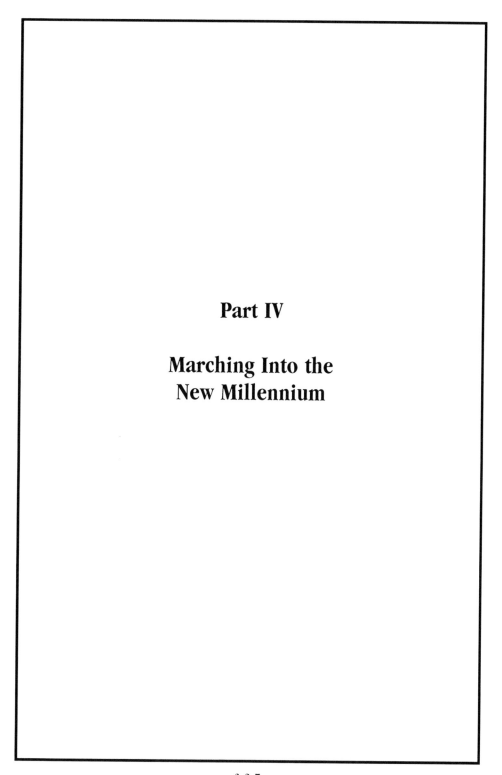

Part IV

Marching Into the
New Millennium

CHAPTER 12

15

Free Will Baptists Facing the Twenty-First Century

The last section of the study begins with Jubilee and ends with a new century and a new millennium. In 1985, the National Association of Free Will Baptists celebrated its fiftieth birthday in Nashville, Tennessee, the city of its birth. But this time, Cofer's Chapel, the church that hosted the first national convention, had to give way to the city's municipal auditorium in order to accommodate the crowds that came to enjoy the denomination's Jubilee celebration. The theme of the conference, "Focusing on Free Will Baptists," set the tone for the entire week of meetings. Ralph Staten, Mrs. Luther Reed, Agnes Frazier, Mary Elizabeth Griffith, Ethel Burroughs and Jessie Parsons were honored for having attended both the first sitting of the convention and the Jubilee event.[1]

During the second session of the new National Association in 1938, J. C. Griffin, the denomination's statistician, bemoaned the fact that an accurate statistical report was all but impossible. "The only solution to the problem is to get all associations to use our report blanks. We have offered this time after time but we are slow to take hold of the work."[2] The statistics that were available revealed a total of 1,143 churches, 82,752 members, and 1,095 ministers.[3]

The minutes for the National Association in 1985 mirrored Griffin's earlier problem as only 2,093 of the denomination's 2,548 churches reported to the annual meeting. But the figures offered that year were encouraging, noting that by the Jubilee year of the movement's history, the membership had almost tripled, the number of ministers had grown by 75 percent, and the number of churches had more than doubled.[4]

But, at the same time, the statistics were disturbing. The denomination's growth rate was far below that of other similar bodies. The Southern Baptists, many of the Pentecostal groups, and numerous independent movements were experiencing phenomenal growth while that of the Free Will Baptists could only be described as steady and less than exciting. It was time for change. The end of the century and the end of the millennium must be marked by new vision, new adventures, new goals, new advancements.

And so it would be. The annual minutes for the National Association during the last fifteen years of the century would reflect the denomination's new expectations and its new optmism—growth campaigns, new mission fields and new missionaries, an expanded outreach for Randall House Publications, a new look at education. By default, as many of the older leaders grew to retirement age, the denomination also would see the passing of the torch of leadership to a new and younger generation. And it would affect every facet of the group's ministry—national administration, publishing, missions, education. The transition would be a gradual one, but it would play a significant role in the direction the denomination would take as it moved into the new millennium.

Facing the New Millennium—The National Scene

At the national level, the last fifteen years of the millennium would be marked by a series of ambitious programs that would reflect the denomination's determination to minister to the needs of a changing world in desperate times, to reverse patterns of growth that had hindered effectiveness in earlier years, to speak to contemporary issues intelligently and boldly, and to prepare itself to meet the challenges of a rapidly changing culture.

A New Look for a Maturing Denomination

It was natural to assume that new attitudes and expectations from within and evolving cultural challenges from without would demand changes and adjustments that would give the denomination a new look as it faced the future. But the excitement of new adventures and new conquests could not allow the Free Will Baptists to abandon the core values that had marked their identity from the very beginning—commitment to Scripture, blood bought redemption, general atonement, a conservative, careful lifestyle. The last days of the century indeed would be marked by change, but within traditional boundaries that were considered non-negotiable.

Setting the Boundaries—Reaffirmation of the Covenant

The era covered by Part III of our text saw two major conflicts that visibly shook the denomination, resulting in one formal parting of the ways and in one less formal, but no less disturbing internal period of unrest.

The first conflict focused on questions of denominational polity and more specifically on the question of the autonomy of the local congregation. A committee report completed in 1955 called upon Free Will Baptists to reaffirm the denomination's traditional commitment to "Baptistic polity," but events later in that same decade and in the early years of the next would lead to open conflict. The context was that of an internal struggle in the Edgemont Free Will Baptist Church in Durham, North Carolina. Leaders of the North Carolina State Convention, contending for a tradition of "connectional" or conference controlled polity, determined that a small minority of the church was the true church at Edgemont. The conflict grew larger and finally was submitted to the local court. The appeal of the North Carolina State Convention was upheld by the courts and the church property was awarded to the minority represented by the convention. By 1962, North Carolina Free Will Baptists found themselves formally divided as the connectional group withdrew from the National Association and the remnant petitioned for membership in the national body as the new North Carolina Association of Free Will Baptists. The group that left the denomination became the North Carolina State Convention of the Original Free Will Baptists.[5]

The second conflict focused on biblical interpretation. Did Jesus make wine for the marriage at Cana or was it simply the juice of the vine? Suggesting that it was illogical to assume that the wedding wine was less than that normally used in first century Palestine, Leroy Forlines, professor of Systematic Theology at Free Will Baptist Bible College, publically defended Jesus' first miracle as a "real wine" creation. Reaction to the announcement was immediate and forceful as numbers of opponents countered with the argument that Jesus would never have tolerated intoxicating ingredients in a wine of His making.

The issue actually surfaced some years earlier, but it was given full attention by the National Association in its yearly meeting in July 1983. For that year, the Resolutions Committee re-port repeated the resolution that had been adopted by the association in its 1982 meeting. That resolution recognized the problem, admitted the gravity of the situation, and acknowledged that both sides of the controversy were in agreement on most of the elements that made up the issue—that teetotalism was the best lifestyle for the Christian, that the use of alcoholic beverages should always be condemned, that Jesus Christ was absolutely sinless. In addition, the resolution assumed that attempts to agree on all scriptural references to wine would lead to divisiveness and that the best approach to the problem would be a reaffirmation of the denomination's covenant and the agreement that all teaching on the issue would take into account the sensitive nature of the issue.[6] The body refused to consider an additional resolution that called for a 10 person committee to consider the question and return the next year with a statement of agreement acceptable to the association.

Resolution number four of the committee's report asked that the delegates determine an official denominational position on the wine question, and that if the body decided that Jesus did not make fermented wine then ". . . those that believe that he did who hold positions as teachers in our college or are board members resign or be dismissed."[7] Again, the association refused to consider the resolution.

Both of the conflicts offered an excellent context for power struggle and the developing confrontations suggested that control was as much a concern as was principle. In both cases, the association showed itself to be aware of the issues, cognizant of the underlying and guiding principles that must determine its responses, and willing to make peace where compromise was not required. The two conflicts would force the denomination to revisit its traditional convictions—biblical authority, local church autonomy, congregational government, and to learn to work together within the framework of a national association. Successful and mature response to the conflicts would leave the denomination with a sense of unity, of purpose, and of hope.

The 1990s would reveal a new face for the National Association. While ordained delegates still registered the larger majority of votes, lay delegates representing local churches and associations now were exercising their right to speak out on matters of concern for the denomination. Rubber stamping of decisions from committees and boards was not to be expected or tolerated. It was becoming increasingly difficult to anticipate decisions that might result from votes from the floor. But this was not to suggest that the denomination was moving away from its core values. It simply meant that every issue would be carefully considered and weighed against the traditions and principles that had guided the movement through the years.

In 1991, recognizing that the world was rapidly changing, that America could no longer be considered a Christian nation, that modernism was giving way to postmodernism, that the church was playing a much smaller role in the shaping of contemporary culture, that the denomination itself was more internally diverse than it had been in the past, that change must come if the movement was to continue to minister to its culture, the National Association agreed that it was time to reaffirm its commitment to those values that had served them well through the years.

> Whereas, researchers believe there will be an increase in non-Biblical religions in America in this decade; and

> Whereas, Free Will Baptists have been dedicated and loyal to the Holy Scriptures and the doctrines we have embraced for more than 26 decades; and

> Whereas, we are a diverse denomination coming from many roots and have continued to progress and grow amidst such through tolerance, courtesy and love;

> Therefore, be it resolved that we affirm our loyalty to God, His Son, His cause, His Word, to each other, and to the denomination that has brought us this far, and that we continue to prefer one another in love and godly compassion and be found faithful in these as we continue forward.[8]

A New Home for the New Millennium

Denominational growth in the last half of the twentieth century is reflected in the number of times the national offices have found it necessary to rebuild or relocate. The first permanent national office was established in a two-story single family home purchased on May 22, 1953, for the grand sum of $19,000. This small building served all of the departments of the National Association except the Bible College until 1965 when a new and larger building was constructed at 1134 Murfreesboro Road in southeast Nashville. The new building was constructed at a cost of $163,000. In 1967, the Sunday School Department added a new building to the complex in an attempt to meet the needs of their growing literature ministry. But by 1978, this building too was in-adequate. After donating their addition to the National Association, the Sunday School Department purchased a new building at 114 Bush Road. This property was free of debt by 1997. Finally, the entire national office found it necessary to again expand. The Murfreesboro Road property was sold for $725,000 and new facilities were built at 5233 Mt. View Road in Antioch, Tennessee, just outside the city of Nashville.[9] Except for the Bible College and the Sunday School and Church Training Department, the national office building continues to serve all of the different ministries of the denomination.

A New Hymnbook

A brief note in the General Board report for the 1985 sitting of the National Association was the first reference to the possibility of a new hymnbook for the denomination. By 1987 the committee was reporting directly to the National Association. In its report for that year it proudly announced that the new hymnbook, *Rejoice: The Free Will Baptist Hymnbook*, would be available for shipment by November 23, 1987. It was suggested that Sunday, December 6 be set aside as a day of celebration and that it be designated as "Rejoice 87: Hymn Book Dedication Sunday."[10]

Early response to the hymnbook was phenomenal and the report to the National in July 1988, spoke of the possibility of the sale of the entire first printing of 100,000 copies. In addition, other denominational groups had expressed interest in the publication and the committee already was dreaming of the addition of a generic hymnbook that ". . . could give us the opportunity to influence other groups' worship and singing for years to come."[11]

In 1988, at the request of the Hymnbook Committee, the National expanded the work of the committee to that of a full commission. During that meeting, delegates elected Blaine Hughes, Vernon Whaley, Rodney Whaley, R. Douglas Little, and Bill Gardner to serve on the new commission and to oversee the denomination's response to musical needs of its members.[12]

A New Plan for Denominational Funding

The old Cooperative Plan served the denomination well for a number of decades but the 1990's would demand that the funding programs of the denomination be revisited. As early as 1990, the national Budget Committee was instructed to evaluate the present financial program and to especially give attention to the needs of the Executive Office. In response, a Stewardship Committee was appointed to work with the Budget Committee on the project, and the annual leadership conference for 1991 was designated as a "Stewardship Summit." The new committee on stewardship included Tom Lilly, Clarence Burton, Don Walker, Alton Loveless, Jeff Crabtree, Connie Cariker, David Joslin, John Edwards, David Shores, and Norwood Gibson.[13]

At the National Association in 1992, the joint committee submitted a detailed proposal for denominational funding to the delegates. The proposal, entitled "Stewardship Philosophy for Denominational Support," called on the denomination to adopt a new funding program that would be known as "The Together Way Plan." The basic principle of the plan was that all participating churches would equitably support all denominational agencies. Each church was asked to give a general offering that would be divided among the different ministries of the denomination according to a percentage schedule approved by the National Association or a designated offering that assigned equitable gifts for each of the various ministries of the national body. In either case, the offerings were to constitute ten percent of the budget of the local church plus additional offerings above the minimum that would assure a balanced income program for all of the ministries being supported.[14]

The new "Together Way Plan" proposal related the giving plan to the mission statement of the denomination and included a five year educational plan designed to encourage ownership of the program by the entire membership of the denomination.

Something New, Something Old

The reader should not assume that all the new—new attitudes, new national offices, new hymnbook, new funding policies—would remove the old from memory. The denomination was still acutely aware of its heritage and of those elements of its character that helped shape it during the long years of its history—a conservative Arminian theology, a strong emphasis on a biblical lifestyle, extreme care in seeking and achieving relationships with other bodies, a heart for world evangelization, and its name. Recognizing that other denominations and religious groups were directing attention away from their names as an attempt to encourage growth, the Free Will Baptists determined that their name, like their theology was non-negotiable. In 1952, the General Board of the National Association included this resolution:

Whereas, Free Will Baptists are and wish to remain a distinct denomination in doctrine and title, and in recent days there is a trend toward carrying generic titles by some of our churches, we urge all churches who are members of the National Association of Free Will Baptists to visibly acknowledge and display their association with Free Will Baptists in all forms communicating the title.[15]

But, at the same time, it was evident that change was necessary if the Free Will Baptists were to enjoy effective ministry in the context of the evolving culture of the late twentieth century and of the coming twenty-first. What changes were necessary? In the light of Free Will Baptist tradition and conviction, what changes were possible? The new directions already mentioned in this chapter have been promising. And new achievements, expectations, and dreams in missions, education, evangelism, and national leadership during the past few years have added to the promise. The denomination seems ready to face the future with excitement about the possibilities, determination to allow God to do all He wants to do in and through the Free Will Baptists, and the willingness to allow change where change is necessary as long as that change can come without compromise.

The National and Its Relationships

As noted in chapter 14, the denomination did not share the ecumenical spirit that had characterized Free Will Baptists in the North. A growing attitude of isolationism was evident in the last half of the twentieth century.

The last days of the century would find little change in the mindset of the denomination and its leaders. Anti-Catholic and anti-liberal convictions continue to separate the denomination from many, if not most, outside religious groups and movements.

The most significant issue faced during the last fifteen years was that of the Promise Keepers movement. During the 1996 sitting of the National Association, the Resolutions Committee sent two conflicting resolutions to the floor without their recommendation, leaving the body of delegates with the task of sorting out the difficulties. Resolution five had appealed for rejection of the Promise Keepers while resolution six had asked for alliance. The delegates were unwilling to make an immediate judgment and passed the responsibility to the Commission for Theological Integrity, asking that the commission return the following year with a written report indicating the doctrinal beliefs of the Promise Keepers' board and field representatives and that clearly revealed the stated goals and practices of the movement as they related to doctrinal purity.[16] And report they did—a thirty-nine page document that included a history and characterization of the movement along with suggestions as to how believers should deal with differing opinions and with recommendations to the National Association for consideration by the delegates. The report was accepted by the body and a second motion, approved by the delegates, indicated the convictions of the majority.

The Free Will Baptist denomination historically has defended the faith against the subtle and insidious movements that would undermine the Word of God and His Church.

In recognition of the work that the committee has done and in light of the study that has been done this past year and a report given by the Commission for Theological Integrity concerning the Promise Keepers movement, and whereas, their report is not in favor of endorsing nor embracing the Promise Keepers movement, I move that the National Association of Free Will Baptists go on record at this annual session as being opposed to the Promise Keepers movement, and that we encourage member churches and pastors to avoid contact and involvement with the movement, and that the National Association of Free Will Baptists direct all national departments and their directors and personnel to adhere to this motion and that no department director or personnel will promote the Promise Keepers movement in any way, and that the National Association of Free Will Baptists take this action as an opportunity to reaffirm our commitment to earnestly contend for the truth through sound, biblical preaching, holy living, and continued ecclesiastical separation from false doctrines and movements.[17]

The last sentence of the motion characterized the mind-set of the denomination from the very beginning and that attitude must be considered one of the factors that limited growth during the denomination's long history. In those cases where compromise was evidently required the delegates remained firm in their convictions. During the National Association in 1988, a resolution called for sanctions against Universal Studios for their production of the film entitled, "The Last Tempation of Christ." The resolution asked the members of the denomination to refuse to support the productions of Univeresal and the theaters that would show them.[18] Later, in 1996, the National would call for a boycott against the Walt Disney Corporation because of its open door policy toward homosexuals.[19] But while earlier fears demanded separation from literally everyone outside, the latter part of the twentieth century gave evidence of a more mature attitude that allowed new alliances if, after careful investigation, it was clear that no compromise was required. The new attitude was revealed in the denomination's support of the "See You at the Pole" youth prayer movement[20] and in the establishment of the "International Fellowship of Free Will Baptists," a new organization that was intended to draw together and to maximize the efforts of Free Will Baptists in different parts of the world. The General Board called on the Executive Committee to do a feasibility study of such an organization in 1986 and by 1992, an International Consultation Committee was ready to report to the national body. An organizational meeting August 24-28, 1992, drew representatives from Free Will Baptist churches in Japan, Canada, Mexico, Brazil, Panama, Uruguay, and the United States and produced a working document for organization that was entitled, "The Panama Declaration, 1992." The declaration reaffirmed basic denominational beliefs and set guidelines for agreement in areas such as the Charismatic Movement, the Ecumenical Movement, separate and holy lifestyles, and the necessity for evangelism.[21]

A more ambitious program of cooperation encouraged by the Resolution Committee in 1989 did not fare so well. In that year, resolution four called upon the denomination to overlook insignificant differences with other Free Will Baptist bodies and to encourage them to attend the National Association the next year.

Be it resolved that we instruct our Executive Committee of the General Board of the National Association of Free Will Baptists to extend an invitiation to all unaffiliated groups of Free Will Baptist churches and the United American Free Will Baptists to send representatives to our meeting in Phoenix, Ariz., July 15-19, 1990.[22]

In 1990, C. H. Overman, General Secretary of the North Carolina State Convention of Original Free Will Baptists was introduced to the National Association and was allowed to bring greetings from his organization. The following year, Dr. Melvin Worthington, Executive Secretary for the National Association, reciprocated by representing the National at the yearly meeting of the North Carolina State Convention. Any expectations of renewed cooperation were quickly ended, however, when those North Carolina Free Will Baptists affiliated with the National asked that no further negotiations with the State Convention be pursued.

Whereas, the National Executive Committee was instructed in Tampa, Florida, to extend invitations to unaffiliated groups of Free Will Baptists and send representatives to Phoenix in 1990; and

Whereas, such invitations were extended to the North Carolina State Convention (unaffiliated); and

Whereas, the North Carolina Association of Free Will Baptists (affiliated) did hereby pass a unanimous resolution at their 29th annual convention that the National Association "be asked to cease any further negotiations in any manner with the State Convention";

Therefore, be it resolved that the Executive Committee be instructed not to enter any negotiations with the North Carolina State Convention. (Adopted as amended and here written.)[25]

The implications were clear. The denomination had grown and matured and was willing to entertain the possibility of new alliances, but only within the boundaries that had been set years before, boundaries that were sacred and non-negotiable.

Growing Programs and Growing Patterns

The last fifteen years of the century and the millennium were good years for the Free Will Baptists. The new headquarters building, the growing crowds at the annual national meetings, the opening of new ministries in distant parts of the world (to be visited later in this chapter), the arrival of a new and younger generation of leaders were all positive signs of growth and denominational maturity and gave birth to a new sense of expectation and hope for the future. But lack of significant growth in national membership continued to be a problem. Earlier in the text, the author attempted to rationalize lack of growth by pointing to the group's demand for a rigid lifestyle, its conservative Arminian theology, and its rural character. But one must wonder if the tendency to lag behind other denominations in response to cultural, theological, and social issues might also play a part in the group's failure to grow.

In its report, a committee appointed by the National Association to look at the new millennium reminded Free Will Baptists that while some hindrances to growth are matters of principle and are, therefore, non-negotiable, others might be areas in which change and adjustment could open doors to growth in the new millennium.

In a section of the report entitled, "Are We Ready for the Changes Before Us?" the committee concludes:

> . . . we, God's people, the church, must be cognizant of the tremendous changes that have taken place in the last few decades in the world's population. It is also important that we recognize that change is still the order of the day. But it is even more important to our task of evangelizing the world to comprehend, as best we can, what world population changes will be in place at the beginning of the 21st century and beyond.
>
> The spiritual trends of our time are a double helix between forces of renewal and emergence, and forces of stability and habit. We will have to become a generation of bridge builders in a world where certainty and chaos, potentiality and stability dance co-creatively. . . . Never before have we been more aware of the existence of 'other people' than we are today. The next century will be even more challenging.[24]

Challenge indeed! Will the Free Will Baptists be ready to meet that challenge? Will they effectively play their role in world evangelization? Is growth possible?

Growth Programs

Growth and effective ministry were clearly on the minds of both leadership and laity in the last years of the millennium. Two strategic growth plans were drafted and implemented between 1985 and the year 2000.

Target 90—Target 90 was approved by the delegates and launched at the 1985 National Association. Goals for the five year growth program included the founding of 100 new churches and a net increase of 50,000 members for the denomination. While the latter goal was not reached, denominational leaders were encouraged by the number of baptisms and church births recorded during the five year period of the project. Totals reported in 1990 included an impressive 41,458 baptisms and 103 new churches. The only disappointment came in the failure to reach the goal assigned to membership growth. That statistic showed a net increase of 27,440 new members, a little more than half of the goal that had been set in 1985.[25]

Double in a Decade Campaign—In 1991, a new growth project was introduced to the denomination. In its initial report to the National Association, the project committee began its report, "The five-year Target 90 campaign to increase net membership by 50,000 and plant 100 new churches is history."[26] The new program would seek to double membership in the group by the year

2000. That first report in 1991 congratulated the Target 90 program for a job well done and admitted that lessons learned from the earlier campaign would serve the new one well.

For the first few years, excitement was evident and hope was possible. The 1993 report noted plans for numbers of planned events—"Roll Call Sunday, 1995", Double in a Decade seminars led by Home Mission staff members—which were designed to encourage pastors and their churches to become actively involved in the growth campaign. But by 1995, the annual committee report was folded into the Executive Secretary's, and it was evident that projected goals were not being met. Again, the number of baptisms was impressive, averaging 8,464 per year from 1988 to 1997. And, indeed, the increases in membership were encouraging. Reports to the Double in a Decade committee showed a net increase of 50,805 in the ten year period mentioned above.[27] Statistics, however, can be confusing. While the Executive Secretary's report listed a total membership of 261,169 in 1997, the recorded statistics in the Yearbook for 1999, listed only 206,397. Maybe history does repeat itself. In 1938, J. C. Griffin, the statistician for the denomination, bemoaned the fact that few churches were careful to send accurate reports to the National. His solution had been to draft a number of standard forms that would make reporting a simple task. Much pleading with local church clerks, however, did not bring about the desired results. These pleas were repeated in the 1999 Yearbook, as local, district, and state clerks were encouraged to "…take the time necessary to fill out the National Association's reporting forms."[28] While accuracy demands that the lower official membership totals be accepted, it is quite possible that both lists were correct. The "Decade" figures were based on actual yearly reports that included baptisms, members gained, and members lost. The net gains were carefully documented. The official lists record only those figures that were reported to the National and while less exciting, are, nevertheless, the figures that must be used.[29] In any case, the final results of the Double in a Decade campaign revealed that the denomination was still characterized by a slow and steady growth but one that fell short of dreams and expectations.

Outreach 21—The New Millennium Committee ended their report with an ambitious ten year program designed to launch the denomination into the next century and the new millennium. Containing strategies for the local church as well as for the global responsibilities of the denomination, the plan focused on a new theme for each year in the target decade.

> OUTREACH 2000 – Obedience to Our Loving God
> OUTREACH 2001 – Unity for His Church
> OUTREACH 2002 – Teach and Train to Equip the Saints
> OUTREACH 2003 – Revive for the Time Is Close
> OUTREACH 2004 – Evangelize! Evangelize!
> OUTREACH 2005 – Announce He cometh
> OUTREACH 2006 – Consecrate: Our Preparation
> OUTREACH 2007 – Honor God for His Goodness Toward All Men
> OUTREACH 2008 – 2 – duplicate – 1000 New Churches from 1999 to 2009
> OUTREACH 2009 – 1 – united – 50,000 New Members by 2009[30]

Committee expectations were great. "**Outreach 21** will bring all parts of the church together as believers unite in prayer, form common goals, and share in making these goals attainable. As we enter the twenty-first century, and the next millennium, we must look at different means of ministry and outreach to those whose cultures, languages, and lifestyles differ from ours."[31] But for some reason, the vision did not capture the attention of the larger body and, in 1999, it was decided that the plan should be set aside.[32]

The Free Will Baptists, Missions, and the New Millennium
Church Planting at Home

While concern for church planting at home had been in the hearts and minds of Free Will Baptists from the beginning, a formal program of home missions was slow in coming. The first salaried home missionaries were appointed by the denomination in 1954. But the latter part of the century would be characterized by new excitement and new growth in this arena of denomination-al ministry. In 1984, the Home Missions Department approved eight new missionary families, cele-brated the attainment of full self-support for two churches, supported seven national pastors in Mexico, reported eight Free Will Baptist chaplains in the armed forces, and placed a Director of Evangelism and Church Growth on the field who would lead 23 "Revival-Time" conferences in dif-ferent parts of the country. The conferences focused on evangelism and church growth at the local level. In addition, the department sponsored a number of church enlargement campaigns, hired a missionary builder who was to be available to new churches and their building programs, and enjoyed its best year in terms of gifts and income. Gifts totaling $1,704,537 made this the greatest income year in the department's history.[33]

In an attempt to involve laymen in the task of Home Missions on the one hand, and to meet the financial needs of struggling home missionaries on the other, the department introduced two new programs in 1987. The "Aquila and Priscilla Program" was to serve the former need and the "Tentmaker Program," the second. During that year, five lay families served with veteran mission-aries on the field and twelve families enjoyed the benefits of the funds issued by the "Tentmaker Program."[34]

Over the next few years to the end of the decade, the Home Missions Department enjoyed sig-nificant growth in the number of new missionaries, the amount of money available to new church-es through the Church Extension Loan fund, the number of mission churches becoming self-sup-porting, and in gift income from the denomination. The loan fund, along with Missionary Builder Howard Gwartney and his crew of volunteer construction workers known as the "Master's Hands," made it possible for small, new groups of believers to construct buildings for worship. Further aid was made available through the Department in the form of free blueprints offered in notebook form.[35] In 1990, Richard Adams assumed the office of Director of Development for the department and immediately launched a fund raising campaign designed to add $1,000,000 to the loan fund. The General Director's report to the National for that year reminded the delegates that "This money will never be spent, but will always be used to build Home Missions Church buildings. As one church pays it back, it will be loaned to another, and continue to build churches until the Lord comes!"[36]

In reflecting back over the four years of his ministry as the new General Director of Home Missions, Trymon Messer noted that one of the most important steps taken under his leadership was the appointment of a Director of Missionary Assistance. This was a new office that was to offer training, encouragement, and assistance to the missionaries as well as drafting and administrating an evaluation program for the department. The new officer was in place by 1996.[37]

Other events closing out the millennium included "Operation Saturation," a joint effort by the Master's Men, Women Nationally Active for Christ, Randall House Publications, and the Home Missions Department intended to place the gospel in homes near home mission ministries and a Free Will Baptist Cross-Cultural Ministry recognized Christian ministry in America could not overlook the importance of reaching across ethnic lines in the task of home missions. Even a cursory look at the American scene at the beginning of the new millennium reminds us that the diversity here is as pronounced as it is in many countries in Europe. The latter ministry was launched via a Cross-Cultural Extension Conference conducted by Hillsdale Free Will Baptist College on the campus of Seminary of the Cross in Reynosa, Mexico. Initial sites for cross-cultural outreach included Hispanic ministries in Tennessee and Florida as well as the already established work in Mexico.[38]

Failure to gain approval for the "Outreach 21" proposal offered by the New Millennium Committee in 1999, left the denomination with a vacuum in the area of planning and vision for the future. A new proposal entitled, "Advancing into the Millennium," was submitted to denominational personnel during their annual Leadership Conference in December 1999. During their meeting in Nashville, Tennessee, conference members heard Trymon Messer, General Director for the Home Missions Department, outline a master plan for evangelism and church growth in the denomination over the first few years of the new millennium. A national goal of gospel exposure for 1,000,000 homes during the year 2000 was to be met through the active involvement of local churches and State Associations. Each church would be asked to present the gospel in 1000 homes and state leaders would be encouraged to oversee, promote, and encourage the work among their churches. At the time of the conference, Free Will Baptists in Alabama already had committed to reach 100,000 homes in their state before the end of the next year.[39] Other state organizations were asked to join them. The plan was approved by the members of the conference and it was determined that the proposal should be formally presented to the National Association during its next meeting in July 2000.[40]

Finally, the Department changed the name of its major publication to *AIM*. The Director reminds the reader that this acronym gives clear evidence of the direction of the department for the new millennium, "Advancing in Missions."[41] The advance was to focus on the founding of new churches. The last item of business for the department's board meeting, December 1-3, 1997, approved the motion that ". . . the Home Missions Board goes on record as adopting church planting as our priority."[42]

Church Planting Across the World

The Foreign Missions report to the National Association for the Jubilee Celebration in 1985 boasted an increase from 1 to 110 missionaries in active ministry and a budget that had grown from a grand total of $475 to a proposed sum of $2,895,498 for 1986.[43] The year of Jubilee was marked by an "Advance Celebration" designed to ". . . stimulate an outburst of praise to God for what He has done through Free Will Baptists in nine countries of the world since 1935."[44] The praise focused on newly opened doors in Spain and on successful yearly conferences in Panama, India, and the Ivory Coast of Africa. More than 500 attended the conference in India.[45] But the celebration embraced far more than simple praise. Designed to meet ". . . special opportunities for helping develop our young overseas Free Will Baptist churches," it was used to raise funds to provide evangelistic tools, training for national workers, funds for the building of new churches (a loan fund much like that employed by the Home Missions Department), and to provide money for the commissioning of 30 new missionaries.[46]

Growth and Expansion—For the most part, the latter years of the century were characterized by steady growth and effective ministry. By 1988, Free Will Baptists missionaries were to be found in Brazil, Uruguay, Panama, Ivory Coast, France, India, Spain, and Japan. One of the most encouraging notes during these years was that of the continuing ministry in Cuba. Though missionaries had been removed from the country during Fidel Castro's rise to power, the church there continued to survive under difficult circumstances. In 1983, Mrs. Mabel Willey traveled to Cuba as guest speaker for the fortieth anniversary of the Cuban Association of Free Will Baptists. During the conference the 400 delegates voted to raise $10,000 for the renovation of the Cedars of Lebanon Seminary. "I sat on the platform and wept," said Mrs. Willey, "That out of their poverty, they gave!"[47] In 1987, the government finally gave permission for renovations of the seminary to begin. In that year, the Cuban church reported 91 conversions and 40 baptisms.[48]

By 1989, the department staff and the Foreign Missions Board were beginning to realize that the century and the millennium were coming to an end and that the future would offer new challenges that must be anticipated and addressed. Progress to this point had been dramatic. The denomination's cross-cultural ministry efforts now included training institutes in Brazil, Cuba, Panama, and Ivory Coast. Membership in Free Will Baptist churches outside the United States had reached more than 7000, and the yearly department budget had grown to more than $4,000,000.[49] But what of the future? Pointing to the expected retirement of thirteen career missionaries by the year 2000, the 12,000 people groups who still had never heard the gospel, and the new opportunities promised by the end of communism and the fall of the iron curtain in eastern Europe, the department appealed to the denomination for 83 new missionaries over the next few years. Final concerns focused on the importance of establishing "Great Commission" churches at home and that of wise leadership for the churches away from home as they made plans for sending out their own missionaries to proclaim the gospel to a lost world.[50]

The ministry of the Foreign Missions Department in the decade of the 1990's was marked by two movements: (1) a strong focus on the development of national churches; and (2) entry into a number of new countries where Free Will Baptists had never before served. During this period, denominational missionaries entered and set up ministries in China, Mongolia, Russia, Central Asia, and Korea while Indian Free Will Baptists were founding seven new churches in Nepal.[51]

One of the highlights for the last decade of the century was the introduction of the Free Will Baptist message in Russia. The board agreed in 1993 that opportunities for ministry in Russia should be explored as soon as possible and by 1995, the former Soviet Union had been declared a viable mission field for the Foreign Missions Department. Approved actions by the board included the sending of copies of the denominational Treatise to Russia and the Ukraine, sending copies of Free Will Baptist commentaries to four Russian Baptist Union Seminaries and to the Autonomous Baptist Bible Institute in Kiev, providing professors for brief, intensive study programs, supporting national church planters especially in areas that were needy and unevangelized, and investigating the possibility of translating Leroy Forlines' *Systematics* into Russian.[52] Later, Professor Leroy Forlines and his wife, Dr. Fay Forlines, would spend six months teaching and preaching in both Russia and the Ukraine as short-term appointees of the Free Will Baptist Foreign Mission Board. The couple was joined by their son James Forlines, Randy Wilson, Jimmy Aldridge and Jim Turnbough for a pastors' conference in Chelyabinsk, Russia, April 1-5, 1996.[53] The ministry of Professor Forlines and his wife was so effective that they were asked to travel to India late in 1999 to teach among the Free Will Baptists there.

Time for Retrenchment—By 1992, the estimated number of retiring missionaries by the year 2000 had risen to 25. It was clearly evident that steps had to be taken to meet the personnel needs that would accompany the coming of the new millennium. Beyond a continuing effort to encourage stateside churches to become "sending churches," the department increased its focus on the training of national leaders on the field. In addition, the board approved the "TEAM" program, a teen group (Teens Equipped and Active in Ministry), designed to give potential young missionaries exposure to and brief experience on the field as an incentive to life-time ministry. The first team consisted of ten young people who were to spend three weeks in Brazil during the summer of 1992.[54]

The years 1997 and 1998 gave clear warning of the need for denominational recruitment of new missionaries and for commitment to generous support of the entire Foreign Missions Program. During these two years, five veteran missionaries passed away and three couples officially retired. The deceased included Mrs. Mabel Willey who, with her husband, Thomas (Pop) Willey, had opened both Panama and Cuba to Free Will Baptist missions. All three of the retiring couples had served 35 years or more with Fred Hersey ending 43 years of ministry in Japan.[55]

But the reader would be mistaken in assuming that the Free Will Baptists had not been faithful in their support of the global ministry of the denomination. Gifts to foreign missions efforts in 1997 totaled $4,974,279. Depending on which statistics are used—the "actual" membership of the denomination in the official listing which is limited to those churches and associations that reported to the National Association or the more optimistic figures compiled by the "Double in a Decade Committee"—total gifts for the year represented an average donation of $24.10 or $19.04 per member in the denomination.[56] Those figures are more than impressive and they compare favorably with the per member giving figures of other denominations. The statistics, however, do not tell the full story. The minutes for the Foreign Missions Board from 1985 to 1987 are full of references to those who had partnered with the department in their fund raising efforts during the those years. The National Youth Conference, the Women Nationally Active for Christ, the Master's Men, local churches and associations all played an important role in financing the work of world evangelization. Between 1994 and 1996, the women's group gave a grand total of $588,000[57] in basic offerings plus providing household items for missionary families through their "Missionary

Provision Closet." In 1997, 67 local churches provided gifts of more than $10,000 with seven sur-passing $40,000 each.[58] During this same period the Master's Men gave aid in the form of the con-struction of church buildings through their "Helping Hands" organization while the youth of the denomination prepared "Love Boxes" containing school supplies and hygiene items for children in Bosnia. Department reports to the National did not neglect to express appreciation for the work of these partners in reaching the world for Christ.

Pulling It All Together—During the last days of the century, churches and mission works sponsored by and administrated by the Foreign Missions Department ". . . grew to 362 with an an-nual average attendance of 11,236. . . , led by 365 pastors and lay preachers."[59] In that same time frame, seventy-three new missionaries were appointed.

Upon the retirement of General Director Eugene Waddell in 1998, the Foreign Missions Board began a search for a new leader who would be given the task of ". . . staff reorganization in order to accomplish the (Board's) strategy of total mobilization of Free Will Baptists for world evange-lization."[60] In a brief summary of the department's ministry, staff member Jimmy Aldridge remem-bered:

> Since the founding of our modern Free Will Baptist movement in 1935, we have sent out 288 missionaries in both career, special and short-term assignments. One hun-dredfifteen of them are on the fields today. That means that 39.9% of all the mission-aries we have ever commissioned are in service now. And we need many more to take advantage of the open doors God is placing before us.[61]

The Free Will Baptists and Their Literature
Setting the Stage

Events between 1965 and 1985 gave some portent of the exciting progress Randall House Publications would enjoy in the last years of the millennium.

In 1967, Dr. Robert Picirilli's commentary, *Pauline Epistles*, launched the book publication ministry for the denomination. This type of service had been long in coming but it would prove to be one of the most rewarding and rapidly growing aspects of the Sunday School Department's larg-er ministry. By 1974, the number of books published by Randall House had grown to 150. In 1969, the first adult Sunday School curriculum was completed, giving the denomination a teaching course for every age level. The purchase of a new building and nine acres of property at 114 Bush Road in Nashville, gave evidence of the rapid growth the department had enjoyed. This new home also has proven to be a wise and rewarding investment. The property that was purchased for $178,000 in 1971, was reappraised at approximately $3,000,000 in 1997.[62]

Attempts at streamlining the entire ministry included the introduction of an umbrella organi-zation, Randall House Publications, and the merging of the Sunday School and the Church Training Service departments. The first occurred in 1971 and the latter in 1978. These two strategic steps would bring all the major book and curriculum publishing under one board.[63]

Final preparations for continuing ministry for the Department gave birth to a new youth division in 1983 that would quickly grow into the National Youth Conference. By the end of the century, annual youth conferences would draw more than 2,000 young Free Will Baptists to the National Association where they would stage their own competition, worship, and recreational activities. This new organization has proven to be a continuing source of excitement, encouragement, and pride for the denomination.

The Drama Unfolds

The latter years of the century would witness continued building on the strong foundations laid earlier. The most obvious progress is noted in the literature itself. Randall House now prides itself in its professionally produced, colorful literature that ranks with much larger publishing houses in other denominations. Recent purchases of powerful computers, up-to-date graphic arts equipment, quality color presses, and a growing presence on the Internet have prepared Randall House for the challenges of ministry in a new millennium.[64] Reaching beyond the boundaries of the denomination, Randall House now provides literature for more than 40 other religious bodies[65] and publishes materials in English, Spanish, Korean, and Russian.

Three notable publications during the last twenty-five years of the century illustrate the growing capabilities of the department in the arena of book-length publishing. In 1975, the publication of Leroy Forlines' *Systematics* marked the first offering of a theology text from a purely Free Will Baptist perspective.[66] In another first, William Davidson's *The Free Will Baptists in America, 1727-1984*, gave to the denomination an all-inclusive, documented record of its history. The present publication revisits the earlier history of the denomination as well as reviews the progress of the movement from the time of the first printing to the present moment. The most ambitious book project for the publishing house began in 1986 and is still in process. Since that time, several authors have contributed to a series of commentaries that have, for the first time, offered Free Will Baptist pastors biblical study aids that reflect their own convictions and understanding of the Scriptures. By 1997, six commentaries on New Testament books had been published and two more were nearing completion.

In 1996, Randall House entered the international market by introducing an entire curriculum in Spanish. This new work was the product of Casa Randall de Publicaciones, a new division of the ministry under the direction of the editor for Spanish literature, Mrs. Lucy Lima Hyman. Offices were first opened in McAllen, Texas, but now are located in Albany, Georgia.[67]

Stable and capable leadership played a large role in the success of this ministry. Only two men have served as director of the department since 1962. Before retiring in 1993, after 31 years of service, Dr. Roger C. Reeds watched the department grow from infancy to a significant level of maturity. During his tenure, he supervised the first book publications, the development of Sunday School and Church Training curricula for all age groups, and the move from the space limitations of the national offices building to new and separate housing that continues to serve Randall House Publications to the present time. On January 1, 1994, Dr. Reeds was succeeded by Dr. Alton Loveless, a twelve year veteran of the department's Board. Dr. Loveless also served as a denominational administrator in Ohio for some twenty years and came with experience as a regional marketing director for a large religious publishing house. His vision for the future of the department and its ministry to the denomination is seen in his optimistic twenty-five year plan designed to guide the work through the year 2025. Short term goals involve the updating of study curricula for all ages as well as a strategic battle for Sunday school growth. Long-term goals ". . . involve producing a full color curriculum and increasing our distribution into more Arminian believing churches."[68]

The Free Will Baptists and Education

Educationally, the Free Will Baptists entered the new millennium with four colleges, one seminary, and a brand new Educational Task force that had been approved by the National Association during its 1999 meeting in Atlanta, Georgia.

Free Will Baptist Bible College

Free Will Baptist Bible College in Nashville, Tennessee, the flagship of educational institutions for the denomination, had, like the parent National, watched as its leadership had grown older and moved toward retirement age. And it could be that the timing was providential. A changing world, a changing educational market, a changing denominational constituency, new challenges to graduates that intended to serve in cross-cultural fields, prospects for a new campus with new opportunities for expansion all suggested that if transition must come, then this was the opportune time. Leroy Forlines, the institution's uniquely talented theology professor, had already moved to partial retirement and Dr. Robert Picirilli, who had served so ably in New Testament and Greek studies and in varied administrative offices, had, during the institution's Board of Trustees' meeting in May 1998, submitted his resignation from his long term duties as Academic Dean.[69] Again, as was true for the parent body, the passing of the torch of ministry to a new and younger generation would surely have far reaching and significant impact upon both the institution and the denomination which it represents.

Looking Toward a New Campus—In the meantime, plans for sale of the West Nashville property and move to larger, more serviceable facilities were in process. In his report to the National Association for 1997, President Tom Malone reminded the delegates that plans were in place for "Step 2" which included the building of an access road to the campus as well as the establishment of a capital campaign designed to raise funds for construction of the new campus.[70] By the next year, two offices had been established to oversee the fund raising process. Roy Harris was assigned as Director of Advancement to handle preparations for the move to the new campus, and Tim Campbell was appointed as Director of Stewardship Development.[71]

Attaining Accreditation—A significant highlight of the latter years of the century was the achievement of accreditation by the Southern Association of Colleges and Schools (SACS) in December 1996.[72] Though the college already enjoyed accreditation by the Accrediting Association of Bible Colleges (AABC), this new honor would credential existing education and teaching programs offered by the school.

Encouraging Enrollment Trends—Rising applications for enrollment, increasing gifts for the general fund, and a record income for the Paul Ketteman Christmas Drive provided a new level of optimism for the 1997-98 school year. But declining enrollments for the following year and bleak prospects for the next, left many concerned, especially in the light of mushrooming educational costs and continuing plans for a new campus. Final matriculation numbers for the 1999-2000 year, however, would renew hopeful expectations for the future.

Looking Toward a New Name—In response to appeals from the denomination's Foreign Missions Department and in the interest of appeal to a larger student market, the school's Board of Trustees ended the millennium with a bold recommendation for a name change for the institution. The decision was affirmed by a unanimous vote of the Board in its December 1999, meeting in Nashville, Tennessee. In explaining the rationale for the change, Trustee Steve Ashby remarked:

> About five years ago, then Foreign Missions director, Eugene Waddell, began making the National Association aware that the name, 'Free Will Baptist Bible College,' was causing our graduates to be excluded from access as missionaries to many of the world's least evangelized countries. Upon learning this, the FWBBC Board and administration began to consider a name change.[73]

Evidently anticipating the fears that might surface as a result of the announcement, Ashby assured the denomination that "Free Will Baptist" would continue to be a part of the name and that "the modification is not a precursor to converting the school from a Bible college to a Christian liberal arts institution."[74]

School president, Tom Malone, echoed his board member's sentiment as he reminded his people that discussions regarding a name change had been in progress for a number of years. "I assure the denomination that modifying the college's name does not change who or what the college is. We are 100% Free Will Baptist and we are 100% a Bible college. It is not my intention that either be changed."[75]

The name change might not come easily. The tone of the news release hinted that some might view the move as a radical one and that opposition to the change probably should be expected. In the context of Free Will Baptist church polity, the final decision must rest with the ministers, deacons, and laypersons that serve as delegates to the National Association. Protocol dictated that the proposal be presented to the delegates when the National met in July 2000, and that the vote would take place the following year.

Southeastern Free Will Baptist College

Southeastern Free Will Baptist College in Wendell, North Carolina, faces the new millennium from the enviable position of a debt free program. A gift of 2.4 million dollars in April 1999, allowed the school to set aside one million dollars for student scholarships and to apply the remainder to institutional indebtedness.[76] A new building, completed in August 1998, provided a chapel, classrooms, offices, and a gymnasium for the school's 150 plus students. Billy Bevan, on staff since 1989, served as the institution's president on a part-time basis from 1990 to 1996 and has filled that office full-time since 1996. Though the school was chartered as a Christian liberal arts college in 1983, it has been moving more recently toward a Bible College program format.[77] During the Fall Semester, 1999, almost half of the students were enrolled in the Bible/Mission/Pastoral Theology study track while another 11% were training for vocational Christian ministry in music. Even so, the institution has continued to offer liberal arts programs in business and in elementary and secondary education.[78] An external study program serves approximately 130 students with 50 of those being resident students and the remainder non-resident.

A "Master Plan," now in progress, is being drafted to give direction for the institution's ministry in the first ten years of the new millennium.

Hillsdale Free Will Baptist College

Hillsdale Free Will Baptist College in Moore, Oklahoma, had ". . . operated for over twenty-five years as a part of the Oklahoma Higher Education system under the authority of the Oklahoma State Regents for Higher Education,"[79] when the state decided to end its accreditation activities. Forced to seek approval elsewhere for its three degree programs, Hillsdale applied for and received candidacy status with the Transnational Association of Christian Colleges and Schools (TRACS) in 1995. Full accreditation was awarded in 1999. The college also maintains membership status in the National Association of Independent Colleges and Universities.[80]

Traditional programs of study offered by the institution include an Associate of Arts Degree track with sixteen subject concentrations as well as Bachelor's degree tracks in Arts and Science. Bachelor of Arts students choose from concentrations in Christian Education, Interdisciplinary Studies (Honors Program), Missions, Music, Pastoral Theology, Theology, and Youth Ministry while those in the Bachelor of Science program focus on business studies. Both four-year degree tracks offer an additional course of study in an adult degree completion program, the Bachelor of Arts in Leadership and Ministry and the Bachelor of Science in Business and Leadership. The opportunities offered in adult education are part of a larger non-traditional package that also includes courses by correspondence and through on-line courses on the internet. A long and successful experience with external training through the medium of correspondence prepared the institution's leadership to recognize the advantages offered by new and advancing technology. The school has been proud of its role as a pacesetter in this type of non-traditional educational ministry.[81] Finally, Hillsdale students have access to dual enrollments and cooperating degree programs with twenty institutions of higher learning in the Oklahoma City area, allowing them an unusual number of options as they plan their educational agendas.

But the school also has made its mark outside the academic arena. Hillsdale teams won a total of six national sports titles during the years 1990-1999. Competing in the National Christian College Athletic Association, school teams have achieved top honors in Men's Baseball and Basketball and in Women's Basketball.[82]

Three presidents have given the institution guidance and direction in the last decades of the twentieth century: Edwin Wade (1982-1988); Jim Shepherd (1989-1997); and Carl Cheshier (1997-). The present chief officer also serves as Moderator for the National Association of Free Will Baptists.[83]

California Christian College

California Christian College enjoys the distinction of being the only Bible College in the state's San Joaquin valley, and when students arrive on campus for Fall enrollment in the year 2000, the college will mark its forty-fifth year of service to the Free Will Baptist denomination.[84]

The entire history of the denomination's most western educational institution has been one of struggle. A decision in 1969 to purchase property and bring all of the school's ministries together on one campus in Fresno, California, offered prospects of better days, but by 1985 the college again was in trouble. During that year, the school was closed as "...the governing board reevaluated the college's needs and mission."[85]

But California Free Will Baptists were not ready to give in to adversity. "Classes resumed in the Fall of 1986 under the presidency of Rev. James McAllister."[86]

In the last decade of the twentieth century, two major events took place that would aid significantly in the task of student recruitment. In 1991, a new gymnasium made it possible to add intercollegiate basketball and baseball to the school's program, and in 1998, the Transnational Association of Christian Colleges and Schools (TRACS) awarded full academic accreditation. The latter achievement now allows the institution to offer both Associate and Bachelor degrees in Christian Ministries.[87] These two important events took shape under the direction of President James McAllister and Dean Greg McAllister, but both of these leaders retired in May 1999. The fate of the college as it moved into the new millennium would rest in the hands of the newly elected president, Wendell Walley, and his Academic Dean, E. T. Hyatt.

In addition to its traditional offerings—Associate of Arts degrees in Bible and Christian Ministry and in Sacred Music, and a Bachelor of Arts degree in Bible and Theology—the school also has introduced an innovative educational program that has provided training for "...Slavic refugees that began coming into this country 8-10 years ago."[88] Courses in the "Russian Degree Completion Program", administered by Leonid Morgun, Director, and Parush Parushev, are all taught in the Slavic (Russian) language and are offered at both the main campus and at an extension site. Since most of the students must work full-time, most of the courses are offered as intensive modules on a Friday-Saturday schedule. Both of the professors in the program came to America from the former Soviet Union and both have degrees from their homeland and from institutions in the United States.[89]

This unique program has proven to be an unusually effective vehicle for Free Will Baptist missions among Slavic refugees in the state of California. "California State Home Missions and National Home Missions have started several Russian speaking churches in the last couple (of) years. Most, if not all of those pastors are students or former students of this program."[90] But as is often true, difficulty has been partner to innovation. At least partly because of the uniqueness of the degree program, the college has found it difficult to obtain state approval. A present "conditional" approval is in place through June 30, 2000. Recognizing that the status of the program is tenuous at best, institutional leaders are seeking permanent approval for the present curriculum and, as an alternative, approval for an English as Second Language (ESL) curriculum that would allow Russian speaking students to move into the regular degree programs offered in English.[91]

An attempt at an additional "International Student Program" designed to meet the needs of Korean students in California did not meet with success, but it, like the Russian program, underlined the determination of the school's leadership to go beyond the traditional as it sought to carry out the mandate placed upon it by the Free Will Baptists of California.

Seminario De La Cruz

Under the administrative direction of Coordinator James Munsey, Home Mission work in Mexico was both exciting and productive in the latter years of the twentieth century and within the context of the larger work, one of the most significant developments was that of The Seminary of the Cross. In 1995, in response to soil contamination of school property by a nearby oil storage facility and the difficulties that accompanied location in an isolated area of Mexico, the Home Missions Board voted to move the seminary campus from Altamira, near Tampico, to a more suitable twenty-five acre site in Reynosa.[92] The vision of the members of the Board anticipated an educational institution capable of ". . . training pastoral personnel to reach out to Spanish speaking people on both sides of the border."[93] The new campus—a central two story building housing the ladies' dorm, kitchen and dining area, classrooms and library, and a second building serving as a men's dorm—was designed to meet the needs of the school for the immediate future. Projected plans included housing for married students and additional classrooms. In 1997, the original vision was expanded to allow the introduction of cross-cultural courses for American students who desire to work with minority students in the United States. Curricular options offered by the seminary include a three year Bible degree program and a four year program that is considered to be equal to a Bachelor of Arts degree in the states.[94]

In 1999, Dr. Thomas Marberry, a veteran Free Will Baptist educator from Hillsdale Free Will Baptist College, left Oklahoma to assume leadership of the denomination's educational program in Mexico. The new President, with the help of Academic Dean, Marco Mendoza, and an additional staff of five, has the enviable, if formidable task of leading The Seminary of the Cross into the new millennium.

Higher Education Task Force

Prompted by resolutions from both Arkansas and Georgia Free Will Baptists, the delegates at the 1999 National Association meeting in Atlanta, Georgia, created a National Higher Education Task Force and assigned it the dual tasks of evaluation of the present status of education in the denomination and the drafting of a vision for its future. The two state resolutions called for the development of a ". . . long-range, comprehensive plan for Christian higher education among Free Will Baptists. . . ."[95]

The Task Force, chaired by Dr. Melvin Worthington, Executive Secretary of the denomination, and consisting of the Presidents and Deans of the various Free Will Baptist educational institutions along with five at-large members, met for its organizational meeting in Nashville, Tennessee, December 11-13, 1999.[96] Working from the knowledge that denominational institutions of higher learning were reaching less than ten percent of Free Will Baptist high school graduates, the Task Force identified six questions that would guide the discussions of this first meeting.

[1] Why aren't our colleges attracting 90%+ of Free Will Baptist college students?
[2] How can we cooperate more and foster more . . . sharing among our colleges?
[3] How can we cooperatively employ creative, entrepreneurial means to increase our

level of educational effectiveness (e.g., educational technology, adult education, cross-cultural education)?

[4] What steps must we take to establish a Free Will Baptist seminary to educate our pastors more effectively for ministry?

[5] How can we better fund our educational institutions?

[6] How do we view Christian education as a denomination?[97]

First steps for the Task Force included clarification of its mandate from the National Association as well as identification of the boundaries within which the group was expected to work. The "comprehensive plan" of the mandate was defined as ". . . An inclusive system of higher education designed to address the growing educational needs of our denomination," while the "long-range plan" was explained in terms of ". . . An incremental plan for the first decade of the twenty-first century."[98] The former task allowed discussion of present circumstances—factors hindering growth, perceptions of higher education in denominational institutions, institutional funding, and cooperation between schools, while the second task demanded that attention be given to finding solutions to perceived problems and to offering counsel for the future. With those guidelines established, the members of the Task Force affirmed the purpose for their continued ministry: "(1) to define the educational needs and problems with the current system and (2) to formulate a strategy with which to address them."[99]

One clear conviction of the group was that any successful educational program for the denomination would include a national Free Will Baptist Seminary, a graduate school designed to prepare pastors and educational leaders who are, in turn, capable of training others as leaders for the denomination's schools and churches in the new millennium.[100]

Conclusion

The employment of frequent summaries at the end of individual chapters and major segments of the study has made an extensive review unnecessary, but the investigation of the sources has led to a number of important conclusions that must be considered.

For more than a century and a half, the Free Will Baptists of America have claimed a definite historical connection with the General Baptist movement of North Carolina begun by Paul Palmer in 1727. Though a number of scholars agreed with the Free Will Baptist claim, conclusions were based on tradition and on a few inadequate sources. A thorough investigation of the sources has shown that the claim is not destitute of support.

Tradition argued that the General Baptist name disappeared before 1800, and that the new name was not used until the end of the first quarter of the nineteenth century. Contemporary sources, however, have revealed that the name was used before the death of William and Joseph Parker, that the old name still was used as a proper title as late as 1812, and that the new name was applied to the remnant of the old General Baptist movement.

S. J. Wheeler and R. K. Hearn revealed that the Parkers established preaching points in the tiny communities of Little Creek, Louson Swamp, Grimsley, Wheat Swamp, and Gum Swamp. It was more than coincidence that Free Will Baptist churches sprang up in the same communities early in the denomination's history. The same thing occurred in at least ten communities that the Parkers evangelized. R. K. Hearn was born in 1819 and knew individuals who had lived during the time of Parker's ministry. They remembered Gum Swamp as a Free Will Baptist church throughout their lifetime. Recently discovered land surveys have shown that a church of the General or Free Will persuasion has existed on the property of Joseph Parker at Scuffleton, North Carolina, since 1761.

As early as 1812, the Free Will Baptists indicated a relationship to the old General Baptists, and by 1829, they openly defended their claim. At that time, individuals were still living that were eyewitnesses to the events of the transition period. At least one leader has been traced through the transition period and established a solid link between the old movement and the new. In 1772, James Roach was living in Craven County, North Carolina, but shortly after that, he moved to Greene County and succeeded the Parkers in their work at Little Creek, Gum Swamp, Grimsley, Louson Swamp, and Wheat Swamp. He became a leading figure in the development of the new identity.

The documents of the period have confirmed the Free Will Baptist claim that they have had a continuing witness in America since 1727.

In addition, discovery of three English documents made it possible for the denomination to claim a much closer relationship to the General Baptists in that country than earlier had been supposed. A 1611 pamphlet published by Thomas Helwys, one of the first General Baptists in England, along with two additional documents published in 1659 and 1660, have revealed that the General Baptists also were known as Free Will Baptists from the very beginning. The 1659 document, *A Declaration of a Small Society of Baptized Believers, Undergoing the Name of Free-Willers About the City of London*, was composed by General Baptist authors, while the 1660 publication, *A Loving Salutation to All People Who Have Any Desires After the Living God: But Especially to the Free-Will-Anabaptists*, was written by an opponent of the young movement.

A look at early developments in North Carolina, Kentucky, Tennessee, and Arkansas confirmed presuppositions that were introduced in the Preface. The denomination cannot be traced to any one background or source. Though the General Baptists probably have played the larger role in the ancient history of the denomination, Free Will Baptists also find themselves indebted to the Congregationalists, the Separate Baptists of Virginia and Tennessee, the United Baptists, and the old Randallite Freewill Baptists of New England.

The nineteenth century was characterized by evolution. The denomination moved from a loosely organized, poorly educated, predominantly rural character to a carefully organized, theologically orthodox, conservative denomination. The potential for reaching across social class lines and barriers to meet the needs of men in every walk of life became reality.

By 1828, Yearly Meetings were organized in both the North and the South, and by the middle of the century, guidelines and parameters were established in theology and lifestyle that would continue to give direction to the denomination into the late twentieth century.

The evolution was more dramatic and more painful in the South. Poorly trained leaders and a firmly entrenched rural character made progress more difficult in those areas that were not touched by New England's influence.

When Jesse Heath wrote to the New England Freewill Baptists in 1829, he admitted that there were no scholars in the movement in North Carolina. Training, such as it was, was obtained in the local church.

It was this tradition that was to have the larger impact on the later denomination. Heath's statement could have been repeated again and again in the decades that followed. Except for brief attempts at the Bible Institute level, the denomination did not initiate a successful educational program until 1942 when the Free Will Baptist Bible College was established in Nashville, Tennessee. Even then it was many years before the denomination as a whole recognized the necessity of trained leadership and an educated clergy.

The denomination's second century of progress witnessed the development of a strict code of conduct and a conservative platform of theology. These early patterns have not changed in the movement's more than two hundred years of existence. The denomination still pleads for consecrated, separated membership, and has never feared the terms "conservative" and "fundamental."

At the end of the nineteenth century, the denomination could have been characterized as Arminian and conservative in theology, severe in lifestyle, revivalistic, mission-minded (though no actual program of cross-cultural ministry had yet been established), somewhat anti-intellectual, fearful of alliances with other like movements, and predominantly rural in orientation.

The denomination came by its tendency toward isolation quite honestly. For the last quarter of the century, the New England segment of the movement courted numerous denominations and finally, in 1911, united with the Northern Baptist Convention. Except for a few associations in Ohio, West Virginia, Kentucky, Nebraska, Texas, and Missouri, the largest single element of the denomination was lost to the movement's continuing development.

The death and subsequent loss of identity of the New England segment of the denomination in the merger of 1911 suggested that the movement could be ignored in any continuing history of the denomination, but the larger study has denied that approach. Remnants of the Randall faction in West Virginia, Ohio, Kentucky, Illinois, Nebraska, Texas, Missouri, and Oklahoma remained loyal to the Free Will Baptist cause. The entire Co-operative General Association as well as numerous other local associations can be traced directly to a New England heritage. Even those churches and associations that can be traced to other sources have been indebted to the Freewill Baptists of the North for their theology and statement of faith.

Though most of the denomination's theological questions were settled by 1900, a few individual doctrines continued to give cause for discussion. Most often, the discussions centered around the doctrines of perseverance and the washing of the saints' feet. Peace was to come only when East and West agreed to disagree within the bonds of fellowship.

The middle of the twentieth century found the Free Will Baptists somewhat less fearful of cooperative fellowship, and strong ties were developed with the American Bible Society and with the National Association of Evangelicals. But the memory of earlier cooperation-related disasters and the continuing influence of fundamentalism caused the old fears to recur. Ties were officially broken with the American Bible Society in 1967 and with NAE in 1972.

The formal break with these two bodies gave clear indication of the direction in which the denomination was moving. The term "evangelical" could no longer describe or define its character.

Always conservative and fundamental in its theology, it now had firmly adopted fundamentalism's additional characteristic of second and third degree separation. The old tendency toward isolation began to surface anew.

But isolationism is a difficult stance to support over a long period of time. Even second and third degree levels of separation allow some relationship with others who are firmly committed to the same types of separation. In addition, the experience of two decades has revealed that there are hidden drawbacks in a commitment to advanced separation. Most of the role models in the movement came from an independent background and some within the denomination began to fear that there are dangers here, though unlike those in evangelicalism, that are just as frightening and potentially devastating.

Finally, in the area of denominational relationships, the possibility of a new shift has been suggested. The clearest example of the shift is found in a new respect for the missions training offered by Columbia Biblical Seminary and School of Missions, the graduate division of Columbia International University in Columbia, South Carolina. Many, if not most, of the veteran missionaries on the field at this time were trained at the Seminary in the early mid-fifties, but in the decades between 1960 and 1980, the school was considered off limits for Free Will Baptist students. The difficulties between the school and the denomination were related to attitudes toward separation rather than to questions of theology. The school's firm commitment to the fundamentals of the faith were not questioned. In any case, by 1985, Free Will Baptist students were being encouraged by denominational leaders to choose the Seminary's curriculum as preparation for cross-cultural ministry.

It still is too early to predict what the new trend promises. It is very well possible that the suggestion of a shift in denominational policy is an overstatement and that the new relationship with Columbia is simply the product of a new respect for this one institution fostered by its recent graduates.

The last decade of the twentieth century was characterized by both hope and optimism. Annual minutes for the National Association revealed a continuing focus of growth plans and campaigns and a growing conviction that the denomination was to play a significant role in the task of world evangelization in the new millennium.

And there were moments of success. Admittedly, growth expectations fell short, but giving to denominational ministries saw phenomenal growth, larger and larger crowds traveled to annual National Association meetings, a new school was founded in Mexico, baptisms multiplied, and new churches were born.

As is often true, however, the real story is not found in numbers and statistics. The end of the century also was marked by new attitudes, a new spirit of cooperation between national departments, and the passing of the torch from one generation to the next.

A new openness toward change allowed the appointment of a National Higher Education Task Force designed to investigate possible avenues of cooperation between existing educational institutions as well as plans and programs that would maximize the denomination's resources, the introduction of a Spanish ministry through Randall House Publications and a Russian ministry through California Christian College, and the adoption of new methods of cross-cultural ministry that would open doors to countries that once had been firmly closed—Russia, China, Nepal.

At the same time, a new spirit of cooperation was manifested in report after report to the National Association as denominational departments recognized and admitted their mutual need for each other. Joint mission enterprises sponsored by Home and Foreign Mission offices, fund raising projects for missions by Women Nationally Active for Christ and the National Youth Conference, the new "Together Way" program for departmental funding, and a growing concern for cooperation among the denomination's educational institutions all spoke to a new conviction that ministry in the new millennium could only be effective as Free Will Baptists worked together in the task of reaching the world for Christ.

The more significant innovation, however, might have come by default. Time alone will tell what direction the denomination will take as those leaders who gave guidance to and shaped the movement in the latter part of the twentieth century pass the torch of leadership to the younger generation that will lead the Free Will Baptists as they march into the twenty-first century and the new millennium.

Jack Williams, editor of *Contact*, the official publication for the denomination, has expressed well the confidence with which Free Will Baptists face the future.

> The twenty-first century holds the brightest promise for Free Will Baptists since the days of Paul Palmer and Benjamin Randall. A new college campus will soon rise off I-24 just a few miles down the road. New mission fields are opening in Korea, China, Russia and all over Asia. Doors closed to the gospel during the twentieth century are swinging open.
>
> New leadership is taking hold at local, state and national levels. . . . Who are these new leaders? God bless them—they're our children!
>
> They sat in our Sunday schools, watched us conduct the Lord's business in our meetings and graduated from our colleges. They set their sails by the sure compass of the Almighty.
>
> Look around. They're everywhere. They're in their 20s and 30s, some in their 40s and 50s. They're ready to take the reins of responsibility. They believe they can pay the bills and build a better future. Their motive is holy, their faith strong, their vision contagious.
>
> . . . I can hardly wait to see what God does through Free Will Baptists as new hands touch the helm in the twenty-first century.[101]

One matter yet demands attention. In many ways—basic theology, commitment to separation, mission concern—the denomination has remained the same. But in others, it has seen significant change. Of those changes, the most evident and noteworthy is the evolution from a purely rural character to a more flexible nature that has allowed ministry to a broader spectrum of the society. Beginning with innovative mission strategies, specifically in South America, the denomination found itself capable of reaching the cities and of ministering vertically across social barriers. Again, it is too early to determine the degree of impact this change will have on the denomination, but it does, without question, offer the most promising potential for growth that the denomination has known in its long history.

Notes for Chapter 15

[1]*The 1986 Free Will Baptist Yearbook* (Nashville: The Executive Office, National Association of Free Will Baptists, Inc., 1986), 22.

[2]*Minutes of the Second Session of the National Association of the Original Free Will Baptists of the United States* (Ayden, N.C.: Free Will Baptist Press, 1938), 6.

[3]Ibid.

[4]*Yearbook, 1986*, 140.

[5]See Chapter 14 for a complete summary.

[6]*The 1984 Free Will Baptist Yearbook* (Nashville: The Executive Office, National Association of Free Will Baptists, Inc., 1984), 109.

[7]*Yearbook, 1984*, 110, 111.

[8]*The 1992 Free Will Baptist Yearbook* (Nashville: The Executive Office, National Association of Free Will Baptists, 1992), p. A-204, 205.

[9]Bill Evans, Trymon Messer, and Alton Loveless. "Report of the New Millennium Committee." (Nashville: Unpublished report, 1997), p. 6; Alton Loveless. E-mail Letter to William F. Davidson, December 29, 1999.

[10]*The 1988 Free Will Baptist Handbook* (Nashville: The Executive Office, National Association of Free Will Baptists, 1988), 133.

[11]*The 1989 Free Will Baptist Handbook* (Nashville: The Executive Office, National Association of Free Will Baptists, 1989), 137.

[12]Ibid., 23, 138.

[13]*The 1993 Free Will Baptist Handbook* (Nashville: The Executive Office, National Association of Free Will Baptists, 1993), A-207.

[14]Ibid, A-208-212.

[15]Ibid, A-198.

[16]*The 1997 Free Will Baptist Yearbook* (Nashville: The Executive Office, National Association of Free Will Baptists, 1997), A-24, 25.

[17]*The 1998 Free Will Baptist Yearbook* (Nashville: The Executive Office, National Association of Free Will Baptists, 1998), A-24.

[18]*Yearbook, 1989*, 134.

[19]*Yearbook, 1997*, A-274.

[20]*Yearbook, 1993*, A-26, 201.

[21]*The 1994 Free Will Baptist Yearbook* (Nashville: The Executive Office, National Association of Free Will Baptists, 1994), A-234, 235.

[22]*The 1990 Free Will Baptist Yearbook* (Nashville: The Executive Office, National Association of Free Will Baptists, 1990), 142,143.

[23]*Yearbook, 1992*, A-206.

[24]*Millenium Report*, 37.

[25]*The 1991 Free Will Baptist Yearbook.* (Nashville: The Executive Office, National Association of Free Will Baptists, 1991), p. 155; *Yearbook, 1992,* A-147.

[26]*Yearbook, 1992,* A-147.

[27]*The 1999 Free Will Baptist Yearbook* (Nashville: The Executive Office, National Association of Free Will Baptists, 1999), A-34.

[28]Ibid., pp. A-34, 247.

[29]Ibid; personal phone call with Melvin Worthington, Executive Secretary of the National Association of Free Will Baptists, January 5, 2000.

[30]*Millennium Report,* 43.

[31]Ibid.

[32]E-mail from Alton Loveless, Committee member, New Millennium Report Committee, December 29, 1999.

[33]*Yearbook, 1984,* 89, 90.

[34]*The 1988 Free Will Baptist Yearbook* (Nashville: The Executive Office, National Association of Frcc Will Baptists, 1988), 87.

[35]*Yearbook, 1990,* 92; *Yearbook, 1991,* 54.

[36]*Yearbook, 1992,* A-115.

[37]E-mail from Trymon Messer to William Davidson, January 4, 2000. Reference to the establishment of this new office did not appear in the Minutes of the National Association, but 1996 was the first year that the Home Missions Department reported a salary for that level of administration.

[38]*Yearbook, 1999,* A-119; E-mail from Trymon Messer, January 4, 2000.

[39]Trymon Messer, "Advancing into the Millennium" (unpublished proposal submitted to the Free Will Baptist Leadership Conference, Nashville, Tennessee, December 1999), 1,2.

[40]Ibid.

[41]E-mail from Trymon Messer, January 4, 2000.

[42]*Yearbook, 1999,* A-121.

[43]*Yearbook, 1986,* 44.

[44]Ibid., 46.

[45]Ibid.

[46]*The 1987 Free Will Baptist Yearbook* (Nashville: The Executive Office, National Association of Free Will Baptists, 1987), 80.

[47]*Yearbook, 1984,* 51.

[48]*Yearbook, 1989,* 77.

[49]*Yearbook, 1991,* 90-94.

[50]Ibid, 94.

[51]Jimmy Aldridge, "E-Mail Letter to William F. Davidson," January 20, 2000.

[52]*The 1996 Free Will Baptist Yearbook* (Nashville: The Executive Office, National Association of Free Will Baptists, 1996), pp. A-99, 100.

[53]*Yearbook, 1997,* A-185, 186.

[54]*Yearbook, 1993,* A-126, 127

[55]*Yearbook, 1999,* A-176, 177.

[56]*Yearbook, 1999,* A-34; A-247.

[57]*Yearbook, 1996,* A-97; *Yearbook, 1997,* A-191; *Yearbook, 1998,* A-98.

[58]*Yearbook, 1999,* A-171-174.

[59]Aldridge, "Letter."

[60]Ibid.

[61]Ibid.

[62]"Report of the Millennium Committee," 14.

[63]Ibid.

[64]Ibid, 15. Dr. Alton Loveless, General Director for Randall House Publications, has given primary attention to the upgrading of publications and equipment for the Department.

[65]Ibid.

[66]*Quest for Truth,* an extensive revision and expansion of *Biblical Systematics,* is available from Randall House Publications.

[67]"Report of the Millennium Committee," 14, 15.

[68]Ibid., 15-17.

[69]*Yearbook, 1999,* A-196.

[70]*Yearbook, 1998,* A-66.

[71]*Yearbook, 1999,* A-196.

[72]*Yearbook, 1998,* A-66.

[73]"Bible College Trustees Propose to Modify Name," Free Will Baptist Bible College News Release, January 7, 2000.

[74]Ibid.

[75]Ibid.

[76]Personal interview with Rev. Billy Bevan, Wendell, North Carolina, January 13, 2000.

[77]"Spring 2000 Program of Studies," student enrollment list by program, Southeastern Free Will Baptist College, Spring Semester, 2000.

[78]Ibid.; *Southeastern Free Will Baptist College Catalog, 1999-2001,* Vol. 12 (Wendell, N. C.: Center Cross Publishing, 1999), 24.

[79]Tim Eaton, "Update of History, Hillsdale Free Will Baptist College, 1985-1999." E-mail memo to William F. Davidson, January 20, 2000.

[80]Ibid.

[81]Ibid.

[82]Ibid.

[83]Ibid.

[84]Wendell Walley, E-mail letter to William F. Davidson, January 23, 2000. Walley is President of California Christian College.

[85]*California Christian College Catalog, 1999-2000,* 2. Quoted in e-mail to William F. Davidson from Dr. E. T. Hyatt, Acting Academic Dean, California Christian College, January 22, 2000.

[86]Ibid.

[87]Ibid.

[88]Walley, "Letter."

[89]Ibid.

[90]Ibid.

[91]Ibid.

[92]"Free Will Baptist Work in Mexico, Seminary of the Cross." Internet Web Page; http://www. Mexicofwb.org/ school/school.shtml, January 24, 2000.

[93]Ibid.

[94]Ibid.

[95]"Resolutions to the National Association of Free Will Baptists: Georgia and Arkansas." Presented to the General Board by the Arkansas and Georgia delegations. Approved and presented to the National Association, as Item #3 of the General Board Report, July 21, 1999 (unpublished copy of the 1999 National Association Minutes faxed to William F. Davidson from the Office of the Executive Secretary, January 20, 2000), 3.

[96]Task Force members included five college presidents: Tom Malone, Carl Cheshier, Wendell Walley, Billy Bevan, and Thomas Marberrry; five Academic Deans: Milton Fields, Tim Eaton, E. T. Hyatt, A. B. Brown, and Marco Antonio Mendoza Gonzales; and five at large members: William Davidson, Douglas Simpson, Daniel Parker, Matthew Pinson, and Randy Sawyer ("Minutes of the First Meeting of the Free Will Baptist Educational Task Force" unpub-

lished minutes, Nashville, Tennessee, December 11-13, 1999, p. 1; addendum).

97Ibid., 4.

98Ibid., 3.

99Ibid.

100Ibid., 2.

101Jack Williams, "What a Century!" In "Briefcase," *Contact,* February 2000.

Bibliography

A. Primary
Published

A Brief Confession of Faith. Quoted in William L. Lumpkin, *Baptist Confessions of Faith.* Philadelphia: The Judson Press, 1959.

Allen, I. M. *The Triennial Baptist Register.* Philadelphia: Baptist General Tract Society, No. 2, 1836.

An Abstract of the Former Articles of Faith Confessed by the Original Baptist Church Holding the Doctrine of General Provision With a Proper Code of Discipline. 2nd ed. Newbern, N.C.: Printed by Salmon Hall, 1814.

Asplund, John. *The Annual Register of the Baptist Denomination in North America to the First of November, 1790.*

_____. *The Universal Register of the Baptist Denomination in North America, For the Years 1790, 1791, 1792, 1793, and Part of 1794.* Boston: Printed by John W. Folsom, for the Author, 1794.

A Treatise of the Faith of the Freewill Baptists. Dover, N.H.: Published by David Marks for the Freewill Baptist Connection, 1834.

A Treatise of the Faith of the Free-Will Baptists. Dover, N.H.: Published by the Free-Will Baptist Printing Establishment, 1850.

A Treatise of the Faith of the Free-Will Baptists, 6th ed. Dover, N.H.: Published by the Free-Will Baptist Printing Establishment, 1854.

A Treatise of the Faith and Government For the Original Free Will Baptists of North Carolina, 1949.

A Treatise of the Faith and Practices of the Freewill Baptists. Dover, N.H.: Published by the Freewill Baptist Historical Society, 1869.

A Treatise of the Faith and Practice of the Freewill Baptists. Dover, N.H.: Published by the Freewill Baptist Printing Establishment, 1871.

A Treatise of the Faith and Practices of the Freewill Baptists. Dover, N.H.: Published by the Freewill Baptist Printing Establishment, 1874.

A Treatise of the Faith and Practice of the Freewill Baptists. Boston: The F. B. Printing Establishment, 1887.

A Treatise of the Faith and Practice of the Freewill Baptists, Adopted by the Cooperative General Association, December 29, 1917. Tecumseh, OK.: The New Morning Star Printing Co., 1917.

A Treatise of the Faith and Practices of the Original Free Will Baptists. 1973 Revision. Nashville: Published by the Executive Office of the National Association of Free Will Baptists, 1974.

A Treatise of the Faith and Practice of the Freewill Baptists, Written under the Direction of the General Conference. Portsmouth, Ohio: Compton Engraving & Printing Company, 1949.

Barrows, C. Edwin, ed. *The Diary of John Comer.* Philadelphia: American Baptist Publication Society, 1892.

Battle, Kemp Plummer, ed. "Minutes of the Kehukee Association (Baptist), 1772-1777." *James Sprunt Historical Monograph* (No. 5, 1904).

Benedict, David. *A General History of the Baptist Denomination in America and Other Parts of the World.* 2 vols. Boston: Lincoln & Edmands, 1813.

"Bible College Trustees Propose to Modify Name." Free Will Baptist Bible College News Release. January 7, 2000.

Biographical Memoirs of the Late John Gano. New York: Printed by the Southwick and Hardcastle for John Tiebout, 1806.

Boyd, William K. *Some Eighteenth Century Tracts Concerning North Carolina.* Raleigh: Edwards & Broughton Company, 1927.

Bricknell, John. *The Natural History of North Carolina (1703)*.

Broughton, Carrie L. *Marriage and Death Notices in the Raleigh Register and North Carolina State Gazette, 1826-1845*. Baltimore: Genealogical Publishing Co., 1968.

Burkitt, Lemuel and Read, Jesse. *A Concise History of the Kehukee Baptist Association From Its Original Rise to the Present Time*. Halifax, N.C.: Printed by A. Hodge, 1803.

Burrows, J. Lansing, ed. *American Baptist Register (1851)*. Philadelphia: American Baptist Publication Society, 1853.

Butler, John J. *Thoughts on the Benevolent Enterprises, Embracing the Subjects of Missions, Sabbath Schools, Temperance, Abolition of Slavery, and Peace*. Dover, N.H.: Published by the Trustees of the Freewill Baptist Connection, 1840.

Buzzell, John. *Life of Elder Benjamin Randall*. Limerick, Me.: Hobbs, Woodman & Co., 1827.

_____. "An Extract of the Experience of Elder Benjamin Randal. (Taken From a Manuscript) Written by Himself, Corrected by the Editor." *A Religious Magazine*, VI (February 1822), 206-216.

_____. "A Short History of the Church of Christ, Gathered at New Durham, N.H., 1780." *A Religious Magazine*, I (January, 1811–July 1812).

Byrd, William. *A Journey to the Land of Eden*. [New York] Macy-Massius, The Vanguard Press, 1928.

Charter for Free Will Baptist University of Nashville, Tennessee. (Copy held by the Free Will Baptist Historical Collection, Free Will Baptist Bible College, Nashville, Tennessee, Loose Collections, "C-18").

"Circular Letter," *Minutes of the Nolynn Association of Separate Baptists, 1820*.

Clark, Elmer T. *The Journal and Letters of Francis Asbury*. Vol. 1, The Journal, 1771 to 1783. London: Epworth Press, 1859.

Cooper, Thomas, ed. *Statutes at Large of South Carolina, 1716-1752*. Vol 3. Columbia, S.C.: Printed by A. S. Johnson, 1838.

Crosby, Tho. *The History of the English Baptists, From the Reformation to the Beginning of the Reign of King George I*. 4 vols. London: Printed for the Author, 1739.

Cumming, William P. *North Carolina in Maps*. Raleigh: State Department of Archives and History, 1966.

_____. *The South East in Early Maps*. Chapel Hill: The University of North Carolina Press, 1962.

Davis, J. *History of the Welsh Baptists from the Year Sixty-Three to the Year One Thousand Seven Hundred and Seventy*. Pittsburgh: Published by D. M. Hogan, 1835.

Deeds, Charleston, SC, 1747-48, "Joshua Toomer." Book DD.

Deed Index, Davidson County, Tennessee, 1784-1871. Held by Tennessee Historical Commission, Nashville, Tennessee.

Deed Records for Muscogee County, Georgia. "Indenture between Champaign Travis Turner and James Edward Broadnax. (Copy held by Mrs. Geraldine Waid, Archivist, Georgia Free Will Baptist Historical Society).

"Description of the Province of Carolina, 1666." Quoted in Hugh Lefler, *North Carolina History as Told by Contemporaries*. 3rd ed., rev. Chapel Hill: The University of North Carolina, 1956.

Dunn, Ransom. "Letter to the General Conference." *Minutes of the General Conference, 1889*.

"Letter to the General Conference." *Minutes of the Freewill Baptist General Conference, 1899*.

Early Tennessee Tax Lists, Davidson County (Before 1805). Microfilm copies of the Original. Film held by the Tennessee State Historical Commission, Nashville, Tennessee.

Edwards, Morgan. "Materials Toward a History of the Baptists in the Provinces of Maryland, Virginia, North Carolina, South Carolina, Georgia." MS, 1772.

"Materials Toward a History of the Baptists in Delaware State." *Pennsylvania Magazine of History and Biography* IX (1885), 45-61; 197-213.

"Tour of Rev. Morgan Edwards of Pennsylvania, To the American Baptists in North Carolina in 1772-73."

Fifth Annual Report of the Freewill Baptist Anti-Slavery Society. Dover, N.H.: Wm. Burr, Printer, 1851.

Fifth Census of the United States, 1830: Population Schedules, South Carolina. Vol. 4, File Microcopies of Records in the National Archives. No. 39, Roll 172.

Free Will Baptist Home Missions Survey. Nashville: Board of Home Missions-Church Extension, National Association of Free Will Baptists [1979].

Free Will Baptist Register and Year Book, 1911. Hillsdale, Mich.: General Conference Free Baptists, 1911.

Free Will Baptist Yearbook, 1983. Nashville: Published by the Executive Office of the National Association of Free Will Baptists, 1983.

Foote, William Henry. *Sketches of North Carolina.* New York: Robert Carter, 1846.

_____. *Sketches of Virginia.* Richmond: John Knox Press, 1850.

Gillette, A. D., ed. *Minutes of the Philadelphia Baptist Association, From A.D. 1707, to A.D. 1807.* Philadelphia: American Baptist Publication Society, 1851.

Grimes, J. Bryan, ed. *Abstracts of North Carolina Wills Compiled from Original and Recorded Wills in the Office of the Secretary of State.* Raleigh: E. M. Uzzell and Company, 1910.

Hammerstley, John. "Personal letter to Nicholas Eyres, dated 1742." Quoted in Robert B. Semple, *A History of the Rise and Progress of the Baptists in Virginia.* Richmond: John Lynch, Printer, 1810.

Handwritten Notes of the Joint Committee of Education Meeting Held during the First session of the National Association in 1935. Original Held by the Free Will Baptist Historical Collection, Free Will Baptist Bible College, Nashville, Tennessee.

Hathaway, J. R. B. *The North Carolina Genealogical Register.* 3 vols (January, 1900–July 1903.)

Hearn Family Bible in the possession of Mrs. J. E. W. Sugg, II.

Hearn, R. K. "Origin of the Free Will Baptist Church in North Carolina." Quoted in D. B. Montgomery, *General Baptist History.* Evansville: Courier Company, 1882.

Heath, Jesse. Personal letter to the Senior Editor of *The Morning Star,* May 29, 1827. *The Morning Star,* June 28, 1827.

Letter to *The Morning Star,* April 25, 1828. *The Morning Star,* May 28,1828.

Letter to Elder John Buzzell, November 18, 1830. Quoted in *The Morning Star,* December 22, 1830.

Heaton, Robert. "Unpublished Ministerial Record." Original in the Free Will Baptist Historical Collection, Free Will Baptist Bible College, Nashville, Tennessee.

Hillsdale Free Will Baptist College Catalog, 1982-1984.

"History of the College." *California Christian College Catalog, 1972-1974.*

Hotten, John Camden. *The Original Lists of Persons of Quality; Emigrants; Religious Exiles; Political Rebels; Serving Men Sold for a Term of Years; Apprentices, Children Stolen; Maidens Pressed; and Others Who Went From Great Britain to the American Plantations, 1600-1700.* New York: G. A. Baker & Co., Inc., 1931.

Hutchins, Elias. Letter to *The Morning Star,* October 26, 1829. *The Morning Star,* November 11, 1829.

_____. Letter to *The Morning Star,* November 25, 1829. *The Morning Star,* December 23, 1829.

_____. Letter to *The Freewill Baptist Magazine* (January 1830). Quoted in *The Freewill Baptist Magazine,* III (March 1830).

Letter, dated June 20, 1830. *The Morning Star,* July 18, 1830.

Letter to the Editors of *The Morning Star,* January 22, 1833, in *The Morning Star,* February 14, 1833.

Letter to *The Morning Star,* March 25,1833. *The Morning Star,* April 8,1833. Personal letter to the North Carolina Free Will Baptist Conference. Quoted in Thad Harrison and J. M. Barfield, *History of the Free Will Baptists of North Carolina.* 2 vols. Ayden, N.C.: The Free Will Baptist Press [1897].

Hyde County, North Carolina. Will Book I.

Knight, Richard D. *History of the General or Six Principle Baptists in Europe and America.* Providence, R.I.: Smith and Parmenter, Printers, 1827.

Latham, Thomas J. Letter to *The Morning Star,* December 23, 1830. *The Morning Star,* January 19, 1831.

Lawson, John. *Lawson's History of North Carolina.* Richmond: Garrett and Massie, Publishers, 1937 [1714].

Lefler, Hugh Talmage. *North Carolina History as Told by Contemporaries.* 3rd ed., rev., Chapel Hill: The University of North Carolina, 1956.

Lumpkin, William L. *Baptist Confessions of Faith.* Philadelphia: The Judson Press, 1959.

MacRae, John and Brazier, H. B. *A New Map of the State of North Carolina, Constructed from Actual Surveys, Authentic Documents and Private Contributions*. Published under the Patronage of the Legislature, by John MacRae, 1833.

Hymns for Christian Melody. Boston: Published by David Marks for the Free-will Baptist Connection, 1832.

Marion County, South Carolina, Deed Book I, p. 109-110, March 5, 1816, p. 122. Probated June 1, 1816 before Turner Bryan, JP. (no recording date).

Marks, David. *Life of David Marks*. Limerick, Me.: Printed at the Office of The Morning Star, 1831.

Marks, David, Compiler. *The Conference Meeting Hymn Book for the Use of All Who Love Our Lord and Saviour Jesus Christ*. Rochester: Printed for Friend Marks, by E. Peck & Co., 1828.

Marks, Marilla. *Memoirs of the Life of David Marks*. Dover, N.H.: Published by the Free-Will Baptist Printing Establishment, 1846.

Mercer, Jesse. *Ten Letters Addressed to the Rev. Cyrus White, In Reference to His Scriptural View of the Atonement*. Washington, Ga.: Printed at the News Office, 1830.

Minutes

ALABAMA

Minutes, Mt. Moriah Free Will Baptist Church, McShan, Alabama, 1850-1880. (Original handwritten document, held by Mr. M. P. Gore, McShan, Alabama.)

Minutes of the One Hundred and Thirtieth Annual Session of the Mount Moriah Association of Free Will Baptists, 1980.

Minutes of the Seventeenth Annual Session of the Mount Moriah Free-Will Baptist Association, 1874. Carrollton, Ala.: Printed at the West Alabamian Office, 1874.

Minutes of the Thirty-First Annual Session of the Mount Moriah Free-Will Baptist Association, 1881. LaGrange, N.C.: Printed at the Baptist Review Job Office, 1881.

Minutes of the Tuscaloosa Baptist Association, 1841-1900. Microfilm held by the Library, Samford University, Birmingham, Alabama.

Minutes of the Union Baptist (Later Pickens County) Association, 1836-1967.

ARKANSAS

Minutes of the Annual Convention of the Free Will Baptists of Arkansas. (Sixth, Twenty-First, Twenty-Eighth, Twenty-Ninth, Thirty-First, and Thirty-Sixth Annual Sessions—1903, 1918, 1925, 1926, 1928, 1933.)

Minutes of the Free Will Baptist Association of Carroll County, 1896. Jasper, Ark.: Herald Print, 1896.

Minutes of the Fourth Annual Session of the State Association of Free Will Baptists (Arkansas), 1901. Campbell, Ill.: Illinois Free Baptist Print, 1901.

CO-OPERATIVE ASSOCIATION

Minutes of the First Adjourned Session of the Co-operative General Association of Freewill Baptists, 1917. Tecumseh, Okla.: The New Morning Star Publishing House, 1918.

Minutes of the First Triennial Session of the Co-operative General Association of Freewill Baptists, 1916. Weatherford, Tex.: The New Morning Star, 1917.

Minutes of the Second Adjourned Meeting of the First Triennial Session of the Co-operative General Association of Freewill Baptists, 1918. Tecumseh, Okla.: The New Morning Star Publishing House, 1919.

Minutes of the Second Regular Session of the Western General Association of Free Will Baptists. Purdy, Mo.: Free Will Baptist Gem Print, 1937.

Minutes of the Seventh Triennial Session of the General Co-operative Association of the Free Will Baptists, 1934. Wanette, Ok.: Wanette Printing Co., 1934.

GENERAL CONFERENCE—NEW ENGLAND

Minutes of the Freewill Baptist General Conference, 1869, 1892. Original Minutes held by the American Baptist Historical Society, Rochester, N.Y.

Minutes of the General Conference of the Freewill Baptist Connection. Vol. 2. Boston: F. B. Printing Establishment, 1887.

Minutes of the General Conference of the Freewill Baptist Connection (1827-1859). Dover, N.H.: Published by the Freewill Baptist Printing Establishment, 1859.

Minutes of the Thirty-Fifth General Conference of Free Baptists. Auburn, Me.: Merrill & Webber Company, Printers and Bookbinders, 1913.

Minutes of the Thirty-Sixth General Conference of Free Baptists, 1917. Auburn, Me.: Merrill & Webber Company, 1917.

Minutes of the Twenty-Fifth General Conference of the Freewill Baptist Connection, 1883. Dover, N.H.: The Morning Star Job Printing House, 1883.

Minutes of the Twenty-Fourth General Conference of the Freewill Baptist Connection, 1880. Dover, N.H.: The Morning Star Job Printing House, 1880.

GEORGIA

Minutes of the Chattahoochee United Baptist Association, 1850.

Minutes of the Fifty-Third Annual Session of the Chattahoochee United Freewill Baptist Association, 1888. Montezuma, Ga.: The Record Book and Job Print, 1888.

Minutes of the Richland Creek and Tired Creek Baptist Church, 1830, 1835.

Minutes of the Fiftieth Annual Session of the Chattahoochee United Free-Will Baptist Association. October 3rd and 4th, 1885. Savannah, Ga.: Morning News Team Printing House, 1885.

Minutes of the First, Recess, and Second Sessions of the Georgia State Association of the Original Free Will Baptist Church of Jesus Christ. Alabaha Church, Blackshear, Ga., August 31, 1937; Ebenezer Church, November 2-3, 1937; Midway Church, Moultrie, Ga., November 9-10, 1938.

Minutes of the Fourth Annual Session of the Georgia State Association of the Original Free Will Baptist Church of Jesus Christ. Greenwood Church, Mitchell County, Camilla, Ga., November 12-14, 1940.

MISCELLANEOUS

Minutes of the Bethlehem Free Will Baptist Church (Tennessee). Original handwritten Minutes, 1847-1874.

Minutes of the Central Illinois Yearly Meeting of Free Baptist, 1901, 1902, 1903, 1909, 1915.

Minutes of the Concord Association, 1812-1846. Copy in the Free Will Baptist Historical Collection, Free Will Baptist Bible College, Nashville, Tennessee.

Minutes of the Cumberland Association of Separate Baptists, 1843.

Minutes of the First Annual Session of the Mississippi State Association of Free Will Baptists, October 1942.

Minutes of the First Session, Mississippi State Association of Free Will Baptists, April 1942.

Minutes of the Johnson County (Ky.) Quarterly Meeting, MS, 1925-1982.

Minutes of the Missouri State Association of Free Will Baptists, 1914. Typewritten copy held by the Free Will Baptist Historical Collection, Free Will Baptist Bible College, Nashville, Tennessee.

Minutes of the Nebraska Yearly Meeting of Free Will Baptists, 1883-1922. Original Minutes held by the Free Will Baptist Historical Collection, Free Will Baptist Bible College, Nashville, Tennessee.

Minutes of the Nebraska Yearly Meeting of Free Baptists, 1908. Handwritten Minutes held by the Free Will

Baptist Historical Collection, Free Will Baptist Bible College, Nashville, Tennessee.

Minutes of the Nolynn Association of Separate Baptists (Ky.), 1819-1883. Copy held by the Free Will Baptist Historical Collection, Free Will Baptist Bible College, Nashville, Tennessee.

Minutes of the Northeast Yearly Association of Free Will Baptists (Missouri), 1910-1934. Original Minutes held by the Free Will Baptist Historical Collection, Free Will Baptist Bible College, Nashville, Tennessee.

Minutes (Original) and Membership of the Old Kyger Free-Will Baptist Church, 1895-1940. (Ohio)

Minutes (Original) of the Meigs County Quarterly Meeting, Meigs County, Ohio, 1901-1929.

Minutes of the Perquimans Monthly Meeting, 1680-1762. Vol. I. Indexed by Dorothy Lloyd, Gilbert and Mildred Marlette. Microfilmed from the Original by Charles E. Rush, Librarian for the University of North Carolina Library, 1942. Copy held by the Friends Historical Collections, Guilford College, Greensboro, North Carolina.

Minutes of the Porter Free Will Baptist Church, Scioto County, Ohio, 1896-1931. Original Record Book held by the Free Will Baptist Historical Collection, Free Will Baptist Bible College, Nashville, Tennessee.

Minutes of the Second Annual Session of the Missouri State Association, 1915.

Minutes of the Sixth Annual Session of the Missouri State Conference of Free-Will Baptists, 1896. Minneapolis: Western Free Baptist Publishing Society, 1896.

Minutes of the Sixty-Fifth Annual Session of the Central Illinois Yearly Meeting of Free Will Baptists, 1915.

Minutes of the Sixty-Fourth Annual Session of the Cumberland Association of Freewill Christian Baptist, 1907. Clarksville, Tenn.: W. P. Titus, Printer and Binder, 1907.

Minutes of the South Carolina General Conference of Free Will Baptists, 1858 to 1929. Original Minutes held by the Free Will Baptist Historical Collection, Free Will Baptist Bible College, Nashville, Tennessee.

Minutes of the South District Association of Baptists (Ky.), 1807-1857. Microfilm of Printed Copies. Film held by Southern Baptist Historical Commission, Nashville, Tennessee.

Minutes of the South Kentucky Association of Separate Baptists, 1785-1872. Microfilm copy of Manuscript. Film held by Southern Baptist Historical Commission, Nashville, Tennessee.

Minutes of the Texas State Association of Free Will Baptists, 1915-1951. Original Minutes held by the Free Will Baptist Historical Collection, Free Will Baptist Bible College, Nashville, Tennessee.

Minutes of the Third Annual Session of the First Free Will Baptist Association of California, 1946.

Minutes of the Thirteenth Annual Session of the Free Will Baptists—South West Convention. Normangee, Texas: Star Print, 1913.

Minutes of the Thirtieth Annual Session of Freewill Baptists (Mt. Zion Association—Arkansas). Conway, Ark.: Arkansas Freewill Baptist Publishing House, 1898.

Minutes of the Tom's Creek Free Will Baptist Church, 1893-1982. Original Minutes held by the Tom's Creek Church, Paintsville, Kentucky.

Minutes of the Tow River Association of Free Will Baptists, 1851-1886. Original Minutes held by the Free Will Baptist Historical Collection, Free Will Baptist Bible College, Nashville, Tennessee.

Minutes of the Tri-State Association of Free Will Baptists—West Virginia, Kentucky, and Ohio, 1931.

Minutes of the Wayne County (Illinois) Quarterly Meeting of Free Will Baptists, 1882 to 1920. Original Minutes held by the Free Will Baptist Historical Collection, Free Will Baptist Bible College, Nashville, Tennessee.

Moore, Elder B. "Preface." *Records of Bethel Church [SC], July 14, 1901.*

"New Durham Church Records." Vol. 11. Original held by the New Durham Library, New Durham, New Hampshire.

NATIONAL ASSOCIATION

Minutes of the First Session of the National Association of the Original Free Will Baptists of the United States, 1935. Ayden, N.C.: Free Will Baptist Press, 1935.

Minutes of the Free Will Baptist Bodies of the United States, 1941. Ayden, N.C.: Free Will Baptist Press, 1941.

Minutes of the National Association of Free Will Baptists. Nashville: Published by the Executive Department, National Association of Free Will Baptists, 1961, 1962, 1969, 1970, 1978.

Minutes of the National Free Will Baptist Bodies of the United States, 1942. Ayden, N.C.: Free Will Baptist Press, 1942.

Minutes of the Nineteenth Annual Session of the National Association of Free Will Baptists, 1955.

Minutes of the Second Session of the National Association of the Original Free Will Baptists of the United States. Ayden, N.C.: Free Will Baptist Press, 1938.

Minutes of the Seventh Annual Session of the National Association of Free Will Baptists of the United States, 1943. Ayden, N.C.: Free Will Baptist Press, 1943.

Minutes of the Thirty-Second Annual Session of the National Association of Free Will Baptists, 1968. Nashville: Published by the Executive Department, National Association of Free Will Baptists, 1968.

Minutes of the National Association of Free Will Baptists, 1999. Unpublished copy of the 1999 Minutes faxed to William F. Davidson from the Office of the Executive Secretary, January 20, 2000.

Minutes of the First Meeting of the Free Will Baptist Educational Task Force. Unpublished Minutes, Nashville, Tennessee, December 11-13, 1999.

The 1984 Free Will Baptist Yearbook. Nashville: The Executive Office, National Association of Free Will Baptists, Inc., 1984.

The 1986 Free Will Baptist Yearbook. Nashville: The Executive Office, National Association of Free Will Baptists, Inc., 1986.

The 1987 Free Will Baptist Yearbook. Nashville: The Executive Office, National Association of Free Will Baptists, Inc., 1987.

The 1988 Free Will Baptist Yearbook. Nashville: The Executive Office, National Association of Free Will Baptists, Inc., 1988.

The 1989 Free Will Baptist Yearbook. Nashville: The Executive Office, National Association of Free Will Baptists, Inc., 1989.

The 1990 Free Will Baptist Yearbook: Nashville: The Executive Office, National Association of Free Will Baptists, Inc., 1990.

The 1991 Free Will Baptist Yearbook: Nashville: The Executive Office, National Association of Free Will Baptists, Inc., 1991.

The 1992 Free Will Baptist Yearbook: Nashville: The Executive Office, National Association of Free Will Baptists, Inc., 1992.

The 1993 Free Will Baptist Yearbook: Nashville: The Executive Office, National Association of Free Will Baptists, Inc., 1993.

The 1994 Free Will Baptist Yearbook: Nashville: The Executive Office, National Association of Free Will Baptists, Inc., 1994.

The 1995 Free Will Baptist Yearbook: Nashville: The Executive Office, National Association of Free Will Baptists, Inc., 1995.

The 1996 Free Will Baptist Yearbook: Nashville: The Executive Office, National Association of Free Will Baptists, Inc., 1996.

The 1997 Free Will Baptist Yearbook: Nashville: The Executive Office, National Association of Free Will Baptists, Inc., 1997.

The 1998 Free Will Baptist Yearbook. Nashville: The Executive Office, National Association of Free Will Baptists, Inc., 1998.

The 1999 Free Will Baptist Yearbook: Nashville: The Executive Office, National Association of Free Will Baptists, Inc., 1999.

NORTH CAROLINA

Minutes of the Annual Conference of the Original Free Will Baptists of North Carolina, 1887-1895.

Minutes of the Annual Conference of Free Will Baptists of North Carolina, Bethel Conference, 1829-1843. Quoted in Thad Harrison and J. M. Barfield, *History of North Carolina.* Ayden, N.C.: The Free Will Baptist Press, 1897.

Minutes of the Central Conference of the Original Free Will Baptists of North Carolina, 1896-1921. Held by the Free Will Baptist Historical Collection, Mount Olive College, Mount Olive, N.C.

Minutes of the Eleventh Annual Session of the Eastern Conference of the Original Free Will Baptist, 1906. Ayden, N.C.: Free Will Baptist Print, 1907.

Minutes of the Free-Will Baptist Association, 1829. Salisbury, N.C.: Printed by Philo White, 1830.

Minutes of the Free-Will Baptist Association, 1830. Salisbury, N.C.: Printed by Philo White, 1830.

Minutes of the Free-Will Baptist Association, 1834. Salisbury, N.C.: Roswell Elmer, Printer, 1834.

Minutes of the Kehukee Association, North Carolina, 1769-1778. MS.

Minutes of the Kehukee Baptist Association (North Carolina), 1794. Held by the Free Will Baptist Historical Collection, Mount Olive College, Mount Olive, N.C.

Minutes of the North Carolina General Conference of Free Will Baptists, 1843-1886. Held by the Free Will Baptist Historical Collection, Mount Olive College, Mount Olive, N.C.

Minutes of the North Carolina Free Will Baptist General Conference, 1845. Copy in the archives of the Free Will Baptist Historical Collection, Free Will Baptist Bible College, Nashville, Tennessee.

Minutes of the North Carolina Primitive Baptist Association, 1769-1959. Microfilm copies of the Original. Film held by the Historical Commission of the Southern Baptist Convention, Nashville, Tennessee.

Minutes of the Pantego-Concord Free Will Baptist Church, 1849-1855. Original Minutes held by the Free Will Baptist Historical Collection, Mount Olive College, Mount Olive, N. C.

Minutes and Records, Pasquotank Monthly Meeting of the Religious Society of Friends in North Carolina, 1722-1725. MS.

Minutes and Records, Perquimans Monthly Meeting of the Religious Society of Friends in North Carolina, 1680-1762. MS.

Minutes of the United Baptist Association Formerly Called the Kehuky Association, 1879.

Minutes of the Western Conference of the Free Will Baptists of North Carolina, 1886-1887.

TRIENNIAL GENERAL CONFERENCE

Minutes of the Eighteenth Annual Session of the Eastern General Association of the Original Free Will Baptists of the United States. Ayden, N.C.: Free Will Baptist Press. 1938.

Minutes of the Annual Sessions of the General Conference of the Original Free Will Baptist of the United States. Ayden, N.C.: Free Will Baptist Press, 1921, 1922, 1923, 1925, 1930, 1931, 1933, 1934, 1935, 1937.

Minutes of the Twelfth Annual Session of the General Conference of the Original Free Will Baptist of the United States, 1932. Blackshear, Ga.: The Times, 1932.

Minutes of the Thirty-First Session of the Free Will Baptist Triennial General Conference, 1901. Ayden, N.C.: The Free Will Baptist Publishing Company, 1903.

Minutes of the Thirty-Second Session of the Free Will Baptist General Conference of the Original Free Will Baptists of the United States, 1904. Ayden, N.C.: Free Will Baptist Print, 1905.

Moore, Emily E. *Travelling with Thomas Story, The Life and Travels of an Eighteenth Century Quaker.* Hertfordshire, Eng.: Letchworth Printers, Ltd., 1947.

Moseley, Edward. *A New and Correct Map of the Province of North Carolina, 1733.*

Mouzon, Henry. *An Accurate Map of North and South Carolina With Their Indian Frontiers.* London: Printed for Robt. Sayer and J. Bennett, Map and Printsellers, 1775.

North Carolina, Colonial Court Records: Craven County Records, Minutes of the Pleas and Quarter

Sessions. Raleigh: State Department of Archives and History.

North Carolina, Craven County Deed Books. Deed recording the Sale of Property on Little Contentnea Creek to Joseph Parker by Jacob Blount. Deed Book 10, December 25, 1756.

Olds, Fred A. *An Abstract of North Carolina Wills From About 1760 to 1800.* Baltimore: Genealogical Publishing Co., 1965.

Parker, Mattie Erma, ed., *The Colonial Records of North Carolina: Higher Court Records.* 2 vols. Raleigh: Department of Archives and History, 1963.

Patterson, Lucretia. *The Experience of Lucretia Patterson.* Nashville: Printed at the Republican Office, 1825.

"Petition to the Court of Pasquotank Precinct for Registration of a Meeting House at the Home of William Burgess." September 5,1729. Copied from the Original, now a part of the Ruth Hathaway Jones Papers in the Southern Historical Collection of the University of North Carolina Library.

"Petition from the Protestant Dissenters of Bay and Neuse Rivers." April 15, 1742. Copied from the Original in the *General Court Records,* now held by the University of North Carolina Library.

"Petition to the General Court of North Carolina for Permission to Build a Meeting House." June 19, 1740. Copied from the original, now held by the University of North Carolina Library.

"Pitt County: 1762 Tax List." *North Carolina Genealogy.* XIV (Winter, 1968).

Proceedings of the One Hundred Twenty-Ninth Annual Session of the Union Association of United Baptists, 1979.

Rippon, John. *The Baptist Register for 1790, 1791, 1792, and Part of 1793.* London: Sold by Mr. Rippon.

Rippon, John. *The Baptist Annual Register for 1794, 1795, 1796, 1797.* London: Sold by Messrs. Dilly and Button.

"Records of the Ohio River Yearly Meeting Called Free Will Baptists." Vol. 1, 1833 to 1897. Original minutes held by the Ohio Historical Society, Columbus, Ohio.

"Records of the Ohio River Yearly Meeting Called Free Will Baptists." Vol. 2, 1898-1911. Original minutes held by the Ohio Historical Society, Columbus, Ohio.

Sacred Melodies for Conference and Prayer Meetings and for Social and Private Devotions. 3rd ed., Dover, N.H.: Published by the Trustees of the Freewill Baptist Connection, 1839.

_____. 4th ed., 1841; 5th ed., 1842; 8th ed., Revised and amended, 1847; cloth ed., Revised and amended, 1851.

Saunders, William L., ed. *The Colonial Records of North Carolina.* 10 vols. Raleigh: P. M. Hale, Printer to the State, 1886.

Semple, Robert B. *A History of the Rise and Progress of the Baptists in Virginia.* Richmond: John Lynch, Printer, 1810.

Sixth US Census, Alabama, 1840.

"Slavery As It Is." Quoted in John J. Butler, *Thoughts on the Benevolent Enterprises.* Dover, N.H.: Published by the Trustees of the Freewill Baptist Connection, 1840.

Smith, F. L. "Rise and Progress of Mt. Moriah Church and Mt. Moriah Association with Some of Their Labor." July 10, 1888. Handwritten manuscript held by Mr. M. P. Gore, McShan, Alabama.

Southeastern Free Will Baptist College, Catalog, 1983-84.

Survey for Benjamin Hooker, November 8, 1797.

Survey for Joseph Parker, 1761.

Sutton, Amos. *A Narrative of the Mission to Orissa.* Boston: Published by David Marks for the Free-Will Baptist Connexion, 1833.

"System of Co-operation of the Nebraska Yearly Meeting of Freewill Baptists." Unpublished manuscript held by the Free Will Baptist Historical Collection, Free Will Baptist Bible College, Nashville, Tennessee.

"Tax Lists," Davidson County, Tennessee, 1805. Held by the Tennessee Historical Commission, Nashville, Tennessee.

Tax Digest, Putnam County, Ga., 1812, 1823.

Tecumseh College Catalog and Announcements, 1921-22.

The American Baptist Almanac, 1855-1861. Philadelphia: The American Baptist Publication Society.

The Church Member's Book or Admonitions and Instructions For All Classes of Christians. Dover, N.H.: Published by the Free-Will Baptist Printing Establishment, 1847.

The Colonial Records of South Carolina: The Journal of the Common House of Assembly, February 20, 1744 to May 25, 1745. Columbia: South Carolina Archives Department, 1955.

The Psalmody: A Collection of Hymns for Public and Social Worship. Dover, N.H.: Freewill Baptist Printing Establishment, 1853.

The Second or 1807 Land Lottery of Georgia. Vidalia, Ga.: Georgia Genealogical Reprints, The Rev. Silas Emmett Lucas, Jr., 1968.

The Third and Fourth or 1820 and 1821 Land Lotteries of Georgia. Easley, S.C.: Georgia Genealogical Reprints and Southern Historical Press, 1973.

The Wolverine Association of Free Will Baptists, 1941.

Thirty-Fourth Annual Report of the Freewill Baptist Home Mission Society, 1867. Dover, N.H.: Published by the Freewill Baptist Printing Establishment, 1868.

Thirty-Seventh Annual Report of the Freewill Baptist Education Society. Dover, N.H.: Published by the Freewill Baptist Printing Establishment, 1876.

Thirty-Third Annual Report of the Freewill Baptist Home Mission Society. Dover, N.H.: Published by Freewill Baptist Printing Establishment, 1867.

Transcript of Wills, Charleston, County, S.C. Vol. 4, PC, 1736-1740, "Joseph Elliott," "William Elliott," "Thomas Elliott."

US Census, 1850-1860, Pope County, Arkansas. Published by Capitola Glazner and Bobbie J. McLane, 1966.

US Census, 1850, Franklin County, Arkansas. Transcribed from microfilm by Ted R. Worley. Held by Arkansas State Historical Commission.

United States Coast Survey: Virginia, North Carolina, South Carolina. H. Lindenkohl & C. G. Krebs, Lith., 1865.

Urner, Clarence H. "Early Baptist Records in Prince George County, Virginia." *The Virginia Magazine of History and Biography,* XLI (April 1933).

US Department of Commerce, US Bureau of the Census. Heads of Families at the First Census of the United States Taken in the Year, 1790, North Carolina. Washington: Government Printing Office, 1908.

US Department of Commerce, Bureau of the Census. Population Schedules of the Second Census of the United States, 1800—for the Counties of Beaufort, Duplin, Hyde, Lenoir, and Pitt. Washington: The National Archives, 1957.

US Department of Commerce, Bureau of the Census. Population Schedules of the Third Census of the United States, 1810—for the Counties of Beaufort, Duplin, Hyde, Lenoir, and Pitt. Washington: The National Archives, 1957.

Wheeler, John H. *Historical Sketches of North Carolina From 1581 to 1851.* 2 vols. Philadelphia: Lippincott, Grambo and Co., 1851.

Wheeler, S. J. *History of the Baptist Church Worshipping at Parker's Meeting House Called Meherrin.* By the Clerk. Raleigh: Printed at the Recorder Office, 1847.

Whitley, W. T. *Minutes of the General Assembly of the General Baptist Churches in England, with Kindred Records.* 2 vols. London: Printed for the Society by the Kingsgate Press, 1910.

_____. *The Works of John Smyth, Fellow of Christ's College, 1594-8.* 2 vols. Cambridge: at the University Press, 1915.

Will of Benjamin Lakaro (Laker). Perquimans Precinct, Files of the North Carolina Secretary of State, April 7, 1701.

Will of Churchill Reading. Bath County, Files of the North Carolina Secretary of State, September 19, 1734.

Will of Juliana Laker. Perquimans Precinct, Files of the North Carolina Secretary of State, September 24, 1735.

Will of Matthew Markes, August 15, 1719. Quoted in Clarence Urner, "Early Baptist Records in Prince George County, Virginia." *The Virginia Magazine of History and Biography,* XLI (April 1933).

Will of Redding Moore. Transcript of Wills (WPA), Marion County, S. C. Vol. I.

Wood, Virginia S. and Wood, Ralph V., transcribers,. *Georgia Land Lottery.* Cambridge, Mass.: The Greenwood Press, 1964.

B. Secondary

Ahlstrom, Sydney E. *A Religious History of the American People.* New Haven: Yale University Press, 1972.

Albee, John. *New Castle. Historic and Picturesque—Bi-centennial Souvenir, 1693-1893.* Hampton, N.H.: Peter E. Randall, Publisher, 1974.

Allen, William B. *A History of Kentucky.* Louisville: Bradley & Gilbert, Publishers, 1872.

Ashe, Samuel A'Court. *History of North Carolina.* Greensboro: Charles L. Van Nappen, Publisher, 1925.

Bailey, J. D., Reverends Philip Mulkey and James Fowler. *The Story of the First Baptist Church Planted in Upper South Carolina.*

Ballard, Jerry. *Never Say Can't.* Carol Stream, Ill.: Creation House, 1971.

Baxter, Norman Allen. *History of the Freewill Baptists.* Rochester: American Baptist Historical Society, 1957.

Bean, Raymond J. "Social Views of the Freewill Baptists." *The Freewill Baptist Centennial Papers, 1780-1980.* The Bicentennial Committee, The American Baptist Churches of New Hampshire, 1980.

Biographical and Historical Memoirs of Mississippi. 2 vols. Chicago: The Goodspeed Publishing Company, 1891.

California Christian College, Catalog, 1999-2000. Quoted in E-mail to William F. Davidson from Dr. E. T. Hyatt, Academic Dean, January 22, 2000.

Campbell, Jesse H. *Georgia Baptists. Historical and Biographical.* Richmond: H. K. Ellyson, 1847.

Carroll, H. K. *The Religious Forces of the United States.* New York: Charles Scribner's Sons, 1912.

Centennial Souvenir of the New Hampshire Yearly Meeting of Free Baptists, 1792-1892. Laconia: N.H.: Published by the Board of Directors, 1892.

Cheshire, Joseph Blount, ed. *Sketches of Church History in North Carolina.* Wilmington, N.C.: Wm. L. De Rosset, Jr., Printer, 1892.

Clanahan, James F. *The History of Pickens County, Alabama, 1540-1920.* Carrollton, Ala.: Clanahan Publication, 1964.

Connor, R. D. W. *History of North Carolina.* 3 vols. Vol. 1, *The Colonial and Revolutionary Periods, 1584-1783.* Chicago: The Lewis Publishing Co., 1919.

Corbitt, David Leroy. *The Formation of North Carolina Counties, 1663-1943.* Raleigh: State Department of Archives and History, 1950.

Crismon, Leo Taylor, ed. *Baptists in Kentucky, 1776-1976.* Middletown, Ky.: Kentucky Baptist Convention, 1975.

Cross, Whitney. *The Burned Over District.* Ithaca, N.Y.: Cornell University Press, 1950.

Crowley, John G. *Primitive Baptists of the Wiregrass South, 1815 to Present.* Gainesville, Fla.: University of Florida Press, 1998.

Davis, Mary A. *History of the Free Baptist Woman's Missionary Society.* Boston: The Morning Star Publishing House, 1900.

Delke, James A., Comp. *History of the North Carolina Chowan Baptist Association, 1896-1881.* Raleigh: Edwards and Broughton, 1882.

Devin, Robert I. *A History of the Grassy Creek Baptist Church, From its Foundation to 1880.* Raleigh: Edwards and Broughton & Co., 1880.

Dodd, Damon C. *Marching Through Georgia: A History of the Free Will Baptists in Georgia.* Published by the author, 1977.

_____. *The Free Will Baptist Story.* Nashville: Executive Department of the National Association of Free Will Baptists, 1956.

Dortch, D. E., ed. *Zion Freewill Baptist Gospel Voices.* Ayden, N.C.: Freewill Baptist Publishing Co., 1901.

Duncan, J. M. *A Brief History of the Meherrin Church, 1729-1929.* Raleigh: Bynum Printing Co., 1929.

Ely, William. *Big Sandy Valley.* Catlettsburg, Ky.: Central Methodist, 1887.

Footer, Henry B. *History of the Tuscaloosa County Baptist Association, 1834-1934.* Tuscaloosa, Ala.; Weatherford Printing Company, 1934.

Gaustad, Edwin Scott. *The Great Awakening in New England.* New York: Harper & Brothers, 1957.

Grime, J. H. *History of Middle Tennessee Baptists.* Nashville: Baptist Reflector, 1902.

Goen, C. C. *Revivalism and Separatism in New England, 1740-1800.* New Haven: Yale University Press, 1962.

Hall, C. Mitchell. *Jenny Wiley Country. A History of the Big Sandy Valley in Kentucky's Highlands and Genealogy of the Region's People.* 3 vols. Kingsport, Tenn.: Kingsport Press, Inc., 1972.

Handy, W. W. *United Baptist Churches, Who Are They?* Piedmont, Mo.: Published by the Author, 1973

Harrison, Harrold D., ed. *Who's Who Among Free Will Baptists.* Nashville: Randall House Publications, 1978.

Harrison, Thad and Barfield, J. M. *History of the Free Will Baptists of North Carolina.* 2 vols. Ayden, N.C.: The Free Will Baptist Press [1897].

Hawks, Francis L. *History of North Carolina.* 2 vols. Fayetteville, N.C.: Published by E. J. Hale & Son, 1858.

History of Adair, Sullivan, Putnam, and Schuyler Counties, Missouri. Astoria, Ill.: Stevens Publishing Co., 1972 [1888].

"History of Parsonsfield Seminary." Parsonsfield Seminary Sesquicentennial, August 21,1982.

Holcombe, Hosea. *A History of the Rise and Progress of Baptists in Alabama.* Philadelphia: King and Baird, Printers, 1840.

History of Tennessee. Nashville: The Goodspeed Publishing Co., 1886.

Huggins, M. A. *A History of North Carolina Baptists, 1727-1932.* Raleigh: The General Board, Baptist State Convention of North Carolina, 1967.

Jamison, A. Leland. "Religions in the Perimeter," *The Shaping of American Religion.* Vol. 1: *Religion in American Life.* Edited by James Ward Smith and A. Leland Jamison. 4 vols. Princeton: Princeton University Press, 1961.

King, Joe M. *A History of South Carolina Baptists.* Columbia: The General Board of the South Carolina Baptist Convention, 1964.

Latch, Ollie. *History of the General Baptists.* Poplar Bluff, Mo.: The General Baptist Press, 1954.

Lee, Lawrence. *The Lower Cape Fear in Colonial Days.* Chapel Hill: The University of North Carolina Press, 1965.

Lefler, Hugh Talmage and Newsome, Albert Ray. *North Carolina.* Chapel Hill: The University of North Carolina Press, 1954.

_____. *The History of a Southern State, North Carolina.* Chapel Hill: The University of North Carolina Press, 1954.

Little, Lewis Peyton. *Imprisoned Preachers and Religious Liberty in Virginia.* Lynchburg, Va.: J. P. Bell Co., Inc., 1938.

Marini, Stephen A. *Radical Sects of Revolutionary New England.* Cambridge, Mass.: Harvard University Press, 1982.

Martin, John H., Comp. *Columbus, Geo., From Its Selection as a "Trading Town" in 1827, to its Partial Destruction by Wilson's Raid in 1865.* Vol. 1. Columbus, Ga.: Published by Thomas Gilbert, 1874.

Masters, Frank M. *A History of Baptists in Kentucky.* Louisville: Kentucky Historical Society, 1953.

McKinney, J. W. *A Brief History of Free Baptists in Southern Illinois.* Marion, Ill.: 1939.

Mead, Frank S. *Handbook of Denominations in the United States.* 4th ed. New York: Abingdon Press, 1965.

Million, G. W. and Barrett, G. A. *A Brief History of the Liberal Baptist People in England and America from 1606 to 1911.* Pocahontas, Ark.: Liberal Baptist Book and Tract Company, 1911.

Million, G. W. *A History of Free Will Baptists.* Nashville: Board of Publication and Literature, National Association of Free Will Baptists, 1958.

Minard, B. *A Remarkable Experience of Elder Benjamin Randall, Founder of the Free Baptist Denomination.* 2nd ed. Houlton, Me.: Published by the Author, 1890.

Montgomery, D. B. *General Baptist History*. Evansville, Ind.: Courier Company, Book and Job Printers, 1882.

Moore, John W. *Sketches of Pioneer Baptist Preachers in North Carolina*. Sketches found pasted over text in old German text book.

Newman, A. H. *A History of the Baptist Churches in the United Sta*tes. Philadelphia: American Baptist Publication Society, 1894.

Parramore, Thomas C. *The Ancient Maritime Village of Murfreesboro, 1787-1825*. Murfreesboro, N.C.: Johnson Publishing Co., 1969.

Paschal, George Washington. *History of North Carolina Baptists*. 2 vols. Raleigh: The General Board, North Carolina Baptist State Convention, 1930.

Pelt, Michael. *A History of Ayden Seminary and Eureka College*. Mount Olive, N.C.: 1983.

Pennington, Edgar Legare. *The Church of England and the Rev. Clement Hall in Colonial North Carolina*. Hartford: Church Missions Publishing Co., 1937.

Picirilli, Robert E., ed. *History of Free Will Baptist State Associations*. Nashville: Randall House Publications, 1976.

Pittman, R. F. and Dunn, C. K., Sr., eds. *Hymns of Adoration*. Ayden, N.C.: Free Will Baptist Press, 1934.

Pittman, R. F. and Loftin, Floyd F. *Hymns of Praise*. Ayden, N.C.: Free Will Baptist Press, 1921.

Pittman, R. F. and Tripp, R. E., eds. *His Service Songs*. Ayden, N.C.: Free Will Baptist Printing Company, 1928.

Powell, William S. *Dictionary of North Carolina Biography*. Vols. 4, 5. Chapel Hill and London: University of North Carolina Press, 1994.

_____. *North Carolina Gazeteer*. Chapel Hill: University of North Carolina Press, 1968.

Pugh, Jesse Forbes. *Three Hundred Years Along the Pasquotank: A Biographical History of Camden County*. Durham: Seeman Printery, Inc.

Purefoy, George W. *History of the Sandy Creek Baptist Association—From its Organization in A.D. 1758 to A.D. 1858*. New York: Sheldon & Co., Publishers, 1859.

Ray, Worth S. *Old Albemarle and Its Absentee Landlords*. Baltimore: Genealogical Publishing Co., 1960.

Riley, B. F. *A History of the Baptists in the Southern States East of the Mississippi*. Philadelphia: American Baptist Publication Society, 1898.

Religious Bodies, 1906. Vol. II. *Separate Denominations*. Washington: United States Government Printing Office, 1910.

Religious Bodies, 1916. Vol. II. *Separate Denominations*. Washington: United States Government Printing Office, 1919.

Religious Bodies, 1926. Vol. II. *Separate Denominations*. Washington: Government Printing Office, 1929.

Religious Bodies, 1936. Vol. II,. *U.S. Department of Commerce, Bureau of the Census*, Dr. T. F. Murphy. Washington: U.S. Government Printing Office, 1941.

Ryland, Garnett. *The Baptists of Virginia, 1699-1926*. Richmond: The Virginia Baptist Board of Missions and Education, 1955.

Scott, Morgan. *History of the Separate Baptist Church*. Indianapolis: Printed at the Hollenbeck Press, 1901.

Southeastern Free Will Baptist College Catalog, 1999-2001. Vol. 12. Wendell, N.C.: Center Cross Publishing, 1999.

Spencer, J. H. *A History of Kentucky Baptists From 1769 to 1885*. 2 vols. Cincinnati: J. R. Baumes, 1885.

Stevenson, George. "Benjamin Laker." In Powell, William S. *Dictionary of North Carolina Biography*. Vol. 4. Chapel Hill and London: University of North Car-olina Press, 1994.

_____. "Paul Palmer." In Powell, William S. *Dictionary of North Carolina Biography*. Vol. 5. Chapel Hill and London: University of North Carolina Press, 1994.

_____. Personal letter to Ronald Creech. Handwritten, March 25, 1968.

Stewart, I. D. *The History of the Freewill Baptists for Half a Century*. Dover, N.H.: Freewill Baptist Printing Establishment, 1862.

Sweet, William Warren. *Religion on the American Frontier*: The Baptists. New York: Cooper Square Publishers, Inc., 1964.

_____. *Revivalism in America*. Gloucester, Mass.: Peter Smith, 1965.

Taylor, Adam. *The History of the General Baptists*. Vol. I, *The English General Baptists of the Seventeenth Century*. London: Printed for the Author, by T. Bore, Raven Row, Mile-End Turnpike, 1818.

Telfair Nancy, *A History of Columbus, Georgia, 1828-1928*. Columbus, Ga.: The Historical Publishing Co., 1929.

The Centennial Record of Freewill Baptists, 1780-1880. Rev. ed. Dover, N.H.: The Freewill Baptist Printing Establishment, 1881.

The Goodspeed Biographical and Historical Memoirs of Northeastern Arkansas. Chicago: The Goodspeed Publishing Company, 1889.

Torbet, Robert G. *A History of the Baptists*. Philadelphia: The Judson Press, 1950.

Torrence, Clayton. *Old Somerset on the Eastern Shore of Maryland*. Baltimore: Regional Publishing Co., 1966.

Townsend, Leah. *South Carolina Baptists, 1670-1805*. Florence, S.C.: The Florence Printing Co., 1935.

Tupper, H. A. *Two Centuries of the First Baptist Church of South Carolina, 1683-1883*. Baltimore: R. H. Woodward and Company, 1889.

Turner, J. Kelly and Bridgers, Jno. L., Jr. *History of Edgecombe County, North Carolina*. Raleigh: Edwards & Broughton Printing Co., 1920.

Underwood, A. C. *A History of the English Baptists*. London: The Baptist Union Publication Department, Kingsgate Press, 1947.

Vedder, Henry C. *A Short History of the Baptists*. Philadelphia: The American Baptist Publication Society, 1907.

Ware, Charles Crossfield. *North Carolina Disciples of Christ*. St. Louis: Christian Board of Publication, 1927.

Watts, Joseph T. *The Rise and Progress of Maryland Baptists*. Maryland State Mission Board of the Maryland Baptist Union Association.

Wheeler, John Hill. *Reminiscences and Memoirs of North Carolina and Eminent North Carolinians*. Baltimore: Genealogical Publishing Co., 1966.

Wiley, Frederick L. *Life and Influence of Rev. Benjamin Randall*. Philadelphia: American Baptist Publication Society, 1915.

Williams, Abby Brown, ed. *100 Years With the Social Band Association of Free Will Baptists*. Published by the Centennial Committee-Dewey Thompson, Carl High, Estalene Winfrey, Abby Brown, and Birdie Boatner, 1975.

Williams, Chas. B. *A History of the Baptists in North Carolina*. Raleigh: Presses of Edwards & Broughton, 1901.

Wood, John Elliott. *Year Book, Pasquotank Historical Society*. 2 vols., 1956.

Woolsey, Paul. *God A Hundred Years and A Free Will Baptist Family*. Chuckey, Tenn.: The Union Free Will Baptist Association, 1949.

C. Pamphlets and Periodicals

Anthony, Alfred Williams. *Getting Together. Baptists and Free Baptists for Two Years*. Pamphlet. Report of Special Joint Secretary, October 15, 1913.

_____. "Twenty Years After: The Story of the Union of Baptists and Free Baptists During the Period of Negotiation and Realization, 1904-1924." *Christian Work*, (October 18, 1904).

"Apostolic Succession and Religion of the Spirit, Exemplified in the Life and Times of Benjamin Randall." *The Morning Star* (April-July 1859).

Babcock, Rufus, Jr. and Peck, John M. "Brief View of the Baptist Interest in Each of the United States." Published in installments in the *Congregational Quarterly Register,* 13:57-67, 182-195, 307-316 for 1840-1841; 14:42-58, 173-186 for 1841-1842. (Typed from microfilm by Donna Trent.)

Battle, Kemp Plummer, ed. "Minutes of the Kehukee Association (Baptist), 1772-1777." *James Sprunt*

Historical Monograph (No. 5, 1904).

Bean, Raymond J. "Benjamin Randall and the Baptists." *The Chronicle*, XV (July 1952), 99-109.

"Biographical Sketch of Rev. Elias Hutchins." *The Morning Star*, XXXIV (October 5, 1859).

"Births, Deaths, and Marriages in Berkeley, Later Perquimans Precinct, N.C." Quoted in J. R. B. Hathaway, *The North Carolina Genealogical Register*, 111, 366.

Bordin, Ruth B. "The Sect to Denomination Process in America: the Freewill Baptist Experience." *Church History*, XXXIV (March 1965).

Buzzell, John. "Short History of the Church of Christ, Gathered at New Durham, N.H., 1780." *A Religious Magazine*, I (January 1811–July 1812).

_____. "An Extract of the Experience of Elder Benjamin Randal (Taken from a Manuscript) Writen by Himself, Corrected by the Editor." *A Religious Magazine*, VI (February 1822), 206-216.

Castelloe, Woodrow. "The Kehukee Baptist Association, North Carolina." *The Chronicle*, III (October 1940), 164-178.

Cate, Carter E. *Free Baptist Gifts to the World*. Auburn, Me.: Merrill & Webber Company, 1913.

Chappell, C. Raymond. "Benjamin Randall—'Frail But Unafraid.'" *The Chronicle*, IV (July 1941), 97-110.

"Chattahoochee United Baptist Association, Ala. and Ga." *The Christian Index*. Vol. 11, No. 2 (Friday, January 13, 1843).

Cobb, N. B. "The Colonial Period of North Carolina Baptist History." *North Carolina Baptist Historical Papers*, *I* (January 1897), 79-100.

Contact. (December 1953).

Edwards, Morgan. "Materials Toward a History of the Baptists in Delaware State." *Pennsylvania Magazine of History and Biography*, IX (1885), 45-61; 197-213.

"Free Will Baptist General Conference." *Free Will Baptist Advocate*, Vol. 15 (May 27, 1896).

Gardner, Robert G. "The Forgotten General Baptist Association in the South." *The Quarterly Review*, Vol. 39, No. 1 (October, November, December 1978).

"Rev. Ellis Gore, Obituary." *West Alabamian* (October 15,1883). Quoted in *The Baptist Review*, LaGrange, N.C.

Griffin, Z. F. *History of Our India Mission Field*. N.D. Pamphlet held by the American Baptist Historical Society, Rochester, N.Y.

Hasty, Steven R. "Zion Bible School." *The Time Machine*, Vol. 1, Number 1, 1982.

Hathaway, J. R. B. *The North Carolina Genealogical Register*. 3 vols. (January 1900-July 1903).

"Hillsdale Registers 175 for Fall Semester." *Contact*, Vol. XXX, No. 11 (November 1983).

Huffman, J. D. "The Baptists in North Carolina." First Paper, *North Carolina Baptist Historical Papers, I* (July 1897), 217-244.

_____. "The Baptists in North Carolina." Fourth Paper, *North Carolina Baptist Historical Papers, II* (October 1897).

_____. "The Baptists in North Carolina." Fifth Paper, *North Carolina Baptist Historical Papers, II* (January 1898).

_____. "The Baptists in North Carolina." Sixth Paper, *North Carolina Baptist Historical Papers, II* (April 1898).

_____. "The Baptists in North Carolina." Part II, First Paper, *North Carolina Baptist Historical Papers, II* (July 1898).

Joslin, David A. "A Look Into the Past: Arkansas and its District Associations." *The Arkansas Vision*, (May 1972).

"A Look Into the Past: Arkansas and its Relationship to National Bodies." *The Arkansas Vision* (June 1972).

_____. "A Look Into the Past: Publications of the State Association." *The Arkansas Vision* (January-February 1973).

_____. "A Look Into the Past: Record Attendance." *The Arkansas Vision* (February 1974).

_____. "A Look Into the Past: The Campbellite Influence on Early Free Will Baptists." *The Arkansas Vision* (October 1972).

_____. "A Look Into the Past: The Origin of Arkansas Free Will Baptists." *The Arkansas Vision* (July-August 1972).

_____. "A Look Into the Past: The State Evangelist." *The Arkansas Vision* (May 1973).

_____. "A Look Into the Past: Toward More Picturesque Speech." *The Arkansas Vision* (November 1972).

_____. "A Look Into the Past: Travel to the Early Session of the State Association." *The Arkansas Vision* (September 1973).

_____. "A Profile From the Past: Rev. John Crafton, 1836-1914." *The Arkansas Vision* (April 1974).

_____. "Editorial." *The Arkansas Vision* (October 1978).

Lane, Jesse. "Letter to The Freewill Baptist Magazine, Dated Evansville, Vanderburg County, Indiana, August 28, 1829." *The Freewill Baptist Magazine*, Vol. 3., No. 5 (October 1829).

Loveless, Alton. "Brief History of Ohio Free Will Baptists." *The Ambassador* (July-August 1975).

"Medals on Sale at Charleston." *Southwest Times Record* (April 7, 1974).

"Minister's Meeting, United Baptist." *The Christian Index*, Vol. 11, No. 33 (August 18, 1843).

Moore, Frank, ed. Rebellion Record: *A Diary of American Events*, 12 vols. New York: 1861-1868. Quoted in C. C. Goen, "Broken Churches, Broken Nation: Regional Religion and North-South Alienation in Antebellum America." *Church History*, Vol. 52, No. 1 (March 1983).

Morris, E. C. "Personal Letter to the Editors of 'The History Corner.'" *Contact* (December 18,1971).

"Ohio Free Will Baptist State Convention and Ohio River Yearly Meeting." *The Free Will Baptist*, Vol. 29, No. 29 (September 6, 1911).

Oliver, David D. "The Society for the Propagation of the Gospel in the Province of North Carolina." *James Sprunt Historical Publications*, IX (1910), 9-23.

Paschal, G. W. "Morgan Edwards' Materials Toward a History of the Baptists in the Province of North Carolina." *The North Carolina Historical Review*, Vol. II, No. 3 (July 1930).

Pelt, Michael. "The Former Articles of Faith and the Present Statement of Faith of the Original Free Will Baptists in North Carolina." *The Free Will Baptist*, Vol. 75, No. 29 (July 27, 1960).

Pierce, Wiley. "Letter to the Editor." *The Primitive Baptist*, Vol. 3, No. 6, March 1, 1838.

"Pitt County: 1762 Tax List." *North Carolina Genealogy, XIV* (Winter, 1968).

Pittman, Thomas M. "The Preparation for Baptist Work in North Carolina." *North Carolina Baptist Historical Papers, III* (January 1900).

Place, Enoch. "Journal." *The Free Will Baptist* (Wednesday, May 27, 1896).

"Religious Intelligence." *The Morning Star.* Vol. I, No. 1 (Wednesday, May 7, 1834).

Scribner, J. Woodbury. "Elias Hutchins." Centennial Paper for the New Hampshire Yearly Meeting, MS, 1892.

Smith, Henry A. M. "The Baronies of South Carolina." *The South Carolina Historical and Genealogical Magazine*, Vol. XV, No. 4 (October 1914), 149-165.

Stewart, I D. "The Anti-Slavery Record of the Freewill Baptists." *The Freewill Baptist Quarterly*, XVI (January 1868), 41-68.

"Support of the Ministry in the Freewill Baptist Denomination." *The Free-Will Baptist Quarterly*, Vol. II, No. 8 (October 1854).

"Sustaining the Christian Ministry," N.D. Pamphlet held by the American Baptist Historical Society, Rochester, New York. *The Freewill Baptist Magazine. Providence: II* (May 1829).

The Freewill Baptist Register. Limerick, Me.: Published by Elder Samuel Burbank for the Conference, 1831-1841.

"The General Conference of Free Baptists: Information Respecting the Basis of Union and Proceedings Relating Thereto." Pamphlet, issued by order of the Conference Board, 1910.

"The General Conference of Free Baptists: Information Respecting the Action of the General Conference in Regard to the Union of Baptists and Free Baptists in Missionary Work and in Other Denominational Activities." Pamphlet, issued by the Committee on Conference with Other Christian People, 1910.

"The Ministry." *The Morning Star*, Vol. IX, No. 12 (July 23, 1834); Vol. IX, No. 23 (November 12, 1834).

"The Six-Principle Baptists in America." *The Chronicle*, III (January 1940), 3-9.

"Two Denominations Uniting. An Historical and Explanatory Statement of Co-operation and Union of Baptists and Free Baptists." Pamphlet. New York: Printed by Authorization of a Special Committee Representing the American Baptist Foreign Mission Society, the American Baptist Home Mission Society, and the American Baptist Publication Society, 1913.

"United Baptist Association, Ga." *The Christian Index,* Vol. 11, No. 48, (December 1, 1843).

"United Baptist Association." *The Christian Index,* Vol. 10, No. 38, (September 1842).

"United Baptist Association." *The Christian Index,* Vol. 11, No. 11 (Friday, March 17, 1843). Available in the Stetson Memorial Library, Special Collections, Mercer University, Macon, Georgia.

Urner, Clarence H. "Early Baptist Records in Prince George County, Virginia." *The Virginia Magazine of History and Biography, XLI* (April 1933), 97-101.

Western Free Baptist Quarterly. Vol. IV, No. 2 (January 1888), and Vol. III, No. 4 (July 1887).

Whitley, W. T. "General Baptists in Carolina and Virginia." *Crozer Quarterly,* XIII (January 1936).

Wiley, Frederick L. *Free Baptists in Temperance Reform,* Boston: The Morning Star Publishing House, 1901.

Williams, Jack. "What a Century!" *Contact,* (February 2000).

D. Encyclopedias

Burgess, G. A. and Ward, J. T. *Free Baptist Cyclopaedia.* Chicago: Free Baptist Cyclopedia Co., 1889.

Hinshaw, William Wade, ed. *Encyclopedia of American Quaker Genealogy.* 7 vols. Vol. I, North Carolina. Ann Arbor: Edwards Brothers, Inc., 1936.

"North Carolina." *Encyclopaedia Britannica.* 1969, Vol. 16, 609-616.

E. Bibliographical Works

Starr, Edward C., ed. *A Baptist Bibliography.* 16 vols. Rochester: American Baptist Historical Society, 1963.

Thornton, Mary Lindsay. *A Bibliography of North Carolina, 1589-1956.* Chapel Hill: University of North Carolina Press, 1958.

F. Unpublished Works

Allen, W. C. "A Brief History of the Baptists in South Carolina." MS, 1934.

Barefoot, Gary Fenton. "A Proposed List of Free Will Baptist Subject Headings." Unpublished Thesis for M.A. Degree. Chapel Hill: University of North Carolina, 1968.

Barnard, Laura Belle. "Joy On a Rugged Path." Manuscript.

Broadnax Family Bible, "Flyleaf."

Davidson, J. R. "Some Experiences in Early History of Free Will Baptist Bible College." N.D. Unpublished manuscript held by the Free Will Baptist Historical Collection, Free Will Baptist Bible College, Nashville, Tennessee.

Dodd, Damon. "Free Will Baptists in Georgia." N.D. Unpublished manuscript held by the Stetson Memorial Library, Special Collections, Mercer University, Macon, Georgia.

Eaton, Tim. "Update of History, Hillsdale Free Will Baptist College, 1985-1989." E-mail memo letter to William F. Davidson, January 20, 2000.

Evans, Bill; Messer, Trymon; and Loveless, Alton. "Report of the New Millennium Committee." Nashville: Unpublished report, 1997.

Gardner, Robert G. "E-Mail Memo," September 6, 1999.

Handwritten Notes of the Joint Committee of Education Meeting held during the first session of the National Association in 1935. Original held by the Free Will Baptist Historical Collection, Free Will Baptist Bible College, Nashville. Tennessee.

Loveless, Alton. "E-mail letter to William F. Davidson," December 29, 1999.

Messer, Trymon. "Advancing into the Millennium." Unpublished proposal submitted to the Free Will Baptist Leadership Conference, Nashville, Tennessee, December 1999.

_____. "Home Missions Since 1984." E-mail letter to William F. Davidson, January 4, 2000.

Million, G. W. "English General Baptists." Nashville: Unpublished handwritten notes, N.D. Held by the Free Will Baptist Historical Collection, Free Will Baptist Bible College, Nashville, Tennessee.

_____. "Free Will Baptists in Oklahoma." Unpublished handwritten notes, N.D. Held by the Free Will Baptist Historical Collection, Free Will Baptist Bible College, Nashville, Tennessee.

_____. "Spread of the Randall Movement Westward." Unpublished handwritten notes, N.D. Held by the Free Will Baptist Historical Collection, Free Will Baptist Bible College, Nashville, Tennessee.

"Notes on the History of the Free Will Baptists in Wright County, Missouri." Typed copy, N.D. Held by the Free Will Baptist Historical Collection, Free Will Baptist Bible College, Nashville, Tennessee.

Olson, Gordon C. The Formative Influences, Rise, and Early History of the General Baptists in England. Unpublished thesis, 1957.

Personal interview granted to Geraldine Waid by Broadnax family member.

Personal interview with Rev. Billy Bevan, Southeastern Free Will Baptist College, Wendell, North Carolina, January 13, 2000.

Picirilli, Robert. "Interview of Rev. John L Welch." Unpublished transcript from tape, April 25, 1971. Held by the Free Will Baptist Historical Collection, Free Will Baptist Bible College, Nashville, Tennessee.

Picirilli, Robert E. and Wisehart, Mary R. "Brief History of the Cumberland Association." Unpublished manuscript held by Free Will Baptist Historical Collection, Free Will Baptist Bible College, Nashville.

Pinson, J. Matthew. Personal letter to William F. Davidson, May 11, 1995.

_____. "The Diversity of Arminian Soteriology: Thomas Grantham, John Goodwin, and Jacobus Arminius." Unpublished manuscript, 1999. Article will constitute a chapter in a proposed dissertation on the varieties of Arminianism in the seventeenth and eighteenth centuries.

Skiles, Lonnie Ray. "A Short History of Free Will Baptist Bible College, 1942-1972." Unpublished thesis, March 1972.

Stevenson, George. "Materials Towards a History of Free Will Baptists in Lenoir County and Kinston, North Carolina, 1769-1919." MS.

Thomley, J. J. "A Brief History of the United Free-will Baptist Church of Christ." N.D. Held by the Free Will Baptist Historical Collection, Free Will Baptist Bible College, Nashville, Tennessee.

Thomley, L. M. "Notes on Freewill Baptist History." N.D. Held by the Free Will Baptist Historical Collection, Free Will Baptist Bible College, Nashville, Tennessee.

[Welch, Mary]. "Early Efforts Toward a Centrally Located School for Free Will Baptists." N.D. Unpublished manuscript held by the Free Will Baptist Historical Collection, Free Will Baptist Bible College, Nashville, Tennessee.

Letter from M. P. Gore, dated McShan, Alabama, November 12, 1971.

Letter from Dr. Barry White, postmarked Regent's Park College, Oxford, May 1, 1972.

Mann, C. E. Personal letter to B. F. Brown, N.D.

Pelt, Michael. Letter to George Stevenson, June 29, 1960. Held by the Free Will Baptist Historical Collection, Mount Olive College, Mount Olive, North Carolina.

_____. Personal interview, February 3, 1983.

_____. Telephone interview, July 21, 1983.

Personal interview with Mr. Ashton Phelps, Sr., Attorney at Law, New Orleans, Louisiana, April 21, 1972.

"Spring 2000 Program of Studies." Student Enrollment list by program, Southeastern Free Will Baptist College, Spring Semester, 2000.

Telephone interview with Dr. Charles Holloman, Raleigh, North Carolina, April 1972.

Telephone interview with Rev. Price, Pastor of the First Kyger Free Will Baptist Church, Cheshire, Ohio, July 13, 1983.

Walley, Wendell. E-mail letter to William F. Davidson, January 23, 2000.

Williams, Jack. Telephone interview, November 17, 1983.

Index